The Civil War and Reconstruction

A DOCUMENTARY COLLECTION

The Civil War and Reconstruction

A DOCUMENTARY COLLECTION

Edited by

WILLIAM E. GIENAPP

W · W · NORTON & COMPANY   NEW YORK · LONDON

ISBN 0-393-97555-X (pbk.)
W. W. Norton & Company, Inc., 500 Fifth Avenue, New York, N.Y. 10110
www.wwnorton.com
W. W. Norton & Company Ltd., 10 Coptic Street, London WC1A 1PU
1 2 3 4 5 6 7 8 9 0

For my mother,
June B. Gienapp,
and the memory of my father,
William H. Gienapp,
who taught me the importance of being a teacher

CONTENTS

The Naval War

Union Politics, 1861–1862

Confederate Politics, 1861–1863

Diplomacy

The Military Struggle, 1863

Union Politics, 1863

The Union Home Front

The Confederate Home Front

African Americans

Common Soldiers

The Military Struggle, 1864

Union Politics, 1864

Confederate Politics, 1864–1865

The End of the War

Part 3: *Reconstruction*

Presidential Reconstruction

Johnson's Clash with Congress

The End of Reconstruction

Appendix

PREFACE

"The real war," Walt Whitman once said of the Civil War, "will never get in the books." Whitman's remark is justly famous and has become one of the most widely quoted comments about the war. For Whitman, the real war was not military strategy, battlefield tactics, or great battles; instead, it was the valor and suffering, the passion and doubt of ordinary Americans, not just rank-and-file soldiers but civilians on the home front as well. Whitman grasped the difficulty of incorporating the ordinary and the personal into the larger story of the conflict, what he called "the minutiae of deeds and passions" with "the official surface" of the war. Although he insisted that he never left those stirring days, he was never able in the end to write a history of what he considered the real war. In his poetry and prose writings, he provided only glimpses of the all-encompassing struggle to which he had been an eyewitness.

The war was so vast in its sweep, it involved so many Americans in so many ways that, like Whitman, historians have found it difficult to comprehend it in all its dimensions. We know a great deal about the war, its causes, and its consequences, and our knowledge increases every year in important ways, and yet somehow it remains elusive to us, just as it was to Whitman and the generation that lived it. The causes of a war in which Americans fought their fellow Americans, its evolving nature and the reasons for its outcome, and the problem of reconstructing the Union after the war ended remain difficult historical problems.

The Civil War was the most important event in American history. Certainly no event in our national past has had a greater and longer-lasting impact on the country or more decisively changed the course of national development. Mark Twain once aptly observed that the war "uprooted institutions that were centuries old, changed the politics of a people, transformed the social life of half the country, and wrought so profoundly upon the entire national character that the influence cannot be measured short of two or three generations." Not surprisingly, no other event has had as powerful a hold on the popular imagination as the Civil War. Viewed from many different angles, it remains the great American epic, even when divorced from the romanticism that has for so long distorted its popular image. Together, the Civil War and Reconstruction constitute the greatest single crisis in American history.

In this book, I have assembled documents from the period 1830 to 1877 that deal with some of the key issues of the Civil War era. This collection is meant to be a representative sample and is far from exhaustive. I have deliberately chosen to include longer excerpts from fewer documents in order to give the reader a better sense of the flavor of the documents included in this collection. In selecting these documents from a much larger set I put together, I have aimed for breadth rather than in-depth coverage of one or two themes. Thus I have sought to cover social and economic developments as well as the traditional political, military, and diplomatic events. In addition, in the documents on the military struggle, I have sought to provide accounts from both the Union and Confederate perspective, of both large-scale strategy and the experiences of ordinary soldiers, and of both the eastern and the western theater. Because of space limitations, I could not cover every important battle, so I have relied on a smaller selection of documents to convey the experience of combat and the nature of the struggle waged between the two armies. Similarly, in the sections on the sectional conflict and Reconstruction, I have combined individual accounts with national developments and documents on social and economic as well as political and constitutional history. By this approach, I have aimed to illustrate the variety of experiences that were part of this larger transforming historical event.

The originals of some of these documents were very difficult to read, but I have striven to accurately reproduce the documents included in this book. Except at the beginning and end of a document, omissions have been marked with ellipses, and any explanatory information that has been supplied is either within brackets or, in a few cases, in footnotes. I have followed the spelling of the original documents, and in order to enhance readability have minimized the use of *sic*. In a few cases in which the paragraphing has been modified to improve clarity, this fact is noted in the introduction. In no case has the order of sentences been altered. The format of diary entries has been standardized, but otherwise they are unchanged. The introductions that accompany each document are intended to situate it in a larger context and aid in understanding and interpretation.

In the course of producing this book, I have incurred a number of personal obligations that I wish to acknowledge. The present book grew out of a sourcebook I assembled for my course on the Civil War that is part of the Core Curriculum at Harvard University. I am deeply indebted to Susan W. Lewis, director of the Core Program, for her constant support and encouragement with respect to this course. Over the years, she has provided funds to produce and revise this sourcebook, without which creating the present volume would have been a much more difficult and time-consuming task. A number of graduate students at Harvard served as research assistants for the original sourcebook, and I would like to recognize the critical contributions of Fred Dalzell, Pearl Ponce, James Sellman, and Silvana Siddali. I am also grateful to the many graduate students who have served as teaching fellows in my Core course over the past decade and offered many valuable suggestions about the use of documents in teaching the Civil War to undergraduates. It has been a privilege to work with such talented students.

Several of my graduate students kept an eye out for useful documents while doing research on the Civil War for their dissertations. In particular, I would like to thank Andy Coopersmith, Christine Dee, Libra Hilde, Michael Vorenberg, and especially Lisa Laskin and Chandra Miller. Within the department of history, Adriana Forte, Mary McConnell, and Cory Paulsen were especially helpful with copying and scanning documents.

Several scholars provided important advice or answered my inquires about various matters pertaining to the period. I owe a particular debt of gratitude to Joe Glatthaar, who not only gave this project a strong endorsement when it was being considered for publication but who has provided me with crucial information about the military aspects of the war. I would also like to thank David Blight, Tom Brown, Larry Buell, Michael Holt, Stephen Maizlish, Kenneth M. Stampp, and Heather Cox Richardson, all good friends who rendered vital assistance in one way or another. I especially wish to acknowledge the help of Jean Baker, who in the early stages of this project sent me a number of suggestions and subsequently helped me track down several elusive documents. Her contribution has been invaluable.

Steve Forman invited me to prepare this volume and has never flagged in his enthusiasm for the project. Moreover, he has always used the greatest tact in reminding me of deadlines or when asking for changes in the manuscript. Since the project began, I have shared several wonderful lunches with him, although somehow we always found it impossible to keep the rivalry between the Yankees and the Red Sox out of our conversation.

I am also grateful to publishers and libraries that have given permission to reproduce copyrighted materials or items in their collection. They are listed individually elsewhere.

Finally, I would like to acknowledge the contribution of my family. For more than thirty years, my wife Erica has been a constant source of encouragement and support, and she took on additional tasks at home without complaint in order to allow me to finish this book. She also rendered vital assistance with the proofreading. My older son Bill helped in assembling and checking documents. My younger son Jonathan contributed in a less direct but equally important way: not only did his Babe Ruth baseball team win the league championship while I was working on this book, he did not voice a single complaint when I had to miss most of his summer season in order to finish it. The book's dedication reflects another personal debt I cannot repay but nevertheless wish to acknowledge. As Abraham Lincoln wrote in 1863, thanks to all.

William E. Gienapp
Father's Day 2000
Lincoln, Massachusetts

PART 1

The Sectional Conflict

1

ALEKSANDR BORISOVICH LAKIER

The Rush of Life in New York City (1857)

Aleksandr Borisovich Lakier, who was a member of the Russian gentry, came to the United States in 1857. While European travellers were common in the United States before the Civil War, visitors from Russia were unusual. Lakier published an account of his journey in 1859, from which this translation was made. In this selection, he describes the bustle and pace of life in New York City.

Starting in the morning until late in the evening, Broadway and the adjoining streets are crowded with magnificently dressed women and with Americans rushing about on business. Despite the wide sidewalks, the crush is so great that one cannot take a step without poking someone with elbows or body. If you want to excuse yourself or if you wait for apologies, the American has long since flown by like an arrow. It dawns on you that an American cannot tell a lamp post from a person and you end up like him—forcing your way through all obstacles and pushing with no less effort. Meanwhile there is the noise on the street from the thousands of carriages, omnibuses, and loaded wagons, from the din of youngsters hawking newspapers, the rattle of toys being demonstrated by street vendors, from whistles and squeaks and the hoarse shouts of auctioneers by their shops; notices and announcements are thrust in your hands, huge boards pasted with gigantic posters are being carried on their shoulders by men and women hired for this purpose; on some streets there are rails for American horse-drawn cars, and enormous coaches scurry back and forth. In the midst of this whirlpool the pale, lean American walks briskly to the pier at the port, or to the courts, or to Wall Street and the banks and offices of the commercial houses and companies. On the streets along the way American flags are stretched from one house to the other, painted all in long red and white stripes, studded with stars on a blue field. And there goes a detachment of militia in a full-dress parade marching in step to the music, or some kind of procession moving along. Who keeps order? How does all this move about and disperse without a word? To count how many carriages and how many people pass by a given place on Broadway in one hour is positively impossible. Apparently no one pays any attention to the interests of anyone else. Here and there policemen are visible, dressed in the manner of English police. But the main part of their day, it seems, is spent in guiding ladies across the street from one sidewalk to another, protecting the spoiled American woman from jolts and bruises. But then the American, keeping order himself, sees to it, as it were, that his neighbor does not disturb the peace either. Hence there are no police in America for the preservation of quiet and tranquility.

FROM Arnold Schrier and Joyce Story, trans. and eds., *A Russian Looks at America: The Journey of Aleksandr Borisovich Lakier in 1857* (Chicago: University of Chicago Press, 1979), pp. 65–66.

The buildings on Broadway are striking by their height, and the speed with which they have been erected is amazing. The most recently constructed are similar and resemble one another, to the detriment of architecture and art. The American does not want to be bothered with external opulence, and he has devised ways to build houses quickly and relatively cheaply. It is remarkable that when the lower floor is not yet ready, the upper is already available: the whole building rests on cast-iron pillars with floors, roofs, and foundations of the same metal; when people are already living and working in the upper stories, the lower is still a row of columns on which the house sits. . . .

In the evening Broadway presents a different scene, illuminated by gaslight from street lamps and from rows of magnificent stores, confectioners' shops, amusement and entertainment places. It is then that you think the American can, indeed, enjoy himself. The broad sidewalk is again congested with people, in the midst of whom the richly attired ladies appear in bursts of gay colors; couples swing off the main street either to the theater or to a sumptuously lighted confectioner's; at various places of entertainment flags are fluttering and music is playing; everywhere there are immense playbills and dreadful signs with portrayals of beasts and fantastic wonders. Go into any theater (there are about ten on Broadway) and all are full of people and everyone is enjoying himself in his own way. Parades by militia and especially the fire brigades with their equipment, music, flags, and fireworks are also frequent in the evening.

2

ANONYMOUS

The Manufacturing City of Lowell (1847)

Lowell, Massachusetts, was famous as the center of the textile industry in the United States before the Civil War. As this article from Hunt's Magazine *indicates, Lowell experienced a remarkable growth since its founding in 1821. In some ways, Lowell was unusual as an industrial town. Its factories were much larger and employed many more operatives, and the work was much more thoroughly mechanized, than was true of most manufacturing operations before the war. In addition, Lowell initially relied on young women from New England farm families for its labor force; only in the 1840s and 1850s did large numbers of Irish immigrants, including men and children, begin to enter the mills. Yet in one sense, visitors, both native and foreign, were justified in wanting to see Lowell: its large-scale factory operations would become increasingly the norm in this country after 1860. And there was no place like it, either in terms of economic organization or urban development, in the South in these years.* Hunt's Magazine, *which was published in New York City, was the most important commercial magazine in the North during these years.*

The city of Lowell, from the number and extent of its manufacturing establishments, is one of the most prominent settlements of New England. As it has attained its present position altogether from the existence of those establishments, we design . . . to show the general progress of the place, as well as its condition, and incidentally to make some remarks respecting that particular branch of industry which constitutes the main feature of its enterprise. It is only about 25 years since the foundations of the settlement were laid. The first portion of the land, constituting its present site, was obtained in the year 1821; a tract of 400 acres, on which the most densely populated part of the city now stands, having been purchased at the cost of about $100,000. The purchasers of this property were incorporated, as the "Merrimack Manufacturing Company," on the 6th day of February, 1822. During that year, the first mill was erected. From such a commencement, the city has gradually advanced—not only through periods of great commercial prosperity, but even when disaster seems to have settled upon most of the manufacturing establishments throughout the country—down to the present time.

A railroad, connecting Lowell with Boston, was opened in 1835, through which, the two places are separated by the distance of a ride of only one hour; and other improvements were also made, relating either to the manufacturing enterprise of the place, or to the condition of the population. . . .

At the present time its population is 28,841.

Of its population of 29,000, about one-third are connected with the manufacturing and mechanical establishments, constituting 6,320 females, and 2,915 males. Besides the print works, and about 550 houses belonging to the corporations, there are 33 mills; the capital stock, invested in manufacturing and mechanical enterprise, being about $12,000,000. There are 1,459,100 yards of cloth, amounting during the year to 75,868,000 yards, manufactured in the place during each week; and, in each year, 61,100 bales of southern cotton are worked up. 14,000,000 yards of printed calico are also here annually made . . . and more than $1,500,000 are paid out annually for labor. Important improvements have been projected, and many have already been completed, with a view to the extension of the business and manufacturing operations of the place.

The city was incorporated on the 30th of March, 1836; and from that period the most strenuous measures have been adopted for the improvement of the city, by the construction of side-walks and by lighting the streets, as well as for the benefit of the public health and the public morals, and for the erection of edifices of various sorts for the purposes of religious instruction, benevolence, and education.

FROM *Hunt's Magazine* 16 (1847): 356–62.

3

WILLIAM LLOYD GARRISON

I Will Be Heard (1831)

The Boston editor William Lloyd Garrison was the most famous abolitionist in the country before the Civil War, and his newspaper, The Liberator, *was an important source of antislavery opinion. Initially a colonizationist, Garrison had gone to Baltimore to help edit a moderate antislavery paper in that city, but his strong opinions and forceful prose soon led to his arrest and imprisonment. Following his release, he returned to Boston, determined to edit a new and much more vigorous antislavery journal. In the columns of* The Liberator *Garrison defined the central tenets of the new, more militant movement known as* abolitionism. *Garrison quickly became the most hated man in the South, and rewards were offered to anyone who would kidnap him and bring him to the South for trial. The following editorial, which appeared in his paper's first issue, makes clear his new tone and commitment.*

During my recent tour for the purpose of exciting the minds of the people by a series of discourses on the subject of slavery, every place that I visited gave fresh evidence of the fact, that a greater revolution in public sentiment was to be effected in the free states—*and particularly in New England*—than at the south. I found contempt more bitter, opposition more active, detraction more relentless, prejudice more stubborn, and apathy more frozen, than among slave owners themselves. Of course, there were individual exceptions to the contrary: This state of things afflicted, but did not dishearten me. I determined, at every hazard, to lift up the standard of emancipation in the eyes of the nation, *within sight of Bunker Hill and in the birth place of liberty.* That standard is now unfurled; and long may it float, unhurt by the spoliations of time or the missiles of a desperate foe—yea, till every chain be broken, and every bondman set free! Let southern oppressors tremble—let their secret abettors tremble—let their northern apologists tremble—let all the enemies of the persecuted blacks tremble.

I deem the publication of my original Prospectus unnecessary, as it has obtained a wide circulation. The principles therein inculcated will be steadily pursued in this paper, excepting that I shall not array myself as the political partisan of any man. In defending the great cause of human rights, I wish to derive the assistance of all religions and of all parties.

Assenting to the "self-evident truth" maintained in the American Declaration of Independence, "that all men are created equal, and endowed by their Creator with certain inalienable rights—among which are life, liberty and the pursuit of happiness," I shall strenuously contend for the immediate enfranchisement of our slave population. In Park-street Church, on the Fourth of July, 1829, in an address on slavery, I unreflectingly assented to the popular but pernicious doctrine of *gradual* abolition. I seize this opportunity to make a full and unequivocal recantation, and thus publicly to ask pardon of my God, of my country, and of my brethren the poor slaves, for having uttered a sentiment so full of timidity, injustice and absurdity.

I am aware, that many object to the severity of my language; but is there not cause for severity? I *will be* as harsh as truth, and as uncompromising as justice. On this subject, I do not wish to think, or speak, or write, with moderation. No! no! Tell a man whose house is on fire, to give a moderate alarm; tell him to moderately rescue his wife from the hands of the ravisher; tell the mother to gradually extricate her babe from the fire into which it has fallen;—but urge me not to use moderation in a cause like the present. I am in earnest—I will not equivocate—I will not excuse—I will not retreat a single inch—AND I WILL BE HEARD.

FROM *The Liberator*, 1 January 1831.

Declaration of Sentiments of the American Anti-Slavery Convention (1833)

Various abolitionists came together in Philadelphia in December 1833 to form the American Anti-Slavery Society (AASS). Until its rupture in 1840, it was the most important abolitionist organization in the country. Uniting the more radical Garrisonians with those abolitionists who wished to work through the churches and established institutions, the AASS served as an umbrella group for the many local antislavery societies in the North. The society issued a declaration, written by William Lloyd Garrison, explaining its principles and methods.

More than fifty-seven years have elapsed since a band of patriots convened in this place [Philadelphia], to devise measures for the deliverance of this country from a foreign yoke. The corner-stone upon which they founded the TEMPLE OF FREEDOM was broadly this—"that all men are created equal; that they are endowed by their Creator with certain inalienable rights; that among these are life, LIBERTY, and the pursuit of happiness." . . .

We have met together for the achievement of an enterprise, without which, that of our fathers is incomplete, and which, for its magnitude, solemnity, and probable results upon the destiny of the world, as far transcends theirs, as moral truth does physical force.

In purity of motive, in earnestness of zeal, in decision of purpose, in intrepidity of action, in steadfastness of faith, in sincerity of spirit, we would not be inferior to them.

Their principles led them to wage war against their oppressors, and to spill human blood like water, in order to be free. *Ours* forbid the doing of evil that good may come, and lead us to reject, and to entreat the oppressed to reject, the use of all carnal weapons for deliverance from bondage—relying solely upon those which are spiritual, and mighty through God to the pulling down of strong holds.

Their measures were physical resistance—the marshalling in arms—the hostile array—the mortal encounter. *Ours* shall be such only as the opposition of moral purity to moral corruption—the destruction of error by the potency of truth—the overthrow of prejudice by the power of love—and the abolition of slavery by the spirit of repentance.

Their grievances, great as they were, were trifling in comparison with the wrongs and sufferings of those for whom we plead. Our fathers were never slaves—never bought and sold like cattle—never shut out from the light of knowledge and religion—never subjected to the lash of brutal taskmasters.

But those, for whose emancipation we are striving,—constituting at the present time at least one-sixth part of our countrymen,—are recognised by the laws, and treated by their fellow beings, as marketable commodities—as goods and chattels—as brute beasts;—are plundered daily of the fruits of their toil without redress;—really enjoy no constitutional nor legal protection from licentious and murderous outrages upon their persons;—are ruthlessly torn asunder—the tender babe from the arms of its frantic mother—the heart-broken wife from her weeping husband—at

FROM *The Liberator,* 14 December 1833.

the caprice or pleasure of irresponsible tyrants;—and, for the crime of having a dark complexion, suffer the pangs of hunger, the infliction of stripes, and the ignominy of brutal servitude. They are kept in heathenish darkness by laws expressly enacted to make their instruction a criminal offence.

These are the prominent circumstances in the condition of more than TWO MILLIONS of our people, the proof of which may be found in thousands of indisputable facts, and in the laws of the slave-holding States.

Hence we maintain— . . .

That no man has a right to enslave or imbrute his brother—to hold or acknowledge him, for one moment, as a piece of merchandise—to keep back his hire by fraud—or to brutalize his mind by denying him the means of intellectual, social and moral improvement.

The right to enjoy liberty is inalienable. . . . Every man has a right to his own body—to the products of his own labor—to the protection of law—and to the common advantages of society. It is piracy to buy or steal a native African, and subject him to servitude. Surely the sin is as great to enslave an AMERICAN as an AFRICAN.

Therefore we believe and affirm—

That there is no difference, *in principle*, between the African slave trade and American slavery;

That every American citizen, who retains a human being in involuntary bondage, is a MAN-STEALER;

That the slaves ought instantly to be set free, and brought under the protection of law; . . .

That all those laws which are now in force, admitting the right of slavery, are therefore before God utterly null and void; being an audacious usurpation of the Divine prerogative, a daring infringement on the law of nature, a base overthrow of the very foundations of the social compact, a complete extinction of all the relations, endearments and obligations of mankind, and a presumptuous transgression of all the holy commandments—and that therefore they ought to be instantly abrogated.

We further believe and affirm—

That all persons of color who possess the qualifications which are demanded of others, ought to be admitted forthwith to the enjoyment of the same privileges, and the exercise of the same prerogatives, as others; and that the paths of preferment, of wealth, and of intelligence, should be opened as widely to them as to persons of a white complexion.

We maintain that no compensation should be given to the planters emancipating their slaves—

Because it would be a surrender of the great fundamental principle that man cannot hold property in man;

Because SLAVERY IS A CRIME, AND THEREFORE IT IS NOT AN ARTICLE TO BE SOLD;

Because the holders of slaves are not the just proprietors of what they claim;—freeing the slaves is not depriving them of property, but restoring it to the right owner;—it is not wronging the master, but righting the slave—restoring him to himself; . . .

Because if compensation is to be given at all, it should be given to the outraged and guiltless slaves, and not to those who have plundered and abused them.

We regard, as delusive, cruel and dangerous, any scheme of expatriation which pretends to aid, either directly or indirectly, in the emancipation of the slaves, or to be a substitute for the immediate and total abolition of slavery.

We fully and unanimously recognise the sovereignty of each State, to legislate exclusively on the subject of the slavery which is tolerated within its limits. We concede that Congress, *under the present national compact*, has no right to interfere with any of the slave States, in relation to this momentous subject.

But we maintain that Congress has a right, and is solemnly bound, to suppress the domestic slave trade between the several States, and to abolish slavery in those portions of our territory which the Constitution has placed under its exclusive jurisdiction.

We also maintain that there are, at the present time, the highest obligations resting upon the people of the free States, to remove slavery by moral and political action, as prescribed in the Constitution of the United States. They are now living under a pledge of their tremendous physical force to fasten the galling fetters of tyranny upon the limbs of millions in the southern States;—they are liable to be called at any moment to suppress a general insurrection of the slaves;—they authorise the slave owner to vote for three-fifths of his slaves as property, and thus enable him to perpetuate his oppression;—they support a standing army at the south for its protection;—and they seize the slave who has escaped into their territories, and send him back to be tortured by an enraged master or a brutal driver.

This relation to slavery is criminal and full of danger; IT MUST BE BROKEN UP.

These are our views and principles—these, our designs and measures. With entire confidence in the overruling justice of God, we plant ourselves upon the Declaration of our Independence, and upon the truths of Divine Revelation, as upon the EVERLASTING ROCK.

We shall organize Anti-Slavery Societies, if possible, in every city, town and village of our land.

We shall send forth Agents to lift up the voice of remonstrance, of warning, of entreaty and rebuke.

We shall circulate, unsparingly and extensively, anti-slavery tracts and periodicals.

We shall enlist the PULPIT and the PRESS in the cause of the suffering and the dumb.

We shall aim at a purification of the churches from all participation in the guilt of slavery.

We shall encourage the labor of freemen over that of the slaves, by giving a preference to their productions;—and

We shall spare no exertions nor means to bring the whole nation to speedy repentance.

Our trust for victory is solely in GOD. *We* may be personally defeated, but our principles never. TRUTH, JUSTICE, REASON, HUMANITY, must and will gloriously triumph. Already a host is coming up to the help of the Lord against the mighty, and the prospect before us is full of encouragement.

. . . We will do all that in us lies, consistently with this Declaration of our principles, to overthrow the most execrable system of slavery that has ever been witnessed upon earth—to deliver our land from its deadliest curse—to wipe out the foulest stain which rests upon our national escutcheon—and to secure to the colored population of the United States all the rights and privileges which belong to them as men and as Americans—come what may to our persons, our interests, or our reputations—whether we live to witness the triumph of JUSTICE, LIBERTY and HUMANITY, or perish untimely as martyrs in this great, benevolent and holy cause.

5

FREDERICK LAW OLMSTED

The South's Lack of a Spirit of Progress (1861)

Frederick Law Olmsted was a member of an old and prosperous Hartford family. Ill health prevented him from enrolling in Yale University, and after several years of drifting and career changes he settled down as a gentleman farmer on Staten Island. Olmsted eventually turned his attention to landscape architecture and gained lasting fame from his various projects (he designed Central Park, among other civic works). In 1852 the New York Times *hired him to travel through the South and report on his observations. Olmsted eventually made three separate trips to the South in the 1850s, each of which resulted in a book describing his travels. At the request of his English publisher, Olmsted condensed his three books into a single volume, to which he added a new introduction. Published in 1861,* The Cotton Kingdom *is arguably the most perceptive, and certainly the most famous, of all the travelers' accounts of the Old South. Olmsted was not especially concerned with the plight of African Americans and opposed slavery primarily because he believed it was an inefficient labor system that retarded the South's social and economic development. In this selection from the introduction he wrote for the 1861 volume, Olmsted discusses what he considered the South's lamentable lack of a spirit of progress and innovation compared to the North.*

I went on my way into the so-called cotton States, within which I travelled over, first and last, at least three thousand miles of roads, from which not a cotton plant was to be seen, and the people living by the side of which certainly had not been made rich by cotton or anything else. And for every mile of road-side upon which I saw any evidence of cotton production, I am sure that I saw a hundred of forest or waste land, with only now and then an acre or two of poor corn half smothered in weeds; for every rich man's house, I am sure that I passed a dozen shabby and half-furnished cottages, and at least a hundred cabins—mere hovels, such as none but a poor farmer would house his cattle in at the North. And I think that, for every man of refinement and education with whom I came in contact, there were a score or two superior only in the virtue of silence, and in the manner of self-complacency, to the sort of people we should expect to find paying a large price for a place from which a sight could be got at a gallows on an execution day at the North, and a much larger number of what poor men at the North would themselves describe as poor men: not that they were destitute of certain things which are cheap at the South,—fuel for instance,—but that they were almost wholly destitute of things the possession of which, at the North, would indicate that a man had begun to accumulate capital—more destitute of these, on an average, than our day-

labourers. In short, except in certain limited districts, mere streaks by the side of rivers, and in a few isolated spots of especially favoured soil away from these, I found the same state of things which I had seen in Virginia, but in a more aggravated form.

. . . White men seldom want an abundance of coarse food in the cotton States: the proportion of the free white men who live as well in any respect as our working classes at the North, on an average, is small, and the citizens of the cotton States, as a whole, are poor. They work little, and that little, badly; they earn little, they sell little; they buy little; and they have little—very little—of the common comforts and consolations of civilized life. Their destitution is not material only; it is intellectual and it is moral.

. . . Let a man be absent from almost any part of the North twenty years, and he is struck, on his return, by what we call the "improvements" which have been made. Better buildings, churches, school-houses, mills, railroads, etc. In New York city alone, for instance, at least two hundred millions of dollars have been reinvested merely in an improved housing of the people; in labour-saving machinery, waterworks, gasworks, etc., as much more. It is not difficult to see where the profits of our manufacturers and merchants are. Again, go into the country, and there is no end of substantial proof of twenty years of agricultural prosperity, not alone in roads, canals, bridges, dwellings, barns and fences, but in books and furniture, and gardens, and pictures, and in the better dress and evidently higher education of the people. But

FROM Frederick Law Olmsted, *The Cotton Kingdom*, vol. 1 (New York: Mason Brothers, 1861), pp. 12–13, 25–26.

where will the returning traveller see the accumulated cotton profits of twenty years in Mississippi? Ask the cotton-planter for them, and he will point in reply, not to dwellings, libraries, churches, school-houses, mills, railroads, or anything of the kind; he will point to his negroes—to almost nothing else. Negroes such as stood for five hundred dollars once, now represent a thousand dollars. We must look then in Virginia and those Northern Slave States which have the monopoly of supplying negroes, for the real wealth which the sale of cotton has brought to the South. But where is the evidence of it? where anything to compare with the evidence of accumulated profits to be seen in any Free State? If certain portions of Virginia have been a little improving, others unquestionably have been deteriorating, growing shabbier, more comfortless, less convenient. The total increase in wealth of the population during the last twenty years shows for almost nothing. One year's improvements of a Free State exceed it all.

6

LOUIS T. WIGFALL

We Are an Agricultural People (1861)

Louis T. Wigfall was a senator from Texas with a well-deserved reputation as a political brawler; impulsive, acerbic, and outspoken, he was a skillful impromptu debater who relished exchanging insults and taunts with antislavery senators. Mary Chesnut, who observed him close-up, aptly termed him a "stormy Petrel," after the small dark seabird fond of strife. When Texas seceded, Wigfall resigned his Senate seat and became a prominent Confederate leader. In 1861 William Russell, a reporter for the London Times *(see p. 67), had a conversation with Wigfall in which the latter made the following comment when boasting about the South's unique civilization.*

We are a peculiar people, sir! You don't understand us, and you can't understand us, because we are known to you only by Northern writers and Northern papers, who know nothing of us themselves, or misrepresent what they do know. We are an agricultural people; we are a primitive but a civilised people. We have no cities—we don't want them. We have no literature—we don't need any yet. We have no press—we are glad of it. We do not require a press, because we go out and discuss all public questions from the stump with our people. We have no commercial marine—no navy—we don't want them. We are better without them. Your ships carry our produce, and you can protect your own vessels. We want no manufactures: we desire no trading, no mechanical or manufacturing classes. As long as we have our rice, our sugar, our tobacco, and our cotton, we can command wealth to purchase all we want from those nations with which we are in amity, and to lay up money besides.

FROM William Howard Russell, *My Diary North and South*, vol. 1 (London: Bradbury and Evans, 1863), pp. 258–59.

7

HINTON ROWAN HELPER

Slavery Impedes the Progress and Prosperity of the South (1857)

Hinton Rowan Helper's was a unique voice before the Civil War. The son of a North Carolina farmer, he published a book in 1857, The Impending Crisis of the South, *analyzing the South's economic and social condition. Helper's book was unusual in that it was an attack on slavery by a non-slaveholding southern white. In his book, Helper marshaled a number of statistics from the U.S. Census in order to demonstrate to his satisfaction that slavery retarded the South's economic development and economically harmed the non-slaveholding white majority. An inveterate foe of the slaveholding aristocracy, he urged non-slaveholders to take political control of the South and abolish slavery. Despite urging the end of slavery, Helper was a strong racist with no sympathy for blacks, whom he wanted removed from the South. He later explained that his book "was* not *written in behalf of the negroes . . . but in behalf of the* whites." *While roundly condemned in the South as insurrectionary and banned by some southern states, Helper's book attracted little notice until the Republican party decided to issue it as a campaign tract for the 1860 presidential election. In the following selection, he discusses slavery and the South's economic condition.*

It is a fact well known to every intelligent Southerner that we are compelled to go to the North for almost every article of utility and adornment, from matches, shoepegs and paintings up to cotton-mills, steamships and statuary; that we have no foreign trade, no princely merchants, nor respectable artists; that, in comparison with the free states, we contribute nothing to the literature, polite arts and inventions of the age; that, for want of profitable employment at home, large numbers of our native population find themselves necessitated to emigrate to the West, whilst the free states retain not only the larger proportion of those born within their own limits, but induce, annually, hundreds of thousands of foreigners to settle and remain amongst them; . . . that, owing to the absence of a proper system of business amongst us, the North becomes, in one way or another, the proprietor and dispenser of all our floating wealth, and that we are dependent on Northern capitalists for the means necessary to build our railroads, canals and other public improvements; . . . and that nearly all the profits arising from the exchange of commodities, from insurance and shipping offices, and from the thousand and one industrial pursuits of the country, accrue to the North, and are there invested in the erection of those magnificent cities and stupendous works of art which dazzle the eyes of the South, and attest the superiority of free institutions!

. . . All the world sees . . . that, in comparison with the Free States, our agricultural resources have been greatly exaggerated, misunderstood and mismanaged; and that, instead of cultivating

FROM Hinton R. Helper, *The Impending Crisis of the South,* ed. George Frederickson (orig. 1857; Cambridge: Harvard University Press, 1968), pp. 21–33, 40–41.

among ourselves a wise policy of mutual assistance and co-operation with respect to individuals, and of self-reliance with respect to the South at large, instead of giving countenance and encouragement to the industrial enterprises projected in our midst, and instead of building up, aggrandizing and beautifying our own States, cities and towns, we have been spending our substance at the North, and are daily augmenting and strengthening the very power which now has us so completely under its thumb.

. . . The causes which have impeded the progress and prosperity of the South, which have dwindled our commerce, and other similar pursuits, into the most contemptible insignificance; sunk a large majority of our people in galling poverty and ignorance, rendered a small minority conceited and tyrannical, and driven the rest away from their homes, entailed upon us a humiliating dependence on the Free States; disgraced us in the recesses of our own souls, and brought us under reproach in the eyes of all civilized and enlightened nations—may all be traced to one common source . . . *Slavery!*

Reared amidst the institution of slavery, believing it to be wrong both in principle and in practice, and having seen and felt its evil influences upon individuals, communities and states, we deem it a duty, no less than a privilege, to enter our protest against it, and to use our most strenuous efforts to overturn and abolish it! . . . We are not only in favor of keeping slavery out of the territories, but, carrying our opposition to the institution a step further, we here unhesitatingly declare ourself in favor of its immediate and unconditional abolition, in every state in this confederacy, where it now exists! Patriotism makes us a freesoiler; state pride makes us an emancipationist; a profound sense of duty to the South makes us an abolitionist; a reasonable degree of fellow feeling for the negro, makes us a colonizationist.

. . . Nothing short of the complete abolition of slavery can save the South from falling into the vortex of utter ruin. Too long have we yielded a submissive obedience to the tyrannical domination of an inflated oligarchy; too long have we tolerated their arrogance and self-conceit; too long have we submitted to their unjust and savage exactions. Let us now wrest from them the sceptre of power, establish liberty and equal rights throughout the land, and henceforth and forever guard our legislative halls from the pollutions and usurpations of pro-slavery demagogues.

. . . It is not so much in its moral and religious aspects that we propose to discuss the question of slavery, as in its social and political character and influences. To say nothing of the sin and the shame of slavery, we believe it is a most expensive and unprofitable institution; and if our brethren of the South will but throw aside their unfounded prejudices and preconceived opinions, and give us a fair and patient hearing, we feel confident that we can bring them to the same conclusion. Indeed, we believe we shall be enabled—not alone by our own contributions, but with the aid of incontestable facts and arguments which we shall introduce from other sources—to convince all true-hearted, candid and intelligent Southerners . . . that slavery, and nothing but slavery, has retarded the progress and prosperity of our portion of the Union; depopulated and impoverished our cities by forcing the more industrious and enterprising natives of the soil to emigrate to the free states; brought our domain under a sparse and inert population by preventing foreign immigration; made us tributary to the North, and reduced us to the humiliating condition of mere provincial subjects in fact, though not in name.

. . . Agriculture, it is well known, is the sole boast of the South; and, strange to say, many pro-slavery Southerners, who, in our latitude, pass for intelligent men, are so puffed up with the idea of our importance in this respect, that they speak of the North as a sterile region, unfit for cultivation, and quite dependent on the South for the necessaries of life! Such rampant ignorance ought to be knocked in the head! We can prove that the North produces greater qualities of bread-stuffs than the South! Figures shall show the facts. Properly, the South has nothing left to boast of; the North has surpassed her in everything, and is going farther and farther ahead of her every day.

. . . We have two objects in view; the first is to open the eyes of the non-slaveholders of the South, to the system of deception, that has so long been practiced upon them, and the second is to show slaveholders themselves—we have reference only to those who are not too perverse, or ignorant, to perceive naked truths—that free labor is far more respectable, profitable, and productive, than slave labor. In the South, unfortunately, no kind of labor is either free or respectable. Every white man who is under the necessity of earning his bread, by the sweat of his brow, or by manual labor, in any ca-pacity, no matter how unassuming in deportment, or exemplary in morals, is treated as if he was a loathsome beast, and shunned with the utmost dis-dain. His soul may be the very seat of honor and integrity, yet without slaves—himself a slave—he is accounted as nobody, and would be deemed in-tolerably presumptuous, if he dared to open his mouth, even so wide as to give faint utterance to a three-lettered monosyllable, like yea or nay, in the presence of an august knight of the whip and the lash.

8

J. D. B. DE BOW

Why Non-Slaveholders Should Support Slavery (1861)

James De Bow grew up in undistinguished circumstances in Charleston. He was an outstanding student at the College of Charleston, which he attended as a scholarship student. After a brief foray into the law, he turned to journalism, and in 1845 he moved to New Orleans to establish De Bow's Review, *the most important business and commercial magazine in the Old South. Under his guidance, the* Review *advocated the economic development of the South. He was an important spokesman for southern economic diversification, greater industrialization, and the development of southern-controlled shipping and commercial services. Despite its commercial focus, the magazine also devoted considerable space to social and political developments, in which De Bow was keenly interested. Unlike many southern proponents of economic modernization, however, De Bow politically became increasingly radical in the decade of the 1850s, and by 1860 he was advocating southern secession. During the secession crisis, some southern leaders voiced concern about the loyalty of non-slaveholders to slavery and southern institutions. De Bow responded to this concern in the following essay, in which he emphasized southern non-slaveholders' self-interest in the preservation of slavery. In many ways, this essay, which was first delivered as a speech in Nashville in 1860, was a reply to Hinton Rowan Helper's earlier book. It was also published as a pamphlet by a pro-secessionist organization in South Carolina in 1860.*

I will proceed to present several general considerations, which must be found powerful enough to influence the non-slaveholders, if the claims of patriotism were inadequate to resist any attempt to overthrow the institutions and industry of the section to which they belong.

1. *The non-slaveholder of the South is assured that the remuneration afforded by his labor, over and above the expense of living, is larger than that which is afforded by the same labor in the free States.* To be convinced of this, he has only to compare the value of labor in the Southern cities with those of the North, and to take note annually of the large number of laborers who are represented to be out of employment there, and who migrate to our shores, as well as to other sections. No white laborer, in return, has been forced to leave our midst, or remain without employment. . . .

2. *The non-slaveholders, as a class, are not reduced by the necessity of our condition, as is the case in the free States, to find employment in crowded cities, and come into competition in close and sickly workshops and factories, with remorseless and untiring machinery.* They have but to compare their condition, in this particular, with the mining and manufacturing operatives of the North and Europe, to be thankful that God has reserved them for a better fate. Tender women, aged men, delicate children, toil and labor there from early dawn until after candle-light, from one year to another, for a miserable pittance, scarcely above the starvation point; and without hope of amelioration. . . .

3. *The non-slaveholder is not subjected to that competition with foreign pauper labor which has degraded the free labor of the North, and demoralized it to an extent which perhaps can never be estimated.* . . .

4. *The non-slaveholder of the South preserves the status of the white man, and is not regarded as an inferior or a dependant.* He is not told that the Declaration of Independence, when it says that all men are born free and equal, refers to the negro equally with himself. It is not proposed to him that the free negro's vote shall weigh equally with his own at the ballot-box, and that the little children of both colors shall be mixed in the classes and benches of the schoolhouse, and embrace each other filially in its outside sports. . . . No white man at the South serves another as a body-servant, to clean his boots, wait on his table, and perform the menial services of his household! His blood revolts against this, and his necessities never drive him to it. He is a companion and an equal. . . . The poor white laborer at the North is at the bottom of the social ladder, while his brother here has ascended several steps, and can look down upon those who are beneath him at an infinite remove!

5. *The non-slaveholder knows that as soon as his savings will admit, he can become a slaveholder, and thus relieve his wife from the necessities of the kitchen and the laundry, and his children from the labors of the field.* This, with ordinary frugality, can in general be accomplished in a few years, and is a process continually going on. . . .

6. *The large slaveholders and proprietors of the South begin life in great part as non-slaveholders.* . . . Cheap lands, abundant harvests, high prices, give the poor man soon a negro. His ten bales of cotton bring him another, a second crop increases his purchases, and so he goes on, opening land and adding labor, until in a few years his draft for $20,000 upon his merchant becomes a very marketable commodity.

7. *But should such fortune not be in reserve for the non-slaveholder, he will understand that by honesty and industry it may be realized to his children.* . . .

8. *The sons of the non-slaveholder are and have always been among the leading and ruling spirits of the South, in industry as well as in politics.* . . . Nowhere else have intelligence and virtue, disconnected from ancestral estates, the same opportunities for advancement, and nowhere else is their triumph more speedy and signal.

9. *Without the institution of slavery the great staple products of the South would cease to be grown, and the immense annual results which are distrib-*

FROM J. D. B. De Bow, "The Non-Slaveholders of the South: Their Interest in the Present Sectional Controversy Identical with That of the Slaveholders," *De Bow's Review* 30 (January 1861): 67–77.

uted among every class of the community, and which give life to every branch of industry, would cease. The world furnishes no instances of these products being grown upon a large scale by free labor. . . .

10. *If emancipation be brought about, as will, undoubtedly be the case, unless the encroachments of the fanatical majorities of the North are resisted now, the slaveholders, in the main, will escape the degrading equality which must result, by emigration, for which they have the means, by disposing of their personal chattels, while the non-slaveholders, without these resources, would be compelled to remain and endure the degradation.* This is a startling consideration. In Northern communities, where the free negro is one in a hundred of the total population, he is recognized and acknowledged often as a pest, and in many cases even his presence is prohibited by law. What would be the case in many of our States, where every other inhabitant is a negro, or in many of our communities, . . . where there are from twenty to one hundred negroes to each white inhabitant? Low as would this class of people sink by emancipation in idleness, superstition, and vice, the white man compelled to live among them would, by the power exerted over him, sink even lower. . . .

. . . They [southern non-slaveholders] fully understand the momentous questions which now agitate the land in all their relations. They perceive the inevitable drift of Northern aggression, and know that if necessity impel to it, as I verily believe it does at this moment, the establishment of a Southern confederation will be a sure refuge from the storm. In such a confederation our rights and possessions would be secure, and the wealth being retained at home, to build up our towns and cities, to extend our railroads, and increase our shipping, which now goes in tariffs or other involuntary or voluntary tributes to other sections, opulence would be diffused throughout all classes, and we should become the freest, the happiest, and the most prosperous and powerful nation upon earth.

9

ANONYMOUS

A Traveler Describes the Lives of Non-Slaveholders in Georgia (1849)

The large majority of southern whites did not own a single slave. Primarily members of land-owning farm families, they had a decent standard of living, yet they led more isolated lives, had less access to education, and lacked many of the refinements and comforts enjoyed by ordinary northern farmers. In an article on the interior areas of Georgia, a traveler describes two non-slaveholding families he stayed with on his journey. The crude lifestyle he recounts was not limited to yeoman farmers, as his subsequent stay with a planter family illustrates.

Mounted on horseback, . . . I set off alone to wander for a few days among the mountains of Georgia, filled with high anticipations of a pleasant and novel excursion. . . .

Toward evening I overtook a man, who from his dress, a home-spun suit, mud-color, and a broad-brimmed wool hat, I took to be a "native." We jogged along together, and in half an hour I knew him well: with the frankness and confidence of a southerner, he had, un-asked, told me his whole history. He frankly acknowledged that he could neither read nor write; which by the way is no uncommon thing in Georgia, even among people of considerable wealth. And his greatest pride seemed to be his "faculty for a horse swap": in this he considered himself *par excellence,* to use his own expression, "right smart." Yes, and he strode a "right smart chance of a critter," that couldn't be beat in "them diggins," if you'd believe him.

Having ridden ninety miles, over an exceedingly rough road, and through a monotonous country, stopping the first night in Gainsville, the second in Clarksville, I arrived on the morning of the third day at Toccoa Falls, twelve miles from Clarksville. . . .

. . . I lingered here long after the sun had departed, . . . and then hastened on to find lodgings for the night. A ride of a mile brought me to a log-cabin, the only house near the falls.

I was soon quite at home in my new and humble habitation, sitting before a blazing lightwood fire, conversing familiarly with mine host: around us were playing four bright-eyed, rosy-cheeked little children. . . .

After partaking heartily of a venison supper, . . . and drinking a gourd of water, feeling fatigued by the day's exposure, I asked where I was to sleep. They led me into an unoccupied part of the house, and up into the second loft, reached only by a ladder. I did not like its open-work looks, for the night was bitter cold, but as my only alternative was this or nothing, I wrapped myself up in my blanket, piled the bed-clothes over me a foot high, and tried to find the soft side of a corn-shuck mattress.

Lulled by the roar of the distant cataract, I strove to sleep, but strove in vain. I tried to forget my woes by counting the stars which glistened through the many cracks in the roof; but through those same cracks the wind, cold and chilling, came whistling through two holes, cut to let in the light, in which there was no sign of glass. Shivering, shaking, was my song during the whole long night, and happy was I when morning dawned. . . .

It was morning when I left Tallula, and before nightfall I had ridden thirty miles. No pleasant villages, with neat white cottages and ornamented gardens, so many of which one sees in a day's ride through New-England, greeted my vision; but the log-cabins of the "squatters" scattered here and there, with an occasional frame-house of the rudest construction, were seen.

I met no one walking: all ride, however poor. Sometimes two are seen on the same animal; a man and woman, perhaps, on one poor doleful-looking mule, or on some antiquated horse, more cadaverous-looking than themselves. I met also large wagons, canvass-covered, drawn by four or six mules, and driven by negroes. . . .

Being anxious to see how the poorest class of people lived in the interior, at night I stopped at the door-way of a very small and rudely-constructed hut, and inquired if I could "get stay" for the night. At first I was refused; but upon representing myself a stranger in the country, and fearing to go farther, as there were "forks in the road" and "creeks to cross" before reaching another house, they finally consented to my staying.

The cabin contained but one room, with no windows; the chimney, built of mud and stones, was, as is usual in the South, outside the house. The furniture of the house was scanty in the extreme; a roughly-constructed frame, on which was laid a corn-shuck mattress, a pine table, and a few shuck-bottomed "cha'rs."

I had not been long in this place, before preparations for supper commenced. An iron vessel—a "spider," so called—was brought and set over the

FROM "Interior Georgia Life and Scenery by a Southern Traveler," *Knickerbocker Magazine* 34 (August 1849): 113–18.

fire; in this dish was roasted some coffee; afterward, in the same dish, a "corn cake" was baked, and still again some rank old ham was fried, and the corn-cake laid in the ashes to have it "piping hot." This constituted our supper, which, being placed on the table, three of us sat down to partake of, while Cynthia, the youngest daughter, held a blazing light-wood knot for us to see by, and the "gude woman" sat in the corner "rubbing snuff," or "dipping," with her infant in her arms. A pet deer stalked in through the open door-way, and helped himself from the table without molestation.

Bed-time coming, one by one the family retired to the corner, and all lay together on the corn-shucks, sleeping as soundly as on "downy couch." Taking my saddle-bags for a pillow, and wrapping my blanket around me, I laid down before the fast dying embers, and was soon in the embrace of "tired nature's sweet restorer." Morning came, and as I was to leave early, all were up "by sun." I asked the hostess for a wash, and the vessel which had served for roasting, baking and frying the evening previous was now brought; and . . . I washed myself in the dish out of which twelve hours before I had eaten a hearty supper. I paid them well, and thanked them kindly, for they had given me the best they had. Destitute as they were, they seemed contented and happy: "Where ignorance is bliss, 't is folly to be wise." . . .

The night after leaving Dahlonega I stayed at the house of a very old and very wicked wretch, who, although worth forty negroes (at the South a man's wealth is reckoned by the negroes he owns,) lived in a log-house, and could neither read nor write. His family consisted of an idiot son and two daughters, who at supper-time sat down to eat with hat and bonnets on, their faces and hands betokening confirmed cases of hydrophobia, from evident dread of water. Rather than eat the food such hands had touched, I took from my saddle-bags some provisions which I was preserving for to-morrow's dinner, and, with a gourd of water, made a palatable meal. Frequent potations from a whiskey-bottle served to keep the old man in good humor during the evening, and his conversation was amusing if not instructive.

Hardly had we all retired to our beds, before the "voices of the night" commenced. The geese and hogs in the yard kept up a continual cackling and grunting, which was promptly responded to by a cat and dog in the house; the latter under my bed. These sounds, mingled with the asthmatic snoring of the old whiskey-drinker, and the muttered curses of the idiot, who could sleep no better than myself, served to "make night hideous."

It was long past midnight, as I lay awake, that I saw the old man rise slowly and softly from his couch, and gradually approach my bed. My heart beat quicker, and I unconsciously grasped my pistol, which was by my side; for I could see no honest purpose to call him up at such an hour. My fears were soon allayed, however, by seeing him pass by me, and take from the shelf just above my head his—whiskey-bottle.

10

WILLIAM HARPER

Slavery Is the Cause of Civilization (1838)

William Harper was a prominent South Carolina politician and proslavery writer. Born in the British colony of Antigua, he grew up in Charleston, attended South Carolina College, and was admitted to the bar in 1813. After briefly removing to Missouri, he returned to South Carolina in 1823 and subsequently held several pub-

lic offices, including chancellor of the state. He was a leading proponent of the doctrine of states' rights and was one of the early contributors in the 1830s to the emerging proslavery argument. His famous work, Memoir on Slavery, *grew out of an oration he delivered in 1837 to the South Carolina Society for the Advancement of Learning. He published it in pamphlet form the following year. In this work, Harper examines slavery as an abstract question and advances many of the ideas found in later proslavery tracts.*

The institution of domestic slavery exists over far the greater portion of the inhabited earth. Until within a very few centuries, it may be said to have existed over the whole earth—at least in all those portions of it which had made any advances towards civilization. We might safely conclude then that it is deeply founded in the nature of man and the exigencies of human society. . . .

President [Thomas] Dew has shown that the institution of Slavery is a principal cause of civilization. Perhaps nothing can be more evident than that it is the sole cause. If any thing can be predicated as universally true of uncultivated man, it is that he will not labour beyond what is absolutely necessary to maintain his existence. Labour is pain to those who are unaccustomed to it, and the nature of man is averse to pain. Even with all the training, the helps and motives of civilization, we find that this aversion cannot be overcome in many individuals of the most cultivated societies. The coercion of Slavery alone is adequate to form man to habits of labour. Without it, there can be no accumulation of property, no providence for the future, no taste for comforts or elegancies, which are the characteristics and essentials of civilization. He who has obtained the command of another's labour, first begins to accumulate and provide for the future, and the foundations of civilization are laid. We find confirmed by experience that which is so evident in theory. Since the existence of man upon the earth, with no exception whatever, either of ancient or modern times, every

society which has attained civilization, has advanced to it through this process. . . .

That the African negro is an inferior variety of the human race, is, I think, now generally admitted, and his distinguishing characteristics are such as peculiarly mark him out for the situation which he occupies among us. And these are no less marked in their original country, than as we have daily occasion to observe them. . . .

Slavery, as it is said in an eloquent article published in a Southern periodical work, . . . "has done more to elevate a degraded race in the scale of humanity; to tame the savage; to civilize the barbarous; to soften the ferocious; to enlighten the ignorant, and to spread the blessings of christianity among the heathen, than all the missionaries that philanthropy and religion have ever sent forth." Yet unquestionable as this is, and though human ingenuity and thought may be tasked in vain to devise any other means by which these blessings could have been conferred, yet a sort of sensibility which would be only mawkish and contemptible, if it were not mischievous, affects still to weep over the wrongs of "injured Africa." Can there be a doubt of the immense benefit which has been conferred on the race, by transplanting them from their native, dark, and barbarous regions, to the American Continent and Islands? . . .

We believe that the tendency of Slavery is to elevate the character of the master. No doubt the character—especially of youth—has sometimes received a taint and premature knowledge of vice, from the contact and association with ignorant and servile beings of gross manners and morals. Yet still we believe that the entire tendency is to inspire disgust and aversion towards their peculiar vices. . . . We flatter ourselves that the view of this

---

FROM William Harper, "Memoir on Slavery," in *The Pro-Slavery Argument as Maintained by the Most Distinguished Writers of the Southern States* (Charleston: Walker, Richards & Co., 1852), pp. 1–98.

degradation, mitigated as it is, has the effect of making probity more strict, the pride of character more high, the sense of honor more strong, than is commonly found where this institution does not exist. Whatever may be the prevailing faults or vices of the masters of slaves, they have not commonly been understood to be those of dishonesty, cowardice, meanness or falsehood. . . . Our institutions would indeed be intolerable in the sight of God and man, if, condemning one portion of society to hopeless ignorance and comparative degradation, they should make no atonement by elevating the other class by higher virtues, and more liberal attainments—if, besides degraded slaves, there should be ignorant, ignoble, and degraded freemen. . . .

I am sure that it is unnecessary to say to an assembly like this, that the conduct of the master to his slave should be distinguished by the utmost humanity. That we should indeed regard them as wards and dependants on our kindness, for whose well being in every way we are deeply responsible. This is no less the dictate of wisdom and just policy, than of right feeling. It is wise with respect to the services to be expected from them. I have never heard of an owner whose conduct in their management was distinguished by undue severity, whose slaves were not in a great degree worthless to him. . . . Public opinion should, if possible, bear even more strongly and indignantly than it does at present, on masters who practise any wanton cruelty on their slaves. The miscreant who is guilty of this, not only violates the law of God and of humanity, but as far as in him lies, by bringing odium upon, endangers the institutions of his country, and the safety of his countrymen. . . .

I would by no means be understood to intimate, that a vigorous, as well as just government, should not be exercised over slaves. This is part of our duty towards them, no less obligatory than any other duty, and no less necessary towards their well being than to ours. I believe that at least as much injury has been done and suffering inflicted by weak and injudicious indulgence, as by inordinate severity. He whose business is to labor, should be made to labor, and that with due diligence, and

should be vigorously restrained from excess or vice. This is no less necessary to his happiness than to his usefulness. The master who neglects this, not only makes his slaves unprofitable to himself, but discontented and wretched—a nuisance to his neighbors and to society.

. . . It is matter of familiar remark that the tendency of warm climates is to relax the human constitution and indispose to labor. The earth yields abundantly—in some regions almost spontaneously—under the influence of the sun, and the means of supporting life are obtained with but slight exertion; and men will use no greater exertion than is necessary to the purpose. . . . Nothing but the coercion of slavery can overcome the repugnance to labor under these circumstances, and by subduing the soil, improve and render wholesome the climate.

It is worthy of remark that there does not now exist on the face of the earth, a people in a tropical climate, or one approaching to it, where slavery does not exist, that is in a state of high civilization, or exhibits the energies which mark the progress towards it. . . . In short, the uncontradicted experience of the world is, that in Southern States where good government and predial and domestic slavery are found, there are prosperity and greatness; where either of these conditions is wanting, degeneracy and barbarism. . . .

I have hitherto, as I proposed, considered it as a naked, abstract question of the comparative good and evil of the institution of slavery. Very far different indeed is the practical question presented to us, when it is proposed to get rid of an institution which has interwoven itself with every fibre of the body politic; which has formed the habits of our society, and is consecrated by the usage of generations. If this be not a vicious prescription, which the laws of God forbid to ripen into right, it has a just claim to be respected by all tribunals of man. . . . But if it can be made to appear, even probably, that no good will be obtained, but that the results will be evil and calamitous as the process, what can justify such innovations? . . .

In one thing I concur with the abolitionists; that if emancipation is to be brought about, it is better that it should be immediate and total. But let us suppose it to be brought about in any manner, and then enquire what would be the effects.

The first and most obvious effect, would be to put an end to the cultivation of our great southern staple. . . . The cultivation of the soil on an extensive scale, can only be carried on where there are slaves, or in countries super-abounding with free labour. No such operations are carried on in any portions of our own country where there are not slaves. . . . I need hardly say that these staples cannot be produced to any extent where the proprietor of the soil cultivates it with his own hands. He can do little more than produce the necessary food for himself and his family.

And what would be the effect of putting an end to the cultivation of these staples, and thus annihilating at a blow, two thirds or three fourths of our foreign commerce? Can any sane mind contemplate such a result without terror? I speak not of the utter poverty and misery to which we ourselves would be reduced, and the desolation which would overspread our own portion of the country. Our slavery has not only given existence to millions of slaves within our own territories, it has given the means of subsistence and therefore existence to millions of freemen in our confederate States; enabling them to send forth their swarms, to overspread the plains and forests of the West and appear as the harbingers of civilization. The products of the industry of those States are in general similar to those of the civilized world, and are little demanded in their markets. By exchanging them for ours, which are every where sought for, the people of these States are enabled to acquire all the products of art and industry, all that contributes to convenience or luxury, or gratifies the taste or the intellect, which the rest of the world can supply. . . . Does not *self defence* then demand of us, steadily to resist the abrogation of that which is productive of so much good? . . .

. . . After President Dew, it is unnecessary to say a single word on the practicability of colonizing our slaves. The two races, so widely seperated from each other by the impress of nature, must remain together in the same country. Whether it be accounted the result of prejudice or reason, it is certain that the two races will not be blended together so as to form a homogenous population. To one who knows any thing of the nature of man and human society, it would be unnecessary to argue that this state of things cannot continue, but that one race must be driven out by the other, or exterminated, or again enslaved. . . . Aggression would beget retaliation, until open war—and that a war of extermination were established. From the still remaining superiority of the white race, it is probable that they would be the victors, and if they did not exterminate, they must again reduce the others to slavery—when they could be no longer fit to be either slaves or freemen. It is not only in self defence, in defence of our country and of all that is dear to us, but in defence of the slaves themselves that we refuse to emancipate them.

11

SOLOMON NORTHUP

The New Orleans Slave Mart (1853)

Solomon Northup was a free black man who lived in upstate New York. In 1841, while working as a musician, he was kidnapped in Washington by unscrupulous slave dealers and sent to New Orleans, the major slave market of the United States, to be sold. While Northup's friends vainly tried to trace his whereabouts, he worked for over a decade on several Louisiana plantations. In 1853, after twelve years of bondage, Northup was finally identified and freed. With the help of a New York lawyer, he wrote an account of his experiences, Twelve Years a Slave. *In the following selection, he describes the sale of slaves in New Orleans.*

The very amiable, pious-hearted Mr. Theophilus Freeman, a partner or consignee of James H. Burch, and keeper of the slave pen in New-Orleans, was out among his animals early in the morning. With an occasional kick of the older men and women, and many a sharp crack of the whip about the ears of the younger slaves, it was not long before they were all astir, and wide awake. Mr. Theophilus Freeman bustled about in a very industrious manner, getting his property ready for the sales-room, intending, no doubt, to do that day a rousing business.

In the first place we were required to wash thoroughly, and those with beards, to shave. We were then furnished with a new suit each, cheap, but clean. The men had hat, coat, shirt, pants and shoes; the women frocks of calico, and handkerchiefs to bind about their heads. We were now conducted into a large room in the front part of the building to which the yard was attached, in order to be properly trained, before the admission of customers. The men were arranged on one side of the room, the women on the other. The tallest was placed at the head of the row, then the next tallest, and so on in the order of their respective heights. Emily was at the foot of the line of women. Freeman charged us to remember our places; exhorted us to appear smart and lively,—sometimes threatening, and again, holding out various inducements. During the day he exercised us in the art of "looking smart," and of moving to our places with exact precision. . . .

Next day many customers called to examine Freeman's "new lot." The latter gentleman was very loquacious, dwelling at much length upon our several good points and qualities. He would make us hold up our heads, walk briskly back and forth, while customers would feel of our hands and arms and bodies, turn us about, ask us what we could do, make us open our mouths and show our teeth, precisely as a jockey examines a horse which he is about to barter for or purchase. Sometimes a man or woman was taken back to the small house in the yard, stripped, and inspected more minutely. Scars upon a slave's back were considered evidence of a rebellious or unruly spirit, and hurt his sale.

One old gentleman, who said he wanted a coachman, appeared to take a fancy to me. From his conversation with Freeman, I learned he was a resident in the city. I very much desired that he would buy me, because I conceived it would not be difficult to make my escape from New-Orleans on some northern vessel. Freeman asked him fifteen hundred dollars for me. The old gentleman insisted it was too much, as times were very hard. Freeman, however, declared that I was sound and healthy, of good constitution, and intelligent. He made it a point to enlarge upon my musical attainments. The old gentleman argued quite adroitly that there was nothing extraordinary about the nigger, and finally, to my regret, went out, saying he would call again. During the day, however, a number of sales were made. David and Caroline were purchased together by a Natchez planter. They left us, grinning broadly, and in the most happy state of mind, caused by the fact of their not being separated. Lethe was sold to a planter of Baton Rouge, her eyes flashing with anger as she was led away.

The same man also purchased Randall. The little fellow was made to jump, and run across the floor, and perform many other feats, exhibiting his activity and condition. All the time the trade was going on, Eliza was crying aloud, and wringing her hands. She besought the man not to buy him, unless he also bought herself and Emily. She

FROM Solomon Northup, *Twelve Years a Slave* (Auburn, N.Y.: Derby and Miller, 1853), pp. 78–82.

promised, in that case, to be the most faithful slave that ever lived. The man answered that he could not afford it, and then Eliza burst into a paroxysm of grief, weeping plaintively. Freeman turned round to her, savagely, with his whip in his uplifted hand, ordering her to stop her noise, or he would flog her. He would not have such work—such snivelling; and unless she ceased that minute, he would take her to the yard and give her a hundred lashes. Yes, he would take the nonsense out of her pretty quick—if he didn't, might he be d——d. Eliza shrunk before him, and tried to wipe away her tears, but it was all in vain. She wanted to be with her children, she said, the little time she had to live. All the frowns and threats of Freeman could not wholly silence the afflicted mother. She kept on begging and beseeching them, most piteously, not to separate the three. Over and over again she told them how she loved her boy. A great many times she repeated her former promises—how very faithful and obedient she would be; how hard she would labor day and night, to the last mo-

ment of her life, if he would only buy them all together. But it was of no avail; the man could not afford it. The bargain was agreed upon, and Randall must go alone. Then Eliza ran to him; embraced him passionately; kissed him again and again; told him to remember her—all the while her tears falling in the boy's face like rain.

Freeman damned her, calling her a blubbering, bawling wench, and ordered her to go to her place, and behave herself, and be somebody. He swore he wouldn't stand such stuff but a little longer. He would soon give her something to cry about, if she was not mighty careful, and *that* she might depend upon.

The planter from Baton Rouge, with his new purchases, was ready to depart.

"Don't cry, mama. I will be a good boy. Don't cry," said Randall, looking back, as they passed out of the door.

What has become of the lad, God knows. It was a mournful scene indeed. I would have cried myself if I had dared.

12

Frederick Douglass Fights a Slave-Breaker (1845)

Frederick Douglass was the most famous black abolitionist in the country. Born a slave in Maryland, he never knew who his white father was. He grew up on a large plantation, where he learned the deprivation and privilege that slavery represented. When he was eight, he had what he considered the good fortune to be sent to Baltimore, where he was first a house servant and then a skilled worker in the city's shipyards. His Baltimore mistress taught him to read and write, and afterwards he continued his self-education. Following his Baltimore owner's death, however, he returned to the country to work on the farm of his new master. Accustomed to the relative freedom and excitement of the city, Douglass was unhappy on the plantation and increasingly rebelled. His owner finally hired Edward Covey, a professional slave-breaker, to transform Douglass into a willing and obedient slave. A clash of wills ensued, and in the following passage Douglass discusses his final confrontation with Covey, from which he dated his determination to be free. During his distinguished life, Douglass wrote three autobiographies. This excerpt is taken from the first one, A Narrative of the Life of Frederick Douglass, *published in 1845.*

Master Thomas at length said he would stand it no longer. I had lived with him nine months, during which time he had given me a number of severe whippings, all to no good purpose. He resolved to put me out, as he said, to be broken; and, for this purpose, he let me for one year to a man named Edward Covey. . . .

I left Master Thomas's house, and went to live with Mr. Covey, on the 1st of January, 1833. I was now, for the first time in my life, a field hand. . . .

I lived with Mr. Covey one year. During the first six months, of that year, scarce a week passed without his whipping me. I was seldom free from a sore back. My awkwardness was almost always his excuse for whipping me. We were worked fully up to the point of endurance. Long before day we were up, our horses fed, and by the first approach of day we were off to the field with our hoes and ploughing teams. Mr. Covey gave us enough to eat, but scarce time to eat it. We were often less than five minutes taking our meals. We were often in the field from the first approach of day till its last lingering ray had left us; and at saving-fodder time, midnight often caught us in the field binding blades. . . .

If at any one time of my life more than another, I was made to drink the bitterest dregs of slavery, that time was during the first six months of my stay with Mr. Covey. We were worked in all weathers. It was never too hot or too cold; it could never rain, blow, hail, or snow, too hard for us to work in the field. Work, work, work, was scarcely more the order of the day than of the night. The longest days were too short for him, and the shortest nights too long for him. I was somewhat unmanageable when I first went there, but a few

months of this discipline tamed me. Mr. Covey succeeded in breaking me. I was broken in body, soul, and spirit. . . .

I have already intimated that my condition was much worse, during the first six months of my stay at Mr. Covey's, than in the last six. The circumstances leading to the change in Mr. Covey's course toward me form an epoch in my humble history. You have seen how a man was made a slave; you shall see how a slave was made a man. . . .

. . . Long before daylight, I was called to go and rub, curry, and feed, the horses. I obeyed, and was glad to obey. But whilst thus engaged, whilst in the act of throwing down some blades from the loft, Mr. Covey entered the stable with a long rope; and just as I was half out of the loft, he caught hold of my legs, and was about tying me. As soon as I found what he was up to, I gave a sudden spring, and as I did so, he holding to my legs, I was brought sprawling on the stable floor. Mr. Covey seemed now to think he had me, and could do what he pleased; but at this moment—from whence came the spirit I don't know—I resolved to fight; and, suiting my action to the resolution, I seized Covey hard by the throat; and as I did so, I rose. He held on to me, and I to him. My resistance was so entirely unexpected, that Covey seemed taken all aback. He trembled like a leaf. This gave me assurance, and I held him uneasy, causing the blood to run where I touched him with the ends of my fingers. Mr. Covey soon called out to Hughes for help. Hughes came, and, while Covey held me, attempted to tie my right hand. While he was in the act of doing so, I watched my chance, and gave him a heavy kick close under the ribs. This kick fairly sickened Hughes, so that he left me in the hands of Mr. Covey. This kick had the effect of not only weakening Hughes, but Covey also. When he saw Hughes bending over with pain, his courage quailed. He asked me if I meant to persist in my re-

FROM *A Narrative of the Life of Frederick Douglass: An American Slave. Written by Himself* (Boston: Anti-Slavery Office, 1845), pp. 56–73.

sistance. I told him I did, come what might; that he had used me like a brute for six months, and that I was determined to be used so no longer. With that, he strove to drag me to a stick that was lying just out of the stable door. He meant to knock me down. But just as he was leaning over to get the stick, I seized him with both hands by his collar, and brought him by a sudden snatch to the ground. By this time, Bill came. Covey called upon him for assistance. Bill wanted to know what he could do. Covey said, "Take hold of him, take hold of him!" Bill said his master hired him out to work, and not to help to whip me; so he left Covey and myself to fight our own battle out. We were at it for nearly two hours. Covey at length let me go, puffing and blowing at a great rate, saying that if I had not resisted, he would not have whipped me half so much. The truth was, that he had not whipped me at all. I considered him as getting entirely the worst end of the bargain; for he had drawn no blood from me, but I had from him. The whole six months afterwards, that I spent with Mr. Covey, he never laid the weight of his finger upon me in anger. He would occasionally say, he didn't want to get hold of me again. "No," thought I, "you need not; for you will come off worse than you did before."

This battle with Mr. Covey was the turning-point in my career as a slave. It rekindled the few expiring embers of freedom, and revived within me a sense of my own manhood. It recalled the departed self-confidence, and inspired me again with a determination to be free. . . . He only can understand the deep satisfacton which I experienced, who has himself repelled by force the bloody arm of slavery. I felt as I never felt before. It was a glorious resurrection, from the tomb of slavery, to the heaven of freedom. My long-crushed spirit rose, cowardice departed, bold defiance took its place; and I now resolved that, however long I might remain a slave in form, the day had passed forever when I could be a slave in fact.

1

DAVID WILMOT

I Plead the Cause of White Freemen (1847)

David Wilmot was an obscure and somewhat lazy Democratic congressman from Pennsylvania when, in 1846, he gained instant notoriety by introducing an amendment to an appropriation bill requested by President James K. Polk to promote peace negotiations with Mexico. Wilmot's amendment, which reflected growing northern resentment over the proslavery policies of Polk and his advisors, prohibited slavery from any territory acquired from Mexico as a result of the Mexican War. Known henceforth as the Wilmot Proviso, his amendment attracted considerable support from northern congressmen and passed the House several times, although it was always rejected by the Senate. In the following speech, delivered in the House in early 1847, Wilmot outlined his reasons for opposing the further expansion of slavery.

I make no war upon the South nor upon slavery in the South. I have no squeamish sensitiveness upon the subject of slavery, nor morbid sympathy for the slave. I plead the cause of the rights of white freemen. I would preserve for free white labor a fair country, a rich inheritance, where the sons of toil, of my own race and own color, can live without the disgrace which association with negro slavery brings upon free labor. I stand for the inviolability of free territory. It shall remain free, so far as my voice or vote can aid in the preservation of its character.

This, sir, is what we ask, and all we ask. Yet the majority of this House, reflecting the will of a vast majority of the freemen of this Republic, a majority of the Republicans of the North, are called upon to yield—what? To make concession of things that ought to be conceded? No; they are required to surrender the dearest rights, to violate the most sacred obligations. Where is the northern man prepared to do it? I am a man of concession, of compromise; but to compromise on this question is to surrender the right and establish the wrong. It is to carry slavery where it does not now exist, to subjugate free territory. If we refuse to convert free into slave territory, is that an invasion of the rights of the South? . . . The future greatness and glory of this Republic demands that the progress of domestic slavery should be arrested now and forever. Let it remain where it now is, and leave to time and a merciful Providence its results.

Sir, upon this subject, the North has yielded until there is no more to give up. We have gone on, making one acquisition after another, until we have acquired and brought into the Union every inch of slave territory that was to be found upon this Continent. Now, sir, we have passed beyond the boundaries of slavery and reached free-soil. Who is willing to surrender it? Men of the North—representatives of northern freedom, will you con-

FROM *Congressional Globe*, 29th Cong., 2d sess., 1847, Appendix, p. 317.

summate such a deed of infamy and shame? I trust in God not. O, for the honor of the North—for the fair fame of our green hills and valleys, be firm in this crisis—be true to your country and your race. The white laborer of the North claims your service; he demands that you stand firm to his interests and his rights; that you preserve the future homes of his children, on the distant shores of the Pacific, from the degradation and dishonor of negro servitude. Where the negro slave labors, the free white man cannot labor by his side without sharing in his degradation and disgrace.

2

HOWELL COBB

The South Is at Your Mercy (1847)

A classic political insider accustomed to the trappings of power and influence, Howell Cobb of Georgia was a leading southern moderate. He served as Speaker of the House, was elected governor in Georgia on a Unionist ticket in 1851, and was secretary of the treasury in James Buchanan's cabinet. Following Lincoln's election, the paunchy Cobb suddenly flip-flopped and became a secessionist, but up until that point he had been a spokesman in national politics for compromise and sectional moderation. Invoking a sense of equity, he made the following remarks opposing the Wilmot Proviso in the House in 1847.

Upon this subject of the institution of slavery—this peculiar subject of sectional jealousy—there is a spirit of compromise running through the Constitution, not confined to isolated paragraphs, but breathing throughout the whole instrument. That spirit of compromise recognised the existence of these sectional interests. The object was to guard them, to protect them, to make the one a check upon the other. The inducement held out to the South, at the time this Constitution was framed, was the spirit of compromise upon this question. She asked, and she had granted to her at that time, such power and such influence as would enable her to be a check upon the North; so that no attempt could ever be made successfully to interfere with the rights of the South. But where is that spirit now? Where is that regard, on the part of the North, for the rights of the South? And where are those rights, when the views presented by the gentlemen who advocate this amendment are carried out? Where is the check which the South was induced by this Constitution to believe she would always be enabled to hold upon her sister States of the North? This amendment [Wilmot Proviso] provides that no territory which may hereafter be acquired, from whatever quarter, from whatever section of the country it may come, shall ever be made subject to settlement by the people of the slaveholding States. You of the North extend your territory, your government, your power, strength, and influence, day by day, and year by year; but here stands the South, her limits fixed, bound hand and foot, subject to your mercy, and to such legislation as you may think proper upon the subject of her institutions and her rights to make. . . .

FROM *Congressional Globe*, 29th Cong., 2d sess., 1847, pp. 361–62.

The gentleman from Pennsylvania [David Wilmot] said that all the North asked was, that this Government should occupy a position of neutrality. What kind of neutrality? To allow the people of this country to settle this territory, and then to determine for themselves the form of its government, the character of its institutions? That, sir, would be neutrality in fact, upon the part of this Government. That would be taking no part or lot in the matter. And does the South step forward to ask any single enactment on the part of this Government, in regard to what shall be the character of the institutions of this territory? How is it that the gentleman from Pennsylvania can charge southern Representatives here, and the people of the South, with an intention or wish to violate the spirit of neutrality on the part of the General Government, when they have not raised their voice for the first time to ask a single provision of law in reference to this subject?

But is the gentleman from Pennsylvania himself willing that the Government should observe that spirit of neutrality which he professes to approve? Is he willing to trust the American people, the settlers upon this territory, to determine for themselves the nature of the institution under which they shall live, and the form of Government to which they shall be subject? No, sir. He steps forward and calls upon this Government to array itself upon the part of the strength of the Union against the weakness of the Union, (for such is the condition of the North and South upon this matter, considered numerically.) And this is the "neutrality" which gentlemen from the North desire.

3

JOHN C. CALHOUN

The Cords of Union Are Snapping One by One (1850)

John C. Calhoun of South Carolina was one of the political giants of the antebellum period. He had served in the House and the Senate, in the cabinet as both secretary of war and secretary of state, and as vice president. Initially a nationalist, Calhoun by the 1830s had become an ardent proponent of states' rights and strict construction of the Constitution. Over the years he became increasingly consumed with the slavery issue. He distrusted the two major parties as unreliable on this issue, and he labored diligently—and unsuccessfully—to get southerners to leave the two parties and unite in a southern party under his leadership. Only a southern sectional party, Calhoun was convinced, could protect the rights of the minority South and thus preserve the Union. By 1850 Calhoun had been in public life for four decades and was near death. In this selection, his final speech to the Senate (which a colleague had to read for him), he opposed Clay's compromise proposals and warned that unless southern rights were protected, the destruction of the Union was inevitable.

I have, Senators, believed from the first that the agitation of the subject of slavery would, if not prevented by some timely and effective measure, end in disunion. Entertaining this opinion, I have, on all proper occasions, endeavored to call the attention of both the two great parties which divide the country to adopt some measure to prevent so great a disaster, but without success. The agitation has been permitted to proceed, with almost no attempt to resist it, until it has reached a point when it can no longer be disguised or denied that the Union is in danger. You have thus had forced upon you the greatest and the gravest question that can ever come under your consideration—How can the Union be preserved?

To give a satisfactory answer to this mighty question, it is indispensable to have an accurate and thorough knowledge of the nature and the character of the cause by which the Union is endangered. . . . What is it that has endangered the Union?

To this question there can be but one answer,—that the immediate cause is the almost universal discontent which pervades all the States composing the Southern section of the Union. This widely-extended discontent is not of recent origin. It commenced with the agitation of the slavery question, and has been increasing ever since. . . . What has caused this widely diffused and almost universal discontent?

. . . It will be found in the belief of the people of the Southern States, as prevalent as the discontent itself, that they cannot remain, as things now are, consistently with honor and safety, in the Union. The next question to be considered is—What has caused this belief?

One of the causes is, undoubtedly, to be traced to the long-continued agitation of the slave question on the part of the North, and the many aggressions which they have made on the rights of the South during the time. . . .

There is another lying back of it—with which this is intimately connected—that may be regarded as the great and primary cause. This is to be found in the fact that the equilibrium between the two sections, in the Government as it stood when the constitution was ratified and the Government put in action, has been destroyed. At that time there was nearly a perfect equilibrium between the two, which afforded ample means to each to protect itself against the aggression of the other; but, as it now stands, one section has the exclusive power of controlling the Government, which leaves the other without any adequate means of protecting itself against its encroachment and oppression. . . .

It is a great mistake to suppose that disunion can be effected by a single blow. The cords which bound these States together in one common Union, are far too numerous and powerful for that. Disunion must be the work of time. It is only through a long process, and successively, that the cords can be snapped, until the whole fabric falls asunder. Already the agitation of the slavery question has snapped some of the most important, and has greatly weakened all the others, as I shall proceed to show.

The cords that bind the States together are not only many, but various in character. Some are spiritual or ecclesiastical; some political; others social. Some appertain to the benefit conferred by the Union, and others to the feeling of duty and obligation. . . .

The first of these cords which snapped, under its explosive force, was that of the powerful Methodist Episcopal Church. The numerous and strong ties which held it together, are all broken, and its unity gone. They now form separate churches; and, instead of that feeling of attachment and devotion to the interests of the whole church which was formerly felt, they are now arrayed into two hostile bodies, engaged in litigation about what was formerly their common property.

The next cord that snapped was that of the Baptists—one of the largest and most respectable of the denominations. That of the Presbyterian is not entirely snapped, but some of its strands have given way. That of the Episcopal Church is the

FROM Richard K. Crallé, ed., *Speeches of John C. Calhoun*, vol. 4 (New York: D. Appleton and Company, 1854), pp. 542–44, 551–57, 570–72.

only one of the four great Protestant denominations which remains unbroken and entire.

The strongest cord, of a political character, consists of the many and powerful ties that have held together the two great parties which have, with some modifications, existed from the beginning of the Government. They both extended to every portion of the Union, and strongly contributed to hold all its parts together. But this powerful cord has fared no better than the spiritual. It resisted, for a long time, the explosive tendency of the agitation, but has finally snapped under its force—if not entirely, in a great measure. Nor is there one of the remaining cords which has not been greatly weakened. To this extent the Union has already been destroyed by agitation, in the only way it can be, by sundering and weakening the cords which bind it together.

If the agitation goes on, the same force, acting with increased intensity, as has been shown, will finally snap every cord, when nothing will be left to hold the States together except force. . . .

. . . I return to the question with which I commenced, How can the Union be saved? There is but one way by which it can with any certainty; and that is, by a full and final settlement, on the principle of justice, of all the questions at issue between the two sections. The South asks for justice, simple justice, and less she ought not to take. She has no compromise to offer, but the constitution; and no concession or surrender to make. She has already surrendered so much that she has little left to surrender. Such a settlement would go to the root of the evil, and remove all cause of discontent, by satisfying the South, she could remain honorably and safely in the Union, and thereby restore the harmony and fraternal feelings between the sections, which existed anterior to the Missouri agitation. Nothing else can, with any certainty, finally and for ever settle the questions at issue, terminate agitation, and save the Union.

. . . The North has only to will it to accomplish it—to do justice by conceding to the South an equal right in the acquired territory, and to do her duty by causing the stipulations relative to fugitive slaves to be faithfully fulfilled—to cease the agitation of the slave question, and to provide for the insertion of a provision in the constitution, by an amendment, which will restore to the South, in substance, the power she possessed of protecting herself, before the equilibrium between the sections was destroyed by the action of this Government.

4

DANIEL WEBSTER

I Speak Today for the Preservation of the Union (1850)

Henry Clay made a personal plea to his old adversary, Senator Daniel Webster of Massachusetts, to support his compromise plan in 1850. Webster announced his support for Clay's effort in his famous Seventh of March speech. In this speech, Webster abandoned his earlier support for the Wilmot Proviso, terming it unnecessary to protect the territories for freedom. Climate and soil, he insisted, would keep southern staple crops—and slavery—out of the arid southwest. A skilled orator and spokesman for nationalism, Webster had increasingly clashed with the antislavery movement in his home state of Massachusetts. The suspicion of antislavery leaders ripened into intense hatred following this speech, and they bitterly denounced Webster for betraying the North and the cause of free soil. For his part, Webster was determined to purge the Whig party of its advanced antislavery elements, and in the aftermath of the passage of the Compromise of 1850, he laid plans to seek the party's 1852 presidential nomination on a pro-Union, pro-Compromise platform.

I wish to speak to-day, not as a Massachusetts man, nor as a Northern man, but as an American, and a member of the Senate of the United States.... I speak to-day for the preservation of the Union. "Hear me for my cause." I speak to-day, out of a solicitous and anxious heart, for the restoration to the country of that quiet and that harmony which make the blessings of this Union so rich, and so dear to us all....

... The annexation of Texas, upon the conditions and under the guaranties upon which she was admitted, did not leave within the control of this government an acre of land, capable of being cultivated by slave labor, between this Capitol and the Rio Grande or the Nueces, or whatever is the proper boundary of Texas; not an acre. From that moment, the whole country, from this place to the western boundary of Texas, was fixed, pledged, fastened, decided, to be slave territory for ever, by the solemn guaranties of law. And I now say, Sir, as the proposition upon which I stand this day, and upon the truth and firmness of which I intend to act until it is overthrown, that there is not at this moment within the United States, or any territory of the United States, a single foot of land, the character of which, in regard to its being free territory or slave territory, is not fixed by some law, and some irrepealable law, beyond the power of the action of the government....

Now, as to California and New Mexico, I hold slavery to be excluded from those territories by a law even superior to that which admits and sanctions it in Texas. I mean the law of nature, of physical geography, the law of the formation of the earth. That law settles for ever, with a strength beyond all terms of human enactment, that slavery cannot exist in California or New Mexico.... It is as impossible that African slavery, as we see it among us, should find its way, or be introduced, into California and New Mexico, as any other natural impossibility....

I look upon it, therefore, as a fixed fact, to use the current expression of the day, that both California and New Mexico are destined to be free, so far as they are settled at all, which I believe, in regard to New Mexico, will be but partially for a great length of time; free by the arrangement of things ordained by the Power above us. I have therefore to say, in this respect also, that this country is fixed for freedom, to as many persons as shall ever live in it, by a less repealable law than that which attaches to the right of holding slaves in Texas; and I will say further, that, if a resolution or a bill were now before us, to provide a territorial government for New Mexico, I would not vote to put any prohibition into it whatever. Such a prohibition would be idle, as it respects any effect it would have upon the territory; and I would not take pains uselessly to reaffirm an ordinance of nature, nor to reënact the will of God. I would put in no Wilmot Proviso for the mere purpose of a taunt or a reproach. I would put into it no evidence of the votes of superior power, exercised for no purpose but to wound the pride ... of the citizens of the Southern States....

... Sir, wherever there is a substantive good to be done, wherever there is a foot of land to be prevented from becoming slave territory, I am ready to assert the principle of the exclusion of slavery. I am pledged to it from the year 1837; I have been pledged to it again and again; and I will perform those pledges; but I will not do a thing unnecessarily that wounds the feelings of others, or that does discredit to my own understanding.

FROM J. W. Paige, ed., *The Works of Daniel Webster*, vol. 5 (Boston: Charles C. Little and James Brown, 1851), pp. 325–26, 340, 350–53, 365–66.

Now, Mr. President, I have established, so far as I proposed to do so, the proposition with which I set out, and upon which I intend to stand or fall; and that is, that the whole territory within the former United States, or in the newly acquired Mexican provinces, has a fixed and settled character, now fixed and settled by law which cannot be repealed; in the case of Texas without a violation of public faith, and by no human power in regard to California or New Mexico; that, therefore, under one or other of these laws, every foot of land in the States or in the Territories has already received a fixed and decided character.

5

Appeal of the Independent Democrats (1854)

When Stephen A. Douglas introduced the Kansas-Nebraska bill in January, 1854, six Free-Soil congressmen quickly issued an appeal to northern public opinion to oppose the attempt to overthrow the Missouri Compromise of 1820, which had prohibited slavery from this region of the Louisiana Purchase. Primarily written by Salmon P. Chase, the Free-Soil senator from Ohio, the appeal generated controversy, in part because the signers rushed it to print rather than modify its language to attract more signers, and in part for its charge that the bill was part of a "plot" to expand slavery. The idea of a conspiracy to expand slavery would become an increasingly important component of the antislavery movement in the 1850s. The appeal was widely published in northern newspapers that opposed Douglas's bill.

As Senators and Representatives in the Congress of the United States, . . . it is our duty to warn our constituents, whenever imminent danger menaces the freedom of our institutions or the permanency of the Union.

Such danger, as we firmly believe, now impends, and we earnestly solicit your prompt attention to it. . . .

At the present session a new Nebraska Bill has been reported by the Senate Committee on Territories, which, should it unhappily receive the sanction of Congress, will open all the unorganized Territories of the Union to the ingress of slavery.

We arraign this bill as a gross violation of a sacred pledge; as a criminal betrayal of precious rights; as part and parcel of an atrocious plot to exclude from a vast unoccupied region immigrants from the Old World and free laborers from our own States, and convert it into a dreary region of despotism, inhabited by masters and slaves. . . .

This immense region, occupying the very heart of the North American Continent, and larger, by thirty-three thousand square miles, than all the existing free States—including California; this immense region, well watered and fertile, through which the middle and northern routes from the Atlantic to the Pacific must pass, this immense region, embracing all the unorganized territory of the nation, except the comparatively insignificant district of Indian Territory north of Red River and between Arkansas and Texas, and now for more than thirty years regarded by the common consent of the American people as consecrated to freedom by statute and by compact—this immense region the bill now before the Senate, without reason and

FROM J. W. Schuckers, *The Life and Public Services of S. P. Chase* (New York: D. Appleton and Co., 1874), pp. 140–47.

without excuse, but in flagrant disregard of sound policy and sacred faith, purposes to open to slavery. . . .

. . . [In 1820] Missouri was allowed to come into the Union with slavery; but a section was inserted in the act authorizing her admission, excluding slavery forever from all the territory acquired from France, not included in the new State, lying north of 36° 30'. . . .

The question of the constitutionality of this prohibition was submitted by President Monroe to his cabinet. John Quincy Adams was then Secretary of State; John C. Calhoun was Secretary of War; William H. Crawford was Secretary of the Treasury; and William Wirt was Attorney-General. Each of these eminent gentlemen—three of them being from the slave States—gave a written opinion, affirming its constitutionality, and thereupon the act received the sanction of the President himself, also from a slave State.

. . . Nothing is more certain than that this prohibition has been regarded and accepted by the whole country as a solemn compact against the extension of slavery into any part of the territory acquired from France lying north of 36° 30', and not included in the new State of Missouri. The same act—let it be ever remembered—which authorized the formation of a constitution by the State, without a clause forbidding slavery, consecrated, beyond question and beyond honest recall, the whole remainder of the Territory to freedom and free institutions forever. For more than thirty years—during more than half our national existence under our present Constitution—this compact has been universally regarded and acted upon as inviolable American law. In conformity with it, Iowa was admitted as a free State and Minnesota has been organized as a free Territory.

It is a strange and ominous fact, well calculated to awaken the worst apprehensions and the most fearful forebodings of future calamities, that it is now deliberately proposed to repeal this prohibition, by implication or directly—the latter cer-

tainly the manlier way—and thus to subvert the compact, and allow slavery in all the yet unorganized territory. . . .

We appeal to the people. We warn you that the dearest interests of freedom and the Union are in imminent peril. Demagogues may tell you that the Union can be maintained only by submitting to the demands of slavery. We tell you that the Union can only be maintained by the full recognition of the just claims of freedom and man. The Union was formed to establish justice and secure the blessings of liberty. When it fails to accomplish these ends it will be worthless, and when it becomes worthless it cannot long endure.

We entreat you to be mindful of that fundamental maxim of Democracy—EQUAL RIGHTS AND EXACT JUSTICE FOR ALL MEN. Do not submit to become agents in extending legalized oppression and systematized injustice over a vast territory yet exempt from these terrible evils.

We implore Christians and Christian ministers to interpose. Their divine religion requires them to behold in every man a brother, and to labor for the advancement and regeneration of the human race.

Whatever apologies may be offered for the toleration of slavery in the States, none can be offered for its extension into Territories where it does not exist, and where that extension involves the repeal of ancient law and the violation of solemn compact. Let all protest, earnestly and emphatically, by correspondence, through the press, by memorials, by resolutions of public meetings and legislative bodies, and in whatever other mode may seem expedient, against this enormous crime.

For ourselves, we shall resist it by speech and vote, and with all the abilities which God has given us. Even if overcome in the impending struggle, we shall not submit. We shall go home to our constituents, erect anew the standard of freedom, and call on the people to come to the rescue of the country from the domination of slavery. We will not despair; for the cause of human freedom is the cause of God.

6

NEW YORK TIMES

The Causes of the
Know-Nothing Movement (1854)

The New York Times *was the voice of Whig (and later Republican) respectability and moderation in the nation's metropolis. It never supported the nativist Know-Nothing movement, although it granted that some of the party's concerns were legitimate. In late 1854, following the Know-Nothings' remarkable showing in the recent elections in New York and other northern states, the* Times *offered an unusually balanced and perceptive discussion of the reasons for the movement's popular strength.*

It is generally conceded by every one who understands history, that there is never a great popular movement without some deep reason for it. The mind of multitudes of men cannot be stirred on a great scale by a mere fancy. The idea which they proclaim as the party watchword may be foolish, or bigoted or narrow;—it may not be the one which really moves them. Still there is at the basis *some* great impelling cause which is worth careful consideration. More than this;—these movements do not always produce the effects which were intended by the men who supposed they were the authors and leaders of them. They aim at one thing, and may suppose they are all the while working towards it; but one who looks calmly at them from a distance can see,—what the event generally proves,—that they are guided to a very different result. . . .

. . . We believe these principles will be found equally true of this new popular movement, which is vibrating over the country. Those who sneer at it as the fruit of a sudden conspiracy of disappointed office-seekers, or as an ingenious device of petty politicians on a large scale, to secure places, will see by the issue that they do not understand the peo-

ple. They do not remember what this movement has done within the space of a few months, in the most intelligent and high-minded population of the Union. Without presses, without electioneering, with no prestige or power, it has completely overthrown and swamped the two old historic parties of the country, paralyzed their action, deprived them to a greater or less extent of influence and of office, and now sways public sentiment even where it has not yet absorbed political power. . . . Such a vast popular movement cannot proceed from any such petty motive as the mere hunting of office. The great surges of the people are not impelled by any such mean cause.

Nor is it to be supposed that such a movement rests upon no broader basis, than hatred of men because they were born on a different soil, and still less because they hold a religious faith different from our own. The day has passed, we trust forever, for religious warfares. On this free soil, won with the blood of men of all creeds; under a Republic which boasts that it shelters, unmolested, every human opinion, the party could not live, could never arise, which should have as its great object the persecution a particular religion or sect. It is not an unreasoning religious bigotry which has principally aroused this great hidden popular movement. Nor do we believe any exclusive Native

American prejudice has been its principal impulse. Our houses are yet full of the memorials of those men who left but two centuries ago *their country* to build a free government on a foreign shore. . . . Our own fathers were foreigners. The blood of strangers—of the chivalric French and the heroic Pole—was poured out in our cause. It was the boast and the inspiration of those men that they were building up a State, not for Anglo-Saxons, but for humanity. . . . Since then, foreigners have incessantly poured in. Their labor has aided in our public works; they have performed the lower tasks, giving an opportunity for the more inventive genius and the bolder spirit of the leading race to secure the grand and more valuable labors of the country. Their toil and their lives have been also contributed in erecting this noble structure of our prosperity. There would be a glaring inconsistency between our principles and our practices, if we were now to abandon the broad liberty for all which has been our boast, and hedge ourselves and our institutions around with the high walls of exclusion. . . . And it would certainly be the height of inconsistency to meet them [immigrants] when they arrive, with the repelling claim that "America is for the Americans"—that they are not of us,—that they may *labor* here, but shall have no share in our birthright. Such a course would be un-American,—hostile to all our history and to the whole spirit of our institutions. . . .

The present movement is due to a deeper, juster, profounder sentiment than that which would counsel such exclusiveness. Bigotry and hostility to foreigners *as such* have had much to do with it; they may have mingled with its tide and given strength to its swell and its sweep. But they are not its main elements. It owes its origin, and will owe its success, to other influences. We believe the present movement is due mainly to the conviction that the liberty we grant to aliens of becoming American citizens has been grossly abused;—that under cover of this privilege the pauperism, the ignorance, the crime of the old countries have been emptied out upon our shores with hostile recklessness of our interests and our rights,—that the Roman Catholic vote has been held in a com-

pact, disciplined mass, under the immediate and supreme control of a hierarchy whose interests and sympathies lead them to resist and denounce every attempt at freedom for the people of Europe, and who hold these votes for the political party that will bid the highest for them,—and that this element, foreign in its origin, ignorant and irresponsible in its character, and secret in its operation, has long been courted by political parties, and has more than once decided the policy and the career of the country at large. This conviction comes, moreover, just at a time when the old political parties have lost their hold upon the confidence of the people,—when the issues that have divided them have been decided or have died out,—when their machinery of intrigue, their shuffling evasions, the dodges, the chicanery and the deception of their leaders have excited universal disgust, and have created a general readiness in the public mind for any new organization that shall promise to shun their vices and combine the elements that have hitherto given them strength. The Know-Nothing movement comes just in time to satisfy those vague but powerful cravings of the public mind. It finds support in the profoundest convictions of the public heart, in the patriotism and public spirit, as well as in the passions and prejudices, of the American people. Many vicious elements undoubtedly mingle in this heterogeneous party. There is the love of mystery and of secret organization; there are the new political hopes from a new combination; there is the hatred of the lowest American operatives and tradespeople for foreigners who are their rivals, and above all, the old ineradicable Saxon bigotry, which periodically likes a crusade against the Pope. But all these are subordinate to the influences we have already noted, as in our judgment at the bottom of the movement, and will in due time give peace to them. . . .

If we had any right to offer counsel to the leaders and the guides of this new and potent organization, or any hope that it would be heeded, we should caution them against the danger of being pushed into extremes fatal to their cause, because hostile to the public good. They have at heart, we do not doubt, the welfare of our Republic—the stability of our Union—the perpetuity and the enlargement of our Freedom. Let them be careful, then, how they light the fires of sectarian hatred, or the jealousies of nationality, in a country like ours. . . . The Union, to last, must be a *fusion of the peoples* who live under the shelter of its laws and the shadow of its flag. To permanently disfranchise any race of men among us is utterly at war with Democratic principles. The only basis of our general suffrage has always been the principle that giving a privilege fits men for using it. That time should be required, before the foreigner is allowed to vote, seems a common-sense principle; but against anything like disfranchisement or proscription from office, every true Republican must earnestly appeal. Indeed, in this day of the world, we are sure no party would dare uphold such a principle long on American soil. The tide of the age—the dictate of reason—sets against them.

Let us adopt such precautions as may seem necessary against the temporary evils which the overwhelming influx of foreign ignorance and superstition and crime may threaten. Let our naturalization laws be amended if they need it,—let secret organizations, controlled by a central head, for purposes other than the public good, be met and offset by other societies using the same instruments, if such a course shall seem best adapted to the emergency;—but let us bear in mind that our free schools, our free press, our open churches, our atmosphere of civil and religious liberty, and the natural progress of human society, give us the best of all assurance for the preservation of our institutions alike from religious bigotry and from the ignorance and crime which are poured out so lavishly upon our shores. Let us protect *them* from invasion, and we need have no fears for the final result.

MOBILE REGISTER

The South Asks Only for Equal Rights in the Territories (1856)

The following editorial from an Alabama newspaper analyzes the controversy between the North and the South over the status of slavery in the territories from the perspective of the South. While its tone is calm and rational, it insists that the northern position is unfair to the South, which is seeking the same rights in the territories.

The great quarrel going on between the North and South must strike a disinterested observer (if there be such a thing in the world, on a question that has engaged all minds on one side or the other,) with astonishment, at the arrogance of the demands on one side, and the unheeded plea on the other side, for simple justice. What does the

South ask? Anything that the North cannot give and ought not to give? Do we demand that no more *free* States shall be admitted to the Union? Do we ask to be permitted officiously to intermeddle with the domestic polity of the free States?— Do we claim that the common territories shall be given up exclusively to the use, occupation and enjoyment of the people and institutions of the South? Nothing of the kind. We simply say to the North, we are your equals in the Union, attend to

FROM *Mobile Register*, 1 February 1856.

your affairs and leave us quietly to manage ours. The territories are a common acquisition and a common property. Do not destroy this community, by Federal legislation, the effect of which is to exclude us and to make over the whole domain to you. When a territory passes from its embryo condition, . . . the South does not declare in advance that the new State shall be excluded from the Union, if it chooses to adopt a free labor Constitution. But it leaves this question to be determined by the free will of the new sovereign, and accepts their decision as final. The position of the two sections is clearly illustrated in the following article from the Richmond Enquirer, which shows that if the South could so far forget what is due to its confederates, and were to retort upon them in kind, the demands which are made upon her, she could do so with great show of reason, though at the expense of an immense hubbub from the North:

NO MORE SLAVE STATES.—Suppose the South should insist that there should be no more free States; would not there be far more of good sense, of humanity and justice, in her position, than in that of the North?

First—slavery excludes, neither in theory or practice, any law-abiding citizens of free States from the States where it exists. Slave States are equally open to all the people of the Union with all of their property.

Secondly—All the territory out of which new States are to be formed, was either ceded to the Union by slave States, or acquired chiefly by Southern counsels, Southern arms, Southern soldiers and Southern Statesmen. . . .

Thirdly—Slave society is the oldest, the most common, and the most natural form of society; whilst free society is a little experiment, small in extent, and short in duration, yet which has been attended (by the showing of its own authors,) with a thousand times greater evils, than slavery has inflicted on mankind, throughout all ages, and all countries. . . .

In view of these facts, would it not be more reasonable for the South to object to the admission of free States, than for the North to refuse to admit slave States.

We do not intend to imitate the North, become speculative philanthropists and try to set the world to rights, else we might well insist there should be no more free States. We do not wish to abolish free society, nor to prevent its introduction into a fair proportion of the new States, nor do we wish to introduce slavery into any State whose people exclude it when prepared to be admitted as States. Such exclusion is a gross act of injustice to the South; but we are practical men, and will not quarrel about abstractions. If Southern institutions are admitted into a sufficient number of the new States, we shall be satisfied.

8

NEW YORK EVENING POST

Are We Too Slaves? (1856)

Edited by the famous writer and poet William Cullen Bryant, the New York Evening Post *had originally been a Democratic newspaper. Its antislavery principles, however, led it to abandon the Democratic party in the mid-1850s and support the new Republican party. It was the organ of the former Democrats who joined the Republican party in New York. In the following editorial, which appeared the day after Brooks's attack on Sumner, it comments on the significance of this event.*

The excuse for this base assault is, that Mr. Sumner, on the Senate floor, in the course of debate had spoken disrespectfully of Mr. Butler, a relative of Preston S. Brooks, one of the authors of this outrage. No possible indecorum of language on the part of Mr. Sumner could excuse, much less justify, an attack like this; but we have carefully examined his speech to see if it contains any matter which could even extenuate such an act of violence, and find none. He had ridiculed Mr. Butler's devotion to slavery it is true, but the weapon of ridicule in debate is by common consent as fair and allowable a weapon as argument. . . .

Has it come to this, that we must speak with bated breath in the presence of our Southern masters; that even their follies are too sacred a subject of ridicule; that we must not deny the consistency of their principles or the accuracy of their statements? If we venture to laugh at them, or question their logic, or dispute their facts, are we to be chastised as they chastise their slaves? Are we too, slaves, slaves for life, a target for their brutal blows, when we do not comport ourselves to please them? If this be so, it is time that the people of the free states knew it, and prepared themselves to acquiesce in their fate. They have labored under the delusion hitherto that they were their own masters.

. . . The sudden attack made with deadly weapons upon an unarmed man in the Senate Chamber, where he could not expect it or have been prepared for it, was the act of men who must be poltroons as well as ruffians. It was as indecent, also, as it was cowardly; the Senate floor should be sacred from such outrages; or, if they are committed at all, it should only be by Senatorial blackguards. It is true that the Senate had just adjourned, but the members were still there, many of them in their places; it was their chamber, and this violence committed in their presence was an insult to their body. Yet we have no expectation that the Senate will do anything to vindicate the sacredness and peace of their chamber, or the right of their members not to be called to account for words spoken in debate. There will be a little discussion; some will denounce and some will defend the assault, and there the matter will end.

The truth is, that the pro-slavery party, which rules in the Senate looks upon violence as the proper instrument of its designs. Violence reigns in the streets of Washington; they are not safe for the man who speaks his mind without reserve. . . . It had been supposed that the Senate Chamber, the room dedicated to the sittings of that "dignified body," as it has been called, was at least free from the intrusion of outside bullies, but violence has now found its way into the Senate chamber. Violence lies in wait on all the navigable rivers and all the railways of Missouri, to obstruct those who pass from the free states to Kansas. Violence overhangs the frontier of that territory like a storm-cloud charged with hail and lightning. Violence has carried election after election in that territory, violence has imposed upon the inhabitants a fictitious legislature and a tyrannical code of laws, and violence is mustering her myrmidons to put that code in execution. In short, violence is the order of the day; the North is to be pushed to the wall by it, and this plot will succeed if the people of the free states are as apathetic as the slaveholders are insolent.

Since we can expect nothing from Congress, the people of the free states must speak out in their public meetings, and denounce the plot and its authors. Here is an attempt to silence a bold and fearless representative of the free states, whose only offence was that he repelled the attacks upon the rights of his constituents with too much plainness of speech. Will the people of the free states stand by him, or will they desert him like cowards, and own that a northern man, who is above fear in the discharge of his duty, deserves to be beaten like a hound? It is idle to wait for what the Senate may do—the Senate will do nothing—it never does anything on such occasions; the people must take the matter into their own hands.

FROM "The Outrage on Mr. Sumner," *New York Evening Post*, 23 May 1856.

9

They Must Be Lashed into Submission (1856)

Preston S. Brooks's attack on Charles Sumner produced sharply divergent reactions in the North and South. While some voiced minor criticisms, in general southern papers strongly backed Brooks's action. One of the most vehement endorsements appeared in the influential and widely respected Richmond Enquirer. *Already stunned by the fact that a senator had been assaulted in the Senate chamber, northerners were shocked by the language of the southern press in discussing this incident. Because of the* Enquirer's *national stature, its views commanded particular attention in both sections of the country.*

In the main, the press of the South applaud the conduct of Mr. Brooks, without condition or limitation. Our approbation at least is entire and unreserved. We consider the act good in conception, better in execution, and best of all in consequence. These vulgar abolitionists in the Senate are getting above themselves. They have been humored until they forget their position. They have grown saucy, and dare to be impudent to gentlemen! Now, they are a low, mean, scurvy set, with some little book learning, but as utterly devoid of spirit or honor as a pack of curs. Intrenched behind "privilege," they fancy they can slander the South and insult its Representatives, with impunity. The truth is they have been suffered to run too long without collars. They must be lashed into submission. . . . These men are perpetually abusing the people and representatives of the South, for tyrants, robbers, ruffians, adulterers, and what not. Shall we stand it? Can gentlemen sit still in the Senate and House of Representatives, under an incessant stream of denunciation from wretches who avail themselves of the privilege of place, to indulge their devilish passions with impunity? In the absence of an adequate law, Southern gentlemen must protect their own honor and feelings. It is an idle mockery to challenge one of these scullions. It is equally useless to attempt to disgrace them. They are insensible to shame; and can be brought to reason only by an application of cowhide or gutta percha. Let them once understand that for every vile word spoken against the South, they will suffer so many stripes, and they will soon learn to behave themselves, like decent dogs—they can never be gentlemen. Mr. Brooks has initiated this salutary discipline, and he deserves applause for the bold, judicious manner, in which he chastised the scamp Sumner. It was a proper act, done at the proper time, and in the proper place. Of all places on earth the Senate chamber, the theatre of his vituperative exploits, was the very spot where Sumner should have been made to suffer for his violation of the decencies of decorous debate, and for his brutal denunciation of a venerable statesman. It was literally and entirely proper, that he should be stricken down and beaten just beside the desk against which he leaned as he fulminated his filthy utterances through the capitol. It is idle to talk of the sanctity of the Senate Chamber, since it is polluted by the presence of such fellows as [Henry] Wilson and Sumner and [Benjamin F.] Wade. They have desecrated it, and cannot now fly to it as to a sanctuary from the lash of vengeance.

FROM *Richmond Enquirer*, 2 June 1856.

We trust other gentlemen will follow the example of Mr. Brooks, that so a curb may be imposed upon the truculence and audacity of abolition speakers.—If need be, let us have a caning or cowhiding every day. If the worse come to the worse, so much the sooner so much the better.

10

Chief Justice Roger B. Taney Rules against Dred Scott (1857)

Andrew Jackson appointed Roger B. Taney to be chief justice of the Supreme Court in 1835. A citizen of Maryland, Taney had emancipated his slaves some years before, yet he remained extremely sensitive to the security of slavery, bitterly resented the antislavery movement in the North, and was anxious to erect additional constitutional safeguards for the institution. Although every justice issued an opinion in the Dred Scott case, Taney's was considered the most important majority opinion. Certainly his opinion attracted the most attention and stirred up the greatest controversy, particularly his assertion that blacks could not be citizens of the United States and his pronouncement that Congress had no power to prohibit slavery from a territory. In his opinion, Taney did not adopt Calhoun's argument that in governing the territories Congress acted as the agent of all the states. Instead, he relied on the constitutional protection of property and the due process clause of the Fifth Amendment.

When a plantiff sues in a court of the United States, it is necessary that he should show, in his pleading, that the suit he brings is within the jurisdiction of the court, and that he is entitled to sue there. . . . And if the plaintiff claims a right to sue in a Circuit Court of the United States, under that provision of the Constitution which gives jurisdiction in controversies between citizens of different States, he must distinctly aver in his pleading that they are citizens of different States; and he cannot maintain his suit without showing that fact in the pleadings. . . .

It becomes necessary, therefore, to determine who were citizens of the several States when the Constitution was adopted. And in order to do this, we must recur to the Governments and institutions of the thirteen colonies, when they separated from Great Britain and formed new sovereignties, and took their places in the family of independent nations. We must inquire who, at that time, were recognised as the people or citizens of a State, whose rights and liberties had been outraged by the English Government; and who declared their independence, and assumed the powers of Government to defend their rights by force of arms.

In the opinion of the court, the legislation and histories of the times, and the language used in the Declaration of Independence, show, that neither the class of persons who had been imported as slaves, nor their descendants, whether they had be-

FROM *Dred Scott v. John F. A. Sanford*, 19 Howard (1857), pp. 393–454.

come free or not, were then acknowledged as a part of the people, nor intended to be included in the general words used in that memorable instrument.

It is difficult at this day to realize the state of public opinion in relation to that unfortunate race, which prevailed in the civilized and enlightened portions of the world at the time of the Declaration of Independence, and when the Constitution of the United States was framed and adopted. But the public history of every European nation displays it in a manner too plain to be mistaken.

They had for more than a century before been regarded as beings of an inferior order, and altogether unfit to associate with the white race, either in social or political relations; and so far inferior, that they had no rights which the white man was bound to respect; and that the negro might justly and lawfully be reduced to slavery for his benefit. . . . This opinion was at that time fixed and universal in the civilized portion of the white race. It was regarded as an axiom in morals as well as in politics, which no one thought of disputing, or supposed to be open to dispute. . . .

This state of public opinion had undergone no change when the Constitution was adopted, as is equally evident from its provisions and language.

. . . There are two clauses in the Constitution which point directly and specifically to the negro race as a separate class of persons, and show clearly that they were not regarded as a portion of the people or citizens of the Government then formed.

One of these clauses reserves to each of the thirteen States the right to import slaves until the year 1808, if it thinks proper. . . . And by the other provision the States pledge themselves to each other to maintain the right of property of the master, by delivering up to him any slave who may have escaped from his service, and be found within their respective territories. . . .

And upon a full and careful consideration of the subject, the court is of opinion, that . . . Dred Scott was not a citizen of Missouri within the meaning of the Constitution of the United States, and not entitled as such to sue in its courts; and,

consequently, that the Circuit Court had no jurisdiction of the case, and that the judgment on the plea in abatement is erroneous. . . .

We proceed, therefore, to inquire whether the facts relied on by the plaintiff entitled him to his freedom. . . .

In considering this part of the controversy, two questions arise: 1. Was he, together with his family, free in Missouri by reason of the stay in the territory of the United States hereinbefore mentioned? And 2. If they were not, is Scott himself free by reason of his removal to Rock Island, in the State of Illinois, as stated in the above admissions?

We proceed to examine the first question.

The act of Congress, upon which the plaintiff relies, declares that slavery and involuntary servitude, except as a punishment for crime, shall be forever prohibited in all that part of the territory ceded by France, under the name of Louisiana, which lies north of thirty-six degrees thirty minutes north latitude, and not included within the limits of Missouri. And the difficulty which meets us at the threshold of this part of the inquiry is, whether Congress was authorized to pass this law under any of the powers granted to it by the Constitution. . . .

The counsel for the plaintiff has laid much stress upon that article in the Constitution which confers on Congress the power "to dispose of and make all needful rules and regulations respecting the territory or other property belonging to the United States;" but, in the judgment of the court, that provision has no bearing on the present controversy, and the power there given, whatever it may be, is confined, and was intended to be confined, to the territory which at that time belonged to, or was claimed by, the United States, and was within their boundaries as settled by the treaty with Great Britain, and can have no influence upon a territory afterwards acquired from a foreign Government. . . .

. . . The Territory being a part of the United States, the Government and the citizen both enter it under the authority of the Constitution, with their respective right defined and marked out; and the Federal Government can exercise no power over his person or property, beyond what that instrument confers, nor lawfully deny any right which it has reserved. . . .

. . . The rights of private property have been guarded with equal care. Thus the rights of property are united with the rights of person, and placed on the same ground by the fifth amendment to the Constitution, which provides that no person shall be deprived of life, liberty, and property, without due process of law. And an act of Congress which deprives a citizen of the United States of his liberty or property, merely because he came himself or brought his property into a particular Territory of the United States, and who had committed no offence against the laws, could hardly be dignified with the name of due process of law.

. . . If the Constitution recognises the right of property of the master in a slave, and makes no distinction between that description of property and other property owned by a citizen, no tribunal, acting under the authority of the United States, whether it be legislative, executive, or judicial, has a right to draw such a distinction, or deny to it the benefit of the provisions and guarantees which have been provided for the protection of private property against the encroachments of the Government.

. . . The right of property in a slave is distinctly and expressly affirmed in the Constitution. The right to traffic in it, like an ordinary article of merchandise and property, was guarantied to the citizens of the United States, in every State that might desire it, for twenty years. And the Government in express terms is pledged to protect it in all future time, if the slave escapes from his owner. This is done in plain words—too plain to be misunderstood. And no word can be found in the Constitution which gives Congress a greater power over slave property, or which entitles property of that kind to less protection than property of any other description. The only power conferred is the power coupled with the duty of guarding and protecting the owner in his rights.

Upon these considerations, it is the opinion of the court that the act of Congress which prohibited a citizen from holding and owning property of this kind in the territory of the United States north of the line therein mentioned, is not warranted by the Constitution, and is therefore void; and that neither Dred Scott himself, nor any of his family, were made free by being carried into this territory; even if they had been carried there by the owner, with the intention of becoming a permanent resident.

11

Associate Justice Benjamin R. Curtis Dissents in the Dred Scott Case (1857)

The most important dissent in the Dred Scott case was filed by Justice Benjamin R. Curtis of Massachusetts. Curtis's opinion, which was carefully researched and precisely argued, effectively challenged Taney's arguments by invoking both historical fact and judicial precedent. Stung by Curtis's rigorous argument, Taney, in an unusual move, inserted additional material in his original opinion as delivered from the bench before publishing it. He also personally assailed his judicial colleague, which led a disgusted Curtis to resign from the Supreme Court. Curtis insisted that African Americans could be citizens of the United States and affirmed the long-accepted power of Congress to prohibit slavery from the territories.

Under the allegations contained in this plea, and admitted by the demurrer, the question is, whether any person of African descent, whose ancestors were sold as slaves in the United States, can be a citizen of the United States. . . .

To determine whether any free persons, descended from Africans held in slavery, were citizens of the United States under the Confederation, and consequently at the time of the adoption of the Constitution of the United States, it is only necessary to know whether any such persons were citizens of either of the States under the Confederation, at the time of the adoption of the Constitution.

Of this there can be no doubt. At the time of the ratification of the Articles of Confederation, all free native-born inhabitants of the States of New Hampshire, Massachusetts, New York, New Jersey, and North Carolina, though descended from African slaves, were not only citizens of those States, but such of them as had the other necessary qualifications possessed the franchise of electors, on equal terms with other citizens. . . .

I can find nothing in the Constitution which . . . deprives of their citizenship any class of persons who were citizens of the United States at the time of its adoption, or who should be native-born citizens of any State after its adoption. . . . And my opinion is, that, under the Constitution of the United States, every free person born on the soil of a State, who is a citizen of that State by force of its Constitution or laws, is also a citizen of the United States. . . .

I dissent, therefore, from that part of the opinion of the majority of the court, in which it is held that a person of African descent cannot be a citizen of the United States; and I regret I must go further, and dissent both from what I deem their assumption of authority to examine the constitutionality of the act of Congress commonly called the Missouri compromise act, and the grounds and conclusions announced in their opinion. . . .

_____

FROM *Dred Scott v. John F. A. Sanford*, 19 Howard (1857), pp. 571–633.

The residence of the plaintiff in the State of Illinois, and the residence of himself and his wife in the territory acquired from France lying north of latitude thirty-six degrees thirty minutes, and north of the State of Missouri, are each relied on by the plaintiff in error. As the residence in the territory affects the plaintiff's wife and children as well as himself, I must inquire what was its effect.

The general question may be stated to be, whether the plaintiff's *status*, as a slave, was so changed by his residence within that territory, that he was not a slave in the State of Missouri, at the time this action was brought. . . .

But if the acts of Congress on this subject are valid, the law of the Territory of Wisconsin, within whose limits the residence of the plaintiff and his wife, and their marriage and the birth of one or both of their children, took place, falls under the first category, and is a law operating directly on the *status* of the slave. By the eighth section of the act of March 6, 1820, (3 Stat. at Large, 548,) it was enacted that, within this Territory, "slavery and involuntary servitude, otherwise than in the punishment of crimes, whereof the parties shall have been duly convicted, shall be, and is hereby, forever prohibited: *Provided, always*, that any person escaping into the same, from whom labor or service is lawfully claimed in any State or Territory of the United States, such fugitive may be lawfully reclaimed, and conveyed to the person claiming his or her labor or service, as aforesaid."

By the act of April 20, 1836, (4 Stat. at Large, 10,) passed in the same month and year of the removal of the plaintiff to Fort Snelling, this part of the territory ceded by France, where Fort Snelling is, together with so much of the territory of the United States east of the Mississippi as now constitutes the State of Wisconsin, was brought under a Territorial Government, under the name of the Territory of Wisconsin. By the eighteenth section of this act, it was enacted, "That the inhabitants of this Territory shall be entitled to and enjoy all and singular the rights, privileges, and advantages, granted and secured to the people of the Territory of the United States northwest of the river Ohio, by the articles of compact contained in the ordinance for the government of said Territory, passed on the 13th day of July, 1787; and shall be subject to all the restrictions and prohibitions in said articles of compact imposed upon the people of the said Territory." The sixth article of that compact is, "there shall be neither slavery nor involuntary servitude in the said Territory, otherwise than in the punishment of crimes, whereof the party shall have been duly convicted." . . .

It would not be easy for the Legislature to employ more explicit language to signify its will that the *status* of slavery should not exist within the Territory, than the words found in the act of 1820, and in the ordinance of 1787. . . .

I have thus far assumed, merely for the purpose of the argument, that the laws of the United States, respecting slavery in this Territory, were constitutionally enacted by Congress. It remains to inquire whether they are constitutional and binding laws.

. . . It is insisted, that whatever other powers Congress may have respecting the territory of the United States, the subject of negro slavery forms an exception.

The Constitution declares that Congress shall have power to make "*all* needful rules and regulations" respecting the territory belonging to the United States.

The assertion is, though the Constitution says all, it does not mean all—though it says all, without [sic] qualification, it means all except such as allow or prohibit slavery. It cannot be doubted that it is incumbent on those who would thus introduce an exception not found in the language of the instrument, to exhibit some solid and satisfactory reason, drawn from the subject-matter or the purposes and objects of the clause, the context, or from other provisions of the Constitution, showing that the words employed in this clause are not to be understood according to their clear, plain, and natural signification. . . .

. . . [In] eight distinct instances, beginning with the first Congress, and coming down to the year 1848, . . . Congress has excluded slavery from the territory of the United States; and six distinct instances in which Congress organized Governments of Territories by which slavery was recognised and continued, beginning also with the first Congress, and coming down to the year 1822. These acts were severally signed by seven Presidents of the United States, beginning with General Washington, and coming regularly down as far as Mr. John Quincy Adams, thus including all who were in public life when the Constitution was adopted.

If the practical construction of the Constitution contemporaneously with its going into effect, by men intimately acquainted with its history from their personal participation in framing and adopting it, and continued by them through a long series of acts of the gravest importance, be entitled to weight in the judicial mind on a question of construction, it would seem to be difficult to resist the force of the acts above adverted to. . . .

Looking at the power of Congress over the Territories as of the extent just described, what positive prohibition exists in the Constitution, which restrained Congress from enacting a law in 1820 to prohibit slavery north of thirty-six degrees thirty minutes north latitude?

The only one suggested is that clause in the fifth article of the amendments of the Constitution which declares that no person shall be deprived of his life, liberty, or property, without due process of law. . . .

Slavery, being contrary to natural right, is created only by municipal law. This is not only plain in itself, and agreed by all writers on the subject, but is inferable from the Constitution, and has been explicitly declared by this court. . . .

Is it conceivable that the Constitution has conferred the right on every citizen to become a resident on the territory of the United States with his slaves, and there to hold them as such, but has neither made nor provided for any municipal regulations which are essential to the existence of slavery?

Is it not more rational to conclude that they who framed and adopted the Constitution were aware that persons held to service under the laws of a State are property only to the extent and under the conditions fixed by those laws; that they must cease to be available as property, when their owners voluntarily place them permanently within another jurisdiction, where no municipal laws on the subject of slavery exist; and that, being aware of these principles, and having said nothing to interfere with or displace them, . . . and having empowered Congress to make all needful rules and regulations respecting the territory of the United States, it was their intention to leave to the discretion of Congress what regulations, if any, should be made concerning slavery therein?

. . . I am of opinion that so much of the several acts of Congress as prohibited slavery and involuntary servitude within that part of the Territory of Wisconsin lying north of thirty-six degrees thirty minutes north latitude, and west of the river Mississippi, were constitutional and valid laws.

12

JAMES HENRY HAMMOND

Cotton Is King (1858)

James Henry Hammond was a South Carolina congressman, governor, and U.S. senator in the three decades before the Civil War. The son of a schoolmaster, the talented and ambitious Hammond graduated from South Carolina College determined to establish himself in South Carolina's aristocracy. By marrying the daughter of a wealthy South Carolina planter for her money, he acquired a large plantation and almost 150 slaves. He set himself up as a country gentleman and threw himself into improving his plantation, systematically increasing his fortune and becoming a very successful planter. The gifted Hammond was too mercurial to be an influential politician, but he was an important proslavery polemicist. In the following speech, delivered in the U.S. Senate in March, 1858, he discussed the economic importance of cotton as the basis of the South's power in the nation and the world. The idea that England could not survive economically without southern cotton pervaded southern thought on the eve of the Civil War and strengthened the hand of secessionists (see p. 143).

But if there were no other reason why we should never have war, would any sane nation make war on cotton? Without firing a gun, without drawing a sword, should they make war on us we could bring the whole world to our feet. The South is perfectly competent to go on, one, two, or three years without planting a seed of cotton. I believe that if she was to plant but half her cotton, for three years to come, it would be an immense advantage to her. I am not so sure but that after three years' entire abstinence she would come out stronger than ever she was before, and better prepared to enter afresh upon her great career of enterprise. What would happen if no cotton was furnished for three years? I will not stop to depict what every one can imagine, but this is certain: England would topple headlong and carry the whole civilized world with her, save the South. No, you dare not make war on cotton. No power on earth dares to make war upon it. Cotton *is* king. . . . Who can doubt, that has looked at recent events, that cotton is supreme? When the abuse of credit had destroyed credit and annihilated confidence;

FROM "Speech on the Admission of Kansas, Under the Lecompton Constitution," *Selection from the Letters and Speeches of the Hon. James H. Hammond, of South Carolina* (New York: John F. Trow & Co., 1866), pp. 311–17.

when thousands of the strongest commercial houses in the world were coming down, and hundreds of millions of dollars of supposed property evaporating in thin air; when you came to a dead lock, and revolutions were threatened, what brought you up? Fortunately for you it was the commencement of the cotton season, and we have poured in upon you one million six hundred thousand bales of cotton just at the crisis to save you from destruction. That cotton, but for the bursting of your speculative bubbles in the North, which produced the whole of this convulsion, would have brought us $100,000,000. We have sold it for $65,000,000, and saved you.

13

The Lincoln-Douglas Debates (1858)

In 1858 the Illinois Republican party took the unusual step of designating Abraham Lincoln the party's candidate for the U.S. Senate seat currently held by Stephen A. Douglas, who was up for re-election. As the underdog in the senatorial race, Lincoln challenged Douglas to a series of debates on the issues confronting the nation. Douglas was reluctant to provide a forum for his less well-known adversary, but he finally agreed to participate in seven joint debates in the state's remaining congressional districts (the two candidates had already spoken on successive days in Chicago and Springfield). The resulting Lincoln-Douglas debates have entered the folklore of American politics. For the modern reader, Lincoln's subsequent importance overshadows this confrontation on the Illinois prairie, but at the time it was Douglas who was the more famous leader and received the bulk of the coverage in the press; indeed, the debates attracted considerable attention outside of the state precisely because of Douglas's national importance and his well-known presidential aspirations. Yet as Douglas had predicted, Lincoln was a formidable opponent as a debater. In the following selections from their famous debates, the two candidates outline their positions on slavery and the sectional conflict.

Popular Sovereignty

[Lincoln at Ottawa, Illinois, August 21, 1858]

What is Popular Sovereignty? Is it the right of the people to have Slavery or not have it, as they see fit, in the territories? I will state . . . my understanding is that Popular Sovereignty, as now applied to the question of Slavery, does allow the people of a Territory to have Slavery if they want to, but does not allow them *not* to have it if they *do not* want it. I do not mean that if this vast concourse of people were in a Territory of the United States, any one of them would be obliged to have a slave if he did not want one; but I do say that, as I understand the Dred Scott decision, if any one man wants slaves, all the rest have no way of keeping that one man from holding them.

FROM Roy P. Basler, et al., eds., *The Collected Works of Abraham Lincoln*, vol. 3 (New Brunswick, N.J.: Rutgers University Press, 1953), pp. 9–10, 18–19, 145–46, 220, 286, 296–97, 312–15, 322, 325.

[Douglas at Alton, Illinois, October 15, 1858].

This government was made upon the great basis of the sovereignty of the States, the right of each State to regulate its own domestic institutions to suit itself, and that right was conferred with understanding and expectation that inasmuch as each locality had separate interests, each locality must have different and distinct local and domestic institutions, corresponding to its wants and interests. Our fathers knew when they made the government, that the laws and institutions which were well adapted to the green mountains of Vermont, were unsuited to the rice plantations of South Carolina. They knew then, as well as we know now, that the laws and institutions which would be well adapted to the beautiful prairies of Illinois would not be suited to the mining regions of California. They knew that in a Republic as broad as this, having such a variety of soil, climate and interest, there must necessarily be a corresponding variety of local laws—the policy and institutions of each State adapted to its condition and wants. For this reason this Union was established on the right of each State to do as it pleased on the question of slavery, and every other question; and the various States were not allowed to complain of, much less interfere, with the policy of their neighbors.

. . . If the people of all the States will act on that great principle, and each State mind its own business, attend to its own affairs, take care of its own negroes and not meddle with its neighbors, then there will be peace between the North and the South, the East and the West, throughout the whole Union.

Slavery

[Lincoln at Alton, Illinois, October 15, 1858]

The real issue in this controversy—the one pressing upon every mind—is the sentiment on the part of one class that looks upon the institution of slavery *as a wrong*, and of another class that *does not* look upon it as a wrong. The sentiment that contemplates the institution of slavery in this country as a wrong is the sentiment of the Republican party. It is the sentiment around which all their actions—all their arguments circle—from which all their propositions radiate. They look upon it as being a moral, social and political wrong; and while they contemplate it as such, they nevertheless have due regard for its actual existence among us, and the difficulties of getting rid of it in any satisfactory way and to all the constitutional obligations thrown about it. Yet having a due regard for these, they desire a policy in regard to it that looks to its not creating any more danger. They insist that it should as far as may be, *be treated* as a wrong, and one of the methods of treating it as a wrong is to *make provision that it shall grow no larger*. They also desire a policy that looks to a peaceful end of slavery at sometime, as being wrong. These are the views they entertain in regard to it as I understand them; and all their sentiments—all their arguments and propositions are brought within this range. I have said and I repeat it here, that if there be a man amongst us who does not think that the institution of slavery is wrong in any one of the aspects of which I have spoken, he is misplaced and ought not to be with us. And if there be a man amongst us who is so impatient of it as a wrong as to disregard its actual presence among us and the difficulty of getting rid of it suddenly in a satisfactory way, and to disregard the constitutional obligations thrown about it, that man is misplaced if he is on our platform. We disclaim sympathy with him in practical action. He is not placed properly with us. . . .

On the other hand, I have said there is a sentiment which treats it as *not* being wrong. That is the Democratic sentiment of this day. I do not mean to say that every man who stands within that range positively asserts that it is right. That class will include all who positively assert that it is right, and all who like Judge Douglas treat it as indifferent and do not say it is either right or wrong. . . .

That is the real issue. That is the issue that will continue in this country when these poor tongues of Judge Douglas and myself shall be silent. It is the eternal struggle between these two principles—right and wrong—throughout the world. . . . The one is the common right of humanity and the other the divine right of kings. . . . No matter in what shape it comes, whether from the mouth of a king who seeks to bestride the people of his own nation and live by the fruit of their labor, or from one race of men as an apology for enslaving another race, it is the same tyrannical principle.

[Douglas at Alton, Illinois, October 15, 1858]

Mr. Lincoln . . . says that he looks forward to a time when slavery shall be abolished everywhere. I look forward to a time when each State shall be allowed to do as it pleases. If it chooses to keep slavery forever, it is not my business, but its own; if it chooses to abolish slavery, it is its own business—not mine. I care more for the great principle of self-government, the right of the people to rule, than I do for all the negroes in Christendom. I would not endanger the perpetuity of this Union. I would not blot out the great inalienable rights of the white men for all the negroes that ever existed. Hence, I say, let us maintain this government on the principles that our fathers made it, recognizing the right of each State to keep slavery as long as its people determine, or to abolish it when they please. . . .

My friends, if, as I have said before, we will only live up to this great fundamental principle there will be peace between the North and the South. Mr. Lincoln admits that under the constitution on all domestic questions, except slavery, we ought not to interfere with the people of each State. What right have we to interfere with slavery any more than we have to interfere with any other question. He says that this slavery question is now the bone of contention. Why? Simply because agitators have combined in all the free States to make war upon it.

The Declaration of Independence

[Lincoln at Galesburg, Illinois, October 7, 1858]

The Judge has alluded to the Declaration of Independence, and insisted that negroes are not included in that Declaration; and that it is a slander upon the framers of that instrument, to suppose that negroes were meant therein; and he asks you: Is it possible to believe that Mr. Jefferson, who penned the immortal paper, could have supposed himself applying the language of that instrument to the negro race, and yet held a portion of that race in slavery? Would he not at once have freed them? I only have to remark upon this part of the Judge's speech . . . that I believe the entire records of the world, from the date of the Declaration of Independence up to within three years ago, may be searched in vain for one single affirmation, from one single man, that the negro was not included in the Declaration of Independence. I think I may defy Judge Douglas to show that he ever said so, that Washington ever said so, that any President ever said so, that any member of Congress ever said so, or that any living man upon the whole earth ever said so, until the necessities of the present policy of the Democratic party, in regard to slavery, had to invent that affirmation.

[Douglas at Alton, Illinois, October 15, 1858]

But the Abolition party really think that under the Declaration of Independence the negro is equal to the white man, and that negro equality is an inalienable right conferred by the Almighty, and hence, that all human laws in violation of it are null and void. . . . I hold that the signers of the Declaration of Independence had no reference to negroes at all when they declared all men to be created equal. They did not mean negro, nor the savage Indians, nor the Fejee Islanders, nor any other barbarous race. They were speaking of white men. They alluded to men of European birth and European descent—to white men, and to none others, when they declared that doctrine. I hold that this government was established on the white basis. It was established by white men for the benefit of white men and their posterity forever, and should be administered by white men, and none others.

Race

[Douglas at Ottawa, Illinois, August 21, 1858]

We are told by Lincoln that he is utterly opposed to the Dred Scott decision, and will not submit to it, for the reason that he says it deprives the negro of the rights and privileges of citizenship. . . . I ask you, are you in favor of conferring upon the negro the rights and privileges of citizenship? Do you desire to strike out of our State Constitution that clause which keeps slaves and free negroes out of the State, and allow the free negroes to flow in, and cover your prairies with black settlements? Do you desire to turn this beautiful State into a free negro colony, in order that when Missouri abolishes slavery she can send one hundred thousand emancipated slaves into Illinois, to become citizens and voters, on an equality with yourselves? If you desire negro citizenship, if you desire to allow them to come into the State and settle with the white man, if you desire them to vote on an equality with yourselves, and to make them eligible to office, to serve on juries, and to adjudge your rights, then support Mr. Lincoln and the Black Republican party, who are in favor of the citizenship of the negro. For one, I am opposed to negro citizenship in any and every form. . . . I am in favor of confining citizenship to white men, men of European birth and descent, instead of conferring it upon negroes, Indians and other inferior races.

. . . I do not question Mr. Lincoln's conscientious belief that the negro was made his equal, and hence is his brother, but for my own part, I do not regard the negro as my equal, and positively deny that he is my brother or any kin to me whatever.

[Lincoln at Charleston, Illinois, September 8, 1858]

While I was at the hotel to-day an elderly gentleman called upon me to know whether I was really in favor of producing a perfect equality between the negroes and white people. While I had not proposed to myself on this occasion to say much on that subject, yet as the question was asked me I thought I would occupy perhaps five minutes in saying something in regard to it. I will say then that I am not, nor ever have been in favor of bringing about in any way the social and political equality of the white and black races, that I am not nor ever have been in favor of making voters or jurors of negroes, nor of qualifying them to hold office, nor to intermarry with white people; and I will say in addition to this that there is a physical difference between the white and black races which I believe will for ever forbid the two races living together on terms of social and political equality. And inasmuch as they cannot so live, while they do remain together there must be the position of superior and inferior, and I as much as any other man am in favor of having the superior position assigned to the white race. I say upon this occasion I do not perceive that because the white man is to have the superior position the negro should be denied everything. I do not understand that because I do not want a negro woman for a slave I must necessarily want her for a wife. My understanding is that I can just let her alone.

14

The Freeport Doctrine (1858)

In their debate at Freeport on August 27, 1858, Abraham Lincoln asked Stephen A. Douglas a series of questions. The second interrogatory read, "Can the people of a United States Territory, in any lawful way, against the wish of any citizen of the United States, exclude slavery from its limits prior to the formation of a State Constitution?" In effect, the Republican candidate challenged Douglas to reconcile his doctrine of popular sovereignty with the Supreme Court's Dred Scott decision, which declared Congress could not prohibit slavery from a territory. In earlier speeches, Douglas had already indicated what his answer would be, but by forcing Douglas to address this issue directly, Lincoln sought to deepen the existing division in the Democratic party between Douglas and his opponents. Douglas's answer became known as the Freeport Doctrine. Lincoln criticized this position at their subsequent debate in Jonesboro, Illinois.

[Douglas at Freeport, Illinois, August 27, 1858]

I answer emphatically, as Mr. Lincoln has heard me answer a hundred times from every stump in Illinois, that in my opinion the people of a territory can, by lawful means, exclude slavery from their limits prior to the formation of a State Constitution. . . . It matters not what way the Supreme Court may hereafter decide as to the abstract question whether slavery may or may not go into a territory under the constitution, the people have the lawful means to introduce it or exclude it as they please, for the reason that slavery cannot exist a day or an hour anywhere, unless it is supported by local police regulations. Those police regulations can only be established by the local legislature, and if the people are opposed to slavery they will elect representatives to that body who will by unfriendly legislation effectually prevent the introduction of it into their midst. If, on the contrary, they are for it, their legislation will favor its extension. Hence, no matter what the decision of the Supreme Court

may be on that abstract question, still the right of the people to make a slave territory or a free territory is perfect and complete under the Nebraska bill.

[Lincoln at Jonesboro, Illinois, September 15, 1858]

I hold that the proposition that slavery cannot enter a new country without police regulations is historically false. It is not true at all. I hold that the history of this country shows that the institution of slavery was originally planted upon this continent *without* these "police regulations" which the Judge now thinks necessary for the actual establishment of it. Not only so, but is there not another fact—how came this Dred Scott decision to be made. It was made upon the case of a negro being taken and actually held in slavery in Minnesota Territory, claiming his freedom because the act of Congress prohibited his being so held there. *Will the Judge pretend that Dred Scott was not held there without police regulations?* There is at least one matter of record as to his having been held in slavery in the Territory, not only without police reg-

FROM Roy P. Basler, et al., eds., *The Collected Works of Abraham Lincoln*, vol. 3 (New Brunswick, N.J.: Rutgers University Press, 1953), pp. 51–52, 130.

ulations, but in the teeth of Congressional legislation supposed to be valid at the time. This shows that there is vigor enough in Slavery to plant itself in a new country even against unfriendly legislation. It takes not only law but the *enforcement* of law to keep it out.

15

John Brown Addresses the Court (1859)

Up until the time of his raid on Harpers Ferry, Virginia, John Brown had led a life of repeated failure. Brown's sanity has been a subject of debate ever since, and certainly his invasion of Virginia was ill-conceived and ineptly executed. He planned to seize the weapons from the government armory, arm the slaves, and lead an insurrection to overthrow slavery in Virginia, but no slaves joined Brown's band, the townspeople soon pinned the raiders down in a few buildings where they were holed up, and before long Brown and most of his men were either killed or captured by U.S. troops. But if Brown demonstrated his military incompetence in the attack on Harpers Ferry, he subsequently displayed a genius for playing the role of an antislavery martyr. He vetoed any plans to attempt to rescue him from the Charleston, Virginia, jail and used the trial to publicize his strong antislavery convictions. To his wife he wrote from his jail cell, "I have been whiped as the saying is, but am sure I can recover all lost capital occasioned by that disaster, by only hanging a few moments by the neck; & I feel quite determined to make the utmost possible out of a defeat." His finest moment occurred at his sentencing when he made the following statement to the court. Brown's statement was not entirely forthright, but it produced widespread admiration, even among his enemies. One jurist reported that Brown spoke "with perfect calmness of voice and mildness of manner, winning the respect of all for his courage and firmness."

I have, may it please the Court, a few words to say.

In the first place, I deny everything but what I have all along admitted: of a design on my part to free slaves. I intended certainly to have made a clean thing of that matter, as I did last winter, when I went into Missouri and there took slaves without the snapping of a gun on either side, moving them through the country, and finally leaving them in Canada. I designed to have done the same thing again on a larger scale. That was all I intended. I never did intend murder, or treason, or the destruction of property, or to excite or incite slaves to rebellion, or to make insurrection.

I have another objection, and that is that it is unjust that I should suffer such a penalty. Had I interfered in the manner which I admit, and which I admit has been fairly proved— . . . had I so interfered in behalf of the rich, the powerful, the intelligent, the so-called great, or in behalf of any of their friends, either father, mother, brother, sister, wife or children, or any of that class, and suffered and sacrificed what I have in this interference, it would

FROM Oswald Garrison Villard, *John Brown, 1800–1859* (Boston: Houghton Mifflin Company, 1911), pp. 498–99.

have been all right. Every man in this Court would have deemed it an act worthy of reward rather than punishment.

This Court acknowledges, too, as I suppose, the validity of the law of God. I see a book kissed, which I suppose to be the Bible, or at least the New Testament, which teaches me that all things whatsoever I would that men should do to me, I should do even so to them. It teaches me, further, to remember them that are in bonds as bound with them. I endeavored to act up to that instruction. I say I am yet too young to understand that God is any respecter of persons. I believe that to have interfered as I have done, as I have always freely admitted I have done, in behalf of His despised poor, I did no wrong, but right. Now, if it is deemed necessary that I should forfeit my life for the furtherance of the ends of justice, and mingle my blood further with the blood of my children and with the blood of millions in this slave country whose rights are disregarded by wicked, cruel, and unjust enactments, I say, let it be done.

16

RICHMOND ENQUIRER

The Harpers Ferry Invasion Has Advanced the Cause of Disunion (1859)

As soon as John Brown was captured in his abortive raid on Harpers Ferry, *Virginia, southern whites became convinced that the Republican party was behind Brown's invasion, and they persisted in this belief even when a subsequent senatorial investigation failed to implicate any prominent Republican party leader in the attack. The following editorial from the* Richmond Enquirer *reflects this widespread southern viewpoint. It also notes the connection between the raid and growing disunion sentiment in the South, fueled by the fear that the Republicans would triumph in the 1860 presidential election.*

The Harper's Ferry Invasion as Party Capital

The tone of the conservative press of the North evinces a determination to make the moral of the Harper's Ferry invasion an effective weapon to rally all men not fanatics against that [Republican] party whose leaders have been implicated directly with this midnight murder of Virginia citizens, and the destruction of Government property. This is certainly legitimate—and we do most sincerely hope that the horror with which the whole country is justly filled, may be the means of opening the eyes of all men to the certain result of the triumph of an "irrepressible conflict" leader, or of any man, by an alliance with the Black Republican Ossawattomites of the North. This great wrong and outrage has been perpetrated by men from the North. It is but just and proper that a disclaimer should be made by the Northern press, but the voice of the press is not enough, the voice of the *people* at the North, through the polls, is necessary to restore confidence and to dispel the belief that the Northern people have aided and abetted this treasonable invasion of a Southern State.

If the success of a party is of more importance than the restoration of good feeling and attach-

FROM *Richmond Enquirer*, 23 October 1859.

ment to the Union, let that fact go forth from the polls of New York at her approaching election. . . . The vile clamor of party, the struggle of Republicanism for power, has given an impetus to the abolition zeal of old Brown and his comrades, that impelled them forward in their mad career of treason and bloodshed. The leader of the Republican forces [William Henry Seward] gave utterance to the treasonable declaration of "an irrepressible conflict," and if the people of New York really repudiate the dogma that has vitalized pillage, robbery and murder, and raised up a body of men to initiate the "irrepressible conflict," let them send from the polls greetings of overthrow that shall, if possible, restore confidence, and cement the broken fragments of attachment for the Union. The triumph of the Black Republicans in the State of New York will be encouragement to future Ossawatomites, to again attempt the plunder and invasion of Virginia; the defeat of this "irrepressible conflict" party will speak thunder tones of encouragement and hope to the people of the Southern States; such a defeat will tend to allay that excitement which now slumbers under inexpressible in-

dignation, and which a spark may light into a conflagration destructive to the Union.

The voice of the Southern people has not been heard. . . . Let not the people of the North mistake this silence for indifference. There exists a horror and indignation which neither press nor public meetings can express; a feeling that has weakened the foundations of the Union, and which may at any moment rase the superstructure. . . .

The Harper's Ferry invasion has advanced the cause of Disunion, more than any other event that has happened since the formation of the Government; it has rallied to that standard men who formerly looked upon it with horror; it has revived, with ten fold strength the desire of a Southern Confederacy. The, heretofore, most determined friends of the Union may now be heard saying, "if under the form of a Confederacy, our peace is disturbed, our State invaded, its peaceful citizens cruelly murdered, and all the horrors of servile war forced upon us, by those who should be our warmest friends; if the form of a Confederacy is observed, but its spirit violated, *and the people of the North sustain the outrage*, then let disunion come."

17

CHARLES ELIOT NORTON

I Have Seen Nothing
Like the Intensity of Feeling (1859)

Born into a prosperous and notable Cambridge, Massachusetts, family, Charles Eliot Norton was a well-known writer, scholar, and editor. As part of the literary circle that shone so brightly in prewar Boston, he was a frequent contributor to the Atlantic Monthly, *edited by his friend James Russell Lowell. Like most members of polite Boston society, he was in sentiment antislavery, but his opposition stemmed more from what he considered the institution's negative impact on whites than from any egalitarian zeal or racial concern. During the war, Norton was a leading figure in the Loyal Publication Society, which disseminated prowar propaganda, and also served as an editor of the* North American Review. *In this letter to a cousin in England, dated December 13, 1859, a week after Brown's execution, he discusses with particular acuteness John Brown's impact on northern public opinion.*

You can hardly have formed an idea of the intensity of feeling and interest which has prevailed throughout the country in regard to John Brown. I have seen nothing like it. We get up excitements easily enough, but they die away usually as quickly as they rose, beginning in rhetoric and ending in fireworks; but this was different. The heart of the people was fairly reached, and an impression has been made upon it which will be permanent and produce results long hence.

. . . There was at first no word of sympathy either for Brown or his undertaking. But soon came the accounts of the panic of the Virginians, of the cruelty with which Brown's party were massacred; of his noble manliness of demeanour when, wounded, he was taken prisoner, and was questioned as to his design; of his simple declarations of his motives and aims, which were those of an enthusiast, but not of a bad man,—and a strong sympathy began to be felt for Brown personally, and a strong interest to know in full what had led him to this course. Then the bitterness of the Virginia press, the unseemly haste with which the trial was hurried on,—and all the while the most unchanged, steady, manliness on the part of "Old Brown," increased daily the sympathy which was already strong. The management of the trial, the condemnation, the speech made by Brown, the letters he wrote in prison, the visit of his wife to him,—and at last his death, wrought up the popular feeling to the highest point. Not, indeed, that feeling or opinion have been by any means unanimous; for on the one side have been those who have condemned the whole of Brown's course as utterly wicked, and regarded him as a mere outlaw, murderer, and traitor, while, on the other, have been those who have looked upon his undertaking with satisfaction, and exalted him into the highest rank of men. But, if I am not wrong, the mass of the people, and the best of them, have agreed with neither of these views. They have, while condemning Brown's scheme as a criminal attempt to right a great wrong by violent measures, and as equally ill-judged and rash in execution, felt for the man himself a deep sympathy and a fervent admiration. They have admitted that he was guilty under the law, that he deserved to be hung as a breaker of the law,—but they have felt that the gallows was not the fit end for a life like his, and that he died a real martyr in the cause of freedom.

. . . The earnestness of his moral and religious convictions and the sincerity of his faith made him single-minded, and manly in the highest degree. There was not the least sham about him; no whining over his failure; no false or factitious sentiment, no empty words;—in everything he showed himself simple, straightforward and brave. . . . And game he was to the very last. He said to the sheriff as he stepped onto the platform of the gallows, "Don't keep me waiting longer than is necessary,"—and then he was kept waiting for more than ten minutes while the military made some movement that their officers thought requisite. This gratuitous piece of cruel torture has shocked the whole country. But Brown stood perfectly firm and calm through the whole. . . .

What its results will be no one can tell, but they cannot be otherwise than great. One great moving fact remains that here was a man, who, setting himself firm on the Gospel, was willing to sacrifice himself and his children in the cause of the oppressed, or at least of those whom he believed unrighteously held in bondage. And this fact has been forced home to the consciousness of every one by Brown's speech at his trial, and by the simple and most affecting letters which he wrote during his imprisonment. The events of this last month or two (including under the word events the impression made by Brown's character) have done more to confirm the opposition to Slavery at the North, and to open the eyes of the South to the danger of taking a stand upon this matter opposed to the moral convictions of the civilized world,—than anything which has ever happened before, than all the anti-slavery tracts and novels that ever were written.

FROM Sara Norton and M. A. DeWolfe Howe, eds., *Letters of Charles Eliot Norton*, vol. 1 (Boston: Houghton Mifflin Company, 1913), pp. 197–201.

1

ROBERT TOOMBS

The South Must Strike
while There Is Yet Time (1860)

The most famous public debate over secession occurred in Georgia in late November 1860. Over the course of a week, some of the state's most important political leaders, including both Unionists and secessionists, spoke in the legislative hall at Milledgeville, the state capital. Public opinion in the state was closely divided on the question of secession, and the prominence of the speakers ensured that the debate would attract widespread attention. One of the first speakers was Senator Robert Toombs, who spoke on the evening of November 13. After a period of indecision, the flamboyant Toombs had become an outspoken secessionist. Toombs's speech, which is more impressive for its emotional power than its logical rigor, effectively expressed the fears and foreboding of the future that energized the secessionist movement. In this excerpt, he explains why Lincoln's election justifies Georgia's secession.

The Abolitionists say you are raising a clamor because you were beaten in the election. The falsity of this statement needs no confirmation. Look to our past history for its refutation. Some excellent citizens and able men in Georgia say the election of any man constitutionally is no cause for a dissolution of the Union. That position is calculated only to mislead, and not to enlighten. It is not the issue. I say the election of Lincoln, with all of its surroundings, is sufficient. What is the significance of his election? It is the indorsement, by the non-slaveholding States, of all those acts of aggression upon our rights by all these States, legislatures, governors, judges, and people. He is elected by the perpetrators of these wrongs with the purpose and intent to aid and support them in wrong-doing.

Hitherto the Constitution has had on its side the Federal Executive, whose duty it is to execute the laws and Constitution against these malefactors. It has earnestly endeavored to discharge that duty. . . . The Executive has been faithful—the Federal judiciary have been faithful—the President has appointed sound judges, sound marshals, and other subordinate officers to interpret and to execute the laws. With the best intentions, they have all failed—our property has been stolen, our people murdered; felons and assassins have found sanctuary in the arms of the party which elected Mr. Lincoln. The Executive power, the last bulwark of the Constitution to defend us against these enemies of the Constitution, has been swept away, and we now stand without a shield, with bare bosoms presented to our enemies. . . . Therefore, redress

FROM Frank H. Moore, ed., *The Rebellion Record*, vol. 1 suppl. (New York: G. P. Putnam, 1861), pp. 366–67.

for past and present wrongs demands resistance to the rule of Lincoln and his Abolition horde over us; he comes at their head to shield and protect them in the perpetration of these outrages upon us, and, what is more, he comes at their head to aid them in consummating their avowed purposes by the power of the Federal Government. Their main purpose, as indicated by all their acts of hostility to slavery, is its final and total abolition. His party declare it; their acts prove it. He has declared it; I accept his declaration. The battle of the irrepressible conflict has hitherto been fought on his side alone. We demand service in this war. Surely no one will deny that the election of Lincoln is the indorsement of the policy of those who elected him, and an indorsement of his own opinions. . . . Since the promotion of Mr. Lincoln's party, all of them speak with one voice, and speak trumpet-tongued their fixed purpose to outlaw four thousand millions of our property in the Territories, and to put it under the ban of the empire in the States where it exists. They declare their purpose to war against slavery until there shall not be a slave in America, and until the African is elevated to a social and political equality with the white man. Lincoln in-

dorses them and their principles, and in his own speeches declares the conflict irrepressible and enduring, until slavery is everywhere abolished.

Hitherto they have carried on this warfare by State action, by individual action, by appropriation, by the incendiary's torch and the poisoned bowl. They were compelled to adopt this method because the Federal executive and the Federal judiciary were against them. They will have possession of the Federal executive with its vast power, patronage, prestige of legality, its army, its navy, and its revenue on the fourth of March next. Hitherto it has been on the side of the Constitution and the right; after the fourth of March it will be in the hands of your enemy. . . . Nothing but ruin will follow delay. The enemy on the fourth of March will intrench himself behind a quintuple wall of defence. Executive power, judiciary, (Mr. Seward has already proclaimed its reformation,) army, navy, and treasury. Twenty years of labor, and toil, and taxes all expended upon preparation, would not make up for the advantage your enemies would gain if the rising sun on the fifth of March should find you in the Union. Then strike while it is yet time.

2

ALEXANDER H. STEPHENS

Lincoln's Election Does Not Justify Secession
(1860)

On the evening after Toombs spoke, Alexander H. Stephens rose to reply for the Unionists. The diminutive, reserved Stephens, who weighed less than a hundred pounds, offered a sharp contrast with the physically imposing, gregarious Toombs. Nonetheless, the two men had been close friends and political allies for two decades, going back to their early years together in the Whig party. On this issue, however, they parted company. Indeed, Stephens would lead the Unionist forces at the subsequent popular convention in a vain effort to keep Georgia in the Union. Stephens, who had been present for Toombs's address, delivered a carefully prepared, dispassionate speech denying that Georgia had sufficient cause following Lincoln's election to break up the Union. His address lacked the fire of Toombs's oration but surpassed it in logical acuity.

The first question that presents itself is, Shall the people of the South secede from the Union in consequence of the election of Mr. Lincoln to the Presidency of the United States? My countrymen, I tell you frankly, candidly, and earnestly, that I do not think they ought. In my judgment, the election of no man, constitutionally chosen to that high office, is sufficient cause for any State to separate from the Union. It ought to stand by and aid still in maintaining the Constitution of the country. To make a point of resistance to the Government, to withdraw from it because a man has been constitutionally elected, puts us in the wrong. We are pledged to maintain the Constitution. Many of us have sworn to support it. Can we, therefore, for the mere election of a man to the Presidency, and that too in accordance with the prescribed forms of the Constitution, make a point of resistance to the Government, without becoming the breakers of that sacred instrument ourselves by withdrawing ourselves from it? Would we not be in the wrong? Whatever fate is to befall this country, let it never be laid to the charge of the people of the South, and especially to the people of Georgia, that we were untrue to our national engagements. Let the fault and the wrong rest upon others. If all our hopes are to be blasted, if the Republic is to go down, let us be found to the last moment standing on the deck with the Constitution of the United States waving over our heads. Let the fanatics of the North break the Constitution, if such is their fell purpose. Let the responsibility be upon them. I shall presently speak more of their acts; but let not the South—let us not be the ones to commit the aggression. We went into the election with this people. The result was different from what we wished; but the election has been constitutionally held. Were we to make a point of resistance to the Government and go out of the Union on that account, the record would be made up hereafter against us.

But it is said that Mr. Lincoln's policy and principles are against the Constitution, and that, if he carries them out, it will be destructive of our rights. Let us not anticipate a threatened evil. If he violates the Constitution, then will come our time to act. Do not let *us* break it, because, forsooth, *he* may. If he does, that is the time for us to strike. I think it would be injudicious and unwise to do this sooner. I do not anticipate that Mr. Lincoln will do anything to jeopard[ize] our safety or security, whatever may be his spirit to do it; for he is bound by the constitutional checks which are thrown around him, which at this time render him powerless to do any great mischief. This shows the wisdom of our system. The President of the United States . . . is clothed with no absolute power. He can do nothing unless he is backed by power in Congress. The House of Representatives is largely in a majority against him. In the very face and teeth of the heavy majority which he has obtained in the Northern States, there have been large gains in the House of Representatives to the Conservative Constitutional party of the country, which here I will call the National Democratic party, because that is the cognomen it has at the North. . . . In the present Congress there were one hundred and thirteen Republicans, when it takes one hundred and seventeen to make a majority. The gains in the Democratic party in Pennsylvania, Ohio, New Jersey, New York, Indiana, and other States, notwithstanding its distractions, have been enough to make a majority of near thirty in the next House against Mr. Lincoln. . . . Is this the time, then, to apprehend that Mr. Lincoln, with this large majority in the House of Representatives against him, can carry out any of his unconstitutional principles in that body?

In the Senate he will also be powerless. There will be a majority of four against him. . . . Mr. Lincoln cannot appoint an officer without the consent of the Senate,—he cannot form a cabinet without the same consent. . . . Then how can Mr. Lincoln obtain a cabinet which would aid him, or allow him, to violate the Constitution. Why, then, I say, should we disrupt the ties of the Union when his hands are tied,—when he can do nothing against us?

FROM Richard M. Johnson and William H. Brown, *Life of Alexander H. Stephens* (Philadelphia: J. B. Lippincott and Co., 1878), pp. 564–68.

I have heard it mooted that no man in the State of Georgia who is true to her interests could hold office under Mr. Lincoln. But I ask who appoints to office? Not the President alone; the Senate has to concur. No man can be appointed without the consent of the Senate. Should any man, then, refuse to hold office that was given him by a Democratic Senate? . . .

My honorable friend who addressed you last night (Mr. Toombs), and to whom I listened with the profoundest attention, asks if we would submit to Black Republican rule? I say to you and to him, as a Georgian, I never would submit to any Black Republican aggression upon our Constitutional rights.

I will never myself consent, as much as I admire this Union, for the glories of the past or the blessings of the present, as much as it has done for civilisation; as much as the hopes of the world hang upon it; I would never submit to aggression upon my rights to maintain it longer; and if they cannot be maintained in the Union standing on the Georgia platform [of 1850], where I have stood from the time of its adoption, I would be in favor of disrupting every tie which binds the States together. I will have equality for Georgia and for the citizens of Georgia in this Union, or I will look for new safeguards elsewhere. This is my position. The only question now is, Can this be secured in the Union? This is what I am counselling with you to-night about. Can it be secured? In my judgment it may be; but it may not be; but let us do all we can, so that in the future, if the worst comes, it may never be said we were negligent in doing our duty to the last.

3

South Carolina Justifies Secession (1860)

The popular convention in South Carolina issued a "Declaration of Causes which Induced the Secession of South Carolina," justifying the state's decision to leave the Union. Written by Christopher Memminger, one of the less radical secessionist leaders, this statement was designed to rally support for secession in other southern states. It places heavy emphasis on the importance of the slavery issue in the breakup of the Union.

The people of the State of South Carolina in Convention assembled, on the 2d day of April, A. D. 1852, declared that the frequent violations of the Constitution of the United States by the Federal Government, and its encroachments upon the reserved rights of the States, fully justified this State in their withdrawal from the Federal Union; but in deference to the opinions and wishes of the other Slaveholding States, she forbore at that time to exercise this right. Since that time these encroachments have continued to increase, and further forbearance ceases to be a virtue.

And now the State of South Carolina having resumed her separate and equal place among nations, deems it due to herself, to the remaining United States of America, and to the nations of the world, that she should declare the immediate causes which have led to this act. . . .

[During the Revolutionary War] were established the two great principles asserted by the Colonies, namely, the right of a State to govern itself; and the right of a people to abolish a Government when it becomes destructive of the ends for which it was instituted. . . .

FROM Frank H. Moore, ed., *The Rebellion Record*, vol. 1 (New York: G. P. Putnam, 1861), pp. 3–4.

In 1787, Deputies were appointed by the States to revise the articles of Confederation; and on 17th September, 1787, these Deputies recommended, for the adoption of the States, the Articles of Union, known as the Constitution of the United States. . . .

Thus was established, by compact between the States, a Government with defined objects and powers, limited to the express words of the grant. . . . We hold that the Government thus established is subject to the two great principles asserted in the Declaration of Independence; and we hold further, that the mode of its formation subjects it to a third fundamental principle, namely, the law of compact. We maintain that in every compact between two or more parties, the obligation is mutual; that the failure of one of the contracting parties to perform a material part of the agreement, entirely releases the obligation of the other; and that, where no arbiter is provided, each party is remitted to his own judgment to determine the fact of failure, with all its consequences.

In the present case, that fact is established with certainty. We assert that fourteen of the States have deliberately refused for years past to fulfil their constitutional obligations [to return fugitive slaves], and we refer to their own statutes for the proof. . . .

. . . The States of Maine, New Hampshire, Vermont, Massachusetts, Connecticut, Rhode Island, New York, Pennsylvania, Illinois, Indiana, Michigan, Wisconsin, and Iowa, have enacted laws which either nullify the acts of Congress, or render useless any attempt to execute them. In many of these States the fugitive is discharged from the service of labor claimed, and in none of them has the State Government complied with the stipulation made in the Constitution. . . . Thus the constitutional compact has been deliberately broken and disregarded by the non-slaveholding States; and the consequence follows that South Carolina is released from her obligation. . . .

We affirm that these ends for which this Government was instituted have been defeated, and the Government itself has been destructive of them by the action of the non-slaveholding States. Those States have assumed the right of deciding upon the propriety of our domestic institutions; and have denied the rights of property established in fifteen of the States and recognized by the Constitution; they have denounced as sinful the institution of Slavery; they have permitted the open establishment among them of societies, whose avowed object is to disturb the peace of and eloin [i.e., carry away] the property of the citizens of other States. They have encouraged and assisted thousands of our slaves to leave their homes; and those who remain, have been incited by emissaries, books, and pictures, to servile insurrection.

For twenty-five years this agitation has been steadily increasing, until it has now secured to its aid the power of the common Government. Observing the *forms* of the Constitution, a sectional party has found within that article establishing the Executive Department, the means of subverting the Constitution itself. A geographical line has been drawn across the Union, and all the States north of that line have united in the election of a man to the high office of President of the United States whose opinions and purposes are hostile to Slavery. . . .

On the 4th of March next this party will take possession of the Government. It has announced that the South shall be excluded from the common territory, that the Judicial tribunal shall be made sectional, and that a war must be waged against Slavery until it shall cease throughout the United States.

The guarantees of the Constitution will then no longer exist; the equal rights of the States will be lost. The Slaveholding States will no longer have the power of self-government, or self-protection, and the Federal Government will have become their enemy.

Sectional interest and animosity will deepen the irritation; and all hope of remedy is rendered vain, by the fact that the public opinion at the North has invested a great political error with the sanctions of a more erroneous religious belief.

We, therefore, the people of South Carolina, by our delegates in Convention assembled, appealing to the Supreme Judge of the world for the rectitude of our intentions, have solemnly declared that the Union heretofore existing between this State and the other States of North America is dissolved, and that the State of South Carolina has resumed her position among the nations of the world, as separate and independent state, with full power to levy war, conclude peace, contract alliances, establish commerce, and to do all other acts and things which independent States may of right do.

4

ABRAHAM LINCOLN

I Hold That the Union Is Perpetual (1861)

Abraham Lincoln wrote his first inaugural address before he left Springfield, Illinois, in February 1861. It was directed simultaneously to northerners who were increasingly angry over the secession movement in the South, and to southern whites fearful of the future now that the Republicans controlled the executive branch of the federal government. The result was a carefully crafted document, designed to uphold the permanency of the Union while at the same time trying to assure southerners about his intentions and their security in the Union. When he reached Washington, Lincoln showed it to several advisers, who recommended some verbal changes to soften its language. He incorporated most of these suggestions in his final text. He also added a new conclusion, based on a draft by William Henry Seward, who was to be secretary of state in his cabinet. Lincoln's skill as a writer and his ability to use words carefully are readily apparent in this address. So, too, is his extraordinary literary grace, most obviously displayed in the memorable final paragraph.

Fellow-Citizens of the United States:

In compliance with a custom as old as the Government itself, I appear before you to address you briefly and to take in your presence the oath prescribed by the Constitution of the United States to be taken by the President "before he enters on the execution of his office."

I do not consider it necessary at present for me to discuss those matters of administration about which there is no special anxiety or excitement.

Apprehension seems to exist among the people of the Southern States that by the accession of a Republican Administration their property and their peace and personal security are to be endangered. There has never been any reasonable cause for such apprehension. Indeed, the most ample evidence to the contrary has all the while existed and been open to their inspection. It is found in nearly all the published speeches of him who now addresses you. I do but quote from one of those speeches when I declare that "I have no purpose, directly or indirectly, to interfere with the institution of slavery in the States where it exists. I believe I have no lawful right to do so, and I have no inclination to do so." . . .

I now reiterate these sentiments, and in doing so I only press upon the public attention the most conclusive evidence of which the case is susceptible that the property, peace, and security of no section

FROM James D. Richardson, ed., *A Compilation of the Messages and Papers of the Presidents*, vol. 6 (Washington, D.C.: Government Printing Office, 1907), pp. 1–12.

are to be in any wise endangered by the now incoming Administration. I add, too, that all the protection which, consistently with the Constitution and the laws, can be given will be cheerfully given to all the States when lawfully demanded, for whatever cause—as cheerfully to one section as to another.

There is much controversy about the delivering up of fugitives from service or labor. The clause I now read is as plainly written in the Constitution as any other of its provisions: "No person held to service or labor in one State, under the laws thereof, escaping into another, shall in consequence of any law or regulation therein be discharged from such service or labor, but shall be delivered up on claim of the party to whom such service or labor may be due."

It is scarcely questioned that this provision was intended by those who made it for the reclaiming of what we call fugitive slaves; and the intention of the lawgiver is the law. All members of Congress swear their support to the whole Constitution—to this provision as much as to any other. . . . Now, if they would make the effort in good temper, could they not with nearly equal unanimity frame and pass a law by means of which to keep good that unanimous oath? . . .

Again: In any law upon this subject ought not all the safeguards of liberty known in civilized and humane jurisprudence to be introduced, so that a free man be not in any case surrendered as a slave? And might it not be well at the same time to provide by law for the enforcement of that clause in the Constitution which guarantees that "the citizens of each State shall be entitled to all privileges and immunities of citizens in the several States"? . . .

It is seventy-two years since the first inauguration of a President under our National Constitution. During that period fifteen different and greatly distinguished citizens have in succession administered the executive branch of the Government. . . . I now enter upon the same task for the brief constitutional term of four years under great and peculiar difficulty. A disruption of the Federal Union, heretofore only menaced, is now formidably attempted.

I hold that in contemplation of universal law and of the Constitution the Union of these States is perpetual. Perpetuity is implied, if not expressed, in the fundamental law of all national governments. It is safe to assert that no government proper ever had a provision in its organic law for its own termination. Continue to execute all the express provisions of our National Constitution, and the Union will endure forever, it being impossible to destroy it except by some action not provided for in the instrument itself.

Again: If the United States be not a government proper, but an association of States in the nature of contract merely, can it, as a contract, be peaceably unmade by less than all the parties who made it? One party to a contract may violate it—break it, so to speak—but does it not require all to lawfully rescind it?

Descending from these general principles, we find the proposition that in legal contemplation the Union is perpetual confirmed by the history of the Union itself. The Union is much older than the Constitution. It was formed, in fact, by the Articles of Association in 1774. It was matured and continued by the Declaration of Independence in 1776. It was further matured, and the faith of all the then thirteen States expressly plighted and engaged that it should be perpetual, by the Articles of Confederation in 1778. And finally, in 1787, one of the declared objects for ordaining and establishing the Constitution was "*to form a more perfect Union.*"

But if destruction of the Union by one or by a part only of the States be lawfully possible, the Union is *less* perfect than before the Constitution, having lost the vital element of perpetuity.

It follows from these views that no State upon its own mere motion can lawfully get out of the Union; that *resolves* and *ordinances* to that effect are legally void, and that acts of violence within any State or States against the authority of the United States are insurrectionary or revolutionary, according to circumstances.

I therefore consider that in view of the Constitution and the laws the Union is unbroken, and to the extent of my ability I shall take care, as the Constitution itself expressly enjoins upon me, that the laws of the Union be faithfully executed in all the States. Doing this I deem to be only a simple duty on my part, and I shall perform it so far as practicable unless my rightful masters, the American people, shall withhold the requisite means or in some authoritative manner direct the contrary. I trust this will not be regarded as a menace, but only as the declared purpose of the Union that it *will* constitutionally defend and maintain itself.

In doing this there needs to be no bloodshed or violence, and there shall be none unless it be forced upon the national authority. The power confided to me will be used to hold, occupy, and possess the property and places belonging to the Government and to collect the duties and imposts; but beyond what may be necessary for these objects, there will be no invasion, no using of force against or among the people anywhere. Where hostility to the United States in any interior locality shall be so great and universal as to prevent competent resident citizens from holding the Federal offices, there will be no attempt to force obnoxious strangers among the people for that object. . . .

. . . To those . . . who really love the Union may I not speak?

Before entering upon so grave a matter as the destruction of our national fabric, with all its benefits, its memories, and its hopes, would it not be wise to ascertain precisely why we do it? Will you hazard so desperate a step while there is any possibility that any portion of the ills you fly from have no real existence? Will you, while the certain ills you fly to are greater than all the real ones you fly from, will you risk the commission of so fearful a mistake?

All profess to be content in the Union if all constitutional rights can be maintained. Is it true, then, that any right plainly written in the Constitution has been denied? I think not. . . . If by the mere force of numbers a majority should deprive a minority of any clearly written constitutional right, it might in a moral point of view justify revolution; certainly would if such right were a vital one. But such is not our case. . . .

. . . If the minority will not acquiesce, the majority must, or the Government must cease. There

is no other alternative, for continuing the Government is acquiescence on one side or the other. If a minority in such case will secede rather than acquiesce, they make a precedent which in turn will divide and ruin them, for a minority of their own will secede from them whenever a majority refuses to be controlled by such minority. . . .

Plainly the central idea of secession is the essence of anarchy. A majority held in restraint by constitutional checks and limitations, and always changing easily with deliberate changes of popular opinions and sentiments, is the only true sovereign of a free people. Whoever rejects it does of necessity fly to anarchy or to despotism. Unanimity is impossible. The rule of a minority, as a permanent arrangement, is wholly inadmissible; so that, rejecting the majority principle, anarchy or despotism in some form is all that is left. . . .

One section of our country believes slavery is *right* and ought to be extended, while the other believes it is *wrong* and ought not to be extended. This is the only substantial dispute. The fugitive-slave clause of the Constitution and the law for the suppression of the foreign slave trade are each as well enforced, perhaps, as any law can ever be in a community where the moral sense of the people imperfectly supports the law itself. . . . It would be worse in both cases *after* the separation of the sections than before. The foreign slave trade, now imperfectly suppressed, would be ultimately revived without restriction in one section, while fugitive slaves, now only partially surrendered, would not be surrendered at all by the other.

Physically speaking, we can not separate. We can not remove our respective sections from each other nor build an impassable wall between them. A husband and wife may be divorced and go out of the presence and beyond the reach of each other, but the different parts of our country can not do this. They can not but remain face to face, and intercourse, either amicable or hostile, must continue between them. Is it possible, then, to make that intercourse more advantageous or more satisfactory *after* separation than *before*? . . .

This country, with its institutions, belongs to the people who inhabit it. Whenever they shall grow weary of the existing Government, they can exercise their *constitutional* right of amending it or their *revolutionary* right to dismember or overthrow it. . . . I understand a proposed amendment to the Constitution . . . has passed Congress, to the effect that the Federal Government shall never interfere with the domestic institutions of the States, including that of persons held to service. To avoid misconstruction of what I have said, I depart from my purpose not to speak of particular amendments so far as to say that, holding such a provision to now be implied constitutional law, I have no objection to its being made express and irrevocable.

The Chief Magistrate derives all his authority from the people, and they have conferred none upon him to fix terms for the separation of the States. The people themselves can do this also if they choose, but the Executive as such has nothing to do with it. His duty is to administer the present Government as it came to his hands and to transmit it unimpaired by him to his successor.

Why should there not be a patient confidence in the ultimate justice of the people? Is there any better or equal hope in the world? In our present differences, is either party without faith of being in the right? If the Almighty Ruler of Nations, with His eternal truth and justice, be on your side of the North, or on yours of the South, that truth and that justice will surely prevail by the judgment of this great tribunal of the American people. . . .

In *your* hands, my dissatisfied fellow-countrymen, and not in *mine*, is the momentous issue of civil war. The Government will not assail *you*. You can have no conflict without being yourselves the aggressors. *You* have no oath registered in heaven to destroy the Government, while *I* shall have the most solemn one to "preserve, protect, and defend it."

I am loath to close. We are not enemies, but friends. We must not be enemies. Though passion may have strained it must not break our bonds of affection. The mystic chords of memory, stretching from every battlefield and patriot grave to every living heart and hearthstone all over this broad land, will yet swell the chorus of the Union, when again touched, as surely they will be, by the better angels of our nature.

5

GEORGE TEMPLETON STRONG

The Outbreak of War Galvanizes New York City

(1861)

George Templeton Strong was a wealthy New York City lawyer who kept an extensive diary during the Civil War era. Elitist and conservative, he was a Republican, although he was not always active politically. He was one of the directors of the U.S. Sanitary Commission, which raised money and medical supplies for military hospitals during the war. In the following entries, he describes the public reaction in the city to the beginning of the Civil War.

April 13 [*1861*]. Here begins a new chapter of my journal, entitled WAR. . . .

This morning's papers confirmed last night's news; viz., that the rebels opened fire at Sumter yesterday morning. . . .

So Civil War is inaugurated at last. God defend the Right. . . .

The Northern backbone is much stiffened already. Many who stood up for "Southern rights" and complained of wrongs done the South now say that, since the South has fired the first gun, they are ready to go all lengths in supporting the government. . . .

April 14, Sunday. . . . There is no doubt that Fort Sumter has surrendered. . . .

From all I can learn, the effect of this on Democrats, heretofore Southern and quasi-treasonable in their talk, has fully justified the sacrifice. I hear of [prominent conservative Democrats] denouncing rebellion and declaring themselves ready to go all lengths in upholding government. If this class of men has been secured and converted to loyalty, the gain to the country is worth ten Sumters. . . .

April 15. Events multiply. The President is out with a proclamation calling for 75,000 volunteers and an extra session of Congress July 4. It is said 200,000 more will be called within a few days. Every man of them will be wanted before this game is lost and won. Change in public feeling marked, and a thing to thank God for. We begin to look like a United North. . . .

April 18. . . . We are living a month of common life every day . . . the attitude of New York and the whole North at this time is magnificent. Perfect unanimity, earnestness, and readiness to make every sacrifice for the support of law and national life. . . .

Went to the [City] Hall. The [Sixth] Massachusetts Regiment, which arrived here last night, was marching down on its way to Washington. Im-

mense crowd; immense cheering. My eyes filled with tears, and I was half choked in sympathy with the contagious excitement. God be praised for the unity of feeling here! It is beyond, very far beyond, anything I hoped for. If it only last, we are safe. . . .

April 19. . . . After long waiting and watching, the Seventh Regiment appeared, far up Broadway—a bluish steel-grey light on the blackness of the dense mob that filled the street. . . . As they came nearer and passed by, the roar of the crowd was grand and terrible. It drowned the brass of the regimental band.

April 20, Saturday. . . . Broadway crowded and more crowded as one approached Union Square. Large companies of recruits in citizen's dress parading up and down, cheered and cheering. Small mobs round the headquarters of the regiments that are going to Washington, staring at the sentinel on duty. Every other man, woman, and child bearing a flag or decorated with a cockade. Flags from almost every building. The city seems to have gone suddenly wild and crazy.

The Union mass-meeting was an event. Few assemblages have equalled it in numbers and unanimity. Tonight's extra says there were 250,000 present. That must be an exaggeration. But the multitude was enormous. All the area bounded by Fourteenth and Seventeenth Streets, Broadway and Fourth Avenue, was filled. In many places it was densely packed, and nowhere could one push his way without difficulty. . . . There were several stands for orators, and scores of little speechifying ganglia besides, from carts, windows, and front stoops. [Major Robert] Anderson appeared and was greeted with roars that were tremendous to hear. The crowd, or some of them, and the ladies and gentlemen who occupied the windows and lined the housetops all round Union Square, sang "The Star-Spangled Banner," and the people generally hurrahed a voluntary after each verse. . . .

FROM Allan Nevins and Milton Halsey Thomas, eds., *The Diary of George Templeton Strong*, vol. 3 (New York: The Macmillan Company, 1952), pp. 117–28.

6

WILLIAM HOWARD RUSSELL

The Popular Mood in Charleston at the Start of the Civil War (1861)

William Russell was a reporter for the London Times, *who arrived in the United States in March 1861 in order to report on the growing crisis in the United States. He visited both the North and the South in the first weeks after he landed and conducted interviews with both Abraham Lincoln and Jefferson Davis. Russell soon offended the North, both by his conviction that the Union could never be restored to what it had been and by his harsh description of the Union defeat at the Battle of Bull Run. The War Department subsequently refused to allow him to visit the front, and so in 1862 Russell, feeling he could no longer accurately report on the war, returned to England. He immediately published his observations as* My Diary North and South *(1863). In the following selection, he reports on popular sentiment in Charleston, which he hastened back to following the surrender of Fort Sumter in April 1861, now that the war had begun. (Paragraphing has been slightly modified.)*

April 17 [*1861*]. The streets of Charleston present some such aspect of those of Paris in the last revolution. Crowds of armed men singing and promenading the streets. The battle-blood running through their veins—that hot oxygen which is called "the flush of victory" on the cheek; restaurants full, revelling in barrooms, club-rooms crowded, orgies and carousing in tavern or private house, in tap-room, from cabaret—down narrow alleys, in the broad highway. Sumter has set them distraught; never was such a victory; never such brave lads; never such a sight. There are pamphlets already full of the incident. It is a bloodless Waterloo or Solferino.

After breakfast I went down to the quay, with a party of the General's staff, to visit Fort Sumter. The senators and governors turned soldiers wore blue military caps, with "palmetto" trees embroidered thereon; blue frockcoats, with upright col-lars, and shoulder straps edged with lace and marked with two silver bars, to designate their rank of captain; gilt buttons, with the palmetto in relief; blue trowsers, with a gold-lace cord, and brass spurs—no straps. . . . The streets were crowded with lanky lads, clanking spurs, and sabres, with awkward squads marching to and fro, with drummers beating calls, and ruffles, and points of war; around them groups of grinning Negroes delighted with the glare and glitter, a holiday and a new idea for them—secession flags waving out of all the windows. . . . As we walked down towards the quay, where the steamer was lying, numerous traces of the unsettled state of men's minds broke out in the hurried conversations of the various friends who stopped to speak for a few moments. "Well, governor, the old Union is gone at last!" "Have you heard what Abe is going to do?" "I don't think [General Pierre] Beauregard will have much more fighting for it. What do you think?" And so on. . . .

There was a large crowd around the pier. . . . As we got on deck, . . . I was presented to many

FROM William Howard Russell, *My Diary North and South,* vol. 1 (London: Bradbury and Evans, 1863), pp. 143–44, 146–48, 153, 159–61.

judges, colonels, and others of the mass of society on board, and "after compliments," . . . I was generally asked in the first place, what I thought of the capture of Sumter, and in the second, what England would do when the news reached the other side. Already the Carolinians regard the Northern States as an alien and detested enemy, and entertain, or profess, an immense affection for Great Britain. . . .

Secession is the fashion here. Young ladies sing for it; old ladies pray for it; young men are dying to fight for it; old men are ready to demonstrate it. The founder of the school was St. Calhoun. Here his pupils carry out their teaching in thunder and fire. States' Rights are displayed after its legitimate teaching, and the Palmetto flag and the red bars of the Confederacy are its exposition. The utter contempt and loathing for the venerated Stars and Stripes, the abhorrence of the very words United States, the intense hatred of the Yankee on the part of these people, cannot be conceived by anyone who has not seen them. I am more satisfied than ever that the Union can never be restored as it was, and that it has gone to pieces, never to be put together again in the old shape, at all events by any power on earth. . . .

. . . It was near nightfall before we set foot on the quay of Charleston. The city was indicated by the blaze of lights, and by the continual roll of drums, and the noisy music, and the yelling cheers which rose above its streets. . . .

But listen! There is a great tumult, as of many voices coming up the street, heralded by blasts of music. It is a speech-making from the front of the hotel. Such an agitated, lively multitude! How they cheer the pale, frantic man, limber and dark-haired, with uplifted arms and clenched fists, who is perorating on the balcony! "What did he say?" "Who is he?" "Why it's he again!" "That's Roger Pryor[1]—he says that if them Yankee trash don't listen to reason and stand from under, we'll march to the North and dictate the terms of peace in Faneuil Hall [in Boston]! Yes, sir—and so we will, certa-i-n su-re!" "No matter, for all that; we have shown we can whip the Yankees wherever we meet them—at Washington or down here." How much I heard of all this to-day—how much more this evening!

---

[1]Roger Pryor, who had recently resigned from Congress, was editor of the *Richmond Enquirer* and a strong secessionist.

PART 2

The Civil War

1

ALEXANDER H. STEPHENS

Slavery Is the Cornerstone of the Confederacy

(1861)

As we have seen, Alexander H. Stephens opposed secession following Lincoln's election (see p. 58). Indeed, he was the leader of the Unionist forces in the Georgia secession convention in 1861 and embraced southern independence only after his state seceded. Nevertheless, he was elected vice president of the Confederacy. In a speech delivered in Savannah in March 1861, shortly after his election, he discussed the central importance of slavery to the Confederacy. Jefferson Davis was dismayed by Stephens's blunt identification of the Confederacy with slavery, not because he disagreed with this point, but because he believed that it would hurt Confederate efforts to win European diplomatic recognition.

But not to be tedious in enumerating the numerous changes for the better, allow me to allude to one other—though last, not least: the new Constitution has put at rest *forever* all the agitating questions relating to our peculiar institutions— African slavery as it exists among us—the proper *status* of the negro in our form of civilization. *This was the immediate cause of the late rupture and present revolution.* JEFFERSON, in his forecast, had anticipated this, as the "rock upon which the old Union would split." He was right. What was conjecture with him, is now a realized fact. But whether he fully comprehended the great truth upon which that rock *stood* and *stands*, may be doubted. *The prevailing ideas entertained by him and most of the leading statesmen at the time of the formation of the old Constitution were, that the enslavement of the African was in violation of the laws*

FROM Frank H. Moore, ed., *The Rebellion Record*, vol. 1 (New York: G. P. Putnam, 1861–1868), pp. 45–46.

of nature; that it was wrong in principle, socially, morally and politically. It was an evil they knew not well how to deal with; but the general opinion of the men of that day was, that, somehow or other, in the order of Providence, the institution would be evanescent and pass away. This idea, though not incorporated in the Constitution, was the prevailing idea at the time. The Constitution, it is true, secured every essential guarantee to the institution while it should last, and hence no argument can be justly used against the constitutional guarantees thus secured, because of the common sentiment of the day. *Those ideas, however, were fundamentally wrong. They rested upon the assumption of the equality of races. This was an error.* It was a sandy foundation, and the idea of a Government built upon it—when the "storm came and the wind blew, it *fell.*"

Our new Government is founded upon exactly the opposite ideas; its foundations are laid, its cornerstone rests, upon the great truth that the negro is not equal to the white man; that slavery, subordination to the superior race, is his natural and moral condition. This, our new Government, is the first, in the history of the world, based upon this great physical, philosophical, and moral truth. . . .

. . . It is the first Government ever instituted upon principles in strict conformity to nature, and the ordination of Providence, in furnishing the materials of human society. Many Governments have been founded upon the principles of certain classes; but the classes thus enslaved, were of the same race, and in violation of the laws of nature. Our system commits no such violation of nature's laws. The negro by nature, or by the curse against Canaan, is fitted for that condition which he occupies in our system. . . . The substratum of our society is made of the material fitted by nature for it, and by experience we know that it is the best, not only for the superior but for the inferior race, that it should be so.

2

JEFFERSON DAVIS

Our Cause Is Just (1861)

In his message to the Confederate Congress on April 29, 1861, Jefferson Davis attributed the war to the aggressions of the North and the Lincoln administration against slavery and the rights of the South. He devoted particular attention to the constitutional theory of secession in order to repel the charge that the southern states had acted illegally in leaving the Union or were responsible for the war that had now begun. (The paragraphing has been slightly modified.)

Montgomery, April 29, 1861.

Gentlemen of the Congress:

. . . The declaration of war made against this Confederacy by Abraham Lincoln, the President of the United States, in his proclamation issued on the 15th day of the present month, rendered it necessary, in my judgment, that you should convene at the earliest practicable moment to devise the measures necessary for the defense of the country. The occasion is indeed an extraordinary one. It justifies me in a brief review of the relations heretofore existing between us and the States which now unite in warfare against us and in a succinct statement of the events which have resulted in this warfare, to the end that mankind may pass intelligent and impartial judgment on its motives and objects. . . .

. . . The people of the Southern States, whose almost exclusive occupation was agriculture, early perceived a tendency in the Northern States to render the common government subservient to their own purposes by imposing burdens on commerce as a protection to their manufacturing and shipping interests. Long and angry controversies grew out of these attempts, often successful, to benefit one section of the country at the expense of the other. And the danger of disruption arising from this cause was enhanced by the fact that the Northern population was increasing, by immigration and other causes, in a greater ratio than the population of the South. By degrees, as the Northern States gained preponderance in the National Congress, self-interest taught their people to yield ready assent to any plausible advocacy of their right as a majority to govern the minority without

FROM James D. Richardson, ed., *A Compilation of the Messages and Papers of the Confederacy*, vol. 1 (Nashville: United States Publishing Company, 1905), pp. 63–66.

control. They learned to listen with impatience to the suggestion of any constitutional impediment to the exercise of their will, and so utterly have the principles of the Constitution been corrupted in the Northern mind that, in the inaugural address delivered by President Lincoln in March last, he asserts as an axiom, which he plainly deems to be undeniable, that the theory of the Constitution requires that in all cases the majority shall govern. . . . This is the lamentable and fundamental error on which rests the policy that has culminated in his declaration of war against these Confederate States.

In addition to the long-continued and deep-seated resentment felt by the Southern States at the persistent abuse of the powers they had delegated to the Congress, for the purpose of enriching the manufacturing and shipping classes of the North at the expense of the South, there has existed for nearly half a century another subject of discord, involving interests of such transcendent magnitude as at all times to create the apprehension in the minds of many devoted lovers of the Union that its permanence was impossible. When the several States delegated certain powers to the United States Congress, a large portion of the laboring population consisted of African slaves imported into the colonies by the mother country. . . . This property was recognized in the Constitution, and provision was made against its loss by the escape of the slave. The increase in the number of slaves by further importation from Africa was also secured by a clause forbidding Congress to prohibit the slave trade anterior to a certain date, and in no clause can there be found any delegation of power to the Congress authorizing it in any manner to legislate to the prejudice, detriment, or discouragement of the owners of that species of property, or excluding it from the protection of the Government.

The climate and soil of the Northern States soon proved unpropitious to the continuance of slave labor, whilst the converse was the case at the South. . . . As soon, however, as the Northern States that prohibited African slavery within their limits had reached a number sufficient to give their representation a controlling voice in the Congress, a persistent and organized system of hostile measures against the rights of the owners of slaves in the Southern States was inaugurated and gradually extended. A continuous series of measures was devised and prosecuted for the purpose of rendering insecure the tenure of property in slaves. Fanatical organizations, supplied with money by voluntary subscriptions, were assiduously engaged in exciting amongst the slaves a spirit of discontent and revolt; means were furnished for their escape from their owners, and agents secretly employed to entice them to abscond; the constitutional provision for their rendition to their owners was first evaded, then openly denounced as a violation of conscientious obligation and religious duty; men were taught that it was a merit to elude, disobey, and violently oppose the execution of the laws enacted to secure the performance of the promise contained in the constitutional compact; owners of slaves were mobbed and even murdered in open day solely for applying to a magistrate for the arrest of a fugitive slave; the dogmas of these voluntary organizations soon obtained control of the Legislatures of many of the Northern States, and laws were passed providing for the punishment, by ruinous fines and long-continued imprisonment in jails and penitentiaries, of citizens of the Southern States who should dare to ask aid of the officers of the law for the recovery of their property. Emboldened by success, the theater of agitation and aggression against the clearly expressed constitutional rights of the Southern States was transferred to the Congress; . . . the transaction of public affairs was impeded by repeated efforts to usurp powers not delegated by the Constitution, for the purpose of impairing the security of property in slaves, and reducing those States which held slaves to a condition of inferiority. Finally a great party was organized for the purpose of obtaining the administration of the Government, with the avowed object of using its power for the total exclusion of the slave States from all participation in the benefits of the public domain acquired by all the States in common, whether by conquest or purchase; of surrounding them entirely by States in which slavery should be prohibited; of thus rendering the property in slaves so insecure as to be comparatively worthless, and thereby annihilating in effect property worth thousands of millions of dollars. This party, thus organized, succeeded in the month of November last in the election of its candidate for the Presidency of the United States.

. . . With interests of such overwhelming magnitude imperiled, the people of the Southern States were driven by the conduct of the North to the adoption of some course of action to avert the danger with which they were openly menaced. With this view the Legislatures of the several States invited the people to select delegates to conventions to be held for the purpose of determining for themselves what measures were best adapted to meet so alarming a crisis in their history. . . . In the exercise of a right so ancient, so well-established, and so necessary for self-preservation, the people of the Confederate States, in their conventions, . . . passed ordinances resuming all their rights as sovereign and independent States and dissolved their connection with the other States of the Union.

Having done this, they proceeded to form a new compact amongst themselves by new articles of confederation. . . . They have organized their new Government in all its departments; the functions of the executive, legislative, and judicial magistrates are performed in accordance with the will of the people, as displayed not merely in a cheerful acquiescence, but in the enthusiastic support of the Government thus established by themselves; and but for the interference of the Government of the United States in this legitimate exercise of the right of a people to self-government, peace, happiness, and prosperity would now smile on our land. That peace is ardently desired by this Government and people has been manifested in every possible form. . . .

. . . We feel that our cause is just and holy; we protest solemnly in the face of mankind that we desire peace at any sacrifice save that of honor and independence; we seek no conquest, no aggrandizement, no concession of any kind from the States with which we were lately confederated; all we ask is to be let alone; that those who never held power over us shall not now attempt our subjugation by arms. This we will, this we must, resist to the direst extremity. The moment that this pretension is abandoned the sword will drop from our grasp, and we shall be ready to enter into treaties of amity and commerce that cannot but be mutually beneficial. So long as this pretension is maintained, with a firm reliance on that Divine Power which covers with its protection the just cause, we will continue to struggle for our inherent right to freedom, independence, and self-government.

3

ABRAHAM LINCOLN

This Is a People's Contest (1861)

Throughout the conflict, Abraham Lincoln repeatedly emphasized the larger issues at stake in the Civil War. Whereas Jefferson Davis in his message to the Confederate Congress focused on specific grievances of the southern states, Lincoln in his special message of July 4, 1861, placed the war in a broader ideological perspective. He concluded with a discussion of what was at stake for the Union in this struggle.

This issue embraces more than the fate of these United States. It presents to the whole family of man the question whether a constitutional republic, or democracy—a government of the people by the same people—can or can not maintain its territorial integrity against its own domestic foes. It presents the question whether discontented individuals, too few in numbers to control administration according to organic law in any case, can always, upon the pretenses made in this case, or on any other pretenses, or arbitrarily without any pretense, break up their government, and thus practically put an end to free government upon the earth. . . .

This is essentially a people's contest. On the side of the Union it is a struggle for maintaining in the world that form and substance of government whose leading object is to elevate the condition of men; to lift artificial weights from all shoulders; to clear the paths of laudable pursuit for all; to afford all an unfettered start and a fair chance in the race of life. Yielding to partial and temporary departures, from necessity, this is the leading object of the Government for whose existence we contend. . . .

Our popular Government has often been called an experiment. Two points in it our people have already settled—the successful *establishing* and the successful *administering* of it. One still remains— its successful *maintenance* against a formidable internal attempt to overthrow it. It is now for them to demonstrate to the world that those who can fairly carry an election can also suppress a rebellion; that ballots are the rightful and peaceful successors of bullets, and that when ballots have fairly and constitutionally decided there can be no successful appeal back to bullets; that there can be no successful appeal except to ballots themselves at succeeding elections. Such will be a great lesson of peace, teaching men that what they can not take by an election neither can they take it by a war; teaching all the folly of being the beginners of a war. . . .

It was with the deepest regret that the Executive found the duty of employing the war power in defense of the Government forced upon him. He could but perform this duty or surrender the existence of the Government. No compromise by public servants could in this case be a cure; not that compromises are not often proper, but that no popular government can long survive a marked precedent that those who carry an election can only save the government from immediate destruction by giving up the main point upon which the people gave the election. The people themselves, and not their servants, can safely reverse their own deliberate decisions.

As a private citizen the Executive could not have consented that these institutions shall perish; much less could he in betrayal of so vast and so sacred a trust as these free people had confided to him. . . . He sincerely hopes that your views and your action may so accord with his as to assure all faithful citizens who have been disturbed in their rights of a certain and speedy restoration to them under the Constitution and the laws.

FROM James D. Richardson, ed., *A Compilation of the Messages and Papers of the Presidents*, vol. 6 (Washington, D.C.: Government Printing Office, 1907), pp. 23, 30–31.

4

The Resources of the Union
and the Confederacy (1861)

At the beginning of the war, the Union enjoyed an enormous advantage over the Confederacy in terms of population, economic resources, transportation, and mining and manufacturing. These resources would play an important role in the Union's eventual military victory, and after the war southerners traditionally emphasized economic factors in explaining the defeat of the Confederacy. Yet these differences between the two sides were well known before the war, and impartial observers (as well as southerners) did not believe that such discrepancies would be significant in the war's outcome. As the first modern war in history, however, the Civil War would demonstrate the importance of industrialization and other economic resources in modern warfare.

	Union	*Confederacy*	*Union Advantage*
Total population	22,300,000	9,100,000[a]	2.5 to 1
White male population (18–45 years)	4,600,000	1,100,000	4.2 to 1
Bank deposits	$207,000,000	$47,000,000	4.4 to 1
Bank capital	$330,000,000	$27,000,000	12 to 1
Capital investment	$850,000,000	$95,000,000	9 to 1
Value of manufactured goods	$1,730,000,000	$156,000,000	11 to 1
Manufacturing establishments	110,000	18,000	6 to 1
Industrial workers	1,300,000	110,000	12 to 1
Railroad mileage	22,000	9,000	2.4 to 1
Shipping tonnage	4,600,000	290,000	16 to 1
Value of textiles produced	$181,000,000	$10,000,000	18 to 1
Value of firearms produced	$2,290,000	$73,000	31 to 1
Pig iron production (tons)	951,000	37,000	26 to 1
Coal production (tons)	13,680,000	650,000	21 to 1

Corn and wheat production (bushels)	698,000,000	314,000,000	2.2 to 1
Draft animals	5,800,000	2,900,000	2 to 1
Cotton production (bales)	43,000	5,344,000	1 to 124

[a]Slaves accounted for 3,500,000, or 40 percent of the total population.

FROM U.S. Census, 1860.

5

Abraham Lincoln Calls for Troops (1861)

Throughout the conflict, the federal government maintained the legal position that the war was a rebellion and not a struggle between separate nations. Reflective of this view was Abraham Lincoln's call for 75,000 troops on April 15, 1861. Portraying this action as essentially defensive in nature, Lincoln carefully pledged to respect the rights and property (which would include slaves) of civilians in the seceded states. This document, which reflected Lincoln's continuing belief that many residents of the Confederacy were still Unionists, offered the first statement of Union war aims and strategy. The proclamation also summoned Congress to assemble in a special session on July 4, 1861.

Whereas the laws of the United States have been for some time past, and now are opposed, and the execution thereof obstructed, in the States of South Carolina, Georgia, Alabama, Florida, Mississippi, Louisiana and Texas, by combinations too powerful to be suppressed by the ordinary course of judicial proceedings, or by the powers vested in the Marshals by law,

Now therefore, I, Abraham Lincoln, President of the United States, in virtue of the power in me vested by the Constitution, and the laws, have thought fit to call forth, and hereby do call forth, the militia of the several States of the Union, to the aggregate number of seventy-five thousand, in order to suppress said combinations, and to cause the laws to be duly executed. . . .

I appeal to all loyal citizens to favor, facilitate and aid this effort to maintain the honor, the integrity, and the existence of our National Union, and the perpetuity of popular government; and to redress wrongs already long enough endured.

I deem it proper to say that the first service assigned to the forces hereby called forth will probably be to re-possess the forts, places, and property which have been seized from the Union; and in every event, the utmost care will be observed, consistently with the objects aforesaid, to avoid any devastation, any destruction of, or interference with, property, or any disturbance of peaceful citizens in any part of the country.

And I hereby command the persons composing the combinations aforesaid to disperse, and retire peaceably to their respective abodes within twenty days from this date.

FROM Roy P. Basler, et al., eds., *The Collected Works of Abraham Lincoln*, vol. 4 (New Brunswick, N.J.: Rutgers University Press, 1953), pp. 331–32.

6

Abraham Lincoln Institutes
a Blockade of the Confederacy (1861)

On April 19, 1861, a few days after he called for troops to suppress the southern rebellion, Abraham Lincoln ordered the United States Navy to blockade the southern coast. The initial proclamation did not include Virginia or North Carolina, which had not yet formally seceded (they were added later). The Supreme Court would subsequently designate this action, rather than the president's call for troops, as marking the beginning of the war. It was also tantamount to extending the rights of belligerency to the Confederacy, since legally a nation cannot blockade its own coast (instead, it can simply close some or all of its ports). Lincoln's threat at the end of the proclamation to treat captured Confederate sailors as pirates instead of prisoners of war was never carried out.

Whereas an insurrection against the Government of the United States has broken out in the States of South Carolina, Georgia, Alabama, Florida, Mississippi, Louisiana, and Texas, and the laws of the United States for the collection of the revenue cannot be effectually executed therein conformably to that provision of the Constitution which requires duties to be uniform throughout the United States:

And whereas a combination of persons engaged in such insurrection, have threatened to grant pretended letters of marque to authorize the bearers thereof to commit assaults on the lives, vessels, and property of good citizens of the country lawfully engaged in commerce on the high seas, and in waters of the United States: And whereas an Executive Proclamation has been already issued, requiring the persons engaged in these disorderly proceedings to desist therefrom, calling out a militia force for the purpose of repressing the same, and convening Congress in extraordinary session, to deliberate and determine thereon:

FROM Roy P. Basler, et al., ed., *The Collected Works of Abraham Lincoln*, vol. 4 (New Brunswick, N.J.: Rutgers University Press, 1953), pp. 338–39.

Now, therefore, I, Abraham Lincoln, President of the United States, with a view to the same purposes before mentioned, and to the protection of the public peace, and the lives and property of quiet and orderly citizens pursuing their lawful occupations, until Congress shall have assembled and deliberated on the said unlawful proceedings, or until the same shall have ceased, have further deemed it advisable to set on foot a blockade of the ports within the States aforesaid, in pursuance of the laws of the United States, and of the law of Nations, in such case provided. For this purpose a competent force will be posted so as to prevent entrance and exit of vessels from the ports aforesaid. If, therefore, with a view to violate such blockade, a vessel shall approach, or shall attempt to leave either of the said ports, she will be duly warned by the Commander of one of the blockading vessels, who will endorse on her register the fact and date of such warning, and if the same vessel shall again attempt to enter or leave the blockaded port, she will be captured and sent to the nearest convenient port, for such proceedings against her and her cargo as prize, as may be deemed advisable.

And I hereby proclaim and declare that if any

person, under the pretended authority of the said States, or under any other pretense, shall molest a vessel of the United States, or the persons or cargo on board of her, such person will be held amenable to the laws of the United States for the prevention and punishment of piracy.

7 Kentucky Declares Its Neutrality (1861)

Kentucky residents, like those of the other border states, were deeply divided over the war. At the beginning of the conflict, Governor Beriah Magoffin of Kentucky, in an action backed by the legislature, officially declared the state's neutrality. Despite his proclamation, Magoffin was a strong secessionist and began secretly cooperating with the Confederacy in hopes of taking the state out of the Union.

Frankfort, Ky., Monday, May 20, 1861

Whereas, . . . every indication of public sentiment shows a determined purpose of the people to maintain a fixed position of self-defence, proposing and intending no invasion or aggression towards any other State or States, forbidding the quartering of troops upon her soil by either hostile section, but simply standing aloof from an unnatural, horrid, and lamentable strife, for the existence whereof Kentucky, neither by thought, word, nor act, is in anywise responsible; and whereas, this policy is, in judgment, wise, peaceful, safe, and honorable, and most likely to preserve the peace and amity between the neighboring border States on both shores of the Ohio, and protect Kentucky from deplorable civil war; and whereas, the arms distributed to the Home Guard are not to be used against the Federal or Confederate States, but to resist and prevent encroachment on her soil, rights, honor, and sovereignty, by either of the belligerent parties, and hoping Kentucky may become a successful mediator between them, and in order to remove a founded distrust and suspicion of purposes to force Kentucky out of the Union at the point of the bayonet, which may have been strongly and wickedly engendered in the public mind in regard to my own position and that of the State Guard;

Now, therefore, I hereby notify and warn all other States, separated or united, especially the United and Confederate States, that I solemnly forbid any movement upon Kentucky soil, or occupation of any post or place therein for any purpose whatever, until authorized by invitation or permission of the legislative and executive authorities. I especially forbid all citizens of Kentucky, whether incorporated in the State Guard or otherwise, making any hostile demonstrations against any of the aforesaid sovereignties, to be obedient to the orders of lawful authorities, to remain quietly and peaceably at home, when off military duty, and refrain from all words and acts likely to provoke a collision, and so otherwise conduct that the deplorable calamity of invasion may be averted; but meanwhile to make prompt and efficient preparation to assume the paramount and supreme law of self-defence, and strictly of self-defence alone.

FROM Frank H. Moore, ed., *The Rebellion Record*, vol. 1 (New York: G. P. Putnam, 1861), pp. 264–65.

8

JOHN B. GORDON

The Raccoon Roughs Go to War (1903)

John B. Gordon of Georgia became one of the prominent military leaders of the Confederacy. Although he lacked formal military training, he rose to the rank of lieutenant general and was one of Lee's most capable subordinates in the Army of Northern Virginia. In the following account from his reminiscences, Gordon recalls his experience as the captain of a group of eager volunteers from northern Georgia at the beginning of the war. Their impatience to go to war was so great that they joined an Alabama regiment when Georgia could not immediately accept their services. In the spring of 1861, both sides had much to learn about the realities of war. Gordon became a major political figure in Georgia after the war.

This company of mounted men was organized as soon as a conflict seemed probable and prior to any call for volunteers. They were doomed to a disappointment, "No cavalry now needed" was the laconic and stunning reply to the offer of our services. What was to be done, was the perplexing question. The proposition to wait until mounted men were needed was promptly negatived by the suggestion that we were so far from any point where a battle was likely to occur, and so hidden from view by the surrounding mountains, that we might be forgotten and the war might end before we had a chance.

"Let us dismount and go at once as infantry." This proposition was carried with a shout and by an almost unanimous vote. My own vote and whatever influence I possessed were given in favor of the suggestion[.] . . . [I]t was to me, as well as to my men, a sad descent from dashing cavalry to a commonplace company of slow, plodding foot-soldiers. Reluctantly, therefore, we abandoned our horses, and in order certainly to reach the point of action before the war was over, we resolved to go at once to the front as infantry, without waiting for orders, arms, or uniforms. Not a man in the com-

pany had the slightest military training, and the captain himself knew very little of military tactics.

The new government that was to be formed had no standing army as a nucleus around which the volunteers could be brought into compact order, with a centre of disciplined and thoroughly drilled soldiery; and the States which were to form it had but few arms, and no artisans or factories to supply them. The old-fashioned squirrel rifles and double-barrelled shot-guns were called into requisition. . . .

. . . My company, dismounted and ready for infantry service, did not wait for orders to move, but hastily bidding adieu to home and kindred, were off for Milledgeville, then capital of Georgia. At Atlanta a telegram from the governor met us, telling us to go back home, and stay there until our services were needed. Our discomfiture can be better imagined than described. In fact, there broke out at once in my ranks a new rebellion. These rugged mountaineers resolved that they would not go home; that they had a right to go to the war, had started to the war, and were not going to be trifled with by the governor or any one else. Finally, after much persuasion, and by the cautious exercise of the authority vested in me by my office of captain, I prevailed on them to get on board the home-bound train. As the engine-bell rang and the whis-

FROM John B. Gordon, *Reminiscences of the Civil War* (New York: Charles Scribner's Sons, 1903), pp. 4–9.

tle blew for the train to start, the rebellion broke loose again with double fury. The men rushed to the front of the train, uncoupled the cars from the engine, and gravely informed me that they had reconsidered and were not going back; that they intended to go to the war, and that if Governor Brown would not accept them, some other governor would. . . .

They disembarked and left the empty cars on the track, with the trainmen looking on in utter amazement. There was no course left me but to march them through the streets of Atlanta to a camp on the outskirts. The march, or rather straggle, through that city was a sight marvellous to behold and never to be forgotten. Totally undisciplined and undrilled, no two of these men marched abreast; no two kept the same step; no two wore the same colored coats or trousers. The only pretence at uniformity was the rough fur caps made of raccoon skins, with long, bushy, streaked raccoon tails hanging from behind them. The streets were packed with men, women, and children, eager to catch a glimpse of this grotesque company. . . . In a moment there came to me the . . . inquiry, "What company is that, sir?" Up to this time no name had been chosen—at least, none had been announced to the men. I had myself, however, selected a name which I considered both poetic and appropriate, and I replied to the question, "This company is the Mountain Rifles." Instantly a tall mountaineer said in a tone not intended for his captain, but easily overheard by his companions and the bystanders: "Mountain hell! we are no Mountain Rifles; we are the Raccoon Roughs." It is scarcely necessary to say that my selected name was never heard of again.

9

The *London Times* Foresees a Confederate Victory in the War (1861)

The London Times, *which represented urban and commercial interests in England and reflected official opinion, was the most important newspaper in the country. Scornful of democracy, it voiced the viewpoint of the British upper class and sympathized with the Confederate cause. In the following article, which was published shortly after the war began, it emphasized the enormous military challenge confronting the Union and predicted that the Confederacy would prevail in its struggle for independence.*

The President's Message is strongly war-like. He calls on Congress for 400,000 men and $400,000,000." Such is the last news from the United States, and it does not look like flinching, or even like a disposition to limit the objects of the war to the recovery of Federal property. It is a straightforward and old-fashioned appeal to the loyalty and pugnacity of the majority of Northerners against the fears and scruples of some and the pockets of all. . . .

. . . It remains to be seen how the public spirit of the North will respond to the very severe test to which it will now be subjected, and whether the passionate desire to maintain the integrity of the Union will be supported by the patient self-

FROM *London Times*, 18 July 1861.

sacrifice that can alone reconcile a commercial people to the prospect of war prices and diminished wealth. . . . The capture of Fort Sumter fired the dormant patriotism of the Northern towns; Volunteers were hurried off from New York and Boston, foreign nations were abused for not falling in heartily enough with the Federal enthusiasm, and civil war was organized on a really grand scale. This time no one can doubt the sincerity of the sentiment. But, then, it seems to have been taken for granted that the issue would be decided in a single campaign. Even General Scott did not discourage this anticipation, and up to the present we suspect that the most clamorous members of the war party have counted on the South being subjugated or conciliated, somehow or other, before the end of the Winter. The imposition of taxes on articles of universal consumption, reaching every household, will put the matter in a new light, and may, perhaps, lead them to reconsider their repudiations of any compromise.

The military movements hitherto reported are ludicrously disproportioned to the magnitude of the result to be achieved. The skirmish at Great Bethel was a very trifling affair, except so far as it must have: shaken the confidence of the Federal troops in their officers. It is one thing to drive the "rebels" from the south bank of the Potomac, or even to occupy Richmond, but another to reduce and hold in permanent subjection a tract of country nearly as large as Russia in Europe and inhabited by Anglo-Saxons. We have never questioned the superiority of the North for purposes of warfare, but no war of independence ever terminated unsuccessfully, except where the disparity of force was far greater than it is in this case. Besides, so far as we can at present judge, the Southerners are more earnest and unanimous, and more deeply pledged to their cause, than their opponents, with all their ostentation of union, can possibly be. So long as the slaves remain faithful the Southerners can give their personal services with less difficulty, and the further they are driven back the more they fight on their own ground, and the greater the difficulties of their enemy. But it is idle to multiply reasons for concluding that this controversy must ultimately be settled by some other arbitrament than that of arms. A victory on either side in the battle which was expected when the last telegrams were despatched might give the victorious party an advantage in negotiation, but it could no more turn the scale than the Battle of Edge-hill determined the fate of the English Civil Wars.

1

WINFIELD SCOTT

The Anaconda Plan (1861)

At the beginning of the war, General Winfield Scott prepared a military plan to subdue the seceded states and restore the Union. Although a Virginian, Scott never wavered in his loyalty to the United States, but he had no desire to fight an aggressive, destructive war that would inflame sectional hatreds and make governing a restored Union costly and difficult. Instead, he advocated a war of limited objectives that would minimize bloodshed and facilitate reunion. Therefore, he proposed surrounding the South and, by strangling it economically, forcing the Confederacy to surrender. The northern press dubbed his proposal "the Anaconda Plan," after the large snake that squeezes its prey. In the following letter to General George McClellan, Scott outlined the basic tenets of his plan. Lincoln never fully accepted Scott's strategy, but incorporated parts of it into his plan for a more aggressive war.

Headquarters of the Army,
Washington, May 3, 1861.

Maj. Gen. George B. McClellan,
   Commanding Ohio Volunteers,
   Cincinnati, Ohio:

Sir:

I have read and carefully considered your plan for a campaign, and now send you confidentially my own views, supported by certain facts of which you should be advised.

First. It is the design of the Government to raise 25,000 additional regular troops, and 60,000 volunteers for three years. It will be inexpedient either to rely on the three-months' volunteers for extensive operations or to put in their hands the best class of arms we have in store. The term of service would expire by the commencement of a regu-

FROM *Official Records*, ser. I, vol. 51, pt. 1, pp. 369–70.

lar campaign, and the arms not lost be returned mostly in a damaged condition. . . .

Second. We rely greatly on the sure operation of a complete blockade of the Atlantic and Gulf ports soon to commence. In connection with such blockade we propose a powerful movement down the Mississippi to the ocean, with a cordon of posts at proper points, and the capture of Forts Jackson and Saint Philip; the object being to clear out and keep open this great line of communication in connection with the strict blockade of the seaboard, so as to envelop the insurgent States and bring them to terms with less bloodshed than by any other plan. I suppose there will be needed from twelve to twenty steam gun-boats, and a sufficient number of steam transports (say forty) to carry all the personnel (say 60,000 men) and material of the expedition; most of the gun-boats to be in advance to open the way, and the remainder to follow and protect the rear of the expedition, &c.

This army . . . should be composed of our best regulars for the advance and of three-years' volunteers, all well officered, and with four months and a half of instruction in camps prior to (say) November 10. In the progress down the river all the enemy's batteries on its banks we of course would turn and capture, leaving a sufficient number of posts with complete garrisons to keep the river open behind the expedition. Finally, it will be necessary that New Orleans should be strongly occupied and securely held until the present difficulties are composed.

Third. A word now as to the greatest obstacle in the way of this plan—the great danger now pressing upon us—the impatience of our patriotic and loyal Union friends. They will urge instant and vigorous action, regardless, I fear, of consequences—that is, unwilling to wait for the slow instruction of (say) twelve or fifteen camps, for the rise of rivers, and the return of frosts to kill the virus of malignant fevers below Memphis. I fear this; but impress right views, on every proper occasion, upon the brave men who are hastening to the support of their Government. . . . I commend these views to your consideration, and shall be happy to hear the result.

With great respect, yours, truly,

Winfield Scott.

2

LYMAN TRUMBULL

The Most Shameful Rout You Can Conceive Of

(1861)

Joined by several other members of Congress, Republican Senator Lyman Trumbull of Illinois jaunted out to Manassas, Virginia, on July 21, 1861, to witness the first important battle of the war. The initial developments were encouraging, and he sat down to enjoy a picnic lunch while the battle to end the rebellion raged. Later in the afternoon he found himself, along with a number of other civilians from Washington, unexpectedly caught up in the maelstrom of the frantic Union retreat. In this letter to his wife, he describes the Union's debacle and his subsequent mortification. (Paragraphing has been modified.)

Washington, July 22nd, 1861.

We started over into Virginia about 9 o'clock A.M., and drove to Centreville, which is a high commanding position and a village of perhaps fifty houses. Bull Run, where the battle occurred, is South about 3 miles and the creek on the main road, looking West, is about 4½ miles distant. . . .

At Centreville, [Senator James] Grimes and I got saddles and rode horseback down the main road towards the creek about three miles toward a hospital where were some few wounded soldiers and a few prisoners who had been sent back. This was about half-past three o'clock P.M. . . . On the hill at Centreville we could see quite beyond the timber of the creek off towards Manassas and see the smoke and hear the report of the artillery, but not very rapid as I thought. This we observed before leaving Centreville, and were told it was our main

FROM Horace White, *The Life of Lyman Trumbull* (Boston: Houghton Mifflin Company, 1913), pp. 165–67.

army driving the enemy back, but slowly and with great difficulty.

. . . We returned on the road towards Centreville and turned up towards a house fifty or a hundred yards from the road, where we quietly took our lunch, the firing continuing about as before. Just as we were putting away the things we heard a great noise, and looking up towards the road saw it filled with wagons, horsemen and footmen in full run towards Centreville. We immediately mounted our horses and galloped to the road, by which time it was crowded, hundreds being in advance on the way to Centreville and two guns of the Sherman battery having already passed in full retreat. We kept on with the crowd, not knowing what else to do. On the way to Centreville many soldiers threw away their guns, knapsacks, etc. Gov. Grimes and I each picked up a gun. I soon came up to Senator [Henry S.] Lane of Indiana, and the gun being heavy to carry and he better able to manage it, I gave it to him. Efforts were made to rally the men by civilians and others on their way to Centreville, but all to no purpose. Literally, three could have chased ten thousand. All this stampede was occasioned, as I understand, by a charge of not exceeding two hundred cavalry upon [General Robert] Schenck's column down in the woods, which, instead of repulsing as they could easily have done (having before become disordered and having lost some of their officers), broke and ran, communicating the panic to everybody they met. . . . It was the most shameful rout you can conceive of. I suppose two thousand soldiers came rushing into Centreville in this disorganized condition. The cavalry which made the charge I did not see, but suppose they disappeared in double-quick time, not dreaming that they had put a whole division to flight. Several guns were left down in the woods, though I believe two were brought off. . . .

Whether other portions of our army were shamefully routed just at the close of the day, after we had really won the battle, it seems impossible for me to learn, though I was told that McDowell was at Centreville when we were there and that his column had also been driven back. If this be so it is a terrible defeat. At Centreville there was a reserve of 8000 or 10,000 men under Col. [Dixon] Miles who had not been in the action and they were formed in line of battle when we left there, but the enemy did not, I presume, advance to that point last night, as we heard no firing. We fed our horses at Centreville and left there at six o'clock last evening. Came on to Fairfax Court House, where we got supper, and leaving there at ten o'clock reached home at half-past two this morning, having had a sad day and witnessed scenes I hope never to see again.

Not very many baggage wagons, perhaps not more than fifty, were advanced beyond Centreville. From them the horses were mostly unhitched and the wagons left standing in the road when the stampede took place. This side of Centreville there were a great many wagons, and the alarm if possible was greater than on the other. Thousands of shovels were thrown out upon the road, also axes, boxes of provisions, etc. In some instances wagons were upset to get them out of the road, and the road was full of four-horse wagons retreating as fast as possible, and also of flying soldiers who could not be made to stop at Centreville. The officers stopped the wagons and a good many of the retreating soldiers by putting a file of men across the road and not allowing them to pass. In this way all the teams were stopped, but a good many stragglers climbed the fences and got by. I fear that a great, and, of course, a terrible slaughter has overtaken the Union forces—God's ways are inscrutable. I am dreadfully disappointed and mortified.

3

GEORGE McCLELLAN

I Have Become the Power in the Land (1861)

When thirty-four-year-old George McClellan was brought to Washington in the summer of 1861 to take charge of the Union's main army, political leaders and journalists heaped praise on the young commander. In this letter to his wife, written shortly after he assumed his new post, McClellan describes this public flattery and its impact on his vanity. Almost immediately, McClellan, his head swirling with dreams of military grandeur, completely lost grasp of reality and concluded that he was irreplaceable. When Lincoln expressed concern that he had given McClellan too many responsibilities, the general confidently replied, "I can do it all."

July 27/61 Washington D.C. Saturday

To Mary Ellen McClellan

. . . I find myself in a new & strange position here—Presdt, Cabinet, Genl Scott & all deferring to me—by some strange operation of magic I seem to have become the power of the land. I almost think that were I to win some small success now I could become Dictator or anything else that might please me—but nothing of that kind would please me—*therefore* I *won't be* Dictator. Admirable self denial! I see already the main causes of our recent failure—I am *sure* that I can remedy these & am confident that I can lead these armies of men to victory once more. I start tomorrow very early on a tour through the lines on the other side of the river—it will occupy me all day long & a rather fatiguing ride it will be—but I will be able to make up my mind as to the state of things. Refused invitations to dine today from Genl Scott & four Sectys—had too many things to attend to. . . .

I will endeavor to enclose with this the "Thanks of Congress" which please preserve. I feel very proud of it. Genl Scott objected to it on the ground that it ought to be accompanied by a gold medal. I cheerfully acquiesce in the Thanks by themselves, hoping to win the medal by some other action, & the sword by some other fait d'éclat.

FROM Stephen W. Sears, ed., *The Civil War Papers of George B. McClellan* (New York: Ticknor & Fields, 1989), p. 70.

4

GEORGE McCLELLAN

The President Is Nothing More Than a Well Meaning Baboon (1861)

McClellan's good relations with Union political leaders soon soured when, content with drilling his massive army, he failed to make any important military movement in the fall of 1861. The Union general did not understand that, in a democracy, military commanders can never exercise a completely free hand in their operations. Instead, he resented politicians' inquiries, which he considered to be meddling. In the following letter, McClellan expresses his contempt for Lincoln and the members of the Cabinet. These attitudes did not bode well for McClellan's ability to deal with the political as well as military realities he confronted as the Union commander.

[Washington] Friday [c. October 11, 1861]

To Mary Ellen McClellan

. . . I can't tell you how disgusted I am becoming with these wretched politicians—they are a most dispicable set of men & I think Seward is the meanest of them all—a meddling, officious, incompetent little puppy—he has done more than any other one man to bring all this misery upon the country & is one of the least competent to get us out of the scrape. The Presdt is nothing more than a well meaning baboon. Welles is weaker than the most garrulous old woman you were ever annoyed by. Bates is a good inoffensive old man[1]—so it goes—only keep these complimentary opinions to yourself, or you may get me into premature trouble. I believe I have choked off Seward already—& have strong hopes that he will keep himself to his own business hereafter. . . .

FROM George B. McClellan Papers, Library of Congress.

[1]The references are to Secretary of State William Henry Seward, Secretary of the Navy Gideon Welles, and Attorney General Edward Bates.

5

Abraham Lincoln Explains His Ideas on Military Strategy (1862)

Following the Union defeat at Bull Run, Lincoln began reading works on military strategy, for which he displayed a striking aptitude. In the following letter to Don Carlos Buell, one of the Union's main generals in the western theater, the president outlined his ideas of the strategy the Union should pursue. In the wake of the Union's military defeats in the East in the spring and summer of 1862, Lincoln assumed a more forceful role in determining Union strategy.

Executive Mansion,
Washington, Jan. 13, 1862.

Brig. Genl. Buell.
My dear Sir:

. . . For my own views, I have not offered, and do not now offer them as orders; and while I am glad to have them respectfully considered, I would blame you to follow them contrary to your own clear judgment—unless I should put them in the form of orders. . . . With this preliminary, I state my general idea of this war to be that we have the greater numbers, and the enemy has the greater facility of concentrating forces upon points of collision; that we must fail, unless we can find some way of making our advantage an over-match for his; and that this can only be done by menacing him with superior forces at different points, at the same time; so that we can safely attack, one, or both, if he makes no change; and if he *weakens* one to strengthen the other, forbear to attack the strengthened one, but seize, and hold the weakened one, gaining so much.

FROM Roy P. Basler, et al., eds., *The Collected Works of Abraham Lincoln*, vol. 5 (New Brunswick, N.J.: Rutgers University Press, 1953), p. 98.

6

CYRUS F. BOYD

An Iowa Soldier "Sees the Elephant" at Shiloh
(1862)

In the antebellum period, the phrase "seeing the elephant" meant getting all you had paid for and more. Hence, Civil War soldiers invoked this phrase in describing their first experience in combat. For Cyrus F. Boyd, this test came at Shiloh, Tennessee.

Accompanied by a group of fellow Iowa farmhands, Boyd enlisted in October 1861, at the age of twenty-four. In explaining this decision, he noted that "times are dull at home," that he feared he would "lose a great deal by not going," and that he believed it was his "patriotic duty" to serve. He was made first sergeant in Company G of the Fifteenth Iowa Volunteer Infantry. Like many volunteers, he worried that the war would be over before he ever saw the enemy. After a dull winter in camp at Keokuk, Iowa, Boyd's regiment departed to join Grant's army in Tennessee.

When the regiment arrived by steamboat at Pittsburgh Landing, its members were entirely green. In fact, they had received their rifles only ten days before and had never fired them. Disembarking, they loaded their weapons for the first time and were promptly thrown into one of the bloodiest engagements of the war. (In the following excerpt Boyd's spelling and abbreviations have been retained, but for purposes of clarity periods, which Boyd used only occasionally, have been inserted at the end of sentences.)

Battle of Shiloh or Pittsburgh Landing

April 6th Sunday—At 6 o'clock we arrived at a point known as "Pittsburgh Landing" on the West bank of the Tenn[essee] river. . . .

At 10 o'clock we are ordered ashore with all our equipments including 40 rounds of ammunition. . . . When we had got into something like a line we were presented with several boxes of ammunition and each man ordered to fill up to the extent of 100 rounds. . . .

The wounded men were by this time coming in freely and were being carried right through our ranks. And we could see hundreds of soldiers running through the woods. . . . We started on the double quick in the direction of the heavy firing which was mostly of musketry. . . . Thus we kept on for at least three miles meeting hundreds—yes thousands of men on the retreat who had thrown away their arms and were rushing toward the Landing—most of these were *hatless* and had nothing on them except their clothes. . . . The woods were full of Infantry, cavalry, Artillery and all arms of the service were flying toward the River in countless numbers. Men yelled as they passed us "Don't go out there" "You'll catch hell" "We are all cut to pieces" "We are whipped." . . .

There was also Infantry officers with swords drawn and trying to head off the flying troops and make them halt. There was Cavalrymen galloping

FROM Mildred Throne, ed., *The Civil War Diary of C. F. Boyd* (Iowa City: State Historical Society of Iowa, 1953), pp. 27–39.

after men and threatening to shoot them if they did not *stop*. But I saw no one stop. But on we went facing all these discouraging circumstances to take our turn at failure to stop the Rebel tide which was coming in like a wave of the sea unresisted and irresistable.

Here we were a new Regt which had never until this morning heard an enemies gun fire thrown into this *hell* of battle—without warning. The hot sun and the dreadful load we had carried through three miles of dust and battle smoke had so exhausted us that there was no strength left in the men. . . .

We came to the edge of a large field and as we crossed a little Ravine the bullets and a few shells passed over us making some of us dodge. Here we deployed by the right flank to come into line of battle but did not get that accomplished until we were out in the open field and in fair view of the enemy. . . . Here I noticed the first man shot. . . . He was close to us and sprang high in the air and gave one groan and fell *dead*. Our Company had to pass over him and each man as he came up seemed to hesitate and some made a motion to pick him up—but the officers sternly ordered them "forward." The men all gave a cheer and rushed on in line of battle with bayonets fixed.

The enemy lay in ambush at the farther side of the field. We at first could not see them only the puffs of white smoke came from the thickets and brush and every log and tree. We reached some scattering trees. . . . It was every man for himself. We knew nothing about orders or officers. Indeed the Companies now became all mixed up and without organization. . . .

At last we could see the enemy and they were advancing around our left flank and the woods seemed alive with *gray coats* and their victorious cheer and unearthly *yells* and the concentrated fire which they had upon us caused somebody to give the order for *retreat*. . . .

As we started down the Ravine a wounded rebel caught me by the leg as I was passing and looking up at me said ["]My friend for God's sake give me a *drink* of water.["] He had been shot

about the head and was covered with blood to his feet. I at once thought of that command "If thine enemy thirst give him drink" and I halted and tried to get my canteen from under my accouterments—but I could not and pulled away from him and said "I have not time to help you." . . .

In the meantime . . . the enemies Cavalry came dashing around on our right flank . . . and followed us almost to the ravine where we made a temporary stand and with a few shots the Cav fell back. Here Jeff Hocket ran to me and said that my brother Scott had given out and was lying upon the ground some distance back. I ran to him and tried to get him upon his feet. But he said I should go on as he never could go any farther and that I had better save myself and let him go. . . . I now took him by the *nap of the neck* and jerked him upon his feet and told him to *come* or I should help him with my *boot*. At this he stood up and I managed to work him along down the ravine and left him to rally on the hill. . . .

Cavalrymen were riding in all directions with drawn sabers and revolvers threatening to shoot and "Cut mens heads off" if they did not stop and rally. Officers were coaxing praying and exhorting men for "God's sake" to stop and all make a stand together. But in most cases their orders and appeals were not heard by these demoralized men who kept going like a flock of sheep. All the terrors of hell would not have stoped them until they got to the River. Hundreds lay in the woods on the ground completely overcome with the heat smoke and dust and fatigue. . . .

Riderless horses came thundering through the woods with empty saddles and artillery horses with caisons attached ran through the squads of men and striking trees caused the percussion shells to explode blowing horses caisons and everything around to atoms. Cannon balls were flying in all directions. . . . Every indication seemed to point to a great and *terrible defeat*. . . .

About 5 o'clock the enemy came on in solid masses for the final *charge*. . . . We were massed upon the surrounding bluffs about the landing. General Grant and Genl Buell rode along the line and urged every man to stand *firm* . . . and pointed to the opposite side of the river where we could see a long line of blue coats far as the eye could reach—and that was *Buells Army. This sight was all that saved Grants Army.* . . .

As the smoke clears away we can see the enemy coming on in long dark lines and seem to spring out of the ground in countless thousands. This is to be the grand and final charge by which they hope to sweep us from the face of the earth or capture the entire army. This *death like stillness* is worse than *murder.* Our Artillery opens with about 40 pieces (all we have left) then nothing more can be seen.

The very earth trembles with the fearful explosions. The enemy charged to the very mouth of our cannon and hundreds of them fell—filled with whiskey and gun powder. The battle raged for the possession of this hill which we held. If we would have lost this *all would have been lost.* Every man seemed nerved beyond human strength to do his utmost and he did. Acres of dead and wounded told the fearful tale of sacrifice.

. . . At dark we found ourselves crowded like a flock of sheep on the bluffs around the Landing just able to keep the Wolf at bay while the favoring night that settled down on friend and foe put an end to the fearful slaughter for the day a parallel to which this Continent had never before witnessed.

Battle of Shiloh or Pittsburgh Landing Second Day's Battle

Farther on the dead and wounded became more numerous. . . . I saw five *dead* Confederates all killed by one six pound solid shot—no doubt from one of our cannon. They had been behind a log and all in a row. The ball had raked them as they crouched behind the log. . . . One of them had his *head* taken off. One had been struck at the right shoulder and his chest lay open. One had been cut in two at the bowels and nothing held the carcass together but the spine. One had been hit at the thighs and the legs were torn from the body. The fifth and last one was piled up into a mass of skull, arms, some toes and the remains of a butternut suit. . . . [1]

I counted 26 dead battery horses on a few square rods of ground and the men were lying almost in heaps. Blue and gray sleep together. Oh my God! Can there be anything in the *future* that *compensates* for this slaughter? Only Thou knowest.

Around these batteries men have died at their posts beside the guns. Some are torn all to pieces leaving nothing but their heads or their boots. Pieces of clothing and *strings of flesh* hang on the limbs of the trees round them. . . .

The trees are just bursting into leaf and the little flowers are covering the ground—but their fragrance is lost in the pall of death which has settled down on this bloody field.

"This is the valley and the shadow of death."

[1]Poor whites from rural areas of the South often wore homespun clothing colored with a yellowish dye made from butternuts.

7

ULYSSES S. GRANT

I Gave Up All Idea of Saving the Union Except by Complete Conquest (1885)

Following his capture of Fort Henry and Fort Donelson, Grant believed the Confederacy was a house of cards that would soon collapse. Overconfident, he rapidly pushed south but was badly surprised at Shiloh, Tennessee, where he barely managed to stave off a crushing defeat. For Grant, who was deeply impressed by the morale and fighting spirit the enemy soldiers had displayed, Shiloh was a turning point, not just professionally but also in terms of his conception of the war. In his Memoirs, *he described the impact this battle—the fiercest fought in the West—had on his thinking.*

Up to the battle of Shiloh I, as well as thousands of other citizens, believed that the rebellion against the Government would collapse suddenly and soon, if a decisive victory could be gained over any of its armies. Donelson and Henry were such victories. An army of more than 21,000 men was captured or destroyed. Bowling Green, Columbus and Hickman, Kentucky, fell in consequence, and Clarksville and Nashville, Tennessee, the last two with an immense amount of stores, also fell into our hands. The Tennessee and Cumberland rivers, from their mouths to the head of navigation, were secured. But when Confederate armies were collected which not only attempted to hold a line farther south, from Memphis to Chattanooga, Knoxville and on to the Atlantic, but assumed the offensive and made such a gallant effort to regain what had been lost, then, indeed, I gave up all idea of saving the Union except by complete conquest. Up to that time it had been the policy of our army, certainly of that portion commanded by me, to protect the property of the citizens whose territory was invaded, without regard to their sentiments, whether Union or Secession. After this, however, I regarded it as humane to both sides to protect the persons of those found at their homes, but to consume everything that could be used to support or supply armies. Protection was still continued over such supplies as were within lines held by us and which we expected to continue to hold; but such supplies within the reach of Confederate armies I regarded as much contraband as arms or ordnance stores. Their destruction was accomplished without bloodshed and tended to the same result as the destruction of armies. I continued this policy to the close of the war.

FROM Ulysses S. Grant, *Personal Memoirs of U. S. Grant*, vol. 1 (New York: Charles L. Webster & Co., 1885), pp. 368–69.

8

ABRAHAM LINCOLN

But You Must Act (1862)

McClellan never comprehended the importance of public opinion in shaping military strategy in a democratic society. As an experienced politician, Lincoln, on the other hand, was extremely sensitive to the growing public impatience over McClellan's slow progress in Virginia. In the following letter, written in early April 1862, shortly after McClellan's peninsula campaign got under way, Lincoln defended his decision to detach part of McClellan's invasion force to protect Washington, repeated his reservations about McClellan's strategic plan, and stressed the importance of McClellan moving quickly and aggressively. This was a lesson that the cautious, obtuse general never absorbed.

Washington,
April 9. 1862

Major General McClellan.
My dear Sir.

Your despatches complaining that you are not properly sustained, while they do not offend me, do pain me very much. . . .

After you left, I ascertained that less than twenty thousand unorganized men, without a single field battery, were all you designed to be left for the defence of Washington, and Manassas Junction; and part of this even, was to go to Gen. Hooker's old position. . . . This presented, (or would present, when McDowell and Sumner should be gone) a great temptation to the enemy to turn back from the Rappahanock, and sack Washington. My explicit order that Washington should, by the judgment of *all* the commanders of Army corps, be left entirely secure, had been neglected. It was precisely this that drove me to detain McDowell.

I do not forget that I was satisfied with your arrangement to leave Banks at Mannassas Junc-

tion; but when that arrangement was broken up, and *nothing* was substituted for it, of course I was not satisfied. I was constrained to substitute something for it myself. And now allow me to ask "Do you really think I should permit the line from Richmond, *via* Mannassas Junction, to this city to be entirely open, except what resistance could be presented by less than twenty thousand unorganized troops?" This is a question which the country will not allow me to evade. . . .

I suppose the whole force which has gone forward for you, is with you by this time; and if so, I think it is the precise time for you to strike a blow. By delay the enemy will relatively gain upon you— that is, he will gain faster, by *fortifications* and *re-inforcements*, than you can by re-inforcements alone.

And, once more let me tell you, it is indispensable to *you* that you strike a blow. *I* am powerless to help this. You will do me the justice to remember I always insisted, that going down the Bay in search of a field, instead of fighting at or near Mannassas, was only shifting, and not surmounting, a difficulty—that we would find the same enemy, and the same, or equal, intrenchments, at either place. The country will not fail to note—is now

FROM Roy P. Basler, et al., eds., *The Collected Works of Abraham Lincoln*, vol. 5 (New Brunswick, N.J.: Rutgers University Press, 1953), pp. 184–85.

noting—that the present hesitation to move upon an intrenched enemy, is but the story of Manassas repeated.

I beg to assure you that I have never written you, or spoken to you, in greater kindness of feeling than now, nor with a fuller purpose to sustain you, so far as in my most anxious judgment, I consistently can. *But you must act.*

Yours very truly

A. Lincoln

9

GEORGE McCLELLAN

You Have Done Your Best to Sacrifice This Army (1862)

In very heavy fighting that marked the beginning of Seven Days' battles, Robert E. Lee, the new Confederate commander, attacked part of McClellan's army at Gaines Mill in Virginia. McClellan effectively parried this blow (while leaving the bulk of his army inactive) but was forced to retreat from a position that would turn out to be the closest the Army of the Potomac would get to Richmond until its capture in April 1865. McClellan's defeatist psychology was readily apparent. Although he outnumbered Lee (his complaints to the contrary notwithstanding), McClellan characteristically sought to place the blame on others, and in this telegram he lashed out at Secretary of War Edwin Stanton, and by clear implication Lincoln, for failing to meet his every request. Edward S. Sanford, head of the War Department's telegraphic office, was shocked by the tone of McClellan's dispatch and deleted the final two sentences before delivering a copy to Stanton. The full text was not published until McClellan presented his report on the campaign. Sanford's action had unfortunate consequences. When Lincoln and Stanton failed to respond to his harsh accusation (which, of course, they had not seen), McClellan believed that they had meekly accepted his rebuke, and his conviction of his indispensability to the Union cause correspondingly increased.

Savage Station
June 28, 1862 12.20 a.m.

To Edwin M. Stanton

I now know the full history of the day [June 27]. On this side of the river (the right bank) we repulsed several very strong attacks. On the left bank our men did all that men could do, all that soldiers could accomplish—but they were overwhelmed by vastly superior numbers, even after I brought my last reserves into action. The loss on both sides is terrible. I believe it will prove to be the most desperate battle of the war.

The sad remnants of my men behave as men. Those battalions who fought most bravely and suffered most are still in the best order. My regulars were superb, and I count upon what are left to turn another battle in company with their gallant com-

FROM *Official Records*, Ser. I, vol. 11, pt. 1, p. 61.

rades of the volunteers. Had I 20,000 or even 10,000 fresh troops to use to-morrow I could take Richmond, but I have not a man in reserve, and shall be glad to cover my retreat & save the material and *personnel* of the army.

If we have lost the day we have yet preserved our honor, & no one need blush for the Army of the Potomac. I have lost this battle because my force was too small.

I again repeat that I am not responsible for this, and I say it with the earnestness of a general who feels in his heart the loss of every brave man who has been needlessly sacrificed to-day. I still hope to retrieve our fortunes, but to do this the Govt must view the matter in the same earnest light that I do. You must send me very large re-inforcements, and send them at once. . . .

In addition to what I have already said, I only wish to say to the President that I think he is wrong in regarding me as ungenerous when I said that my force was too weak. I merely intimated a truth which to-day has been too plainly proved. If, at this instant, I could dispose of 10,000 fresh men, I could gain the victory to-morrow. I know that a few thousand men more would have changed this battle from a defeat to a victory. As it is, the government must not and cannot hold me responsible for the result.

I feel too earnestly to-night. I have seen too many dead and wounded comrades to feel otherwise than that the Government has not sustained this Army. If you do not do so now the game is lost.

If I save this Army now, I tell you plainly that I owe no thanks to you or any other persons in Washington. You have done your best to sacrifice this army.

George B. McClellan

10

GEORGE McCLELLAN

The War Should Be Conducted upon the Highest Principles of Christian Civilization

(1862)

In late June 1862, following the Army of the Potomac's repulse in Virginia, McClellan wrote a letter outlining the strategy of a limited war, which he handed to Lincoln in early July when the president visited the army along the James River. Lincoln accepted the letter without comment, but by now he had lost faith both in this strategy and in McClellan. In his letter, McClellan repeated the standard arguments in favor of a limited war, including a forceful statement of his opposition to emancipation.

Camp near Harrison's Landing, Va.
July 7, 1862

Mr President

You have been fully informed, that the rebel army is in our front, with the purpose of overwhelming us by attacking our positions or reducing us by blocking our river communications. I can not but regard our condition as critical, and I earnestly desire, in view of possible contingencies, to lay before your excellency, for your private consideration, my general views concerning the existing state of the rebellion, although they do not strictly relate to the situation of this army or strictly come within the scope of my official duties. These views amount to convictions and are deeply impressed upon my mind and heart. Our cause must never be abandoned; it is the cause of free institutions and self-government. The Constitution and the Union must be preserved, whatever may be the cost in time, treasure, and blood. If secession is successful other dissolutions are clearly to be seen in the future. Let neither military disaster, political faction, nor foreign war shake your settled purpose to enforce the equal operation of the laws of the United States upon the people of every state.

The time has come when the government must determine upon a civil and military policy, covering the whole ground of our national trouble.

The responsibility of determining, declaring and supporting such civil and military policy, and of directing the whole course of national affairs in regard to the rebellion, must now be assumed and exercised by you, or our cause will be lost. The Constitution gives you power sufficient even for the present terrible exigency.

This rebellion has assumed the character of a war; as such it should be regarded, and it should be conducted upon the highest principles known to Christian Civilization. It should not be a war looking to the subjugation of the people of any State in any event. It should not be at all a war upon popu-

lation; but against armed forces and political organizations. Neither confiscation of property, political executions of persons, territorial organization of States, or forcible abolition of slavery should be contemplated for a moment. In prosecuting the war all private property and unarmed persons should be strictly protected, subject only to the necessities of military operations. All private property taken for military use should be paid or receipted for; pillage and waste should be treated as high crimes; all unnecessary trespass sternly prohibited, and offensive demeanor by the military towards citizens promptly rebuked. Military arrests should not be tolerated, except in places where active hostilities exist, and oaths not required by enactments constitutionally made should be neither demanded nor received. Military government should be confined to the preservation of public order and the protection of political rights. Military power should not be allowed to interfere with the relations of servitude, either by supporting or impairing the authority of the master, except for repressing disorder, as in other cases. Slaves contraband under the act of Congress, seeking military protection, should receive it. The right of the government to appropriate permanently to its own service claims to slave labor should be asserted, and the right of the owner to compensation therefor should be recognized.

This principle might be extended upon grounds of military necessity and security, to all the slaves within a particular State, thus working manumission in such State; and in Missouri, perhaps in Western Virginia also, and possibly even in Maryland, the expediency of such a military measure is only a question of time.

A system of policy thus constitutional and conservative, and pervaded by the influences of Christianity and freedom, would receive the support of almost all truly loyal men, would deeply impress the rebel masses and all foreign nations, and it might be humbly hoped that it would commend itself to the favor of the Almighty.

Unless the principles governing the further conduct of our struggle shall be made known and approved, the effort to obtain requisite forces will

FROM George B. McClellan, *McClellan's Own Story* (New York: Charles L. Webster and Company, 1887), p. 487–89.

be almost hopeless. A declaration of radical views, especially upon slavery, will rapidly disintegrate our present armies. The policy of the government must be supported by concentrations of military power. The national forces should not be dispersed in expeditions, posts of occupation, and numerous armies, but should be mainly collected into masses and brought to bear upon the armies of the Confederate States. Those armies thoroughly defeated, the political structure which they support would soon cease to exist. . . .

I may be on the brink of eternity; and as I hope forgiveness from my Maker, I have written this letter with sincerity towards you and from love for my country.

Very respectfully, your obedient servant,
Geo. B. McClellan,
Maj.-Gen. Commanding.

11

John Pope Adopts Harsher Policies against Southern Civilians (1862)

Following the failure of McClellan's invasion of Virginia, Lincoln brought General John Pope from the West and put him in command of a newly organized army in that state. An advocate of waging a harder war against the Confederacy, Pope issued a series of controversial orders outlining harsher policies against southern civilians. Henry Halleck, the new general-in-chief, believed Pope's orders were counterproductive, but Lincoln, who had decided sterner measures were required, read and approved these orders before they were published. Terming Pope a "miscreant," Lee formally protested these orders and threatened retaliation by the Confederacy. Unpopular with the army and militarily inept, Pope did not remain in command for long, but his orders nevertheless were evidence of the escalation in Union war policy.

Headquarters Army of Virginia,
Washington, July 18, 1862.

General Orders, No. 5.

Hereafter, as far as practicable, the troops of this command will subsist upon the country in which their operations are carried on. In all cases supplies for this purpose will be taken by the officers to whose department they properly belong under the orders of the commanding officer of the troops for whose use they are intended. Vouchers will be given to the owners, stating on their face that they will be payable at the conclusion of the war, upon sufficient testimony being furnished that such owners have been loyal citizens of the United States since the date of the vouchers. Whenever it is known that supplies can be furnished in any district of the country where the troops are to operate the use of trains for carrying subsistence will be dispensed with as far as possible.

By command of Major-General Pope.

Headquarters Army of Virginia,
Washington, July 10 [?], 1862.

General Orders, No. 7.

The people of the valley of the Shenandoah and throughout the region of operations of this army

FROM *Official Records*, ser. I, vol. 12, pt. 2, pp. 50–52; pt. 3, p. 509.

living along the lines of railroad and telegraph and along the routes of travel in rear of the United States forces are notified that they will be held responsible for any injury done to the track, line, or road, or for any attacks upon trains or straggling soldiers by bands of guerrillas in their neighborhood. No privileges and immunities of warfare apply to lawless bands of individuals not forming part of the organized forces of the enemy nor wearing the garb of soldiers, who, seeking and obtaining safety on pretext of being peaceful citizens, steal out in rear of the army, attack and murder straggling soldiers, molest trains of supplies, destroy railroads, telegraph lines, and bridges, and commit outrages disgraceful to civilized people and revolting to humanity. Evil-disposed persons in rear of our armies who do not themselves engage directly in these lawless acts encourage them by refusing to interfere or to give any information by which such acts can be prevented or the perpetrators punished.

Safety of life and property of all persons living in rear of our advancing armies depends upon the maintenance of peace and quiet among themselves and upon the unmolested movements through their midst of all pertaining to the military service. They are to understand distinctly that this security of travel is their only warrant of personal safety.

It is therefore ordered that wherever a railroad, wagon road, or telegraph is injured by parties of guerrillas the citizens living within 5 miles of the spot shall be turned out in mass to repair the damage, and shall, beside, pay to the United States in money or in property, to be levied by military force, the full amount of the pay and subsistence of the whole force necessary to coerce the performance of the work during the time occupied in completing it.

If a soldier or legitimate follower of the army be fired upon from any house the house shall be razed to the ground, and the inhabitants sent prisoners to the headquarters of this army. If such an outrage occur at any place distant from settlements, the people within 5 miles around shall be held accountable and made to pay an indemnity sufficient for the case.

Any persons detected in such outrages, either during the act or at any time afterward, shall be shot, without awaiting civil process. No such acts can influence the result of this war, and they can only lead to heavy afflictions to the population to no purpose.

It is therefore enjoined upon all persons, both for the security of their property and the safety of their own persons, that they act vigorously and cordially together to prevent the perpetration of such outrages.

Whilst it is the wish of the general commanding this army that all peaceably disposed persons who remain at their homes and pursue their accustomed avocations shall be subjected to no improper burden of war, yet their own safety must of necessity depend upon the strict preservation of peace and order among themselves; and they are to understand that nothing will deter him from enforcing promptly and to the full extent every provision of this order.

By command of Major-General Pope.

Headquarters Army of Virginia,
Washington, July 23, 1862.

General Orders, No. 11.

Commanders of army corps, divisions, brigades, and detached commands will proceed immediately to arrest all disloyal male citizens within their lines or within their reach in rear of their respective stations.

Such as are willing to take the oath of allegiance to the United States and will furnish sufficient security for its observance shall be permitted to remain at their homes and pursue in good faith their accustomed avocations. Those who refuse shall be conducted South beyond the extreme pickets of this army, and be notified that if found again anywhere within our lines or at any point in rear they will be considered spies, and subjected to the extreme rigor of military law.

If any person, having taken the oath of allegiance as above specified, be found to have violated it, he shall be shot, and his property seized and applied to the public use.

All communication with any person whatever living within the lines of the enemy is positively prohibited, except through the military authorities and in the manner specified by military law; and any person concerned in writing or in carrying letters or messages in any other way will be considered and treated as a spy within the lines of the United States Army.

By command of Major-General Pope.

Headquarters Army of Virginia,
Washington, July 25, 1862.

General Orders, No. 13.

Hereafter no guards will be placed over private houses or private property of any description

whatever. Commanding officers are responsible for the conduct of the troops under their command, and the Articles of War and Regulations of the Army provide ample means for restraining them to the full extent required for discipline and efficiency.

Soldiers were called into the field to do battle against the enemy, and it is not expected that their force and energy shall be wasted in protecting private property of those most hostile to the Government.

No soldier serving in this army shall hereafter be employed in such service.

By command of Major-General Pope.

12

Abraham Lincoln Authorizes the Army to Seize Private Property in the Confederacy (1862)

At the same time he approved of Pope's orders, Lincoln directed the War Department to draw up orders instructing the Union army to seize private property in the Confederacy for supplies or that could be used for other military purposes. General Order No. 109 was issued on August 16, 1862. This document marked a significant step on the part of the Union government toward a harsher, more punitive military strategy.

War Department, Washington, July 22.

First. Ordered that military commanders within the States of Virginia, North-Carolina, Georgia, Florida, Alabama, Mississippi, Louisiana, Texas and Arkansas, in an orderly manner seize and use any property, real or personal, which may be necessary or convenient for their several commands,

FROM Adjutant General, *General Orders 1862* (Washington, D.C.: Government Printing Office, 1863), p. 559.

for supplies, or for other military purposes; and that while property may be destroyed for proper military objects, none shall be destroyed in wantonness or malice.

Second. That military and naval commanders shall employ as laborers, within and from said States, so many persons of African descent as can be advantageously used for military or naval purposes, giving them reasonable wages for their labor.

Third. That, as to both property, and persons of African descent, accounts shall be kept sufficiently accurate and in detail to show quantities and amounts, and from whom both property and such persons shall have come, as a basis upon which compensation can be made in proper cases; and the several departments of this Government shall attend to and perform their appropriate parts toward the execution of these orders.

By order of the President.

Edwin M. Stanton,
Secretary of War.

13

Robert E. Lee Proposes to Invade the North

(1862)

In early September 1862, Robert E. Lee wrote to Jefferson Davis, outlining his plan to invade Maryland. As Lee explained, his invasion would necessarily be a great raid rather than an occupying force, since the Confederacy lacked the logistical capacity to supply his army over long distances. Still, for reasons he noted, he believed the risk was justified. This letter also is an early statement of Lee's single-minded focus on Virginia and the eastern theater of the conflict.

Headquarters Alexandria and Leesburg Road,
Near Dranesville,
September 3, 1862

Mr. President:

The present seems to be the most propitious time since the commencement of the war for the Confederate Army to enter Maryland. The two grand armies of the United States that have been operating in Virginia, though now united, are much weakened and demoralized. Their new levies, of which I understand 60,000 men have already been posted in Washington, are not yet organized, and will take some time to prepare for the field. If it is ever desired to give material aid to Maryland and afford her an opportunity of throwing off the oppression to which she is now subject, this would seem the most favorable.

After the enemy had disappeared from the vicinity of Fairfax Court House, and taken the road to Alexandria and Washington, I did not think it would be advantageous to follow him farther. I had

no intention of attacking him in his fortifications, and am not prepared to invest them. If I possessed the necessary munitions, I should be unable to supply provisions for the troops. I therefore determined, while threatening the approaches to Washington, to draw the troops into Loudoun, where forage and some provisions can be obtained, menace their possession of the Shenandoah Valley, and, if found practicable, to cross into Maryland. The purpose, if discovered, will have the effect of carrying the enemy north of the Potomac, and, if prevented, will not result in much evil.

The army is not properly equipped for an invasion of an enemy's territory. It lacks much of the material of war, is feeble in transportation, the animals being much reduced, and the men are poorly provided with clothes, and in thousands of instances are destitute of shoes. Still, we cannot afford to be idle, and though weaker than our opponents in men and military equipments, must endeavor to harass if we cannot destroy them. I am aware that the movement is attended with much risk, yet I do not consider success impossible, and shall endeavor to guard it from loss. As long as the

FROM *Official Records*, ser. I, vol. 19, pt. 2, pp. 590–91.

army of the enemy are employed on this frontier I have no fears for the safety of Richmond, yet I earnestly recommend that advantage be taken of this period of comparative safety to place its defense, both by land and water, in the most perfect condition. A respectacle force can be collected to defend its approaches by land, and the steamer *Richmond*, I hope, is now ready to clear the river of hostile vessels.

Should General [Braxton] Bragg find it impracticable to operate to advantage on his present frontier, his army, after leaving sufficient garrisons, could be advantageously employed in opposing the overwhelming numbers which it seems to be the intention of the enemy now to concentrate in Virginia. . . .

What occasions me most concern is the fear of getting out of ammunition. I beg you will instruct the Ordnance Department to spare no pains in manufacturing a sufficient amount of the best kind, and to be particular, in preparing that for the artillery, to provide three times as much of the long-range ammunition as of that for smooth-bore or short-range guns. The points to which I desire the ammunition to be forwarded will be made known to the Department in time. If the Quartermaster Department can furnish any shoes, it would be the greatest relief. . . .

I have the honor to be, with high respect, your obedient servant,

R. E. LEE,
General

14

General Edward Alexander Criticizes Lee at Antietam (1899)

A distinguished graduate of West Point, General Edward Porter Alexander (his friends called him Porter) was only in his mid-twenties when the war began. Despite his youth, he became head of ordinance for the Army of Northern Virginia and commanded the artillery in the First Corps of that army. He served in all the major campaigns in Virginia, from Bull Run to the surrender at Appomattox, and was closely associated with many of the Confederacy's most important military leaders. At his family's urging, late in life he wrote a personal account of his service for their use. Alexander's recollections, which were written in 1897–1899 but remained unpublished for many years, are remarkable for their frank assessment of individuals and their honest portrayal of events. Unlike many Confederate generals, he was largely unaffected by the Lost Cause, a postwar movement that extolled southern superiority in the war, and did not write to glorify the Confederacy or to justify every action Robert E. Lee took. In the following selection, he criticizes Lee's costly decision to fight at Antietam (Sharpsburg) rather than withdraw.

So that now our whole army was back on the Va. side of the Potomac except Longstreet's & Hill's divisions. These could have been easily retired across the river, & we would, indeed, have left Maryland without a great battle, but we would nevertheless have come off with good prestige & a very fair lot of prisoners & guns, & lucky on the whole to do this, considering the accident of the "lost order." And that seems to have been, perhaps at first, Gen. Lee's intention. For Jackson was first ordered to halt on the Va. side, but early on [the] 16th the orders were changed & he & every body else was ordered to come across the river to deliver battle. For the onus was on McClellan to attack. And this, I think, will be pronounced by military critics to be the greatest military blunder that Gen. Lee ever made. I have referred to it briefly once before, but I will give the reasons now more fully.

In the first place Lee's inferiority of force was too great to hope to do more than to fight a sort of drawn battle. Hard & incessant marching, & camp diseases aggravated by irregular diet, had greatly reduced his ranks, & I don't think he mustered much if any over 40,000 men. McClellan had over 87,000, with more & better guns & ammunition, &, besides that, fresh troops were coming to Washington & being organised & sent him almost every day. A drawn battle, such as we did actually fight, was the best *possible* outcome one could hope for. Even that we only accomplished by the Good Lord's putting it into McClellan's heart to keep Fitz John Porter's corps entirely out of the battle, & Franklin's nearly all out. I doubt whether many hearts but McClellan's would have accepted the suggestions, even from a Divine source. For Common Sense was just shouting, "Your adversary is backed against a river, with no bridge & only one ford, & that the worst one on the whole river. If you whip him now, you destroy him utterly, root & branch & bag & baggage. Not twice in a life time

does such a chance come to any general. Lee for once has made a mistake, & given you a chance to ruin him if you can break his lines, & such game is worth great risks. Every man must fight & keep on fighting for all he is worth."

For no military genius, but only the commonest kind of every day common sense, was necessary to appreciate that. . . .

When at last night put a welcome end to the bloody day the Confederate army was worn & fought to a perfect frazzle. There had been no reserves all day. But on the Federal side Porter's corps had hardly pulled a trigger & Burnside's was comparatively fresh. In view of this, it seems strange that Gen. Lee did not take advantage of the night & recross the river into Virginia. For he knew too that McClellan had reinforcements coming to him & liable to arrive at any hour. But with sublime audacity the only question he debated with his generals, when they met at his headquarters after dark, was whether or not he should himself attack McClellan in the morning. Fortunately for somebody he decided to stand on the defensive. But surely military historians will say that McClellan again threw away a chance which no other Federal commander ever had, before or since. For he decided to wait for the considerable reinforcements now within a day's march. And when Lee appreciated his game he saw that there was nothing left to do but to return to Va. So all preparations were duly made & during the night of the 18th the whole army recrossed without accident, loss, or trouble. But I have always been proud of the fact that Gen. Lee did dare to stand & defy McClellan on the 18th. It not only showed his audacity as a commander, & his supreme confidence in his army; but it showed that in spite of distance from railroads, & of the excessive amount of fighting in the previous three weeks, his chief of ordnance still had plenty of ammunition at hand.

FROM Gary W. Gallagher, ed., *Fighting for the Confederacy: The Personal Recollections of General Edward Porter Alexander* (Chapel Hill: University of North Carolina Press, 1989), pp. 145–46, 153–54.

15

RUFUS R. DAWES

The Most Dreadful Slaughter (1890)

Antietam has aptly been called America's bloodiest day. More than 5,000 Americans were killed in the fighting on September 17, 1862, the greatest loss of life on a single day in all American wars. It was also one of the most ferocious battles in the war. As happened only a few other times in the war, the men seemed seized by demoniacal fury as the two armies slugged it out along Antietam creek near the Potomac in Maryland. Lee was barely able to beat back the Union assaults throughout the day and preserve his army. The battle opened at dawn with General Joseph Hooker's assault on the Confederate left, and for several hours the fighting surged back and forth across a cornfield. The following account by Major Rufus R. Dawes of the Sixth Wisconsin, describing the fighting in the cornfield, details the gruesome losses on both sides and conveys a sense of what the men in both armies experienced that day. Hooker's assault was only the opening phase of a day-long struggle. (Paragraphing has been modified.)

Our lines on the left now came sweeping forward through the corn and the open fields beyond. I ordered my men up to join in the advance, and commanded: "Forward—guide left—march!" We swung away from the turnpike, and I sent the sergeant-major (Howard J. Huntington) to Captain Kellogg, commanding the companies on the turnpike, with this order: "If it is practicable, move forward the right companies, aligning with the left wing." Captain Kellogg said: "Please give Major Dawes my compliments, and say it is impracticable; the fire is murderous."

As we were getting separated, I directed Sergeant Huntington to tell Captain Kellogg that he could get cover in the corn, and to join us, if possible. Huntington was struck by a bullet, but delivered the order. Kellogg ordered his men up, but so many were shot that he ordered them down again at once. While this took place on the turnpike, our companies were marching forward through the thick corn, on the right of a long line of battle. Closely following was a second line. At the front edge of the corn-field was a low Virginia rail fence. Before the corn were open fields, beyond which was a strip of woods surrounding a little church, the Dunkard church. As we appeared at the edge of the corn, a long line of men in butternut and gray rose up from the ground. Simultaneously, the hostile battle lines opened a tremendous fire upon each other. Men, I can not say fell; they were knocked out of the ranks by dozens. But we jumped over the fence, and pushed on, loading, firing, and shouting as we advanced. There was, on the part of the men, great hysterical excitement, eagerness to go forward, and a reckless disregard of life, of every thing but victory. Captain Kellogg brought his companies up abreast of us on the turnpike.

The Fourteenth Brooklyn Regiment, red legged Zouaves, came into our line, closing the awful gaps. Now is the pinch. Men and officers of New York and Wisconsin are fused into a common mass, in the frantic struggle to shoot fast. Every body tears cartridges, loads, passes guns, or shoots.

FROM Rufus R. Dawes, *Service with the Sixth Wisconsin Volunteers* (Marietta, Ohio: E. R. Alderman & Sons, 1890), pp. 90–92.

Men are falling in their places or running back into the corn. The soldier who is shooting is furious in his energy. The soldier who is shot looks around for help with an imploring agony of death on his face. After a few rods of advance, the line stopped and, by common impulse, fell back to the edge of the corn and lay down on the ground behind the low rail fence.

Another line of our men came up through the corn. We all joined together, jumped over the fence, and again pushed out into the open field. There is a rattling fusilade and loud cheers. "Forward" is the word. The men are loading and firing with demoniacal fury and shouting and laughing hysterically, and the whole field before us is covered with rebels fleeing for life, into the woods. Great numbers of them are shot while climbing over the high post and rail fences along the turnpike. We push on over the open fields half way to the little church. The powder is bad, and the guns have become very dirty. It takes hard pounding to get the bullets down, and our firing is becoming slow. A long and steady line of rebel gray, unbroken by the fugitives who fly before us, comes sweeping down through the woods around the church. They raise the yell and fire. It is like a scythe running through our line. "Now, save, who can." It is a race for life that each man runs for the cornfield. A sharp cut, as of a switch, stings the calf of my leg as I run. Back to the corn, and back through the corn, the headlong flight continues.

At the bottom of the hill, I took the blue color of the state of Wisconsin, and waving it, called a rally of Wisconsin men. Two hundred men gathered around the flag of the Badger state. Across the turnpike just in front of the haystacks, two guns of Battery "B," 4th U.S. artillery were in action. The pursuing rebels were upon them. General John Gibbon, our brigade commander, who in regular service was captain of this battery, grimed and black with powder smoke in himself sighting these guns of his old battery, comes running to me, "Here, major, move your men over, we must save these guns." I commanded "Right face, forward march," and started ahead with the colors in my hand into the open field, the men following. As I entered the field, a report as of a thunderclap in my ear fairly stunned me. This was Gibbon's last shot at the advancing rebels. The cannon was double charged with canister. The rails of the fence flew high in the air. A line of union blue charged swiftly forward from our right across the field in front of the battery, and into the corn-field. They drove back the rebels who were firing upon us. . . .

I gathered my men on the turnpike, reorganized them, and reported to General Doubleday, who was himself there. He ordered me to move back to the next woods in the rear, to remain and await instruction. Bullets, shot, and shell, fired by the enemy in the corn-field, were still flying thickly around us, striking the trees in this woods, and cutting off the limbs. I placed my men under the best shelter I could find, and here we figured up, as nearly as we could, our dreadful losses in the battle. . . . Of two hundred and eighty men who were at the corn-field and turnpike, one hundred and fifty were killed or wounded. This was the most dreadful slaughter to which our regiment was subjected in the war.

16

HARPER'S WEEKLY

Northern Despair after the Battle of Fredericksburg (1862)

At the Battle of Fredericksburg on December 13, 1862, Union General Ambrose Burnside launched a series of suicidal assaults against an impregnable Confederate line. The Union lost almost 13,000 men in the battle, more than twice the number of Confederate casualties. This horrendous slaughter, which brought no military gain, produced a tremendous public outcry in the North. The winter of 1862–1863 was the North's Valley Forge, as the defeat at Fredericksburg, Virginia, brought Union morale—both in the army and on the home front—to its low point during the war. Harper's Weekly normally voiced the viewpoint of the Republican party, but the mismanagement of the battle at Fredericksburg, which it termed a "disastrous reverse," badly shook its confidence in the government, as the following comment from its December 27, 1862, issue indicates.

We are indulging in no hyperbole when we say that these events are rapidly filling the heart of the loyal North with sickness, disgust, and despair. Party lines are becoming effaced by such unequivocal evidences of administrative imbecility; it is the men who have given and trusted the most, who now feel most keenly that the Government is unfit for its office, and that the most gallant efforts ever made by a cruelly tried people are being neutralized by the obstinacy of their leaders. Where this will all end no one can see. But it must end soon. The people have shown a patience during the past year, quite unexampled in history. They have borne, silently and grimly, imbecility, treachery, failure, privation, loss of friends and means, almost every suffering which can afflict a brave people. But they can not be expected to suffer that such massacres as this at Fredericksburg shall be repeated. Matters are rapidly ripening for a military dictatorship.

FROM *Harper's Weekly*, 27 December 1862.

1

G. J. VAN BURNT

The *Monitor* Challenges the *Merrimack* (1862)

Captain G. J. Van Burnt watched the first battle of ironclads at Hampton Roads, Virginia, on March 9, 1862, from the deck of the U.S. frigate Minnesota, *which he commanded. In the previous day's fighting, the* Minnesota *had run aground while futilely trying to repel the Confederacy's new ironclad, the* Merrimack *(renamed the* Virginia*). When the* Merrimack *returned the following day to destroy the helpless ship, the* Monitor, *the new federal ironclad that had just arrived, steamed out to offer battle. Noting the* Monitor's *small, unimpressive appearance and limited armament, one reporter commented, "Never was a greater hope placed upon more insignificant means." By the end of the day, the age of wooden ships had passed. (Paragraphing has been supplied.)*

At six A.M. the enemy again appeared. . . . The Merrimac ran down near the Rip Raps, and then turned into the channel through which I had come. Again all hands were called to quarters, and opened upon her with my stern-guns, and made signal to the Monitor to attack the enemy. She immediately ran down in my wake, right within the range of the Merrimac, completely covering my ship, as far as was possible with her diminutive dimensions, and, much to my astonishment, laid herself right alongside of the Merrimac, and the contrast was that of a pigmy to a giant.

Gun after gun was fired by the Monitor, which was returned with whole broadsides from the rebels, with no more effect, apparently, than so many pebble-stones thrown by a child. After a while they commenced manœuvring, and we could see the little battery point her bow for the rebel's,

with the intention, as I thought, of sending a shot through her bow-porthole; then she would shoot by her, and rake her through her stern. In the mean time the rebels were pouring broadside after broadside, but almost all her shot flew over the little submerged propeller; and when they struck the bomb-proof tower, the shot glanced off without producing any effect, clearly establishing the fact that wooden vessels cannot contend successfully with iron-clad ones, for never before was anything like it dreamed of by the greatest enthusiast in maritime warfare.

The Merrimac, finding that she could make nothing of the Monitor, turned her attention once more to me in the morning. She had put one eleven-inch shot under my counter, near the water-line, and now, on her second approach, I opened upon her with all my broadside-guns and ten-inch pivot—a broadside which would have blown out of water any timber-built ship in the world. She returned my fire with her rifled bow-gun, with a shell which passed through the chief

FROM Frank H. Moore, ed., *The Rebellion Record*, vol. 4 (New York: G. P. Putnam, 1862), pp. 267–68.

engineer's state-room, through the engineer's mess-room amidships, and burst in the boatswain's room, tearing four rooms all into one, in its passage exploding two charges of powder, which set the ship on fire, but it was promptly extinguished by a party headed by my first lieutenant. Her second went through the boiler of the tugboat Dragon, exploding it, and causing some consternation on board my ship for the moment, until the matter was explained. This time I had concentrated upon her an incessant fire from my gun-deck, spar-deck and forecastle pivot-guns, and was informed by my marine officer, who was stationed on the poop, that at least fifty solid shot struck her on her slanting side, without producing any apparent effect.

By the time she had fired her third shell, the little Monitor had come down upon her, placing herself between us, and compelled her to change her position, in doing which she grounded, and again I poured into her all the guns which could be brought to bear upon her. As soon as she got off, she stood down the bay, the little battery chasing her with all speed, when suddenly the Merrimac turned around, and ran full speed into her antagonist. For a moment I was anxious, but instantly I saw a shot plunge into the iron roof of the Merrimac, which surely must have damaged her, for some time after the rebels concentrated their whole battery upon the tower and pilot-house of the Monitor, and soon after the latter stood down for Fortress Monroe, and we thought it probable she had exhausted her supply of ammunition, or sustained some injury.

2

HORATIO WAIT

The United States Navy Blockades the Confederacy (1898)

When the war began, Abraham Lincoln ordered the navy to blockade the Confederacy. With over 3,500 miles of southern shoreline, several major ports, and countless rivers and inlets, this was a staggering assignment. Horatio Wait, paymaster of the United States Navy, discusses the navy's unprecedented achievement in this regard. The blockade was hardly leakproof, but it tightened with each year of the war. While a large number of foreign ships successfully made it to Confederate ports, the amount of cargo they carried was small, since speed was essential to run the blockade. By the last year of the war, shortages of basic essentials had made scarcity a way of life in the Confederacy.

At the beginning of the war in 1861, a perplexing question arose as to whether it would be best for the government to declare all the Southern

FROM Horatio Wait, "The Blockade of the Confederacy," *Century Magazine*, 34 (October 1898): 914–19.

ports of entry to be closed, or to proclaim a blockade. Many facts made public since the war indicate that this was the chief question that affected the European nations in their attitude toward us, and it certainly influenced the character of the struggle in our own country. The urgency of the case caused President Lincoln to act promptly. On

April 19, 1861, six days after the surrender of Fort Sumter, he issued a proclamation declaring a blockade of the entire coast of the Confederacy, from South Carolina to Texas; and on April 27 extended it to cover Virginia and North Carolina, making a coast-line of over three thousand miles to be blockaded, greater in extent than the Atlantic coast of Europe—an undertaking without precedent in history.

. . . When Mr. Lincoln issued this proclamation we had only forty-two ships in commission in our navy. Most of them were absent on foreign stations, and only one efficient war-ship, the *Brooklyn*, was available for immediate service. The days of paper blockades had long since passed away. The universally recognized rule of international law on this subject was that "blockades, to be binding, must be effectual. There must be a squadron lying off the harbor to be blockaded, and it must be strong enough to constitute an actual blockade of the port. The neutral must have had due notice of its existence, and to affect a neutral vessel she must have been guilty of an act of violation, by passing, or attempting to pass, in or out of the port, with a cargo laden after the commencement of the blockade. The neutral must be ready to prove himself that which he professes to be; therefore he is subject to the right of visitation and search."

A more serious difficulty now presented itself. How was it possible to undertake such a blockade as this, along such a vast extent of coast, when so few ships of any kind were available, without its being open to the charge of being a mere paper blockade? In the early part of the century European powers had attempted to enforce paper blockades, but the same nations were now the first to make merry over the subject of our paper blockade. Some of the most prominent European statesmen publicly declared it a "material impossibility to enforce it." To avoid any chance of technical complications, a special notice was given by our vessels at the entrance of each port actually closed by them, in addition to the general diplomatic notice, so that for a time one warning was allowed every ship touching at a blockaded port before she was liable

to capture. Thus each port was brought under the full operation of the proclamation only when it was actually blockaded by one or more armed vessels.

By degrees, as the blockading force was increased, and the blockade became more extended and stringent, it was assumed that the general notice rendered the special notice unnecessary; it was finally discontinued entirely, and capture took place without warning. The magnitude of the task of establishing and maintaining the blockade was not realized by the people generally, public attention being absorbed by the raising of many large armies from the body of the people.

When the Secretary of the Navy asked the principal shipping merchants and ship-owners of New York to aid him in procuring vessels for the blockade, it is related that their committees decided that thirty sailing-ships would be needed. As it took over six hundred ships, mostly steamers, to do the work, it is manifest that they had a very faint conception of what was to be done. There were twenty-eight old ships of war lying dismantled at the various navy-yards. Those that were worth repairing were fitted for sea as rapidly as possible. All the available merchant vessels that could be made to carry a battery, including tugs and old New York ferry-boats, were purchased and converted into fighting ships as hastily as the limited facilities of the Northern ports would permit. The scanty resources of the navy-yards were inadequate. All the private ship-yards were crowded with work. There were not enough skilled workmen to meet this sudden demand, and the naval officers found it necessary personally to direct the unskilled artisans, or to assist with their own hands in fitting these nondescript vessels for the mounting and working of heavy guns. As fast as the vessels could be purchased, altered, and equipped, they were stationed along the coast or sent to sea. Many such vessels, by the tact and skill of the officers in charge of them, were made to do good service. One of the most important prizes captured, the steamer *Circassian*, was taken near the harbor of Havana by one of the old Fulton Ferry boats.

The lack of men was as great an embarrassment as the want of vessels. Three hundred and twenty-two officers of the old navy joined the insurgent forces, many of them having already distinguished themselves in service. One of these, Commander John M. Brooke, rendered very important services to the Southerners by converting the ten-inch columbiads captured by them into rifled guns. They proved to be very effective pieces, and were said to be the best converted guns ever made. He also aided in devising the simplest and best of the many kinds of torpedoes and fuses used by the Confederates, as well as in designing the ram *Merrimac.*

The total number of seamen at all the Northern naval stations available for immediate detail amounted to only two hundred and seven; and it must be remembered that it was as important that they should be trained to handle heavy guns at sea as that they should be good seamen. The true sailor will soon make himself efficient on board any ship, as far as the handling of the vessel is concerned; but in the effective use of the battery only the trained man-o'-war's-man can safely be relied upon; and there are many other minor matters, such as the division of duties, the exercise at quarters and in boats, forming essential features of the system on a man-o'-war, that are unknown outside the naval service. Officers and men from the merchant service freely offered themselves. Gunnery schools were established at the naval stations for their instruction. As fast as the volunteers could be given an elementary training in the handling of heavy guns, they were sent to sea. This was continued for three years, by which time we had six hundred and fifty vessels and over fifty thousand men afloat.

The service to be performed by this hastily improvised force was as unique as the fleet itself. The entire outer coast-line of the Confederacy was 3549 miles in extent, with several large seaports. To guard the ordinary entrances to these ports was comparatively a simple task. There was, however, a greater difficulty to be met; for the outer coast-line is only the exterior edge of a series of islands between which and the mainland there is an elaborate network of navigable sounds and passages, having numerous inlets communicating with the sea. These inlets were frequently changing under the influence of the great storms; new channels would be opened and old ones filled up. As soon as we closed a port, by stationing vessels at the main entrance thereto, the blockade-runners would slip in at some of the numerous remote inlets, reaching their destination by the inside passages; so that blockade-running flourished until we were able to procure as many blockaders as there were channels and inlets to be guarded. The extreme diversity of the services required of these blockading vessels made it difficult to obtain ships that could meet the varying necessities. They must be heavy enough to contend with the enemy's rams, or they would be driven away from the principal ports. They must be light enough to chase and capture the swift blockade-runners. They must be deep enough in the water to ride out in safety the violent winter gales, and they must be of such light draft as to be able to go near enough to the shallow inlets to blockade them efficiently. . . .

. . . Many of the islands controlled by foreign governments, and lying conveniently near our coast, had good harbors that afforded admirable places of rendezvous for the blockade-runners, where they could safely refit, and remain unmolested until a favorable time came for them to slip out and make a quick run over to the forbidden port; and if unsuccessful in their illicit attempt, they could return as quickly to the protection of the neutral port. . . .

Supplies were brought to the South from various sources, but principally from European ports. At the beginning of the war the blockade-running was carried on from Chesapeake Bay to the mouth of the Rio Grande, by vessels of all sorts, sizes, and nationalities. The steamers formerly engaged in the coasting-trade, that had been interrupted in their regular business by the war, were at first the most successful. The small sailing-vessels did well for some time before the blockade became vigorous; but as the number of our war-ships increased, the earlier groups of blockade-runners were either captured, destroyed, or drawn off. This diminished the volume of supplies to the Confederates just at the time when the demand was greatly increased by the emergencies of warfare, caus[ed] general distress and embarassment in the Confederacy. Prices reached an unprecedented height. Cotton was as low as eight cents a pound in the Confederacy, as high as sixty cents a pound in England, and over one dollar a pound in New York. The moment this state of affairs became known, the science, ingenuity, and mechanical skill of the British seemed to be directed to the business of violating our blockade. Stock companies were formed, by whom the swiftest steamers in the European merchant service were quickly freighted with the supplies that would bring the highest prices in the Confederacy. Officers of rank in the royal navy, under assumed names; officers of the Confederate navy, who had but just resigned from the United States navy; and adventurous spirits from all quarters, flocked to this new and profitable, though hazardous, occupation. . . .

When the blockade-running was at its height, in 1863, a Confederate officer stated that the arrivals and departures were equal to one steamer a day, taking all of the Confederate ports together. Prior to this no such attempts had ever been made to violate a blockade. The industrial necessities of the principal maritime nations stimulated them to unusual efforts, in return for which they looked forward to a rich harvest. The British especially had abundant capital, the finest and swiftest ships ever built, manned by the most energetic seamen.

They felt confident that they could monopolize the Southern cotton and the markets of the Confederacy; but when it was found that neither swift steamers, skilled officers, nor desperate efforts could give security to their best investments of capital, and that the perils to their beautiful vessels and precious cargoes increased as fast as their efforts to surmount them, ultimately becoming even greater in proportion than the enormous gains of the traffic when successful, . . . they finally gave up the business, admitting that the blockade was a success. . . .

This signal defeat of that extraordinary development of our Civil War has been spoken of as one of the great moral lessons of our struggle. After the war British officers frankly stated to our naval officers that they considered the blockade and its enforcement the great fact of the war. This was the first time in the history of naval warfare that a steam navy had been kept at sea for so long a period. . . .

During the war our navy captured or destroyed 1504 blockade-runners, besides causing many valuable cargoes to be thrown overboard by the long-continued and close pursuit of fugitives, who escaped capture by resorting to this expedient to lighten the vessels. A Confederate officer stated that all the approaches to Wilmington harbor were as thickly paved with valuable merchandise as a certain place is said to be with "good intentions."

3

THOMAS TAYLOR

Aboard a Blockade-Runner (1896)

Blockade-running was an exciting and very lucrative business. Both qualities attracted Thomas Taylor, who worked for a British firm engaged in running supplies to the Confederacy through the Union blockade. At the tender age of twenty-one, he took charge of one of the company's blockade-runners operating out of Nassau. There was a certain amount of danger inherent in entering southern ports at high speed at night, but otherwise, foreign nationals such as Taylor incurred limited risk since the Union navy routinely released any foreigners it captured trying to evade the blockade. Here Taylor recounts the tense excitement of his initial voyage on the Banshee, *a blockade-runner, to the port of Wilmington, North Carolina, in 1863.*

Wilmington was the first port I attempted; in fact with the exception of one run to Galveston it was always our destination. It had many advantages. Though furthest from Nassau it was nearest to headquarters at Richmond, and from its situation was very difficult to watch effectively. . . .

At one entrance of the river lies Fort Fisher, a work so powerful that the blockaders instead of lying in the estuary were obliged to form roughly a semicircle out of range of its guns, and the falling away of the coast on either side of the entrance further increased the extent of ground they had to cover. The system they adopted in order to meet the difficulty was extremely well conceived, and, did we not know to the contrary, it would have appeared complete enough to ensure the capture of every vessel so foolhardy as to attempt to enter or come out.

Across either entrance an inshore squadron was stationed at close intervals. In the daytime the steamers composing this squadron anchored, but at night they got under weigh and patrolled in touch with the flagship, which, as a rule, remained at anchor. Further out there was a cordon of cruisers, and outside these again detached gun-boats keeping at such a distance from the coast as they calculated a runner coming out would traverse between the time of high water on Wilmington bar and sunrise, so that if any blockade-runner coming out got through the two inner lines in the dark she had every chance of being snapped up at daybreak by one of the third division.

Besides these special precautions for Wilmington there must not be forgotten the ships engaged in the general service of the blockade, consisting, in addition to those detailed to watch Nassau and other bases, of free cruisers that patrolled the Gulfstream. From this it will be seen readily, that from the moment the *Banshee* left Nassau harbour till

she had passed the protecting forts at the mouth of Cape Fear river, she and those on board her could never be safe from danger or free for a single hour from anxiety. . . .

The *Banshee*'s engines proved so unsatisfactory that under ordinary conditions nine or ten knots was all we could get out of her; she was therefore not permitted to run any avoidable risks, and to this I attribute her extraordinary success where better boats failed. As long as daylight lasted a man was never out of the cross-trees, and the moment a sail was seen the *Banshee*'s stern was turned to it till it was dropped below the horizon. . . .

Following these tactics we crept noiselessly along the shores of the Bahamas, invisible in the darkness, and ran on unmolested for the first two days out, though our course was often interfered with by the necessity of avoiding hostile vessels; then came the anxious moment on the third, when, her position having been taken at noon to see if she was near enough to run under the guns of Fort Fisher before the following daybreak, it was found there was just time, but none to spare for accidents or delay. Still the danger of lying out another day so close to the blockaded port was very great, and rather than risk it we resolved to keep straight on our course and chance being overtaken by daylight before we were under the Fort.

Now the real excitement began, and nothing I have ever experienced can compare with it. . . . Perhaps my readers can sympathise with my enthusiasm when they consider the dangers to be encountered, after three days of constant anxiety and little sleep, in threading our way through a swarm of blockaders, and the accuracy required to hit in the nick of time the mouth of a river only half a mile wide, without lights and with a coast-line so low and featureless that as a rule the first intimation we had of its nearness was the dim white line of the surf.

FROM Thomas Taylor, *Running the Blockade* (London: John Murray, 1896), pp. 44–54.

There were of course many different plans of getting in, but at this time the favourite dodge was to run up some fifteen or twenty miles to the north of Cape Fear, so as to round the northernmost of the blockaders, instead of dashing right through the inner squadron; then to creep down close to the surf till the river was reached: and this was the course the *Banshee* intended to adopt.

We steamed cautiously on until nightfall: the night proved dark, but dangerously clear and calm. No lights were allowed—not even a cigar; the engine-room hatchways were covered with tarpaulins, at the risk of suffocating the unfortunate engineers and stokers in the almost insufferable atmosphere below. But it was absolutely imperative that not a glimmer of light should appear. Even the binnacle was covered, and the steersman had to see as much of the compass as he could through a conical aperture carried almost up to his eyes.

With everything thus in readiness we steamed on in silence except for the stroke of the engines and the beat of the paddle-floats, which in the calm of the night seemed distressingly loud; all hands were on deck, crouching behind the bulwarks; and we on the bridge, namely, the captain, the pilot, and I, were straining our eyes into the darkness. . . . As we crept in not a sound was heard but that of the regular beat of the paddle-floats still dangerously loud in spite of our snail's pace. Suddenly [the pilot Tom] Burroughs gripped my arm,—

"There's one of them, Mr. Taylor," he whispered, "on the starboard bow."

In vain I strained my eyes to where he pointed, not a thing could I see; but presently I heard [Captain] Steele say beneath his breath, "All right, Burroughs, I see her. Starboard a little, steady!" was the order passed aft.

A moment afterwards I could make out a long low black object on our starboard side, lying perfectly still. Would she see us? that was the question; but no, though we passed within a hundred yards of her we were not discovered, and I breathed again. Not very long after we had dropped her Burroughs whispered,—

"Steamer on the port bow."

And another cruiser was made out close to us.

"Hard-a-port," said Steele, and round she swung, bringing our friend upon our beam. Still unobserved we crept quietly on, when all at once a third cruiser shaped herself out of the gloom right ahead and steaming slowly across our bows.

"Stop her," said Steele in a moment, and as we lay like dead our enemy went on and disappeared in the darkness. It was clear there was a false reckoning somewhere, and that instead of rounding the head of the blockading line we were passing through the very centre of it. However, Burroughs was now of opinion that we must be inside the squadron and advocated making the land. So "ahead slow" we went again, until the low-lying coast and the surf line became dimly visible. Still we could not tell where we were, and, as time was getting on alarmingly near dawn, the only thing to do was to creep down along the surf as close in and as fast as we dared. It was a great relief when we suddenly heard Burroughs say, "It's all right, I see the 'Big Hill'!"

The "Big Hill" was a hillock about as high as a full-grown oak tree, but it was the most prominent feature for miles on that dreary coast, and served to tell us exactly how far we were from Fort Fisher. And fortunate it was for us we were so near. Daylight was already breaking, and before we were opposite the fort we could make out six or seven gunboats, which steamed rapidly towards us and angrily opened fire. Their shots were soon dropping close around us: an unpleasant sensation when you know you have several tons of gunpowder under your feet. To make matters worse, the North Breaker shoal now compelled us to haul off the shore and steam further out. It began to look ugly for us, when all at once there was a flash from the shore followed by a sound that came like music to our ears—that of a shell whirring over our heads. It was Fort Fisher, wide awake and warning the gunboats to keep their distance. With a parting broadside they steamed sulkily out of range, and in half an hour we were safely over the bar. . . . Blockade-running seemed the pleasantest and most exhilarating of pastimes. I did not know then what a very serious business it could be.

Benjamin F. Butler Encounters the Contrabands (1892)

In May 1861, General Benjamin F. Butler was assigned command of the Union forces at Fortress Monroe, on the Virginia coast. Almost immediately, slaves from the area began entering his military lines. Since the federal government had not devised any policy concerning such slaves, Butler relied on his own resourcefulness in handling the problem. In the following account from his autobiography, he described how he came to declare these slaves to be contraband of war. Butler's action garnered great publicity and received general approval in the North, and the War Department declined to overturn his policy. But as Butler notes at the end of this passage, he recognized that legally it was not a satisfactory solution, since many of the slaves in his custody, including women and children, had not been used for military purposes by the Confederate army. Still, Butler's action marked the first step on the long road that would lead to emancipation.

On the day after my arrival at the fort, May 23, three negroes were reported coming in a boat from Sewall's Point, where the enemy was building a battery. Thinking that some information as to that work might be got from them, I had them before me. I learned that they were employed on the battery on the Point, which as yet was a trifling affair. There were only two guns there, though the work was laid out to be much larger and to be heavily mounted with guns captured from the navy-yard. The negroes said they belonged to Colonel Mallory, who commanded the Virginia troops around Hampton, and that he was now making preparation to take all his negroes to Florida soon, and that not wanting to go away from home they had escaped to the fort. I directed that they should be fed and set at work.

On the next day I was notified by an officer in charge of the picket line next Hampton that an officer bearing a flag of truce desired to be admitted to the fort to see me. . . . Accompanied by two gentlemen of my staff, Major Fay and Captain Haggerty, neither now living, I rode out to the picket line and met the flag of truce there. It was under charge of Major Carey, who introduced himself, at the same time pleasantly calling to mind that we last met at the Charleston convention. Major Carey opened the conversation by saying: "I have sought to see you for the purpose of ascertaining upon what principles you intend to conduct the war in this neighborhood." I expressed my willingness to answer. . . .

"I am informed," said Major Carey, "that three negroes belonging to Colonel Mallory have es-

FROM Benjamin F. Butler, *Butler's Book* (Boston: A. M. Thayer and Co., 1892), pp. 256–59.

caped within your lines. I am Colonel Mallory's agent and have charge of his property. What do you mean to do with those negroes?"

"I intend to hold them," said I.

"Do you mean, then, to set aside your constitutional obligation to return them?"

"I mean to take Virginia at her word, as declared in the ordinance of secession passed yesterday. I am under no constitutional obligations to a foreign country, which Virginia now claims to be."

"But you say we cannot secede," he answered, "and so you cannot consistently detain the negroes."

"But you say you have seceded, so you cannot consistently claim them. I shall hold these negroes as contraband of war, since they are engaged in the construction of your battery and are claimed as your property. The question is simply whether they shall be used for or against the Government of the United States. Yet, though I greatly need the labor which has providentially come to my hands, if Colonel Mallory will come into the fort and take the oath of allegiance to the United States, he shall have his negroes, and I will endeavor to hire them from him."

"Colonel Mallory is absent," was Major Carey's answer.

We courteously parted. On the way back, the correctness of my law was discussed by Major Haggerty, who was, for a young man, a very good lawyer. He said that he doubted somewhat upon the law, and asked me if I knew of that proposition having been laid down in any treatise on international law.

"Not the precise proposition," said I; "but the precise principle is familiar law. Property of whatever nature, used or capable of being used for warlike purposes, and especially when being so used, may be captured and held either on sea or on shore as property contraband of war. Whether there may be a property in human beings is a question upon which some of us might doubt, but the rebels cannot take the negative. At any rate, Haggerty, it is a good enough reason to stop the rebels' mouths with, especially as I should have held these negroes anyway."

At headquarters and in the fort nothing was discussed but the negro question, and especially this phase of it. The negroes came pouring in day by day, and the third day from that I reported the fact that more than $60,000 worth of them had come in; that I had found work for them to do, had classified them and made a list of them so that their identity might be fully assured, and had appointed a "commissioner of negro affairs" to take this business off my hands, for it was becoming onerous.

I wrote the lieutenant-general that I awaited instructions but should pursue this course until I had received them. On the 30th I received word from the Secretary of War, to whom I had duplicated my letter to General Scott. His instructions gave me no directions to pursue any different course of action from that which I had reported to him, except that I was to keep an accurate account of the value of their work.

. . . I do not claim for the phrase "contraband of war," used in this connection, the highest legal sanction, because it would not apply to property used or property for use in war, as would be a cargo of coal being carried to be burned on board an enemy's ship of war. To hold that contraband, as well might be done, by no means included all the coal in the country. . . . The truth is, as a lawyer I was never very proud of it, but as an executive officer I was very much comforted with it as a means of doing my duty.

2

The Crittenden Resolution
Defines Union War Aims (1861)

On July 22, 1861, following the Union defeat at Bull Run, the House of Representatives passed a resolution offered by John J. Crittenden of Kentucky enunciating Union war aims. The purpose of this resolution (and a similar one passed by the Senate) was to reassure public opinion in the border slave states by denying any intention to interfere with slavery ("the established institutions of those States"). Only two members of the House voted against this resolution, which northern public opinion strongly supported.

*R*esolved by the House of Representatives of the Congress of the United States, That the present deplorable civil war has been forced upon the country by the disunionists of the Southern States now in revolt against the constitutional Government and in arms around the capital; that in this national emergency Congress, banishing all feelings of mere passion or resentment, will recollect only its duty to the whole country; that this war is not waged upon our part in any spirit of oppression, nor for any purpose of conquest or subjugation, nor purpose of overthrowing or interfering with the rights or established institutions of those States, but to defend and maintain the supremacy of the Constitution and to preserve the Union, with all the dignity, equality, and rights of the several States unimpaired; and that as soon as these objects are accomplished the war ought to cease.

FROM James D. Richardson, *A Compilation of the Messages and Papers of the Presidents*, vol. 6 (Washington, D.C.: Government Printing Office, 1907), p. 430.

3

FREDERICK DOUGLASS

Cast Off the Mill-Stone (1861)

Frederick Douglass was the most prominent black abolitionist in the country before the war. Initially he was a follower of William Lloyd Garrison, but he eventually broke with Garrison and moved to Rochester to publish his own antislavery newspaper. In the 1850s, Douglass increasingly countenanced the idea of using violence to overthrow slavery, and once the war began, he became one of the leading advocates of using the war to destroy slavery. In the following editorial in his monthly paper, Douglass called for a war of abolition. While advancing many of the same arguments other abolitionists put forward, Douglass also emphasized the importance of rallying slaves to the Union cause.

We are determined that our readers shall have line upon line and precept upon precept. Ours is only one humble voice; but such as it is, we give it freely to our country, and to the cause of humanity. That honesty is the best policy, we all profess to believe, though our practice may often contradict the proverb. The present policy of our Government is evidently to put down the slave-holding rebellion, and at the same time protect and preserve slavery. This policy hangs like a mill-stone about the neck of our people. It carries disorder to the very sources of our national activities. Weakness, faint heartedness and inefficiency is the natural result. The mental and moral machinery of mankind cannot long withstand such disorder without serious damage. This policy offends reason, wounds the sensibilities, and shocks the moral sentiments of men. It forces upon us in consequent conclusions and painful contradictions, while the plain path of duty is obscured and thronged with multiplying difficulties. Let us look this slavery-preserving policy squarely in the face, and search it thoroughly.

Can the friends of that policy tell us why this should not be an abolition war? Is not abolition plainly forced upon the nation as a necessity of national existence? Are not the rebels determined to make the war on their part a war for the utter destruction of liberty and the complete mastery of slavery over every other right and interest in the land?—And is not an abolition war on our part the natural and logical answer to be made to the rebels? We all know it is. But it is said that for the Government to adopt the abolition policy, would involve the loss of the support of the Union men of the Border Slave States. Grant it, and what is such friendship worth? We are stronger without than with such friendship. It arms the enemy, while it

disarms its friends. The fact is indisputable, that so long as slavery is respected and protected by our Government, the slaveholders can carry on the rebellion, and no longer.—Slavery is the stomach of the rebellion. The bread that feeds the rebel army, the cotton that clothes them, and the money that arms them and keeps them supplied with powder and bullets, come from the slaves, who, if consulted as to the use which should be made of their hard earnings, would say, give it to the bottom of the sea rather than do with it this mischief. Strike here, cut off the connection between the fighting master and the working slave, and you at once put an end to this rebellion, because you destroy that which feeds, clothes and arms it. Shall this not be done, because we shall offend the Union men in the Border States?

But we have good reasons for believing that it would not offend them. The great mass of Union men in all those Border States are intelligently so. They are men who set a higher value upon the Union than upon slavery. In many instances, they recognize slavery as the thing of all others the most degrading to labor and oppressive towards them. They dare not say so now; but let the Government say the word, and even they would unite in sending the vile thing to its grave, and rejoice at the opportunity. Such of them as love slavery better than their country are not now, and have never been, friends of the Union. They belong to the detestable class who do the work of enemies in the garb of friendship, and it would be a real gain to get rid of them. Then look at slavery itself—what good thing has it done that it should be allowed to survive a rebellion of its own creation? Why should the nation pour out its blood and lavish its treasure by the million, consent to protect and preserve the guilty cause of all its troubles? The answer returned to these questions is, that the Constitution does not allow the exercise of such power. As if this were a time to talk of constitutional power!

FROM *Douglass' Monthly*, September 1861.

When a man is well, it would be mayhem to cut off his arm. It would be unconstitutional to do so. But if the arm were shattered and mortifying, it would be quite unconstitutional and criminal not to cut it off. The cause is precisely so with Governments. The grand object, end and aim of Government is the preservation of society, and from nothing worse than anarchy. When Governments, through the ordinary channels of civil law, are unable to secure this end, they are thrown back upon military law, and for the time may set aside the civil law precisely to the extent which it may be necessary to do so in order to accomplish the grand object for which Governments are instituted among men. The power, therefore, to abolish slavery is within the objects sought by the Constitution. But if every letter and syllable of the Constitution were a prohibition of abolition, yet if the life of the nation required it, we should be bound by the Constitution to abolish it, because there can be no interest superior to existence and preservation. . . .

Another evil of the policy of protecting and preserving slavery, is that it deprives us of the important aid which might be rendered to the Government by the four million slaves. These people are repelled by our slaveholding policy. They have their hopes of deliverance from bondage destroyed. They hesitate now; but if our policy is pursued, they will not need to be compelled by Jefferson Davis to fight against us. . . .

A third evil of this policy, is the chilling effect it exerts upon the moral sentiment of mankind. Vast is the power of the sympathy of the civilized world. . . . Our policy gives the rebels the advantage of seeming to be merely fighting for the right to govern themselves. We divest the war on our part of all those grand elements of progress and philanthropy that naturally win the hearts and command the reverence of all men, and allow it to assume the form of a meaningless display of brute force. . . .

Another evil arising from this mischievous slaveholding policy, is that it invites the interference of other Governments with our blockade. . . . Let the war be made an abolition war, and no statesman in England or France would dare even, if inclined, to propose any disturbance of the blockade. Make this an abolition war, and you at once unite the world against the rebels, and in favor of the Government.

4

ABRAHAM LINCOLN

To Lose Kentucky Is to Lose the Whole Game (1861)

At the end of August 1861, John C. Frémont, who was the Union military commander in Missouri, issued a proclamation on his own authority establishing martial law and freeing the slaves of disloyal residents. Frémont's proclamation received substantial support in the North, and when Lincoln subsequently revoked the general's emancipation edict, he was subjected to a torrent of criticism. Surely the most surprising critic of Lincoln's action, however, was Senator Orville H. Browning of Illi-

nois. A conservative Republican, Browning had been a good friend of Lincoln's for years, dating from their association in the Illinois Whig party, and he had never been a strong antislavery man. In the following letter, Lincoln patiently explained the reasons for his action but was unable to hide his astonishment at Browning's endorsement of Frémont's action.

Private & confidential.

Executive Mansion
Washington Sept 22d 1861.

Hon. O. H. Browning
My dear Sir

Yours of the 17th is just received; and coming from you, I confess it astonishes me. That you should object to my adhering to a law, which you had assisted in making, and presenting to me, less than a month before, is odd enough. But this is a very small part. Genl. Fremont's proclamation, as to confiscation of property, and the liberation of slaves, is *purely political*, and not within the range of *military* law, or necessity. If a commanding General finds a necessity to seize the farm of a private owner, for a pasture, an encampment, or a fortification, he has the right to do so, and to so hold it, as long as the necessity lasts; and this is within military law, because within military necessity. But to say the farm shall no longer belong to the owner, or his heirs forever; and this as well when the farm is not needed for military purposes as when it is, is purely political, without the savor of military law about it. And the same is true of slaves. If the General needs them, he can seize them, and use them; but when the need is past, it is not for him to fix their permanent future condition. That must be settled according to laws made by law-makers, and not by military proclamations. The proclamation in the point in question, is simply "dictatorship." It assumes that the general may do *anything* he pleases—confiscate the lands and free the slaves of *loyal* people, as well as of disloyal ones. And going the whole figure I have no doubt

would be more popular with some thoughtless people, than that which has been done! But I cannot assume this reckless position; nor allow others to assume it on my responsibility. You speak of it as being the only means of *saving* the government. On the contrary it is itself the surrender of the government. Can it be pretended that it is any longer the government of the U.S.—any government of Constitution and laws,—wherein a General, or a President, may make permanent rules of property by proclamation?

I do not say Congress might not with propriety pass a law, on the point, just such as General Fremont proclaimed. I do not say I might not, as a member of Congress, vote for it. What I object to, is, that I as President, shall expressly or impliedly seize and exercise the permanent legislative functions of the government.

So much as to principle. Now as to policy. No doubt the thing was popular in some quarters, and would have been more so if it had been a general declaration of emancipation. The Kentucky Legislature would not budge till that proclamation was modified; and Gen. Anderson telegraphed me that on the news of Gen. Fremont having actually issued deeds of manumission, a whole company of our Volunteers threw down their arms and disbanded. I was so assured, as to think it probable, that the very arms we had furnished Kentucky would be turned against us. I think to lose Kentucky is nearly the same as to lose the whole game. Kentucky gone, we can not hold Missouri, nor, as I think, Maryland. These all against us, and the job on our hands is too large for us. We would as well consent to separation at once, including the surrender of this capitol. On the contrary, if you will give up your restlessness for new positions, and back me manfully on the grounds upon which you and other kind friends gave me the election, and

FROM Roy P. Basler, et al., eds., *The Collected Works of Abraham Lincoln*, vol. 5 (New Brunswick, N.J.: Rutgers University Press, 1953), pp. 531–33.

have approved in my public documents, we shall go through triumphantly.

You must not understand I took my course on the proclamation *because* of Kentucky. I took the same ground in a private letter to General Fremont before I heard from Kentucky. . . .

There has been no thought of removing Gen. Fremont on any ground connected with his proclamation. . . . I hope no real necessity for it exists on any ground. . . .

A. Lincoln

5

SAMUEL S. COX

A Democratic Congressman Attacks Emancipation (1862)

Samuel S. Cox was an important Democratic leader and congressman from Ohio. Like many War Democrats, Cox initially supported the war effort, but he strongly opposed making emancipation a Union war aim and hence became increasingly disaffected. In the following speech, entitled "Emancipation and Its Results—Is Ohio to Be Africanized?," Cox marshalled constitutional, economic, and racist arguments against any policy of emancipation. Cox's racist arguments were forcefully expressed, but his language was generally not as crude as that of rabid Copperhead sheets. (Copperhead was a Republican epithet for northern opponents of the war.) His speech, which was delivered on June 3, 1862, was widely circulated as a Democratic campaign document that fall.

Mr. Chairman: At the beginning of our civil conflict this House passed almost unanimously a resolution offered by the gentleman from Kentucky [Mr. Crittenden] as to the character of the war. It was a pledge that the war should not be waged in hostility to the institutions of any of the States. On the faith of its pledge men and money were voted. Since then that pledge has been broken both in this House and out of it. . . .

Measures . . . which would create equality of black and white, such as passed the Senate, in carrying the mails; which abolished slavery in this District; which, like the acts of confiscation and emancipation here urged, are to free the whole or a

portion of the black population; all these measures, sir, are subversive of the institutions of the States, and have created apprehension and distrust. . . .

There is something needed in making successful civil war besides raising money and armies. You must keep up the confidence and spirit of the people. It must not only be animated by a noble passion at the outset, but it must be sustained by confidence in the cause. You dispirit the Army and destroy its power, if you give forth an uncertain sound. Is there a member here who dare say that Ohio troops will fight successfully or fight at all, if the result shall be the flight and movement of the black race by millions northward to their own State? . . .

You wish to put down this rebellion; yet you despise the counsels of the Union men of the South, who tell you that your anti-slavery crusade

FROM *Congressional Globe*, 37th Cong., 2d sess., 1862, Appendix, pp. 242–49.

adds to the rebel army day after day thousands of soldiers and to the southern treasury millions of money. You presume on their forbearance, not caring to know that their lips are often sealed here, because by denouncing you, the secession element, which is kept alive by your action in their States, will point to their denunciations of their conduct as a justification of the rebellion. You will justify this crime to history, provided only your vengeance and your election are made sure.

Sir, I fear and distrust much which I cannot, from motives of prudence and patriotism, utter. Is it the policy here, as it would seem to be, to force the Union men South into some rash expression or act, by such proclamations as [General David] Hunter's, and such legislation as we have had, and then to charge this rashness as an excuse for converting the war into a St. Domingo–insurrection, turning the South into one utter desolation? Is it in anticipation of this that we have arms for negroes sent to South Carolina and Louisiana?—We can get no information on these subjects, though we strive for it. Are we to be deceived by the prevarication of this Congress in regard to extreme measures? In the mean time, are these extreme measures to be taken as the Army advances with its triumphant flag? In the name of God, is no man's hand to be raised to retard the downward, hellward course of these extreme men? Will not the President at once leap to fill the niche in history pointed out to him by my friend from Kentucky [Mr. Crittenden]? He has done so many noble acts, in spite of the lashings of his friends, will he not change this equivocal situation and give us reassurance in our doubt and trouble, like that which inspired his proclamation, and like that which dictated the Crittenden resolve? Such assurance would make the country ring with his praises. It would make our taxation light, our duty clear, and our patriotism resplendent beyond all that is written in the annals of man.

I trace the murmurs of discontent which come to us from Army and people to the alliance between Republicans and abolitionists. That alliance may be natural, but it is not patriotic. The Philadelphia platform of no more slave States, and Republicanism with its Chicago dogma of no more slave territory, may be innocent in intention, but, allied with abolitionism, with its raids and war upon slavery everywhere, and its defiance of the Constitution, it is crime.

Is this alliance the forerunner of that perfect Union when "liberty shall be proclaimed throughout all the land and to all the inhabitants thereof?" Is it the dawn of that millennial day which shall reflect back the saber, the musket, and the torch in the hands of the enfranchised African, already urged and voted for by thirty members of this House?

We want no more poetry about striking off chains and bidding the oppressed go. Plain people want to know whether the chains will not be put upon white limbs; and *whither* the oppressed are to go. If the industry of the North is to be fettered with their support; if they are to go to Ohio and the North, we want to know it. Nay, we want, if we can, to stop it. . . .

It is beyond doubt that a large number of the four millions of slaves will be freed incidentally by the war. . . . It has been computed that already some seventy thousand blacks are freed by the war. . . . These are being scattered North, are becoming resident in this District and supported by the largesses of the Federal Treasury. It is said that eighteen thousand rations are daily given out to negroes by our Government. This is but a small number of those who are freed, or to be freed, by these bills. The mildest confiscation bill proposed will free not less than seven hundred thousand slaves. The bill which is before us frees three millions, at least. The bills which receive the favor of the majority of the Republican party will free four millions. . . .

It may have been wrong to have held them in slavery. Is it right to set them free, to starve? What is to be done with them? This is the riddle, more difficult than that of the Ethiopian Sphynx. . . .

Slavery may be an evil, it may be wrong for southern men to use unpaid labor, but what will be the condition of the people of Ohio when the free jubilee shall have come in its ripe and rotten maturity? If slavery is bad, the condition of the State of

Ohio, with an unrestrained black population, only double what we now have[,] partly subservient, partly slothful, partly criminal, and all disadvantageous and ruinous, will be far worse.

I do not speak these things out of any unkindness to the negro. It is not for the interest of the free negroes of my State that that class of the population should be increased. I speak as their friend when I oppose such immigration.

Neither do I blame the negro altogether for his crime, improvidence, and sloth. He is under a sore calamity in this country. He is inferior, distinct, and separate, and he has, perhaps, sense enough to perceive it. The advantages and equality of the white man can never be his. . . .

I lay down the proposition that the white and black races thrive best apart; that a commingling of these races is a detriment to both; that it does not elevate the black, and it only depresses the white. . . . The character of these mixed races is that of brutality, cowardice, and crime, which has no parallel in any age or land. If you permit the dominant and subjugated races to remain upon the same soil, and grant them any approach to social and political equality, amalgamation, more or less, is inevitable. . . .

Is this the fate to be commended to the Anglo-Saxon-Celtic population of the United States? Tell me not that this amalgamation will not go on in the North. What means the mulattoes in the North, far exceeding, as the census of 1850 shows, the mulattoes of the South? There are more free mulattoes than there are free blacks in the free States. . . .

The mixture of the races tends to deteriorate both races. Physiology has called our attention to the results of such intermarriages or connections. These results show differences in stature and strength, depending on the parentage, with a corresponding difference in the moral character, mental capacity, and worth of labor. . . . But how long before the manly, warlike people of Ohio, of fair hair and blue eyes, in a large preponderance, would become, in spite of Bibles and morals, degenerate under the wholesale emancipation and immigration favored by my colleague?

The free negroes will become equal, or will continue unequal to the whites. Equality is a condition which is self-protective, wanting nothing, asking nothing, able to take care of itself. It is an absurdity to say that two races as dissimilar as black and white, of different origin, of unequal capacity, can succeed in the same society when placed in competition. There is no such example in history of the success of two separate races under such circumstances. . . .

Prejudice, stronger than all principles, though not always stronger than lust, has imperatively separated the whites from the blacks. In the schoolhouse, the church, or the hospital, the black man must not seat himself beside the white; even in death and at the cemetery the line of distinction is drawn.

To abolish slavery the North must go still further and forget that fatal prejudice of race which governs it, and which makes emancipation so illusory. To give men their liberty, to open to them the gates of the city, and then say, "there, you shall live among yourselves, you shall marry among yourselves, you shall form a separate society in society," is to create a cursed caste, and replace slaves by pariahs.

How will this immigration of the blacks affect labor in Ohio and in the North?

First, directly, it affects our labor, as all unproducing classes detract from the prosperity of a community. Ohio is an agricultural State. Negroes will not farm. They prefer to laze or serve around towns and cities. . . .

But suppose they do work, or work a little, or a part of them work well; what then is the effect upon our mechanics and laboring men? It is said that many of them make good blacksmiths, carpenters, &c., and especially good servants. If that be so, there are white laborers North whose sweat is to be coined into taxes to ransom these negroes; and the first effect of the ransom is to take the bread and meat from the families of white laborers. If the wages of white labor are reduced, they will ask the cause. That cause will be found in the delusive devices of members of Congress. The helps of German and Irish descent, the workmen and mechanics in the shop and field, will find some, if not all, of these negroes, bought by their toil, competing with them at every turn. Labor will then go down to a song. It will be degraded by such association. Our soldiers, when they return, one hundred thousand strong, to their Ohio homes, will find these negroes, or the best of them, filling their places, felling timber, plowing ground, gathering crops, &c. How their martial laurels will brighten when they discover the result of their services! Labor that now ranges at from one to two dollars per day, will fall to one half. Already, in this District the Government is hiring out the fugitives at from two to eight dollars per month, while white men are begging for work. Nor is the labor of the most of these negroes desirable. No system of labor is so unless it be steady. They will get their week's wages, and then idle the next week away. Many will become a charge and a nuisance upon the public charity and county poor tax. . . .

And for this result *directly* to northern labor, what compensation is there to the southern half of our country by their removal? Herein lies the indirect effect of their immigration upon northern labor. By this emancipation, the labor system of the South is destroyed. The cotton, which brought us $200,000,000 per annum, a good part of which came to Ohio to purchase pork, corn, flour, beef, machinery, &c., where is it? Gone. What of the cotton fabric, almost as common as bread among the laboring classes! With four millions of indolent negroes, its production is destroyed, and the ten millions of artisans in the world who depend on it for employment, and the hundred million who depend on it for clothing will find the fabric advanced a hundred per cent. So with sugar, and other productions of slave labor. For all these results, labor will curse the jostling elements which thus disturb the markets of the world.

In conclusion, then, if the negro cannot be colonized without burdens intolerable, and plans too delusive; if he cannot be freed and left South without destroying its labor, and without his extermination; if he cannot come North without becoming an outcast and without ruin to northern industry and society, what shall be done? Where shall he go? . . .

What shall be done? I answer, Representatives! that our duty is written in our oath! IT IS IN THE CONSTITUTION OF THE UNITED STATES! Leave to the States their own institutions where that instrument leaves them, keep your faith to the Crittenden resolution, be rid of all ambiguous schemes and trust under God for the revelation of His will concerning these black men in our land, and the overthrow by our power of this rebellion.

6

JOHN SHERMAN

Support for Emancipation Is Increasing (1862)

John Sherman was a Republican senator from Ohio who belonged to the moderate wing of the party. He had never been a radical on the slavery issue, but like many northerners, he found his ideas undergoing rapid change in 1862. In a letter written in late summer of that year to his brother, the famous Union general William Tecumseh Sherman, he signaled his support for emancipation as a Union war aim.

Mansfield, Ohio, Aug. 24, 1862.

Dear Brother:

. . . You can form no conception at the change of opinion here as to the Negro Question. Men of all parties who now appreciate the magnitude of the contest and who are determined to preserve the unity of the government at all hazards, agree that we must seek the aid and make it the interests of the negroes to help us. Nothing but our party divisions and our natural prejudice of caste has kept us from using them as *allies* in the war, to be used for all purposes in which they can advance the cause of the country. Obedience and protection must go together. When rebels take up arms, not only refuse obedience but resist our force, they have no right to ask protection in any way. And especially that protection should not extend to a local right inconsistent with the general spirit of our laws and the existence of which has been from the beginning the chief element of discord in the country. I am prepared for one to meet the broad issue of universal emancipation. . . .

We all wait with intense anxiety the events impending in Virginia. We all fear results for a month to come. Now is the chance for the rebels.

Affectionately yours,

John Sherman.

FROM Rachel Sherman Thorndike, *The Sherman Letters* (New York: Charles Scribner's Sons, 1894), pp. 156–58.

7

ABRAHAM LINCOLN

I Would Save the Union (1862)

On August 19, 1862, Horace Greeley published an editorial in the New York Tribune, *which he modestly entitled "The Prayer of Twenty Millions," harshly criticizing Lincoln's policy on slavery and calling on the president to adopt emancipation as a war aim. Because the* Tribune *was the most widely circulated Republican newspaper in the country, with a broad following among northern reform elements, Greeley's outburst attracted considerable attention.*

Greeley was personally eccentric and politically unreliable, as he had a penchant for riding particular hobbies and sometimes flip-flopped on critical issues. But Lincoln knew the peevish New York editor could not safely be ignored, so he wrote a careful reply to Greeley's editorial. Lincoln's letter, which was intended for publication, was his most famous statement about his policy on slavery and the Union prior to his issuing the preliminary Emancipation Proclamation. Yet ironically, its real purpose was to prepare the northern public to accept emancipation as a Union war aim, for the president had already drafted his proclamation and discussed it with the Cabinet. A month later, when he issued the preliminary proclamation, Lincoln officially made emancipation a Union war aim, precisely the policy that Greeley advocated in his editorial. Nevertheless, Lincoln never lost sight of his original purpose to save the Union.

Executive Mansion,
Washington, August 22, 1862.

Hon. Horace Greely:
Dear Sir

I have just read yours of the 19th. addressed to myself through the New-York Tribune. If there be in it any statements, or assumptions of fact, which I may know to be erroneous, I do not, now and here, controvert them. If there be in it any inferences which I may believe to be falsely drawn, I do not now and here, argue against them. If there be perceptable in it an impatient and dictatorial tone, I waive it in deference to an old friend, whose heart I have always supposed to be right.

As to the policy I "seem to be pursuing" as you say, I have not meant to leave any one in doubt.

I would save the Union. I would save it the shortest way under the Constitution. The sooner the national authority can be restored; the nearer the Union will be "the Union as it was." If there be those who would not save the Union, unless they could at the same time *save* slavery, I do not agree with them. If there be those who would not save the Union unless they could at the same time *destroy* slavery, I do not agree with them. My paramount object in this struggle *is* to save the Union, and is *not* either to save or to destroy slavery. If I could save the Union without freeing *any* slave I would do it, and if I could save it by freeing *all* the slaves I would do it; and if I could save it by freeing some and leaving others alone I would also do that. What I do about slavery, and the colored race, I do because I believe it helps to save the Union; and what I forbear, I forbear because I do *not* believe it would help to save the Union. I shall do *less* whenever I shall believe what I am doing hurts the cause, and I shall do *more* whenever I shall believe doing more will help the cause. I shall try to correct errors when shown to be errors; and I shall adopt new views so fast as they shall appear to be true views.

I have here stated my purpose according to my view of *official* duty; and I intend no modification of my oft-expressed *personal* wish that all men every where could be free.

Yours,

A. Lincoln

FROM Roy P. Basler, et al., eds., *The Collected Works of Abraham Lincoln*, vol. 5 (New Brunswick, N.J.: Rutgers University Press, 1953), pp. 388–89.

8

Harper's Weekly Gauges the Northern Response to Emancipation (1862)

In the following editorial, which appeared shortly after Lincoln issued the preliminary Emancipation Proclamation, Harper's Weekly *analyzed northern public opinion on the issue of emancipation and noted the significant change that had occurred since the war commenced. It particularly noticed—and then dismissed—the fear of northern workers that emancipated slaves would compete for jobs in the North. Yet the magazine did not speak for the working class.*

And how will negro emancipation be viewed at the North? There was a time, not very long since, when a large majority of the Northern people would have opposed it strenuously—not so much from any admiration for slavery, as from a belief that, under the Constitution, we had no right to meddle with it, and that its abolition involved dangers and inconveniences perhaps as formidable as those which were created by its existence. Even at the present time a mortal antipathy for the negro is entertained by a large class of persons at the North—as is evidenced by the recent vote against negroes in Illinois, the riots in Cincinnati and Brooklyn, and the unkind treatment of the negro fugitives at Hilton Head by the regiments of General Hunter's army. At the same time, the war has produced a remarkable change in the opinions of educated and liberal men at the North. Such leading men as General [Lew] Wallace of Illinois [i.e., Indiana], Daniel S. Dickinson of New York, General [Benjamin F.] Butler of Massachusetts, and nine-tenths of the generals in the field—who, a year ago, really believed that slavery was the true station for the negro—have lately freely expressed what used to be called "abolition views." How long it will take for these liberal views to permeate society, and stamp themselves on the mind of the working-class, remains to be seen. We do not, for our part, apprehend any serious opposition at the North to the President's policy, except in circles whose loyalty to the country may well be questioned.

Demagogues will of course endeavor to excite our working-classes against the Government by threatening them with the competition of free negro labor. It seems hardly worth while to reply to so shallow and so mean an argument as this. Our laboring class in this country is intelligent enough to know that what we want in every part of this country is not fewer but more laborers. For years we at the North have been moving heaven and earth to get more labor from Europe, and we have succeeded in getting a very large number of men every year; yet wages have steadily advanced instead of falling. . . . So at the South. They have increased their stock of labor steadily by every means, lawful and unlawful, for thirty years, and yet the price of slaves has steadily risen from $400 to $1500 for adult field hands, and the cry—before the war—was still for more labor. The man who tries to frighten the North with threats of competition by emancipated negroes insults the understanding of our laboring class.

FROM *Harper's Weekly*, 4 October 1862.

9

NEW YORK TIMES

The 1862 Elections Are a Repudiation of the Administration's Conduct of the War (1862)

The Republican party experienced a series of defeats in the 1862 northern state and congressional elections. While the party did well in some states, it suffered major defeats in several key northern states, including New York, Indiana, and Illinois. In the following editorial, which appeared as soon as these elections were over, the New York Times, a leading Republican paper that generally supported the administra-

tion, analyzed the reasons for these defeats and called for a more vigorous prosecution of the war. Lincoln was accustomed to such criticism from the Radicals, but coming as it did from the Times, *it documented the northern home front's growing frustration over the war.*

The Election and the War.

The heaviest load which the friends of the Government have been compelled to carry through this canvass has been the inactivity and inefficiency of the Administration. We speak from a knowledge of public sentiment in every section of the State, when we say that the failure of the Government to prosecute the war with the vigor, energy and success which the vast resources at its command warranted the country in expecting at its hands, has weighed like an incubus upon the public heart. With every disposition to sustain the Government—with the most profound conviction that the only hope of the country lies in giving it a cordial and effective support—its friends have been unable to give a satisfactory answer to the questions that have come up from every side: Why has the war made so little progress? Why have our splendid armies achieved such slight successes? Why have they lain idle so long, and why have the victories they have won been so utterly barren of decisive results? The war has dragged on for a year and a half. The country has given the Government over a million of men, and all the money they could possibly use; yet we have made scarcely any progress toward crushing the rebellion. The rebel armies still menace the capital. Their privateers defy our navy, and spread increasing terror among our peaceful traders on the seas. What is the use of trying to sustain an Administration which lags so far behind the country, and seems so indifferent and incompetent to the dreadful task committed to its hands?

It has been impossible to lift the public heart out of the terrible despondency which such reflections, fortified by the inexorable logic of facts, have brought upon it. The people of this State are thoroughly loyal to the Union and the Constitution.

FROM *New York Times*, 5 November 1862.

They desire and demand that this rebellion shall be *crushed*. They desire no half-way measures—they will tolerate no base and degrading compromise—they will never consent to any peace which involves the disruption of the Union and the overthrow of the Constitution. They demand a vigorous prosecution of the war; and the fact that they have not had it, and that they have seen no fair prospect of getting it, has bred in them a degree of discouragement and despair which has left them an easy prey to the demagogues who are always ready to profit by the calamities of their country. If the Government had given them victories—if it had even shown any just appreciation of the need of victories, and had taken the most ordinary means of exacting them at the hands of its Generals in the field, the people would have rallied as one man to its support. They would have spurned with indignation the base attempts of demagogues to sap their faith in the Administration, and to array them in hostility against it.

. . . The vote in this State, as in Pennsylvania and the West, indicates a profound dissatisfaction with the method of the Administration in carrying on this war,—and a peremptory demand for the adoption of one better adapted to the awful emergencies of the case. The President must not hesitate an hour to respond to this demand. Whatever may have been the results of these elections, all the powers of the Government are still in his hands—all the fearful responsibilities of the crisis still rest upon his shoulders. He must not suffer them to depress his courage or enfeeble his energies;—he must the rather meet them with fresh vigor and redoubled resolution. Let the popular verdict just pronounced dispel whatever of hesitation or of timidity may have hampered his movements. He must have more self-confidence,—more of that reliance upon his own strength and resources which, though it might be reckless audacity in a private individual, is only a necessary and becoming courage in the ruler of a mighty nation, in a great and terrible crisis of its fate.

President Lincoln has now in his hands everything which he can possibly require for the completion of the great work that devolves upon him. He has a more powerful army under his command than any monarch of Europe. The finances of the country are on a safe basis, and he has all the money he will require. He has a navy adequate to any service that may be demanded of it. With these abundant and overflowing resources at his command—sustained and stimulated to the most vigorous efforts by the fervid patriotism of the people, and by every motive which can animate a loyal heart, he can make no excuse to his conscience or his country if he fails to push this war to a speedy and successful end. He must instantly put in motion every arm of the National power. There must be an end of excuses, of apologies and of delays. The country will not longer tolerate half-hearted counsels in the Cabinet, or half-hearted leadership in the field. The fate of the nation must no longer be committed to Generals who, like Essex in the English Revolution, "next to a great defeat, *dread a great victory*." The Government must no longer be content with defending itself against a rebellion. It must act upon the offensive—and act with the vigor and determination that insure a victory. If the recent elections shall inspire the Administration with this spirit, and prompt it to such action, they will be of more service than results which might have betrayed it into a delusive and fatal confidence in the fruitless policy it has hitherto pursued.

10

Abraham Lincoln Replies to a Republican Critic after the 1862 Elections (1862)

When the Republicans suffered a series of defeats in the northern state and congressional elections in the fall of 1862, some party leaders blamed Lincoln and his policies for these setbacks. One who did so was Carl Schurz, the famous German Republican leader who was a Union general and notable antislavery spokesman. Lincoln replied to Schurz's criticisms in the following letter, which stresses the necessity of gaining the support of Democrats for the war effort by giving them political and military appointments. In the process, the exasperated president offered his own assessment of the recent elections. As this letter demonstrates, Lincoln's patience and tact in dealing with critics was virtually limitless.

Private & confidential

Executive Mansion,
Washington, Nov. 10. 1862.

Gen. Schurz.
My dear Sir

Yours of the 8th. was, to-day, read to me by Mrs. S[churz]. We have lost the elections; and it is natural that each of us will believe, and say, it has been because his peculiar views was not made sufficiently prominent. I think I know what it was, but I may be mistaken. Three main causes told the whole story. 1. The democrats were left in a majority by our friends going to the war. 2. The democrats observed this & determined to re-instate themselves in power, and 3. Our newspaper's, by vilifying and disparaging the administration, furnished them all the weapons to do it with. Certainly, the ill-success of the war had much to do with this.

You give a different set of reasons. If you had not made the following statements, I should not have suspected them to be true. "The defeat of the administration is the administrations own fault." (opinion) "It admitted its professed opponents to its counsels" (Asserted as a fact) "It placed the Army, now a great power in this Republic, into the hands of its' enemys" (Asserted as a fact) "In all personal questions, to be hostile to the party of the Government, seemed, to be a title to consideration." (Asserted as a fact) "If to forget the great rule, that if you are true to your friends, your friends will be true to you, and that you make your enemies stronger by placing them upon an equality with your friends." "Is it surprising that the opponents of the administration should have got into their hands the government of the principal states, after they have had for a long time the principal management of the war, the great business of the national government."

I can not dispute about the matter of opinion.

On the the [sic] three matters (stated as facts) I shall be glad to have your evidence upon them when I shall meet you. The plain facts, as they appear to me, are these. The administration came into power, very largely in a minority of the popular vote. Notwithstanding this, it distributed to it's party friends as nearly all the civil patronage as any administration ever did. The war came. The administration could not even start in this, without assistance outside of it's party. It was mere nonsense to suppose a minority could put down a majority in rebellion. Mr. Schurz (now Gen. Schurz) was about here then & I do not recollect that he then considered all who were not republicans, were enemies of the government, and that none of them must be appointed to to [sic] military positions. He will correct me if I am mistaken. It so happened that very few of our friends had a military education or were of the profession of arms. It would have been a question whether the war should be conducted on military knowledge, or on political affinity, only that our own friends (I think Mr. Schurz included) seemed to think that such a question was inadmissable. Accordingly I have scarcely appointed a democrat to a command, who was not urged by many republicans and opposed by none. It was so as to McClellan. He was first brought forward by the Republican Governor of Ohio, & claimed, and contended for at the same time by the Republican Governor of Pennsylvania. I received recommendations from the republican delegations in congress, and I believe every one of them recommended a majority of democrats. But, after all many Republicans were appointed; and I mean no disparagement to them when I say I do not see that their superiority of success has been so marked as to throw great suspicion on the good faith of those who are not Republicans.

Yours truly,

A. Lincoln

FROM Roy P. Basler, et al., eds., *The Collected Works of Abraham Lincoln*, vol. 5 (New Brunswick, N.J.: Rutgers University Press, 1953), pp. 493–95.

Governor Joseph Brown Obstructs Conscription in Georgia (1862)

In a series of increasingly acerbic letters to Jefferson Davis, Governor Joseph Brown attacked the conscription law recently passed by the Confederate Congress as unconstitutional and announced his intention to prevent the conscription of state civil and military officials. Unable to placate the governor, Davis finally dispatched Howell Cobb, a former Georgia political leader, to the state as military commander in order to try to secure Brown's cooperation. Cobb, however, had no more luck in dislodging the obstinate governor from his obstructionism. Cobb finally complained in frustration that Brown exempted many more state officials than were needed to perform the work, including countless officials in county courts that no longer even convened because of the war's disruptions as well as men of military age who had gotten themselves elected to offices that had been vacant for years prior to the war. Knowledge that Brown earlier had instituted a state conscription program without any constitutional warrant to do so no doubt intensified the Confederate president's exasperation.

Milledgeville, Ga.
May 8, 1862

Dear Sir:

I have the honor to acknowledge the receipt of your favor of the 28th ult., in reply to my letter to you upon the subject of the Conscription Act. I should not trouble you with a reply, were it not that principles are involved of the most vital character, upon the maintenance of which, in my opinion, depend not only the rights and sovereignty of the States, but the very existence of State Government.

While I am always happy as an individual to render you any assistance in my power . . . and while I am satisfied you will bear testimony that I have never, as the executive of this State, failed in a single instance to furnish all the men, and more than you have called for, and to assist you with all the other means at my command, I cannot consent to commit the State to a policy which is, in my judgment, subversive of her sovereignty, and at war with all the principles for the support of which Georgia entered into this revolution.

It may be said that this is no time to discuss constitutional questions in the midst of revolution, and that State rights and State sovereignty must yield for a time to the higher law of necessity. If this is a safe principle of action, it cannot certainly

FROM Allen D. Candler, *The Confederate Records of the State of Georgia*, vol. 3 (Atlanta: Charles P. Byrd, 1910), pp. 212–21.

apply until the necessity is shown to exist; and I apprehend it would be a dangerous policy to adopt, were we to admit that those who are to exercise the power of setting aside the Constitution, are to be the judges of the necessity for so doing. But did the necessity exist in this case? The Conscription Act cannot aid the Government in increasing its supply of arms or provisions, but can only enable it to call a larger number of men into the field. The difficulty has never been to get men. The States have already furnished the Government more than it can arm, and have, from their own means, armed and equipped very large numbers for it. Georgia has not only furnished more than you have asked, and armed and equipped from her own treasury, a large proportion of those, she has sent to the field, but she stood ready to furnish promptly her quota (organized as the Constitution provided)[1] of any additional number called for by the President. . . .

Feeling satisfied that the Conscription Act, and such other Acts of Congress as authorize the President to appoint or commission the officers of the militia of the State, when employed in the service of the Confederate States "to repel invasion," are in palpable violation of the Constitution, I can consent to do no act which commits Georgia to willing acquiescence in their binding force upon her people. I cannot therefore consent to have anything to do with the enrollment of the conscripts in this State; nor can I permit any commissioned officer of the militia to be enrolled, who is necessary to enable the State to exercise her reserved right of training her militia, according to the discipline prescribed by Congress, at a time, when to prevent troubles with her slaves, a strict military police is absolutely necessary to the safety of her people. Nor can I permit any other officer, civil or military, who is necessary to the maintenance of the State Government, to be carried out of the State as a conscript. . . .

Your obedient servant,

Joseph E. Brown

---

[1]Brown contended that, under the Confederate Constitution, military officers were to be elected by the troops and commissioned by the state, not the Confederate government. Brown's position was intended to enhance the state's control over its own troops, and this ongoing dispute was another reason he resisted conscription in Georgia.

2

The Twenty Negro Law (1862)

After the Confederate Congress adopted conscription in April 1862, it enacted a long list of exemptions, mostly occupations that were designated as essential to the war effort. In reality, many of those exempted did not perform crucial war work, but the most controversial exemption was the so-called twenty Negro law, which allowed some slave owners and overseers to escape military service. Critics noted that similar protection was not offered to non-slaveholding farmers in the South. Congress revised this provision in 1863 (to protect against fraud) and 1864 (reducing the number of slaves to fifteen). The text of the original law, approved on October 11, 1862, follows.

The Congress of the Confederate States of America do enact . . . to secure the proper police of the country, one person, either as agent, owner or overseer on each plantation on which one white person is required to be kept by the laws or ordinances of any State, and on which there is no white male adult not liable to do military service, and in States having no such law, one person as agent, owner or overseer, on each plantation of twenty negroes, and on which there is no white male adult not liable to military service; *And furthermore,* For additional police for every twenty negroes on two or more plantations, within five miles of each other, and each having less than twenty negroes, and of which there is no white male adult not liable to military duty, one person, being the oldest of the owners or overseers on such plantations; . . . are hereby exempted from military service in the armies of the Confederate States; . . . *Provided, further,* That the exemptions hereinabove enumerated and granted hereby, shall only continue whilst the persons exempted are actually engaged in their respective pursuits or occupations.

FROM James M. Matthews, *Public Laws of the Confederate States of America, Passed at the Second Session of the First Congress* (Richmond: R. M. Smith, 1862), pp. 77–79.

3

A Georgia Soldier Condemns the Exemption of Slaveholders (1862)

A Georgia soldier wrote the following letter to the Atlanta Southern Confederacy *discussing conscription in the Confederacy. In this communication, the author emphasized the growing hardships the war inflicted on the poor in the Confederacy. In calling for the war's burdens to be shared equally, he criticized in particular the exemption of slaveholders from conscription.*

"Are We Whipped? Must We Give Up?"

Messrs Editors:

I notice in your issue, of the 25th inst., an editorial with the above caption, which contained many good suggestions and some wise counsel. It is but too true that many are skulking and hiding, hatching excuses to avoid conscription. I will admit for the sake of argument that their reason is as you assign it a fear to contend on the field of battle. But as to the justice of the clause of the Exemption Bill to which you refer, I must say that your ideas of justice and equity are quite different from mine. I cannot for my life see how it is, that because the institution of slavery elevates the social position of the poor man, that therefore the poor should fight the battles of our country, while the rich are allowed to remain at home and to enjoy ease and pleasure. You say that it is proper and right for some persons to remain at home. I grant it. But is it just that each conscript, who happens to own ten negroes of certain age should be exempt from military duty?—Why sir, what say you to the poor white man who has *ten children* all dependant upon him for succor and support? Shall he be exempt? No, you answer, "go fight for the negroes of

FROM *Atlanta Southern Confederacy*, 30 October 1862.

your neighbor, because it elevates you in society." You say that the negroes must work to support our army. Why sir, have you not learned that of all men left at home, the man who owns ten negroes or more is the last to help either the soldier or his family.

It is but too true. I tell you that the worst enemy our young republic has is the spirit that pervades our land to an alarming extent of extorting from the poor and needy to build up the rich and powerful. Our army is composed of poor men— men who listened to that old cry, "*We* pay the taxes, *we* are the bone and sinew of the country. *Our* business is too large and complicated to leave. *You* go; you have nothing to leave but your family and they will be taken care of."

It is easy to be a soldier, to leave home and its endearments, *on paper*. But when the reality is tested it is something different. I have seen the soldier in the heat of battle and in the monotony of camp. I have seen him in pleasure and in melancholy; in prosperity and in adversity, but the source of most trouble and anxiety to his mind, is the ill treatment of his family by the very men who are, by the clause referred to, exempt from duty. The soldier can meet the enemy of his country in dreadful battle, but the thought that his family are suffering at the hands of the rich for whom he is fighting, unnerves the strongest arm and sickens the stoutest heart. The men of wealth are erecting new mills, tan-yards, shoe-shops, &c., and are filling them with their sons. This will be done and

other means will be resorted to until the army will be composed of poor men exclusively. Their families will be left to the scanty charities of Extortion and Speculation. Then, sir, you may well ask, "Shall we be whipped?" The answer then would not be difficult. Sir, I have already heard it argued that the *poor* man could not be injured by Lincoln's proclamation. Say they, "it is true, we might lose our negro or two, but what is that to life, to continued exposure, to prolonged absence from wife and children." If poor men must fight, the rich ought to pay the expenses of the fight. The poor men who are now in the army are patriots. They deem no sacrifice too great to be made; no privation too severe to be borne for liberty. They leave home and friends for *country's* sake. Let the appeal be made to their patriotism, to the justice of our cause, but for God's sake don't tell the poor soldier who now shivers in a Northern wind while you snooze in a feather bed, that it is *just* and *right* that the men, whom Congress has exempted, should enjoy ease at home, amassing untold riches, while *he* must fight, bleed, and even die, for their ten negroes. If we are ever whipped, it will be by violations of our own constitution, infringements of justice and right. When burdens are borne equally, *dangers* must be also. People's eyes may be closed by glaring newspaper pleas of *necessity* and *right*, but they will at some time be opened. Then, if ever, *we will be whipped.*

A Soldier.
Jonesboro, Georgia.

An Atlanta Paper Defends the Exemption of Slaveholders (1862)

The Atlanta Southern Confederacy *responded to the previous letter in the same issue. In its reply, the paper defended the exemption of slaveholders by invoking a set of traditional racial arguments.*

The Negroes and the Poor.

We cheerfully lay before our readers today, the communication of "A Soldier," in opposition to our views upon that section of the Exemption Bill which exempts a white man to take care of plantations having a certain number of negroes. "A Soldier" has made the best of his case. His pleadings are plausible. His language is pretty strong, but he is entirely courteous and respectful . . .

We regret to find that he misapprehends one of our positions. . . . We were contending for the wisdom and justice of that provision of the law which exempts *somebody* to take care of and control the negroes and make them work.—We don't advocate the exemption of the rich and the conscription of the poor, because they happen to be rich or poor, but that the negroes must have some white person to remain with and care for them and cause them to make bread. That's all.

And we will here remark that the law does not exempt the owner specially. It says, "To secure *the proper police* of the country *one person*, either as agent, owner or overseer" shall be kept on each plantation of 20 negroes or any number which State laws require one white man to be kept with, provided there is no white male adult on the place, not liable to do military duty. A rich man can't keep an overseer and stay at home too. A rich man fifty, sixty or seventy years old with half a dozen sons over 18 must send them all to the war and oversee his own plantation.

FROM *Atlanta Southern Confederacy,* 30 October 1862.

The poor of the country would be very unsafe in their property and to some extent in their persons, if the negroes were left without any one to keep them at work and regulate their conduct.

But, "A Soldier" inquires if a rich man with ten negroes is exempt, why not a poor man with ten children? Simply because ten white children are not negroes. The "proper police of country" don't require a white man to stay at home to control his children.

The negro has intelligence and brutality combined, enough to make him very troublesome, and even very dangerous, if left without proper control; but he has not enough of intelligence with high moral development, to leave him among us without absolute control. The poor man can leave his ten children with his wife. She can keep them at work and control them—if not as well as the husband and father, at least enough to prevent their being a pest—a terror to the country—lazy, thieving, vicious, brutal—to say nothing more. But a man's negroes can't be thus left. They must have a man to control and take care of them. This "A Soldier;" we have no doubt, will admit. It is one of the *accidents* of that provision of the law that it exempts a rich man occasionally while it does not a poor man. That is not the *design.* It is intended to have the negroes looked after. It *must be done*; hence, this is a wise provision of the law. It may be the misfortune of the poor man to be conscribed while a few rich men are not, but the law does not make that distinction or contemplate any such gross injustice or inequality, in its operation.

The accidents or misfortunes of any provision

of law, or any man upon which it operates, must not be used to condemn the law. . . . The enacting of laws that will mete out equal and exact justice to all persons in all cases and under all circumstances, is impossible.—Laws must be enacted for the *whole* people and must be framed so as to secure "the greatest good to the greatest number." . . .

"A Soldier," and all who think as he does, must recollect that there are thousands of rich men in our army who have gone voluntarily into the ranks and are daily performing the labors of the camp; and fight the battles of freedom, whenever the Yankees are met. He is too sweeping in his criticisms.—He will find this out by looking round among his own neighbors; and his remark that the rich at home will not do anything for the families of the soldiers is also, we are very sure too broad. There may be, and doubtless are some hoggish rich men who refuse to do their duty in this respect. It would be strange if there were not, for the world has bad and selfish men in every community—both rich and poor. We have no doubt the rich in all communities are more liberal towards the poor than our correspondent seems to suppose.

5

Jefferson Davis Defends His Policies (1862)

Unlike Abraham Lincoln, who delivered few formal speeches and made no speaking tours during the war, Jefferson Davis left Richmond several times to rally popular support to the Confederate government. On December 26, 1862, he delivered a major speech to the state legislature of his home state of Mississippi, in which he discussed the war and defended his policies from the criticisms of his opponents.

You have been involved in a war waged for the gratification of the lust of power and aggrandizement, for your conquest and your subjugation, with a malignant ferocity, and with a disregard and a contempt of the usages of civilisation, entirely unequalled in history. Such, I have ever warned you, were the characteristics of the Northern people—of those with whom our ancestors entered into a Union of consent, and with whom they formed a constitutional compact. . . . After what has happened during the last two years, my only wonder is, that we consented to live for so long a time in association with such miscreants, and have loved so much a Government rotten to the core. . . .

You in Mississippi have but little experienced as yet the horrors of the war. You have seen but little of the savage manner in which it is waged by your barbarous enemies. It has been my fortune to witness it in all its terrors; in a part of the country where old men have been torn from their homes, carried into captivity, and immured in distant dungeons, and where delicate women have been insulted by a brutal soldiery, and forced even to cook for the dirty Federal invaders; where property has been wantonly destroyed, the country ravaged, and every outrage committed. And it is with these people that our fathers formed a union and a solemn contract. There is indeed a difference between the two peoples. Let no man hug the delusion that there can be renewed association between them. . . .

Having been hurried into a war with a people so devoid of every mark of civilisation, you have no doubt wondered that I have not carried out the policy, which I had intended should be our policy, of fighting our battles on the fields of the enemy,

FROM Frank H. Moore, ed., *The Rebellion Record*, vol. 6 (New York: G. P. Putnam, 1864), pp. 295–301.

instead of suffering him to fight them on ours. This was not the result of my will, but of the power of the enemy. They had at their command all the accumulated wealth of seventy years—the military stores which had been laid up during that time. They had grown rich from the taxes wrung from you for the establishing and supporting their manufacturing institutions. We have entered upon a conflict with a nation contiguous to us in territory, and vastly superior to us in numbers. In the face of these facts the wonder is not that we have done little, but that we have done so much. . . . At the end of twelve months of the war, it was still necessary for us to adopt some expedient to enable us to maintain our ground. The only expedient remaining to us was to call on those brave men who had entered the service of the country at the beginning of the war, supposing that the conflict was to last but a short time, and that they would not be long absent from their homes. The only expedient, I say, was to call on these gallant men; to ask them to maintain their position in front of the enemy, and to surrender for a time their hopes of soon returning to their families and friends. And nobly did they respond to the call. They answered that they were willing to stay; that they were willing to maintain their position, and to breast the tide of invasion. But it was not just that they should stand alone. They asked that the men who had staid at home—who had thus far been sluggards in the cause—should be forced, likewise, to meet the enemy.

From this resulted the law of Congress, which is known as the conscription act, which declared all men, from the age of eighteen to the age of thirty-five, to be liable to enrolment in the confederate service. I regret that there has been some prejudice excited against the act, and that it has been subjected to harsher criticism than it deserves. And here I may say that an erroneous impression appears to prevail in regard to this act. It is no disgrace to be brought into the army by conscription. . . . We assess the property of the citizen—we appoint tax-gatherers; why should we not likewise distribute equally the labor, and enforce equally the obligation of defending the country from its enemies? . . . Thus resulted the conscription act; and thence arose the necessity for the conscription act. The necessity was met; but when it was found that under these acts enough men were not drawn into the ranks of the army to fulfil the purpose intended, it became necessary to pass another conscription act, and another conscription act. It is only of this latter that I desire to speak. Its policy was to leave at home those men needed to conduct the administration, and those who might be required to support and maintain the industry of the country—in other words, to exempt from military service those whose labor, employed in other avocations, might be more profitable to the country and to the government, than in the ranks of the army.

I am told that this act has excited some discontent, and that it has provoked censure, far more severe, I believe, than it deserves. It has been said that it exempts the rich from military service, and forces the poor to fight the battles of the country. The poor do, indeed, fight the battles of the country. It is the poor who save nations and make revolutions. But is it true that in this war the men of property have shrunk from the ordeal of the battle-field? Look through the army; cast your eyes upon the maimed heroes of the war whom you meet in your streets and in the hospitals; remember the martyrs of the conflict; and I am sure you will find among them more than a fair proportion drawn from the ranks of men of property. The object of that portion of the act which exempts those having charge of twenty or more negroes, was not to draw any distinction of classes, but simply to provide a force, in the nature of a police force, sufficient to keep our negroes in control. This was the sole object of the clause. Had it been otherwise, it would never have received my signature. As I have already said, we have no cause to complain of the rich. All our people have done well, and, while the poor have nobly discharged their duties, most of the wealthiest and most distinguished families of the South have representatives in the ranks. . . .

In considering the manner in which the war has been conducted by the enemy, nothing arrests the attention more than the magnitude of the preparations made for our subjugation. Immense navies have been constructed, vast armies have been accumulated, for the purpose of crushing out the rebellion. It has been impossible to meet them in equal numbers; nor have we required it. . . . But troops must be disciplined in order to develop their efficiency, and in order to keep them at their posts. Above all, to assure this result, we need the support of public opinion. We want public opinion to frown down those who come from the army with sad tales of disaster and prophecies of evil, and who skulk from the duties they owe their country. We rely on the women of the land to turn back these deserters from the ranks. . . .

The issue before us is one of no ordinary character. We are not engaged in a conflict for conquest or for aggrandizement, or for the settlement of a point of international law. The question for you to decide is: "Will you be slaves or will you be independent?" Will you transmit to your children the freedom and equality which your fathers transmitted to you, or will you bow down in adoration before an idol baser than ever was worshipped by Eastern idolaters? Nothing more is necessary than the mere statement of this issue. . . . Those men

who now assail us, . . . when left to themselves, have shown that they are incapable of preserving their own personal liberty. They have destroyed the freedom of the press; they have seized upon and imprisoned members of State Legislatures and of municipal councils, who were suspected of sympathy with the South; men have been carried off into captivity in distant States without indictment, without a knowledge of the accusations brought against them, in utter defiance of all rights guaranteed by the institutions under which they live.

. . . I invoke you not to delay a moment, but to rush forward and place yourself at the disposal of the State. I have been one of those who, from the beginning, looked forward to a long and bloody war; but I must frankly confess that its magnitude has exceeded my expectations. The enemy have displayed more power, and energy, and resources than I had attributed to them. Their finances have held out far better than I imagined would be the case. But I am also one of those who felt that our final success was certain, and that our people had only to be true to themselves to behold the confederate flag among the recognized nations of the earth.

6

RICHMOND EXAMINER

A Richmond Paper Calls for a Tax-in-Kind (1863)

The Confederate government lacked sufficient revenues to finance the war. There was little specie in the South when the war began, the Confederate Congress was reluctant to approve taxes, and foreign and domestic loans were disappointing. In addition, the Union blockade reduced the exports of staple crops, which had been the basis of southern wealth before the war, to a fraction of their prewar levels. To pay the cost of the war, therefore, the Treasury Department in Richmond printed huge amounts of paper money, as did the states. The result was rampant inflation, which steadily eroded the southern people's standard of living. In response, the Richmond Examiner *advocated enactment of a tax-in-kind to provision the army and also reduce the amount of paper money in circulation. Shortly thereafter, the Confederate*

Congress approved such a law, but the paper's optimistic predictions about how this tax would function were not borne out by experience. Instead, the tax-in-kind became one of the major grievances of the rural population and a source of growing popular disaffection.

Inflation of the currency is the source of the chief evils which now disturb us. It is specially the cause of that perturbation of mind which is in fact the greatest evil the country suffers. Except the war, nearly all other troubles are imaginary. . . . Except in localities where the lines of transportation have been being monopolized by the Government, the real price of provisions is not higher now than it was in the first year of the war.

But it seems so when counted in paper money. If the currency stood still, the evil of its depreciation would soon correct itself. But it is progressive. Hence it unsettles everything and produces countless real inequalities, which are real evils. If Congress could reduce the volume of the currency and keep it to one point, that would relieve the country of more than half its suffering. Of this it is well convinced, and the aim of all its measures is the reduction of the currency. It is not ready, nor is the public mind prepared, for compulsory funding, and has exhausted ingenuity in the construction of more complicated and less effective machinery to attain its results. . . .

If the currency was already reduced to its proper limits, these measures would be abundantly sufficient to keep it there. They would themselves reduce it, if the expenditure of the Government did not flood the country with Treasury notes even faster than the Funds and the Taxes can absorb. Unfortunately, they are powerless in face of the enormous sum which the extent of the army and the present high comparative price of all that it requires, oblige the Treasury to issue. The taxes will absorb several hundred millions in the year; but the Government continues to issue *many* hundred millions in the year. Hence the volume of the currency will never grow less; will always grow larger.

The inflation will go on despite of all measures for the encouragement of absorption (short of compulsion) which the wit of man can devise; and none need be told where it is going to end. . . .

There is but a single remedy . . . which promises relief. It is to make a levy of *taxes in kind.*—This will at once take the Government out of the market as a purchaser of the heaviest part of its stores and supplies. Consequently, the issue of Treasury notes will be so much diminished, that the absorption caused by the Tax and Currency Bills will be greater than the quantity of new paper thrown on the markets.—The volume of the currency will be rapidly diminished to a manageable amount, and the relative values of gold and everything else restored to their usual state.

. . . Let us endeavor to explain in a word what is meant by a *tax in kind.* It signifies the payment to the Government of a certain portion of all that the labor or property of the citizen produces . . . without its previous conversion into money. . . . The producer would make a direct gain by paying his tax in produce, without changing it into the shape of money. . . . The Government would receive this great benefit and advantage from a tax in kind: that it would then be able to stop the issue of new Treasury notes.— . . . The articles of produce received as the tax of producers would supply the chief, if not the entire consumption of its troops; and what remained of cotton, tobacco, and the like would be so much cash in its hands to purchase in Europe the means of war.—The printing presses which now deluge the land with oceans of paper money which commerce does not require, would rest. . . .

To such a tax it will be objected that it is cumbrous, inconvenient, and that it cannot be collected by the ordinary agencies which collect the tax money. But it will be discovered that it requires no machinery or operation which the Government

FROM *Richmond Examiner,* 3 April 1863.

is not already obliged to ha[v]e, to supply itself with the necessaries of a vast army in a blockaded country, where interior transportation by individuals has become nearly impossible. The Government has only to unite the agencies which collect the money tax with those which gather the supplies of its armies, and it possesses all the machinery necessary to ascertain and collect a tax in kind.

7

EDWARD POLLARD

A Richmond Editor Denounces Davis's Leadership (1869)

Edward Pollard was editor of the Richmond Examiner *during the war. He was captured in 1864 trying to run the blockade and was imprisoned by Union authorities until exchanged in January 1865, when he returned to Richmond. An advocate of secession prior to the war, Pollard was a fiery champion of the Confederacy, but he quickly concluded that Jefferson Davis was unfit for his office and became the president's bitter and unrelenting critic. A prolific writer, he published a number of books on the war, all of which blamed Davis for the Confederacy's defeat.*

It is remarkable that to those who make a boast of the patriotic devotion of the South in the war, and are intent to display it as an ornament of a lost cause, the thought has never occurred how this claim can consist with the necessities of conscription and impressment, the amount of force necessary to raise armies in the Confederacy, the amount of fraud by which the public service was cheated of men and material, the extent of desertions and of evasions of military duty, and all the other peculiar incidents we have mentioned of unwilling service and forced contribution in the war. . . . The only possible hypothesis on which that honor can be saved is that the people of the South acted in the manner we have described, grudging the demands of the war from the conviction of the unworthiness and misdirection of their government, rather than from that of any demerit or de-

cline of their cause. It is certain that they had a great and noble cause to fight for, and that in the first part of the contest they had displayed unbounded devotion and courage, the admiration of the world. The cause had lost none of its merits, the war none of its just inspiration; these rather had been increased; and yet at a time when the people of the South had in no degree diminished their desire for independence, and long before they thought the war for any natural reason hopeless, and when all that was thought necessary for its success was well-directed effort—when the disasters that had occurred were considered only of that measure which reinspires and strengthens the courageous spirit rather than reduces it—we find them yielding the war an uncertain and niggardly support, displaying nothing of a former devotion, and disposed to deny or to cheat every contribution which the government required of them. The only explanation can be that that government had in some way wounded them, in some way forfeited their confidence—either this, or that the people of

FROM Edward Pollard, *The Life of Jefferson Davis* (Philadelphia: National Publishing Co., 1869), pp. 330–36.

the South had some inherent defect of cowardice or irresolution:—either Jefferson Davis unworthy, or the whole population of the South in fault and disgrace. . . .

When Mr. Davis, after the disasters of Gettysburg and Vicksburg, found his appeals for volunteers unavailing, and when he must have been sensible of his loss of the popular confidence, we find him at once taking a new breadth of despotism in his government—a measure, indeed, calculated to produce a certain re-animation of the war, and this for a certain period, but having no depth of public spirit in it, and although postponing the catastrophe, yet making it more certain and disastrous at the last. We refer to the enlargement of the conscription law. First, on the 15th of July, 1863, came a proclamation of the President extending the limits of the conscription, which in the former year had been of persons between the ages of eighteen and thirty-five, to include all up to the age of forty-five; then an act of Congress extending the term of the conscript age to fifty-five years; added to this a law repealing all substitutions in the military service, and actually compelling the seventy or eighty thousand persons who had furnished substitutes to take up arms themselves, and that without returning them the money they had paid or releasing the substitutes they had employed—an example of the very effrontery of fraud and despotism; and lastly, at the close of the year, a law to clinch the whole matter, declaring every man between eighteen and fifty-five years of age to belong to the army, subject at once to the articles of war, military discipline and military penalties, and requiring him to report within a certain time, or be liable to death as a deserter. The whole people of the South were made soldiers under martial law. The country was converted into a vast camp, and the government of Jefferson Davis into one of the most thorough military despotisms of the age.

But the levy *en masse* was not all. The twin measure of conscription, that which completed the despotic character of the government at Richmond, was impressment. They were logical correspondents; they made as a whole a government in which the lives of the citizens and all the production and labor of the country, were put under military control. It was the maximum of the demands of a despotism.

After the disasters of 1863, complaints of the want of food arose simultaneously with those of the deficiency of men; and it was evident to the intelligent that the same decay of public spirit that denied the claims of military service, also withheld the meaner contributions of food and supply for the army. Both necessities grew out of the same unwilling spirit in the Confederacy. There was really no scarcity of food to the absurd extent represented by Mr. Davis when he declared that it was "*but the one* danger to be regarded with apprehension"—as if in an extensive and fruitful land like the South, there could be danger of the starvation of a whole population! What necessities did really exist were mostly artificial, or of the government's own creation. There was plenty of food in the South; but it was badly distributed by a Commissary who was unwise and rapacious; who had no idea of equalizing the supplies of the country, or conciliating the generosity of the people. Again, the apparent deficiency was greatly due to the wretched currency of the Confederacy; and that by a law certain and irresistible in its effects. . . . When a currency depreciates there is a general disposition to withhold from market and to hoard supplies which would otherwise be converted into money. These results were excessively realized in the Confederacy, where the currency was rapidly verging to worthlessness, and where hoarders and engrossers were found in every department of industry and in every class of society.

In the early months of the war, when General Beauregard was preparing to fight the battle of Manassas, he had written a letter to a farmer in Orange county, representing that the army was in need of sixty wagon-loads of corn and provisions, and engaging to pay for the same and the expense of hauling, as soon as the funds could be obtained from Richmond. The letter was read the following Sunday to all the churches in Orange county. The response was that the next day the sixty wagons, loaded with corn, were sent to General Beauregard, free of charge, and with the message that he should also keep the wagons and teams for the use of his army. Such was the patriotic generosity of a single county in Virginia; it was indicative of public spirit in the Confederacy. How great a change must have befallen that spirit, when, two years later, we find the same class of producers who then hastened with donations for the army, avaricious and chaffering traders in the life-blood of their own country, refusing to sell their grain to the government, perhaps haggling about the price of pork per pound, when their sons and brothers in the army were living on a quarter of a pound of meat a day, and sometimes had none at all.

Truly the patriotism of the Confederacy had wofully declined—had fallen by a whole heaven—in view of a government compelled to recruit supplies for its army in a war for its existence on the alternative of begging to buy them or of taking them with a ruthless hand. The army was badly fed; it was worse clothed. . . . Thousands of these poor fellows were clothed in the Federal uniforms which had been captured. Thousands were destitute of shoes; and it was reported that nearly half of Longstreet's corps were barefoot, when the snows laid on the ground at the close of the year 1863. Meanwhile the railway system of the Confederacy was giving out; even if supplies were found it was difficult to transport them; and thus distress from every point stared the people of the South, while the enemy continued to invade their towns and States, to offer liberty to their slaves, to enrol them in his armies, and to defy their retaliation.

Great and bitter as were the wants of the government for supplies, nothing could have been worse than the law into which it wildly and madly plunged for a remedy. The law of impressment was excessive; it alarmed the sentiment of the whole country; it destroyed the last vestiges of civil rights in the Confederacy. To show to what extent the government of Mr. Davis contemplated its powers, it may be mentioned that his dull creature, Northrop, the Commissary-General had proposed

to him to seize plantations throughout the South, and to work them on government account; and that the President had, only after hesitation, declined this high-handed scheme to adopt the more uniform, but scarcely less cruel law of impressments. This law authorized the government to seize or impress all the produce necessary for the army. It provided that a board of commissioners should be appointed in each State who should determine, every sixty days, the prices which the government should pay for each article of produce impressed within the State. A central board of commissioners was also appointed for all the States. The act authorized the agents of the government to seize all the produce of the farmer, except so much as was necessary to sustain himself and family.

Denunciations of the law arose on all sides. It was inseparable from abuses. The newspapers complained of the rude and rapacious action of "the press-gangs." The meaner citizens resorted to all possible methods to save their property from impressment; many of them were driven to sell clandestinely or openly their stores to non-producers out of the army, who were willing and anxious to pay fifty or a hundred per cent. more than the government paid. On the other hand the few who were really patriotic and disposed to contribute to the war, who still maintained a romantic enthusiasm in the contest, had their feelings hurt; they were touched in their pride and sense of justice that the government should treat them with rudeness and suspicion. Yet another and more important class of citizens resented the law in a more serious light—as an act of unexampled despotism. There were men even in the Confederate Congress who were bold enough to declare that impressment and other acts of misrule and oppression in the administration of Mr. Davis had extracted all virtue from the cause, and that the war simply remained as a choice of despots, one at Washington and one at Richmond.

1

ANONYMOUS

Southerners' Faith in King Cotton Diplomacy
(1861)

After traveling in the South early in the war, a reporter for Blackwood's Magazine, *which was published in Edinburgh, Scotland, described the popular sentiment in the Confederacy concerning the power of cotton in world affairs. Like William Russell, the* London Times *reporter who preceded him, he was amazed at the faith southerners placed in the idea of King Cotton diplomacy.*

The [Confederate] Government have not prohibited the export of cotton, except to the Northern States; but self-constituted authorities have, in more than one instance that we know of, made it impossible for ships to load which had run the blockade, and whose owners were desirous of doing so again. The popular feeling which has dictated these violent acts is caused, first, by the desire that the North should be made to suffer for enforcing the blockade, and the apprehension that, if any cotton were to be allowed to leave the country, Massachusetts would manage to obtain it; and, secondly, by the impression that in laying on a general embargo they would incline European governments to recognise the Confederacy. Amongst the enlightened this latter motive was always repudiated; but there can be no doubt that the prevalent conviction throughout the South is that England cannot do without the "king;" that all cotton, except American, is either too short or too long; and that the medium is the only staple which Manchester cares to have. In vain we would tell them that our manufacturers would soon change their machinery, and adapt it to the necessities of the times; that our Government was making great exertions to procure cotton from India and Africa; that it was our interest to foster our own colonies, and to produce it there if possible; and that the longer we were deprived of America as a market, the more strenuous would our efforts be to render ourselves independent of it. But it was no use; they were ineradicably impressed with the conviction that they can command the market at any time; and that the distance from England at which its rivals are placed must always give the Confederacy a great advantage.

FROM "A Month with the Rebels," *Blackwood's Edinburgh Magazine* 90 (December 1861): 762–63.

CHARLES FRANCIS ADAMS

The *Trent* Affair Has Almost Wrecked Us (1862)

In November 1861, Captain Charles Wilkes of the United States Navy precipitated an international crisis when he stopped the British merchant ship Trent *and seized two Confederate diplomats, James Mason and John Slidell, who were aboard on their way to Europe. Eager for any triumph over the Confederacy, northern public opinion hailed Wilkes's action, but Lincoln finally concluded that Wilkes had acted illegally and released the Confederate envoys. In the following letter to his son, Charles Francis Adams, who was the American minister to Great Britain during the war, recounted the danger that the* Trent *affair posed abroad to the United States and described the change of opinion in London after Mason and Slidell were freed. At the same time, he emphasized the critical influence of the military situation, particularly Lee's position in the eastern theater, on the diplomatic situation in Europe.*

London, January 10, 1862

. . . Captain Wilkes has not positively shipwrecked us, but he has come as near to it without succeeding as he could. Thus far the country has been at least saved the danger of setting up military idols. This reconciles me a little to the slowness of our operations. Another consideration is the crushing nature of our expenditure which must stop this war, if something effective does not follow soon. It is idle to talk of putting down the rebellion whilst our power is resisted successfully within a dozen miles of the capital. This idea prevails so much here that it will undoubtedly become the basis of a movement for recognition before long. . . .

The first effect of the surrender of Messrs. Mason and Slidell has been extraordinary. The current which ran against us with such extreme violence six weeks ago now seems to be going with equal fury in our favor. The reaction in the city was very great yesterday, and even the most violent of the presses, the Times and the Post, are for the moment a little tamed. Possibly, if nothing else should intervene to break its force, this favoring gale may carry us through the first half of the session of Parliament, in other words, until the first of May. If by that time we shall have made no decided progress towards a result, we may as well make up our minds to disbelieve in our power to do it at all. Foreign nations will come to that conclusion if we do not. . . .

FROM Worthington Chauncey Ford, *A Cycle of Adams Letters, 1861–1865,* vol. 2 (Boston: Houghton Mifflin Company, 1920), p. 99.

3

Jefferson Davis Complains of Europe's Refusal to Recognize the Confederacy (1863)

The failure of the Confederacy's intensive diplomatic efforts in European capitals in the fall of 1862 greatly frustrated Jefferson Davis and other Confederate leaders. In his January 12, 1863, message to Congress, the Confederate president criticized the refusal of European nations to recognize the Confederacy and come to its assistance.

During nearly two years of struggle, in which every energy of our country has been evoked for maintaining its very existence, the neutral nations of Europe have pursued a policy which, nominally impartial, has been practically most favorable to our enemies and most detrimental to us. The exercise of the neutral right of refusing entry into their ports to prizes taken by both belligerents was eminently hurtful to the Confederacy. It was sternly asserted and maintained. The exercise of the neutral right of commerce with a belligerent whose ports are not blockaded by fleets sufficient really to prevent access to them would have been eminently hurtful to the United States. It was complacently abandoned. The duty of neutral states to

FROM *Official Records,* ser. IV, vol. 2, p. 343.

receive with cordiality and recognize with respect any new confederation that independent states may think proper to form was too clear to admit of denial, but its postponement was eminently beneficial to the United States and detrimental to the Confederacy. It was postponed.

In this review of our relations with the neutral nations of Europe it has been my purpose to point out distinctly that this Government has no complaint to make that those nations declared their neutrality. It could neither expect nor desire more. The complaint is that the neutrality has been rather nominal than real, and that recognized neutral rights have been alternately asserted and waived in such manner as to bear with great severity on us, and to confer signal advantages on our enemy.

4

CHARLES FRANCIS ADAMS

This Is War (1863)

Unable to build commerce raiders in its own ports, the Confederate government sought to construct these ships overseas, particularly in England. While English law prohibited such activity, Confederate representatives easily evaded the law. The Confederate cruisers the Florida *and the* Alabama, *which were built in England, in-*

flicted great losses on Union shipping during the war. Encouraged by their successes, Confederate agents hired the Laird brothers, an important British shipbuilding firm, to build two powerful ironclad rams. These rams were more powerful than any ship in the Union navy and posed a serious threat to the Union blockade. Charles Francis Adams, the American minister to Great Britain, presented evidence of Confederate ownership and strenuously pressed the British government to seize the ships before completion. In the following note to Lord John Russell, the British foreign minister, Adams warned that the escape of these ships could lead to war. Unbeknownst to Adams, Russell had already decided to detain the ironclads, which were eventually purchased by the British navy.

Legation of the United States, London,
September 5, 1863.

My Lord,

At this moment, when one of the iron-clad war-vessels is on the point of departure from this kingdom on its hostile errand against the United States, I am honoured with the reply of your Lordship to my notes of the 11th, 16th, and 25th of July and of the 14th of August. I trust I need not express how profound is my regret at the conclusion to which Her Majesty's Government have arrived. I can regard it no otherwise than as practically opening to the insurgents free liberty in this kingdom to execute a policy described in one of their late publications in the following language:—

"In the present state of the harbour-defences of New York, Boston, Portland, and smaller Northern cities, such a vessel as the 'Warrior' would have little difficulty in entering any of those ports, and inflicting a vital blow upon the enemy. The destruction of Boston alone would be worth a hundred victories in the field. . . . Vessels of the 'Warrior' class would promptly raise the blockade of our ports, and would, even in this respect, confer advantages which would soon repay the cost of their construction."

It would be superfluous in me to point out to your Lordship that this is war. No matter what may be the theory adopted of neutrality in a struggle, when this process is carried on in the manner indicated from a territory and with the aid of the subjects of a third party, that third party, to all intents and purposes, ceases to be neutral. Neither is it necessary to show that any Government which suffers it to be done fails in enforcing the essential conditions of international amity towards the country against whom the hostility is directed. In my belief it is impossible that any nation retaining a proper degree of self-respect could tamely submit to a continuance of relations so utterly deficient in reciprocity. I have no idea that Great Britain would do so for a moment.

After a careful examination of the full instructions with which I have been furnished in preparation for such an emergency, I deem it inexpedient for me to attempt any recurrence to arguments for effective interposition in the present case. The fatal objection of impotency which paralyzes Her Majesty's Government seems to present an insuperable barrier against all further reasoning. Under these circumstances I prefer to desist from communicating to your Lordship even such further portions of my existing instructions as are suited to the case, lest I should contribute to aggravate difficulties already far too serious. I therefore content myself with informing your Lordship that I transmit by the present steamer a copy of your note for the consideration of my Government, and shall await the more specific directions that will be contained in the reply. . . .

I pray, &c.

Charles Francis Adams

FROM House of Commons, *Parliamentary Papers, State Papers, North America,* 1864, vol. 62, no. 5, pp. 17–18.

1

Abraham Lincoln Counsels General Joseph Hooker (1863)

When he appointed General Joseph Hooker to be commander of the Army of the Potomac in January 1863, Lincoln wrote a letter of advice, which he handed to Hooker when they met at the White House. Lincoln adopted a fatherly tone in counseling his erratic general. As the letter reveals, Lincoln was disturbed by reports of the loose-talking Hooker having called for a dictatorship; before long, the president was more worried about Hooker's constant boasting about what he would do to Lee once campaigning resumed. "My plans are perfect," the Union commander bragged. "May God have mercy on General Lee for I will have none." Lincoln had heard similar bluster before from McClellan, with no positive results. Hooker's abysmal generalship in the Battle of Chancellorsville would solidify Lincoln's growing unease with "Fighting Joe," who shortly thereafter was removed from command of the Army of the Potomac.

Executive Mansion,
Washington, January 26, 1863.

Major General Hooker:
General.

I have placed you at the head of the Army of the Potomac. Of course I have done this upon what appear to me to be sufficient reasons. And yet I think it best for you to know that there are some things in regard to which, I am not quite satisfied with you. I believe you to be a brave and a skilful soldier, which, of course, I like. I also believe you do not mix politics with your profession, in which you are right. You have confidence in yourself, which is a valuable, if not an indispensable quality.

You are ambitious, which, within reasonable bounds, does good rather than harm. But I think that during Gen. Burnside's command of the Army, you have taken counsel of your ambition, and thwarted him as much as you could, in which you did a great wrong to the country, and to a most meritorious and honorable brother officer. I have heard, in such way as to believe it, of your recently saying that both the Army and the Government needed a Dictator. Of course it was not *for* this, but in spite of it, that I have given you the command. Only those generals who gain successes, can set up dictators. What I now ask of you is military success, and I will risk the dictatorship. The government will support you to the utmost of it's ability, which is neither more nor less than it has done and will do for all commanders. I much fear that the spirit which you have aided to infuse into the Army, of criticising their Commander, and

FROM Roy P. Basler, et al., eds., *The Collected Works of Abraham Lincoln,* vol. 6 (New Brunswick, N.J.: Rutgers University Press, 1953), pp. 78–79.

withholding confidence from him, will now turn upon you. I shall assist you as far as I can, to put it down. Neither you, nor Napoleon, if he were alive again, could get any good out of an army, while such a spirit prevails in it.

And now, beware of rashness. Beware of rashness, but with energy, and sleepless vigilance, go forward, and give us victories.

Yours very truly

A. Lincoln

HENRY HALLECK

The Character of the War Has Very Much Changed (1863)

In the following letter to Ulysses S. Grant, Henry W. Halleck, the Union's chief general, discussed the government's policy toward slaves and the necessity of the army to carry out this policy. This concern was especially strong for the army's operations in the Mississippi valley, since the bulk of the slaves under Union control were located in this region, and where, as Halleck's letter makes clear, it was rumored that many officers opposed the government's policy. A loyal soldier, Grant was prepared to carry out this policy in any case, but in fact he harbored no personal misgivings over it.

Headquarters of the Army,
Washington, March 31, 1863.

Maj. Gen. U.S. Grant,
Commanding Department of the Tennessee,
   near Vicksburg:

General:

It is the policy of the Government to withdraw from the enemy as much productive labor as possible. So long as the rebels retain and employ their slaves in producing grains, &c., they can employ all the whites in the field. Every slave withdrawn from the enemy is equivalent to a white man put *hors de combat.*

Again, it is the policy of the Government to use the negroes of the South, as far as practicable, as a military force, for the defense of forts, depots, &c. If the experience of General Banks near New Orleans should be satisfactory, a much larger force will be organized during the coming summer; and if they can be used to hold points on the Mississippi during the sickly season, it will afford much relief to our armies. They certainly can be used with advantage as laborers, teamsters, cooks, &c., and it is the opinion of many who have examined the question without passion or prejudice, that they can also be used as a military force. It certainly is good policy to use them to the very best advantage we can. Like almost anything else, they may be made instruments of good or evil. In the hands of the enemy, they are used with much effect against us; in our hands, we must try to use them with the best possible effect against the rebels.

It has been reported to the Secretary of War that many of the officers of your command not only discourage the negroes from coming under our protection, but by ill-treatment force them to return to their masters. This is not only bad policy in itself, but is directly opposed to the policy adopted by the Government. Whatever may be the individual opinion of an officer in regard to the

FROM *Official Records,* ser. I, vol. 24, pt. 3, pp. 156–57.

wisdom of measures adopted and announced by the Government, it is the duty of every one to cheerfully and honestly endeavor to carry out the measures so adopted. Their good or bad policy is a matter of opinion before they are tried; their real character can only be determined by a fair trial. When adopted by the Government, it is the duty of every officer to give them such a trial, and to do everything in his power to carry the orders of his Government into execution.

It is expected that you will use your official and personal influence to remove prejudices on this subject, and to fully and thoroughly carry out the policy now adopted and ordered by the Government. That policy is to withdraw from the use of the enemy all the slaves you can, and to employ those so withdrawn to the best possible advantage against the enemy.

The character of the war has very much changed within the last year. There is now no possible hope of reconciliation with the rebels. The Union party in the South is virtually destroyed. There can be no peace but that which is forced by the sword. We must conquer the rebels or be conquered by them. . . .

This is the phase which the rebellion has now assumed. We must take things as they are. The Government, looking at the subject in all its aspects, has adopted a policy, and we must cheerfully and faithfully carry out that policy. . . .

Very respectfully, your obedient servant,

H. W. Halleck

3

Robert E. Lee Proposes to Take the Offensive

(1863)

In the following letters, written shortly after fighting resumed in 1863 in the Virginia theater, Robert E. Lee advocated taking the offensive by invading the North. Several considerations entered Lee's thinking, but one important purpose, as the second letter to Jefferson Davis indicates, was to strengthen the peace movement in the North. His letter also provides an often overlooked context for Lincoln's letter to Erastus Corning (see p. 172) concerning civil liberties in the Union. Under Jefferson Davis, who actively supervised the war effort, the Confederate secretary of war was essentially a clerk. Consequently Secretary of War James Seddons's reply represented Davis's approval of Lee's plan.

Headquarters Army of Northern Virginia,
June 10, 1863.

His Excellency Jefferson Davis, Richmond:

Mr. President: . . .

Conceding to our enemies the superiority claimed by them in numbers, resources, and all the means and appliances for carrying on the war, we have no right to look for exemptions from the military consequences of a vigorous use of these advantages, excepting by such deliverance as the mercy of Heaven may accord to the courage of our soldiers, the justice of our cause, and the constancy and prayers of our people. While making the most we can of the means of resistance we possess, and gratefully accepting the measure of success with which God has blessed our efforts as an earnest of

FROM *Official Records,* ser. I, vol. 27, pt. 3, pp. 880–82, 888–89.

His approval and favor, it is nevertheless the part of wisdom to carefully measure and husband our strength, and not to expect from it more than in the ordinary course of affairs it is capable of accomplishing. We should not, therefore, conceal from ourselves that our resources in men are constantly diminishing, and the disproportion in this respect between us and our enemies, if they continue united in their efforts to subjugate us, is steadily augmenting.

The decrease of the aggregate of this army, as disclosed by the returns, affords an illustration of this fact. Its effective strength varies from time to time, but the falling off in its aggregate shows that its ranks are growing weaker and that its losses are not supplied by recruits.

Under these circumstances, we should neglect no honorable means of dividing and weakening our enemies, that they may feel some of the difficulties experienced by ourselves. It seems to me that the most effectual mode of accomplishing this object, now within our reach, is to give all the encouragement we can, consistently with truth, to the rising peace party of the North.

Nor do I think we should, in this connection, make nice distinction between those who declare for peace unconditionally and those who advocate it as a means of restoring the Union, however much we may prefer the former.

We should bear in mind that the friends of peace at the North must make concessions to the earnest desire that exists in the minds of their countrymen for a restoration of the Union, and that to hold out such a result as an inducement is essential to the success of their party.

Should the belief that peace will bring back the Union become general, the war would no longer be supported, and that, after all, is what we are interested in bringing about. When peace is proposed to us, it will be time enough to discuss its terms, and it is not the part of prudence to spurn the proposition in advance, merely because those who wish to make it believe, or affect to believe, that it will result in bringing us back to the Union. We entertain no such apprehensions, nor doubt that the desire of our people for a distinct and independent national existence will prove as steadfast under the influence of peaceful measures as it has shown itself in the midst of war. . . .

I am, with great respect,
your obedient servant,

R. E. Lee,
General.

War Department, C. S. A.,
Richmond, Va., June 10, 1863.

General R. E. Lee, Commanding, &c.:

General:

I have the honor to acknowledge yours of the 8th instant, just received. I concur entirely in your views of the importance of aggressive movements by your army. Indeed, in my present judgment, such action is indispensable to our safety and independence, and all attendant sacrifices and risks must be incurred. I steadily urge and sustain this view; at the same time, I am most anxious to assure your communications and supplies, and it is in this view I press upon your own consideration some of the dangers to which our destitution of a covering force to this city and the railroad may expose us. I have not hesitated, in co-operating with your plans, to leave this city almost defenseless, and since my letter of yesterday, learning that you had ordered away the small brigade left by General Pickett at Hanover, I have readily concurred in sending Cooke's brigade to the Junction. As General Wise is far down the Peninsula and in King William, this leaves us literally without force, should the enemy make a dash with their transports up the James. I have some apprehension, from intelligence recently received, that they are concentrating a force at Yorktown and Newport News with this view, but we must incur the hazard. The President has not been willing to order Jenkins' brigade from North Carolina, in view of the representations made by Generals Hill and Whiting, but he has communicated your late telegrams to the former, and submitted to his discretion the propriety of the removal. I trust he will concur in the policy of encountering some risk to promote the grand results that may be attained by your successful operations. Our great want here is some cavalry, to scout and give timely notice, and I again invite your attention to this subject and the suggestions made in my letter of yesterday.

With high esteem, very truly, yours,

J. A. Seddon,
Secretary of War.

4

RACHEL CORMANY

A Pennsylvania Woman Encounters Lee's Army
(1863)

Samuel and Rachel Cormany met at Otterbein University, a denominational school run by the United Brethren Church in Ohio, in the 1850s. Both had grown up in farm families, Samuel near Chambersburg, Pennsylvania; Rachel in Ontario, Canada. They were married in 1860, and after living for two years in Canada, they moved to Chambersburg to be near his parents. Shortly thereafter, in September, fearing he would be drafted, Samuel enlisted in the Union army, a decision Rachel felt misgivings about but nevertheless accepted. She worried constantly about her husband's safety, and his absence meant she had to raise their year-old daughter Cora alone. By the time Robert E. Lee launched his invasion of Pennsylvania in 1863, Rachel had moved from the country and was living in the town of Chambersburg. In her diary, Rachel, who was a strong supporter of the Union cause, discussed the interaction between the Confederate soldiers and the town's citizens during the Gettysburg campaign.

June 15, 1863   Monday. This morning pretty early Gen Milroys wagon train (so we were told) came.[1] Contrabands[2] on ahead coming as fast as they could on all & any kind of horses, their eyes fairly protruding with fear—teams coming at the same rate—some with the covers half off—some lost— men without hats or coats—some lost their coats as they were flying, one darky woman astride of a horse going what she could. There really was a real panic. All reported that the rebels were just on their heels. . . . For awhile before dark the excitement abated a little—but it was only like the calm before a great storm. . . .

June 16, 1863   Retired at 11 oclock. All was very quiet, so we concluded that all those reports must be untrue about the Reb's being so near . . . At 11½ I heard the clattering of horses hoofs. I hopped out of bed & ran to the front window & sure enough there the Greybacks were going by as fast as their horses could take them down to the Diamond. . . . But a short time after the whole

---

[1] Over the past several days General Robert Milroy's small force had been skirmishing with the Confederate army, and his supply wagons were retreating from the advancing enemy.

[2] A term applied to freed slaves within the Union lines.

FROM James Mohr, ed., *The Cormany Diaries: A Northern Family in the Civil War* (Pittsburgh: University of Pittsburgh Press, 1982), pp. 328–41.

body came. . . . It took a long time for them all to pass, but I could not judge how many there were—not being accustomed to seeing troops in such a body—At 2 oclock A.M. all was quiet again save an occasional reb. riding past. We went to bed again & slept soundly until 5 the morning. All seemed quiet yet. We almost came to the conclusion that the reb's had left again, leaving only a small guard who took things quite leasurely. Soon however they became more active. Were hunting up the contrabands & driving them off by droves. O! How it grated on our hearts to have to sit quietly & look at such brutal deeds—I saw no men among the contrabands—all women & children. Some of the colored people who were raised here were taken along—I sat on the front step as they were driven by just like we would drive cattle. Some laughed & seemed not to care—but nearly all hung their heads. One woman was pleading wonderfully with her driver for her children—but all the sympathy she received from him was a rough "March along"—at which she would quicken her pace again. It is a query what they want with those little babies—whole families were taken. Of course when the mother was taken she would take her children. I suppose the men left thinking the women & children would not be disturbed. I cannot describe all the scenes. . . .

June 17, 1863 . . . All was so quiet during the night that I veryly thought the Reb's had left—but they are still here. All forenoon they were carrying away mens clothing & darkeys. . . . Some of the officers tipped their hats to us. I answered it with a curl of the lip. I knew they did it to taunt us. The one after he had tipped his hat most graciously & received in answer a toss of the head & curl of the lip took a good laugh over it. There were a few real inteligent good looking men among them. What a pity that they are rebels. After the main body had passed, the news came that our soldiers were coming & just then some ½ doz reb's flew past as fast as their horses could take them. we learned since that one of them fired Oaks warehouse & that he was very near being shot by the citizens. Among the last to leave were some with darkeys on their horses behind them. . . . None of our Soldiers came.

June 22, 1863 . . . The rebels are reported within 8 or 10 miles. Guess there will be nothing to hinder them from coming now—suppose they will be on here by tomorrow which will stop our mail again for some time. . . . Indeed I believe I shall pack up & leave in the morning. I cant bear to think of being shut up without any news another week.

June 23, 1863 . . . It was not long until the reb's really made their appearance—I do not think that they are Cav. but mounted infantry—they most of them have nothing but a musket to fight with. They rode in as leisurely as you please each one having his hand on the trigger though, to fire any minute—so now I judge we are shut out again for awhile—I just wonder what they want this time. . . . Evening—The Reb's have been cutting up high. Sawed down telegraph poles, destroyed the scotland bridge again, took possession of the warehouses & were dealing out flour by the barrel & mollasses by the bucket ful—They made people take them brea[d]—meat—&c to eat—Some dumb fools carried them jellies & the like—Not a thing went from this place. . . .

June 24, 1863 . . . At 10 A.M. the infantry commenced to come & for 3 hours they just marched on as fast as they could. it is supposed that about 15,000 have already passed through, & there are still more coming. . . . This P.M. the Rebs are plundering the stores. some of our merchants will be almost if not entirely ruined. . . . Some of the Rebs seemed quite jolly at the idea of being in Pa. . . .

June 25, 1863 . . . Evening. The other division that was to come today did not come, but those here have not been idle. They must surely expect to set up stores or fill their empty ones judging from the loads they have been hauling away & they take every thing a body can think of. . . .

June 27, 1863 . . . Before we got started [to go to the store] the rebels poured in already. they just marched through. Such a hard looking set I never saw. All day since 7 oclock they have been going through. . . . While I am writing thousands are passing—such a rough dirty ragged rowdyish set one does not often see—Gen's Lee & Longstreet passed through today. A body would think the whole south had broke loose & are coming into Pa.

It makes me feel too badly to see so many men & cannon going through knowing that they have come to kill our men—Many have chickens as they pass—There a number are going with honey—rob[b]ed some man of it no doubt—they are even carrying it in buckets. The report has reached us that . . . at Harisburg the north has congregated en masse to oppose the invaders. Many think this the best thing in the wor[l]d to bring the war to a close—I hope our men will be strong enough to completely whip them—Now it is on our side—While down there our army was in the enemys country & citizens kept the rebels posted in our army movements—now *they* are in the enemys country. Scarcely any are willing to give them anything—in fact none give unless the[y] have to except perhaps the Copperheads.[3] . . . They are going rather fast—wonder whether there is not fighting going on in front. They are poorly clad—many have no shoes on. As they pass along they take the hats off our citizens heads and throw their old ones in exchange. I was at the window up stairs with my baby nearly all day looking at them—at one time one of them said something that I did not like so I curled my lip as disdainful as I could & turned away[.] just look at he[r] he said to another[.] I saw a lot looking up, so I just wheeled & left the window at which they set up a cheer. Once before the same was enacted except the general cheer. I did wish I dared spit at their old flag—I pity some of the men for I am sure they would like to be out. . . .

June 28, 1863 . . . At 8½ A.M. the rebels commenced coming again. Ga. troops. I was told this morning of some of their mean tricks of yesterday & before. They took the hats & boots off the men—Took that off Preacher Farney. Took $50. off Dr. Sneck & his gold watch valued very highly—took the coats off some, tetotally stripped one young fellow not far from town—Mr. Skinner.

We have to be afraid to go out of our houses. A large wagon train & 500 or 600 Cavalry have just passed & it is now about 3½ oclock. . . . Many of the saddles were empty, & any amount of negroes are along. This does not seem like Sunday. No church.

June 29, 1863 . . . Hoke [a local storekeeper] told me that the Reb's had taken about 500 $ worth of sugar & molasses—they went into the private cellar & took Mrs Hokes canned fruit & bread. . . . Evening. A large waggon train headed by 10 pieces of artillery & I judge a regiment of of infantry just passed. The wagons were all well loaded. I judge they are bound for Dixie. . . . I felt real badly to see those poor men going through as they did. likely many of them will be killed. . . .

June 30, 1863 . . . The Rebs are still about doing all the mischief they can. They have everything ready to set fire to the warehouses & machine shops—Tore up the railroad track & burned the crossties—They have cleared out nearly every store so they cannot rob much more—Evening—Quite a number of the young folks were in the parlor this evening singing all the patriotic & popular war songs. Quite a squad of rebels gathered outside to listen & seemed much pleased with the music—"When this cruel war is over" nearly brought tears from some. they sent in a petition to have it sung again which was done. they then thanked the girls very much & left—they acted real nicely.

July 1, 1863 . . . They [the Confederates] are chopping &c at a great rate over at the R.R. all morning. I judge they are breaking up the iron by the sound. . . . Mrs. Fritz was here & told us . . . how the rebels . . . robbed the country people of nearly everything they had & acted very insultingly.

July 2, 1863 At 3 A.M. I was wakened by the yells & howls of this dirty ragged lousy trash—they made as ugly as they could—all day they have been passing—part of the time on the double quick. . . .

July 3, 1863 . . . Daddy Byers . . . came to see how I was getting along & told me how the rebels acted—they robbed him of a good deal—they wanted the horse but he plead so hard for him that they agreed to leave him & while one wrote a paper of securety others plundered the house. I guess

[3]One of Lee's motives in launching his invasion was to strengthen the antiwar movement in the North. Although there was significant opposition to Lincoln and the Republican party in the area around Chambersburg, the civilian population displayed considerable resistance to the Confederate army, as Cormany's diary shows.

Samuels silk hat & all that was in the box is gone. took Ellies best shoes—took towels sheets &c &c— After they were gone others came & took the horse too yet—they did not care for his security. Other of their neighbors fared worse yet. . . . There are no rebels in town today except the sick—& two or three squads passed through, in all not much over a hundred if that many. One squad asked the way to Getysburg & were sent towards Harisburg, they did not go very far until they asked again, when they were told the truth they came back very angry & wanted the man that sent them the wrong way but he was not to be found. Canonading was heard all day.

July 4, 1863 At daybreak the bells were rung— Then all was quiet until about 8 oclock when a flag was hoisted at the diamond. Soon after the band made its appearance & marched from square & played national airs—two rebels came riding along quite leisurely thinking I suppose to find their friends instead of that they were taken prisoners by the citizens—some 13 more footmen came and were taken prisoners. those were willing prisoners they had thrown their guns away before they reached this. . . . Evening. We have had a powerful rain. Wild rumors of a dreadful fight are numerous.

July 5, 1863 . . . I was told that 10, 4 or 6 horse waggons filled with wounded from the late battle were captured by citizens & brought to town—the wounded were put into the hospitals & the waggons & drivers were taken on toward Harisburg. Was also told that a great many more were out toward Greencastle—some went out to capture those but found that it was a train 20 miles long. P.M. . . . It is frightful how those poor wounded rebels are left to suffer. they are taken in large 4 horse waggons—wounds undressed—nothing to eat. Some are only about 4 miles from town & those that are here are as dirty and lousy as they well can be. The condition of those poor rebels all along from Getysburg to as far as they have come yet is reported dreadful. I am told they just beg the people along the road to help them—many have died by the way.

5

JOHN DOOLEY

A Virginia Soldier Survives Pickett's Charge
(1863)

Among the Confederate soldiers who charged the Union center on the third day at Gettysburg was John Dooley. His parents emigrated from Ireland in the 1830s after their marriage and settled in Richmond, where John Dooley (named after his father) grew up. His father was a successful merchant, and the family was prominent in the city's Irish community. He enrolled at Georgetown College when he was only 14 but left before he received a degree. Despite his Irish heritage, Dooley thoroughly identified with the South and the Confederacy, and he left college in 1862 to enlist in the Confederate army. He joined the famous Old First Virginia Infantry Regiment, in which both his father and older brother had served, in August of that year. This regiment was part of Longstreet's corps in the Army of Northern Virginia. Dooley, who enlisted as a private and eventually held the rank of captain, kept a diary during his active military service. Captured at Gettysburg, he rewrote and elaborated on his original diary while a prisoner. What follows is his account of Pickett's charge, written after his capture. (Dooley's headings have been omitted.)

Gettysburg, July 3, 1863

The sun poured down his [*sic*] fiercest beams and added to our discomfort. Genl. Dearing was out in front with his flag waving defiance at the Yankees and now and then rushing forward to take the place of some unfortunate gunner stricken down at his post. The ammunition wagons fly back and forth bringing up fresh supplies of ammunition, and still the air is shaking from earth to sky with every missile of death fired from the cannon's mouth. Around, above, beneath, and on all sides they schreech [*sic*], sing, scream, whistle, roar, whirr, buzz, bang and whizz, and we are obliged to lie quietly tho' frightened out of our wits and unable to do any thing in our own defence or any injury to our enemies. . . .

Our artillery has now ceased to roar and the enemy have checked their fury, too. The time appointed for our charge is come.

I tell you, there is no romance in making one of these charges. You might think so from reading "Charlie O'Malley," that prodigy of valour, or in reading of any other gallant knight who would as little think of riding over *gunners and sich like* as they would of eating a dozen oysters. But when you rise to your feet as we did today, I tell you the enthusiasm of ardent breasts in many cases *ain't there*, and instead of burning to avenge the insults of our country, families and altars and fire-sides, the thought is most frequently, *Oh, if I could just come out of this charge safely how thankful would I be!*

We rise to our feet, but not all. There is a line of men still on the ground with their faces turned, men affected in 4 different ways. There are the gallant dead who will never charge again; the helpless

wounded, many of whom desire to share the fortunes of this charge; the men who have charged on many a battlefield but who are now helpless from the heat of the sun; and the men in whom there is not sufficient courage to enable them to rise,—but of these last there are but few.

Up, brave men! Some are actually *fainting* from the heat and dread. They have fallen to the ground overpowered by the suffocating heat and the terrors of that hour. Onward—steady—dress to the right—give way to the left—steady, not too fast— don't press upon the center—how gentle the slope! steady—keep well in line—there is the line of guns we must take—right in front—but how far they appear! Nearly one third of a mile, off on Cemetery Ridge, and the line stretches round in almost a semicircle. Upon the center of this we must march. Behind the guns are strong lines of infantry. You may see them plainly and now they see us perhaps more plainly.

To the right of us and above the guns we are to capture, black heavy monsters from their lofty mountain sites belch forth their flame and smoke and storms of shot and shell upon our advancing line; while directly in front, breathing flame in our very faces, the long range of guns which must be taken thunder on our quivering melting ranks. Now truly does the work of death begin. The line becomes unsteady because at every step a gap must be closed and thus from left to right much ground is often lost.

Close up! Close up the ranks when a friend falls, while his life blood bespatters your cheek or throws a film over your eyes! Dress to left or right, while the bravest of the brave are sinking to rise no more! Still onward! Capt. Hallinan has fallen and I take his place. So many men have fallen now that I find myself within a few feet of my old Captain (Norton). His men are pressing mine out of place. I ask him to give way a little to the left, and scarcely has he done so than he leaps into the air, falling

FROM Joseph T. Durkin, ed., *John Dooley, Confederate Soldier: His War Journal* (Washington, D.C.: Georgetown University Press, 1945), pp. 105–7.

prostrate. Still we press on—oh, how long it seems before we reach those blazing guns. Our men are falling faster now, for the deadly musket is at work. Volley after volley of crashing musket balls sweeps through the line and mow us down like wheat before the scythe.

On! men, on! Thirty more yards and the guns are ours; but who can stand such a storm of hissing lead and iron? What a relief if earth, which almost seems to hurl these implements of death in our faces, would open now and afford a secure retreat from threatening death. Every officer is in front, Pickett with his long curls streaming in the fiery breath from the cannons' mouth.[1] Garnett on the right, Kemper in the center and Armistead on the left; Cols., Lieut. Cols., Majors, Captains, all press on and cheer the shattered lines.

Just here—from right to left the remnants of our braves pour in their long reserved fire; until now no shot had been fired, no shout of triumph had been raised; but as the cloud of smoke rises over the heads of the advancing divisions the well known southern battle cry which marks the victory gained or nearly gained bursts wildly over the

blood stained field and *all that line of guns is ours.*

Shot through both thighs, I fall about 30 yards from the guns. By my side lies Lt. Kehoe, shot through the knee. Here we lie, he in excessive pain, I fearing to bleed to death, the dead and dying all around, while the division sweeps over the Yankee guns.[2] Oh, how I long to know the result, the end of this fearful charge! We seem to have victory in our hands; but what can our poor remnant of a shattered division do if they meet beyond the guns an obstinate resistance?

There—listen—we hear a new shout, and cheer after cheer rends the air. Are those fresh troops advancing to our support? No! no! That huzza never broke from southern lips. Oh God! Virginia's bravest, noblest sons have perished here today and perished all in vain!

Oh, if there is anything capable of crushing and wringing the soldier's heart it was this day's tragic act and all in vain! But a little well timed support and Gettysburg was ours. The Yankee army had been routed and Pickett's division earned a name and fame not inferior to that of the Old Guard of Bonaparte.

---

[1]Contrary to Dooley's account, Pickett did not lead the charge, nor given his rank and position would it have been appropriate for him to have done so.

[2]In reality, only a couple hundred of the approximately 13,000 who made the charge reached the Union guns, and all of them were killed or, like Dooley, captured.

6

BENJAMIN HIRST

A Connecticut Soldier Helps Repel Pickett's Charge (1863)

Awaiting Dooley and his comrades in the center of the Union line was Sergeant Benjamin Hirst of Connecticut. Hirst was born in England and came to the United States with his family in the late 1840s. Like his father, he was a skilled weaver and found work in the textile mills, first in Pennsylvania and then at Rockville, Connecticut, where he was living when the war began. In the summer of 1862 he enlisted as a member of the Fourteenth Connecticut Volunteer Infantry, in which he served as a sergeant. By July 1863 he was a hardened veteran, having participated in the heavy fighting at Antietam and having survived the Federal defeats at Fredericksburg and Chancellorsville. On the third day at Gettysburg, his regiment was stationed in the center of the Union line near the copse of trees that was the target of the Confederate assault. In addition to the many letters he wrote to his wife Sarah, he also kept a journal narrating what he termed "Important Events." The following excerpt from his journal, written several months after the battle, described the fighting on the third day at Gettysburg and Pickett's charge. (The paragraphing has been supplied.)

July the Third   At early dawn we quietly took our Position in Line, and our Co with Co B were sent out to relieve Co A and F and to push back the Rebel skirmishers who were a little too near our lines for our comfort, however we advanced in good order and took the required position in good shape. This was the first time our Company had been thus engaged, and when I was sent with 10 men, to relieve some other ones further to the Front, I felt a little timid about walking erect, with the Ball whizing about my ears from the Rebel Sharp Shooters. But I made out to Post the men (I found one of the men I was to relieve Dead at his Post, he was shot through the Head and from his position he seemed to be taking aim at a Rebel. I did not know he was Dead until I put my hand upon his shoulder, and spoke to him) and we were soon popping away as lively as Crickets. (I will here tell you of one incident which goes to show how soon we get insensible to danger; my Gun becoming foul, I got a Ball stuck in the Barrel so that I could not get it home or take it out, in this Dilemma, I placed it before me with the Butt resting against a fence rail, and with my shoe string I pulled the trigger fully expecting it to burst, but it came out all right and I was soon firing away again.)

In the mean time the Rebels again occupied the House and Barn I before mentioned, and the remainder of our Regiment were sent to drive them out, and to hold it, which was done in as Gallant a Style as could well be. The Regt held on until they got orders to Burn them down, and the Boys soon had a Fire that effectualy kept the Rebels out for the rest of the Battle. In this affair the Regt lost quite a number of good men, and one or two officers were wounded, and thus the forenoon wore away. [At about 10 A.M. Hirst and his squad were relieved on the advanced skirmish line and returned to the skirmish reserve posted along the Emmitsburg Road.]

About noon commenced the Fiercest Canonading I ever heard, the shot and shell came from Front and Right and Left. It makes my Blood Tingle in my veins now; to think of. Never before did I hear such a roar of Artilery, it seemed as if all the Demons in Hell were let loose, and were Howling through the Air. Turn your eyes which way you will the whole Heavens were filled with Shot and Shell, Fire and Smoke. The Rebels had concentrated about 120 Pieces of Artilery upon us and for 2 long hours they delivered a Rapid and Destructive fire upon our Lines, Principally upon the old Second Corps whom they desired to attack. To add to all this was our own Batteries in full Blaze, every shot from which seemed to pass over our heads; it was a terrible situation to be in between those two fires; how we did Hug the ground expecting every moment was to be our last. And as first one of us got Hit and then another to hear their cries was Awful. And still you dare not move either hand or foot, to do so was Death. Once I ventured to look around and just then I saw one of our Cassions blown up, while the same moment a Rebel one was blown up from the same Battery. But all this could not last much longer, our fire began to lose its vigour for want of Amunition, and as the Smoke

FROM Robert L. Bee, ed., *The Boys from Rockville* (Knoxville: University of Tennessee Press, 1998), pp. 145–52.

lifted from the Crest we saw our Guns leaving one after the other and soon a terrible stillness prevailed so that you could almost hear your heart thud in your bosom.

But what means that shout of derision in our Front. Up men the Rebels are upon us, there they come a Cloud of Skirmishers in front, with one[,] two, three lines of Battle, stretched all along our Front with their Banners flying, and the men carrying their Pieces at trail Arms. It was a Glorious Sight to see, Rebels though they were. The[y] seemed to march as though upon Parade, and were confident of carrying all before them. But away up that mountain slope in our Rear we knew that (biding their time) as Gallant a body of men as ever Rebels could dare to be were awaiting for them. Yes behind that long, low stone Wall is our own Glorious Second Corps so soon to Imortalise themselves by hurling back that Rebelious Crew who brought their Polluting footsteps to our own dear North. Steady men, and Rally on the Reserve cries our Leader, as we take to our feet; we are driven in, but not in confusion. Sometimes we about Face and return their Skirmishers fire. But still we fall back up the Hill and over the Wall bringing our wounded with us.

And now we have a short breathing spell and can Note the Intense anxiety depicted on every countenance. You can see that: One is looking at the Far off Home He will never see again. Another one is looking at his Little ones, and he mechanically empties his Cartridge Box before him determined to part with Life as Dearly as posible. Other ones you can see are communing with Him before whom so many of us will have to shortly appear.

We must hold this Line to the Last Man. The Fate of the whole Army now rests with you. Don't Fire until you get the order, and then fire Low and Sure. It is the Clear Voice of Gen Gibbon as he rides along the Line, and gives a word of cheer to each Regiment as he goes along. A few more words from Gen Hayes, and our own Gallant Col Ellis

and there runs along the Line Ready, up with our Flags, Aim, Fire. And time it was too, for the Rebels seemed to me to be within 150 yards of us, and we could hear their Officers pressing them on to the charge, Fire, Fire, Fire all along our Line. There opened upon them such a Storm of Bullets, Oaths and Imprecations as fully satisfied them we had met before, under circumstances a little more favourable to them. Give them Hell x x x Now We've got you. Sock it to the Blasted Rebels. Fredericksburg on the other Leg. Hurah, Hurah, the first Line is broken. Never mind who is Hit. Give them Hell again. And soon the second Line is sent Howling back after the first one. Right Oblique Fire, Left Oblique Fire, and the supporting Colums are thrown in disorder and soon seek safety in Flight.

Then you ought to have heard the Exhultant Shouts of our Brave Boys as the whole Rebel Force gave way in utter confusion leaving thousands and thousands of Killed, Wounded and Missing in our hands. What a sight it was, where but a short time before had stood the Flower of the Rebel Army in all the Pomp of Pride and Power was now covered with Dead in every conceivable Posture, and such a Wailing Cry, mingled with Groans of the Dieing is past conception. Oh for a thousand or two fresh men to charge upon the discomfited Foe, and push them Home. Could this have been done the Southron Army might have been Anhiliated.

As it was they suffered a Tremendous Defeat. Our Corp alone Captured 30 Stand of Colers, our Division taking 13 of them, 6 of which were captured by our own little Regt, besides this we took more Prisoners then we numbered men. I did not have the oppertunity to see the whole Fruit of our Victory, but I saw a part of them brought in amid the Exhultant shouts of the Boys, and while I was rejoicing with them I was sent rolling in the Dust being Hit for the third time upon this Eventful day and was this time D[is]abled for ever carrying a Gun in Active Service again.

7

ANONYMOUS

Daily Life during the Siege of Vicksburg (1863)

When the Confederate army defending Vicksburg, Mississippi, was forced back into the city's defensive lines, civilian residents found themselves trapped by the ensuing Union siege. Shelling from both Union gunboats on the Mississippi River and Grant's artillery became a constant feature of life in the city; federal gunboats alone fired some 22,000 shells at the city during the siege. Civilians quickly evacuated their homes and dug caves in the sides of the city's many hills for protection from the ceaseless shelling. As the siege continued, supplies quickly dwindled because Confederate General John C. Pemberton, indecisive about his proper strategy, had failed to stockpile adequate provisions. The following entries describing daily life in Vicksburg are from the diary of an unknown woman who was a Unionist. (In a few places, paragraphing has been inserted.)

March 20th [*1863*] . . .—Non-combatants have been ordered to leave or prepare accordingly. Those who are to stay are having caves built. Cave-digging has become a regular business; prices range from twenty to fifty dollars, according to size of cave. Two diggers worked at ours a week and charged thirty dollars. It is well made in the hill that slopes just in the rear of the house, and well propped with thick posts, as they all are. It has a shelf, also, for holding a light or water. When we went in this evening and sat down, the earthy, suffocating feeling, as of a living tomb, was dreadful to me. I fear I shall risk death outside rather than melt in that dark furnace. The hills are so honeycombed with caves that the streets look like avenues in a cemetery. . . .

April 2d.—We have had to move, and thus lost our cave. The owner of the house suddenly returned and notified us that he intended to bring his family back; didn't think there'd be any siege. The cost of the cave could go for the rent. That means he has got tired of the Confederacy

and means to stay here and thus get out of it. . . .

April 28th.—I never understood before the full force of those questions—What shall we eat? what shall we drink? and wherewithal shall we be clothed? . . . Such minute attention must be given the wardrobe to preserve it that I have learned to darn like an artist. Making shoes is now another accomplishment. Mine were in tatters. H—— [her husband] came across a moth-eaten pair that he bought me, giving ten dollars, I think, and they fell into rags when I tried to wear them; but the soles were good, and that has helped me to shoes. A pair of old coat-sleeves saved—nothing is thrown away now—was in my trunk. I cut an exact pattern from my old shoes, laid it on the sleeves, and cut out thus good uppers and sewed them carefully; then soaked the soles and sewed the cloth to them. I am so proud of these home-made shoes, think I'll put them in a glass case when the war is over, as an heirloom. . . . I have but a dozen pins remaining, so many I gave away. Every time these are used they are straightened and kept from rust. All these curious labors are performed while the shells are leisurely screaming through the air. . . . For many nights we have had but little sleep, because the Federal gun-boats have been running past the bat-

FROM George W. Cable, ed., "A Woman's Diary of the Siege of Vicksburg," *Century Illustrated Magazine* 8 (1885): 767–75.

teries. The uproar when this is happening is phenomenal. . . .

May 1st, 1863.—It is settled at last that we shall spend the time of siege in Vicksburg. Ever since we were deprived of our cave, I had been dreading that H—— would suggest sending me to the country, where his relatives lived. As he could not leave his position and go also without being conscripted, and as I felt certain an army would get between us, it was no part of my plan to be obedient. A shell from one of the practicing mortars brought the point to an issue yesterday and settled it. Sitting at work as usual, listening to the distant sound of bursting shells, apparently aimed at the court-house, there suddenly came a nearer explosion; the house shook, and a tearing sound was followed by terrified screams from the kitchen. I rushed thither, but met in the hall the cook's little girl America, bleeding from a wound in the forehead, and fairly dancing with fright and pain, while she uttered fearful yells. I stopped to examine the wound, and her mother bounded in, her black face ashy from terror. "Oh! Miss V——, my child is killed and the kitchen tore up." Seeing America was too lively to be a killed subject, I consoled Martha and hastened to the kitchen. Evidently a shell had exploded just outside, sending three or four pieces through. When order was restored I endeavored to impress on Martha's mind the necessity for calmness and the uselessness of such excitement. Looking round at the close of the lecture, there stood a group of Confederate soldiers laughing heartily at my sermon and the promising audience I had. They chimed in with a parting chorus:

"Yes, it's no use hollerin, old lady." . . .

May 17.— . . . About three o'clock the rush began.[1] I shall never forget that woful sight of a beaten, demoralized army that came rushing back,—humanity in the last throes of endurance. Wan, hollow-eyed, ragged, footsore, bloody, the men limped along unarmed, but followed by siege-guns, ambulances, gun-carriages, and wagons in aimless confusion. At twilight two or three bands on the court-house hill and other points began playing Dixie, Bonnie Blue Flag, and so on, and drums began to beat all about; I suppose they were rallying the scattered army.

May 28th.—Since that day the regular siege has continued. We are utterly cut off from the world, surrounded by a circle of fire. . . . The fiery shower of shells goes on day and night. . . . People do nothing but eat what they can get, sleep when they can, and dodge the shells. There are three intervals when the shelling stops, either for the guns to cool or for the gunners' meals, I suppose,—about eight in the morning, the same in the evening, and at noon. In that time we have both to prepare and eat ours. Clothing cannot be washed or anything else done. On the 19th and 22d, when the assaults were made on the lines, . . . people were sitting, eating their poor suppers at the cave doors, ready to plunge in again. As the first shell again flew they dived, and not a human being was visible. The sharp crackle of the musketry-firing was a strong contrast to the scream of the bombs. I think all the dogs and cats must be killed or starved, we don't see any more pitiful animals prowling around. . . .

The cellar is so damp and musty the bedding has to be carried out and laid in the sun every day, with the forecast that it may be demolished at any moment. The confinement is dreadful. To sit and listen as if waiting for death in a horrible manner would drive me insane. I don't know what others do, but we read when I am not scribbling in this. H—— borrowed somewhere a lot of Dickens's novels, and we reread them by the dim light in the cellar. When the shelling abates H—— goes to walk about a little or get the "Daily Citizen," which is still issuing a tiny sheet at twenty-five and fifty cents a copy. It is, of course, but a rehash of speculations which amuses a half hour. . . .

I am so tired of corn-bread, which I never liked, that I eat it with tears in my eyes. We are lucky to get a quart of milk daily from a family near who have a cow they hourly expect to be killed. I send five dollars to market each morning, and it buys a small piece of mule-meat. Rice and milk is my main food; I can't eat the mule-meat. We boil the rice and eat it cold with milk for sup-

[1]She is describing the retreat of Pemberton's army into the city after the Battle of Big Black.

per. Martha [their servant] runs the gauntlet to buy the meat and milk once a day in a perfect terror. . . .

June 7th. In the cellar.—There is one thing I feel especially grateful for, that amid these horrors we have been spared that of suffering for water. The weather has been dry a long time, and we hear of others dipping up the water from ditches and mud-holes. This place has two large underground cisterns of good cool water, and every night in my subterranean dressing-room a tub of cold water is the nerve-calmer that sends me to sleep in spite of the roar. One cistern I had to give up to the soldiers, who swarm about like hungry animals seeking something to devour. Poor fellows! my heart bleeds for them. They have nothing but spoiled, greasy bacon, and bread made of musty pea-flour, and but little of that. The sick ones can't bolt it. They come into the kitchen when Martha puts the pan of corn-bread in the stove, and beg for the bowl she mixed it in. They shake up the scrapings with water, put in their bacon, and boil the mixture into a kind of soup, which is easier to swallow than pea-bread. When I happen in, they look so ashamed of their poor clothes. I know we saved the lives of two by giving a few meals. . . .

June 9th.—The churches are a great resort for those who have no caves. People fancy they are not shelled so much, and they are substantial and the pews good to sleep in. . . .

June 13th.—Shell burst just over the roof this morning. Pieces tore through both floors down into the dining-room. The entire ceiling of that room fell in a mass. We had just left it. Every piece of crockery on the table was smashed up. . . .

June 18th.—To-day the "Citizen" is printed on wall paper; therefore has grown a little in size. . . .

June 21st.—I had gone upstairs to-day during the interregnum to enjoy a rest on my bed and read the reliable items in the "Citizen," when a shell burst right outside the window in front of me. Pieces flew in, striking all round me, tearing down masses of plaster that came tumbling over me. When H—— rushed in I was crawling out of the plaster, digging it out of my eyes and hair. When he picked up a piece large as a saucer beside my pillow, I realized my narrow escape. The window-frame began to smoke, and we saw the house was on fire. H—— ran for a hatchet and I for water, and we put it out. Another [shell] came crashing near, and I snatched up my comb and brush and ran down here [the cellar]. . . .

June 25th.—A horrible day. The most horrible yet to me, because I've lost my nerve. We were all in the cellar, when a shell came tearing through the roof, burst upstairs, tore up that room, and the pieces coming through both floors down into the cellar. One of them tore open the leg of H——'s pantaloons. This was tangible proof the cellar was no place of protection from them. On the heels of this came Mr. J——, to tell us that young Mrs. P—— had had her thigh-bone crushed. When Martha went for the milk she came back horror-stricken to tell us the black girl there had her arm taken off by a shell. For the first time I quailed. I do not think people who are physically brave deserve much credit for it; it is a matter of nerves. In this way I am constitutionally brave, and seldom think of danger till it is over; and death has not the terrors for me it has for some others. Every night I had lain down expecting death, and every morning rose to the same prospect, without being unnerved. . . . But now I first seemed to realize that something worse than death might come; I might be crippled, and not killed. Life, without all one's powers and limbs, was a thought that broke down my courage. I said to H——, "You must get me out of this horrible place; I cannot stay; I know I shall be crippled." Now the regret comes that I lost control, because H—— is worried, and has lost his composure, because my coolness has broken down. . . .

July 3d.— . . . To-day we are down in the cellar again, shells flying as thick as ever. Provisions so nearly gone, except the hogshead of sugar, that a few more days will bring us to starvation indeed. Martha says rats are hanging dressed in the market for sale with mule meat,—there is nothing else. The officer at the battery told me he had eaten one yesterday. We have tried to leave this Tophet and failed, and if the siege continues I must summon that higher kind of courage—moral bravery—to subdue my fears of possible mutilation.

July 4th.—It is evening. All is still. Silence and night are once more united. I can sit at the table in the parlor and write. . . . We have had wheat supper and wheat bread once more. H—— is leaning back in the rocking-chair; he says:

"G——, it seems to me I can hear the silence, and feel it, too. It wraps me like a soft garment; how else can I express this peace?" . . .

. . . [Last night] when supper was eaten, . . . we crossed the street to the cave opposite. As I crossed a mighty shell flew screaming right over my head. It was the last thrown into Vicksburg.

We lay on our pallets waiting for the expected roar, but no sound came except the chatter from neighboring caves, and at last we dropped asleep.

I woke at dawn stiff. . . . Every one was expressing surprise at the quiet. We started for home and met the editor of the "Daily Citizen." H—— said:

"This is strangely quiet, Mr. L——."

"Ah, sir," shaking his head gloomily, "I'm afraid (?) the last shell has been thrown into Vicksburg."

"Why do you fear so?"

"It is surrender."

8

ALEXANDER S. ABRAMS

The Conduct of the Negroes
Was beyond All Expression (1863)

In the following selection, Alexander St. Clair Abrams of the Vicksburg Whig *described the entry of Union troops into Vicksburg, Mississippi, after its surrender, and their impact on the town's slave population. Confederate propaganda frequently emphasized the alleged familiarity between Union soldiers and black women. In reality, racism and aversion to race mixing ran deep in the Union ranks and, at times, blended with antislavery sentiment.*

On Saturday [July 4th], at twelve o'clock, M., [General John A.] Logan's division of [General James B.] McPherson's corps, of the Federal army, commenced entering the city, and in a quarter of an hour Vicksburg was crammed with them. Their first act was to take possession of the court house, on the spire of which they hoisted the United States flag, amid the exultant shouts of their comrades, and a deep feeling of humiliation on the part of the Confederate soldiers who witnessed the hauling up of the flag which they

had hoped never to see floating over the city they had so long and proudly boasted impregnable, and never to be taken by the enemy of the South. . . .

The conduct of the negroes, after the entrance of their "liberators," was beyond all expression. While the Yankee army was marching through the streets, crowds of them congregated on the sidewalks, with a broad grin of satisfaction on their ebony countenances. The next day, which was Sunday, witnessed a sight, which would have been ludicrous had it not galled our soldiers by the reflection that they were compelled to submit to it. There was a great turn out of the "contrabands," dressed up in the most extravagant style imagin-

FROM A. S. Abrams, *A Full and Detailed History of the Siege of Vicksburg* (Atlanta: Intelligencer Steam Power Presses, 1863), pp. 63–65.

able, and promenading through the streets, as if Vicksburg had been confiscated and turned over [to] them. In familiar conversation with the negro wenches, the soldiers of the Federal army were seen, arm-in-arm, marching through the streets, while the "bucks" congregated on the corners and discussed the happy event that had brought them freedom.

So arrogant did the negroes become after the entrance of the Federal forces, that no white Confederate citizen or soldier dared to speak to them, for fear of being called a rebel, or some other abusive epithet. One of the Confederate soldiers, happening to enter the garden of the house that the author of this work resided in, for the purpose of picking a peach, a negro, belonging to a gentleman of Vicksburg, who had charge of the garden, brought out a gun, and, taking deliberate aim at

the soldier, was about to fire. We immediately threw up the gun, and, drawing a knife, threatened the negro if he fired at the man; no sooner was the threat made, than the negro, with an oath, levelled the gun at us and drew the trigger; luckily the cap snapped without exploding, and we succeeded in getting the gun away and discharging it.

While making these observations about the negroes, we would say that it was confined to the city negroes alone. The slaves brought in by planters, and servants of soldiers and officers, did not appear the least gratified at their freedom. The majority of those connected with our army were very desirous of leaving with their masters, and General Grant at first consented that those who desired it should leave; but as soon as a few passes were made out, he revoked the order, and compelled the balance to remain.

9

JOSIAH GORGAS

The Confederacy Totters to Its Destruction (1863)

Josiah Gorgas, who was head of the Confederate Ordnance Bureau, was one of the Confederacy's most talented administrators. In the following diary entry, he reflects on the stunning change in the military situation in the summer of 1863.

July 28, [*1863*]   Events have succeeded one another with disastrous rapidity. One brief month ago we were apparently at the point of success. Lee was in Pennsylvania, threatening Harrisburgh, and even Philadelphia. Vicksburgh seemed to laugh all Grant's efforts to scorn, & the northern papers had reports of his raising the siege. Port Hudson had beaten off Banks' forces, and "the question" said a northern correspondent was only now, could he save the remnant of his army. Taylor had driven the enemy from the greater part of Louisiana, and

FROM Sarah Woolfolk Wiggins, ed., *The Journals of Josiah Gorgas, 1857–1878* (Tuscaloosa: University of Alabama Press, 1995), p. 75.

had captured immense stores at Brashear. Winchester with 28 pieces of artillery and four thousand prisoners had fallen into our hands. All looked bright. Now the picture is just as sombre as it was bright then. Lee failed at Gettysburg, and has recrossed the Potomac & resumed the position of two months ago, covering Richmond. Alas! he has lost fifteen thousand men and twenty-five thousand stands of arms. Vicksburgh and Port Hudson capitulated, surrendering thirty five thousand men and forty-five thousand arms. It seems incredible that human power could effect such a change in so brief a space. Yesterday we rode on the pinnacle of success—to-day absolute ruin seems to be our portion. The Confederacy totters to its destruction.

ABRAHAM LINCOLN

The Emancipation Proclamation (1863)

This is the text of the Emancipation Proclamation, which Lincoln signed on January 1, 1863. The document contains none of Lincoln's usual appeal to higher moral values and transcendent issues. Instead, its language reflects his view that only as a military act was the proclamation constitutional.

Whereas, on the twentysecond day of September, in the year of our Lord one thousand eight hundred and sixty two, a proclamation was issued by the President of the United States. . . .

Now, therefore I, Abraham Lincoln, President of the United States, by virtue of the power in me vested as Commander-in-Chief, of the Army and Navy of the United States in time of actual armed rebellion against authority and government of the United States, and as a fit and necessary war measure for suppressing said rebellion, do, on this first day of January, in the year of our Lord one thousand eight hundred and sixty three, and in accordance with my purpose so to do publicly proclaimed for the full period of one hundred days, from the day first above mentioned, order and designate as the States and parts of States wherein the people thereof respectively, are this day in rebellion against the United States, the following, towit:

Arkansas, Texas, Louisiana, (except the Parishes of St. Bernard, Plaquemines, Jefferson, St. Johns, St. Charles, St. James[,] Ascension, Assumption, Terrebonne, Lafourche, St. Mary, St. Martin, and Orleans, including the City of New-

Orleans) Mississippi, Alabama, Florida, Georgia, South-Carolina, North-Carolina, and Virginia, (except the fortyeight counties designated as West Virginia, and also the counties of Berkley, Accomac, Northampton, Elizabeth-City, York, Princess Ann, and Norfolk, including the cities of Norfolk & Portsmouth[)]; and which excepted parts are, for the present, left precisely as if this proclamation were not issued.

And by virtue of the power, and for the purpose aforesaid, I do order and declare that all persons held as slaves within said designated States, and parts of States, are, and henceforward shall be free; and that the Executive government of the United States, including the military and naval authorities thereof, will recognize and maintain the freedom of said persons.

And I hereby enjoin upon the people so declared to be free to abstain from all violence, unless in necessary self-defence; and I recommend to them that, in all cases when allowed, they labor faithfully for reasonable wages.

And I further declare and make known, that such persons of suitable condition, will be received into the armed service of the United States to garrison forts, positions, stations, and other places, and to man vessels of all sorts in said service.

And upon this act, sincerely believed to be an

FROM Roy P. Basler, et al., eds., *The Collected Works of Abraham Lincoln*, vol. 6 (New Brunswick, N.J.: Rutgers University Press, 1953), pp. 28–30.

act of justice, warranted by the Constitution, upon military necessity, I invoke the considerate judgment of mankind, and the gracious favor of Almighty God.

In witness whereof, I have hereunto set my hand and caused the seal of the United States to be affixed.

2

Northern Newspapers Debate the Significance of the Emancipation Proclamation (1863)

As he had promised when he issued his preliminary proclamation in September 1862, Lincoln signed the final Emancipation Proclamation on January 1, 1863. In the following editorials, two New York City newspapers discussed the meaning of this action—the World *from the Democratic perspective and the* Times *from a Republican one.*

The President's Proclamation.

President LINCOLN's proclamation, which we publish this morning, marks an era in the history, not only of this war, but of this country and the world. It is not necessary to assume that it will set free instantly the enslaved blacks of the South, in order to ascribe to it the greatest and most permanent importance. Whatever may be its immediate results, it changes entirely the relations of the National Government to the institution of Slavery. Hitherto Slavery has been under the protection of the Government; henceforth it is under its ban. The power of the Army and Navy, hitherto employed in hunting and returning to bondage the fugitive from service, are to be employed in maintaining his freedom whenever and wherever he may choose to assert it. This change of attitude is itself a revolution.

President LINCOLN takes care, by great precision in his language, to define the basis on which this action rests. He issues the Proclamation "as a fit and necessary war measure for suppressing the re-

FROM *New York Times*, 3 January 1863.

bellion." While he sincerely believes it to be an "act of justice warranted by the Constitution," he issues it "upon military necessity." In our judgment it is only upon that ground and for that purpose that he has any right to issue it at all. In his civil capacity as President, he has not the faintest shadow of authority to decree the emancipation of a single slave, either as an "act of justice" or for any other purpose whatever. As Commander-in-Chief of the army he has undoubtedly the right *to deprive the rebels of the aid of their slaves,*—just as he has the right to take their horses, and to arrest all persons who may be giving them aid and comfort,— "as a war measure" and upon grounds of military necessity.

It may seem at first sight a matter of small importance in what capacity the act is done. But its validity may, in the end, depend upon that very point. Sooner or later his action in this matter will come up for review before the Supreme Court; and it is a matter of the utmost importance to the President, to the slaves, and to the country, that it should come in a form to be sustained. . . .

What effect the Proclamation will have remains to be seen. We do not think that it will at once set free any considerable number of slaves beyond the actual and effective jurisdiction of our armies. It will lead to no immediate insurrections, and involve no massacres, except such as the rebels in the blindness of their wrath may themselves set on foot. The slaves have no arms, are without organization, and in dread of the armed and watchful whites. Besides, they evince no disposition to fight for themselves so long as they see that we are fighting for them. They understand, beyond all question, that the tendency of this war is to give them freedom, and that the Union armies, whatever may be their motive, are actually and practically fighting for their liberty. If the war should suddenly end,—if they should see the fighting stop, and the Constitution which protects Slavery restored to full vigor in the Slave States, their disappointment would vent itself in the wrathful explosion of insurrection and violence. But so long as the war continues, we look for nothing of that kind. Whenever our armies reach their immediate vicinity, they will doubtless assert their freedom, and call upon us to "recognize and maintain" it. Until then, they will work for their masters and wait for deliverance.

"The Proclamation of Freedom."

The character of this document was so fully foreshadowed in its September precursor that public interest centers more on the fact of its issue than on the nature of its contents. What principally strikes public attention is the fact that President LINCOLN has fully and finally committed himself to the policy of emancipation. The particular features of the proclamation which seem deserving of remark are these: the President rests the measure *on purely military grounds* with a distinctness which did not appear in the September proclamation; he avows an intention to receive the emancipated slaves into the military and naval service of the United States. . . .

The most important question that can arise relative to this proclamation respects its legal effect. Immediate *practical* effect it has none; the slaves remaining in precisely the same condition as before. They still live on the plantations; tenant their accustomed hovels; obey the command of their master or overseer, eating the food he furnishes and doing the work he requires precisely as though Mr. LINCOLN had not declared them free. Their freedom, then, it is clear, is only a *dormant* freedom; if free at all, they are not actually but only legally free. . . . The original remedy of the slave (if he has any) is in the local courts of the state where he has his domicil. These courts, we know beforehand, will not entertain his suit. They do not recognize the validity of the decree on which he rests his claim. So long, therefore, as the present political and military *status* continues, the freedom declared by this proclamation is a dormant, not an actual freedom. . . .

The slaves might, to be sure, take the vindication of their rights into their own hands, by rising, *en masse*, against their masters. But this they could have done any time within the last fifty years with quite as good advantages and as strong a color of right as now. Mr. LINCOLN's paper proclamation is of no more force than the imprescriptable title to freedom born with every human being who has courage and vigor of character to assert it. There has never been a time when the negroes had so little to hope from an insurrection as at present. The whole white population of the South is in arms. If the slaves were disposed to run away, they are hemmed in by large armies on all the southern frontiers. Whither could they flee? If, assembling in large bodies, they should offer a show of violence, what chance have they, unarmed, against the abundance of improved artillery and firearms in the hands of the superior race. If they resort to the torch of the incendiary, how are they and their little ones to subsist? Whatever small chance they have of gaining their freedom is by a servile insurrection; but they have ten chances to rush on destruction to one of escaping from servitude. It is obvious, therefore, that *for the present*, the proclamation is inoperative and futile. It may strengthen the resistance of the rebels, but it cannot benefit the slaves.

FROM *New York World*, 3 January 1863.

It may be said that the proclamation establishes a legal claim to freedom which the slaves may successfully assert after the military subjugation of the South. But this knocks the bottom out of the proclamation and spoils all its contents. The proclamation is issued as a *war measure*; as an instrument for the subjugation of the rebels. But that cannot be a *means* of military success which presupposes this same military success as the condition of its own existence. It confounds all ideas of means and ends to call emancipation a war measure when emancipation is obviously unattainable until after military resistance is put out of the way. If the war should end in the triumph of the rebellion the proclamation would, of course, amount to nothing. If the rebellion is subdued, the proclamation merely gives a colorable ground for suits for freedom before the tribunals of the country. Its whole efficacy must finally depend on whether it is sustained by the courts. That the courts of the slave states in which the suits must originally be brought will not sustain it admits of no doubt whatever. That the Supreme Court of the United States, to which such suits may be carried for final adjudication, will declare the proclamation void is also morally certain. It is clearly unconstitutional and wholly void unless sustainable as a war measure. A war measure it clearly is not, inasmuch as the previous success of the war is the only thing that can give it validity.

3

HARPER'S WEEKLY

The Work Done by Congress (1863)

The Thirty-seventh Congress, which met in three sessions between 1861 and 1863, passed a series of far-reaching laws to promote the social, economic, and intellectual development of the United States. Following its final session, Harper's Weekly *surveyed some of this legislation and discussed its significance.*

The Thirty-seventh Congress of the United States has expired, having, in the short session which ended on March 4, passed some of the most momentous measures ever placed upon the statute-book. Those measures, as a whole, are equivalent to the step which, in republican Rome, was taken whenever the state was deemed in imminent danger, and which history calls the appointment of a Dictator. The President of the United States has, in effect, been created Dictator, with almost supreme power over liberty, property, and life—a power nearly as extensive and as irresponsible as that which is wielded by the Emperors of Russia, France, or China. And this is well. To succeed in a struggle such as we are waging a strong central Government is indispensable. One great advantage which the rebels have had over us is the unity of their purposes, and the despotic power of their chief. We are now on a par with them in these respects, and we shall see which is the better cause.

The measures which collectively confer upon Mr. Lincoln dictatorial powers consist, 1*st*, of the Conscription Act; 2*d*, of the Finance measures; and, 3*d*, of the Indemnity Act.

The conscription bill enrolls all the males of the loyal States (including Indians and negroes) between the ages of 20 and 45 into a national militia, and empowers the President to call them into the service of the United States for three years or the war. The only exemptions are the President and Vice-President, and one adult male in each family where there are aged parents or infant children dependent on the labor of their adult relative for support. The entire body of the militia, as thus enrolled, is to be divided into two classes: 1*st*, persons between 20 and 35, whether married or single, and persons between 35 and 45 if unmarried; and 2*d*, married men between 35 and 45. It is presumed that the latter class will not be called upon until the former has been exhausted. As according to the census there will remain, in the loyal States, after deducting the army now in the field, some 3,500,000 men liable to enrollment under this Act; and as it is quite certain that under no circumstances can so large a number be required, Congress has wisely empowered the Executive to receive a sum of $300 from any drafted man who prefers paying to serving. This sum, it is believed, will always secure a substitute. Clergymen, professional men, large merchants and manufacturers, and others who are of more use to the country while prosecuting their various peaceful avocations than they would be if forced to carry a musket, will thus be exempted, while the class of men which take their place will receive money enough to keep their families as comfortably as if they had remained at home.

Under the operation of this Act the President will be enabled to recruit our armies to the full standard when the time of the nine months' men expires, and the hopes of the rebels—which have been re-echoed by the correspondents of disloyal journals—that our armies would melt away in the spring will be thoroughly defeated. Under this Act the President may keep a million of men in the field without difficulty.

No allusion is made in the Act to the enlistment of negroes. Other laws are held to cover the case, and to clothe the President with ample power to enroll and arm negroes in any part of the country. Under these laws General Hunter has a brigade, at least, of negro troops at Port Royal; General Banks has several colored regiments at New Orleans and Baton Rouge; General Grant has quite a considerable negro force at Vicksburg, and

General Rosecrans—who appears to arm the negro chiefly with M'Clellan's favorite and trusty weapon—the spade—has several thousand at or near Murfreesboro. In a word, we have armed and are using all the adult negroes we have got, and shall continue to do so. We presume that before the end of the year we shall have 100,000 of them armed, equipped, and in the field.

The second of the measures which have been passed to increase the power of the President is the Financial Bill. This empowers him to issue $550,000,000 more legal tender paper-money—in addition to the $300,000,000 authorized at the last session of Congress; of which $550,000,000 $150,000,000 are to be ordinary United States notes similar to those now in circulation, and $400,000,000 interest-bearing notes, to be either a legal tender themselves or to be exchangeable for legal tender on presentation. He may furthermore negotiate, at any rate which he deems fair, United States Bonds to run for not less than ten and not more than twenty years, and to bear a rate of interest not over six per cent., said interest payable in specie. The money-market and the purse of the country are thus placed absolutely at the disposal of the Government. If the Secretary of the Treasury can borrow, he has every opportunity of doing so. If he can not borrow, he has the right to manufacture money. It is true that such money—manufactured at the fiat of a Government—invariably depreciates in the ratio of its issues. This is one of the evils which are usually involved by great wars, and which are inseparable from the paper-money system. It must be hoped that we may succeed in crushing the rebellion before the point of absolute depreciation is reached.

Besides this measure, another Act—Mr. Chase's Bank Act—transfers the entire control of the bank currency of the country to the General Government. This Act empowers any individual or corporation to bank on the basis of Government securities, and to issue currency, based on the deposit of such securities, to within ten per cent. of their market value. It is not expected that this Act will go fully into effect during the war, though some banks in the West will probably be organized under it. But the purpose of the measure is to institute such a connection between the public credit and the banking interest as shall, on the one hand, give the President virtual control of all the banks in the country, and, on the other, make every stockholder and banknote-holder in the land an underwriter, so to speak, of the Government bonds. Of course, pending the war, any issues of bank-notes under this Act will merely operate to swell the inflation of paper-money. But, as we said, this inflation is one of the necessary drawbacks of war.

The purse and the sword of the country thus placed unconditionally in the President's hands, it only remained to invest him with power to protect the Government from attacks in the rear from insidious traitors at the North. For this purpose, in accordance with the practice of old Rome, of constitutional England, and of the United States themselves, Congress passed an Act empowering the President to suspend the Act of *habeas corpus* whenever and wherever he may deem it necessary. That this Act was necessary no one who has watched the treacherous movements of the Northern Copperheads, or reflected upon the mischief they might do if unrestrained, will venture to deny. At this very moment Southern emissaries and their sympathizers in Indiana are manoeuvring to wrest the control of the State troops out of the hands of the constitutional authorities; and individuals in New York and Connecticut are engaged in sending arms and supplies to the rebels, chiefly for the sake

of gain, but also, in some degree, from love. It is quite evident that in the face of such a state of things, and when the nation is engaged in a death-grapple of which the issue is very doubtful, the slow and cautious remedies which the law provides for the redress of wrongs in time of peace would be out of place. The country might be ruined while we were empanneling a jury to try a traitor. *Inter arma leges silent.*[1]

When we undertook the war we tacitly agreed to accept it with all its evils. Prominent among these are a depreciated currency, a temporary deprivation of personal liberty, and a liability to be taken from one's business to carry a musket in the army. These are grave inconveniences. But they are temporary and bearable; whereas the evils which would result from the disruption of the Union are lasting and intolerable. We may suffer, but our children will benefit by our suffering. Whereas if this country is severed in twain the future which lies before us is plainly depicted in the history of Mexico and Central America: incessant wars, constant subdivisions, a cessation of honest industry and agriculture, a decay of trade, a disappearance of wealth and civilization, and in their stead chronic strife, rapine, bloodshed, and anarchy. To avoid these things we can well afford for a few years to have a strong Government.

---

[1] In the midst of arms, laws are silent.

4 CLEMENT VALLANDIGHAM

One of the Worst Despotisms on Earth (1863)

Clement Vallandigham was a congressman from Ohio and a leader of the peace Democrats. He intensely hated abolitionists and New Englanders, whom he blamed for the war, and increasingly became an outspoken opponent of the war. A bitter critic of the Lincoln administration, Vallandigham condemned the policies of conscription, the suspension of the writ of habeas corpus, and emancipation. He out-

lined his ideas in the following speech in the House of Representatives, on January 14, 1863. A few months later Vallandigham was arrested by military authorities in Ohio and convicted of disloyalty by a military court. Lincoln subsequently altered his sentence from imprisonment to banishment to the Confederacy. Vallandigham eventually went to Canada and then returned to the United States in 1864 to campaign against Lincoln. (Paragraphing has been slightly modified.)

Soon after the war began] the reign of the mob was . . . supplanted by the iron domination of arbitrary power. Constitutional limitation was broken down; habeas corpus fell; liberty of the press, of speech, of the person, of the mails, of travel, of one's own house, and of religion; the right to bear arms, due process of law, judicial trial, trial by jury, trial at all; every badge and muniment of freedom in republican government or kingly government—all went down at a blow; and the chief law-officer of the crown—I beg pardon, sir, but it is easy now to fall into this courtly language—the Attorney-General, first of all men, proclaimed in the United States the maxim of Roman servility: Whatever pleases the President, that is law! Prisoners of state were then first heard of here. Midnight and arbitrary arrests commenced; travel was interdicted; trade embargoed; passports demanded; bastiles were introduced; strange oaths invented; a secret police organized; "piping" began; informers multiplied; spies now first appeared in America. The right to declare war, to raise and support armies, and to provide and maintain a navy, was usurped by the Executive. . . .

On the 4th of July Congress met, not to seek peace; not to rebuke usurpation nor to restrain power; not certainly to deliberate; not even to legislate, but to register and ratify the edicts and acts of the Executive. . . . Free speech was had only at the risk of a prison; possibly of life. Opposition was silenced by the fierce clamor of "disloyalty." . . .

Thus was CIVIL WAR inaugurated in America. Can any man to-day see the end of it?

. . . I have denounced, from the beginning, the usurpations and the infractions, one and all, of law and Constitution, by the President and those under him; their repeated and persistent arbitrary arrests, the suspension of *habeas corpus,* the violation of freedom of the mails, of the private house, of the press and of speech, and all the other multiplied wrongs and outrages upon public liberty and private right, which have made this country one of the worst despotisms on earth for the past twenty months; and I will continue to rebuke and denounce them to the end. . . .

And now, sir, I recur to the state of the Union to-day. What is it? Sir, twenty months have elapsed, but the rebellion is not crushed out; its military power has not been broken; the insurgents have not dispersed. The Union is not restored; nor the Constitution maintained; nor the laws enforced. Twenty, sixty, ninety, three hundred, six hundred days have passed; a thousand millions been expended; and three hundred thousand lives lost or bodies mangled; and to-day the Confederate flag is still near the Potomac and the Ohio, and the Confederate Government stronger, many times, than at the beginning. . . .

Thus, with twenty millions of people, and every element of strength and force at command—power, patronage, influence, unanimity, enthusiasm, confidence, credit, money, men, an Army and a Navy the largest and the noblest ever set in the field, or afloat upon the sea; with the support, almost servile, of every State, county, and municipality in the North and West, with a Congress swift to do the bidding of the Executive; without opposition anywhere at home; and with an arbitrary power which neither the Czar of Russia, nor the Emperor of Austria dare exercise; yet after nearly two years of more vigorous prosecution of war than ever recorded in history; . . . you have utterly, signally, disastrously—I will not say ignominiously—failed to subdue ten mil-

FROM Clement Vallandigham, *Speeches, Arguments, and Letters* (New York: J. Walter and Company, 1864), pp. 418–37.

lions of "rebels," whom you had taught the people of the North and West not only to hate, but to despise. . . . You have not conquered the South. You never will. It is not in the nature of things possible; much less under your auspices. But money you have expended without limit, and blood poured out like water. Defeat, debt, taxation, sepulchres, these are your trophies. . . . The war for the Union is, in your hands, a most bloody and costly failure. The President confessed it on the 22d of September. . . . War for the Union was abandoned; war for the negro openly begun, and with stronger battalions than before. With what success? Let the dead at Fredericksburg and Vicksburg answer. . . .

But slavery is the cause of the war. Why? Because the South obstinately and wickedly refused to restrict or abolish it at the demand of the philosophers or fanatics and demagogues of the North and West. Then, sir, it was abolition, the purpose to abolish or interfere with and hem in slavery, which caused disunion and war. Slavery is only the subject, but Abolition the cause of this civil war. It was the persistent and determined agitation in the free States of the question of abolishing slavery in the South, because of the alleged "irrepressible conflict" between the forms of labor in the two sections . . . that forced a collision of arms at last. . . .

Neither will I be stopped by that other cry of mingled fanaticism and hypocrisy, about the sin and barbarism of African slavery. Sir, I see more of barbarism and sin, a thousand times, in the continuance of this war, the dissolution of the Union, the breaking up of this Government, and the enslavement of the white race, by debt and taxes and arbitrary power. The day of fanatics and sophists and enthusiasts, thank God, is gone at last. . . . Sir, I accept the language and intent of the Indiana resolution, to the full—"that in considering terms of settlement, we will look only to the welfare, peace, and safety of the white race, without reference to the effect that settlement may have upon the condition of the African." And when we have done this, my word for it, the safety, peace, and welfare of the African will have been best secured. Sir, there is fifty-fold less of antislavery sentiment to-day in the West than there was two years ago; and if this war be continued, there will be still less a year hence. The people there begin, at last, to comprehend, that domestic slavery in the South is a question, not of morals, or religion, or humanity, but a form of labor, perfectly compatible with the dignity of free white labor in the same community, and with national vigor, power, and prosperity, and especially with military strength. . . .

5

ABRAHAM LINCOLN

I Think I Shall Be Blamed for Having Made Too Few Arrests (1863)

The army's arrest of Clement Vallandigham provoked outcries from many northern Democrats. When Democrats in Albany held a meeting to protest the administration's policy on civil liberties, Lincoln wrote a public letter in response that defended his suspension of the writ of habeas corpus. The letter was addressed to Erastus Corning, a prominent New York Democratic leader. Lincoln's letter was written in the aftermath of the Union defeat at Chancellorsville and at the time when Lee's army was moving north toward Maryland and Pennsylvania, both states with a large Copperhead element. While Lee's destination was not yet clear, Lincoln had good cause to be concerned about the threat of disloyalty at home. Indeed, one motive for Lee's invasion was to discourage Union morale and strengthen northern opposition to the war (see p. 149). In this context, Lincoln's strong language was understandable.

(see p. 149)

Executive Mansion
Washington [June 12] 1863.

Hon. Erastus Corning & others
Gentlemen

. . . Prior to my installation here it had been inculcated that any State had a lawful right to secede from the national Union; and that it would be expedient to exercise the right, whenever the devotees of the doctrine should fail to elect a President to their own liking. I was elected contrary to their liking; and accordingly, so far as it was legally possible, they had taken seven states out of the Union, had seized many of the United States Forts, and had fired upon the United States' Flag, all before I was inaugurated; and, of course, before I had done any official act whatever. The rebellion, thus began soon ran into the present civil war; and, in certain respects, it began on very unequal terms between the parties. The insurgents had been preparing for it more than thirty years, while the government had taken no steps to resist them. The former had carefully considered all the means which could be turned to their account. It undoubtedly was a well pondered reliance with them that in their own unrestricted effort to destroy Union, constitution, and law, all together, the government would, in great degree, be restrained by the same constitution and law, from arresting their progress. Their sympathizers pervaded all departments of the government, and nearly all communities of the people. From this material, under cover of "Liberty of speech" "Liberty of the press" and "Habeas corpus" they hoped to keep on foot amongst us a

most efficient corps of spies, informers, suppliers, and aiders and abettors of their cause in a thousand ways. They knew that in times such as they were inaugurating, by the constitution itself, the "Habeas corpus" might be suspended; but they also knew they had friends who would make a question as to *who* was to suspend it; meanwhile their spies and others might remain at large to help on their cause. Or if, as has happened, the executive should suspend the writ, without ruinous waste of time, instances of arresting innocent persons might occur, as are always likely to occur in such cases; and then a clamor could be raised in regard to this, which might be, at least, of some service to the insurgent cause. It needed no very keen perception to discover this part of the enemies' programme, so soon as by open hostilities their machinery was fairly put in motion. Yet, thoroughly imbued with a reverence for the guarranteed rights of individuals, I was slow to adopt the strong measures, which by degrees I have been forced to regard as being within the exceptions of the constitution, and as indispensable to the public Safety. Nothing is better known to history than that courts of justice are utterly incompetent to such cases. Civil courts are organized chiefly for trials of individuals, or, at most, a few individuals acting in concert; and this in quiet times, and on charges of crimes well defined in the law. Even in times of peace, bands of horse-thieves and robbers frequently grow too numerous and powerful for the ordinary courts of justice. But what comparison, in numbers, have such bands ever borne to the insurgent sympathizers even in many of the loyal states? Again, a jury too frequently have at least one member, more ready to hang the panel than to hang the traitor. And yet again, he who dissuades one man from volunteering, or induces one

FROM Roy P. Basler, et al., eds. *The Collected Works of Abraham Lincoln*, vol. 6 (New Brunswick, N.J.: Rutgers University Press, 1953), pp. 263–67.

soldier to desert, weakens the Union cause as much as he who kills a union soldier in battle. Yet this dissuasion, or inducement, may be so conducted as to be no defined crime of which any civil court would take cognizance.

Ours is a case of Rebellion—so called by the resolutions before me—in fact, a clear, flagrant, and gigantic case of Rebellion; and the provision of the constitution that "The previlege of the writ of Habeas Corpus shall not be suspended, unless when in cases of Rebellion or Invasion, the public Safety may require it" is *the* provision which specially applies to our present case. This provision plainly attests the understanding of those who made the constitution that ordinary courts of justice are inadequate to "cases of Rebellion"—attests their purpose that in such cases, men may be held in custody whom the courts acting on ordinary rules, would discharge. Habeas Corpus, does not discharge men who are proved to be guilty of defined crime; and its suspension is allowed by the constitution on purpose that, men may be arrested and held, who can not be proved to be guilty of defined crime, "when, in cases of Rebellion or Invasion the public Safety may require it." This is precisely our present case—a case of Rebellion, wherein the public Safety does require the suspension. Indeed, arrests by process of courts, and arrests in cases of rebellion, do not proceed altogether upon the same basis. The former is directed at the small per centage of ordinary and continuous perpetration of crime; while the latter is directed at sudden and extensive uprisings against the government, which, at most, will succeed or fail, in no great length of time. In the latter case, arrests are made, not so much for what has been done, as for what probably would be done. The latter is more for the preventive, and less for the vindictive, than the former. In such cases the purposes of men are much more easily understood, than in cases of ordinary crime. . . . I think the time not unlikely to come when I shall be blamed for having made too few arrests rather than too many.

By the third resolution the meeting indicate their opinion that military arrests may be constitu-

tional in localities where rebellion actually exists; but that such arrests are unconstitutional in localities where rebellion, or insurrection, does not actually exist. They insist that such arrests shall not be made "outside of the lines of necessary military occupation, and the scenes of insurrection[.]" In asmuch, however, as the constitution itself makes no such distinction, I am unable to believe that there is any such constitutional distinction. I concede that the class of arrests complained of, can be constitutional only when, in cases of Rebellion or Invasion, the public Safety may require them; and I insist that in such cases, they are constitutional *wherever* the public safety does require them—as well in places to which they may prevent the rebellion extending, as in those where it may be already prevailing—as well where they may restrain mischievous interference with the raising and supplying of armies, to suppress the rebellion, as where the rebellion may actually be—as well where they may restrain the enticing men out of the army, as where they would prevent mutiny in the army—equally constitutional at all places where they will conduce to the public Safety, as against the dangers of Rebellion or Invasion.

Take the particular case mentioned by the meeting. They assert in substance that Mr. Vallandigham was by a military commander, seized and tried "for no other reason than words addressed to a public meeting, in criticism of the course of the administration, and in condemnation of the military orders of that general[.]" Now, if there be no mistake about this—if this assertion is the truth and the whole truth—if there was no other reason for the arrest, then I concede that the arrest was wrong. But the arrest, as I understand, was made for a very different reason. Mr. Vallandigham avows his hostility to the war on the part of the Union; and his arrest was made because he was laboring, with some effect, to prevent the raising of troops, to encourage desertions from the army, and to leave the rebellion without an adequate military force to suppress it. He was not arrested because he was damaging the political prospects of the administration, or the personal interests of the commanding general; but because he was damaging the army, upon the existence, and vigor of which, the life of the nation depends. He was warring upon the military; and this gave the military constitutional jurisdiction to lay hands upon him. . . .

I understand the meeting, whose resolutions I am considering, to be in favor of suppressing the rebellion by military force—by armies. Long experience has shown that armies can not be maintained unless desertion shall be punished by the severe penalty of death. The case requires, and the law and the constitution, sanction this punishment. Must I shoot a simple-minded soldier boy who deserts, while I must not touch a hair of a wiley agitator who induces him to desert? . . . I think that in such a case, to silence the agitator, and save the boy, is not only constitutional, but, withal, a great mercy.

It I be wrong on this question of constitutional power, my error lies in believing that certain proceedings are constitutional when, in cases of rebellion or Invasion, the public Safety requires them, which would not be constitutional when, in absence of rebellion or invasion, the public Safety does not require them—in other words, that the constitution is not in it's application in all respects the same, in cases of Rebellion or invasion, involving the public Safety, as it is in times of profound peace and public security. The constitution itself makes the distinction; and I can no more be persuaded that the government can constitutionally take no strong measure in time of rebellion, because it can be shown that the same could not be lawfully taken in time of peace, than I can be persuaded that a particular drug is not good medicine for a sick man, because it can be shown to not be good food for a well one. Nor am I able to appreciate the danger, apprehended by the meeting, that the American people will, by means of military arrests during the rebellion, lose the right of public discussion, the liberty of speech and the press, the law of evidence, trial by Jury, and Habeas corpus, throughout the indefinite peaceful future which I trust lies before them. . . .

6

ABRAHAM LINCOLN

The Heaviest Blow Yet Dealt to the Rebellion (1863)

When local Republicans invited him to address a rally in August 1863 in his hometown of Springfield, Illinois, Lincoln declined but sent the following letter to be read to the meeting. In this letter, addressed to his friend James C. Conkling, Lincoln forcefully defended his policy of emancipation and urged men of all parties to support the war effort. This letter appeared as the 1863 election campaigns in the North were getting under way. There was no state election in Illinois that year, but crucial contests were scheduled in the key states of Ohio, Pennsylvania, and New York, and Lincoln's public letter was as much addressed to residents of states with upcoming elections as to those of his home state.

Executive Mansion,
Washington, August 26, 1863.

Hon. James C. Conkling
My Dear Sir.

. . . There are those who are dissatisfied with me. To such I would say: You desire peace; and you blame me that we do not have it. But how can we attain it? There are but three conceivable ways. First, to suppress the rebellion by force of arms. This, I am trying to do. Are you for it? If you are, so far we are agreed. If you are not for it, a second way is, to give up the Union. I am against this. Are you for it? If you are, you should say so plainly. If you are not for force, nor yet for dissolution, there only remains some imaginable compromise. I do not believe any compromise, embracing the maintenance of the Union, is now possible. All I learn, leads to a directly opposite belief. The strength of the rebellion, is its military—its army. That army dominates all the country, and all the people, within its range. Any offer of terms made by any man or men within that range, in opposition to that army, is simply nothing for the present; because such man or men, have no power whatever to enforce their side of a compromise, if one were made with them. . . . But no paper compromise, to which the controllers of Lee's army are not agreed, can, at all, affect that army. In an effort at such compromise we should waste time, which the enemy would improve to our disadvantage; and that would be all. A compromise, to be effective, must be made either with those who control the rebel army, or with the people first liberated from the domination of that army, by the success of our own army. Now allow me to assure you, that no word or intimation, from that rebel army, or from any of the men controlling it, in relation to any peace compromise, has ever come to my knowledge or belief. All charges and insinuations to the contrary, are deceptive and groundless. And I promise you, that if any such proposition shall

FROM Roy P. Basler, et al., eds., *The Collected Works of Abraham Lincoln*, vol. 6 (New Brunswick, N.J.: Rutgers University Press, 1953), pp. 406–10.

hereafter come, it shall not be rejected, and kept a secret from you. I freely acknowledge myself the servant of the people, according to the bond of service—the United States constitution; and that, as such, I am responsible to them.

But, to be plain, you are dissatisfied with me about the negro. Quite likely there is a difference of opinion between you and myself upon that subject. I certainly wish that all men could be free, while I suppose you do not. Yet I have neither adopted, nor proposed any measure, which is not consistent with even your view, provided you are for the Union. I suggested compensated emancipation; to which you replied you wished not to be taxed to buy negroes. But I had not asked you to be taxed to buy negroes, except in such way, as to save you from greater taxation to save the Union exclusively by other means.

You dislike the emancipation proclamation; and, perhaps, would have it retracted. You say it is unconstitutional—I think differently. I think the constitution invests its commander-in-chief, with the law of war, in time of war. The most that can be said, if so much, is, that slaves are property. Is there—has there ever been—any question that by the law of war, property, both of enemies and friends, may be taken when needed? And is it not needed whenever taking it, helps us, or hurts the enemy? Armies, the world over, destroy enemies' property when they can not use it; and even destroy their own to keep it from the enemy. Civilized belligerents do all in their power to help themselves, or hurt the enemy, except a few things regarded as barbarous or cruel. Among the exceptions are the massacre of vanquished foes, and non-combatants, male and female.

But the proclamation, as law, either is valid, or is not valid. If it is not valid, it needs no retraction. If it is valid, it can not be retracted, any more than the dead can be brought to life. Some of you profess to think its retraction would operate favorably for the Union. Why better *after* the retraction, than *before* the issue? There was more than a year and a half of trial to suppress the rebellion before the proclamation issued, the last one hundred days of which passed under an explicit notice that it was coming, unless averted by those in revolt, returning to their allegiance. The war has certainly progressed as favorably for us, since the issue of the proclamation as before. I know as fully as one can know the opinions of others, that some of the commanders of our armies in the field who have given us our most important successes, believe the emancipation policy, and the use of colored roops, constitute the heaviest blow yet dealt to the rebellion; and that, at least one of those important successes, could not have been achieved when it was, but for the aid of black soldiers. Among the commanders holding these views are some who have never had any affinity with what is called abolitionism, or with republican party politics; but who hold them purely as military opinions. I submit these opinions as being entitled to some weight against the objections, often urged, that emancipation, and arming the blacks, are unwise as military measures, and were not adopted, as such, in good faith.

You say you will not fight to free negroes.

Some of them seem willing to fight for you; but, no matter. Fight you, then, exclusively to save the Union. I issued the proclamation on purpose to aid you in saving the Union. Whenever you shall have conquered all resistance to the Union, if I shall urge you to continue fighting, it will be an apt time, then, for you to declare you will not fight to free negroes.

I thought that in your struggle for the Union, to whatever extent the negroes should cease helping the enemy, to that extent it weakened the enemy in his resistance to you. Do you think differently? I thought that whatever negroes can be got to do as soldiers, leaves just so much less for white soldiers to do, in saving the Union. Does it appear otherwise to you? But negroes, like other people, act upon motives. Why should they do any thing for us, if we will do nothing for them? If they stake their lives for us, they must be prompted by the strongest motive—even the promise of freedom. And the promise being made, must be kept.

7

ABRAHAM LINCOLN

A New Birth of Freedom (1863)

Lincoln spent the war in Washington, rarely leaving the city other than to visit the army in the field. He accepted an invitation, however, to deliver a brief address at the ceremonies on November 20, 1863, dedicating a national military cemetary at Gettysburg. The Gettysburg Address lasted only a couple of minutes, but it is the most famous presidential speech ever delivered. In a few immortal words, Lincoln explained the war's larger purpose.

Four score and seven years ago our fathers brought forth on this continent, a new nation, conceived in Liberty, and dedicated to the proposition that all men are created equal.

Now we are engaged in a great civil war, testing

whether that nation, or any nation so conceived and so dedicated, can long endure. We are met on a great battle-field of that war. We have come to dedicate a portion of that field, as a final resting place for those who here gave their lives that that nation might live. It is altogether fitting and proper that we should do this.

But, in a larger sense, we can not dedicate—we can not consecrate—we can not hallow—this

FROM Roy P. Basler, et al., eds., *The Collected Works of Abraham Lincoln,* vol. 7 (New Brunswick, N.J.: Rutgers University Press, 1953), p. 23.

ground. The brave men, living and dead, who struggled here, have consecrated it, far above our poor power to add or detract. The world will little note, nor long remember what we say here, but it can never forget what they did here. It is for us the living, rather, to be dedicated here to the unfinished work which they who fought here have thus far so nobly advanced. It is rather for us to be here dedicated to the great task remaining before us— that from these honored dead we take increased devotion to that cause for which they gave the last full measure of devotion—that we here highly resolve that these dead shall not have died in vain— that this nation, under God, shall have a new birth of freedom—and that government of the people, by the people, for the people, shall not perish from the earth.

Conscription in the Union (1866)

The following table lists the various drafts conducted by the Union and the disposition of the men called. Because of the stigma attached to being a draftee, the real purpose of conscription was to encourage enlistments. Indeed, the figures for the various Union drafts reveal that few men were actually drafted into service.

Union Drafts, 1863–1865

Call	Drawn	Did Not Report[a]	Examined[a]	Exempted	Held to Service	Commuted	Furnished Substitutes	Drafted
Summer, 1863	292,441	39,415	252,566	164,395	88,171	52,288	26,002	9,881
Spring, 1864	113,446	27,193	84,957	39,952	45,005	32,678	8,911	3,416
Fall, 1864	231,918	66,159	138,536	82,531	56,005	1,298	28,502	26,205
Spring, 1865	139,024	28,477	46,128	28,631	17,497	460	10,192	6,845
Totals	776,829	161,244	522,187	315,509	206,678	86,724	73,607	46,347

[a]Columns 2 and 3 do not equal column 1 because some men who reported were discharged without being examined.

FROM Final Report of the Provost Marshal, *Journal of the House of Representatives*, 39th Cong., 1st sess., 1866, vol. 4, House Exec. Doc. 1, pp. 175, 184, 199, 212.

The New York Press Debates the Causes of the Draft Riots (1863)

The press in mid-nineteenth-century America was intensely partisan, and thus it is not surprising that New York City papers were deeply divided over the nature and causes of the draft riots. Below are editorials from two of the most important dailies in the city, the Times *and the* World.

Edited by Manton Marble, the World *was the regular Democratic organ in the city. It endorsed a war to save the Union but bitterly opposed emancipation and was harshly critical of Lincoln's policies and leadership. It was the most influential Democratic paper in the North. The* World *placed the blame for the riot squarely on Lincoln and the Republican party.*

The Times *represented respectable Republican opinion. Its editor was Henry J. Raymond, the party's national chairman, who was close politically to Secretary of State William Henry Seward. The paper loyally supported the moderate policies of the Lincoln administration. Even though the* Times *was less vehement in its discussion of the riot than other Republican papers in New York City, it strongly condemned the rioters and called for the vigorous use of force to restore order.*

Yesterday's Riot.

New-York yesterday saw the saddest sight that she has ever seen since her first foundation stone was laid. . . . Crowds all day marched hither and thither along the streets, reckless, unguided, with a burning sense of wrong toward the government which has undertaken to choose at random from among them the compulsory soldiers of a misconducted war—with a sense of wrong, we say, but wreaking their wrath cowardly and meanly on defenceless, inoffensive negroes, blindly on property-owners whose buildings chanced to be hired by government officials, senselessly on the policemen whose discipline and power day by day

insure them that security and order which guards their labor and lives. The law-abiding citizen hangs his head with shame that a government can so mismanage a struggle for the life of the nation, so wantonly put itself out of harmony and sympathy with the people, so deny itself the support of those whom it represents and serves, as that . . . here, in the chief city and very heart of the nation, such scenes as those of yesterday can shock the sight. . . .

Will the insensate men at Washington now at length listen to our voice? Will they now give ear to our warnings and adjurations? Will they now believe that Defiance of Law in the rulers breeds Defiance of Law in the people? Does the doctrine proclaimed from the Capitol that in war laws are silent please them put in practice in the streets of New-York? Will they continue to stop their ears

FROM *New York World*, 14 July 1863.

and shut their eyes to the voice and will of a loyal people, which for three long years has told them by every act and every word that this war must be nothing but a war for the Union and the Constitution?

Does Mr. Lincoln now perceive what alienation he has put between himself and the men who three years ago thundered out with one voice in Union square—"The Union, it must and shall be preserved?" These are the very men whom his imbecility, his wanton exercise of arbitrary power, his stretches of ungranted authority have transformed into a mob. At the beginning hundreds of thousands of men went willingly to risk their lives at his and the nation's call. Was it impossible for him so to have rested upon the nation's heart, so to have obeyed the nation's will, that if need were still other hundreds of thousands would have gone forth willingly at his bidding? Who believes it? It was not impossible. What has he and his infatuated party done instead? They have framed a Conscription Act, never tolerable to a free people, unconstitutional beyond any manner of doubt in its provisions if not in its very nature, offensive and most unwise in the method of its enforcement, discriminating between rich and poor, unfair, onerous, and most oppressive here where the attrition of discontent was at its height. Does any man wonder that poor men refuse to be forced into a war mismanaged almost into hopelessness, perverted almost into partisanship? Did the President and his cabinet imagine that their lawlessness could conquer, or their folly seduce, a free people?

The Raging Riot—Its Character, and the True Attitude Toward It.

The mob in our City is still rampant. Though the increasing display of armed force has done something to check its more flagrant outrages, it is yet wild with fury, and panting for fresh havoc. The very fact of its being withstood seems only to

FROM *New York Times*, 15 July 1863.

give it, for the time, new malignity; just as the wild beast never heaves with darker rage than when he begins to see that his way is barred. The monster grows more dangerous as he grows desperate. More than ever, everything depends on the energy and vigilance of the authorities, and the sustaining coöperation of all true men. Official duty and public spirit should supremely rule the hour. The man in public place, or in private place, who falters in this dread crisis should stand accursed.

We trust that Gov. SEYMOUR does not mean to falter. We believe that in his heart he really intends to vindicate the majesty of the law, according to his sworn obligations. But, in the name of the dignity of Government and of public safety, we protest against any further indulgence in the sort of speech with which he yesterday sought to propitiate the mob. Entreaties and promises are not what the day calls for. No official, however high his position, can make them, without bringing public authority into contempt. This monster is to be met with a sword, and that only. He is not to be placated with a sop; and, if he were, it would only be to make him all the more insatiate hereafter. In the name of all that is sacred in law and all that is precious in society, let there be no more of this. There is force enough at the command of Gov. SEYMOUR to maintain civil authority. He will do it. He cannot but do it. He is a ruined man if he fails to do it. This mob is not our master. It is not to be compounded with by paying blackmail. It is not to be supplicated and sued to stay its hand. It is to be defied, confronted, grappled with, prostrated, crushed. The Government of the State of New-York is its master, not its slave; its ruler, and not its minion.

It is too true that there are public journals who try to dignify this mob by some respectable appellation. The *Herald* characterizes it as the people, and the *World* as the laboring men of the City. These are libels that ought to have paralyzed the fingers that penned them. . . .

This mob is not the people, nor does it belong to the people. It is for the most part made up of the very vilest elements of the City. . . . It has not even the poor merit of being what mobs usually are—the product of mere ignorance and passion. They talk, or rather did talk at first, of the oppressiveness of the Conscription law; but three-fourths of those who have been actively engaged in violence have been boys and young men under twenty years of age, and not at all subject to the Conscription. Were the Conscription law to be abrogated to-morrow, the controlling inspiration of the mob would remain all the same. It comes from sources quite independent of that law, or any other—from malignant hate toward those in better circumstances, from a craving for plunder, from a love of commotion, from a barbarous spite against a different race, from a disposition to bolster up the failing fortunes of the Southern rebels. All of these influences operate in greater or less measure upon any person engaged in this general defiance of law; and all combined have generated a composite monster more hellish than the triple-headed Cerberus.

It doubtless is true that the Conscription, or rather its preliminary process, furnished the occasion for the outbreak. This was so, simply because it was the most plausible pretext for commencing open defiance. But it will be a fatal mistake to assume that this pretext has but to be removed to restore quiet and contentment. Even if it be allowed that this might have been true at the outset, it is completely false now. A mob, even though it may start on a single incentive, never sustains itself for any time whatever on any one stimulant. . . .

You may as well reason with the wolves of the forest as with these men in their present mood. It is quixotic and suicidal to attempt it. The duties of the executive officers of this State and City are not to debate, or negotiate, or supplicate, but to *execute the laws*. To execute means to enforce *by authority*. This is their *only* official business. Let it be promptly and sternly entered upon with all the means now available, and it cannot fail of being carried through to an overwhelming triumph of public order. It may cost blood—much of it perhaps; but it will be a lesson to the public enemies, whom we always have and must have in our midst, that will last for a generation. Justice and mercy, this time, unite in the same behest:—*Give them grape, and a plenty of it.*[1]

[1]Grape was an antipersonnel artillery shell.

3

GEORGE TEMPLETON STRONG

Jefferson Davis Rules New York Today (1863)

We have already read portions of George Templeton Strong's diary discussing the popular reaction to the attack on Fort Sumter (see p. 65). In the following entries, Strong describes the draft riots in New York City in July 1863 and the response of the city's political and social elite to the crisis. Strong's upper-class elitism, his hostility to Copperheads, his racism, and his deep disdain for the Irish come through vividly in these passages.

July 13 [*1863*], Monday. A notable day. Stopped at the Sanitary Commission office on my way downtown . . . and heard there of rioting in the upper part of the city. . . . I went to Wall Street nevertheless; but the rumors grew more and more unpleasant, so I left it at once and took a Third Avenue car for uptown. At the Park were groups and small crowds in more or less excitement (which found relief afterwards, I hear, in hunting down and maltreating sundry unoffending niggers), but there was nothing to indicate serious trouble. . . . Above Twentieth Street all shops were closed, and many people standing and staring or strolling uptown, not riotously disposed but eager and curious. Here and there a rough could be heard damning the draft. No policemen to be seen anywhere. Reached the seat of war at last, Forty-sixth Street and Third Avenue. Three houses on the Avenue and two or three on the Street were burned down. . . .

The crowd seemed just what one commonly sees at any fire, but its nucleus of riot was concealed by an outside layer of ordinary peaceable lookers-on. . . . At last, it opened and out streamed a posse of perhaps five hundred, certainly less than one thousand, of the lowest Irish day laborers. The rabble was perfectly homogeneous. Every brute in

the drove was pure Celtic—hod-carrier or loafer. They were unarmed. A few carried pieces of fence-paling and the like. They turned off west into Forty-fifth Street and gradually collected in front of two three-story dwelling houses on Lexington Avenue, just below that street, that stand alone together on a nearly vacant block. Nobody could tell why these houses were singled out. Some said a drafting officer lived in one of them, others that a damaged policeman had taken refuge there. The mob was in no hurry; they had no need to be; there was no one to molest them or make them afraid. The beastly ruffians were masters of the situation and of the city. After a while sporadic paving-stones began to fly at the windows, ladies and children emerged from the rear and had a rather hard scramble over a high board fence, and then scudded off across the open, Heaven knows whither. Then men and small boys appeared at rear windows and began smashing the sashes and the blinds and shied out light articles, such as books and crockery, and dropped chairs and mirrors into the back yard; the rear fence was demolished and loafers were seen marching off with portable articles of furniture. And at last a light smoke began to float out of the windows and I came away. I could endure the disgraceful, sickening sight no longer, and what could I *do*?

The fury of the low Irish women in that region was noteworthy. Stalwart young vixens and with-

FROM Allan Nevins and Milton Halsey Thomas, eds., *The Diary of George Templeton Strong*, vol. 3 (New York: The Macmillan Company, 1952), pp. 335–41.

ered old bags were swarming everywhere, all cursing the "bloody draft" and egging on their men to mischief.

Omnibussed down to No. 828, where is news that the Colored Half Orphan Asylum on Fifth Avenue . . . is burned. "*Tribune* office to be burned tonight."[1] Railroad rails torn up, telegraph wires cut, and so on. If a quarter one hears be true, this is an organized insurrection in the interest of the rebellion and Jefferson Davis rules New York today. . . .

Went to Union League Club awhile. No comfort there. Much talk, but no one ready to do anything whatever, not even to telegraph to Washington.

We telegraphed, two or three of us, from General [John] Wool's rooms, to the President, begging that troops be sent on and stringent measures taken. The great misfortune is that nearly all our militia regiments have been despatched to Pennsylvania. All the military force I have seen or heard of today were in Fifth Avenue at about seven P.M. There were two or three feeble companies of infantry, a couple of howitzers, and a squadron or two of unhappy-looking "dragoons."

These wretched rioters have been plundering freely, I hear. Their outbreak will either destroy the city or damage the Copperhead cause fatally. Could we but catch the scoundrels who have stirred them up, what a blessing it would be! God knows what tonight or tomorrow may bring forth. . . .

July 14 [*1863*]. Eleven P.M. Fire bells clanking, as they have clanked at intervals through the evening. Plenty of rumors throughout the day and evening, but nothing very precise or authentic. There have been sundry collisions between the rabble and the authorities, civil and military. Mob fired upon. It generally runs, but on one occasion appears to have rallied, charged the police and

militia, and forced them back in disorder. The people are waking up, and by tomorrow there will be adequate organization to protect property and life. Many details come in of yesterday's brutal, cowardly ruffianism and plunder. Shops were cleaned out and a black man hanged in Carmine Street, for no offence but that of Nigritude. [Mayor George] Opdyke's house again attacked this morning by a roaming handful of Irish blackguards. . . .

Walked uptown perforce, for no cars and few omnibi were running. They are suppressed by threats of burning railroad and omnibus stables, the drivers being wanted to reinforce the mob. . . . (Here I am interrupted by report of a fire near at hand, and a great glare on the houses across the Park. Sally forth, and find the Eighteenth Ward station house, Twenty-second Street, near First Avenue, in full blaze. A splendid blaze it made, but I did not venture below Second Avenue, finding myself in a crowd of Celtic spectators disgorged by the circumjacent tenement houses. They were exulting over the damage to "them bloody police," and so on. . . .)

A good deal of yelling to the eastward just now. . . . There go two jolly Celts along the street, singing a genuine Celtic howl, something about "Tim O'Laggerty." . . . Long live the sovereigns of New York. . . . Paddy . . . reigns in this promised land of milk and honey and perfect freedom. . . .

July 15 [*1863*]. . . . Morning papers report nothing specially grave as occurring since midnight. But there will be much trouble today. Rabbledom is not yet dethroned any more than its ally and instigator, Rebeldom. . . .

Tonight is quieter than the last, though there seems to be a large fire downtown, and we hear occasional gun-shots. . . .

July 16 [*1863*]. Rather quiet downtown. No trustworthy accounts of riot on any large scale during the day. General talk downtown is that the trouble is over. We shall see. It will be as it pleases the scoundrels who are privily engineering the outbreak—agents of Jefferson Davis, permitted to work here in New York.

Omnibusses and railroad cars in full career

---

[1]Horace Greeley's *New York Tribune* was a notable Republican paper. Its advocacy of the policy of emancipation, support for the rights of northern free blacks, and partisanship made it a special target for the rioters.

again. Coming uptown tonight I find Gramercy Park in military occupation. Strong parties drawn up across Twentieth Street and Twenty-first Streets at the east end of the Square, . . . each with a flanking squad, forming an L. Occasional shots fired at them from the region of Second or First Avenue, which were replied to by volleys that seem to have done little execution. . . .

Never knew exasperation so intense, unqualified, and general as that which prevails against these rioters and the politic knaves who are supposed to have set them going, Governor [Horatio] Seymour not excepted. Men who voted for him mention the fact with contrition and self-abasement, and the Democratic Party is at a discount with all the people I meet. . . .

It is not clear that the resources of the conspiracy are yet exhausted. The rioters of yesterday were better armed and organized than those of Monday, and their inaction today may possibly be meant to throw us off our guard, or their time may be employed perfecting plans for a campaign of plundering and brutality in yet greater force. They are in full possession of the western and the eastern sides of the city, from Tenth Street upward, and of a good many districts beside. I could not walk four blocks eastward from this house this minute without peril. . . .

July 19 [*1863*], Sunday. . . . Not half the history of this memorable week has been written. I could put down pages of incidents that the newspapers have omitted, any one of which would in ordinary times be the town's talk. Men and ladies attacked and plundered by daylight in the streets; private houses suddenly invaded by gangs of a dozen ruffians and sacked, while the women and children run off for their lives. Then there is the unspeakable infamy of the nigger persecution. They are the most peaceable, sober, and inoffensive of our poor. . . . This is a nice town to call itself a centre of civilization! Life and personal property less safe than in Tipperary, and the "people" (as the *Herald* calls them) burning orphan asylums and conducting a massacre. . . .

I am sorry to find that England is right about the lower class of Irish. They are brutal, base, cruel, cowards, and as insolent as base. . . .

July 20 [*1863*]. . . . Talking with Americans of the middle and laboring class, even of the lowest social grade, I find they fully appreciate and bitterly resent these Celtic outrages. . . . The Germans have behaved well and kept quiet. Where they acted at all, they volunteered against the rabble, as they did, most effectively, in the Seventh Ward. . . . For myself, personally, I would like to see war made on Irish scum as in 1688.

4

J. W. C. PENNINGTON

This Country Also Belongs to Us (1863)

In the following speech, delivered in Poughkeepsie, New York, on August 14, 1863, the black leader Dr. J. W. C. Pennington discussed the New York City draft riots and their lessons. Blaming the foreign-born for the violence, Pennington stressed the importance of antiblack racism in these disturbances, and carefully identified African Americans with the country and the cause of the Union.

The elements of this mob have been centering and gathering strength in New York, for more than two years. And, as soon as the rebellion broke out, . . . and as it became evident that our sympathies were with the Federal government, we became objects of more marked abuse and insult. From many of the grocery corners, stones, potatoes, and pieces of coal, would often be hurled, by idle young loafers, standing about. . . . The language addressed to colored men, not seemly to record on paper, became the common language of the street, and even of some of the fashionable avenues. . . . In no other country in the world would the streets of refined cities be allowed to be polluted, as those of New-York have been, with foul and indecent language, without a word of the rebuke from the press, the pulpit, or the authorities. . . . What has been the result? Why, just what we might have expected,—the engendering of a public feeling unfriendly toward colored people. This feeling, once created, might at any moment be intensified into an outbreak against its unoffending objects. . . .

The opposition to the draft comes largely from that class of men of foreign birth who had declared their intention to become citizens, but who have not done so. They have been duly notified that they could leave the country within sixty days, or submit to the draft. . . . They do not wish to leave the country, and they do not wish to fight. . . .

Dishonest politicians aim to make these men believe that the war has been undertaken to abolish slavery; and so far as they believe so, their feelings are against colored people. . . .

Let the greedy foreigner know that a part of this country BELONGS TO US; and that we assert the right to live and labor here: That in New York and other cities, we claim the right to buy, hire, occupy and use houses and tenements, for legal considerations; to pass and repass on the streets, lanes, avenues, and all public ways. Our fathers have fought for this country, and helped to free it from the British yoke. We are now fighting to help to free it from the combined conspiracy of Jeff. Davis and Co.; we are doing so with the distinct understanding, that WE ARE TO LEAVE ALL OUR RIGHTS AS MEN AND AS CITIZENS, and, that there are to be no side issues, no RESERVATIONS, either political, civil, or religious. In this struggle we know nothing but God, Manhood, and American Nationality, full and unimpaired. . . .

For all the purposes, therefore, of social, civil, and religious enjoyment, and right, we hold New York solemnly bound to insure us, as citizens, permanent security in our homes. Relief, and damage money, is well enough. But it cannot atone, fully, for evils done by riots. It cannot bring back our murdered dead. It cannot remove the insults we feel; and finally, it gives no proof that the people have really changed their minds, for the better towards us.

FROM *Principia*, 7–14 January 1864.

5

ANONYMOUS

A Rioter Condemns the $300 Commutation Fee
(1863)

The following letter, allegedly written by one of the rioters, attacked the controversial $300 commutation fee as an instrument of class privilege. There is no way of knowing whether the author was a participant in the riot, but this letter accurately reflected the belief among many workers that the draft was unfair and that the war was a poor man's fight.

A Letter from one of the Rioters.

Monday Night   Up Town

To the Editor of the New-York Times:

You will, no doubt, be hard on us rioters tomorrow morning, but that 300-dollar law has made us nobodies, vagabonds and cast-outs of society, for whom nobody cares when we must go to war and be shot down. We are the poor rabble, and the rich rabble is our enemy by this law. Therefore we will give our enemy battle right here, and ask no quarter. Although we got hard fists, and are dirty without, we have soft hearts, and have clean consciences within, and that's the reason we love our wives and children more than the rich, because we got not much besides them; and we will not go and leave them at home for to starve. Until that draft law is repealed, I for one am willing to knock down more such rum-hole politicians as [Police Superintendent John] KENNEDY. Why don't they let the nigger kill the slave-driving race and take possession of the South, as it belongs to them.

A POOR MAN, BUT A MAN FOR ALL THAT.

FROM *New York Times*, 15 July 1863.

6

The *New York Evening Post*
Defends the $300 Commutation Fee (1863)

When Congress instituted conscription in the Union, it provided that anyone subject to military service who paid a $300 commutation fee could avoid being conscripted in the current (although not future) draft calls. Along with substitution, which allowed a draftee to hire someone to take his place in the army, commutation was a very controversial policy. Democrats charged that it allowed the rich and well-born *to avoid military service, while poor working men and farmers, who were unable to pay the commutation fee, were increasingly swept up by the draft. In a discussion of conscription, the* New York Evening Post, *a Republican journal, defended the equity of commutation.*

The Evening Post *was edited by the famous poet and author William Cullen Bryant, and it had a number of famous journalists and literati on its staff. Originally a Democratic journal, it had championed the city's workers and defended the rights of the foreign-born against nativist prejudice, but its strong opposition to the expansion of slavery caused it to endorse the new Republican party in the 1850s. During the war, the paper vigorously supported making emancipation a Union war aim and vehemently assailed the Copperhead movement.*

The Enrollment Law

. . . Concerning the three hundred dollar exemption clause there is much difference of opinion; we still hold the belief, after considerable inquiry, that it should be retained. There is no doubt that it is a boon to the large middle class of industrious mechanics and farmers, who, just beginning life, with families of young children dependent upon them, cannot, in many cases, serve under arms without serious distress to those whom they leave unprovided for at home. Almost every one of this class whose presence at home is really necessary to his family, can raise a sum of three hundred dollars to secure his exemption. But repeal this clause, and force every man to go or procure a substitute, and these men become at once the prey of sharpers and brokers, or are compelled, at every sacrifice, to serve in person. Now this class, which mainly carries on the varied industry of the free states and creates their prosperity, deserves the most careful consideration at the hands of legislators.

The question to be settled is, whether the government shall engage, for a stated sum, to procure substitutes, or whether it shall throw this burden upon those who are drafted. Now if it were difficult or impossible for the government to procure men for the sums it receives under the exemption clause, then it might be urged that this should be done by those persons upon whom the draft falls. But it so happens that there is little or no trouble upon this point. We suggested, some time ago, that some of the states which find it hard to fill their quotas should apply to the general government for permission to recruit among the freedmen in the southern states. It is amongst these that the Provost Marshal General can easily get substitutes for those who pay the exemption fee. We speak now of the blacks in the states over which the Proclamation extends. . . .

Moreover, experience has shown that the characters who offer themselves in the North as substitutes are the lowest and vilest of the population. They cheat those who engage them; cheat the government by running away when they can; and are a vicious element, not fit to form a part of our armies.

For these reasons we hold that the three hundred dollar exemption clause should be retained in the law.

FROM *New York Evening Post,* 19 December 1863.

7

CORNELIA HANCOCK

A Union Nurse at Gettysburg (1863)

When her brother-in-law, who was an army doctor, asked her to help following the Battle of Gettysburg, Cornelia Hancock volunteered to be a Union nurse. A New Jersey Quaker, she was twenty-three years of age when she arrived at Gettysburg to relieve the suffering and care for the wounded. She had intended to work in the hospitals only a short time, but she found the work both patriotic and personally satisfying and ended up working as a nurse for the duration of the war, rejecting her family's entreaties to return home. As a result of her Civil War experiences, Hancock made nursing her vocation, and after the war she worked with southern blacks and among the poor of Philadelphia.

Gettysburg—July 8, 1863

My Dear Sister

We have been two days on the field; go out about eight and come in about six—go in ambulances or army buggies. . . . I feel assured I shall never feel horrified at anything that may happen to me hereafter. There is a great want of surgeons here; there are hundreds of brave fellows, who have not had their wounds dressed since the battle. Brave is not the word; more, more Christian fortitude never was witnessed than they exhibit, always say— "Help my neighbor first he is worse." The Second Corps did the heaviest fighting, and, of course, all who were badly wounded, were in the thickest of the fight, and, therefore, we deal with the very best class of the men—that is the bravest. . . . The reason why they suffer more in this battle is because our army is victorious and marching on after Lee, leaving the wounded for citizens and a very few surgeons. The citizens are stripped of everything they have, so you must see the exhausting state of

FROM Henrietta S. Jacquette, ed., *South after Gettysburg: Letters of Cornelia Hancock from the Army of the Potomac* (New York: Thomas Y. Crowell, 1956), pp. 8–12.

affairs. The Second Army Corps alone had two thousand men wounded, this I had from the Surgeon's head quarters.

. . . I hope you will write. It would be very pleasant to have letters to read in the evening, for I am so tired I cannot write them. Get the Penn Relief to send clothing here; there are many men without anything but a shirt lying in poor shelter tents, calling on God to take them from this world of suffering; in fact the air is rent with petitions to deliver them from their sufferings. . . .

I do not know when I shall go home—it will be according to how long this hospital stays here and whether another battle comes soon. . . . The Christian Committee support us and when they get tired the Sanitary [Commission] is on hand. Uncle Sam is very rich, but very slow, and if it were not for the Sanitary, much suffering would ensue. . . . Old sheets we would give much for. Bandages are plenty but sheets very scarce. We have plenty of woolen blankets now, in fact the hospital is well supplied, but for about five days after the battle, the men had no blankets nor scarce[ly] any shelter.

It took nearly five days for some three hundred surgeons to perform the amputations that occurred here, during which time the rebels lay in a dying condition without their wounds being dressed or scarcely any food. . . . One man died this morning. I fixed him up as nicely as the place will allow; he will be buried this afternoon. We are becoming somewhat civilized here now and the men are cared for well.

. . . We have some plucky boys in the hospital, but they suffer awfully. One had his leg cut off yesterday, and some of the ladies, newcomers, were up to see him. I told them if they had seen as many as I had they would not go far to see the sight again. I could stand by and see a man's head taken off I believe—you get so used to it here. I should be perfectly contented if I could receive my letters. I have the cooking all on my mind pretty much. I have torn almost all my clothes off of me, and Uncle Sam has given me a new suit. William says I am very popular here as I am such a contrast to some of the office-seeking women who swarm around hospitals. I am black as an Indian and dirty as a pig and as well as I ever was in my life—have a nice bunk and tent about twelve feet square. . . .

The suffering we get used to and the nurses and doctors, stewards, etc., are very jolly and sometimes we have a good time. . . . There is all in getting to do what you *want* to do and I am doing that.

Pads are terribly needed here. Bandages and lint are plenty. I would like to see seven barrels of dried rusk [sweetened bread] here. I do not know the day of the week or anything else. Business is slackening a little though—order is beginning to reign in the hospital and soon things will be right. One poor fellow is hollowing fearfully now while his wounds are being dressed.

There is no more impropriety in a *young* person being here provided they are sensible than a sexagenarian. Most polite and obliging are all the soldiers to me.

. . . All is well with me; we do not know much war news, but I know I am doing all I can, so I do not concern [myself] further. Kill the copperheads. Write everything, however trifling, it is all interest here.

From thy affectionate

C. Hancock

8

HARPER'S MONTHLY

The Fortunes of War (1864)

The northern economy boomed during the war, fueling both great profits and lavish expenditures. Those fortunate enough to receive war contracts garnered huge profits, and for the dishonest who sold inferior goods the profits were even greater. The following article from Harper's Monthly *took a critical look at business in wartime and condemned the lavish spending that the war's prosperity stimulated. This self-indulgence was most noticeable in New York City, but similar complaints were voiced in other commercial centers, such as Chicago, during the war.*

The Fortunes of War.
How They Are Made and Spent.

The strangest and most frequently repeated boasts—for boasts we make, such is our national vanity, on all occasions whether of prosperity or adversity—is that *we don't feel this war.* Above the shock of battle, the groans of the wounded and dying, the sobs of the bereaved, the murmurs of defeat, and the shouts of victory, rises the triumphant exclamation, *We don't feel it!* Is this insensibility? Is it the delight in ruin? Is it indifference to failure or success? No! It is worse than either of these, for it embraces them all; it is the chuckling of gain over its pockets filling with the treasure of the country, while our brave soldiers are pouring out their blood in its defense.

We don't feel the war! is the exulting cry of the contractors, money-changers, and speculators, whose shouts of revel stifle the tearful voice of misery. It is in our large cities especially where this boasted insensibility to the havoc of war is found. It is there in the market-place and exchange, where fortunes are being made with such marvelous rapidity, and in the haunts of pleasure, where they are being spent with such wanton extravagance, that *they don't feel this war.* They are at a banquet of abundance and delight, from which they are not to be unseated, though the ghosts of the hundreds of thousands of their slaughtered countrymen shake their gory locks at them.

While the national wealth has been poured out with a profuse generosity in behalf of a cause dear to the national heart, there have been immense fortunes made by enterprising money-getters, seeking only to fill their own pockets.

When the war suddenly burst upon the nation, and before it was able to arouse its gigantic energies, the Government was so helpless that it besought aid at any cost. It was then, as our brave fellow-citizens came forward in multitudes to defend their country, there arose an urgent demand for arms, clothing, and subsistence. Every thing re-

FROM *Harper's Monthly* 29 (July 1864): 227–31.

quired for the use and consumption of the soldier was wanted, and wanted at once. Tents and blankets to protect him from the weather—clothes, from cap to shoe, to dress him—bread and meat and all the varied necessaries of the daily ration, even to the salt, to feed him—the knapsack, haversack, belt, and cartridge box, to equip him—muskets, pistols, cannon, swords, sabres, powder, shot, and percussion caps to fight with—horses and mules, wagons, railways, steam and sailing vessels of all kinds, for transportation.

A hundred thousand men or more in the immediate and continued want not only of all the ordinary necessaries of life, but of the many additional requirements for war, were to be provided for without delay. . . . Another army—the army of contractors—then came forward no less promptly than the hundred thousands of citizen soldiers. These with their lives as their offering asking nothing in exchange, and receiving only a bare subsistence; the former, no less liberal of the contents of their docks, ships, fields, stables, granaries, warehouses, and shops, demanding a great price, and getting it.

Think of the immense activity with which trade was inspired by the numerous and multifarious demands of the Government! Contractors for meat, contractors for bread, contractors for tents, contractors for clothing, contractors for arms, contractors for ammunition, contractors for equipments, contractors for wagons, contractors for horses, contractors for mules, contractors for forage, contractors for railway conveyance, contractors for steamers, contractors for ships, contractors for coal, contractors for hospitals, contractors for surgical instruments, contractions for drugs, and contractors for every thing else required for human use and consumption in order not only to sustain life but to destroy it, suddenly started into existence. The Government, pressed by a necessity which admitted of no hesitation in regard to time, character, quantity, quality, and cost, accepted almost every offer, and paid almost any price. It is true, that political allies and social friends and relatives were favored with the earliest information and the best places in the general race and scramble for the national treasure. . . .

The contractors of all kinds, with their contracts signed and sealed, hastened to pocket the profits. In many cases, with a mere dash of their pens, they transfered their bargains at an advance, and made snug fortunes, without the labor of an hour or the expense of a shilling. In other instances they fulfilled their contracts in a way more profitable to themselves than useful to the Government. The quality of the article they heeded little, provided it bore the name and the semblance of the thing, and could be had for almost nothing, or for much less than they were to receive for it. Thus *shoddy*, a villainous compound, the refuse stuff and sweepings of the shop, pounded, rolled, glued, and smoothed to the external form and gloss of cloth, but no more like the genuine article than the shadow is to the substance, was hastily got up, at the smallest expense, and supplied to the Government at the greatest. Our soldiers, on the first day's march, or in the earliest storm, found their clothes, over-coats, and blankets, scattering to the winds in rags, or dissolving into their primitive elements of dust under the pelting rain. . . . *Shoddy*, with the external gloss and form of a substantial thing but with the inherent weakness and solubility of its reflected image, has ever since become a word, in the vocabulary of the people, always quick in their forcible and incisive rhetoric to catch and appropriate a simple and expressive figure to represent a familiar idea. The ostentatious *nouveau riche,* the fraudulent contractor who makes a display of his ill-gotten gains, and vulgar pretenders of all kinds, will forever, in the popular eye, bear upon their emblazoned coaches, the fronts of their palatial residences, the liveries of their coachmen, and on their own backs of superfine cloths and glistening silks, the broad mark SHODDY. . . .

It was not only in the contracts for clothing, but in those for almost every other supply that Government paying for the substance was mocked by the shadow. For sugar it often got sand; for coffee, rye; for leather, something no better than brown paper; for sound horses and mules, spavined beasts and dying donkeys; and for serviceable muskets and pistols the experimental failures of sanguine inventors, or the refuse of shops and foreign armories. There was, it is true, a show of caution on the part of the authorities in the form of a Governmental inspection; but the object of this was often thwarted by haste, negligence, collusion, or favoritism. . . .

There were fifty millions of dollars spent by the Government in a few months, at the beginning of the war, for arms alone. Out of this a dozen or more contractors enriched themselves for life. Poor men thus became rich between the rising and setting of the same day's sun; while the hundreds of thousands of dollars of the wealthy increased to millions in the same brief space of time. It is said that one of our great merchant princes gained from his transactions with Government two millions of dollars in a single year.

The proprietors of coal-mines came in for a large share of the national treasure. One company made such enormous profits from its supplies of coal to the Government, and the general rise in price in consequence of the increased demand, that it was enabled to declare, in a single year, dividends that, in the aggregate, amounted to two-thirds of its capital. Its stock, which a few years since could hardly tempt a purchaser at ten dollars a share, has arisen since the war to more than two hundred dollars, and is eagerly caught up at that price. . . .

The "good time" of the contractors has, however, now gone. The Government, with the experience of three years' war, and with its commissariat thoroughly organized, is no longer at the mercy of the fraudulent and extortionate. In fact, it is said that in some later contracts the Government, more thanks to its luck than shrewdness, has, with the depreciation of the currency and the consequent rise in prices, got the best of the bargain.

As fortunes can be no longer made in a day out of the national treasury the eager money-seekers have taken to the stock exchange to make them out of each other. The rage of speculation—excitement is too mild a word—which has seized upon the community, and is fast making us a nation of stock-jobbers, has never been equaled since the days of John Law during the French regency of the Duc d'Orleans. The city exchanges and their approaches are already crowded with a frenzied throng of eager speculators. . . . Streets are blocked up by a mass so frenzied by the general passion for gain that almost all regard for individual safety and respect for personal propriety seems lost. . . .

The passion for stock-gambling is fast extending to every class of society. Merchants, mechanics, and traders of all kinds are abandoning their counting-houses, their work-shops, and their stalls, and thronging into Wall Street. The daily industry, the constant self-denial, the vigilant prudence, and the patient expectation necessary to acquire a decent competence are scorned for the chances of making a fortune in a day. The number of brokers has more than quadrupled in a few months, such has been the enormous increase of stock-jobbing. Their aggregate business, in the city of New York alone, has arisen from twenty-five to more than a hundred millions a day. . . .

The old proverb says: "That which comes easy goes easy." The suddenly enriched contractors, speculators, and stock-jobbers illustrate its truth. They are spending money with a profusion never before witnessed in our country, at no time remarkable for its frugality. Our great houses are not big enough for them; they pull them down and build greater. . . .

These Sybarites of "shoddy" buy finer furniture than was ever bought before, and dress in costlier cloths and silks than have been hitherto imported. No foreign luxury, even at the present enormous prices, is too dear for their exorbitant desires and swollen pockets. The importations of the country have arisen to the large amount of thirty millions of dollars a month, chiefly to satisfy the increased appetite for luxurious expense. . . .

If this extravagance and wantonness were confined to the fools of fortune we might leave them to the exhaustion that must come from this waste of means and perversion of the faculties of mind and body. Their ruin would be hardly felt or regretted. But, unfortunately, our people are so imitative that when one simpleton, provided he be rich, leads the way, all follow. Every man and woman thinks he must do as his wealthy neighbor does. The consequence is already shown in the general prevalence of extravagance and dissipation. The shops of the dry-goods man, the jeweler, the dealer in carpets and cabinet-ware, and the gilded establishments of the restaurateur were never so crowded. The tradesman hardly shows any but his most expensive wares, which his greedy customer snatches up without solicitation. Thus camel's-hair shawls, at fifteen hundred dollars or more, go off briskly at the price; rivers of diamonds . . . flow unchecked by any regard for cost. Aubusson and tapestry carpets of fabulous expense are bought unhesitatingly and recklessly trod upon, and dinners are eaten and wine drunk at Delmonico's and the *Maison Dorée* at a price *per* head, in a single sitting, which would support a soldier and his family for a good portion of the year. . . .

Apart from the fatal and permanent effect of the habit of expense and sensual indulgence upon the individual and national character, it may have a disastrous influence upon the war. While the passion for speculation is raging, and the means for gratifying the appetite for luxury and pleasure are abounding, the war is not felt, and is willingly concurred in. Let, however, the reaction come, as it surely will, when fortunes shall scatter more rapidly than they have been gathered, and abundance and delight be no longer so easily purchasable, then the sensibility of our luxurious citizens may be so awakened as to feel the war, and feel it so much that they may wish it at an end before its great purpose is accomplished. . . . Are we deluding ourselves with the idea that this war is to be a continued carnival of abundance and pleasure? If so, we had better awaken at once to the fact that it is a sacrifice demanding the utmost effort of patient endurance. No noble cause, such as we are struggling for, was ever won by men while besotting themselves with excess and dallying pleasure. We must feel this war, and feel it resolutely, or we shall never triumph.

9

Working Women Protest Their Low Wages (1865)

A group of women in Cincinnati, Ohio, who supported themselves by sewing sent the following protest to Abraham Lincoln, complaining of the low wages they received for doing war work while contractors made an exorbitant profit from war contracts. Inflation significantly reduced workers' wartime wages in the North.

Cincinnati, O., Feb. 20, 1865.

To His Excellency, Abraham Lincoln, President of the United States:

The undersigned, wives, widows, sisters, and friends of the soldiers in the army of the United States, depending upon our own labor for bread, sympathizing with the Government of the United States, and loyal to it, beg leave to call the attention of the Government, through his Excellency the President, to the following statement of facts:

1. We are willing and anxious to do the work required by the Government for clothing and equipping the armies of the United States, at the prices paid by the Government.

2. We are unable to sustain life for the price offered by contractors, who fatten on their contracts by grinding immense profits out of the labor of their operatives. As an example, the contractors are paid one dollar and seventy-five cents per dozen for making gray woolen shirts, and they require us to make them for one dollar per dozen. This is a sample of the justice meted out to us, the willing laborers, without whom the armies could not be promptly clothed and equipped.

We most respectfully request that the Government, through the proper officers of the Quartermaster's Department, issue the work required directly to us, we giving ample security for the prompt and faithful execution of the work and return of the same at the time required, and in good order.

We are in no way actuated by a spirit of faction, but desirous of aiding the best government on earth, and at the same time securing justice to the humble laborer.

The manufacture of pants, blouses, coats, drawers, tents, tarpaulins, etc., exhibits the same irregularity and injustice to the operative. Under the system of direct employment of the operative by the Government, we had no difficulty, and the Government, we think, was served equally well.

We hope that the Government, in whose justice we have all confidence, will at once hear us and heed our humble prayer, and we will ever pray, etc.

FROM *Fincher's Trade Review*, 18 March 1865. In *A Documentary History of American Industrial Society*, vol. 9, ed. John R. Commons (Cleveland: A. H. Clarke Company, 1910–1911), pp. 22–23.

10

HARPER'S MONTHLY

Wall Street in Wartime (1865)

Huge government expenditures and the printing of large amounts of paper money stimulated speculation in the North during the war. The price of stocks, bonds, and gold fluctuated with the Union's military situation, tempting individuals to invest in expectation of future price swings. Caught up in the mania, people from all walks of life joined traders and capitalists in the orgy of buying and selling on Wall Street, where stocks traded at a feverish pace. In the following essay, Harper's Monthly *described the speculative fever that gripped Wall Street during the war, and the vast fortunes that could be made as a result.*

The battle of Bull Run," said a late eminent financier, . . . "the battle of Bull Run makes the fortune of every man in Wall Street who is not a natural idiot."

He foresaw a long war, great expenditures, and consequently, taxes being almost unknown, vast issues of paper-money, with their inevitable results, namely, active speculation, an advance in the price of all articles exchangeable for money, and unparalleled vicissitudes of fortune. And he went to work and bought 75,000 shares of stock on the spot. It was moderate, under the circumstances, considering the low prices of stocks, and the improving condition of the railways, to look for an average advance of twenty per cent. This would give him a profit of $1,500,000. But the advance would probably be nearer forty than twenty. Forty would give him three millions. With that he would for the present remain satisfied. . . .

Paper-money brought every one into Wall Street, and interested every family in the ups and downs of stocks. It circulated like fertilizing dew throughout the land, generating enterprise, facilitating industry, developing internal trade; the

railways found their business increase beyond their most sanguine expectations; dividend-paying roads had extra profits to divide; embarrassed enterprises cleared off their debts, and became lucrative to their owners; every body wanted to own railway property. Within a few weeks after the first issue of legal tenders, stocks began to rise, and rose steadily, with slight interruptions, till April, 1864, when Mr. Chase, by selling his surplus gold for legal tenders, created an unexpected money panic, and the whole fabric of stock speculation toppled to the earth, overwhelming in the ruin thousands of unlucky operators.

It is keeping within bounds to say that $250,000,000—in paper-money—was realized as profits by the operators in stocks between 1862 and 1864. The difference between the aggregate price of the railroad and miscellaneous shares and bonds dealt in on our Stock Exchange at mid-summer, 1862, and the price of the same securities on 1st August, 1864, is more than that sum. Many popular shares rose 300 per cent.

This profit was divided among many thousands of people. In 1863, and in the first quarter of 1864, every body seemed to be speculating in stocks. Nothing else was talked of at clubs, in the streets, at the theatres, in drawing-rooms. Ladies

FROM *Harper's Monthly* 29 (April 1865): 615–16.

privately pledged their diamonds as margin with brokers, and astonished their husbands with the display of their gains. Clergymen staked their salary, and some of them realized in a few months more than they could have made by a lifetime of preaching. One man, who had nothing in the world but a horse, sent him to a broker's stable, and persuaded the broker to buy him a hundred shares; he drew from the broker, a few months after, a balance of $300,000. . . . Two or three different people realized a handsome competency by hiring a convenient room for stock gamblers to meet in, and charging a moderate entrance-fee. . . .

The labors and profits of the brokers were enormous. One house checked more than once for $4,000,000 in a day. A day's commissions, in the case of a leading firm, were not unfrequently $5000. Nearly all the leading members of the board lost their voices from constant bawling, and talked in the evening as though they were in the last stage of bronchitis; clerks seldom left their offices before 11 or 12 P.M., a liberal dinner at Delmonico's being allowed by their employers as a stimulus to exertion. The day was not long enough for the gamblers.

At half past 8 A.M. they began to collect in William Street, and by half past 10 the police could hardly keep the thoroughfare open. All day long the crowd ebbed and flowed between the boards and the street, shouting, screaming, swearing, quarreling, tussling, and not a few of them cheating and lying. A man-milliner from up-town, of short stature but prodigious lungs, was always a leading personage in the crowd: his bids rose like muffled thunder from under other men's coat-tails. The little rogue made $100,000, and went off to Europe with it, to study, as he said, "de newe fashions for my emporium." When evening fell the throng adjourned to the Fifth Avenue Hotel, and, the rooms adjacent, which were hired for the purpose. There night was made hideous by discordants bids and offers—often till every one in the neighborhood was or wished to be asleep. The Fifth Avenue Board, on an exciting night, was probably the nearest approach to Pandemonium we can hope to witness on this earth.

1

MONTGOMERY ADVERTISER

Slavery Is a Tower of Strength to the South (1861)

In the following editorial, written early in the war, the Montgomery Advertiser *explained how slavery benefited the Confederate war effort. Certainly the institution of slavery allowed for a greater mobilization of white men of military age in the Confederacy. But as this editorial reveals, southern whites at the beginning of the conflict underestimated the ways in which the war would loosen the bonds of slavery and thereby disrupt the southern economy.*

The total white population of the eleven States now comprising the confederacy is 6,000,000, and therefore to fill up the ranks of the proposed army (600,000) about ten per cent of the entire white population will be required. In any other country but our own such a draft could not be met, but the Southern States can furnish that number of men, and still not leave the material interests of the country in a suffering condition. Those who are incapacitated for bearing arms can oversee the plantation, and the Negroes can go on undisturbed in their usual labors. In the North, the case is different; the men who join the army of subjugation are the laborers, the producers and the factory operatives. Nearly every man from that section, especially those from the rural districts, leaves some branch of industry to suffer during his absence. The institution of slavery in the South alone enables her to place in the field a force much larger in proportion to her white population [than] in the North. The institution is a tower of strength to the South, particularly at the present crisis, and our enemies will be likely to find that the "moral cancer" about which their orators are so fond of prating, is really one of the most effective weapons employed against the union by the South.

FROM *Montgomery Advertiser*, 6 November 1861.

2

SAMUEL L. HOLT

Slave Owners Ought to Bear the Principal Burden of the War (1863)

The war and its mounting hardships placed heavy strains on the traditional class structure of the South. In 1863 impressment officers seized the horse of Samuel L. Holt, a farmer in Randolph County, North Carolina. In response, he fired off an angry letter attacking the impressment law and the entire system of class relations in the Confederacy.

Randolph County
May 24 1863

Govr. Z. Vance

This County has sent many true men to this piratical war and deserves some forbearance on the part of the public authorities. The small number of slaves leaves the amo[un]t of labor for agricultural purposes comparatively much less than in a very large number of the Counties of N.C. The truth is the slave owners ought to bear the principal burden of the war, if not the whole of it. Those who make the law have managed very *notably* to screen their *own carcasses* from Yankee bullets & have made it literally a *Poor-Man's War*. The coxcombs, cowards & puppies among the young dandies of this badly governed land figure largely in the *peace* and *safety* or *back-door* department of the War Service. The last act of this miserable farce is to send unsaddled partisan rangers or runaways—horseless dragoons & would be worthless cavalry out upon the poor farmers of the county—to seize the best of the few remaining horses that they have to cultivate their crops. . . .

This morning . . . a poor man complains that the only horse he had to plough his field was taken from him by a press gang with the usual terms of Billingsgate lexicography. It is not sufficient to take his property without his consent—without adequate consideration; but threats & abuse must be added to legalise the infamous Act. In War the law is silent is the grand axiom to justify every thing. These are not ordinary times—the *Higher Law* to be judged of by selfishness, extortion & villainy of all sorts is the order of the day. Let the antidote be applied from the proceeds of Cuffy's[1] labor & the sale of Cuffy's carcass. Go to the slave holder and draw upon him for his horses & his means first & afterwards upon the poor laboror [*sic*] of North Carolina. . . .

Respy your Obt Servt

Saml. L. Holt

FROM Samuel L. Holt to Zebulon Vance, May 24, 1863, Zebulon Vance Papers, North Carolina Division of Archives and History.

[1]Cuffy was a generic term for slave.

3

A Resident Observes the Richmond Bread Riot
(1863)

The high price of food precipitated a number of riots in different parts of the Confederacy. The largest and most serious occurred on April 2, 1863, in the capital of Richmond, where several thousand people, mostly women, broke into and looted bakeries, groceries, and other stores in the business district before being dispersed by troops.

Sara Rice Pryor was the wife of Roger A. Pryor, a former congressman who was an editor in Richmond and a Confederate Army officer. She included in her published reminiscences the letters of a lifelong friend, who was living in Richmond during the war and whose husband was a colonel in the Confederate Army. Since her friend wished to avoid any notoriety, Sara concealed her identity, referring to her only as "Agnes." In the following letter from Richmond, dated April 4, 1863, "Agnes" recounts a personal interview she had with a young girl who participated in the bread riot in the city.

My Dear:

I hope you appreciate the fact that you are herewith honored with a letter written in royal-red ink upon sumptuous gilt-edged paper. There is not, at the present writing, one inch of paper for sale in the capital of the Confederacy, at all within the humble means of the wife of a Confederate officer. Well is it for her—and I hope for you—that her youthful admirers were few, and so her gorgeous cream-and-gold album was only half filled with tender effusions. Out come the blank leaves, to be divided between her friend and her Colonel. Don't be alarmed at the color of the writing. I have not yet dipped my goose-quill (there are no steel pens) in the "ruddy drops that visit my sad heart,"

nor yet into good orthodox red ink. There are fine oaks in the country, and that noble tree bears a gall-nut filled with crimson sap. One lies on my table, and into its sanguinary heart I plunge my pen.

Something very sad has just happened in Richmond—something that makes me ashamed of all my jeremiads over the loss of the petty comforts and conveniences of life—hats, bonnets, gowns, stationery, books, magazines, dainty food. Since the weather has been so pleasant, I have been in the habit of walking in the Capitol Square before breakfast every morning. Somehow nothing so sets me up after a restless night as a glimpse of the dandelions waking up from their dewy bed and the songs of the birds in the Park. Yesterday, upon arriving, I found within the gates a crowd of women and boys—several hundreds of them, standing quietly together. I sat on a bench near, and one of

FROM Sara Rice Pryor, *Reminiscences of Peace and War* (New York: Macmillan Company, 1904), pp. 237–39.

the number left the rest and took the seat beside me. She was a pale, emaciated girl, not more than eighteen, with a sunbonnet on her head, and dressed in a clean calico gown. "I could stand no longer," she explained. As I made room for her, I observed that she had delicate features and large eyes. Her hair and dress were neat. As she raised her hand to remove her sunbonnet and use it for a fan, her loose calico sleeve slipped up, and revealed the mere skeleton of an arm. She perceived my expression as I looked at it, and hastily pulled down her sleeve with a short laugh. "This is all that's left of me!" she said. "It seems real funny, don't it?" Evidently she had been a pretty girl—a dressmaker's apprentice, I judged from her chafed forefinger and a certain skill in the lines of her gown. I was encouraged to ask: "What is it? Is there some celebration?"

"There *is*," said the girl, solemnly; "we celebrate our right to live. We are starving. As soon as enough of us get together we are going to the bakeries and each of us will take a loaf of bread. That is little enough for the government to give us after it has taken all our men."

Just then a fat old black Mammy waddled up the walk to overtake a beautiful child who was running before her. "Come dis a way, honey," she called, "don't go nigh dem people," adding, in a lower tone, "I's feared you'll ketch somethin' fum dem po'-white folks. I *wonder* dey lets 'em into de Park."

The girl turned to me with a wan smile, and as she rose to join the long line that had now formed and was moving, she said simply, "Good-by! I'm going to get something to eat!"

"And I devoutly hope you'll get it—and plenty of it," I told her. The crowd now rapidly increased, and numbered, I am sure, more than a thousand women and children. It grew and grew until it reached the dignity of a mob—a bread riot. They impressed all the light carts they met, and marched along silently and in order. They marched through Cary Street and Main, visiting the stores of the speculators and emptying them of their contents. Governor Letcher sent the mayor to read the Riot Act, and as this had no effect he threatened to fire on the crowd. The city battalion then came up. The women fell back with frightened eyes, but did not obey the order to disperse. The President then appeared, ascended a dray, and addressed them. It is said he was received at first with hisses from the boys, but after he had spoken some little time with great kindness and sympathy, the women quietly moved on, taking their food with them. General Elzey and General Winder wished to call troops from the camps to "suppress the women," but Mr. Seddon, wise man, declined to issue the order.[1] While I write women and children are still standing in the streets, demanding food, and the government is issuing to them rations of rice.

This is a frightful state of things. I am telling you of it because *not one word* has been said in the newspapers about it. All will be changed, Judge Campbell tells me, if we can win a battle or two (but, oh, at what a price!), and regain the control of our railroads. Your General has been magnificent. He has fed Lee's army all winter—I wish he could feed our starving women and children.

Dearly,

"Agnes."

---

[1] General Arnold Elzey was commander of the Department of Richmond, John Winder was the city's provost marshal, and James A. Seddon was secretary of war.

4

JOHN B. JONES

This Is War, Terrible War (1862–1864)

John B. Jones was the editor of a weekly magazine in Philadelphia when the war began. A native of Baltimore and married to a Virginia woman, he was an ardent southern patriot, so he hurried south to offer his services to the Confederate government and be at the center of the action. At fifty-one, he believed that he was too old to fight, but he secured a position as a clerk in the War Department, from which he recorded his observations in his extensive diary. Unlike many diaries kept during the war, Jones wrote with an eye to future publication. His strong prejudices often colored his observations—he hated Yankees, Jews, and the British—but nevertheless his diary is an invaluable source of the inner workings of the Confederate government and day-to-day life in the capital of Richmond. His diary was originally published in 1866.

January 9, 1862.—Butter is 50 cts. per pound, bacon 25 cts., beef has risen from 13 cts. to 30 cts., wood is selling for $8 per cord, but flour is abundant, and cheap enough, to keep us from starving.

May 23, 1862.—Oh, the extortioners! Meats of all kinds are selling at 50 cts. per pound; butter, 75 cts.; coffee, $1.50; tea, $10; boots, $30 per pair; shoes, $18; ladies' shoes, $15; shirts, $6 each. Houses that rented for $500 last year are $1000 now. . . .

October 1, 1862.—How shall we subsist this winter? There is not a supply of wood or coal in the city—and it is said that there are not adequate means of transporting it hither. Flour at $16 per barrel and bacon at 75 cts. per pound threaten a famine. And yet there are no beggars in the streets.

November 19, 1862.—Salt sold yesterday at auction for $1.10 per pound. Boots are now bringing $50 per pair; candles (tallow) 75 cts. per

pound; butter $2.00 per pound. Clothing is almost unattainable. We are all looking shabby enough.

December 1, 1862.—God speed the day of peace! Our patriotism is mainly in the army and among the ladies of the South. The avarice and cupidity of the men at home, could only be excelled by ravenous wolves; and most of our sufferings are fully deserved. Where a people will not have mercy on one another, how can they expect mercy? They depreciate the Confederate notes by charging from $20 to $40 per bbl. for flour; $3.50 per bushel of meal; $2 per lb. for butter; $20 per cord for wood, etc. When we shall have peace, let the extortionists be remembered! let an indelible stigma be branded upon them.

A portion of the people look like vagabonds. We see men and women and children in the streets in dingy and dilapidated clothes; and some seem gaunt and pale with hunger—the speculators, and thieving quartermasters and commissaries only, looking sleek and comfortable.

January 18, 1863—We are now, in effect, in a state of siege, and none but the opulent, often those who have defrauded the government, can

FROM John B. Jones, *A Rebel War Clerk's Diary* (Philadelphia: J. B. Lippincott and Co., 1866) vol. 1, pp. 104–283 passim; vol. 2, pp. 17–334 passim.

obtain a sufficiency of food and raiment. Calico, which could once be bought for 12½ cts. per yard, is now selling at $2.25, and a lady's dress of calico costs her about $30.00. Bonnets are not to be had. Common bleached cotton shirting brings $1.50 per yard. All other dry goods are held in the same proportion.

January 30, 1863—I cut the following from yesterday's *Dispatch*:

"*The Results of Extortion and Speculation.*—The state of affairs brought about by the speculating and extortion practiced upon the public cannot be better illustrated than by the following grocery bill for one week for a small family, in which the prices before the war and those of the present are compared:

1860			1863	
Bacon, 10 lbs. at 12½	$1.25		Bacon, 10 lbs. at $1	$10.00
Flour, 30 lbs. at 5¢	1.50		Flour, 30 lbs. at 12½¢	3.75
Sugar, 5 lbs. at 8¢	.40		Sugar, 5 lbs. at $1.15	5.75
Coffee, 4 lbs. at 12½¢	.50		Coffee, 4 lbs. at $5	20.00
Tea (green), ½ lb. at $1	.50		Tea (green), ½ lb. at $16	8.00
Lard, 4 lbs. at 12½¢	.50		Lard, 4 lbs. at $1	4.00
Butter, 3 lbs. at 25¢	.75		Butter, 3 lbs. at $1.75	5.25
Meal, 1 pk. at 25¢	.25		Meal, 1 pk. at $1	1.00
Candles, 2 lbs. at 15¢	.30		Candles, 2 lbs. at $1.25	2.50
Soap, 5 lbs. at 10¢	.50		Soap, 5 lbs. at $1.10	5.50
Pepper and salt (about)	.10		Pepper and salt (about)	2.50
Total	$6.55		Total	$68.25

So much we owe the speculators, who have stayed at home to prey upon the necessities of their fellow-citizens."

February 11, 1863—Some idea may be formed of the scarcity of food in this city from the fact that, while my youngest daughter was in the kitchen today, a young rat came out of its hole and seemed to beg for something to eat; she held out some bread, which it ate from her hand, and seemed grateful. Several others soon appeared and were as tame as kittens. Perhaps we shall have to eat them!

March 14, 1863—Bacon now sells for $1.50 per pound in Richmond. Butter $3. I design to cultivate a little garden 20 by 50 feet; but fear I cannot get seeds. I have sought in vain for peas,

beans, corn, and tomatoes seeds. Potatoes are $12 per bushel. Ordinary chickens are worth $3 a piece. My youngest daughter put her earrings on sale to-day—price $25; and I think they will bring it, for which she can purchase a pair of shoes.

March 30, 1863—The gaunt form of wretched famine still approaches with rapid strides. Meal is now selling at $12 per bushel, and potatoes at $16. Meats have almost disappeared from the market, and none but the opulent can afford to pay $3.50 per pound for butter. *Greens*, however, of various kinds, are coming in; and as the season advances, we may expect a diminution of prices. . . .

August 16, 1863—What shall we do for sugar, now selling at $2 per pound? When the little supply this side of the Mississippi is still more reduced it will probably be $5! It has been more than a year since we had coffee or tea. Was it not thus in the trying times of the Revolution? If so, why can we not bear privation as well as our forefathers did? We must!

October 20, 1863—I saw flour sell at auction to-day for $61 per barrel. This, too, when there is an abundant crop of new grain but recently harvested. It is the result of the depreciation of a redundant currency, and not of an ascertained scarcity. . . . Many are becoming very shabby in appearance; and I can get no clothes for myself or my family, unless the government shall very materially increase our salaries.

October 22, 1863—A poor woman yesterday

applied to a merchant in Carey Street to purchase a barrel of flour. The price he demanded was $70.

"My God!" exclaimed she, "how can I pay such prices? I have seven children; what shall I do?"

"I don't know, madam," said he, coolly, "unless you eat your children."

November 20, 1863—Every night robberies of poultry, salt meats, and even of cows and hogs are occurring. Many are desperate.

January 13, 1864—The auctions are crowded—the people seeming anxious to get rid of their money by paying the most extravagant prices for all articles exposed for sale. An old pair of boots, with large holes in them, sold to-day for $7.00—it costs $125 to foot a pair of boots.

February 4, 1864—Eighteen car loads of coffee went up to the army to-day. I have not tasted coffee or tea for more than a year.

February 23, 1864—Meal is the only food now attainable, except by the rich. We look for a healthy year, everything being so cleanly consumed that no garbage or filth can accumulate. We are all good scavengers now, and there is no need of buzzards in the streets. Even the pigeons can scarcely find a grain to eat.

March 12, 1864—My income, including Custis's, is not less now, than $600 per month, or $7200 per annum; but we are still poor, with flour at $300 per barrel; meal, $50 per bushel; and even fresh fish at $5 per pound.

March 18, 1864—My daughter's cat is staggering to-day, for want of animal food. Sometimes I fancy I stagger myself. We do not average two ounces of meat daily; and some do not get any for several days together. Meal is $50 per bushel.

April 8, 1864—. . . It is the day of *fasting*, humiliation, and prayer, and all the offices are closed. May God put it into the hearts of the extortioners to relent, and abolish, for a season, the insatiable greed for gain! I paid $25 for a half cord of wood to-day, new currency. I fear a nation of extortioners are unworthy of independence, and that we must be chastened and purified before success will be vouchsafed us.

What enormous appetites we have now, and how little illness, since food has become so high in price! I cannot afford to have more than an ounce of meat daily for each member of my family of six. . . . The old cat goes staggering about from debility, though Fannie often gives him her share. We see neither rats nor mice about the premises now. This is famine. . . . *And, still, there are no beggars.*

April 11, 1864—An ounce of meat, daily, is the allowance to each member of my family, the cat and parrot included. The pigeons of my neighbor have disappeared. Every day we have accounts of robberies, the preceding night, of cows, pigs, bacon, flour—and even the setting hens are taken from their nests!

June 19, 1864—Every Sunday I see how shabby my clothes have become, as every one else, almost, has a good suit in reserve. During the week all are shabby, and hence it is not noticeable. The wonder is that we are not naked, after wearing the same garments three or four years.

August 13, 1864—Flour is falling. It is now $200 per barrel—$500 a few weeks ago; and bacon is falling in price also, from $11 to $6 per pound. A commission merchant said to me, yesterday, that there was at least eighteen months' supply (for the people) of breadstuffs and meats in the city; and pointing to the upper windows at the corner of Thirteenth and Cary Streets, he revealed the ends of many barrels piled above the windows. He said that flour had been there two years, held for "still higher prices." Such is the avarice of man. Such is war. And such the greed of extortioners, even in the midst of famine—and famine in the midst of plenty!

August 19, 1864—The speculators are on the *qui vive* already, and no flour can be had. I fear *our* flour will be intercepted, delayed, and perhaps lost! The meat we got to-day will supply but two ounces for each member of my family daily for two months. This is war, terrible war!

November 18, 1864—We have now 200 pounds of flour in the house; 3. bushel meal; 1 bushel sweet potatoes; 1 bushel Irish potatoes; 3 half pecks white beans; 4 pumpkins; 10 pounds beef; 2 pounds butter, and 3 pounds sugar, with salt, etc. This seems like moderate stores for a family of seven, but it is a larger supply than we ever had be-fore, and will suffice for a month. At the market price, they would cost $620. Add to this 1½ loads coal and a quarter cord of wood—the first at $75, the last at $20—the total is $762.50. This sum in ordinary times, and in specie, would subsist my family twelve months.

5

Phoebe Yates Pember Becomes
a Hospital Matron (1879)

Phoebe Yates Pember grew up in Charleston, South Carolina, and then Savannah, Georgia, as a member of a prosperous and notable Jewish family. We do not know anything about her schooling, but it is clear from her writings that she was well ed-ucated. Pember became a widow shortly after the war began. After an unhappy year spent living with her parents, she received an offer from George Randolph, the Sec-retary of War, with whose wife she was friends, to become a matron in the Chimbo-razo military hospital in Richmond, reputedly the largest such hospital in the world. She took up her new duties in December 1862. While welcomed by the chief surgeon, other doctors and male attendants in the hospital were openly hostile, but she was undaunted. Her energy and efficiency were immediately apparent; so was her strong will and willingness to defy male authority and cut through bureaucratic red tape. She spent the remainder of the war in Richmond, supervising the care of wounded soldiers. In the following excerpt from her memoirs, she recounted her first day in her new position.

About this time one of these large hospitals was to be opened, and the wife of the then acting secretary of war offered me the superintendence—rather a startling proposition to a woman used to all the comforts of luxurious life. Foremost among the Virginia women, she had given her resources of mind and means to the sick, and her graphic and earnest representations of the benefit a good and determined woman's rule could effect in such a position settled the result in my mind. The natural idea that such a life would be injurious to the deli-cacy and refinement of a lady—that her nature would become deteriorated and her sensibilities blunted, was rather appalling. But the first step only costs, and that was soon taken.

A preliminary interview with the surgeon-in-chief gave necessary confidence. He was ener-getic—capable—skillful. A man with ready oil to pour upon troubled waters. Difficulties melted away beneath the warmth of his ready interest, and mountains sank into mole-hills when his quick comprehension had surmounted and leveled them. However troublesome daily increasing annoyances became, if they could not be removed, his few and ready words sent applicants and grumblers home satisfied to do the best they could. Wisely he de-

FROM Phoebe Yates Pember, *A Southern Woman's Story* (New York: G. W. Carleton and Co., 1879), pp. 14–16.

cided to have an educated and efficient woman at the head of his hospital, and having succeeded, never allowed himself to forget that fact.

The day after my decision was made found me at "headquarters," the only two-story building on hospital ground, then occupied by the chief surgeon and his clerks. He had not yet made his appearance that morning, and while awaiting him, many of his corps, who had expected in horror the advent of female supervision, walked in and out, evidently inspecting me. There was at that time a general ignorance on all sides, except among the hospital officials, of the decided objection on the part of the latter to the carrying out of a law which they prognosticated would entail "petticoat government;" but there was no mistaking the stage-whisper which reached my ears from the open door of the office that morning, as the little contract surgeon passed out and informed a friend he met, in a tone of ill-concealed disgust, that "*one of them had come.*"

6

SALLY PUTNAM

Southern Women Enter the Government Bureaucracy (1867)

Sally Putnam was an upper-class Virginian who lived in Richmond during the war. In her memoir of the war years, she described the eagerness with which women sought government clerkships in order to support themselves.

In various offices under the government, and particularly in those of the Treasury Department, the services of females were found useful. Employment was given and a support secured to hundreds of intelligent and deserving women of the South, who, by the existence of the war, or other misfortunes, had been so reduced in the means of living as to be compelled to earn a support. The Treasury Note Bureau, in which the greatest number of women were employed, was under the supervision of experienced and gentlemanly clerks, and no place in the Confederate Capital was more interesting or attractive than that where these fair operatives were engaged in signing and numbering Mr. Memminger's Confederate bills. The duties were pleasant and profitable, and so much sought after by those in need, that hundreds of applications were placed on file by women to whom it was impossible to furnish employment.

It sometimes required considerable diplomacy and influence to secure an office under our Government, and their fair friends made ample use of the members of Congress, the clergy and the military, for reference as to social position, qualification, worth, and need for such assistance.

A visit to Mr. Memminger, whose stolid and apparently unsympathizing face ever produced an unpleasant impression on the beholder, was sometimes undertaken by a woman more courageous than her sisters, to be attended with nervous apprehension when in his sight, and often by weeping when the ordeal was over. Few could endure the cold phase: "If I find your case more worthy of notice than others I will regard your application favorably," when their hearts were aching under trials so bitter that their drink was mingled with weeping, and their nights restless with the agony of

FROM Sally Putnam, *Richmond During the War* (New York: G. W. Carleton, 1867), pp. 173–75.

the thought, "How am I to live?" But notwithstanding the cold exterior of Mr. Memminger, he was not wanting in that warmth of soul that opens with sympathy for misfortune; but it became extremely difficult for him to discriminate between the applicants, when they were so numerous, and their claims to notice so well substantiated.

From the Treasury Department, the employment of female clerks extended to various offices in the War Department, the Post Office Department, and indeed to every branch of business connected with the government. They were in all found efficient and useful. By this means many young men could be sent into the ranks, and by the testimony of the chiefs of Bureaus, the work left for the women was better done; for they were more conscientious in their attendance upon their duties than the more self-satisfied, but not better qualified, male *attachés* of the government offices.

For offices in the War Department, an examination of qualification for business was required. This, in itself, was extremely simple, but sufficiently formidable to deter many from seeking employment that required such a test of efficiency. The applicants were expected to show a thorough

acquaintance with the primary rules of arithmetic, and some knowledge of fractions; but under the circumstances in which many timid ladies were examined they could scarcely tell whether or not two and two make four, or how many thirds there are in a whole. These examinations, therefore, could not be considered a test of qualification, for there were some so much frightened by the trial that, losing all self-possession, they gave up in despair. The experiment of placing women in government clerkships proved eminently successful, and grew to be extremely popular under the Confederate government.

Many a poor young girl remembers with gratitude the kindly encouragement of our Adjutant General Cooper, our Chief of Ordnance, Colonel Gorges [*sic*], or the First Auditor of the Confederate Treasury, Judge Bolling Baker, or Postmaster General Reagan, and various other officials, of whom their necessities drove them to seek employment. The most high-born ladies of the land filled these places as well as the humble poor; but none could obtain employment under the government who could not furnish testimonials of intelligence and superior moral worth.

7

GIDEON J. PILLOW

A Confederate General Reports on Widespread Resistance to Conscription (1863)

For a brief period in 1863, Confederate General Gideon J. Pillow was authorized to organize a conscript bureau for Tennessee, Alabama, and Mississippi that was independent of the bureau in the War Department in Richmond. Pillow's aggressive tactics in enforcing conscription produced many complaints and soon led to the revocation of his authority. In the following letter, he described the widespread resistance he encountered in enforcing the draft in these states, particularly northern Alabama. Resistance to conscription was especially marked in hill and mountain areas where there were few slaves.

Hdqrs. Vol. and Conscript Bureau, Dept. No. 2,
Marietta, Ga., July 28, 1863.

Col. Benjamin S. Ewell,
Assistant Adjutant-General:

Under the orders of General Johnston I am directed to superintend and direct the enforcement of the conscript law in Tennessee, Alabama, and Mississippi. The officers of the Richmond Bureau in these States having been placed under my orders, I have commenced work. There are, I think, from 8,000 to 10,000 deserters and tory conscripts in the mountains of Alabama, many of whom have deserted the second, third, and (some of them) the fourth time. They cannot be kept in the army so near their homes. As fast as I catch them and send them to the army they desert and bring off their arms and steal all the ammunition of their comrades they can bring away. These deserters and the tory conscripts, for mutual protection against my officers, have banded together and are as vicious as "copperheads." They have killed a number of my officers and in several instances have driven small bodies of cavalry, acting under my orders, from the mountains. It is useless to send them back to the Army of Tennessee. From Virginia they could not so easily return. By filling up the Alabama regiments in the Army of Virginia they would render the general service as much aid. I therefore apply for authority to send them to the Army of Virginia. The application amounts to a transfer of these deserters from Alabama regiments of the Army of Tennessee to Alabama regiments in Virginia. The President has the power to do this. Tennessee has nearly all passed (with her population) from our control. A very large portion of Mississippi has also. From these portions of Tennessee and Mississippi yet within our lines it is almost impossible to get the men out and into our army. They hide and dodge in the thickets and swamps and mountains, and when hard pressed they run into the enemy's lines to elude capture by my officers.

The population of Central and Southern Alabama are nearly all in the Army who are liable. The largest portion of the population remaining to be gathered up are in the mountains of Northern Alabama, and, for the reasons already explained, I propose to send them to the Army of Virginia. You perceive, therefore, that the means of building up the Army of Tennessee and that of Mississippi are most inadequate. Indeed, without authority to draw from other sources than this department, I regard it impossible materially to strengthen those armies. I therefore ask for authority to embrace Georgia in the work of the bureau of this department. To gather up the tory conscripts and stragglers in the mountains of Alabama will require a considerable supporting force of cavalry. All small detachments of cavalry sent into the mountains on this duty are driven out or killed off. I cannot get an adequate force from General Bragg's army. It cannot well be spared. Besides, to be efficient on this duty the detail ought to be permanent. One hundred men who have been on this duty long enough to understand it will do more than 300 freshly detailed troops. I therefore ask the orders of the Government upon the Governor of Alabama to turn over to this bureau one regiment or ten companies of mounted men of the troops called out for local defense. If I am properly supported by the Government I will clear out these mountains of tories and deserters. If not, my labor will profit the general service but little.

Respectfully,

Gid. J. Pillow,
Brigadier-General, C. S. Army, and Supt.
Volunteer and Conscript Bureau, Dept. No. 2.

FROM *Official Records,* ser. IV, vol. 2, pp. 680–81.

8

DANIEL O'LEARY

The War Corrodes Female Virtue (1863)

Daniel O'Leary of Kentucky epitomized the divided loyalties of many border state families. A Unionist, he enlisted in the Fifteenth Kentucky Infantry in the United States Army, where he held the rank of captain. His wife's family, however, was pro-Confederate, and her brother fought in a Kentucky regiment in the Confederate Army. In this letter, O'Leary expressed concern over the war's impact on traditional moral standards in southern rural society.

Chattanooga, Tenn.
December 29th 1863

My dear wife

. . . The sooner peace is restored the better for the southern people as they are the real sufferers, driven from their homes, their property destroyed or taken for the use of the army. And what is worse, yes even than death itself, the Mothers, Wives & daughters of these men [Confederate soldiers] have become strangers to virture and female modesty—which is the greatest ornament of the sex—worse than the most degraded creatures which abound in the cities of the north. I do not Know what the standard of morality was in this country before the rebellion but if it has been the means of bringing about the present state of depravity and vice its authors deserve the execrations of all honest people. . . .

Ere you receive this the year 63 will be numbered with the past. May our sorrows and disappointments too be left behind and with the New Born Year realize fresh hope that we may live to see the day for which we have hoped and prayed during the last year. . . .

I remain ever your
loving husband

Daniel O'Leary

FROM "The Civil War Letters of Daniel O'Leary," *Register of the Kentucky Historical Society* 77 (Summer 1979): 168.

9

THEODORE LYMAN

A Union Officer Marvels at the Endurance of the Southern People (1864)

An upper-class Bostonian, Theodore Lyman had graduated from Harvard in 1855. Lyman spent the first part of the war in Europe, but upon his return in 1863, he accepted the invitation of General George Meade, whom he had met before the war, to join his staff. He spent the remainder of the war working for Meade in the Army of the Potomac. In the following selection from his letters to his wife, written at the end of May 1864, he described the suffering and hardship of the southern people as well as their tenacious resiliency. Note his comments on the relationship between social class and loyalty to the Confederacy. (Paragraphing has been supplied.)

There is, and can be, no doubt of the straits to which these people are now reduced; particularly, of course, in this distracted region;[1] there is nothing in modern history to compare with the conscription they have. They have swept this part of the country of all persons under 50, who could not steal away. I have just seen a man of 48, very much crippled with rheumatism, who said he was enrolled two days ago. He told them he had thirteen persons dependent on him, including three grandchildren (his son-in-law had been taken some time since); but they said that made no difference; he was on his way to the rendezvous, when our cavalry crossed the river, and he hid in the bushes, till they came up. I offered him money for some of his small vegetables; but he said: "If you have any bread, I would rather have it. Your cavalry have taken all the corn I had left, and, as for meat, I have not tasted a mouthful for six weeks." If you had seen his eyes glisten when I gave him a piece of salt pork, you would have believed his

story. He looked like a man who had come into a fortune. "Why," said he, "that must weigh four pounds—that would cost me forty dollars in Richmond! They told us they would feed the families of those that were taken; and so they did for two months, and then they said they had no more meal."

What is even more extraordinary than their extreme suffering, is the incomprehensible philosophy and endurance of these people. Here was a man, of poor health, with a family that it would be hard to support in peace-times, stripped to the bone by Rebel and Union, with no hope from any side, and yet he almost laughed when he described his position, and presently came back with a smile to tell me that the only two cows he had, had strayed off, got into a Government herd, and "gone up the road"—that's the last of *them*. In Europe, a man so situated would be on his knees, tearing out handfuls of hair, and calling on the Virgin and on several saints. There were neighbors at his house; and one asked me if I supposed our people would burn his tenement? "What did you leave it for?" I asked. To which he replied, in a concise way that told the whole: "Because there was right smart of bullets over thaar!"

The poorest people seem usually more or less

---

[1] Union forces were in the vicinity of Cold Harbor, Virginia, less than 10 miles northeast of Richmond.

FROM Theodore Lyman, *Meade's Headquarters, 1863–1865,* ed. George R. Agassiz (Boston: Atlantic Monthly Press, 1922), pp. 132–33.

indifferent or adverse to the war, but their bitterness increases in direct ratio to their social position. Find a well-dressed lady, and you find one whose hatred will end only with death—it is unmistakable, though they treat you with more or less courtesy. Nor is it extraordinary: there is black everywhere; here is one that has lost an only son; and here another that has had her husband killed. People of this class are very proud and spirited; you can easily see it; and it is the officers that they supply who give the strong framework to their army. They have that military and irascible nature so often seen among an aristocracy that was once rich and is now poor; for you must remember that, before the war, most of these land-owners had ceased to hold the position they had at the beginning of this century.

10

ELLA GERTRUDE THOMAS

Until Adversity Tries Us (1861–1865)

Ella Gertrude Thomas (1834–1907) was an upper-class Georgia woman who kept a diary intermittently from 1848 to 1889. She was born to privilege: her father, Turner Clanton, was a large slaveholder and one of the wealthiest planters in the state. As a young girl, she displayed considerable intellectual ability, and her father sent her to Macon, Georgia, to attend Wesleyan Female College, an unusual opportunity even for southern women of the upper class. She graduated in 1851 after three years of study. Through a classmate she met James Jefferson Thomas, who was also a member of a prosperous planter family. In 1852, despite her father's misgivings, they were married. By then the feckless Jefferson had dropped out of medical school to begin a career as a planter, and her father gave them property and slaves worth $30,000 for her dowry. Over the next twenty-two years she bore ten children, seven of whom survived past the age of five. Intellectually curious and desirous of greater social outlets, Gertrude did not like living in the country, so the family spent a good part of each year in nearby Augusta, Georgia. Through her diary, we can trace Gertrude Thomas's changing attitudes toward the war.

*I*n an entry she made shortly after the war began, Gertrude avowed her loyalty to the Confederacy and her faith in the Confederate cause. With pride she discussed her husband's pending departure to Virginia.

FROM Virginia Ingraham Burr, ed., *The Secret Eye: The Journal of Ella Gertrude Clanton Thomas, 1848–1889* (Chapel Hill: University of North Carolina Press, 1990), pp. 183–261 passim.

July 13, 1861 . . . The Richmond Hussars . . . have received orders to hold themselves in readiness to leave— And to this company *my husband* belongs, holding the rank of first Lieutenant and I can write this without one wish for him to remain with me. When Duty and Honour call him it would be strange if I would influence him to remain "in the lap of inglorious ease" when so much is at stake. Our country is invaded—our homes are in danger—We are deprived or they are attempting to deprive us of that glorious liberty for which our Fathers fought and bled and shall we tamely submit to this? Never! My husband will go—My brother Jimmie will leave in the same co so will Jack (Mr. Thomas' younger brother) and I am proud to see them exhibit the noble, manly, spirit which prompts them to go. . . . surely ours is a just cause— We are only asking for self government and freedom to decide our own destinys. We claim nothing of the North but—*to be let alone*—and *they,* a people like ourselves whose republican independence was won by a rebellion, whose liberty was achieved by a secession—to think that they should attempt to coerce us—the idea is preposterous. True, they have a much larger number of men than we have. Yet we are amply able to live within ourselves.

. . . Trusting to the God of Battles, I shall see my husband go, feeling that if one word of mine could keep him home I would not utter it.

As 1862 opened, Gertrude was buoyant about the future and the prospects for southern independence. She believed that reunion with the North was impossible and still hoped for European aid.

January 1, 1862 . . . I wonder if the Northern people still cling to the delusion that such a thing as our being united with them is possible. So far from it I am inclined to believe that each successive day but widens the gulf between [us]. Each man we lose but serves to render more intense our hatred of the Yankee. Some of them may be sincere in their abolition feelings but what consistency is there in the effort to free one Negro if his freedom causes the death of so many whites— Is their love for their Black Brother greater than they experience for their white? Oh they are a miserable fanatic set.

Thomas served as director of the Augusta Ladies' Aid Society, sewed uniforms and made cartridges, and worked in military hospitals. In this glimpse of her wartime attitudes, she discusses her experiences

as a volunteer in a military hospital, the Empire House in Augusta. Her diary records few subsequent such visits, although whether she ceased performing such work is not clear.

April 17, 1862 . . . The halls [of a military hospital in Augusta] were terribly stained with tobacco juice. The convalescents walked through the passages smoking pipes which added to the unholsome atmosphere and there were too many in one room. To a man of refinement and education how horrible the association and promixity of men essentially different from him. No privacy— no seclusion.

By the end of the year, she had become much more gloomy about the Confederacy's prospects. In a long entry written as the year drew to a close, she reflected on a number of matters, both public and private.

December 31, 1863 . . . laying my Journal aside I could . . . reflect upon the disappointment of our sanguine hopes for the coming of peace with the closing of the year. But I will strive against such feelings and hope that the close of 1864 may find us an Independent Nation upon the face of the earth but while I hope so I confess that there is more hope than trust. Our prospects are extremely gloomy. . . .

The human mind is so constituted that it cannot stand a constant pressure—The war has been going on for a much longer time than we could have thought of and our minds are becoming in some degree accustomed to it—It is in this way that we must account for the gayety which appears to prevail in our town. I hear of numerous partys which are being given and a number of sociables. . . .

What boots it now to wonder what the coming year may bring forth? Well for us perhaps that we do not know. . . . But reality calls upon me to look around me, to see our country agonised in a struggle for an existence, and deeper, still deeper settles the conviction that we are upon the eve of some great struggle, the echo of which will reverberate through all time. Fortunately for those who believe in an all ruling Providence we are taught that "he doeth all things well"— . . . but we do not know the stuff of which we are made until adversity tries us. I have great faith in that innate courage which all women are said to possess when great trials come upon them—providential trials—I write despondingly as to our future but indeed I do not think as a mass of people we fully realise the importance of the struggle in which we are engaged—

The war produced doubts in Gertrude's mind about the institution of slavery. Yet she admitted that she was unwilling to give up the wealth and lifestyle that the ownership of slaves brought her.

September 17, 1864 . . . I have sometimes doubted on the subject of slavery. I have seen so many of its evils chief among which is the terribly demoralising influence upon our men and boys but of late I have become convinced the Negro *as a race* is better off with us as he has been than if he were made free, but I am by no means so sure that we would not gain by his having his freedom given him. I grant that I am not so philanthropic as to be willing voluntarily to give all we own for the sake of the principle, but I do think that if we had the same invested in something else as a means of support I would willingly, nay gladly, have the responsibility of them taken off my shoulders.

With Sherman in Georgia, Gertrude desperately continued to hope the Confederacy would survive, but she began to see that her old way of life was drawing to a close, whatever the outcome of the military struggle. Financial worries loomed large as she pondered the future.

September 22, 1864 . . . Shall I dare hope that this new Journal which I am commencing will record Peace, and independent Southern Confederacy? Truly the skies are gloomy and the heavy storm appears ready to discharge its thunders in our very midst. Yet how calm, how indifferent we are—we laugh, we smile, we talk, we jest, just as

tho no enemy were at our door. And yet the idea has several times suggested itself to me that someday I would have to aid in earning my own support. We have made no arrangement whatever for such a contingency. Gold has increased in value and we have *not a dollar*—and yet I am hopeful of the success of our cause, the ultimate success of our Confederacy, while I do not think it improbable that *we* will lose our fortunes before that final success is achieved.

As Sherman prepared to leave Atlanta, Gertrude's doubts about slavery eclipsed her worry that Sherman would come to Augusta.

September 23, 1864 . . . [More than Sherman] I will confess that what troubles me more than anything else is that I am not certain that Slavery is right.

. . . But as to the doctrine of slavery altho I have read very few abolition books (*Uncle Tom's Cabin* making most impression) nor have I read many pro slavery books—yet the idea has gradually become more and more fixed in my mind that the institution of slavery is not right—but I am reading a new book, *Nellie Norton,* by the Rev E W Warren which I hope will convince me that it is right— Owning a large number of slaves as we do I might be asked why I do not free them? This if I could, I would not do, but if Mr. Thomas would sell them to a man who would look after their temporal and spiritual interest I would gladly do so. Those house servants we have if Mr Thomas would agree to it I would pay regular wages but this is a subject upon which I do not like to think and taking my stand upon the moral view of the subject, I can but think that to hold men and women in perpetual bondage is wrong—During my comparatively short life, spent wholly under Southern skies, I have known of and heard too much of its demoralizing influence to consider the institution a blessing—

When rumors circulated that the Georgia troops were being assembled to recapture Atlanta, Gertrude manifested a growing tension between her personal security and Confederate patriotism. After resigning from the army, her husband had enlisted in the state militia to avoid being conscripted. He believed that he might be called out to help recapture Atlanta.

October 21, 1864 . . . Oh God how we sigh and yearn for Peace, honourable Peace—. . .

It would be a brilliant thing to recapture Atlanta. I wish it could be done. I wish Mr Thomas could be engaged in the fight if he could escape safely, but he *might not* and then what? Am I willing to give my husband to gain Atlanta for the Confederacy? No, No, No, a thousand times No!

Gertrude believed Davis's endorsement of recruiting slaves for the Confederate army was a sign of the Confederacy's weakness. Her sagging spirits dropped further.

October 27, 1864 . . . President Davis in his message says that we are better off than we were this time last year, but when President Davis advocates the training of Negroes to aid us in fighting— promising them, as an inducement to do so, *their freedom*, and in the same message intimates that rather than yield we would place every Negro in the Army—he so clearly betrays the weakness of our force that I candidly confess I am disheartened. I take a woman's view of the subject but it does seem strangely inconsistent, the idea of our offering to a Negro the rich boon— the priceless reward of freedom to aid us in keeping in bondage a large portion of his brethren, when by joining the Yankees he will instantly gain the very reward which Mr Davis offers to him after a certain amount of labor rendered and danger incurred. Mr Davis to the contrary, the Negro has had a great deal to do with this war and if—but I fear I grow toryish in my sentiments—

Sherman's men visited one of the Thomas's plantations, burned many of the buildings, plundered the storehouses, and destroyed large amounts of personal property. Moreover, some of the Thomas's slaves either ran away to the Union lines or collaborated with Sherman's raiders. Her world shattered, Gertrude was now anxious for the war simply to end.

December 26, 1864 . . . The fact is the time and circumstances somehow appears to create a reckless, careless feeling, an impatience to have it over—It is impossible to settle quietly down or form plans for the future when everything depends in a great degree upon the whim or caprice of Gen Sherman.

For Gertrude, the war was a sobering experience. She dismissed the idea that war somehow elevated people.

January 3, 1865 . . . War is a terrible demon. It does not elevate—it debases. It does not lift heavenward—it crushes into the dust. I lose faith in humanity when I see such efforts to sink the nobler better part of man's nature in an effort to exterminate the white race at the South in order to elevate the Negro race to a position which I doubt their ability to fill—

Her hope obliterated, Gertrude could barely face the reality of her situation and longed for the end of the war.

March 29, 1865 . . . I know I will regret hereafter that I have made no record of time and events which are fraught with so much interest, record of events which are hourly making history—but I cannot. I shrink from the task. At times I feel as if I was drifting on, on, ever onward to be at last dashed against some rock and I shut my eyes and almost wish it was over, the shock encountered and I prepared to know what destiny awaits me. I am tired, oh so tired of this war. I want to breathe free. I feel the restraint of the blockade and as port after port becomes blockaded, I feel shut up, pent up. . . .

I make no plans for the future. . . . I shrink from what I too much fear will prove a reality. I have seen poverty staring me in the face when I expected Sherman in Augusta and our planting interest was destroyed and God know[s] there was nothing attractive in the gaunt picture presented.

The war destroyed slavery and the Confederacy. But when it finally ended, Gertrude, who had so much at stake socially and economically, felt only re-lief.

May 1, 1865 . . . The war is over and I am glad of it. What terms of agreement may be decided upon I cannot say but if *anything* is left us—if we can count with certainty upon enough to raise and educate our children I shall be grateful. It is humiliating, very indeed to be a conquered people but the sky is so bright, the air so pure, the aspect of nature so lovely that I can but be encouraged, and hope for something which will benefit us.

11

MARY CHESNUT

Is Anything Worth It? (1862–1865)

Mary Boykin Chesnut was a member of South Carolina's slaveholding aristocracy. Her father was a wealthy planter and prominent political leader in the state, and she married James Chesnut, Jr., whose father was also a large slaveholder. Extremely intelligent and well-informed, Mary Chesnut hated plantation life and longed for the social and intellectual excitement of Charleston, where her brilliant wit and vivacious personality made her a much sought-after guest at the city's most refined social gatherings. She was an ardent believer in the Confederacy and spent most of the war in Richmond, where her husband was a government official and where she readily moved among the city's social and political elite. From her vantage point in the Confederate capital she desperately tried to maintain a hopeful outlook toward the war, but with each battle the death toll mounted, and at times she was almost numbed by the pervasiveness of death. In her diary, she recorded the reaction of women of the southern upper class to the constant reality of loss of friends, acquaintances, and loved ones. In the 1880s Chesnut rewrote her wartime diary to make it a more polished and consciously crafted literary work, and it has been published in several versions.

June 9, 1862 . . . When we read of the battles in India, in Italy, in the Crimea—what did we care? Only an interesting topic like any other to look for in the paper.

Now you hear of a battle with a thrill and a shudder. It has come home to us. Half the people that we know in the world are under the enemy's guns.

A telegram comes to you. And you leave it on your lap. You are pale with fright. You handle it, or dread to touch it, as you would a rattlesnake—worse—worse. A snake would only strike you. How many, many, this scrap of paper may tell you, have gone to their death.

When you meet people, sad and sorrowful is the greeting; they press your hand, tears stand in their eyes or roll down their cheeks, as they happen to have more or less self-control. They have brothers, fathers, or sons—as the case may be—in the battle. And this thing now seems never to stop. We

FROM C. Vann Woodward, ed., *Mary Chesnut's Civil War* (New Haven, Conn.: Yale University Press, 1981), pp. 370–71, 377–78, 397–402, 406–7, 412, 607, 625, 628, 702.

have no breathing time given us. It cannot be so at the North, for the papers say gentlemen do not go in the ranks there. They are officers or clerks of departments, &c&c&c. . . . Every company on the field is filled with our nearest and dearest—rank and file, common soldiers.

Miriam's story today:

A woman she knew heard her son was killed— had hardly taken in the horror of it, when they came to say it was all a mistake—mistake of name. She fell on her knees with a shout of joy. "Praise the Lord, oh, my soul!" she cried in her wild delight. The household were totally upset. The swing back of the pendulum from the scene of weeping and wailing of a few moments before was very exciting. In the midst of this hubbub, the hearse drove up with the poor boy in his metallic coffin.

Does anybody wonder so many women die? Grief and constant anxiety kill nearly as many women as men die on the battlefield. Miriam's friend is at the point of death with brain fever; the sudden changes from joy to grief were more than she could bear.

June 4–11, 1862 . . . I know how it feels to die—I have felt it again and again.

For instance. Someone calls out, "Albert Sidney Johnston is killed." My heart stands still. I feel no more. I am for so many seconds, so many minutes—I know not how long—I am utterly without sensation of any kind—dead. And then there is that great throb, that keen agony of physical pain—the works are wound up again, the ticking of the clock begins anew, and I take up the burden of life once more. Someday it will stop too long, or my feeble heart will be too worn out to make that awakening jar, and all will be over. I know not— think when the end comes that there will be any difference except the miracle of the new wind up, throb. . . .

June 27, 1862 . . . Rebecca Haskell is dead—poor little darling! Immediately after her baby was born, she took it into her [head] that Alex was killed. He was wounded, but they had not told her of it.

She surprised them by asking, "Does anyone know how the battle has gone since Alex was killed?"

She could not read for a day or so before she died. Her head was bewildered, but she would not let anyone else touch his letters, so she died with several unopened ones in her bosom.

One needs a hard heart now. Even old Mr. Shand shed tears. Mary Barnwell sat as still as a statue—as white and stony. "Grief which can relieve itself by tears is a thing to pray for," said Rev. Mr. Shand.

June 29, 1862 . . . Victory! Victory heads every telegram now, one reads on the bulletin board. . . .

And now comes the list of killed and wounded.

Victory does not seem to soothe the sore hearts. Mrs. Haskell has five sons before the enemy's illimitable cannon. Mrs. Preston two.

This fair one rejoices that her sons were too young to be soldiers. "Of course, one fretted and worried about one's husband—but then, everyone knew husbands had a way of taking care of themselves. But, oh—the heartbreak and misery if one's son was there, &c&c&c."

July 1, 1862 . . . Edward Cheves—only son of John Cheves—killed. His sister kept crying, "Oh, mother, what shall we do—Edward is killed!" But the mother sat dead still, white as a sheet, never uttering a word or shedding a tear.

Are our women losing the capacity to weep? . . .

July 3, 1862 . . . Arrived at Mrs. McMahon's at the wrong moment. Mrs. Bartow was reading to the stricken mother an account of the death of her son. The letter was written by a man who was standing by him when he was shot through the head. "My God!" That was all—and he fell dead.

July 10, 1862 . . . After all, suppose we do all we hoped. Suppose we start up grand and free—a proud young republic. Think of all these young lives sacrificed! If three for one be killed, what comfort is that? What good will that do Mrs. Hayne or Mary DeSaussure? The best and the bravest of one generation swept away! Henry De-Saussure has left four sons to honor their father's memory and emulate his example. But those poor boys of between 18 and 20 years of age—Haynes, Trezevants, Taylors, Rhetts, &c&c—they are washed away, literally, in a tide of blood. There is nothing to show they ever were on earth.

May 8, 1864 . . . The dreadful work of death is beginning again.

John L. Miller, my cousin, killed at the head of his regiment.

The blows now fall so fast on our heads it is bewildering.

July 26, 1864 . . . When I remember all the true-hearted, the lighthearted, the gay and gallant boys who have come laughing, singing, dancing in my way in the three years past, I have looked into their brave young eyes and helped them as I could every way and then seen them no more forever. They lie stark and cold, dead upon the battlefield or moldering away in hospitals or prisons—which is worse. I think, if I consider the long array of those bright youths and loyal men who have gone to their deaths almost before my very eyes, my heart might break, too.

Is anything worth it? This fearful sacrifice—this awful penalty we pay for war?

August 1, 1864 . . . Forget to weep my dead—feel exalted. Oh, my Confederate heroes fallen in the fight! You are not to be matched in song or story.

We talk so calmly of them.

"Remember, now, was he not a nice fellow? He was killed at Shiloh."

Day after day we read the death roll. Someone holds up her hands. "Oh, here is another of our friends killed. He was such a good fellow."

January 16, 1865 . . . Mrs. McCord and Mrs. Goodwyn had lost each a son—Mrs. McCord her only one. Some had lost their husbands, brothers, sons. The thought that their lives had been given up in vain was very bitter to them. The besom of destruction had swept over every family there. Miss Middleton's only brother, the brave little Oliver, only a child, after all—but he would go.

What a cohort would rise to view, if thoughts took shape. Splendid young life sacrificed—in vain.

12

MARY COOPER

Dear Edward (1906)

With each passing year of the war, more and more southern farm wives wrote to their husbands in the army, detailing their desperate plight at home. Officers complained that these letters undermined morale and precipitated desertions. One such letter to a Confederate soldier follows. Edward Cooper, an artillery man in the Army of Northern Virginia, deserted and went home to look after his family in 1863 after receiving this letter; he subsequently returned to duty, was pardoned for his offense, and was killed in battle.

FROM John L. Underwood, *The Women of the Confederacy* (New York: The Neale Publishing Co, 1906), p. 170.

My dear Edward—

I have always been proud of you, and since your connection with the Confederate army, I have been prouder of you than ever before. I would not have you do anything wrong for the world, but before God, Edward, unless you come home, we must die. Last night I was aroused by little Eddie crying. I called and said, "What is the matter, Eddie?" And he said, "O mamma! I am so hungry." And Lucy, Edward, your darling Lucy, she never complains, but she is getting thinner and thinner every day. And before God, Edward, unless you come home, we must die.

Your Mary.

13

JUDITH McGUIRE

The Revulsion Was Sickening (1865)

Judith McGuire was a member of a prominent and well-connected Virginia family. Along with her husband, who was an Episcopal clergyman, she fled Alexandria shortly after the war began to avoid living under Union occupation. They lived in several towns before her husband was appointed a clerk in the post office and they moved to Richmond, where she eventually got a job in the Commissary Department. Both of her sons served in the Confederate Army and, imbued with a strong Confederate nationalism, she volunteered to work in the military hospitals in the city. She kept a diary during the war discussing her experiences as a war refugee. In the following entry, written early in 1865, she condemned the festive atmosphere in the war-torn city. By this time, one of her sons was a prisoner of war.

January 8, 1865—Some persons in this beleaguered city seem crazed on the subject of gayety. In the midst of the wounded and dying, the low state of the commissariat, the anxiety of the whole country, the troubles of every kind by which we are surrounded, I am mortified to say that there are gay parties given in the city. There are those denominated "starvation parties," where young persons meet for innocent enjoyment, and retire at a reasonable hour; but there are others where the most elegant suppers are served—cakes, jellies, ices in profusion, and meats of the finest kinds in abundance, such as might furnish a meal for a regiment of General Lee's army. I wish these things were not so, and that every extra pound of meat could be sent to the army. When returning

FROM Judith W. McGuire, *Diary of a Southern Refugee* (New York: E. J. Hale and Son, 1867), pp. 328–29.

from the hospital, after witnessing the dying scene of a brother, whose young sister hung over him in agony, with my heart full of the sorrows of hospital-life, I passed a house where there were music and dancing. The revulsion of feeling was sickening. I thought of the gayety of Paris during the French Revolution, of the "cholera ball" in Paris, the ball at Brussels the night before the battle of Waterloo, and felt shocked that our own Virginians, at such a time, should remind me of scenes which we were wont to think only belonged to the lightness of foreign society.

1

JOHN BOSTON

An Escaped Slave Writes His Wife from a Union Camp (1862)

John Boston was a Maryland slave who ran away and found sanctuary in a Union regiment in Virginia. The Union was not yet accepting black recruits, so presumably he performed camp chores and other nonmilitary duties. In the following letter to his wife, Boston announced his safe arrival and described his elation at having escaped from slavery. Boston's reception indicates that long before emancipation became a Union war aim, the army frequently treated runaway slaves as essentially free persons.

Upton Hill [Va.] January the 12th 1862

My Dear Wife

It is with grate joy I take this time to let you know Whare I am i am now in Safety in the 14th Regiment of Brooklyn this Day i can Adress you thank god as a free man   I had a little truble in giting away But as the lord led the Children of Isrel to the land of Canon So he led me to a land Whare fredom Will rain in spite Of earth and hell   Dear you must make your Self content i am free from al the Slavers Lash   and as you have chose the Wise plan Of Serving the lord i hope you Will pray Much and i Will try by the help of god To Serv him With all my hart   I am With a very nice man and have All that hart Can Wish   But My Dear I Cant express my grate desire that i Have to See you   i trust the time Will Come When We Shal meet again   And if We dont met on earth We Will Meet in heven Whare Jesas ranes   Dear Elizabeth tell Mrs Own [Owens] That i trust that She Will Continue Her kindness to you and that god Will Bless her on earth and Save her In grate eternity My Acomplements To Mrs Owens and her Children   may They Prosper through life   I never Shall forget her kindness to me Dear Wife i must Close   rest yourself Contented i am free   i Want you to rite To me Soon as you Can Without Delay Direct your letter to the 14th Reigment New york State malitia   Uptons Hill Virginea   In Care of Mr Cranford Comary   Write my Dear Soon As you C[an] Your Affectionate Husban Kiss Daniel For me

John Boston

Give my love to Father and Mother

FROM Ira Berlin, et al., eds., *Freedom: A Documentary History*, ser. I, vol. 1 (New York: Cambridge University Press, 1982), pp. 357–58.

Frederick Douglass Urges Black Men to Enlist
(1863)

After Abraham Lincoln announced that African Americans would be accepted in the Union Army, Frederick Douglass took the lead in the northern black community in urging black men to volunteer. In the following speech, delivered in Philadelphia on July 6, 1863, he outlined why it was important for blacks to fight for the Union.

Mr. President and Fellow Citizens— . . . There are those among us who say they are in favor of taking a hand in this tremendous war, but they add they wish to do so on terms of equality with white men. They say if they enter the service, endure all the hardships, perils and suffering—if they make bare their breasts, and with strong arms and courageous hearts confront rebel cannons, and wring victory from the jaws of death, they should have the same pay, the same rations, the same bounty, and the same favorable conditions every way afforded to other men.

I shall not oppose this view. There is something deep down in the soul of every man present which assents to the justice of the claim thus made, and honors the manhood and self-respect which insist upon it. I say at once, in peace and war, I am content with nothing for the black man short of equal and exact justice. The only question I have, and the point at which I differ from those who refuse to enlist, is whether the colored man is more likely to obtain justice and equality while refusing to assist in putting down this tremendous rebellion than he would be if he should promptly, generously and earnestly give his hand and heart to the salvation of the country in this day of calamity and peril. Nothing can be more plain, nothing more certain than that the speediest and best possible way open to us

to manhood, equal rights and elevation, is that we enter this service. . . .

. . . Jefferson Davis and his government make no secret as to the cause of this war, and they do not conceal the purpose of the war. That purpose is nothing more nor less than to make the slavery of the African race universal and perpetual on this continent. It is not only evident from the history and logic of events, but the declared purpose of the atrocious war now being waged against the country. Some, indeed, have denied that slavery has anything to do with the war, but the very same men who do this affirm it in the same breath in which they deny it, for they tell you that the abolitionists are the cause of the war. Now, if the abolitionists are the cause of the war, they are the cause of it only because they have sought the abolition of slavery. View it in any way you please, therefore, the rebels are fighting for the existence of slavery— they are fighting for the privilege, the horrid privilege, of sundering the dearest ties of human nature—of trafficking in slaves and the souls of men—for the ghastly privilege of scourging women and selling innocent children.

I say this is not the concealed object of the war, but the openly confessed and shamelessly proclaimed object of the war. Vice-President Stephens has stated, with the utmost clearness and precision, the difference between the fundamental ideas of the Confederate Government and those of the Federal Government. One is based upon the idea that

FROM *The Liberator*, 24 July 1863.

colored men are an inferior race, who may be enslaved and plundered forever, and to the heart's content of any men of a different complexion, while the Federal Government recognizes the natural and fundamental equality of all men. . . .

Now, what is the attitude of the Washington government towards the colored race? What reasons have we to desire its triumph in the present contest? Mind, I do not ask what was its attitude towards us before this bloody rebellion broke out. . . .

. . . I do not ask you about the dead past. I bring you to the living present.—Events more mighty than men, eternal Providence, all-wise, and all-controlling, have placed us in new relations to the government, and the government to us. What that government is to us to-day, and what it will be to-morrow, is made evident by a very few facts. Look at them, colored men! Slavery in the District of Columbia is abolished forever; slavery in all the territories of the United States is abolished forever; the foreign slave trade, with its ten thousand revolting abominations, is rendered impossible; slavery in ten States of the Union is abolished forever; slavery in the five remaining States is as certain to follow the same fate as the night is to follow the day. The independence of Hayti is recognized: her minister sits beside our Prime Minister, Mr. Seward, and dines at his table in Washington, while colored men are excluded from the cars in Philadelphia; showing that a black man's complextion in Washington, in the presence of the Federal government, is less offensive than in the city of brotherly love. Citizenship is no longer denied us under this government. . . .

Such is the Government, fellow-citizens, you are now called upon to uphold with your arms. Such is the Government that you are called upon to cooperate with in burying rebellion and slavery in a common grave. Never since the world began was a better chance offered to a long enslaved and oppressed people. The opportunity is given us to be men. With one courageous resolution we may blot out the hand-writing of ages against us. Once let the black man get upon his person the brass letters U.S.; let him get an eagle on his button, and a musket on his shoulder, and bullets in his pocket, and there is no power on the earth or under the earth which can deny that he has earned the right of citizenship in the United States. . . .

Do not flatter yourselves, my friends, that you are more important to the Government than the Government is to you. You stand but as the plank to the ship. This rebellion can be put down without your help. Slavery can be abolished by white men: but liberty so won for the black man, while it may leave him an object of pity, can never make him an object of respect.

Depend upon it, this is no time for hesitation. Do you say you want the same pay that white men get? I believe that the justice and magnanimity of your country will speedily grant it. But will you be over-nice about this matter? Do you get as good wages now as white men get by staying out of the service? Don't you work for less every day than white men get? You know you do. Do I hear you say you want black officers? Very well, and I have not the slightest doubt that, in the progress of this war, we shall see black officers, black colonels, and generals even. But is it not ridiculous in us in all at once refusing to be commanded by white men in time of war, when we are everywhere commanded by white men in time of peace? . . .

Young men of Philadelphia, you are without excuse. The hour has arrived, and your place is in the Union army. Remember that the musket—the United States musket with its bayonet of steel—is better than all mere parchment guarantees of liberty. In your hands that musket means liberty; and should your constitutional right at the close of this war be denied, which, in the nature of things, it cannot be, your brethren are safe while you have a Constitution which proclaims your right to keep and bear arms.

3

HANNAH JOHNSON

A Mother Calls on the Government
to Protect Black Soldiers (1863)

The black mother of a New Yorker who was serving in the Fifty-fourth Massachu-setts Regiment wrote the following letter to Abraham Lincoln shortly after the regi-ment's assault on Fort Wagner insisting that the government safeguard the rights of black soldiers. Her anxiety was precipitated by the Confederacy's threat to enslave captured black soldiers rather than treat them as prisoners of war. Unbeknownst to Johnson, on the day before she wrote this letter Lincoln had issued an order decree-ing that, for every captured black Union soldier the Confederacy enslaved, a rebel soldier was to be placed at hard labor in retaliation.

Buffalo [New York] July 31 1863

Excellent Sir

My good friend says I must write to you and she will send it[.] My son went in the 54th regiment. I am a colored woman and my son was strong and able to fight for his country and the colored people have as much to fight for as any. My father was a Slave and escaped from Louisiana before I was born morn forty years agone[.] I have but poor ed-ication but I never went to schol, but I know just as well as any what is right between man and man. Now I know it is right that a colored man should go and fight for his country, and so ought to a white man. I know that a colored man ought to run no greater risques than a white, his pay is no greater his obligation to fight is the same. So why should not our enemies be compelled to treat him the same, Made to do it.

My son fought at Fort Wagoner but thank God he was not taken prisoner, as many were[.] I

FROM Ira Berlin, et al., eds., *Freedom: A Documentary His-tory*, ser. II (New York: Cambridge University Press, 1982), pp. 582–83.

thought of this thing before I let my boy go but then they said Mr. Lincoln will never let them sell our colored soldiers for slaves, if they do he will get them back quck[.] he will rettallyate and stop it. Now Mr. Lincoln dont you think you oght to stop this thing and make them do the same by the col-ored men they have lived in idleness all their lives on stolen labor and made savages of the colored people, but they now are so furious because they are proving themselves to be men, such as have come away and got some edication. It must not be so. You must put the rebels to work in State pris-ons to making shoes and things, if they sell our col-ored soldiers, till they let them all go. And give their wounded the same treatment. it would seem cruel, but their [is] no other way, and a just man must do hard things sometimes, that shew him to be a great man. They tell me some do you will take back the Proclamation, don't do it. When you are dead and in Heaven, in a thousand years that ac-tion of yours will make the Angels sing your praises I know it. Ought one man to own another, law for or not, who made the law, surely the poor slave did not. so it is wicked, and a horrible Out-rage, there is no sense in it, because a man has lived by robbing all his life and his father before him, should he complain because the stolen things found on him are taken. Robbing the colored people of their labor is but a small part of the robbery[.] their souls are almost taken, they are made bruits of often. You know all about this[.]

Will you see that the colored men fighting now, are fairly treated. You ought to do this, and do it at once, Not let the thing run along meet it quickly and manfully, and stop this, mean cowardly cruelty. We poor oppressed ones, appeal to you, and ask fair play.

Yours for Christs sake

Hannah Johnson

4

LORENZO THOMAS

A Union General Describes Slaves Entering the Union Lines (1863)

Lorenzo B. Thomas, the adjutant general of the army, was placed in charge of organizing regiments of former slaves in the Mississippi valley in 1863. In the following letter to Secretary of War Edwin Stanton, he describes the condition of runaway slaves entering the Union military lines.

Cairo, Illinois, Augt 23. 1863.

Sir,

. . . On arriving at Lake Providence on my way to Vicksburg, I found upwards of a thousand negroes, nearly all women and children, on the banks of the river, in a most helpless condition, who had left the plantations in consequence of the withdrawal of the troops on account of sickness. They had successfully sustained one attack of guerillas, aided by a gun-boat, but expected another attack. I took them all to Goodrich's Landing where there is a garrison of negro troops. The number of this helpless class in the various camps is very large and daily increasing, and altho' everything is done for their well being, I find that sickness prevails to an alarming extent, and the bills of mortality are very high. This results from their change of life and habits, from daily work to comparative idleness, and also from being congregated in large numbers in camps, which is a matter of necessity. Besides, they will not take care of themselves much less of those who are sick. I have therefore after much reflection and consultation with officers, come to the conclusion that the old men, women and children should be advised to remain on the plantations, especially on those within our lines where we can have an oversight of them. Besides, it is important that the crops on the plantations within our lines should be gathered. A number of those now in our camps express a desire to return to their old homes, and indeed many have already done so. All such will be encouraged to do so, in cases where we are satisfied their former masters will nor run them off or sell them. . . .

It is important that woodyards should be established on the river, and General Grant is encouraging the measure. I will permit persons duly authorized to cut wood for steamboats, to hire woodchoppers from those who are unfit for mili-

FROM Ira Berlin, et al., eds., *Freedom: A Documentary History,* ser. I, vol. 1 (New York: Cambridge University Press, 1982), pp. 308–10.

tary service, including the women. It will be far more for their benefit to support themselves than to sit in idleness in camps depending on the Government for subsistence.

. . . A large amount of clothing will be needed for the women and children, and as such clothing is not provided by the Government, I propose to appeal to the benevolent for a supply. From this point the government boats can transport it without expence, but I desire your authority to pay the transportation to Cairo from the places where the clothing is provided. I have the honor to be, Very respectfully Your Obed. Svt.

L. Thomas

5

SUSANNA CLAY

The Negroes Are Worse Than Free (1863)

Susanna Claiborne Clay was a member of a prominent political family in northern Alabama. Her husband was a leader of the state Democratic party and a former congressman, governor, and senator. In 1860 he owned 70 slaves, making him one of the largest slaveowners in the state. Their son, Clement Claiborne Clay, also served in the U.S. Senate from 1854 to 1861 and was subsequently a Confederate senator and then a Confederate diplomat stationed in Canada. The Clays's primary residence was in Huntsville, but they periodically lived on their plantation outside of town, which Susanna increasingly managed because of her husband's declining health. In this letter, she described the growing independence of the slaves and the lessening power of white authority on the plantation.

Sep. 5th [18]63

My dear son,

. . . The negroes are worse than free—they say they are free. We cannot exert any authority. I beg ours to do what little is done. Lucinda makes the beds, Maria gets the morsel we eat for we have just sufficient to keep us from starvation. She and Crity milk two cows, but grumble and threaten, if Lucinda does not go to get the calves that they will quit. Charles goes to Withers' to make fires in the morning after he has made one here and says he will not go there if he is troubled &c. Alfred does less than Charles. I have to work harder than I ever did, but am patient[,] silent and prayerful. Your

Father cannot realize the times but is led by the overseer who writes to him to see things differently from what is true. The negroes are so bold, that Alfred told me this morning that if your father went to M.V. [Monte Vista plantation] (as he wishes to do with Alfred's horse) and let the overseer attempt to punish for disobedience that some one would kill the overseer! I asked him how he knew. He said Stephen[,] Hannibal, and Sampson said that they would do it if he ever attempted it! . . .

Campbell [a slave] came with an Officer, and men, just as I was preparing for bed. They came to my room[.] I was undressed and beged [*sic*] them not to come in[.] they looked at me while I threw on a Robe. I asked, what they wanted? They said the children. I heard that they had your Father at the gate and followed them down where I met Campbell. He was impudent and told lies. I said

FROM Clay Family Papers, Duke University, Durham, North Carolina.

little to him. He had gone to M.V. and taken Harie to Stephenson before he came here. Harrison took Margaret and Jim two weeks afterwards. Peter and Wesley went, but returned, Peter with a pass for his wife, but said, he did not intend to go but the cars ceased to run, and there were no wagons. One came for Margaret.

Your negroes are free as ours. Where masters are they do better but all I have heard speak, expect that all the negroes able to go will do so when the cars run or the Y's [Yankees] get here. . . .

Oct. 13th. Severs [the overseer] went out but did not take my letter. I suppose he was angry because I advised him not to punish or force Tempe.

She threatened to have his house burned when the Y's came. I beged her to think of the sin &c. . . . The negroes are making molasses slowly. There is no cotton. The overseer is slow and inert. He has no authority. They have no meat except a beef occasionally. Not a grain of salt and they are too lazy to make it out of the smoke house [from salt deposits in the dirt floor]. Milly is the most true one there. Many profess to be so. . . . Milly says that Lydia, Hannah and others are packed to go as soon as they can get news from their friends. . . .

God bless and preserve you,

Mother

6

ISAIAH H. WELCH

A Black Soldier Explains His Motives for Fighting (1863)

In the following letter, Isaiah H. Welch, a member of the black Massachusetts Fifty-fifth Regiment, discussed his motivation for enlisting. Unlike most northern free blacks who lived in urban areas, Welch came from a farm family in Bellfont, Pennsylvania. The twenty-one-year-old Welch was a sergeant in the regiment. His letter was published in the (Philadelphia) Christian Recorder, *the organ of the African Methodist Episcopal Church.*

Folly Island, S.C., October 15, 1863

Dear Brother in Christ:

. . . I will mention a little about the 55th Massachusetts Regiment. They seem to be in good health at present, and are desirous of making a bold dash upon the enemy. I pray God the time will soon come when we, as soldiers of God, and of our race and country, may face the enemy with boldness. For my part, I feel willing to suffer all privations incidental to a Christian and a soldier.

This is the calmest day that I have witnessed on

the Island. Since here I have been for some four weeks or more in bombarding the enemy's forts. Thank God, we have silenced their batteries. . . . I stood upon the parapets surrounding the "Swamp Angel,"[1] and saw men fall around me like hailstones. I stood fast and kept the men that were working upon them together as much as possible. The enemy fired shell and grape into us like hot cakes, but we kept at our work like men of God. In

---

FROM [Philadelphia] *Christian Recorder*, 24 October 1863.

[1]The "Swamp Angel" was a gigantic artillery piece that hurled 200-pound shells great distances. Mounted by the Union forces on Morris Island, it was used to bombard Charleston, South Carolina, several miles away.

conclusion, let me say, If I fall in the battle anticipated, remember, I fall in defense of my race and country. Some of my friends thought it very wrong in me setting aside the work of the Lord to take up arms against our enemy. Certainly I can with as much grace as taking a drink out of Wilberforce spring. Another excuse or reason they offered was, that it is wrong to take that which you cannot restore, but I am fully able to answer all questions pertaining to rebels. If taking lives will restore the country to what it once was, then God help me to slay them on every hand. . . .

I remain yours truly,

I.H. Welch
Orderly Sgt.

7

NEW YORK TIMES

A Prodigious Revolution (1864)

When the Twentieth Regiment United States Colored Troops paraded through New York City to the enthusiastic cheers of the city's residents, the New York Times *on March 6, 1864, hailed its reception as a sign of the social and political progress that the war had produced. Noting that only seven months had elapsed since the draft riots had shaken the city, the paper could not resist adding the ironic observation that the presence of these black men in Union uniforms had the effect of "saving from inevitable and distasteful conscription the same number of those who hunted their persons and destroyed their homes during these days of humiliation and disgrace." On the following day, the* Times *offered these additional comments.*

The Ovation to the Black Regiment.

There has been no more striking manifestation of the marvelous times that are upon us than the scene in our streets at the departure of the first of our colored regiments. Had any man predicted it last year he would have been thought a fool, even by the wisest and most discerning. History abounds with strange contrasts. It always has been an ever-shifting melo-drama. But never, in this land at least, has it presented a transition so extreme and yet so speedy as what our eyes have just beheld.

Eight months ago the African race in this City were literally hunted down like wild beasts. They fled for their lives. When caught, they were shot down in cold blood, or stoned to death, or hung to the trees or the lamp-posts. Their houses were pillaged; the asylum which Christian charity had provided for their orphaned children was burned; and there was no limit to the persecution but in the physical impossibility of finding further material on which the mob could wreak its ruthless hate. Nor was it solely the raging horde in the streets that visited upon the black man the nefarious wrong. Thousands and tens of thousands of men of higher social grade, of better education, cherished precisely the same spirit. It found expression in contumelious speech rather than in the violent act, but it was persecution none the less for that. In fact the mob would never have entered upon that career of outrage but for the fact that it was fired and maddened by the prejudice which had been

FROM *New York Times*, 7 March 1864.

generated by the ruling influences, civil and social, here in New York, till it had enveloped the City like some infernal atmosphere. The physical outrages which were inflicted on the black race in those terrible days were but the outburst of malignant agencies which had been transfusing the whole community from top to bottom, year after year.

How astonishingly had all this been changed! The same men who could not have shown themselves in the most obscure street in the City without peril of instant death, even though in the most suppliant attitude, now march in solid platoons, with shouldered muskets, slung knapsacks, and buckled cartridge-boxes down through our gayest avenues and our busiest thoroughfares to the peal-ing strains of martial music, and are everywhere saluted with waving handkerchiefs, with descending flowers, and with the acclamations and plaudits of countless beholders. They are halted at our most beautiful square, and amid an admiring crowd, in the presence of many of our most prominent citizens, are addressed in an eloquent and most complimentary speech by the President of our chief literary institution, and are presented with a gorgeous stand of colors in the name of a large number of the first ladies of the City. . . .

It is only by such occasions that we can at all realize the prodigious revolution which the public mind everywhere is experiencing. Such developments are infallible tokens of a new epoch.

8

ANONYMOUS

A Black Soldier Protests Unequal Pay (1864)

Black troops encountered persistent discrimination in the Union Army. One example was pay. Like the members of the famous Fifty-fourth Massachusetts Regiment, the soldiers in the black Fifty-fifth Massachusetts Regiment refused to accept less pay than white soldiers received. They had enlisted under the promise of thirteen dollars a month, plus an additional three-dollar clothing allowance; the War Department subsequently ruled that the law authorizing black enlistments stipulated pay of only ten dollars per month, with three dollars deducted for clothing. Members of both regiments repeatedly refused to accept this lesser rate of pay and vigorously agitated for equal treatment. A member of the Fifty-fifth Massachusetts Regiment wrote this letter to the New York Weekly Anglo-African *shortly before the unit departed from Florida, in which he discussed the issue and the sentiment in the regiment.*

Headquarters 55th Reg. Mass. Infantry,
Palatka, Fla., April 10, 1864

Mr. Editor:

This Regiment was mustered into the United States service about the 18th or 20 of June, 1863, conse-

FROM [New York] *Weekly Anglo-African*, 30 April 1864.

quently we have been ten months working for Uncle Sam, not taking into account the time when some of us were sworn in.

The only thing that engrosses our mind now, is the old and troublesome subject of pay.

We have been promised that we would be paid, and a paymaster came (last November) to pay us. He offered us $7 per month. We enlisted for $13 per month, with the promise (and I wish the public to keep this fact before them, to see how these promises are being fulfilled) that we should be treated in all respects like white soldiers, our bounty, rations, and emoluments being the same. The same inducements were held out to us as to all Massachusetts volunteers.

You, sir, no doubt, have copies of the circulars that were distributed through the country to encourage enlistments. . . .

We do not look upon Massachusetts as being responsible for our sufferings; but upon the government of the United States, and how a government with such a lofty reputation can so act, is beyond our conception or comprehension. We know, and the world knows that had we been white men the whole land would have been in a blaze of indignation in regard to the great injustice done us.

How the authorities expect our families to live without the means to buy bread, pay house rent, and meet the other incidental expenses of living in these terrible times, we know not; but if it does not exert its well known power it certainly will not be held guiltless in this matter.

Are our parents, wives, children and sisters to suffer, while we, their natural protectors, are fighting the battles of the nation? We leave the government and Congress to answer.

That they *do* suffer we have abundant evidence.

I have seen a letter from a wife in Illinois to her husband, stating that she had been sick for six months, and begging him to send her the sum of *fifty cents.* Was it any wonder that the tears rolled in floods from that stout-hearted man's eyes?

How can it be expected that men will do their duty consistently with a soldier's training, under such circumstances?

Patience has an end, and with us will soon cease to be a virtue. We would be contented and happy could we but receive our pay.

I have been asked by officers, not connected with our Regiment, why we did not take our pay when we could get it. My answer was that our pay has never been sent to us. True, money has been sent here, but it was not our pay. When the United

States authorities shall send us $13 per month, which is our just due, we will take it, *and not until then, will we take one cent.* . . .

Money has been sent us through different channels which we have refused, and which we must continue to refuse. To accept our pay in this way would degrade us, and mark us as inferior soldiers, and would be a complete annihilation of every vestige of our manhood.

The United States knows our value as soldiers too well to suppose that we will sacrifice the position that we have gained by most arduous labor, and we, thoroughly comprehending our relation to the past glorious history of our race, and the verdict that must fall upon us in the future if we falter; will stand up for our rights, come what may. . . .

It is glorious to see how our noble fellows stand up under their trials. Pride has kept them where they are to-day, and they certainly deserve to be respected.

Promises have no weight with us now, until the past and present is fulfilled—future ones we will not heed. . . .

The words of cheer that we once received from our mothers, wives and sisters, are becoming fainter and fainter, and their cries of want stronger and stronger with each revolving day. Is the picture of our desolate house-holds, and the gaunt figures of our friends now suffering almost the pangs of starvation, to haunt us by day and night in our camp? . . .

Oh, God! most bitter is the cup presented to our lips; but that others may live we will drink it even to the dregs.

Our debasement is most complete. No chances for promotion, no money for our families, and we little better than an armed band of laborers with rusty muskets and bright spades, what is our incentive to duty? Yet God has put it into our hearts to believe that we will survive or perish with the liberty of our country. If she lives, we live; if she dies we will sleep with her, even as our brave comrades now sleep with Col. Shaw within the walls of Wagner.

More anon,

Bay State

9

SPOTSWOOD RICE

A Black Soldier Writes His Daughter's Owner
(1864)

Spotswood Rice of Missouri was serving in a black Union regiment when he wrote this letter to Kitty Diggs, who held Rice's daughter as a slave. Rice's words disclose some of the unique motivations of black soldiers in the war, as well as their growing self-assertion. Rice's free status is revealed by the fact that he tried to buy his daughter from Diggs (under southern law, children followed the status of the mother, so presumably Rice was married to a slave woman). The second letter was written by Diggs's brother to General William Rosecrans, the commander of the Department of Missouri, in response to Rice's letter.

[Benton Barracks Hospital, St. Louis, Mo., September 3, 1864]

I received a leteter from Cariline telling me that you say I tried to steal to plunder my child away from you   now I want you to understand that mary is my Child and she is a God given rite of my own and you may hold on to hear as long as you can but I want you to remembor this one thing that the longor you keep my Child from me the longor you will have to burn in hell and the qwicer youll get their   for we are now makeing up a bout one thoughsand blacke troops to Come up tharough and wont to Come through Glasgow and when we come wo be to Copperhood rabbels and to the Slaveholding rebbels for we dont expect to leave them there root neor branch   but we thinke how ever that we that have Children in the hands of you devels we will trie your [word illegible] the day that we enter Glasgow   I want you to understand kittey diggs that where ever you and I meets we are enmays to each orthere   I offered once to pay you forty dollers for my own Child but I am glad now that you did not accept it   Just hold on now as long as you can and the worse it will be for you   you never in you life befor I came down hear did you give Children any thing not eny thing whatever not even a dollers worth of expencs now you call my children your pro[per]ty   not so with me   my Children is my own and I expect to get them and when I get ready to come after mary I will have bout a powrer and autherity to bring hear away and to exacute vengencens on them that holds my Child   you will then know how to talke to me   I will assure that and you will know how to talk rite too   I want you now to just hold on to hear if you want to   iff your concho-sence tells thats the road go that road and what it will brig you to kittey diggs   I have no fears about geting mary out of your hands   this whole Gov-ernment gives chear to me and you cannot help your self.

Spotswood Rice

FROM Ira Berlin, et al., eds., *Freedom: A Documentary History*, ser. II (New York: Cambridge University Press, 1982), p. 690.

10

RACHEL ANN WICKER

The Hardship of Black Soldiers' Families (1864)

Most African Americans who volunteered to serve in the Union Army had only limited financial means. Hence the refusal of several black regiments to accept unequal pay imposed severe financial hardships on the families of many of these soldiers, as the following letter from the wife of an Ohio free black man serving in the Fifty-fifth Massachusetts Infantry details. She sent the letter to Governor John Andrew of Massachusetts, who forwarded it to the War Department. Shortly after this letter was written, the men in both regiments were finally paid in accordance with the law passed by Congress in June 1864, which provided full pay retroactive to the time of enlistment for black soldiers who had been free before the war. Not until March 1865 did Congress include in these provisions those former slaves who had enlisted.

Piqua Miama Co ohio Sep 12 1864

Sir

I write to you to know the reason why our husbands and sons who enlisted in the 55th Massichusette regiment have not Bin paid off   i speak for my self and Mother and i know of a great many others as well as ourselve are suffering for the want of money to live on   when provision and Clotheing wer Cheap we might have got a long   But Every thing now is thribbl and over what it was some thre year Back   But it matters not if Every thing was at the old Price   i think it a Piece of injustice to have those soldiers there 15 months with out a cent of Money   for my part i Cannot see why they have not th[e] same rite to their 16 dollars per month as th Whites or Even th Coulord Soldiers that went from ohio   i think if Massichusette had left off Comeing to other States for Soldiers th Soldirs would have bin Better off and Massichusette saved her Credit   i wish you if you pleas to Answer this Letter and tell me Why it is that you Still insist upon them takeing 7 dollars a month when you give the Poorest White Regiment that has went out 16 dollars   Answer this if you Pleas and oblige Your humble Servant

Rachel Ann Wicker

FROM Ira Berlin, et al., eds., *Freedom: A Documentary History*, ser. II (New York: Cambridge University Press, 1982), pp. 402–403.

11

Mittie Freeman Meets a Yankee (1937)

In the 1930s, the Works Progress Administration conducted a series of interviews with former slaves about their memories of bondage. Several other institutions, including Fiske University in Nashville, collected similar interviews. Given the elapsed time and the fact most of those interviewed were young children during the war, these interviews are extremely difficult to use but constitute the largest body of first-hand evidence of slaves' experiences available.

Mittie Freeman was born on a plantation in Mississippi around 1850, but before the war her owner moved his slaves to Arkansas. Her father was a driver on the new plantation, a position of prestige and authority. Uncertain of their slaves' loyalty, slaveowners during the war tried to frighten them with descriptions of Yankees that portrayed them as half beasts or even the devil. In this interview, Freeman recalls the first time she encountered a dreaded Yankee soldier.

Old Miss[tress] was name Miss 'liza. She skeered to stay by herself after old master died. I was took to be her companion. . . . One day I was a standing by the window, and I seen smoke—blue smoke a rising over beyond a woods. I heered cannons a-booming and axed her what was it. She say: "Run, Mittie, and hide yourself. It's the Yanks. Theys coming at last, Oh lordy!" I was all incited [excited] and told her I didn't want to hide, I wanted to see 'em. "No," she say, right firm. "Ain't I always told you Yankees has horns on their heads? They'll get you. Go on now, do like I tells you." So I runs out the room and went down by the big gate. A high wall was there and a tree put its branches right over the top. I clim up and hid under the leaves. They was coming, all a marching. The captain opened our big gate and marched them in. A soldier seen me and said "Come on down here; I want to see you." I told him I would, if he would take off his hat and show me his horns.

FROM George P. Rawick, ed., *The American Slave*, vol. 8, pt. 2, (Westport, Conn.: Greenwood, 1972), pp. 347–48.

12

Former Slaves Recall the End of Slavery (1937)

In the Works Progress Administration and other interviews, former slaves discussed many aspects of their experiences during the war. A particularly vivid memory for a number of the black men and women who were interviewed was the time when slavery finally ended. As these individual experiences demonstrate, freedom did not come at the same time, or in the same way, to all slaves.

Charlotte Brown, b. ca. 1855, Woods Crossing, Virginia

De news come on a Thursday, an' all de slaves been shoutin' an' carryin' on tell ev'ybody was all tired out. 'Member de fust Sunday of freedom. We was all sittin' roun' restin' an' tryin' to think what freedom meant an' ev'ybody was quiet an' peaceful. All at once ole Sister Carrie who was near 'bout a hundred started in to talkin':

> Tain't no mo' sellin' today,
> Tain't no mo' hirin' today,
> Tain't no pullin' off shirts today,
> Its stomp down freedom today.
> Stomp it down!

An' when she says, "Stomp it down," all de slaves commence to shoutin' wid her:

> Stomp down Freedom today—
> Stomp it down!
> Stomp down Freedom today.

Wasn't no mo' peace dat Sunday. Ev'ybody started in to sing an' shout once mo'. Fust thing you know dey done made up music to Sister Carrie's stomp song an' sang an' shouted dat song all de res' de day. Chile, dat was one glorious time!

Ambrose Douglas, b. 1845, Brooksville, Florida

I guess we musta celebrated 'Mancipation about twelve times in Hornett County [North Carolina]. Every time a bunch of No'thern sojers would come through they would tell us we was free and we'd begin celebratin'. Before we would get through somebody else would tell us to go back to work, and we would go. Some of us wanted to jine up with the army, but didn't know who was goin' to win and didn't take no chances.

I was 21 when freedom finally came, and that time I didn't take no chances on 'em taking it back again. I lit out for Florida and wound up in Madison County.

John Brown, b. 1860, of Petersburg, Virginia

Didn't know nothin' 'about it [emancipation] till Lee's army surrendered at de apple tree. I never will fergit dat day 'cause all Marsa's seben chillun come runnin' out de house an' yellin': "John, John, you is free, John! De war is over an' dat make you a free man!"

FROM George P. Rawick, ed. *The American Slave*, vol. 4, pt. III and IV (Texas), p. 70 (Westport, Conn.: Greenwood, 1972), vol. 14, pt. I (North Carolina), pp. 24–25; vol. 17 (Florida), pp. 103, 246; Virginia Writers' Project, *The Negro in Virginia* (New York: Hastings House, 1940), pp. 208–209, 212.

An' I made out like I was cryin' an' kivered my face wid both hands an' hollered dat I didn't want to leave Missus, but I was gloryin' jus' de same.

Mary Anderson, b. 1851, Raleigh, N.C.

The war was begun and there were stories of fights and freedom. The news went from plantation to plantation and while the slaves acted natural and some even more polite than usual, they prayed for freedom. Then one day I heard something that sounded like thunder and missus and marster began to walk around and act queer. The grown slaves were whispering to each other. Sometimes they gathered in little gangs in the grove. Next day I heard it again, boom, boom, boom. I went and asked missus "is it going to rain?" . . . In a day or two everybody on the plantation seemed to be disturbed and marster and missus were crying. Marster ordered all the slaves to come to the great house at nine o'clock. Nobody was working and slaves were walking over the grove in every direction. At nine o'clock all the slaves gathered at the great house and master and missus come out on the porch and stood side by side. You could hear a pin drap [*sic*] everything was so quiet. Then marster said, "Good morning," and missus said, "Good morning, children." They were both crying. Then marster said, "Men, women and children, you are free. You are no longer my slaves. The Yankees will soon be here."

Marster and missus then went into the house[,] got two large arm chairs[,] put them on the porch facing the avenue[,] and sat down side by side and remained there watching. In about an hour there was one of the blackest clouds coming up the avenue from the main road. It was the Yankee soldiers, they finally filled the mile long avenue reaching from marster's house to the main Louisburg road and spread out over the mile square grove. The mounted men dismounted. The footmen stacked their shining guns and began to build fires and cook. They called the slaves, saying, "You are free." Slaves were whooping and laughing and acting like they were crazy. Yankee soldiers were shaking hands with the Negroes and calling them Sam, Dinah, Sarah and asking them questions. They busted the door to the smoke house and got all the hams. They went to the icehouse and got several barrels of brandy, and such a time. The Negroes and Yankees were cooking and eating together. The Yankees told them to come on and join them, they were free. Marster and missus sat on the porch and they were so humble no Yankee bothered anything in the great house. The slaves were awfully excited. The Yankees stayed there, cooked, eat, drank and played music until about night, then a bugle began to blow and you never saw such getting on horses and lining up in your life. In a few minutes they began to march, leaving the grove which was soon as silent as a grave yard. They took marster's horses and cattle with them and joined the main army. . . .

When they left the country, lot of the slaves went with them and soon there were none of marster's slaves left. . . .

William Mathews, b. 1848, Galveston, Texas[1]

We went right on workin' after freedom. Old Buck Adams wouldn't let us go. It was way after freedom dat de freedom man come and read de paper, and tell us not to work no more 'less us git pay for it. When he gone, old Mary Adams [the plantation mistress], she come out. I 'lect what she say as if I jes' hear her say it. She say, "Ten years from today I'll have you all back 'gain." Dat ten years been over a mighty long time and she ain't git us back yit and she dead and gone.

Dey makes us git right off de place, jes' like you take an old hoss and turn it loose. Dat how us was. No money, no nothin'.

---

[1]Mathews was a slave in Franklin Parish, Louisiana, during the war. His owner's name was Buck Adams.

13 ❧

ELIZA EVANS

The Slave Eliza Acquires a New Name (1937)

In the following Works Progress Administration interview, Eliza Evans (b. ca. 1850) of McAlester, Oklahoma, describes the effect Yankee soldiers had on her when they arrived at the plantation of her owner, John Mixon, near Selma, Alabama.

Once the Yankee soldiers come. I was big enough to tote pails and piggins then. These soldiers made us chillun tote water to fill their canteens and water their horses. We toted the water on our heads. Another time we heard the Yankee's was coming and old Master had about fifteen hundred pounds of meat. They was hauling it off to bury it and hide it when the Yankees caught them. The soldiers ate and wasted every bit of that good meat. We didn't like them a bit.

One time some Yankee soldiers stopped and started talking to me—they asked me what my name was. I say "Liza," and they say, "Liza who?" I thought a minute and shook my head. "Jest Liza, I ain't got no other name."

He say, "Who live up yonder in dat Big House?" I say, "Mr. John Mixon." He say, "You are Liza Mixon." He say, "Do anybody ever call you nigger?" And I say, "Yes Sir." He say, "Next time anybody call you nigger you tell 'em dat you is a Negro and your name is Miss Liza Mixon." The more I thought of that the more I liked it and I made up my mind to do jest what he told me to.

. . . One evening when I was minding the calves and old Master come along. He say, "What you doin' nigger?" I say real pert like, "I ain't no nigger. I'se a Negro and I'm Miss Liza Mixon." Old Master sho' was surprised and he picks up a switch and starts at me.

Law, but I was skeered! I hadn't never had no whipping so I run fast as I can to Granma Gracie. I hid behind her . . . 'bout that time Master John got there. He say, "Gracie, dat little nigger sassed me." She say, "Lawsie child, what does ail you?" I told them what the Yankee soldier told me to say and Grandma Gracie took my dress and lift it over my head and pins my hands inside, and Lawsie, how she whipped me. . . . I just said dat to the wrong person.

FROM George P. Rawick, ed., *The American Slave*, vol. 7 (Westport, Conn.: Greenwood, 1972), pp. 95–96.

1

RANDOLPH SHOTWELL

The Comforts of a Soldier's Life (1929)

Virginia-born Randolph Shotwell was in school in Pennsylvania when the war began. So intense was his southern patriotism that in August 1861 he left school, slipped through the Union lines, and enlisted in the first Confederate regiment he came upon. He was only sixteen years old at the time. As a member of the Eighth Virginia, he soon learned that soldiering was not the romantic adventure he had envisioned. In the following selection from his autobiography, he described some of the discomforts of a soldier's life in winter camp. Shotwell was captured at Cold Harbor, Virginia, and spent the remainder of the war in prison camp.

Fancy the comforts of such a life as this! Roused at dawn to crawl out and stand half-dressed in a drenching storm while the company-roll was being called; then return to damp blankets—or to rub the skin off of your knuckles, trying to start a fire with green pine poles in the storm; go down to the marsh to break the ice off of a shallow branch or rivulet, and flirt a few handfuls of muddy water upon your face, then wipe it off on the clean corner of a dirty pocket handkerchief, borrow a broken piece of comb (having lost your own, and having no money to replace it) and, after raking the bits of trash out of your stubby locks, devote the next hour to trying to boil a dingy tin-cup of so-called coffee; after which, with a chunk of boiled beef, or broiled bacon (*red*, almost, with rust and skippers) and a piece of cornbread, you are ready to breakfast. But now you have blackened your hands, and are begrimed with the sooty smoke from the snapping, popping, sappy, green pine logs, your eyes are red and smarting, your face burned while your back is drenched and chilled; and you have no place to sit while eating your rough meal.

Around you are dozens of rough, uncouth fellows, whose mingled complaints, coarse jests, quarrels, noise and impatience make you sigh at the prospect of spending the entire day and the next, and the next, and so on *ad infinitum* under precisely similar circumstances.

FROM Randolph Shotwell, "Three Years in Battle," in *The Papers of Randolph Abbott Shotwell*, vol. 1, ed. J. G. de Roulhac Hamilton (Raleigh: North Carolina Historical Commission, 1929), p. 136.

Hard Marching (1863)

Civil War volunteers thought of war in terms of fighting, but as they soon discovered, they spent far more time drilling in camp or marching along country roads than they did in combat. Born in 1839, Wilbur Fisk had grown up on a Vermont farm and was working as a farm hand when he enlisted in 1861 in the Second Vermont Volunteers. He served in the Virginia theater as a private until the war was over. Despite having only a limited formal education, Fisk became a regular correspondent for The Green Mountain Freeman, *a Montpelier paper, and eventually published nearly one hundred letters discussing the war and the experiences of his regiment. Although written for publication, these letters provide an often frank and certainly unglamorous commentary on the war from the viewpoint of the ordinary soldier. The following letter describes a portion of his regiment's marching during the 1862 peninsula campaign. Two years later, Fisk's letters were still recounting his regiment's constant marching while on campaign. Indeed, Fisk encapsulated his war experience as "hard marching every day."*

Vicinity of Richmond
Tuesday, May 20, 1862

The next day we marched on to New Kent Court House, where part of our regiment was detailed for picket. We left our posts the following morning, falling into line as the remainder of the regiment came up, marched to Cumberland or Perham's Landing on the Pamunkey river. This was emphatically a crosslot march, and the distance, if counted by difficulties instead of miles would reach an enormous figure. The route lay through swamps and creeks and thick undergrowth woods—the most difficult place in the world to march. March-

ing in a column a mile or more in length is altogether a different thing from marching alone. If the head of the column comes to a place where but one can pass at a time, those in the rear are obliged to wait till all ahead of them have reached solid ground, so that whenever they have crossed the swamp, or creek, or whatever the obstruction may be, they are far behind and it takes a long time to get the ranks closed up. There is a general order issued to remedy this evil, but it can hardly be said to be effectual. This kind of marching, especially after a rain, may be considered the rule, while good marching on good solid ground is the exception. If some of the boys in Vermont, who think a soldier's life an easy one, had been in the ranks with us during our various marches, they would have found a practical logic in the reality to convince them that marching is fatiguing business, even for soldiers, these hot days—and rainy ones are no better.

FROM Emil Rosenblatt and Ruth Rosenblatt, eds., *Hard Marching Every Day, 1861–1865: The Civil War Letters of Private Wilbur Fisk* (Lawrence: University of Kansas Press, 1992), pp. 27–29.

The word "halt" is always an agreeable command, but there is always a great many annoying preliminaries to go through before we can take advantage of it to rest. Often just as we are about to release our aching shoulders from the galling knapsack strap, the order "attention" is given, and we are moved perhaps six inches and perhaps six rods when we halt again and wait for further orders. Some run the risk and sit down, others throw off their knapsacks, but the majority wait, expecting every minute to move to another position that will square more precisely with military exactness. . . .

When we reached Perham's Landing, we stopped as usual, and of course went through the customary evolutions preliminary to a final halt. The word came at last and not doubting its good faith we eagerly threw off our burdensome knapsacks, hoping to have time to rest and partake of our rations. . . . We had had no coffee that morning, many of us had eaten nothing since the afternoon previous, having come directly from the picket, and as it was close on to noon, we naturally began to feel the keen demands of appetite. One of our company happened to have a paper of tea which he generously distributed as far as it would go, and we repaired to the bushes near by and struck up a fire, and in a short time had it covered with cups of water for our tea. Just as it was beginning to simmer, and we were anticipating a decent breakfast after all, the everlasting order came for the fifth time I believe, to "fall in." We had no means of knowing whether we were to march ten miles or ten feet, but the old Colonel was coming and the order must be obeyed, and promptly too. So away went our tea into the fire, and with it all our labor and expectations, and many I fear lost their patience too in that unlucky moment, for their countenances, which a few minutes before were all aglow with animation, suddenly became darkened with angry scowls, and more than one fierce thunderbolt of wrath, in the shape of oaths and curses, was hurled forth from under that black cloud of frowns, but of no avail. Forward march was soon ordered. We go on 200 yards perhaps and halt, unsling knapsacks and sit down once more, but not long. "Fall in," was the order again and we marched straight back to the place where we were at first. "Such is life," soldiers' life at any rate.

3

SAMUEL E. BURGES

A South Carolina Soldier Confronts His Captain (1862)

Civil War soldiers displayed incredible courage on the battlefield, but compared with modern soldiers they were remarkably undisciplined. Nor did they readily accept the privileges accorded to officers, which clashed with egalitarian principles. The son of a Charleston bookseller, Samuel Edward Burges was farming (with his only slave) and serving as a collector for the Charleston Mercury *when he enlisted in a South Carolina unit shortly before the firing on Fort Sumter. Like many of his fellow soldiers, Burges had difficulty adjusting to military routine and was not shy about voicing his displeasure. The following entry in his diary described a confrontation with his captain.*

February 2, 1862, Quarrel with Capt about break- fast. said if I got none it would be my fault. replied it would be his fault and if I could not get it in my place where I then was it would be his fault, that he never troubled himself to see that the men were properly provided. On inspection said my rifle was

dirty. replied it was clean, having cleaned it 3 days ago and not used it since. gave me an hour to clean it in. replied I would think of it and laughed at him. ordered Lieut to report me. I finally went to him for things to clean it if the State furnished. said it did not. would lend me an oiled rag. I did not borrow. However I soaped over the rust and car- ried it to him. said rifle was in first rate order. I replied that it was no cleaner than before, only soaped over. Went off laughing at him.

FROM Thomas W. Chadwick, ed., "The Diary of Samuel Ed- ward Burges, 1860–1862," *South Carolina Historical and Genealogical Magazine* 48 (October 1947): 216.

4

TALLY SIMPSON

Trading with the Enemy (1863)

Taliaferro (Tally) N. Simpson grew up in the South Carolina upcountry, a member of a prosperous and politically distinguished slaveholding planter family. Indeed, his father was a congressman and had signed the state's ordinance of secession. Tally was in his final year as a student at Wofford College in Spartanburg, South Car- olina, when the war began. As soon as he heard the news of the firing on Fort Sumter, he immediately left college and enlisted in the army (he was hastily granted his diploma by the college).

Simpson, who in spite of his education never rose above the rank of corporal, served in the elite Third South Carolina Volunteers, which were part of Kershaw's Brigade in the Army of Northern Virginia. He was accompanied by his personal slave and fought in all the major engagements in the eastern theater of the war from 1861 through 1863. Despite the escalating violence and destruction of the war, frat- ernization between the troops in the two armies continued unabated whenever there was a lull in the fighting. In writing to his sister Mary on April 10, 1863, from the army's winter quarters along the Rappahannock River, Simpson described the illicit trade carried on by common soldiers on opposite banks of the river.

I was on guard or picket night before last and spent a very pleasant time indeed. A Mississip- pian had a small boat about three inches deep and two feet long, with rudder and sails affixed and

every thing in trim. We took it down to the river, waved our hand [at the Yankees], and received the same signal in return. We then laded her with pa- pers and sent her across. She landed safely and was sent back with a cargo of coffee. The officer of the day is very strict with them (the Yankees), and whenever he is about, they have to keep close. The first time the boat was sent over, he was not there,

FROM Guy R. Everson and Edward W. Simpson, Jr., eds., *"Far, Far from Home"* (New York: Oxford University Press, 1994), pp. 211–12.

and every thing passed off very well. But the next morning when we sent it over, they were detected, and the boat was captured, greatly to the mortification of us all. Before the officer detected them, however, they had taken the papers and tobacco which we sent them and concealed them.

As soon as the officer had gone with the boat to the headquarters of Gen Patrick, they halloed to us that it was too bad, that we must not blame them for not sending it back, and that as soon as they returned to camp they intended to put that d——d stickler [of an] officer up as a target and have a shooting match at him. They then told us they would be back in two or three days (they were going to be relieved in an hour or two from that time) and would bring us plenty of papers &cc.

Our boat gone, we returned to our quarters, but soon saw them waving their handkerchiefs and motioning down the river. We ran out and a little sail was coming across. It came diagonally across, and when about half way, it upset, but luckily drifted ashore. We got it, and it contained a bag of coffee weighing about two pounds and a little note, which I enclose with others I got from them on different occasions. I hope they may interest you, for it looks strange that we [are] so friendly at one time, when in the next moment we may be attempting to draw each other's life's blood. This last boat they sent over was only a temporary affair, being made of a plank (short piece) with a handkerchief attached to it for a sail. Orders from hdqrs prohibit any communication now what ever.

5

CHAUNCEY H. COOKE

Fraternization among Soldiers of the Two Armies (1864)

Chauncey Cooke grew up in a farm family on the Wisconsin frontier. He was only sixteen when he enlisted in the Twenty-fifth Wisconsin Infantry and held stronger antislavery sentiments than many Union soldiers. After serving in the Indian war in Minnesota in 1862, his regiment was sent to the South, where he took part in the Vicksburg, Mississippi, campaign and subsequent campaigns in the western theater. In the following letter, he described the fraternization between soldiers in the two armies during the struggle for Atlanta in 1864.

Hd. Quarters, 25th Wis. Vol. Camp,
Near Kenesaw Mountain, Ga.
June 24th, 1864.

Dear Parents:

Had just nicely finished my notes for yesterday in my diary when we were ordered to fall in for picket

duty on the skirmish line. . . . The rebels had their lines already made. Under cover of the night our lines were pushed close to theirs. We made a bargain with them that we would not fire on them if they would not fire on us, and they were as good as their word. It seems too bad that we have to fight men that we like. Now these southern soldiers seem just like our own boys, only they are on the other side. They talk about their people at home, their mothers and fathers and their sweet-

FROM Chauncey H. Cooke, "Letters of a Badger Boy in Blue," *Wisconsin Magazine of History* 5 (1921–1922): 87–88.

hearts just as we do among ourselves. Both sides did a lot of talking back and forth, but there was no shooting until I came off duty in the morning. . . .

June 25th. When the pickets came off the line this morning they had quite a pretty story to tell of how they chummed it with some Louisiana rebs. A company of our Indiana boys met a company of Louisiana rebels half way between the two lines. They stacked arms, shook hands, exchanged papers, swapped tobacco, told each other a lot of things about their feelings and how they wished the war would end so they might go back to their homes and be good friends again, shook hands once more with tears in their eyes as they bid each other goodbye forever, and after calling to each other to be sure that both sides were ready, commenced a furious fire on each other. . . .

Your boy,

Chauncey

6

T. J. STOKES

Religious Revivals in the Confederate Army
(1864)

Religion was an important source of morale for Civil War soldiers. This was especially the case in the Confederate army once the tide of battle turned against the South. Stimulated by the thinning ranks, the stress of combat, and the increasingly bleak military situation, a series of religious revivals swept through the main Confederate armies in the last two years of the war. These revivals were especially strong in the winter, when the soldiers were largely confined to camp. The Reverend T. J. Stokes, who was a member of the Tenth Texas Regiment, discussed the great revival in the Army of Tennessee in 1864. Similar revivals occurred at the same time in the Army of Northern Virginia in the eastern theater.

Near Dalton, April 5th, 1864.

We have had for some weeks back very unsettled weather, which has rendered it very disagreeable. . . . It has also interfered some with our meetings, though there is preaching nearly every night that there is not rain. Brother Hughes came up and preached for us last Friday night and seemed to give general satisfaction. He was plain and practical, which is the only kind of preaching that does good in the army. . . . Another old brother, named Campbell, whom I heard when I was a boy, preached for us on Sabbath evening. There was much feeling, and at the close of the services he invited mourners to the anxious seat, and I shall never forget that blessed half-hour that followed; from every part of that great congregation they came, many with streaming eyes; and, as they gave that old patriarch their hands, asked that God's people would pray for them. Yes, men who never shrank in battle from any responsibility, came forward weeping. Such is the power of the Gospel of Christ when preached in its purity. . . .

. . . . I have never seen such a spirit as there is now in the army. Religion is the theme. Every-

FROM Mary A. H. Gay, *Life in Dixie during the War*, 4th ed. (Atlanta: Foote and Davies Company, 1901), pp. 79–81.

where, you hear around the campfires at night the sweet songs of Zion. This spirit pervades the whole army. God is doing a glorious work, and I believe it is but the beautiful prelude to peace. I feel confident that if the enemy should attempt to advance that God will fight our battles for us, and the boastful foe be scattered and severely rebuked.

I witnessed a scene the other evening, which did my heart good—the baptism of three men in the creek near the encampment. To see those hardy soldiers taking up their cross and following their Master in His ordinance, being buried with Him in baptism, was indeed a beautiful sight. I really believe . . . that there is more religion now in the army than among the thousands of skulkers, exempts and speculators at home. There are but few now but who will talk freely with you upon the subject of their soul's salvation. What a change, what a change! when one year ago card-playing and profane language seemed to be the order of the day. Now, what is the cause of this change? Manifestly the working of God's spirit. He has chastened His people, and this manifestation of His love seems to be an earnest of the good things in store for us in not a far away future. "Whom the Lord loveth He chasteneth, and scourgeth every son whom He receiveth." Let all the people at home now, in unison with the army, humbly bow, acknowledge the afflicting hand of the Almighty, ask Him to remove the curse upon His own terms, and soon we will hear, so far as our Nation is concerned, "Glory to God in the highest, on earth peace, good will toward men!" . . .

Your affectionate brother,

T. J. Stokes.

7

JOHN A. POTTER

Antiblack Prejudice in the Union Ranks (1897)

As was true in northern society, antiblack prejudice was deeply ingrained in the ranks of the Union Army. Although the war produced some moderation in racial attitudes among those in blue, it fell far short of eradicating racist attitudes. In the following account, John A. Potter, who was a private in an Illinois regiment, described the cruel treatment of some fugitive slaves by a group of Union soldiers. This incident occurred in December 1862, soon after he joined the regiment. Shortly thereafter Potter was captured at Holly Springs, Mississippi, was paroled, and remained inactive until he was officially exchanged.

It was a bitter cold night. My chum and I were compelled to leave our bed in the ambulance and go to a large, blazing fire near by, that the battery boys kept feeding with good, fine lumber, as there were thousands of feet stacked up in a lumber yard close by. I enjoyed the warmth of the fire, but my nature revolted at the wasteful destruction of such valuable lumber. The battery boys were very kind to us. Our rations were rather scant, and they gave us a supply of hard bread, of which they seemed to have no lack. We boiled a kettle of coffee, and were told to make ourselves welcome to their fire and not freeze to death on the cars. We were pleased to share their kind hospitality; but

FROM John A. Potter, *Reminiscences of the Civil War in the United States* (Oskaloosa, Iowa: Globe Presses, 1897), pp. 32–33.

some colored men who had come in to escape the toils of bondage did not fare so well. I never could understand the antipathy of some white men towards the colored race; their detestation of them, on account of color, and their delight in torturing them. Our hosts were men of this type. They were lavish in their kindness to us, but cruel to the unfortunate men of color. These poor runaways begged to stop and warm at the roaring fire. They were told rudely they might warm awhile, and soon depart, for they did not want them there. The poor men sank down by the fire, and, seeming in a very exhausted state, were soon snoring, fast asleep. Soon one of the battery men, annoyed by the loud snoring, said: "Look at them niggers, gone fast asleep! They said they'd go directly, and they've taken up quarters for the night. Come, boys, let's cook them!" and, to my great horror, proceeded to drag the negroes through the blazing fire. I could hardly reconcile their cruelty to them to the great kindness they had shown us. Can the casuist explain how such a streak of the milk of human kindness and such a display of ferocious cruelty unite in one breast? Thus I was touched on two sides of my nature, but was powerless to obviate the cruelty shown the colored men because we had been the recipients of great favors at the hands of the offenders, and all parties were entire strangers to us. Truly the phenomena of human nature is the greatest mystery of the universe.

8

CHAUNCEY WELTON

A Union Soldier's Changing Views on Emancipation (1863–1865)

A resident of Weymouth, Ohio, Chauncey B. Welton enlisted with Company I, 103rd Ohio Volunteer Infantry, in August 1862 when he was only eighteen years of age. He served most of the war in the western theater, primarily in Kentucky and Tennessee, and in 1864 was promoted to the rank of corporal. He participated in Sherman's campaign that captured Atlanta and, after being stationed in Washington for several months, was transferred to North Carolina in the last weeks of the war. The following excerpts from his letters to his family reveal his changing attitudes about slavery and the war. (Paragraphing has been supplied.)

Welton had grown up in a staunchly Democratic family. In the following letter he discussed his reaction to Lincoln's Emancipation Proclamation and its impact on the army.

FROM Chauncey Welton Papers, Southern Historical Collection, University of North Carolina, Chapel Hill.

Frankfort, [Ky]
January 13, 1863

Father I want you to write and tell me what you think of Lincolns proclimation setting all of the negroes free. I can tell you we don't think mutch of it hear in the army for we did not enlist to fight for the negro and I can tell you that *we never shall* or many of us any how[.] *no never*[.] And just so shure as that proclimation becomes a law there will be a general boalting[.] already men are deserting evry day from our regment and some of the best men that we have. how many have left the regment I do not know but there has 8 gone out of our company and the companies will average more than that through the regment and it is so throughout the whole Brigade.

As the following letter indicates, Welton shared the antiblack attitudes that pervaded American culture during this period and had no faith in blacks' ability to live in freedom. He was equally disdainful of Lincoln and his leadership.

Benson five miles from Frankfort
February 11, 1863

excepting sickness we have not seen as hard times as I anticipated when comming into the field. perhaps you will then say why has so many deserted. they have left in disgust at the proceedings of the administration[.] it is because they enlisted to fight for our country the constitution and the union as it was, the glorious old stripes and stars and now insted of that they are kept here to sacrifise thier lives for the liberty of a miserable black race of beings, which when once set at liberty if ever they are will not onely be worse off themselves but those that once wer so anxious to free them will curse the day that the thought of liberty to sutch a race ever entered the mind of any one and if things goes on in this 3 monthes longer you will see not onely single men deserting but whole companies and regments grounding arms and starting for Ohio. but no more about the cursed negroe and this more cursed administration.

A month later in a letter to his uncle, Welton elaborated on his views on emancipation and Union war aims and discussed the Proclamation's effect on the army.

In camp near Frankfort
March 20, 1863

. . . Now although I hate to find fault with the administration, and hate to see this everlasting fault finding with the government and with officers of high rank in the field wich characterizes many at the north of all parties for I always have been opposed to this, yet for all of this at this late date and age of proceedings I cannot help disliking the present Administration or some of his deeds rather. But I will find no fault however with any thing except his proclimation, and that I consider both illegal and unconstitutional. no one can deny that, and no one attempts to[.] Now let us look for one moment on the man himself. . . . honest old abe is the characteristic of this individual and perhaps it might have been applicable and just before he was (through his weakness) under the controll and influence of a vile, demoralized and fanatic cabinet of Republicans or abolitionists. You spoke about my writing that I thought that that the proclimation was in his mind from the beginning. . . . I think that it was a premeditated act. , . With an eye zealous to that one cause he has succeeded to a great extent in charming and deceiving the people. While they supposed that he was agoing to let slavery alone he was onely waiting a proper time when events should afford him a plausiable excuse. . . . like the reptile he has kept his eye on and gradualy come to the point. it has been step by step, inch by inch. . . .

. . . what has been the effect of this proclimation[?] what has it done. It was calculated to rais rebellions and insurrections among the people of the south, the negroes[.] have you heard of a single one yet. can you tell me one instances where it has done any good. It also provides that your *Ammerican citizens of affrican decesent* when comming into any fort or camp be armed if they wish. Negroe regiments have been raised[,] then have been placed along side of white Soldiers and how many complaints do we hear daily about it too. . . .

how was it recd. by those in the field[?] . . . what a bustle an stir there was in the 103d[,] yes and in all the 3rd Brigade. the morning that the news reached nearly a half of the men declared that they would desert and many of them have done as they said. and this was not only the case in this regment but even so with all of the troops that we have yet met with. . . . I honestly believe that ⅔ of the disertions [from the Union army] may be laid to that proclimation.

. . . Before the proclimation there was a good many good union men in Ky but now where are they[?] they are here but thier hearts are with the rebellion. it has made thousand[s] and thousands of union men Secesh [secessionists] . . . .

When that proclimation is annulled we want no compromise[.] we want onely one thing and that is the union preserved exactly as it was, and the constitution as it is. . . . we want no constitution better than the one we have already got. I enlisted to fight for and vindicate the supremacy of the constitution . . . we will ask for peace onely upon one condition and that of unconditional surrender of the rebels.

The growing ascendancy of peace advocates in the Democratic party following Lincoln's adoption of the policy of emancipation, however, disturbed Welton and weakened his earlier loyalty to the party. Under the impact of Clement Vallandigham's nomination for governor, Welton's views began to diverge from those of his father, who continued to support the Democratic party. A different attitude toward Lincoln and emancipation began to emerge in his letters, which also made clear soldiers' detestation of the Copperheads. In this letter Welton replied to his father's recent criticism of his views.

Camp Sterling [KY]
June 15, 1863

You said you thought that I was changing my principals considerable. I think there that you are mistaken a considerable. In all the letters that I have wrote to you you cannot find one single principl which I do not uphold. I am just as far from being an abolitionist as ever and just as good a democrat upholding the same principles that I ever did. But when I see a part of that party seceeding from the true principles of democracy and certainly acting as aliens [allies] of of [*sic*] one of the most damnable rebellion that ever exists[,] am I *changing my* principles because I act not with that part[y]. No I am just the same as I always was

for the preservation of the union without a single blot on it[,] against the abolishment of slavery without colonisation. onely that it be a means of haistening the speedy restoration of the union and the termination of this war, which I now believe it is.

. . . I consider the most accursed of traitors *The Copperheads of the north.* . . . The news reached here last night that Valandingham was nominated for Gov of Ohio. the news fell like a thunderboalt upon this regiment. not that they wer at all fraid of his being elected but that what few loyal men that are left in Ohio would allow sutch a thing to be done in thier midst. Sutch a convention should be dispersed without organizing. *Oh my Country what have ye come to, what will yet be thy Doom.* But Father understand that any man who upholds Vallandigham at all never can be called any thing but my enemy. . . . There is no one on the face of this earth that is dispised and hated by every soldier as mutch as the Copperhead is. . . . You speak with some reflection upon the Administration[.] The onely thing that I can see is its Leniancy with northern traitors[.]

By 1864 the political gap between Welton and his father had widened, as the following letter reveals.

Decatur, Ga
September 19, 1864

It seames by your letter that you are down on old Abe, but you do not tell what for! . . . The only fault I ever heard you find with him was because he was not sevier enough and because he did not croud thing through faster and with more energy. We will admit that at first he was a little lenient and slow, but at that time we wer all deceived in the full determination of the south. And since that time I think every thing has been pressed foreward as fast as it could be and as fast as the *publick sentiment would allow.* What if the emancipation proclimation had been ishued 6 monthes before it was? my opinion always has been that if it had been there would have been a generall revolt both in our armies and at home, but Lincoln wisely witheld it untill public opinion would allow it. . . . It looks to me as if every action and step that he has taken has been ne[a]r exactly the right time.

In the following letter to his father discussing the 1864 presidential contest, Welton explained his support for Lincoln while he severely criticized the Democratic national platform.

Rome, Georgia
October 13, 1864

. . . I like the rest of the soldiers in both armies[,] the Rebel and the union, look forward to it [the 1864 presidential contest] as deciding the great question which we have been contending about for the last four years. I look forward anxiously to it as deciding whether all our toil, bloodshed, misery, suffering, and perills which we have endured for the last four years shall be counted as lost and in vain or whether now when victory is within our grasp we shall reach forth and grasp it. . . . I cannot see what possible plea a good union man can enter against our union candidate [i.e., Lincoln]. he who has guided and steared the ship of state through the peri[l]ous Rough and eventful storm of four years so well! No I cannot see why now as he is about to enter the harbor of peace tryumphant over the rough wave that have tried in vain to sink the old ship, and I cannot see why you would wish him now to be cast overboard and a captain put in who would bore a hole in the bottom and sink that which was so nearly saved. I think that our past administration has been as nigh what it should be as we could ask[.] some measures and steps have been taken of course that in ordinary times you and I might not have liked . . . but all that have come under my observation have been tending to bear against the rebellion and to crush it forever. in one instance an emancipation proclimation was ishued which of course in or under other circumstances would have been inconsis-

tent, but it was intended to weaken the rebellion and I can asshure you it was a great blow to them[.]

October 17

. . . Father when the rebels attacked Altoona . . . they gave three cheers for McClealand and then went forward on the charge. So you can see where thier last hope rests so if Lincoln is defeated or elected by a small majority what will be the result. . . . I ask you to ask yourself the question Shall I who have a son in the ranks of thier enemy incourage and sustain thier last and dying hope. And also think and if Lincoln is elected by so small a majority that it will still contiue thier hopes for a while and prompt them to fight a little longer in hopes that Copperheadism will at length overthrow our government and give them thier independence. . . .
. . . One word about the [Democratic] platform. . . . has there ever been anything printed eaven in the southern papers that was more insulting to the soldiers of this army. no never. It is an insult to every soldier in the field. is there one word of incouragement or of thank[s] to the soldier. no not one. is there one sentence against treason and the rebellion[?] no not one.

Early in 1865 Welton was in Washington, where he would witness Lincoln's second inauguration. The following letter to his parents made clear his complete conversion to the policy of emancipation.

Washington, D.C.
February 18, 1865

. . . dear parents let us trust in Him that never forsakes the faithfull, and never cease to pray . . . that soon we may look upon an undivided Country and that Country *free free free* yes free from that blighting curs[e] Slavery the cause of four years Bloody warfare.

9

REUBEN A. PIERSON

A Louisiana Soldier Links Slavery and Race to the Cause of the Confederacy (1862–1864)

Reuben A. Pierson was a sergeant in the Ninth Louisiana Infantry. He was twenty-six years old and supporting himself as a teacher when he enlisted in 1861. Despite his western residence, he served in the Virginia theater during the war. In these two letters to his father, who owned a moderate-size plantation, he outlined his view of what was at stake in the war and defended the cause of the Confederacy. Pierson was killed in combat in the summer of 1864 in Virginia.

Camp C, Virginia
January 31, 1862

The young men who have not ambition and moral courage to fight for the preservation of that rich legacy bequeathed to them—and purchased for them by the blood of their ancestors will be scoffed at and looked upon as base cowards unworthy [of] the name of southern man and unfit for the enjoyment of our glorious institution [of slavery]. The day is now dawning and will soon open bright and clear as a May morning, when we will be acknowledged as one of the best governments that holds a place in the catalogue of the nations of the earth. Let the unholy and base legions of Lincolndom pour forth their fury and rage in all its power—we will meet them [on the field and] we will defeat them or perish upon the soil of our loved and cherished southern republic. This is what southern men have vowed by their acts and not by words. Let us die a soldiers death or live a freemans life.

Orange County, Virginia
March 22, 1864

I for one am unwilling to accept anything short of a final separation from the fiendish barbarians with whom we have been so long associated. It is true I love peace but give me an everlasting war in preference to a union with a people who condescend to equalize themselves with the poor, ignorant & only half civilized negro. Such a people is base, vile, & altogether unworthy of the honorable and once proud name of Americans. I will not dwell upon this theme. Such thoughts are always exciting my passions of revenge and veng[e]ance.

FROM Thomas W. Cutrer and T. Michael Parrish, eds., *Brothers in Gray: The Civil War Letters of the Pierson Family* (Baton Rouge: Louisiana State University Press, 1997), pp. 77, 228.

10

T. D. KINGSLEY

A Wounded Soldier Describes a Field Hospital (1863)

In a letter to his wife, dated June 27, 1863, T. D. Kingsley, a Union colonel who was wounded at Port Hudson, Louisiana offered a chilling description of the conditions at a field hospital. Wounded soldiers who required immediate treatment were evacuated to hospitals located just behind the military lines. Conditions were more primitive at field hospitals than in the regular hospitals further removed from the battle zone. Notice his reference to an area where the surgeons were working as "the butchering room."

I never wish to see another such time as the 27th of May. The surgeons used a large Cotton Press for the butchering room & when I was carried into the building and looked about I could not help comparing the surgeons to fiends. It was dark & the building lighted partially with candles: all around on the ground lay the wounded men; some of them were shrieking, some cursing & swearing & some praying; in the middle of the room was some 10 or 12 tables just large enough to lay a man on; these were used as dissecting tables & they were covered with blood; near & around the tables stood the surgeons with blood all over them & by the side of the tables was a heap of feet, legs & arms. On one of these tables I was laid & being known as a Col. the Chief Surgeon of the Department was called (Sanger) and he felt of my mouth and then wanted to give me cloriform: this I refused to take & he took a pair of scissors & cut out the pieces of bone in my mouth: then gave me a drink of whiskey & had me laid away.

FROM Bell Wiley, *The Life of Billy Yank* (Indianapolis: Bobbs Merrill, 1951), p. 148.

11

WILLIAM FISHER PLANE

The Scourge of War (1862)

William Fisher Plane was an attorney and planter in Baker County, Georgia, when the war broke out. He promptly enlisted as a member of the Sixth Georgia Volunteers, holding the rank of captain. Plane's letters to his wife reveal a man who was serious, sober, and deeply religious. Like most Civil War soldiers, Plane, who served in the Virginia theater, was not prepared for the reality of war and combat. After his regiment was engaged in hard fighting in the Seven Days' battles (June 26–July 1, 1862), he wrote the following letter to his wife reflecting on the nature of war. Two months later, Plane was killed in the Battle of Antietam.

But dearest, tis one thing to read of battles, another to be an actor in the Strife, & behold the scenes of anguish & of pain, the dead and the dying, & those not mortally wounded, to hear the cries of distress, and untold pain. None can realize the horrors of war, save those actually engaged. The dead lying all around, your foes unburied to the last, horses & wagons & troops passing heedlessly along, rushing to overtake the foe in his retreat, and to give him battle again. The stiffened bodies lie, grasping in death, the arms they bravely bore, with glazed eyes, and features blackened by rapid decay. Here sits one against a tree in motionless stare. Another has his head leaning against a stump, his hands over his head. They have paid the last penalty. They have fought their last battle. The air is putrid with decaying bodies of men & horses. My God, My God, what a scourge is war. . . .

FROM William Fisher Plane to Caroline Plane, July 8, 1862, S. Joseph Lewis, Jr., ed., "Letters of William Fisher Plane, C. S. A. to His Wife," *Georgia Historical Society Quarterly* 48 (June 1964): 223.

Ulysses S. Grant Devises a New Union Strategy

(1885)

After he was appointed commander of all the Union armies in March 1864, Grant devised a strategy to exert maximum pressure on the Confederacy's armies. Discerning that the problem in the past was that Union armies "acted independently and without concert, like a balky team, no two ever pulling together," he planned to launch a series of coordinated attacks against the Confederate armies along a front extending more than one thousand miles. Somewhere, he reasoned, the Union could punch through the overextended Confederate defenses. Instead of strangling the Confederacy into submission, as Scott's Anaconda Plan (see p. 83) had envisioned, Grant intended to defeat the Confederacy with a series of sledgehammer blows. In the following passage from his memoirs, he described his strategy.

The Union armies were now divided into nineteen departments, though four of them in the West had been concentrated into a single military division. The Army of the Potomac was a separate command and had no territorial limits. There were thus seventeen distinct commanders. Before this time these various armies had acted separately and independently of each other, giving the enemy an opportunity often of depleting one command, not pressed, to reinforce another more actively engaged. I determined to stop this. To this end I regarded the Army of the Potomac as the centre, and all west to Memphis along the line described as our position at the time, and north of it, the right wing; the Army of the James, under General Butler, as the left wing, and all the troops south, as a force in rear of the enemy. Some of these latter were occupying positions from which they could not render service proportionate to their numerical strength. All such were depleted to the minimum necessary to hold their positions as a guard against blockade runners; where they could not do this their positions were abandoned altogether. In this way ten thousand men were added to the Army of the James from South Carolina alone, with General Gillmore in command. It was not contemplated that General Gillmore should leave his department; but as most of his troops were taken, presumably for active service, he asked to accompany them and was permitted to do so. Officers and soldiers on furlough, of whom there were many thousands, were ordered to their proper commands; concentration was the order of the day, and to have it accomplished in time to advance at the earliest moment the roads would permit was the problem. . . .

My general plan now was to concentrate all the force possible against the Confederate armies in

FROM Ulysses S. Grant, *Personal Memoirs of U. S. Grant*, vol. 2 (New York: Charles L. Webster and Co., 1885), pp. 127–32.

the field. There were but two such, as we have seen, east of the Mississippi River and facing north. The Army of Northern Virginia, General Robert E. Lee commanding, was on the south bank of the Rapidan, confronting the Army of the Potomac; the second, under General Joseph E. Johnston, was at Dalton, Georgia, opposed to Sherman who was still at Chattanooga. Beside these main armies the Confederates had to guard the Shenandoah Valley, a great storehouse to feed their armies from, and their line of communications from Richmond to Tennessee. Forrest, a brave and intrepid cavalry general, was in the West with a large force; making a larger command necessary to hold what we had gained in Middle and West Tennessee. We could not abandon any territory north of the line held by the enemy because it would lay the Northern States open to invasion. But as the Army of the Potomac was the principal garrison for the protection of Washington even while it was moving on Lee, so all the forces to the west, and the Army of the James, guarded their special trusts when advancing from them as well as when remaining at them. Better indeed, for they forced the enemy to guard his own lines and resources at a greater distance from ours, and with a greater force. Little expeditions could not so well be sent out to destroy a bridge or tear up a few miles of railroad track, burn a storehouse, or inflict other little annoyances. Accordingly I arranged for a simultaneous movement all along the line. Sherman was to move from Chattanooga, Johnston's army and Atlanta being his objective points. Crook, commanding in West Virginia, was to move from the mouth of the Gauley River with a cavalry force and some artillery, the Virginia and Tennessee Railroad to be his objective. Either the enemy would have to keep a large force to protect their communications, or see them destroyed and a large amount of forage and provision, which they so much needed, fall into our hands. Sigel was in command in the Valley of Virginia. He was to advance up the valley, covering the North from an invasion through that channel as well while advancing as by remaining near Harper's Ferry. Every mile he advanced also gave us possession of stores on which Lee relied. Butler was to advance by the James River, having Richmond and Petersburg as his objective. . . .

Banks in the Department of the Gulf was ordered to assemble all the troops he had at New Orleans in time to join in the general move, Mobile to be his objective.

At this time I was not entirely decided as to whether I should move the Army of the Potomac by the right flank of the enemy, or by his left. Each plan presented advantages. If by his right—my left—the Potomac, Chesapeake Bay and tributaries would furnish us an easy line over which to bring all supplies to within easy hauling distance of every position the army could occupy from the Rapidan to the James River. But Lee could, if he chose, detach or move his whole army north on a line rather interior to the one I would have to take in following. A movement by his left—our right—would obviate this; but all that was done would have to be done with the supplies and ammunition we started with. All idea of adopting this latter plan was abandoned when the limited quantity of supplies possible to take with us was considered. The country over which we would have to pass was so exhausted of all food or forage that we would be obliged to carry everything with us.

HORACE PORTER

A Union Officer Depicts the Fury of the Fighting at Spotsylvania (1897)

The Battle of Spotsylvania (May 8–12, 1864) witnessed some of the most savage fighting of the war, particularly at a salient in the Confederate line known as Bloody Angle. One veteran Union officer remarked, "I never expect to be fully believed when I tell what I saw of the horrors of Spottsylvania, because I should be loth to believe it myself, were the case reversed." The Confederate fieldworks at Spotsylvania were the strongest constructed during the entire war, and at places the two lines were only a quarter mile apart. For eighteen hours on May 12, from dawn until past midnight, the battle raged along a few hundred yards of the lines; it was one of the few times during the war that the two armies engaged in hand-to-hand combat. Horace Porter, who served on Grant's staff, described the furious struggle at Bloody Angle.

The battle near the "angle" was probably the most desperate engagement in the history of modern warfare, and presented features which were absolutely appalling. It was chiefly a savage hand-to-hand fight across the breastworks. Rank after rank was riddled by shot and shell and bayonet-thrusts, and finally sank, a mass of torn and mutilated corpses; then fresh troops rushed madly forward to replace the dead, and so the murderous work went on. Guns were run up close to the parapet, and double charges of canister played their part in the bloody work. The fence-rails and logs in the breastworks were shattered into splinters, and trees over a foot and a half in diameter were cut completely in two by the incessant musketry fire. . . . The opposing flags were in places thrust against each other, and muskets were fired with muzzle against muzzle. Skulls were crushed with clubbed muskets, and men stabbed to death with swords and bayonets thrust between the logs in the parapet which separated the combatants. Wild cheers, savage yells, and frantic shrieks rose above the sighing of the wind and the pattering of the rain, and formed a demoniacal accompaniment to the booming of the guns as they hurled their missiles of death into the contending ranks. Even the darkness of night and the pitiless storm failed to stop the fierce contest, and the deadly strife did not cease till after midnight. Our troops had been under fire for twenty hours, but they still held the position which they had so dearly purchased.

My duties carried me again to the spot the next day, and the appalling sight presented was harrowing in the extreme. Our own killed were scattered over a large space near the "angle," while in front of the captured breastworks the enemy's dead, vastly more numerous than our own, were piled upon each other in some places four layers deep, exhibiting every ghastly phase of mutilation. . . . The place was well named the "Bloody Angle."

FROM Horace Porter, *Campaigning with Grant* (New York: The Century Company, 1897), pp. 110–11.

3

ROBERT E. LEE

Our Numbers Are Daily Decreasing (1864)

After the advance units of the Army of the Potomac failed to seize Petersburg, Virginia, before Lee arrived with the main body of his army, Grant settled into a siege. Steadily Grant extended his lines, intending to use his superior numbers to weaken Lee's defensive line to the point where it could be taken by a direct assault. With his army guarding Richmond's last remaining rail links to the south, Lee knew that if he failed to maintain his position, the Confederate capital would have to be evacuated. As he scrambled to maintain his defensive works, Lee stressed the urgency of mobilizing every possible man.

Headquarters Army of Northern Virginia
August 23, 1864.

Hon. Secretary of War [James A. Seddon]

Sir:

The subject of recruiting the ranks of our army is growing in importance and has occupied much of my attention. Unless some measures can be devised to replace our losses, the consequences may be disastrous. I think that there must be more men in the country liable to military duty than the small number of recruits received would seem to indicate. It has been several months since the passage of the last conscript law, and a large number of able-bodied men and officers are engaged in enforcing it. They should by this time, if they have not been remiss, have brought out most of the men liable to conscription, and should have no duty to perform, except to send to the army those who arrive at the legal age of service.

I recommend that the facts of the case be investigated, and that if the officers and men engaged in enrolling have finished their work, with the exception indicated, they be returned to the army, where their presence is much needed. It is evidently inexpedient to keep a larger number out of service in order to get a smaller. I would also respectfully recommend that the list of detailed men be revised, and that all details of arms bearing men be revoked, except in cases of absolute necessity. I have myself seen numbers of men claiming to be detailed in different parts of the country who it seemed to me might well be in service. The corps are generally secured, or beyond the necessity of further labor, and I hope some of the agricultural details may be revoked. Our numbers are daily decreasing, and the time has arrived in my opinion when no man should be excused from service, except for the purpose of doing work absolutely necessary for the support of the army. If we had here a few thousand men more to hold the stronger parts of our lines where an attack is least likely to be made, it would enable us to employ with good effect our veteran troops. Without some increase of our strength, I cannot see how we are to escape the natural military consequences of the enemy's numerical superiority.

Very respectfully, your obedient servant,

R. E. Lee
General.

FROM *Official Records*, ser. I, vol. 42, pt. 2, pp. 1199–1200. Paragraphing supplied.

4

ROBERT STILES

A Confederate Soldier Describes the Pressure of Fighting in the Trenches (1903)

The increased range and accuracy of Civil War weapons literally drove men into the ground to escape the rain of bullets and artillery shells that sprayed across a battlefield. Defending soldiers increasingly fought behind earthworks and other defensive works. Robert Stiles was educated in the North, but soon after the war began he headed south with his brothers and Georgia-born father and enlisted as a private in the Confederate Army. Stiles, who served in the Army of Northern Virginia and rose to the rank of major, described the hardship of living and fighting in the trenches at Cold Harbor, which was a foretaste of the experience of both sides during the drawn-out siege of Petersburg, Virginia, which commenced soon thereafter.

One can readily understand, now, the supreme discomfort and even suffering of "the lines." Thousands of men cramped up in a narrow trench, unable to go out, or to get up, or to stretch or to stand without danger to life and limb; unable to lie down, or to sleep, for lack of room and pressure of peril; night alarms, day attacks, hunger, thirst, supreme weariness, squalor, vermin, filth, disgusting odors everywhere; the weary night succeeded by the yet more weary day; the first glance over the way, at day dawn, bringing the sharpshooter's bullet singing past your ear or smashing through your skull, a man's life often exacted as the price of a cup of water from the spring.

FROM Robert Stiles, *Four Years under Marse Robert* (New York: The Neale Publishing Company, 1903), p. 290.

5

WILLIAM TECUMSEH SHERMAN

War Is Cruelty, and You Cannot Refine It (1864)

Following the capture of Atlanta, Sherman ordered the civilian population to evacuate the city. When the mayor and city council protested his order, Sherman wrote the following reply, discussing the nature of the war. More bluntly than any other commander, Sherman expressed the meaning of total war in the context of the Civil War. When he left the city to begin his famous march to the sea, Sherman burned Atlanta to prevent it from again being used by the Confederacy as a military base.

Headquarters Military Division of the Mississippi,
in the Field, Atlanta, Georgia,
September 12, 1864

*James M. Calhoun, Mayor, E. E. Rawson, and
S. C. Wells, representing City Council of Atlanta.*

Gentlemen:

I have your letter of the 11th, in the nature of a petition to revoke my orders removing all the inhabitants from Atlanta. I have read it carefully, and give full credit to your statements of the distress that will be occasioned, and yet shall not revoke my orders, because they were not designed to meet the humanities of the case, but to prepare for the future struggles in which millions of good people outside of Atlanta have a deep interest. We must have peace, not only at Atlanta, but in all America. To secure this, we must stop the war that now desolates our once happy and favored country. To stop war, we must defeat the rebel armies which are arrayed against the laws and Constitution that all must respect and obey. . . .

You cannot qualify war in the harsher terms than I will. War is cruelty, and you cannot refine it; and those who brought war into our country deserve all the curses and maledictions a people can pour out. . . . But you cannot have peace and a division of our country. If the United States submits to a division now, it will not stop, but will go on until we reap the fate of Mexico, which is eternal war. The United States does and must assert its authority, wherever it once had power; for, if it relaxes one bit to pressure, it is gone, and I believe that such is the national feeling. This feeling assumes various shapes, but always comes back to that of Union. Once admit the Union, once more acknowledge the authority of the national Government, and, instead of devoting your houses and streets and roads to the dread uses of war, I and this army become at once your protectors and supporters, shielding you from danger, let it come from what quarter it may. . . .

You might as well appeal against the thunderstorm as against these terrible hardships of war. They are inevitable, and the only way the people of Atlanta can hope once more to live in peace and quiet at home, is to stop the war, which can only be done by admitting that it began in error and is perpetuated in pride.

We don't want your negroes, or your horses, or your houses, or your lands, or any thing you have, but we do want and will have a just obedience to the laws of the United States. That we will have, and, if it involves the destruction of your improvements, we cannot help it.

. . . By the original compact of Government, the United States had certain rights in Georgia, which have never been relinquished and never will be; that the South began war by seizing forts, arsenals, mints, custom-houses, etc., etc., long before Mr. Lincoln was installed, and before the South had one jot or tittle of provocation. I myself have seen in Missouri, Kentucky, Tennessee, and Mississippi, hundreds and thousands of women and children fleeing from your armies and desperadoes, hungry and with bleeding feet. In Memphis, Vicksburg, and Mississippi, we fed thousands upon thousands of the families of rebel soldiers left on our hands, and whom we could not see starve. Now that war comes home to you, you feel very different. You deprecate its horrors, but did not feel them when you sent car-loads of soldiers and ammunition, and moulded shells and shot, to carry war into Kentucky and Tennessee, to desolate the homes of hundreds and thousands of good people who only asked to live in peace at their old homes, and under the Government of their inheritance. But these comparisons are idle. I want peace, and believe it can only be reached through union and war, and I will ever conduct war with a view to perfect and early success. . . .

Yours in haste,

W. T. Sherman, Major-General commanding.

FROM William T. Sherman, *Memoirs of General William T. Sherman*, vol. 2 (New York: D. Appleton and Co., 1875), pp. 125–27.

6

William Tecumseh Sherman Proposes to March to the Sea (1864)

When Sherman first suggested his unorthodox plan to abandon his communications and supply lines and march his army 300 miles through enemy territory, Grant balked at the idea, believing it too risky. Sherman's men could forage for food, but they would have to take all their military and medical supplies with them; there would be no way to resupply or reinforce his army until it arrived at the coast (the navy was not even certain of Sherman's ultimate destination). But Sherman persisted and Grant finally agreed. In the following dispatch, Sherman explained the political and psychological advantages of his march. When he started on his march, a British military magazine commented that "Sherman has done either one of the most brilliant or one of the most foolish things ever performed by a military leader." Events would justify Sherman's thinking.

Hdqrs. Military Division of the Mississippi,
In the Field, Kingston, Ga., November 6, 1864.

Lieut. Gen. U.S. Grant,
Commander-in-Chief, City Point, Va.:

Dear General:

I have heretofore telegraphed and written you pretty fully, but I still have some thoughts in my busy brain that should be confided to you as a key to future developments. The taking of Atlanta broke upon Jeff. Davis so suddenly as to disturb the equilibrium of his usually well-balanced temper, so that at Augusta, Macon, Montgomery, and Columbia, S. C., he let out some of his thoughts which otherwise he would have kept to himself. As he is not only the President of the Southern Confederacy but also its Commander-in-Chief, we are bound to attach more importance to his words than we would to those of a mere civil chief magistrate. The whole burden of his song consisted in the statement that Sherman's communications

FROM *Official Records*, ser. I, vol. 39, pt. 3, pp. 658–61.

must be broken and his army destroyed. Now, it is a well-settled principle that if we can prevent his succeeding in his threat we defeat him and derive all the moral advantages of a victory. . . .

I have employed the last ten days in running to the rear the sick and wounded and worthless, and all the vast amount of stores accumulated by our army in the advance, aiming to organize this branch of my army into four well-commanded corps, encumbered by only one gun to 1,000 men, and provisions and ammunition which can be loaded up in our mule teams, so that we can pick up and start on the shortest notice. I reckon that by the 10th instant this end will be reached, and by that date I also will have the troops all paid, the Presidential election over and out of our way, and I hope the early storms of November, now prevailing, will also give us the chance of a long period of fine healthy weather for campaigning. Then the question presents itself, What shall be done? On the supposition always that Thomas can hold the line of the Tennessee, and very shortly be able to assume the offensive as against Beauregard, I propose to act in such a manner against the material resources of the South as utterly to negative Davis' boasted threat and promises of protection. If we can march a well-appointed army right through his territory, it is a demonstration to the world, foreign and domestic, that we have a power which Davis cannot resist. This may not be war, but rather statesmanship, nevertheless it is overwhelming to my mind that there are thousands of people abroad and in the South who will reason thus: If the North can march an army right through the South, it is proof positive that the North can prevail in this contest, leaving only open the question of its willingness to use that power.

Now, Mr. Lincoln's election, which is assured, coupled with the conclusion thus reached, makes a complete, logical whole. Even without a battle, the result operating upon the minds of sensible men would produce fruits more than compensating for the expense, trouble, and risk. . . .

I am, with respect,

W. T. Sherman,
Major-General.

7

JAMES CONNOLLY

An Illinois Soldier Marches with Sherman to the Sea and Beyond (1864–1865)

In 1862 James A. Connolly, a young lawyer in Charleston, Illinois, enlisted in the 123rd Illinois Infantry. Serving in the western theater, he wrote a number of letters to his fiancée, Mary Dunn, and then kept a dairy while with Sherman's army on its famous march through Georgia and South Carolina, from which these excerpts are taken. By the end of the war he had attained the rank of lieutenant colonel. He was active in Illinois politics after the war and was elected to Congress.

Atlanta, November 15, 1864 . . . Our Commissaries have been busily engaged all day in loading rations, and our Quarter Masters in issuing clothing and shoes to the troops. Up to about 3 p.m. this issuing was carried on with something like a show of regularity, but about that time fires began to break out in various portions of the city, and it soon became evident that these fires were but the beginning of a general conflagration which would sweep over the entire city and blot it out of existence; so Quartermasters

FROM Paul M. Angle, ed., *Three Years in the Army of the Cumberland* (Bloomington: Indiana University Press, 1959), pp. 301, 311, 314, 318–19, 322–24, 356, 375, 384, 387.

and Commissaries ceased trying to issue clothing or load rations, they told the soldiers to go in and take what they wanted before it burned up. The soldiers found many barrels of whiskey and of course they drank of it until they were drunk; then new fires began to spring up, all sorts of discordant noises rent the air, drunken soldiers on foot and on horseback raced up and down the streets while the buildings on either side were solid sheets of flame, they gathered in crowds before the finest structures and sang "Rally around the Flag" while the flames enwrapped these costly edifices, and shouted and danced and sang again while pillar and roof and dome sank into one common ruin. The night, for miles around was bright as midday; the city of Atlanta was one mass of flame, and the morrow must find it a mass of ruins. . . . All the pictures and verbal descriptions of hell that I have ever seen never gave me half so vivid an idea of it, as did this flame wrapped city to-night.

Near Sand Town, Ga., November 19, 1864 . . . Our men are foraging on the country with the greatest liberality. Foraging parties start out in the morning; they go where they please, seize wagons, mules, horses, and harness; make the negroes of the plantation hitch up, load the wagons with sweet potatoes, flour, meal, hogs, sheep, chickens, turkeys, barrels of molasses, and in fact everything good to eat, and sometimes considerable that's good to drink. Our men are living as well as they could at home and are in excellent health.

Near Murder Creek, Ga., November 21, 1864 . . . Citizens everywhere look paralyzed and as if stricken dumb as we pass them. Columns of smoke by day, and "pillars of fire" by night, for miles and miles on our right and left indicate to us daily and nightly the route and location of the other columns of our army. Every "Gin House" we pass is burned; every stack of fodder we can't carry along is burned; every barn filled with grain is destroyed; in fact everything that can be of any use to the rebels is either carried off by our foragers or set on fire and burned.

Milledgeville, Ga., November 23, 1864 . . . Our soldiers and even some officers have been plundering the State library today and carrying off law and miscellaneous works in armfuls. It is a downright shame. Public libraries should be sacredly respected by all belligerents, and I am sure General Sherman will, some day, regret that he permitted this library to be destroyed and plundered. I could get a thousand dollars worth of valuable law books there if I would just go and take them, but I wouldn't touch them. I should feel ashamed of myself every time I saw one of them in my book case at home. I don't object to stealing horses, mules, niggers and all such *little things*, but I will not engage in plundering and destroying public libraries. Let them alone, to enlarge and increase for the benefit of the loyal generations that are to people this country long after we shall have fought our last battle and gone into our eternal camp.

Near Milledgeville, Ga., November 25, 1864 . . . Our foragers came into camp tonight pretty well loaded, and I can't imagine where they found so much stuff through this country. I suppose the negroes assisted them. Where can all the rebels be? Here we are riding rough shod over Georgia and nobody dares to fire a shot at us. We burn their houses, barns, fences, cotton and everything else, yet none of the Southern braves show themselves to punish us for our vandalism. . . . Georgia is an excellent state for foraging. We are living finely, and the whole army would have no objection to marching around through the State for the next six months. Indeed, the whole trip thus far has been a holiday excursion, but a very expensive one to the rebels.

Near Sandersville, Ga., November 26, 1864 . . . The rebel papers we get hold of from Augusta also call on all the citizens to turn out and fall timber across the roads—destroy their forage and provisions, and do everything possible to harass us and retard our march. Let them do it if they dare. We'll burn every house, barn, church, and everything else we come to; we'll leave their families houseless and without food; their towns will *all* be destroyed, and nothing but the most complete desolation will be found in our track. This army will not be trifled with by citizens. If citizens raise their hands against us to retard our march or play the guerrilla against us, neither youth nor age, nor sex will be respected. Everything must be destroyed. This is the feeling that has settled down over the army in its bivouac tonight. We have gone so far now in our triumphal march that we will not be balked. It is a question of life or death with us, and all considerations of mercy and humanity must bow before the inexorable demands of self preservation.

Effingham County, Ga., 18 miles from Savannah, December 9, 1864 . . . Slaves are not very plenty[ful] amongst them [the residents], but this I think arises from the fact that slave labor cannot be made profitable on this very poor soil. These people through here were not original Secessionists and are now in favor of a reconstruction of the Union on *any* terms.

Savannah, January 19, 1865 . . . I don't care

how soon we get over into South Carolina, for I want to see the long deferred chastisement begin. If we don't purify South Carolina it will be because we *can't get a light.*

Fayetteville, N.C., March 12, 1865 . . . Our entire army is, and has been all the time, in the best possible condition. We have lived just as well as on our march through Georgia. . . . The army burned everything it came near in the State of South Carolina, not under orders, but in spite of orders. The men "had it in" for the State and they took it out in their own way. Our track through the State is a desert waste. Since entering North Carolina the wanton destruction has stopped.

Near Neuse River, N.C., March 21, 1865 . . . Be-fore we marched half way through South Carolina I was perfectly sickened by the frightful devastation our army was spreading on every hand. Oh! It was absolutely terrible! Every house except the church and the negro cabin was burned to the ground; women, children and old men turned out into the mud and rain and their houses and furniture first plundered, then burned. I knew it would be so before we entered the state, but I had no idea how frightful the reality would be. This state is filled with deserters from the rebel army; they flock to us every day; the look upon us as their friends. Hundreds of them have gathered up their families and, with a little bundle of bedding stowed away in an ox car or mule cart, they toil along after our trains.

8

DOLLY LUNT BURGE

The Heavens Were Lit with Flames (1864)

Dolly Lunt left Maine as a young woman and went to Covington, Georgia, to teach school. There she married Thomas Burge, a planter, and became mistress of his plantation. By the time Sherman's army swept through Georgia, she was a widow. The following account from her diary described the arrival of Union troops in November 1864 at her plantation.

November 19, 1864. Slept in my clothes last night, as I heard that the Yankees went to neighbor Montgomery's on Thursday night at one o'clock, searched his house, drank his wine, and took his money and valuables. As we were not disturbed, I walked after breakfast, with Sadai, up to Mr. Joe Perry's, my nearest neighbor, where the Yankees were yesterday. Saw Mrs. Laura [Perry] in the road surrounded by her children. . . . Before we we were done talking, up came Joe and Jim Perry from their hiding-place. Jim was very much excited. Happening to turn and look behind, as we stood there, I saw some blue-coats coming down the hill. . . .

. . . I . . . ran home as fast as I could, with Sadai.

I could hear them cry, "Halt! Halt!" and their guns went off in quick succession. Oh God, the time of trial has come!

. . . I walked to the gate. There they came filing up.

I hastened back to my frightened servants and told them that they had better hide, and then went back to the gate to claim protection and a guard. But like demons they rush in! My yards are full. To

FROM Dolly Lunt Burge, *A Woman's Wartime Journal* (New York: The Century Company, 1918), pp. 20–32.

my smoke-house, my dairy, pantry, kitchen, and cellar, like famished wolves they come, breaking locks and whatever is in their way. The thousand pounds of meat in my smoke-house is gone in a twinkling, my flour, my meat, my lard, butter, eggs, pickles of various kinds—both in vinegar and brine—wine, jars, and jugs are all gone. My eighteen fat turkeys, my hens, chickens, and fowls, my young pigs, are shot down in my yard and hunted as if they were rebels themselves. Utterly powerless I ran out and appealed to the guard.

"I cannot help you, Madam; it is orders."

As I stood there, from my lot I saw driven, first, old Dutch, my dear old buggy horse, who has carried my beloved husband so many miles, and who would so quietly wait at the block for him to mount and dismount, and who at last drew him to his grave; then came old Mary, my brood mare, who for years had been too old and stiff for work, with her three-year-old colt, my two-year-old mule, and her last little baby colt. There they go! There go my mules, my sheep, and, worse than all, my boys [slaves]!

Alas! little did I think while trying to save my house from plunder and fire that they were forcing my boys from home at the point of the bayonet. One, Newton, jumped into bed in his cabin, and declared himself sick. Another crawled under the floor,—a lame boy he was,—but they pulled him out, placed him on a horse, and drove him off. Mid, poor Mid! The last I saw of him, a man had him going around the garden, looking, as I thought, for my sheep, as he was my shepherd. Jack came crying to me, the big tears coursing down his cheeks, saying they were making him go. I said:

"Stay in my room."

But a man followed in, cursing him and threatening to shoot him if he did not go; so poor Jack had to yield. James Arnold, in trying to escape from a back window, was captured and marched off. Henry, too, was taken. . . .

My poor boys! My poor boys! What unknown trials are before you! How you have clung to your mistress and assisted her in every way you knew.

. . . Their cabins are rifled of every valuable, the soldiers swearing that their Sunday clothes were the white people's, and that they never had money to get such things as they had. Poor Frank's chest was broken open, his money and tobacco taken. He has always been a money-making and saving boy; not infrequently has his crop brought him five hundred dollars and more. All of his clothes and Rachel's clothes, which dear Lou gave her before her death and which she had packed away, were stolen from her. Ovens, skillets, coffee-mills, of which we had three, coffee-pots—not one have I left. Sifters all gone!

Seeing that the soldiers could not be restrained, the guard ordered me to have their [the slaves'] remaining possessions brought into my house, which I did, and they all, poor things, huddled together in my room, fearing every movement that the house would be burned.

A Captain Webber from Illinois came into my house. Of him I claimed protection from the vandals who were forcing themselves into my room. . . .

He felt for me, and I give him and several others the character of gentlemen. I don't believe they would have molested women and children had they had their own way. . . .

Sherman himself and a greater portion of his army passed my house that day. All day, as the sad moments rolled on, were they passing not only in front of my house, but from behind; they tore down my garden palings, made a road through my back-yard and lot field, driving their stock and riding through, tearing down my fences and desolating my home—wantonly doing it when there was no necessity for it.

Such a day, if I live to the age of Methuselah, may God spare me from ever seeing again!

As night drew its sable curtains around us, the heavens from every point were lit up with flames from burning buildings. Dinnerless and supperless as we were, it was nothing in comparison with the fear of being driven out homeless to the dreary woods. Nothing to eat! I could give my guard no supper, so he left us. I appealed to another, asking him if he had wife, mother, or sister, and how he should feel were they in my situation. A colonel from Vermont left me two men, but they were Dutch [Germans], and I could not understand one word they said.

My Heavenly Father alone saved me from the destructive fire. My carriage-house had in it eight bales of cotton, with my carriage, buggy, and harness. On top of the cotton were some carded cotton rolls, a hundred pounds or more. These were thrown out of the blanket in which they were, and a large twist of the rolls taken and set on fire, and thrown into the boat of my carriage, which was close up to the cotton bales. Thanks to my God, the cotton only burned over, and then went out. Shall I ever forget the deliverance?

To-night, when the greater part of the army had passed, . . . my room was full, nearly, with the negroes and their bedding. They were afraid to go out. . . . I sat up all night, watching every moment for the flames to burst out from some of my buildings. . . . I could not close my eyes, but kept walking to and fro, watching the fires in the distance and dreading the approaching day, which, I feared, as they had not all passed, would be but a continuation of horrors.

The *New York Times* Is Amazed by the Change in Public Opinion on Slavery (1864)

The New York Times *printed the following editorial early in 1864 remarking on the change in popular attitudes toward the idea of gradual emancipation. Such changes demonstrated the war's corrosive effect on traditional ideas and assumptions.*

No Gradual Emancipation.

A mass convention was held yesterday in Memphis, inaugurating a general movement in Tennessee for the reorganization of the civil government in the State. One of the features of the call, we observe, is that "emancipation *immediate* and *unconditional* is our best and only true policy." The Unionism of the State has settled firmly on that principle.

It is extraordinary how completely the idea of *gradual* emancipation has been dissipated from the public mind everywhere, by the progress of events. Before the rebellion, it was accounted the very extreme of Anti-Slavery fanaticism to believe in the possibility of immediate emancipation without social ruin. The wisest Anti-Slavery men of the day, whether in this country or in Europe, assumed it almost as an axiom that there could be no transition from Slavery to freedom without an apprenticeship, or some other arrangement that should deaden the shock. All of the acts of emancipation by England and the continental nations, and by our own Northern States, whenever they applied to more than a mere handful of slaves, were invari-

ably based on that assumption. It took our own State not less than twenty-eight years to consummate the gradual extinction of the system after the Emancipation Law was passed. Long after the rebellion opened, even when it had become a generally accepted fact that Slavery must come to an end, the idea still adhered that the emancipation must be gradual in order to be safe. President LINCOLN, in his recommendation to Congress of appropriations to induce the Border States to initiate a system of emancipation, was particular to make it apply only to *gradual* emancipation. Even so late as last June, the Missouri Convention passed its emancipation ordinance so framed that no slave should go free before 1870, and the younger ones not until long afterwards.

But all these gradual methods are now hardly more thought of than if they had been obsolete a century. The people of Missouri, through their Legislature, have convened another convention to make a complete end of Slavery without delay. In Maryland immediate emancipation is the order of the day. The convention to frame the Free State Constitution, which is to be elected on the first Wednesday of April, and to meet on the last Wednesday of the same month, will not think of adopting any other plan. In Louisiana, in Arkansas,

FROM *New York Times*, 25 February 1864.

in Florida, and in fact wherever the purpose of emancipation is entertained at all, there seems to be an almost unanimous agreement that immediate emancipation is the wisest, and in fact the only practicable method.

The change of opinion on this subject is a remarkable illustration of the practical aptitude of the American mind. With hardly an effort, theories and prejudices, that had apparently rooted themselves in it so deeply as to become a part of it, are discarded, and new ideas, in keeping with a new condition of affairs, are conceived, and conformed to, almost by universal consent. It is recognised that whatever may be the advantage theoretically of gradual over immediate emancipation, the actual situation permits no option between the two. Gradual emancipation is, in truth, no longer a debatable matter, for there is nothing really left to graduate. Slavery now exists only in name. Its substance has been destroyed by the terrible attrition of the war. . . . When the military arm once has play, there is no such thing as a gradual severance of the bond between the master and slave. The rupture is intantaneous, and complete, and permanent. To undertake to renew the relation between master and slave for the sake of destroying it more scientifically would be only to prolong social confusion, and work unmixed evil to both races.

2

Party Platforms in 1864

Below are the platforms of the two major parties that were adopted for the 1864 presidential campaign. As Lincoln wanted, the Republican (Union) platform endorsed the proposed constitutional amendment to abolish slavery throughout the United States, which was still pending in Congress. The most controversial plank of the Democratic platform, which produced great resentment among the troops, was the one that termed the war a "failure" and called for an armistice and peace negotiations with the Confederacy. This statement was written by Clement Vallandigham, an Ohio delegate and the leader of the peace wing of the Democratic party, who earlier had been banished to the Confederacy for disloyalty (see p. 170). Although after much indecision George McClellan, the Democratic presidential nominee, declined to endorse the idea of an armistice, Republicans nevertheless seized upon the platform to accuse the Democratic party of disloyalty and support for disunion.

The 1864 Republican Platform

1. *Resolved*, That it is the highest duty of every American citizen to maintain against all their enemies the integrity of the Union, and the permanent authority of the Constitution and laws of the United States; and that, laying aside all differences of political opinion, we pledge ourselves as Union men, animated by a common sentiment, and aiming at a common object, to do everything in our power to aid the government in quelling by force of arms the rebellion now raging against its authority, and in bringing to the punishment due to

FROM Edward Stanwood, *A History of Presidential Elections* (Boston: Houghton, Mifflin, and Co., 1896), pp. 237–43.

their crimes the rebels and traitors arrayed against it.

2. *Resolved*, That we approve the determination of the government of the United States not to compromise with rebels, or to offer them any terms of peace, except such as may be based upon an unconditional surrender of their hostility and a return to their just allegiance to the Constitution and laws of the United States; and that we call upon the government to maintain this position, and to prosecute the war with the utmost possible vigor to the complete suppression of the rebellion, in full reliance upon the self-sacrificing patriotism, the heroic valor, and the undying devotion of the American people to their country and its free institutions.

3. *Resolved*, That as slavery was the cause, and now constitutes the strength of this rebellion, and as it must be, always and everywhere, hostile to the principles of republican government, justice and the national safety demand its utter and complete extirpation from the soil of the Republic; and that, while we uphold and maintain the acts and proclamations by which the government, in its own defence, has aimed a deathblow at this gigantic evil, we are in favor, furthermore, of such amendment to the Constitution, to be made by the people in conformity with its provisions, as shall terminate and forever prohibit the existence of slavery within the limits or the jurisdiction of the United States.

4. *Resolved*, That the thanks of the American people are due to the soldiers and sailors of the army and navy who have perilled their lives in defence of their country and in vindication of the honor of its flag; that the nation owes to them some permanent recognition of their patriotism and their valor, and ample and permanent provision for those of their survivors who have received disabling and honorable wounds in the service of the country; and that the memories of those who have fallen in its defence shall be held in grateful and everlasting remembrance.

5. *Resolved*, That we approve and applaud the practical wisdom, the unselfish patriotism, and the unswerving fidelity with which Abraham Lincoln has discharged, under circumstances of unparal-

leled difficulty, the great duties and responsibilities of the presidential office; that we approve and indorse, as demanded by the emergency and essential to the preservation of the nation and as within the provisions of the Constitution, the measures and acts which he has adopted to defend the nation against its open and secret foes; that we approve, especially, the proclamation of emancipation and the employment as Union soldiers of men heretofore held in slavery; and that we have full confidence in his determination to carry these and all other constitutional measures essential to the salvation of the country into full and complete effect.

6. *Resolved*, That we deem it essential to the general welfare that harmony should prevail in the national councils, and we regard as worthy of public confidence and official trust those only who cordially indorse the principles proclaimed in these resolutions, and which should characterize the administration of the government.

7. *Resolved*, That the government owes to all men employed in its armies, without regard to distinction of color, the full protection of the laws of war; and that any violation of these laws, or of the usages of civilized nations in time of war, by the rebels now in arms, should be made the subject of prompt and full redress.

8. *Resolved*, That foreign immigration, which in the past has added so much to the wealth, development of resources, and increase of power to this nation,—the asylum of the oppressed of all nations,—should be fostered and encouraged by a liberal and just policy.

9. *Resolved*, That we are in favor of a speedy construction of the railroad to the Pacific coast.

10. *Resolved*, That the national faith, pledged for the redemption of the public debt, must be kept inviolate, and that for this purpose we recommend economy and rigid responsibility in the public expenditures, and a vigorous and just system of taxation; and that it is the duty of every loyal State to sustain the credit and promote the use of the national currency.

11. *Resolved*, That we approve the position taken by the government, that the people of the United States can never regard with indifference

the attempt of any European power to overthrow by force, or to supplant by fraud, the institutions of any republican government on the western continent; and that they will view with extreme jealousy, as menacing to the peace and independence of their own country, the efforts of any such power to obtain new footholds for monarchical governments, sustained by foreign military force, in near proximity to the United States.

The 1864 Democratic Platform

Resolved, That in the future, as in the past, we will adhere with unswerving fidelity to the Union under the Constitution as the only solid foundation of our strength, security, and happiness as a people, and as a framework of government equally conducive to the welfare and prosperity of all the States, both Northern and Southern.

Resolved, That this convention does explicitly declare, as the sense of the American people, that after four years of failure to restore the Union by the experiment of war, during which, under the pretence of a military necessity, or war power higher than the Constitution, the Constitution itself has been disregarded in every part, and public liberty and private right alike trodden down, and the material prosperity of the country essentially impaired,—justice, humanity, liberty, and the public welfare demand that immediate efforts be made for a cessation of hostilities, with a view to an ultimate convention of the States, or other peaceable means, to the end that, at the earliest practicable moment, peace may be restored on the basis of the Federal union of the States.

Resolved, That the direct interference of the military authorities of the United States in the recent elections held in Kentucky, Maryland, Missouri, and Delaware was a shameful violation of the Constitution; and a repetition of such acts in the approaching election will be held as revolutionary, and resisted with all the means and power under our control.

Resolved, That the aim and object of the Democratic party is to preserve the Federal Union and the rights of the States unimpaired; and they hereby declare that they consider that the administrative usurpation of extraordinary and dangerous powers not granted by the Constitution; the subversion of the civil by military law in States not in insurrection; the arbitrary military arrest, imprisonment, trial, and sentence of American citizens in States where civil law exists in full force; the suppression of freedom of speech and of the press; the denial of the right of asylum; the open and avowed disregard of State rights; the employment of unusual test oaths; and the interference with and denial of the right of the people to bear arms in their defence; are calculated to prevent a restoration of the Union and the perpetuation of a government deriving its just powers from the consent of the governed.

Resolved, That the shameful disregard of the administration to its duty in respect to our fellow-citizens who are now, and long have been, prisoners of war and in a suffering condition, deserves the severest reprobation, on the score alike of public policy and common humanity.

Resolved, That the sympathy of the Democratic party is heartily and earnestly extended to the soldiery of our army and the sailors of our navy, who are and have been in the field and on the sea, under the flag of our country; and, in the event of its attaining power, they will receive all the care, protection, and regard that the brave soldiers and sailors of the Republic have so nobly earned.

ABRAHAM LINCOLN

Events Have Controlled Me (1864)

In late March 1864, Lincoln met with several Kentucky leaders who were angry over the recruitment of Kentucky slaves by the Union Army. In seeking to harmonize their feelings, Lincoln discussed the evolution of his policy toward slavery from the beginning of the war to the present. In this subsequent letter to one of the participants, Lincoln summarized his remarks. Albert Hodges was the editor of a newspaper in Frankfort, Kentucky.

Executive Mansion,
Washington, April 4, 1864.

A. G. Hodges, Esq
Frankfort, Ky.

My dear Sir:

You ask me to put in writing the substance of what I verbally said the other day, in your presence, to Governor Bramlette and Senator Dixon. It was about as follows:

"I am naturally anti-slavery. If slavery is not wrong, nothing is wrong. I can not remember when I did not so think, and feel. And yet I have never understood that the Presidency conferred upon me an unrestricted right to act officially upon this judgment and feeling. It was in the oath I took that I would, to the best of my ability, preserve, protect, and defend the Constitution of the United States. I could not take the office without taking the oath. Nor was it my view that I might take an oath to get power, and break the oath in using the power. I understood, too, that in ordinary civil administration this oath even forbade me to practically indulge my primary abstract judgment on the moral question of slavery. I had publicly declared this many times, and in many ways. And I aver that, to this day, I have done no official

act in mere deference to my abstract judgment and feeling on slavery. I did understand however, that my oath to preserve the constitution to the best of my ability, imposed upon me the duty of preserving, by every indispensable means, that government—that nation—of which that constitution was the organic law. Was it possible to lose the nation, and yet preserve the constitution? By general law life *and* limb must be protected; yet often a limb must be amputated to save a life; but a life is never wisely given to save a limb. I felt that measures, otherwise unconstitutional, might become lawful, by becoming indispensable to the preservation of the constitution, through the preservation of the nation. Right or wrong, I assumed this ground, and now avow it. I could not feel that, to the best of my ability, I had even tried to preserve the constitution, if, to save slavery, or any minor matter, I should permit the wreck of government, country, and Constitution all together. When, early in the war, Gen. Fremont attempted military emancipation, I forbade it, because I did not then think it an indispensable necessity. When a little later, Gen. Cameron, then Secretary of War, suggested the arming of the blacks, I objected, because I did not yet think it an indispensable necessity. When, still later, Gen. Hunter attempted military emancipation, I again forbade it, because I did not yet think the indispensable necessity had come. When, in March, and May, and July 1862 I made earnest, and successive appeals to the border states

FROM Roy P. Basler, et al., eds., *The Collected Works of Abraham Lincoln*, vol. 7 (New Brunswick, N.J.: Rutgers University Press, 1953), pp. 281–82.

to favor compensated emancipation, I believed the indispensable necessity for military emancipation, and arming the blacks would come, unless averted by that measure. They declined the proposition; and I was, in my best judgment, driven to the alternative of either surrendering the Union, and with it, the Constitution, or of laying strong hand upon the colored element. I chose the latter. In choosing it, I hoped for greater gain than loss; but of this, I was not entirely confident. More than a year of trial now shows no loss by it in our foreign relations, none in our home popular sentiment, none in our white military force,—no loss by it any how or any where. On the contrary, it shows a gain of quite a hundred and thirty thousand soldiers, seamen, and laborers. These are palpable facts, about which, as facts, there can be no cavilling. We have the men; and we could not have had them without the measure.

["]And now let any Union man who complains of the measure, test himself by writing down in one line that he is for subduing the rebellion by force of arms; and in the next, that he is for taking these hundred and thirty thousand men from the Union side, and placing them where they would be but for the measure he condemns. If he can not face his case so stated, it is only because he can not face the truth.["]

I add a word which was not in the verbal conversation. In telling this tale I attempt no compliment to my own sagacity. I claim not to have controlled events, but confess plainly that events have controlled me. Now, at the end of three years struggle the nation's condition is not what either party, or any man devised, or expected. God alone can claim it. Whither it is tending seems plain. If God now wills the removal of a great wrong, and wills also that we of the North as well as you of the South, shall pay fairly for our complicity in that wrong, impartial history will find therein new cause to attest and revere the justice and goodness of God.

Yours truly

A. Lincoln

4

HORACE GREELEY

Our Bleeding Country Longs for Peace (1864)

Horace Greeley, the editor of the powerful New York Tribune, *was a frequent thorn in Lincoln's side. An unreliable adviser, the mercurial editor oscillated between extreme and sometimes contradictory positions, and was subject to great mood swings that clouded his judgment and often produced self-doubt. Although a brilliant, slashing writer, he lacked the ability to sway people who were not already committed to his cause. Indeed, following the Union debacle at Bull Run in July 1861, Greeley privately advised Lincoln to abandon the war and recognize the Confederacy. Now in the summer of 1864 he took up the cause of peace negotiations. In the following letter, he urged Lincoln to begin discussions with Confederate leaders to end the war.*

New York, July 7, 1864

My Dear Sir:

I venture to inclose you a letter and telegraphic dispatch that I received yesterday from our irrepressible friend, Colorado Jewett, at Niagara Falls. I think they deserve attention. Of course, I do not indorse Jewett's positive averment that his friends . . . have "full powers" from J.D. [Jefferson Davis], though I do not doubt that *he* thinks they have. I let that statement stand as simply evidencing the anxiety of the Confederates everywhere for peace. So much is beyond doubt.

And thereupon I venture to remind you that our bleeding, bankrupt, almost dying country also longs for peace—shudders at the prospect of fresh conscriptions, of further wholesale devastations, and of new rivers of human blood. And a widespread conviction that the Government . . . are not anxious for Peace, and do not improve proffered opportunities to achieve it, is doing great harm now, and is morally certain, unless removed, to do far greater in the approaching Elections. . . .

I entreat you, in your own time and manner, to submit overtures for pacification to the Southern insurgents which the impartial must pronounce frank and generous. If only with a view to the momentous Election soon to occur in North Carolina, and of the Draft to be enforced in the Free States, this should be done at once.

I would give the safe conduct required by the Rebel envoys at Niagara . . . but *you* may see reasons for declining it. But, whether through them or otherwise, do not, I entreat you, fail to make the Southern people comprehend that you and all of us are anxious for peace. . . .

Mr. President, I fear you do not realize how intently the people desire any peace consistent with the national integrity and honor . . . . With United States stocks worth but forty cents in gold per dollar, and drafting about to commence on the third million of Union soldiers, can this be wondered at?

I do not say that a just peace is now attainable, though I believe it to be so. But I *do* say, that a frank *offer* by you to the insurgents of terms . . . will . . . prove an immense and sorely needed advantage to the national cause; it may save us from a northern insurrection. . . .

I beg you to invite those now at Niagara to exhibit their credentials and submit their ultimatum.

Yours truly,

Horace Greeley

FROM Horace Greeley to Abraham Lincoln, July 7, 1864, Abraham Lincoln Papers, Library of Congress.

5

Abraham Lincoln Outlines His Terms for Peace (1864)

Lincoln came under very heavy pressure in the summer of 1864 to open peace negotiations with the Confederacy, but he realized that such negotiations were futile, since Jefferson Davis would never accept reunion. Hoping to unmask the Confederate government's true position, he sent a reluctant Horace Greeley, who was a persistent party critic, to meet with Confederate representatives in Canada. Lincoln knew that Greeley's trip constituted a wild goose chase, but he thought it might aid the Union cause, and in any case it would certainly embarrass the strident New

York Tribune *editor. After Greeley reached Canada and requested authorization, Lincoln wired him the following statement. Indignant Democrats seized upon Lincoln's insistence on emancipation as part of any peace settlement to condemn the president. They referred to this statement as Lincoln's "To Whom It May Concern" letter, which became one of the catchphrases of the 1864 presidential campaign.*

Executive Mansion,
Washington, July 18, 1864.

To Whom it may concern:

Any proposition which embraces the restoration of peace, the integrity of the whole Union, and the abandonment of slavery, and which comes by and with an authority that can control the armies now at war against the United States will be received and considered by the Executive government of the United States, and will be met by liberal terms on other substantial and collateral points; and the bearer, or bearers thereof shall have safe-conduct both ways.

Abraham Lincoln

FROM Roy P. Basler, et al., eds., *The Collected Works of Abraham Lincoln*, vol. 7 (New Brunswick, N.J.: Rutgers University Press, 1953), p. 451.

6

HENRY J. RAYMOND

The Tide Is Setting Strongly against Us (1864)

Henry J. Raymond was chairman of the Republican National Committee in 1864 as well as editor of the influential New York Times. *In this letter to Lincoln discussing the 1864 presidential campaign, he stressed the widespread belief among northern voters that Lincoln was prolonging the war by insisting on emancipation and urged the necessity of neutralizing the peace issue in the election. Lincoln shared this pessimism and as late as the end of August fully expected to be defeated in November. At a subsequent meeting with Raymond in Washington, however, Lincoln rejected the national chairman's proposal. John G. Nicolay, one of Lincoln's private secretaries, reported that the president and his advisers told Raymond that "to follow his plan of sending a commission to Richmond would be worse than losing the presidential contest—it would be ignominiously surrendering it in advance."*

New York
August 22, 1864

My Dear Sir:—

I feel compelled to drop you a line concerning the political condition of the country as it strikes me. I am in active correspondence with your staunchest friends in every state and from them all I hear but one report. The tide is setting strongly against us. Hon. E. B. Washburne writes that "were an election to be held now in Illinois we should be beaten." Mr. [Simon] Cameron writes that Pennsylvania is against us. Gov. [Oliver P.] Morton writes that nothing but the most strenuous efforts can carry Indiana. This state [New York], according to the best information I can get, would go 50,000 against us to-morrow. And so of the rest. Nothing but the most resolute and decided action on the part of the government and its friends, can save the country from falling into hostile hands.

Two special causes are assigned to this great reaction in public sentiment,—the want of military successes, and the impression in some minds, the fear and suspicion in others, that we are not to have peace *in any event* under this administration until Slavery is abandoned. In some way or other the suspicion is widely diffused that we *can* have peace with Union if we would. It is idle to reason with this belief—still more idle to denounce it. It can only be expelled by some authoritative act, at once bold enough to fix attention and distinct enough to defy incredulity & challenge respect.

Why would it not be wise, under these circumstances, to appoint a Commissioner, in due form, *to make distinct proffers of peace to Davis, as the head of the rebel armies, on the sole condition of acknowledging the supremacy of the constitution,*—all other questions to be settled in a convention of the people of all the States? The making of such an offer would require no armistice, no suspension of active war, no abandonment of positions, no sacrifice of consistency.

If the proffer were *accepted* (which I presume it would not be,) the country would never consent to place the practical execution of its details in any but loyal hands, and in those we should be safe.

If it should be *rejected*, (as it would be,) it would plant seeds of disaffection in the south, dispel all the delusions about peace that prevail in the North, silence the clamors & damaging falsehoods of the opposition, take the wind completely out of the sails of the Chicago craft, reconcile public sentiment to the War, the draft, & the tax as inevitable *necessities*, and unite the North as nothing since firing on Fort Sumter has hitherto done.

I cannot conceive of any answer which Davis could give to such a proposition which would not strengthen you & the Union cause *everywhere*. Even your radical friends could not fail to applaud it when they should see the practical strength it would bring to the common cause.

I beg you to excuse the earnestness with which I have pressed this matter upon your attention. It seems to me calculated to do good—& incapable of doing harm. It will turn the tide of public sentiment & avert pending evils of the gravest character. It will rouse & concentrate the loyalty of the country &, unless I am greatly mistaken, give us an early & a fruitful victory.

Permit me to add that if done at all I think this should be done at once,—as your own spontaneous act. In advance of the Chicago Convention it might render the action of that body, of very little consequence. . . .

I am very respectfully,
Your obt servt

Henry J. Raymond

FROM Roy P. Basler, et al., eds., *The Collected Works of Abraham Lincoln,* vol. 7 (New Brunswick, N.J.: Rutgers University Press, 1953), pp. 517–18.

ILLINOIS STATE REGISTER

A Negotiated Peace with the Confederacy Is Possible (1864)

In the following editorial, the Illinois State Register, *which was the Democratic party organ in Springfield, replied to Republican criticism and argued that negotiations with the Confederacy would end the war.*

The abolition journals and talkers all declare that Jeff. Davis will not consent to honorable terms of peace, upon the basis of the Union of these states. We have every reason to believe the contrary, and that if a democratic president were in power, peace and the Union would be restored on terms honorable and satisfactory to every American citizen. We form this opinion from what the rebels have done to obtain peace; from what their leading journals say in regard to the peace question, and from well-known and universal principles of human nature which always govern human action.

But suppose the abolitionists tell the truth, and that Jeff. Davis should refuse to make peace on other terms than recognition of southern independence. We know that Lincoln has refused to listen to overtures of peace because they did not include the "abandonment of slavery," and says he will receive no propositions which do not make this the first and leading feature. And for this very reason,

the people are going to put him out of office, and put in a man who will agree to make peace so soon as we can have the Union in its original integrity. And as the people of the south are Jeff. Davis' masters in the same sense that we of the north are Lincoln's, if Davis stands between them and honorable peace, they will drive him from his place at the earliest opportunity. . . .

The people at the south . . . must be as anxious for peace; they know that . . . the American people will never again commit the great blunder of placing an abolitionist and a buffoon in the presidential chair, and will be willing and anxious to return to the Union as it was, under the constitution as it is.

. . . We know, for we have Lincoln's official assurance, that we can have no honorable peace while he reigns, and the work before us, therefore, is to replace him by a man who will place the constitution and the Union before abolition and anarchy, and make the rights and liberties of the white race paramount to the freedom of the negro.

FROM *Illinois State Register*, 9 September 1864.

8

NEW YORK TRIBUNE

An Armistice Would Lead to a
Southern Victory (1864)

The Republican New York Tribune *published the following editorial attacking the Democratic platform's call for an armistice and negotiations to restore the Union.*

An Armistice—
How It Would Ruin Us

What is an armistice? Webster defines it to be . . . "a temporary suspension of hostilities *by agreement of the parties.*"

An armistice is the cardinal idea upon which the McClellan movement swings in this Presidential canvass. If McClellan is elected, he will be elected by it.

Suppose he is elected. . . . The expectation of an armistice at a future day certain, would as surely break down and dissolve an American army—an army of volunteers fighting for a principle—as the flow of the Niagara would dissolve and wash away salt. The 4th of March [the date of the inauguration] would inevitably find us in a condition—to do what? To propose an armistice? Oh no! but abjectly, and with just fear and retribution trembling, to receive propositions for a cessation of hostilities. We should be conquered. . . .

Who is to take the initiative in . . . the opening of the negotiation—who is to ask for the "convention" and propose the "agreement" [for an armistice]? Not President Davis—for he has not asked for an armistice, and he won't ask for an armistice, so long as his heart locks within itself the manhood of courage instead of the sheepishness of

cowardice, and so long as his soul remains faithful to the Confederacy which has committed its life to his keeping. . . . Who then, is to take the initiative, and send commissioners to propose an armistice? Why President McClellan, clearly.

His commissioners go. They unfold their credentials, *and in the very act of unfolding them recognize the Rebel Confederacy.*

This legal result of the cowardly and traitorous folly of proposing an armistice, could not possibly be escaped. . . . This fact of recognition by McClellan's administration would immediately be accepted in Paris and London as the solvent of the difficulty which for three years has defeated the application of the Confederate States to be recognized as an independent power. France and Great Britain have consistently replied to [Confederate diplomats John] Slidell and [James] Mason's entreaties: "The American Government treats you as Rebels. Until you can fight yourselves out of it, we can not treat with you as an independent power without getting into war." But the obstacle to this coveted recognition would be removed throughout Europe in an instant by McClellan's proposal of an armistice. France, England, Spain, Austria, and Belgium, would acknowledge the sovereignty of the Confederacy forthwith, and make treaties with them, the commercial classes of which would hourly bribe those powers to help the Rebels while the war lasted. . . .

The argument might well stop here. But let us follow up this negotiation for an armistice.

FROM *New York Tribune,* 27 September 1864.

The first question to be settled after the proposal, would be Jeff. Davis's inquiry . . . , "What is the armistice which you propose?"

"An immediate cessation of hostilities, to the end that peace may be restored on the basis of the Federal Union of the States."[1]

"We will accept the proposal upon the terms and conditions which public law affixes to an armistice. We will withdraw the Confederate troops from every part of your territory; we will suspend the blockade of your coast, and stop privateering on your commerce. You must withdraw the United States troops from every part of our territory; you must suspend the blockade of any and every part of our coast, and cease from capturing merchant vessels bound to our ports. That is, we must be upon terms of equality with you, and free from duress, and relieved from all cercion and restraint, in order to enter into the convention for reunion which you propose."

McClellan's commissioners could not possibly escape from this definition of an armistice, in connection with its object—a convention for reunion. . . .

Through the relaxation or suspension of the blockade, and the demoralization of the pickets, supplies of all sorts . . . would get easy ingress and egress into and out of the Confederacy. And in the train of these commissioners would go Delay—stately, cunning, ceremonious, ingenious, diplomatic Delay . . . and the ships of Liverpool, Marseilles, Bremen, and Trieste would the while flock like pigeons to the Southern ports—the cotton, sugar, and tobacco of the Confederacy would get converted into gold—what the Rebellion needed of arms, munitions, clothing, machinery, and men, would be supplied to her—treaties of amity, as well as commerce, . . . would be snug in the State Department at Richmond. The Rebellion, materially re-invigorated and morally braced by the recognition and promised support of the British, French, Spaniards and Austrians, would be strong enough in September '65, to stalk into the Peace Commission at Richmond in the person of Jeff. Davis, and say: "This affair must come to a conclusion. All negotiations for a peace with the Confederate States must be based upon the recognition of their independence. . . ."

What a condition we would be in? Where would be our army? Desertions consequent on the loss of its spirit, and the destruction of its discipline, sickness and death so sure to run havoc through troops that are idle and demoralized, would have swept it away by whole brigades. Only a decaying skeleton of it would be left. The two hundred thousand black soldiers and employees in the service, would early in March have been kicked out, to appease the beastly rage which shirked in Democratic processions, "This is a white man's war!" The blockade would have to be rescued again by a fleet which had anchored its spirit and vigilance deep down. And when we came to key up the nation to the sacrifice and elasticity necessary to an offensive war—could it be done? Every man in this country out of an idiot asylum knows that it could not be done. The war would be gone. The South would triumph.

---

[1]This statement is from the 1864 Democratic platform.

9

The Republican and Democratic Parties' Final Appeals to the Voters (1864)

Below are the final appeals of both parties in two New York papers on election day 1864. The Republican New York Times *and the Democratic* New York World *agreed on the importance of the election, but otherwise they manifested different strategies. The Times downplayed the importance of the candidates and stressed the larger issues confronting the nation, particularly preservation of the Union. The World, in contrast, focused on Abraham Lincoln himself and condemned his leadership and policies.*

The Momentous Day.

The day has come—the day of fate. Before this morning's sun sets, the destinies of this republic, so far as depends on human agency, are to be settled for weal or for woe. An inevitable choice is this day to be made by the American people, between a policy carrying salvation or a policy carrying ruin to the nation. On the one hand is war, tremendous and terrible, yet ushering in at the end every national security and glory. On the other is the mocking shadow of a peace, tempting us to quit these sacrifices, and sink again into indulgence, and yet sure to rob us of our birthright, and to entail upon our children a disseveered Union and ceaseless strife. As the popular decision of this day is rendered in favor of the principles declared at Baltimore, or the principles declared at Chicago, so must either this or that consequence follow. The two men for whom the votes are to be cast are nothing in the presence of this mighty issue. Whatever their respective merits or faults, and however legitimately these, in ordinary times, might determine which of the two should be accepted and which rejected, such personal considerations are but as the dust in the balance when policies of such dread import are to be weighed. . . . GEORGE B. MC-CLELLAN might be all that his most extravagant

admirers claim him to be, and a thousand times beyond, and yet he would be as helpless as an infant to stay the destruction of the Union in the line of the policy marked out for him by his party at Chicago. It is not within the power of mortal man to abandon the war at this stage, and make terms with the rebellion that will not involve the wreck of all that constitutes us a nation. Every man that casts his vote to-day should keep his eyes on this mighty fact. His choice is to be made, not between persons but between policies. The sovereign question is whether this rebellion, which is assailing the life of the Union, is to be dealt with on the principle of maintaining the national authority, or on the principle of surrendering it—in other words, whether we are to have stability through the ascendancy of law, or subversion through the triumph of lawlessness. We are making this decision not for ourselves simply. We are settling the lot of the generations that shall come after us. . . .

It is almost appalling to reflect that such stupendous interests, stretching far into the coming years, must depend upon our faithfulness or unfaithfulness, our discretion or indiscretion, within the next ten hours. Could the consequences of our doings this day be realized in all their full scope, the universal feeling would be that finite hands are not fit for such measureless trusts, and the universal impulse would be to look for some miraculous direction from Heaven. But no such direction is

FROM *New York Times*, 8 November 1864..

needed if we will but faithfully exercise the attributes of our nature that come from Heaven—our reason and conscience. It is the faith that the majority of the American people will so do, which gives this day its bright promise as a day that will be forever memorable for the reaffirmation and reconsecration of the great principles which alone make a free government possible among men.

Last Words.

The time for argument and discussion on the merits of the candidates who now claim the confidence of America for the chief magistracy of the republic has gone by. The morning breaks upon a day, not of words, but of deeds. All the resources of pen and tongue have been exhausted to set before the people the magnitude of the issues involved in this day's election. By their votes this day, the freemen of America must stand or fall. Whoever casts his vote to-day blindly, casts his vote passionately, casts his vote in obedience to the dictates of party; whoever fails to-day to cast his vote at all, must bear upon his soul forever the damning sense of an inevitable responsibility for all the ills and miseries and shame which an evil choice of the nation's rulers through the next four years must bring upon the land.

What can rhetoric add of force to the overwhelming testimony which events have borne to the utter unfitness of ABRAHAM LINCOLN for this awful trust which he now asks the republic to renew to him?

A rebellion which all the ablest men of his own party concurred in asserting might have been subdued in sixty days has grown beneath his hands into a civil war which shakes and sickens Christendom.

That sovereign majesty of the Constitution, endeared to the hearts of the people by seventy years of prosperity and of peace, which all the ablest men of his party concurred in asserting that a loyal army of seventy-five thousand men would be amply adequate to defend, is still insulted and defied by millions of American citizens over the graves of five hundred thousand loyal soldiers sacrificed in vain by him to maintain it. The commerce which whitened, every sea when ABRAHAM LINCOLN assumed the presidential chair, now shrinks under the cover of foreign flags. Upon the people whom he found, out of all the earth, the least burdened by debt, the least harassed by taxation, his financial policy has imposed such a weight as centuries of war have not laid upon the industries and the energy of the oldest European states. We are asked now to believe that the President through whose incapacity—by none more loudly proclaimed than by those who have most enjoyed his confidence and have most profited by his blunders—the hope of reunion and of peace has been thus fearfully adjourned, will prove himself equal to the task of undoing all the mischief he has done.

Four years ago we gave into his keeping a prosperous and happy nation threatened by incipient treason. Four years of his rule have given us desolation for prosperity, and misery for happiness; and the treason incipient then now meets us over half a continent as with the organized front of a hostile nationality.

What argument for a change in the persons and the policy of the national administration can eloquence supply to those whom the facts of 1861, confronted with the facts of 1864, fail to convince?

Citizens of America! Providence itself has conducted before you the canvass of which this day's setting sun must see the issue decided by your wisdom or your madness. It has set before you in letters of fire and blood, and tears, the contrast between the fatal experiments of a reckless and tyrannical fanaticism, and the ancient guarantees of liberty and of law; of respect for established rights, of justice, and of true humanity.

Choose for yourselves this day! for with this day's setting sun your irrevocable verdict will have been passed; and with it the weal or woe of yourselves and of your children's children assured through years on years to come.

FROM *New York World*, 8 November 1864.

10

J. N. JONES

A Democratic Soldier Votes for Lincoln (1891)

With so many men away at war, a number of northern states made provisions for soldiers to vote in the fields in November 1864. Lincoln demonstrated a remarkable appeal to the men in the Union ranks, and indeed his powerful support from Union soldiers swelled his margin of victory. In the following account, a Union officer described the decision of one New Hampshire enlisted man, who was a lifelong Democrat, to vote for Lincoln, aided by some patriotic rhetoric from his captain.

On the morning of that [election] day, at roll-call, I told the men of my company that there would be no drill, and that at nine o'clock A.M. opportunity to vote would be given all of them who were legal voters in New Hampshire. The law made the three ranking officers in each company judges of election. Having no lieutenant, I invited two sergeants to assist me. My tent was about six feet by seven, and sink into the ground twelve or fifteen inches for greater security against bullets that might come straying around at any time. It was noticed, however, that on that day the rebels were unusually quiet, firing scarcely a shot. A cigar box answered for a ballot box. The state furnished blanks for recording each voter's name, together with that of the town he claimed to be his residence, and for whom he voted. In case, therefore, a man voted who had no right to do so, his vote could be thrown out. The polls having been declared open, and both Democratic and Republican votes placed upon the table, the men came up, were registered, voted, and retired.[1] There was one man, a good specimen of the New Hampshire voter who goes to town-meeting and makes a day of it. He seemed in no hurry to vote, and I invited

him to take a seat on a hard-bread box at the mouth of the tent. He had served almost three years; had been with the regiment in its every battle; had been slightly wounded several times—was, indeed, a good soldier. At last he said,—"Say, captain, what do you think of the election?" To my reply, "I guess it is all right," he responded, "Well, what do you think of voting? I have always been a Democrat, and never voted anything but the Democratic ticket in my life." "All right," said I, "there are Democratic ballots—vote just as you please. If you can't do so after having gone through what you have, we had better all go home. I shall vote for Lincoln, but do you vote just as you choose." "Well," said he, "I have been thinking about voting for Lincoln. I believe he is a pretty good man." Then taking a Republican ballot in one hand and a Democratic ballot in the other, he rested his elbows on his knees and scanned the tickets in silence. Seeing his dilemma, I read aloud and as impressively as I could, the following lines of poetry printed on the back of the Republican ticket, while the listened attentively:

> "What! hoist the white flag when our triumph is nigh!
> What! crouch before treason—make freedom a lie!
> What! spike all our guns when the foe is at bay,
> With his flags and black banners fast dropping away!"

I added the response, "Not much!" and he, without saying a word, put the Lincoln ballot into the box, had his name recorded, and walked away.

[1]In this period, parties printed their own ballots.

FROM Lyman Jackman, *History of the Sixth New Hampshire Regiment* (Concord, N.H.: Republican Press Association, 1891), pp. 344–46.

Company F voted solid for Lincoln, of free choice and without undue influence. And it is gratifying to record the fact that the soldiers' election was likewise a fair one throughout the army.

11

ABRAHAM LINCOLN

The Election Was a Necessity (1864)

Shortly after the election, a group of well-wishers came to the White House and serenaded the president. In response Lincoln read the following brief remarks on the significance of the election, which he had written out. Some advisers had suggested earlier that the election be cancelled or postponed, but Lincoln gave no consideration to such a policy. The United States was the first modern nation to hold a general election in wartime.

November 10, 1864

It has long been a grave question whether any government, not *too* strong for the liberties of its people, can be strong *enough* to maintain its own existence, in great emergencies.

On this point the present rebellion brought our republic to a severe test; and a presidential election occurring in regular course during the rebellion added not a little to the strain. If the loyal people, *united*, were put to the utmost of their strength by the rebellion, must they not fail when *divided*, and partially paralized, by a political war among themselves?

But the election was a necessity.

We can not have free government without elections; and if the rebellion could force us to forego, or postpone a national election, it might fairly claim to have already conquered and ruined us.

The strife of the election is but human-nature practically applied to the facts of the case. What has occurred in this case, must ever recur in similar cases. Human-nature will not change. . . .

But the election, along with its incidental, and undesirable strife, has done good too. It has demonstrated that a people's government can sustain a national election, in the midst of a great civil war. Until now it has not been known to the world that this was a possibility. It shows also how *sound*, and how *strong* we still are. It shows that, even among candidates of the same party, he who is most devoted to the Union, and most opposed to treason, can receive most of the people's votes. It shows also, to the extent yet known, that we have more men now, than we had when the war began. Gold is good in its place; but living, brave, patriotic men, are better than gold.

But the rebellion continues; and now that the election is over, may not all, having a common interest, re-unite in a common effort, to save our common country? For my own part I have striven, and shall strive to avoid placing any ob-

FROM Roy P. Basler, et al., ed., *The Collected Works of Abraham Lincoln*, vol. 8 (New Brunswick, N.J.: Rutgers University Press, 1953), pp. 100–101.

stacle in the way. So long as I have been here I have not willingly planted a thorn in any man's bosom.

While I am deeply sensible to the high compliment of a re-election; and duly grateful, as I trust, to Almighty God for having directed my countrymen to a right conclusion, as I think, for their own good, it adds nothing to my satisfaction that any other man may be disappointed or pained by the result.

May I ask those who have not differed with me, to join with me, in this same spirit towards those who have?

And now, let me close by asking three hearty cheers for our brave soldiers and seamen and their gallant and skilful commanders.

12

CHICAGO TRIBUNE

Lincoln's Election Is a Mandate to Abolish Slavery (1864)

Following the 1864 election, the Chicago Tribune, *a strongly antislavery Republican paper, insisted that Lincoln's re-election represented a popular mandate to abolish slavery.*

The Voice of the People.

In any country no true statesman would fail in deciding upon the policy of the administration, to observe carefully the changes in public sentiment, and to mould his measures to suit the demands of the people. This course of action, the dictate of the soundest political sagacity under every government, is a supreme duty with us, who hold the will and choice of the people to be the source of all power, and to be diligently sought for, and faithfully and intently obeyed as soon as pronounced. It is not always easy to ascertain what public sentiment is, and after an election involving many and various questions and issues, the most candid and fair minds may differ as to the meaning and extent of the popular decision. . . . It is often difficult to ascertain on what subject the popular opinion is united, and in regard to what question its decision is unanimous and determined. As re-

gards the election just terminated, very few if any can be found who doubt that the people have voted with an overwhelming majority, that the rebellion must be subdued by force, that there shall be no compromise or armistice with rebels in arms, that the Union must be restored, and the authority of the Government re-established to its extreme bounds; of the will and determination of the people on all these issues there can be no doubt. There is another subject, that of slavery, which has been a controling one in the canvass, as it always has and will be so long as it exists, and it is most important to know what judgement and purpose the people have expressed at the polls respecting it. If the platform of the party who have been so triumphantly sustained by the people, is to be taken as proof of the popular determination, then beyond a doubt the people demand the destruction of slavery, as the deadliest foe to the country, and the real life and support of the rebellion.

The Administration would be false to its avowed purposes, as given in the platform, and to its solemn pledges to the country, and to the loyal

FROM *Chicago Tribune*, 18 November 1864.

men who re-elected it, if it hesitated or swerved in carrying out a thorough emancipation policy. As regards the form in which such policy could most safely and wisely be carried out, whether it should be immediate or gradual, and under what conditions, securing the most advantage to the slave, or the least injury to the slaveholding sections, there may be room for discussion. But we feel sure that the people who have voted with such unparalleled unanimity to continue the policy of the present Administration, intended to say, and have most emphatically declared, that they believe slavery to be in all ages bad and mischievous; that it was the source of the rebellion, and is now its chief strength and support; that we can have no permanent Union and no enduring peace until it is destroyed; and they demand of their rulers that it shall be extinguished. Of the mode and manner of its taking off, it may be difficult to ascertain any definite expression of the popular voice; but if this popular verdict has any clear meaning at all, its voice rings out in the loudest tones an utter condemnation of slavery, and a demand that it shall be utterly destroyed.

It is well known that one of the strongest points made by the Opposition against the re-election of Lincoln was, that his avowed purpose was to make no peace with the rebels unless they would first consent to the abolition of slavery, rendered it impossible for him ever to subdue the rebellion or end the war. While the policy of the Opposition was to re-establish State Sovereignty, with additional guarantys, meaning slavery. . . . If there was any one single issue which, by the unending and most strenuous efforts of the opposition was most distinctly drawn and plainly presented, it was whether the people of this country would vote for the Lincoln policy to carry on the war, not to save the Union, but to destroy slavery. And the people have recorded their answer, by reelecting Lincoln. There can be no doubt that on this issue the opposition was overwhelmingly defeated. The meaning of the election is, the people have made up their minds that slavery, and the Union with peace, cannot exist together, and they demand the destruction of slavery.

Whatever may be the danger of making the South a united and compact mass, and rousing in them an unconquerable and most malignant fury, if you strike slavery, the people of the North, in full view of all the danger, have emphatically pronounced their determination, that the country cannot be saved unless slavery be destroyed; and whatever may be the cost or sacrifice in blood or treasure, that the war shall go on until both rebellion and slavery are wholly crushed out and ended. The conviction has been growing and ripening with wondrous rapidity in the hot air of this great conflict, that slavery is the life and strength of the rebellion, and that there is no way in which to end rebellion and save the Union but by the utter extinction of slavery, and the overwhelming result of the election is simply the formal utterance of that conviction.

13

Abraham Lincoln Hails the Passage of the Thirteenth Amendment (1865)

After Congress approved the proposed Thirteenth Amendment abolishing slavery, a group of well-wishers came to the White House to cheer the president. In response, Lincoln made the following remarks to the assembled group.

February 1, 1865

The President said he supposed the passage through Congress of the Constitutional amendment for the abolishment of Slavery throughout the United States, was the occasion to which he was indebted for the honor of this call. The occasion was one of congratulation to the country and to the whole world. But there is a task yet before us—to go forward and consummate by the votes of the States that which Congress so nobly began yesterday. He had the honor to inform those present that Illinois had already to-day done the work. Maryland was about half through; but he felt proud that Illinois was a little ahead. He thought this measure was a very fitting if not an indispensable adjunct to the winding up of the great difficulty. He wished the reunion of all the States perfected and so effected as to remove all causes of disturbance in the future; and to attain this end it was necessary that the original disturbing cause should, if possible, be rooted out. He thought all would bear him witness that he had never shrunk from doing all that he could to eradicate Slavery by issuing an emancipation proclamation. But that proclamation falls far short of what the amendment will be when fully consummated. A question might be raised whether the proclamation was legally valid. It might be added that it only aided those who came into our lines and that it was inoperative as to those who did not give themselves up, or that it would have no effect upon the children of the slaves born hereafter. In fact it would be urged that it did not meet the evil. But this amendment is a King's cure for all the evils. It winds the whole thing up. He would repeat that it was the fitting if not indispensable adjunct to the consummation of the great game we are playing. He could not but congratulate all present, himself, the country and the whole world upon this great moral victory.

FROM Roy P. Basler, et al., eds., *The Collected Works of Abraham Lincoln*, vol. 8 (New Brunswick, N.J.: Rutgers University Press, 1953), pp. 254–55.

1

Josiah Gorgas Notes the Achievements of the Confederate Ordnance Bureau (1864)

Despite his Pennsylvania birth, Josiah Gorgas, influenced by his southern-born wife and his strong dislike of abolitionism, sided with the Confederacy during the war. A graduate of West Point, he served in the United States Army's ordnance branch and was named the Confederacy's chief of ordnance in 1861. Gorgas was an extremely capable administrator and achieved remarkable success in supplying Confederate armies with arms and ammunition. In an entry in his diary in 1864, he discussed these achievements.

April 8, [1864] It is three years ago to-day since I took charge of the Ord. department of the Conf. States at Montgomery—three years of constant work and application. I have succeeded beyond my utmost expectations. From being the worst supplied of the Bureaus of the War Dept. it is now the best. Large Arsenals have been organized at Richmond, Fayetteville, Augusta, Charleston, Columbus, Macon, Atlanta, & Selma and Smaller ones at Danville, Lynchburgh and Montgomery, besides other establishments. A superb powder mill has been built at Augusta, the credit of which is due to Col. G. W. Rains. Lead smelting works were established by me at Petersburgh, and turned over to the Nitre & Mining Bureau, when that Bureau was at my request separated from mine. A cannon foundry established at Macon for heavy guns, & bronze foundries at Macon Columbus Ga. and at Augusta. A foundry for shot & shell at Salisbury

N. C. A large shop for leather work at Clarksville Va. Besides the Armories here & at Fayetteville, a manufactory of carbines has been built up here—a rifle factory at Asheville (transferred to Columbia S. C)—a new and very large armory at Macon, including a pistol factory, built up under contract here & sent to Atlanta, & thence transferred under purchase to Macon. A second pistol factory at Columbus Ga. All of these have required incessant toil & attention, but have borne such fruit as relieves the country from fear of want in these respects. Where three years ago we were not making a gun, a pistol nor a sabre—a pound of powder—no shot nor shell (except at the Tredegar Works) we now make all these in quantities to meet the demands of our large armies. In looking over all this I feel that my three years of labor have not been passed in vain.

FROM Sarah Woolfolk Wiggins, ed., *The Journals of Josiah Gorgas, 1857–1878* (Tuscaloosa: University of Alabama Press, 1995), pp. 97–98.

2

ALEXANDER H. STEPHENS

Once Lost, Liberty Is Lost Forever (1864)

As the Confederate vice president, Alexander H. Stephens initially supported Jefferson Davis's policies, but Davis did not consult him on public matters, and eventually the two became politically and personally estranged. With no real responsibility or power, Stephens eventually went home to Georgia, where he joined the growing opposition movement against Davis in that state. As part of the anti-Davis campaign, he delivered a major speech in the Georgia legislature in March 1864, denouncing the Confederate president and his policies. Characterizing Davis as a would-be dictator, Stephens focused in particular on the issues of conscription and civil liberties.

This brings me to the main objects of this address, a review of those acts of Congress to which your attention has been specially called by the governor, and on which your action is invoked—these are, the currency, the military, and the *habeas corpus* suspension acts. . . . In grave and important matters, however disagreeable or even painful it may be to express disapproval, yet sometimes the highest duty requires it. . . . Our opinions in all such discussions of public affairs, should be given as from friends to friends, as from borthers [*sic*] to brothers, in a common cause. We are all launched upon the same boat, and must ride the storm or go down together. Disagreements should never arise, except from one cause—a difference in judgment, as to the best means to be adopted, or course to be pursued, for the common safety. This is the spirit by which I am actuated in the comments I shall make upon these acts of Congress.

As to the first two of these measures, the Tax Act and Funding Act, known together as the financial and currency measures, I simply say, in my judgment, they are neither proper, wise or just. Whether in the midst of conflicting views, in such diversity of opinion and interests, any thing better

could not be obtained, I know not—perhaps not. With that view we may be reconciled to what we do not approve. It is useless now to go into discussions of how better measures might have been obtained, or how bad ones might have been avoided—the whole is a striking illustration of the evils attending first departures from principle. . . . Our present financial embarrassments had their origin in a blunder at the beginning, but we must deal with the present, not the past. . . .

The military act by which conscription is extended so as to embrace all between the ages of seventeen and fifty, and by which the State is to be deprived of so much of its labor, and stripped of the most efficient portion of her enrolled militia, presents a much graver question. This whole system of conscription I have looked upon from the beginning as wrong, radically wrong in principle and in policy. . . . It is for you to say whether you will turn over these forces, and allow them to be conscripted, as is provided, leaving the question of constitutionality for the courts, or whether you will hold them in view of agricultural and other interest, or for the execution of your laws, and to be called out for the public defence in case of emergency by the governor when he sees the necessity, or when they are called for as militia by the President. The act upon its face, in its provisions for details, seems to indicate that its object is not to put

FROM Henry Cleland, ed., *Alexander H. Stephens in Public and Private* (Philadelphia: National Publishing Company, 1866), pp. 761–77.

the whole of them in the field. Nothing could be more ruinous to our cause if such were the object and intention, and should it ever be carried into effect. For if all the white labor of the country, from seventeen to fifty—except the few exemptions stated—be called out and kept constantly in the field, we must fail, sooner or later, for want of subsistence and other essential supplies. To wage war successfully, men at home are as necessary as men in the field. Those in the field must be provided for, and their families at home must be provided for. In my judgment, no people can successfully carry on a long war, with more than a third of its arms-bearing population kept constantly in the field, especially if, cut off by blockade, they are thrown upon their own internal resources for all necessary supplies, subsistence and munitions of war. . . . But can we succeed against the hosts of the enemy unless all able to bear arms up to fifty years of age are called to and kept in the field? Yes, a thousand times yes, I answer, with proper and skilful management. If we cannot without such a call, we cannot with it, if the war last long. . . .

Of all the dangers that threaten our ultimate success, I consider none more imminent than the policy embodied in this act, if the object really be, as its broad terms declare, to put and keep in active service all between the ages of seventeen and fifty, except the exempts named. On that line we will most assuredly, sooner or later, do what the enemy never could do, conquer ourselves. . . .

I come, now, to the last of these acts of Congress. The suspension of the writ of *habeas corpus* in certain cases. This is the most exciting as it is by far the most important question before you. Upon this depends the question . . .[of] other great essential rights enjoyed by us as freemen. This act upon its face, confers upon the President, secretary of war, and the general commanding in the trans-Mississippi department, (the two latter acting under the control and authority of the President,) the power to arrest and imprison any person who may be simply charged with certain acts, not all of them even crimes under any law; and this is to be done without any oath or affirmation alledging probable cause as to the guilt of the party. This is attempted to be done under that clause of the constitution, which authorizes Congress to suspend the privilege of the writ of *habeas corpus*, in certain cases.

In my judgment this act is not only unwise, impolitic and unconstitutional, but exceedingly dangerous to public liberty. Its unconstitutionality does not rest upon the idea that Congress has not got the power to suspend the privilege of this writ, nor upon the idea that the power to suspend it is an implied one, or that clearly implied powers are weaker as a class and subordinate to others, positively and directly delegated. . . .

. . . You have been told that it affects none but the disloyal, none but traitors, or those who are no better than traitors, spies, bridge-burners, and the like, and you have been appealed to and asked, if any such are entitled to your sympathies? I affirm, and shall maintain before the world that this act affects and may wrongfully oppress as loyal and as good citizens and as true to our cause as ever trod the soil or breathed the air of the South. . . . This long list of offences, set forth in such array, in the thirteen specifications, are, as I view them, but rubbish and verbiage, which tend to cover and hide what in its workings will be found to be the whole gist of the act. . . . The real gist of the whole of it lies, so far as appears upon its face, covered up in the fifth specification near the middle of the act. It is embraced in these words—"and attempts to avoid military service!"

Here is a plain indisputable attempt to deny every citizen in this broad land the right, if ordered into service, to have the question whether he is liable to military duty under the laws tried and adjudicated by the courts. . . .

Enough has been said, without dwelling longer upon this point, to show, without the possibility of a doubt, that the act does affect others, and large classes of others, than spies, traitors, bridge-burners, and disloyal persons—that the very gist of the act, whatever may have been the intent or the motive, will operate most wrongfully and oppressively on as loyal, as patriotic, and as true men as ever inherited a freeman's birthright under a southern sky. You have also seen that there is and can be no necessity for the passage of such an act, even if it were constitutional, in the case of spies, traitors, or conspirators. For, if there be a traitor in the confederacy—if such a monster exists—if any well grounded suspicion is entertained that any such exists, why not have him legally arrested, by judicial warrant, upon oath or affirmation, setting forth *probable* cause, and then he can be held under a constitutional suspension of the privileges of the writ—he can be tried, and if found guilty, punished. What more can the public safety by possibility require? Why dispense with the oath? Why dispense with judicial warrants? Why put it in the power of any man on earth to order the arrest of another on a simple *charge*, to which nobody will *swear*? Who is safe under such a law? Who knows, when he goes forth, when or whether he shall ever return? . . .

. . . Conscription has been extended to embrace all between seventeen and fifty years of age. It cannot be possible that the intention and object of that measure was really to call and keep in the field all between those ages. The folly and ruinous consequences of such a policy is too apparent. . . . The effect and the object of this measure, therefore, was not to raise armies or procure soldiers, but to put all the population of the country between those ages under military law. Whatever the object was, the effect is to put much the larger portion of the labor of the country, both white and slave, under the complete control of the President. Under this system almost all the useful and necessary occupations of life will be completely under the control of one man. No one between the ages of seventeen and fifty can tan your leather, make your shoes, grind your grain, shoe your horse, lay your plough, make your wagon, repair your harness, superintend your farm, procure your salt, or perform any other of the necessary vocations of life, (except teachers, preachers, and physicians, and a very few others,) without permission from the President. This is certainly an extraordinary and a dangerous power. In this connection take in view this *habeas corpus* suspension act, by which it has been shown the attempt is made to confer upon him the power to order the arrest and imprisonment of any man, woman or child in the confederacy, on the bare charge, unsupported by oath, of any of the acts for which arrests are allowed to be made. Could the whole country be more completely under the power and control of one man, except as to life or limb? Could dictatorial powers be more complete? . . .

. . . I warn you against that most insidious enemy which approaches with her syren song, "Independence first and liberty afterward." It is a fatal delusion. Liberty is the animating spirit, the soul of our system of government, and like the soul of man, when once lost it is lost forever. . . . Never for a moment permit yourselves to look upon liberty, that constitutional liberty which you inherited as a birthright, as subordinate to independence. The one was resorted to to secure the other. . . . Let them stand together "through weal and through woe," and if such be our fate, let them and us all go down together in a common ruin.

3

RICHMOND EXAMINER

We Are Fighting for Independence, Not Slavery
(1864)

During the summer of 1864, several unofficial emissaries went to Richmond hoping to open peace negotiations between the two governments. After one of these meetings, the Richmond Examiner *published the following editorial, affirming that independence was the South's primary goal. Edited by J. Moncure Daniel and Edward A. Pollard, the* Examiner *was a leading critic of Jefferson Davis and his policies, and the paper could not resist taking the Confederate president to task for his failure to exploit public opinion on this issue. The* Examiner's *stance contrasts sharply with its subsequent vigorous condemnation of Davis's proposal to recruit slaves as soldiers and adopt emancipation.*

Mr. Davis, in conversation with a Yankee spy, named Edward Kirk, is reported by said spy to have said, "We are not fighting for slavery; we are fighting for independence." This is true; and is a truth that has not sufficiently been dwelt upon. It would have been very much to be desired that this functionary had developed the idea in some message, or some other State paper . . . instead of leaving it to be promulgated through the doubtful report of an impudent blockade-runner. . . . The sentiment is true, and should be publicly uttered and kept conspicuously in view; because our enemies have diligently labored to make all mankind believe that the people of these States have set up a pretended State sovereignty, and based themselves upon that ostensibly, while their real object has been only to preserve to themselves the property in so many negroes, worth so many millions of dollars. The direct reverse is the truth. The question of slavery is only one of the minor issues; and the cause of the war, the whole cause, on our part, is the maintenance of the sovereign independence of these States. . . .

The whole cause of our resistance was and is, the pretension and full determination of the Northern States to use their preponderance in the Federal representation, in order to govern the Southern States for their profit. . . . Slavery was the immediate occasion—carefully made so by them—it was not the cause. The tariff . . . would have much more accurately represented, though it did not cover, or exhaust, the real cause of the quarrel. Yet neither tariffs nor slavery, nor both together, could ever have been truly called the cause of the secession and the war. We refuse to accept for a cause any thing . . . than that truly announced, namely, the sovereign independence of our States. This, indeed, includes both those minor questions, as well as many others yet graver and higher. It includes full power to regulate our trade for our *own* profit, and also complete jurisdiction over our own social and domestic institutions; but it further involves all the nobler attributes of national, and even of individual life and character. A community which once submits to be schooled, dictated to, legislated for, by any other, soon grows poor in spirit; . . . its citizens, become a kind of half-men, [and] feel that they have hardly a right to walk in the sun. . . .

FROM *Richmond Examiner,* 2 August 1864.

The people of Virginia do not choose to accept that position for themselves and for their children. They choose rather to die. They own a noble country, which their fathers created, exalted, and transmitted to them. . . . That inheritance we intend to own while we live, and leave intact to those who are to come after us. . . .

It is right to let foreign nations, and "those whom it may concern," understand this theory of our independence. Let them understand that, though we are "not fighting for slavery," we will not allow ourselves to be dictated to in regard to slavery or any other of our internal affairs, not because that would diminish our interest in any property, but because it touches our independence.

4

RICHMOND EXAMINER

We Prefer the Law (1864)

In the following editorial, the Richmond Examiner *criticized the growing concentration of power in the hands of the Confederate president. Complaints about the centralization of power in the Confederate government was a staple of the growing anti-Davis element in Confederate politics.*

The bill to limit exemptions, as reported by the House Military Committee . . . ends by a sweeping clause which is to enable the Secretary of War (that is to say the President) to exempt or detail any other person or persons he, the President, may think proper. . . . He is to exempt such planters, etc., "as he may be satisfied will be more useful to the country in the pursuits of agriculture," and such other persons "as he may be satisfied ought to be exempted . . . on account of publick necessity, justice, or equity." It is always *He* that is to be satisfied; not the law; not the country; only that sentiment profoundly hidden in the bosom of the Chief Magistrate. . . . Thus, in passing this act . . . Congress will pretend to designate who should be exempted . . . and then leave it to an irresponsible individual to nullify that law.

. . . We suppose it will be admitted that nobody should be exempted for his own private profit and ease. We suppose it will be admitted that it should not be left to the President to see the public necessity and justice of exempting, for example, his own historiographer, or the mailing clerks and reporters of his own newspaper; and that in the case of any other of his own flatterers, sycophants or political supporters he might perchance be too easily "satisfied" of the expediency of detailing such complaisant persons for agricultural pursuits and the pleasures of the chase.

In short, the grievance and sore evil of the country is, and has been, that the conscription acts have not been executed; and that there are thousands of persons throughout the Confederate States avoiding their military duty to the country . . . by reasons of details which satisfy the President . . . but are not so well calculated to satisfy the general publick, and . . . those faithful soldiers who have stood in the gap of invasion. . . . Those soldiers know that there are certain laws for putting

FROM *Richmond Examiner*, 15 December 1864.

citizens of fighting age into the army; they know that they are there by virtue of those laws; and they often wonder how and why certain gentlemen of their respective neighborhoods, younger and stronger than they . . . can evade their plain duty. . . . They cannot all be planting and hoeing corn. . . . They cannot all be engaged in Government works; they cannot all be writing histories of the War. No; but they have all contrived somehow to satisfy the feeling deep in the President's bosom that it is right, or expedient, or at any rate convenient, to detail *them* for domestick duties.

The fact that this system enables the Executive to create a large class of personal and political supporters who owe him, perhaps their lives, and at all events their ease and comfort, and who may become ready tools for any enterprise against the liberties of the land, is an evil, indeed. . . . The army needs men; and that so urgently as to raise the question of arming negroes: and the interest at

stake is more than life or death; it is independence and prosperity and honour, or oppression, and beggary and shame, for us *all*. Yet we see a large portion of the flower of the land (physically) sedulously avoiding military duty, through their influence and interest with somebody or other. . . . How many thousands may have been exempted and detailed by the Secretary of War, "under the direction of the President," is to us unknown. And now Congress, instead of carefully revising its list of exemptions and making them a law, and providing that the law shall be enforced, is preparing . . . to abdicate the most important duty it has, and after specifying a few cases of persons who *shall* be exempt . . . to leave all the rest of this vast jurisdiction in the irresponsible hands of the President, who is to satisfy himself—and his friends—and nobody else.

We may be very singular; but we prefer to live under the laws of the land.

5

CHARLESTON MERCURY

We Want No Confederacy without Slavery (1865)

Jefferson Davis's proposal to make slaves soldiers provoked a firestorm of protest from the Confederate press. No paper in the Confederacy was more radical than the Charleston Mercury, *which responded to Davis's suggestion with the following stinging condemnation.*

In 1860 South Carolina seceded alone from the old union of States. Her people, in Convention assembled, invited the *slaveholding* States (none others) of the old Union to join her in erecting a separate Government of *Slave States*, for the protection of their common interests. All of the slave states, with the exception of Maryland and Kentucky, responded to her invitation. The Southern Confederacy of slave States was formed.

It was on account of encroachments upon the institution of *slavery* by the sectional majority of the old Union, that South Carolina seceded from that Union. It is not at this late day, after the loss of thirty thousand of her best and bravest men in battle, that she will suffer it to be bartered away; or ground between the upper and nether mill stones, by the madness of Congress, or the counsels of shallow men elsewhere.

By the compact we made with Virginia and the other States of this Confederacy, South Carolina will stand to the bitter end of destruction. By that

FROM *Charleston Mercury*, 13 January 1865.

compact she intends to stand or to fall. Neither Congress, nor certain makeshift men in Virginia, can force upon her their mad schemes of weakness and surrender. She stands upon her institutions— and there she will fall in their defence. *We want no Confederate Government without our institutions.* And we will have none. Sink or swim, live or die, we stand by them, and are fighting for them this day. That is the ground of our fight—it is well that all should understand it at once. Thousands and tens of thousands of the bravest men, and the best blood of this State, fighting in the ranks, have left their bones whitening on the bleak hills of Virginia in this cause. We are fighting for our system of civilization—not for buncomb, or for Jeff Davis. We

intend to fight for *that,* or nothing. We expect Virginia to stand beside us in that fight, as of old, as we have stood beside her in this war up to this time. But such talk coming from such a source is destructive to the cause. Let it cease at once, in God's name, and in behalf of our common cause! It is paralizing [*sic*] to every man here to hear it. It throws a pall over the hearts of the soldiers from this State to hear it. The soldiers of South Carolina will not fight beside a nigger—to talk of emancipation is to disband our army. We are free men, and we chose to fight for ourselves—we want no slaves to fight for us. . . . Hack at the root of the Confederacy—our institutions—our civilization—and you kill the cause as dead as a boiled crab.

6

RICHMOND ENQUIRER

Slavery and the Cause of the Confederacy (1865)

After the war, proponents of the Lost Cause insisted that the Civil War had nothing to do with slavery and that the Confederacy fought instead for states' rights. In reality, beginning with the justifications of the secessionist conventions in 1860–1861 (see p. 60), leaders of the Confederacy never disguised the central importance of slavery to both the war's origins and the cause of southern independence. Furthermore, states' rights could not be neatly separated from the defense of slavery, since southern whites correctly understood that this constitutional doctrine was the most effective way to protect slavery. Indeed, as the war continued some slaveholders made it quite clear both by their statements and actions that they preferred reunion to the loss of slavery. In the following editorial, published in response to the public discussion, both in the press and in Congress, of Davis's proposal to adopt emancipation, the Richmond Enquirer *forthrightly addressed these issues. This editorial clearly and forcefully linked the desire to preserve slavery with the war's origins, the cause of the Confederacy, and the doctrine of state sovereignty.*

Slaveholding Reconstructionists

It is stated that there are certain members of Congress, representing large slaveholding constituencies, who have openly declared their preference for reconstruction, with Federal guaranty of slavery, to the emancipation of slaves [by the Confederacy] as a means of securing the independence of the Confederate States.

. . . Can it be possible that men representing slaveholding constituencies would prefer returning to the Union to the dedication of their property to the cause of independence.

What constituted the proximate cause of this war? The prohibition of slavery extension and the unwarrantable interference with its institution of slavery within the States.

Why have our people rallied to this cause? Only because they regarded it one form of interference with the rights of property within the States.

Is the army of defence composed exclusively of slaveholders? They have responded nobly in the vindication of the public rights. They have contributed their means and their lives to the common defence. But, as a class, they have enjoyed certain practical exemptions from the general conscription. . . .

Now what contributions to the cause have been made by the non-slaveholding sections of this and other States? Take the Valley of Virginia for instance. There the slave property has been carried away; the houses burned and the country abandoned to conflict between the contending armies. The men from this region have endured the fate of war.—They have been mutilated and beggared by the war. They have lost the special interest which in chief part occasioned the war.—Have they flinched from or abandoned the cause because their interest in the cause has been extinguished? On the contrary, they cling the closer to the principles of independence when their property interest in its preservation has been diminished.

Can it, then, be possible that those so deeply interested in the cause as the slaveholders from the interior of the cotton States should prefer, under any circumstances, the security of their property to the independence of those States? It would be in effect to say to all other interests: "You have fought for the integrity of slave title, your country has been desolated, your lives and limbs have been sacrificed to the success of this object, but we doubt your ability to guarantee, by your valor, the safety of our title. You even propose to sacrifice this title to the success of your cause. As the object of the war was the safety of slave title, we must seek that object by another course. We shall throw ourselves upon the protection of the enemy. They will grant us, at least, the temporary use of our own slaves."

This is the alleged proposition of certain slaveholding members translated. We cannot admit that any sacrifice of interest or institution is too great to be made, if such sacrifice will secure peace and independence. We repeat, that we do not believe emancipation will secure independence and we would not, therefore, make the experiment.

But if any ill-advised slaveholder should resort to reconstruction for the protection of his property, let us see what he would gain. . . . A proposition has been introduced in the Federal Congress for so amending the Constitution as to authorize the abolition of slavery.

. . . It is said . . . that [the U.S.] Congress will adopt the measure during the ensuing session. . . . How long, then, would the protection of slavery last? For how many months or days? Long enough, say some, to reap the profits of their labor for the maintenance of their owner. Then we should have a premature peace to secure to a comparative few this temporary use of their property? These men would have given life, limb, property, and a great cause, for the special gain of a few.

. . . It would be a singular spectacle if it should appear that either one of those States, which invited Virginia into this conflict, finding their interests likely to suffer by the further prosecution of the war, should compound for their own safety, by surrender of the principles of State Sovereignty involved in the war.

FROM *Richmond Enquirer*, 28 January 1865.

7

HOWELL COBB

Opposition and Disloyalty Are Increasing Daily
(1865)

A prominent Georgia political leader before the war, Howell Cobb had served in the House of Representatives, had been Speaker of the House one term, and was a member of James Buchanan's Cabinet. He resigned his post in December 1860 to support secession and served as a member of the Confederate Congress. It was Cobb who introduced Jefferson Davis to the assembled crowd in Montgomery, Alabama, in February 1861 following Davis's election as president of the Confederacy. In the following letter, he surveyed the state of popular feeling in the Confederacy early in 1865 and called on Davis to respond to public opinion with a change in policy.

Augusta, January 20, 1865.
Private and confidential.
Hon. Jefferson Davis,

Dear Sir:

It gives me no pleasure to write this letter, but it is my duty, both to you and our cause, to say what I am about to say. In a former letter I expressed the opinion that the prevailing sentiment in this State would in the end become true and loyal. I regret to say that the feeling becomes worse and more disloyal every day. I am unwilling even now to write the extent of dissatisfaction which exists and is spreading every hour. It could not be worse. I meet every day the men whom I regarded as the last to yield, who come to me to represent their hopelessness and despair. I meet those whom I know to have been the warm and earnest supporters of your Administration, and find them, not in open hostility, but deeply disaffected and under the cloud which our reverses have brought upon us. Let me say to you in all candor and frankness that the opposition to your Administration has become so general that you know not whom to look upon as a

friend and supporter. I tell you unpleasant truths, but you should know them, for the crisis demands that you should be honestly informed of the true state of things. Many of the causes which have produced this state of things are beyond your present control, such as the conduct of Quartermaster's and Commissary Departments in the failure to supply them with money, and the conduct of inefficient subordinates, who have too often taken more pains to trample upon the feelings and rights of citizens than to do their duty. All this is past immediate remedy; but, Mr. President, there are things which you can do, and which I again urge and press you to do. First, respond to the urgent and overwhelming public feeling in favor of the restoration of General [Joseph] Johnston. I assure you that your refusal to do this is doing you more harm and producing more opposition to your Administration than you dream of. Better that you put him in command, admitting him to be as deficient in the qualities of a general as you or any one else may suppose, than to resist a public sentiment which is weakening your strength and destroying your powers of usefulness. Second, rest assured that the conscript law has done its work and you cannot maintain your army if you look to that law to furnish recruits. The law is odious and cannot

FROM *Official Records*, ser. I, vol. 53, pp. 393–94.

be enforced in the present state of public feeling . . . the time is fast passing when anything can be done by volunteering.

This brings me to the main object I have in writing you at this time. By accident I have become possessed of the facts in reference to the proposed action of the Governors of certain States. . . . Some who started this movement are urging State conventions, that steps may be taken to take the control of affairs out of your hands. Others favor the movement because they believe it will lead to peace, and they are willing and, I believe, anxious for peace, even upon the terms of reconstruction, and in the present state of feeling, if a convention should be called in Georgia, it would be an unconditional submission concern. . . . I have no idea that any of them [state governors] will now favor a convention. My opinion is that . . . they will address you an earnest appeal for a change of policy on the part of the Confederate Government on the subject of the conscript laws, impressments, &c. If I have been correctly informed, their effort will be mainly directed to the point of recruiting the army, and will look to the volunteering system and the State machinery for that purpose. Whilst I have no sympathy, as you well know, with those who have made war upon your Administration, I do not hesitate to say to you that the safety of the country and success of our cause requires concession from you on these subjects. The time has come when we must do, not what we prefer, but what is best for the country, and you underestimate the danger by which we are surrounded if you attribute this perhaps unwelcome communication to any other motive than a sincere desire to advance the cause more dear to me than life itself.

I am, with sentiments of sincere regard,
very truly, yours, &c.,

Howell Cobb.

JUDITH MCGUIRE

A Bleak Confederate Christmas (1864)

Even though both Judith McGuire and her husband had government jobs in Richmond, they found it increasingly difficult to make ends meet because of the spiraling cost of living. In the following entries in her diary, she described their Christmas celebration in the beleaguered Confederate capital in 1864.

[*December*] *24th.*— . . . To-morrow is Christmas-day. Our girls and B. have gone to Cedar Hill to spend a week. Our office has suspended its labours, and I am anticipating very quiet holidays. A Christmas present has just been handed me from my sweet young friend S. W.—a box filled with all manner of working materials, which are now so scarce and expensive, with a beautiful mat for my toilet at the bottom of it. Christmas will come on the Sabbath. The "Colonel" is gone, but J. and C. will take their usual Sunday dinner, and I have gotten up a little dessert, because Christmas would not be Christmas without something better than usual; but it is a sad season to me. On last Christmas-day our dear R. T. C. was buried; and yesterday I saw my sweet young cousin E. M. die, and to-morrow expect to attend her funeral. . . .

26th.—The sad Christmas has passed away. J. and C. were with us, and very cheerful. We exerted ourselves to be so too. The Church services in the morning were sweet and comforting. St. Paul's was dressed most elaborately and beautifully with evergreens; all looked as usual; but there is much sadness on account of the failure of the South to keep Sherman back. When we got home our family circle was small, but pleasant. The Christmas turkey and ham were not. We had aspired to a turkey, but finding the prices range from $50 to $100 in the market on Saturday, we contented ourselves with roast-beef and the various little dishes which Confederate times have made us believe are tolerable substitutes for the viands of better days. At night I treated our little party to tea and ginger cakes—two very rare indulgences; and but for the sorghum, grown in our own fields, the cakes would be an impossible indulgence. Nothing but the well-ascertained fact that Christmas comes but once a year would make such extravagance at all excusable. We propose to have a family gathering when the girls come home, on the day before or after New Year's day, (as that day will come on Sunday,) to enjoy together, and with one or two refugee friends, the contents of a box sent the girls by a young officer who captured it from the enemy, consisting of white sugar, raisins, preserves, pickles, spices, etc. They threaten to give us a plum-cake, and I hope they will carry it out, particularly if we have any of our army friends with us. Poor fellows, how they enjoy our plain dinners when they come, and how we love to see them enjoy them! Two meals a day has become the universal system among refugees, and many citizens, from

FROM Judith W. McGuire, *Diary of a Southern Refugee* (New York: E. J. Hale and Son, 1867), pp. 323–24.

necessity. The want of our accustomed tea or cof-fee is very much felt by the elders. The rule with us is only to have tea when sickness makes it neces-sary, and the headaches gotten up about dark have become the joke of the family. A country lady, from one of the few spots in all Virginia where the enemy has never been, and consequently where they retain their comforts, asked me gravely why we did not substitute milk for tea. She could scarcely believe me when I told her that we had not had milk more than twice in eighteen months, and then it was sent by a country friend. It is now $4 a quart.

2

Catherine Edmondston Reflects on the Situation of the Confederacy (1865)

Catherine Ann Devereux married Patrick Edmondston of Charleston, South Car-olina, in 1846. The couple eventually moved to North Carolina to live on a planta-tion named Looking Glass, given to them by her father, a prominent lawyer and planter in the state. The 1860 census indicated that the Edmonstons owned nearly 1,900 acres, along with eighty-eight slaves, putting them in the elite of the slavehold-ing class. In contrast to her father, who was a staunch Unionist in 1861, she and her husband strongly supported secession and southern independence. During the war she lived a typically rural existence of a plantation mistress, concerned with farming and daily tasks, but she was forced to perform more of these tasks herself because of scarcities and her slaves' growing disobedience. Her intellectual horizons were broader than many of her class, and she closely followed public events and the war's developments. In the following entry in her extensive wartime diary, she reflected on the situation in the Confederacy at the beginning of 1865, and particularly the pro-posal to end slavery. This entry blends many themes of the Confederate experience: the centrality of slavery to the war, deepening southern class divisions, mounting scarcities and hardships on the home front, complaints over the oppression of Con-federate laws, bitterness at the course of England and other European powers, and the increasingly dire military situation combined with a desperate clinging to hope that in the end God would sustain the Confederacy.

January 9, 1865. "Out of the abundance of the heart the mouth speaketh," but the hand writeth not. Never were we more absorbed in outward matters, never have we looked on them so anxiously as now, & yet it is days since I have written aught of them. This negro question, this vexed negro question, will if much longer discussed do us more injury than the loss of a battle. Gen Lee advises the Conscription & ultimate Emancipation of 200,000 Slaves to be used as soldiers. One or two rabid partizan papers, Democratic, I might almost say Agrarian to the core, seize on the proposal, hold it up to the people, to the army, in the most attractive lights. They promise the white soldier that if the negro is put in the army, for every negro soldier fifteen white ones will be allowed to return home. They use it as an engine to inflame the passions of one class against another, tell the poor man that the War is but for his rich neighbor's slaves, that his blood is poured out to secure additional riches to the rich, etc., etc., nay one paper, to its shame be it said, the Richmond Enquirer, openly advocates a general Emancipation! as the price for fancied benefits to be obtained by an alliance with England & France. Actually it offers to sell the birthright of the South, not for a mess of pottage, but only for the hope of obtaining one. The Traitor, recreant to principle, lost to every sense of national honour, & blind to what constitutes a true national prosperity—the wonder is that he finds anyone either to read or think seriously of his monstrous proposition. But so it is. Coming as it does on the evacuation of Savannah when we are almost ready to sink under the accumulation of Yankee lies & Yankee bragg, over their boasted Victory over Hood, our money depreciated & depreciating daily more & more, deafened on one side by loud mouthed politicians who advocate "Reconstruction to save Annihilation," "Reconstruction as a choice of Evils," & on the other by the opponents of the Government who expati-

ate with alass too much truth upon the mismanagement, the waste, the oppression which, cast our eyes which way we will we see around us, threatened again with a new suspension of Habeas Corpus, the Constitution daily trampled under foot by Impressment Laws & Government Schedules, what wonder that many unthinking people catch at this straw as at hope of salvation & delivery from present misery without pausing to ask themselves what will be their condition when they have accepted it. But sounder & better councils will prevail. This beaten and crushed Abolitionist, the Enquirer, will find that the body of the people are against him. . . . Slaveholders on principle, & those who hope one day to become slaveholders in their time, will not tacitly yeild their property & their hopes & allow a degraded race to be placed at one stroke on a level with them. But these discussions & these thoughts have occupied us for the past fortnight & such a deluge of gloomy forebodings have been penned out upon us that I almost hailed the frequent mail failures as a blessing.

The tide now seems turning. God has blessed us with a signal victory over the Yankee fleet.[1] God's blessing & God's hand alone it is, for we had but little to do with it. . . .

Better news but still not authentic reaches us from Tenn. We hear that in a second battle we regained some of the prestige lost before Nashville, of which however we have still only Yankee accounts, but I will refrain all but passing mention of them until they are confirmed. Still they influence our spirits wonderfully. What cheers our very hearts is an intimation that Mr Davis has reinstated Gen Joe Johnston in command. The whole nation hails it with acclamation. Gen D H Hill too is ordered to report to Gen Beauregard, so our old dogs of War are unleashed again.

Sherman is reposing himself in Savannah after his leisurely saunter through Geo & bloodless conquest of that city. He makes a magnificent Christmas gift to Mr Lincoln of the City of Savannah

FROM Beth Gilbert Crabtree and James W. Patton, eds., *Journal of a Secesh Lady: The Diary of Catherine Ann Devereux Edmondston, 1860–1866* (Raleigh, N.C.: Division of Archives and History, 1979), pp. 652–55.

[1]This is a reference to the recent Union failure to capture Fort Fisher and close the port of Wilmington, North Carolina.

with arms, munitions of war, cotton, Rice, seige guns, etc., too tedious for me to enumerate. He even includes the 25,000 inhabitants in his munificent donation; so, as other autocrats do, he has now only to enslave & deport them. God help them! The evacuation took them entirely by surprise we hear. Few of them escaped & they with the loss of all their effects. Sherman has a right to his self glorification. Let him indulge it whilst we cherish the hope that Beauregard will yet pluck the Laurel crown from his brow & trample it in the dust. His programme, as announced, is the capture of Branchville and advance along the lines of R R into Va. Nous verrons! No news from Petersburg or Richmond for days. All quiet since the defeat of the demonstration on Gordonsville.

As for ourselves, since the negroes holiday at Christmas, for Christmas shone no holiday to any but them, we have been engaged with our year's supply of meat. Frying up Lard, squeezing out cracklins, & all the, to me, disagreeable et ceteras of "a hog killing" are I beleive a perfect happiness to Cuffee![2] The excitement & interest over the weight of their favorites, the feasting on chitterlings & haslets, the dabbling in grease, seems to constitute a negro paradise, whilst the possession of a "bladder to blow" or better still a hog tail is all a negro child needs of earth's enjoyments. Well we "killed Hogs" here, then we went to Hascosea & did the same thing there.

As usual we were weatherbound & detained 24 hours longer than we intended to remain. Mr E ordered a large box of books, principally farming periodicals (which we had bound the winter before the commencement of the war & which came home whilst we were in great excitement about Ft Sumter & which we have since refrained from opening on account of our unsettled state & the determination we from time to time take to pack up all our books) to be opened, & we passed the time most pleasantly & profitable, rubbing up our old knoledge, forming new plans, agricultural, horticultural, & domestic which this spring & summer we hope to put in execution. I lent an es-

pecial eye to the Poultry yard—am armed with several infalible receipts to cure & to prevent "the gapes," all of which I shall try on my spring chickens. In Vinegar receipts too I have come home quite learned & I now sigh for a peice of genuine Vinegar plant! I have some very fine Vinegar made from the skimmings of last year's Sorghhum, but alas, it is too little for my many uses. I used to be famous for Pickles, but my cunning has departed, as the price of whisky and Apple Brandy has risen, for on them did I rely to give my Vinegar body. I am now making yeast by the pailful and even contemplate malting some corn to supply the deficiency. This war is teaching us many things. Dying, spinning, and weaving are no longer unknown mysteries to me. I think of making a compilation of all my practical knoledge on the subject and I intend for the future Peace or war to let *homespun* be my ordinary dress.[3] The object of my ambition is to have a black watered silk trimmed with black thread lace. Think of it! How shall I feel when I pull off my russet yarn spun & woven on the Plantation & bedeck myself in that style! It seems so long since I wore a silk dress that I begin to doubt if I ever owned one.

I have been reading Motley's "United Netherlands" & have derived great comfort from it.[4] We are not so divided, lean not so much on foreign aid, & are not reduced near so low as they were, & yet by perseverance they triumphed. Their advantage lay in a command of the Sea, however, an ability to export and import as they liked, an assistance we too would have did foreign nations uphold their own international Law on the subject of Blockades! International Law, a humbug & a sham, designed only by the strong as a police code to keep order amongst themselves but ignored & for-

---

[2]A term frequently used to refer to slaves.

[3]Homespun was clothing made out of thread spun and woven on the premises rather than in a textile mill. Before the war, homespun was increasingly a sign of social backwardness and often poverty, and clothing made from factory cloth, which was smoother and more brightly colored, was greatly preferred.

[4]The American historian John L. Motley wrote a widely read history of the successful Dutch revolt against Spanish rule in the seventeenth century.

gotten when a weak power suffers from its infringement. This it is which has changed our once strong love to England into Gall! this & the manner in which her boasted *Neutrality* is maintained. Her *Neutrality*, heaven save the mark, is only another word for *deceit*, for mean low petty trickery, for cringing to the U S, saying to us "Am I not in Peace my brother" & stabbing as Joab-like under the fifth rib.

3

GEORGE WARD NICHOLS

Southerners Have Lost the Will to Resist (1865)

Before setting off on his famous march to the sea, Sherman had boasted that he would make southerners sick of war. After refitting his army in Savannah, Georgia, on February 1, 1865, Sherman turned north and marched thorough South Carolina, the hated symbol of secession. While Sherman's march thorough Georgia is more famous, his army was actually far more destructive in its trek through South Carolina, which culminated in the burning of Columbia. In the following selection, Major George Ward Nichols, who was an aide-de-camp to Sherman, described the impact of Sherman's march on the morale of the residents of South Carolina. Nichols had studied art in Europe and was a journalist in New York when the war began. He held several administrative positions in the army before joining Sherman's staff. His book, which attracted wide attention, was based on a diary he kept during Sherman's campaign in Georgia and the Carolinas.

Columbia will have bitter cause to remember the visit of Sherman's army. Even if peace and prosperity soon return to the land, not in this generation nor the next—no, not for a century—can this city or the state recover from the deadly blow which has taken its life. It is not alone in the property that has been destroyed—the buildings, bridges, mills, railroads, material of every description—nor in the loss of the slaves, who, within the last few days, have joined us by hundreds and thousands—although this deprivation of the means by which they lived is of incalculable importance—that the most blasting, withering blow has fallen. It is in the crushing downfall of their inordinate vanity, their arrogant pride, that the rebels will feel the effects of the visit of our army. Their fancied unapproachable, invincible security has been ruthlessly overthrown. Their boastings, threatenings, and denunciations have passed by us like the idle wind. The feet of one hundred thousand abolitionists, hated and despised, have pressed heavily upon their sacred soil, and their spirit is broken. . . .

By constantly improving many excellent opportunities for conversing with prominent citizens, I have unquestionable evidence of their desire to end the war by submitting to the national authority. While not disguising their belief in the sovereignty of a state, and scarcely concealing their hate for the Yankees, they acknowledge their powerlessness to contend against the might of the idea of nationality embodied in our armies and navies. A citizen, whose name may be found in the earliest

FROM George Ward Nichols, *The Story of the Great March* (New York: Harper and Brothers, 1865), pp. 170–72.

annals of the state, and stands forth in high honor in the war of the Revolution, but whose sons are now in high office in the army of treason, said to me to-day:

"Sir, every life that is now lost in this war is murder; *murder*, sir. We have fought you bravely, but our strength is exhausted; we have no resources; we have no more men. The contest was unequal. You have conquered us, and it is best to submit and make wise use of the future. This is not my opinion because the Union flag is flying upon yonder capitol to-day, but it has been my conviction for many months past—a conviction more than confirmed by recent events. We could have peace, sir, but for that vain, obstinate, ambitious man, Jeff. Davis. I am not in excitement nor anger, sir, when I assure you that I know that a large majority of our people curse him, not only with their hearts, but their lips. His haughty ambition has been our ruin."

The words of this gentleman express the sentiments of nearly all the leading civilians I meet, excepting only that the expression is sometimes more vehement, while the conversation is occasionally interlarded with more violent objurgations against Jeff. Davis. Unhappy chief! failure has brought down upon him hatred and abuse. Were he in South Carolina now, no cheers would greet him, no friendly welcome would meet him; nothing but execrations would be showered upon his head.

4

LUTHER MILLS

Desertion Now Is Not Dishonorable (1865)

A native of Virginia, Luther Rice Mills graduated from Wake Forest College in 1861 and then entered the Confederate Army. He served as a lieutenant in the Twenty-sixth Virginia Infantry and was commander of a sharpshooter unit. He took part in the seige of Petersburg, Virginia, in 1864–1865 and was captured in April 1865 on the retreat from Richmond. In this letter to his brother, Mills discussed the problem of desertions from the Army of Northern Virginia and the influence of the home front in encouraging desertion. After the war, Mills became a professor at Wake Forest.

Trenches Near Crater
March 2nd, 1865.

Brother John:

Something is about to happen. I know not what. Nearly every one who will express an opinion says Gen'l Lee is about to evacuate Petersburg. The authorities are having all the cotton, tobacco &c. moved out of the place as rapidly as possible. This was commenced about the 22nd of February. Two thirds of the Artillery of our Division has been moved out. The Reserved Ordnance Train has been loaded up and is ready to move at any time. I think Gen'l Lee expects a hard fight on the right and has ordered all this simply as a precautionary measure. Since my visit to the right I have changed my opinion about the necessity for the evacuation of Petersburg. If it is evacuated Johnson's Division will be in a bad situation for getting out. Unless we are so fortunate as to give the Yankees the slip many of us will be captured. . . . If Petersburg and Richmond is evacuated—from what I have seen &

FROM *North Carolina Historical Review* 4 (1927): 307–8.

heard in the army—our cause will be hopeless. It is useless to conceal the truth any longer. Many of our people at home have become so demoralized that they write to their husbands, sons and brothers that desertion *now* is not *dishonorable*. It would be impossible to keep the army from straggling to a ruinous extent if we evacuate. I have just received an order from Wise to carry out on picket tonight a rifle and ten rounds of Cartridges to shoot men when they desert. The men seem to think desertion no crime & hence never shoot a deserter when he goes over—they always shoot but never hit. I am glad to say that we have not had but four desertions from our Reg't to the enemy. . . .

Yours truly

L. R. Mills

5

ABRAHAM LINCOLN

With Malice toward None (1865)

Abraham Lincoln's second inaugural address is justly famous. Delivered on the eve of victory, it is remarkable for its compassion, for its profound understanding of the depths of the tragedy the nation had suffered, and for its great humility. In his brief remarks, Lincoln characterized the war as God's punishment for the national sin of slavery and closed with a moving plea for a generous peace. Rarely has the eloquence of this speech been approached in the history of American politics. Noah Brooks, a newspaperman who was present, reported that just as Lincoln rose to speak, "the sun, which had been obscured all day, burst forth in its unclouded meridian splendor," an incident Brooks interpreted as an omen that the darkness of war was passing away.

March 4, 1865

[Fellow Countrymen:]

At this second appearing to take the oath of the presidential office, there is less occasion for an extended address than there was at the first. Then a statement, somewhat in detail, of a course to be pursued, seemed fitting and proper. Now, at the expiration of four years, during which public declarations have been constantly called forth on every point and phase of the great contest which still absorbs the attention, and engrosses the eneergies

FROM Roy P. Basler, et al., eds., *The Collected Works of Abraham Lincoln,* vol. 8 (New Brunswick, N.J.: Rutgers University Press, 1953), pp. 332–33.

[*sic*] of the nation, little that is new could be presented. The progress of our arms, upon which all else chiefly depends, is as well known to the public as to myself; and it is, I trust, reasonably satisfactory and encouraging to all. With high hope for the future, no prediction in regard to it is ventured.

On the occasion corresponding to this four years ago, all thoughts were anxiously directed to an impending civil-war. All dreaded it—all sought to avert it. While the inaugeral address was being delivered from this place, devoted altogether to *saving* the Union without war, insurgent agents were in the city seeking to *destroy* it without war— seeking to dissol[v]e the Union, and divide effects, by negotiation. Both parties deprecated war; but one of them would *make* war rather than let the nation survive; and the other would *accept* war rather than let it perish. And the war came.

One eighth of the whole population were colored slaves, not distributed generally over the Union, but localized in the Southern part of it. These slaves constituted a peculiar and powerful interest. All knew that this interest was, somehow, the cause of the war. To strengthen, perpetuate, and extend this interest was the object for which the insurgents would rend the Union, even by war; while the government claimed no right to do more than to restrict the territorial enlargement of it. Neither party expected for the war, the magnitude, or the duration, which it has already attained. Neither anticipated that the *cause* of the conflict might cease with, or even before, the conflict itself should cease. Each looked for an easier triumph, and a result less fundamental and astounding. Both read the same Bible, and pray to the same God; and each invokes His aid against the other. It may seem strange that any men should dare to ask a just God's assistance in wringing their bread from the sweat of other men's faces; but let us judge not that we be not judged. The prayers of both could not be answered; that of neither has been answered fully. The Almighty has His own purposes. "Woe unto the world because of offences! for it must needs be that offences come; but woe to that man by whom the offence cometh!" If we shall suppose that American Slavery is one of those offences which, in the providence of God, must needs come, but which, having continued through His appointed time, He now wills to remove, and that He gives to both North and South, this terrible war, as the woe due to those by whom the offence came, shall we discern therein any departure from those divine attributes which the believers in a Living God always ascribe to Him? Fondly do we hope—fervently do we pray—that this mighty scourge of war may speedily pass away. Yet, if God wills that it continue, until all the wealth piled by the bond-man's two hundred and fifty years of unrequited toil shall be sunk, and until every drop of blood drawn with the lash, shall be paid by another drawn with the sword, as was said three thousand years ago, so still it must be said "the judgments of the Lord, are true and righteous altogether."

With malice toward none; with charity for all; with firmness in the right, as God gives us to see the right, let us strive on to finish the work we are in; to bind up the nation's wounds; to care for him who shall have borne the battle, and for his widow, and his orphan—to do all which may achieve and cherish a just, and a lasting peace, among ourselves, and with all nations.

6

MARY A. FONTAINE

Bitter Tears Came in a Torrent (1865)

Mary A. Fontaine, who was the daughter of a prominent Baptist minister and the wife of a Confederate officer, lived in Richmond near the Capitol Square with its important public buildings. At the time of the city's fall she had not seen her husband, who was now a prisoner of war, for more than a year. In the following letter, she described the arrival of Union forces in the Confederate capital in April 1865. (The paragraphing has been modified.)

Richmond, Va.
April 30, 1865

My Dear Cousin,

. . . I hardly dare venture a description of the first few days of April, but will attempt to give you an idea. Sunday, the 2nd, was one of those unusually lovely days that the Spring sometimes brings, when delicate silks that look too fine at other times seem just to suit; when invalids and convalescents venture out in the sunshine; when the churches are crowded as never before. So it was on this Sunday. I have never seen a calmer or more peaceful Sabbath morning, and alas! never a more confused evening. During service messengers tiptoed into the churches after prominent military and civil officers, and when the congregation were dismissed, everybody asked, "What is it?" but no one could tell.

Presently there were rumors that Gen. Lee's line was broken, and the enemy had reached the R. R., and Richmond must fall, etc., etc. We ladies were not contented except in the yard, and all were in the street with troubled faces. Major Williamson came to prepare to leave; then, one by one, the gentlemen hurried up with orders to leave that night. Then Mr. Davis, oh, so bowed and anxious, came, and when he told us he feared Richmond must be evacuated by midnight, the truth was forced upon us. We turned to our rooms to prepare those who were to leave. Mrs. Williamson gave herself to a grief which was terrible.

All through that long, long night we worked and wept and bade farewells, never thinking of sleep; in the distance we heard the shouts of the soldiers and mob as they ransacked stores; the rumbling of wagons, and beating of drums, all mixed in a confused medley. Just before dawn explosions of gunboats and magazines shook the city, and glass was shattered, and new houses crumbled beneath the shocks. Involuntarily I closed the shut-

ters, and then everything had become still as death, while immense fires stretched their arms on high all around me. I shuddered at the dreadful silence. Richmond burning and no alarm. It was terrible. I cannot describe my feelings as I stood at a window overlooking the city in that dim dawn. I watched those silent, awful fires, I felt that there was no effort to stop them, but all like myself were watching them, paralyzed and breathless.

After a while the sun rose as you may have seen it, a great, red ball veiled in a mist. Again the streets were alive with hurrying men and women, and the [cry] of "Yankees" reached me. I did not move, I could not, but watched the blue horseman ride to the City Hall, enter, with his sword knocking the ground at every step, and throw the great doors open, and take possession of our beautiful city; watched two blue figures on the Capitol, white men, I saw them unfurl a tiny flag, and then I sank on my knees, and the bitter, bitter tears came in a torrent.

May 7th . . . About eight o'clock, after some thirty Cavalrymen had taken possession of Richmond, hoisted their flag, etc., the Artillery came dashing up Broad street, positively the fat horses came trotting up that heavy hill, dragging the cannon as tho. they were light carriages, the trappings were gay, and I commenced to realize the fearful odds against which our gallant little army had contended. Then the Cavalry thundered at a furious gallop. We haven't been used to that, you know, and it startled us; indeed I imagined that there never was such riding before, unless at Bull Run. Then the Infantry came playing "The Girl I left behind me," that dear old air that we heard our brave men so often play; then the negro troops playing "Dixie." . . .

Then our Richmond servants were completely crazed, they danced and shouted, men hugged each other, and women kissed, and such a scene of confusion you have never seen. Imagine the streets crowded with these wild people, and troops by the thousands, some loaded with plunder from the burning stores, whole rolls of cloth, bags of corn, etc., chairs, one old woman was rolling a great sofa; dozens of bands trying to drown each other it

FROM Mary A. Fontaine to Mrs. Marie B. Sayre, April 30, 1865, Douglas S. Freeman, ed., *A Calendar of Confederate Papers* (Richmond: Confederate Museum, 1908), pp. 249–53.

seemed; gorgeously dressed officers galloping furiously about, men shouting and swearing as I never heard men do before; the fire creeping steadily nearer to us, until houses next to us caught and we prepared to leave; and above all, inconceivably terrible, the 800,000 shells exploding at the laboratory. I say imagine, but you cannot; no one who was not here will ever fully appreciate the horrors of that day. I have heard persons say it was like their idea of the judgment day; perhaps it may be.

So many shells exploding for five hours would be fearful at any time; the heavens were black as with a thunder cloud, great pieces of shells flying about, oh! it was too awful to remember, if it were possible to be erased, but that can not be. By night things quieted down; there were brigade headquarters in the house; so we were protected from stragglers; and the oppressive stillness and darkness (there was no gas) was as fearful as the confusion had been.

7

A. W. BARTLETT

Richmond's Black Residents Welcome Abraham Lincoln (1897)

After the fall of Richmond to Union forces, Abraham Lincoln visited the former capital of the Confederacy on April 4, 1865. The city's white population generally remained indoors, but former slaves joined by a few white Unionists gave him a tumultuous welcome. A New Hampshire soldier described the president's reception.

When it became certain that it was really "Marsa Abraham" that was in their midst, there was such a rush to see and speak with him that it was almost impossible, at times, for his carriage to move. A number of bright eyed and woolly headed urchins, taking advantage of this delay, climbed upon the top of the carriage and took a peep at him over the rim, greatly to the amusement of the President. His reception in a city which, only a day or two before, had been the headquarters and centre of the Rebellion, was most remarkable; and more resembled the triumphant return from, than an entry into the enemy's capital. Instead of the streets being silent and vacated, they were filled with men, women, and children, shouting and cheering wherever he went.

"I'd rather see him than Jesus," excitedly exclaims one woman, as she runs ahead of the crowd to get a full view of his benign countenance. "De kingdom's come, and de Lord is wid us," chants another. "Hallelujah!" shouts a third; and so on through a whole volume of prayers, praises, blessings, and benedictions showered down upon him, the great emancipator of a race, and the saviour of his country, thus redeemed, as he walked slowly forward with smiling face and uncovered head. . . .

But it was not the colored population alone which welcomed the Union troops and their great commander-in-chief into the city of Richmond. Thousands of the white citizens were glad to be again under the protection of the flag of their fathers; and some, who had been true to it from the first, keeping it safely hidden away as a sacred emblem of their loyalty, were more happy, if possible, though less demonstrative, than the negro, as they once more were allowed the privilege of spreading its bright folds to the free air of heaven.

FROM A. W. Bartlett, *History of the Twelfth Regiment New Hampshire Volunteers* (Concord, N.H.: I. C. Evans, 1897), pp. 271–73.

8

JOSHUA L. CHAMBERLAIN

An Awed Stillness (1915)

Few soldiers wrote about their experiences in the war with more eloquence than Joshua L. Chamberlain. A professor of literature at Bowdoin College when the war began, Chamberlain volunteered in 1862 and served as the colonel of the Twentieth Maine. He fought in over twenty engagements, was wounded six times, received the Congressional Medal of Honor, and at the end of the war held the rank of brevet major general and commanded two brigades in the Fifth Corps of the Army of the Potomac. In a singular honor that testified to the great respect his heroism and leadership had earned him, Ulysses S. Grant selected Chamberlain to receive the formal surrender of Lee's army at Appomattox Courthouse, Virginia, on April 12, 1865. After the war he was governor of Maine and president of Bowdoin College.

It was now the morning of the 12th of April. I had been ordered to have my lines formed for the ceremony at sunrise. It was a chill gray morning, depressing to the senses. But our hearts made warmth. Great memories uprose; great thoughts went forward. We formed along the principal street, from the bluff bank of the stream to near the Court House on the left,—to face the last line of battle, and receive the last remnant of the arms and colors of that great army which ours had been created to confront for all that death can do for life. We were remnants also: . . . veterans, and replaced veterans; cut to pieces, cut down, consolidated, divisions into brigades, regiments into one, gathered by State origin; . . . men of near blood born, made nearer by blood shed. Those facing us—now, thank God! the same. . . .

Our earnest eyes scan the busy groups on the opposite slopes, breaking camp for the last time, taking down their little shelter-tents and folding them carefully as precious things, then slowly forming ranks as for unwelcome duty. And now they move. The dusky swarms forge forward into gray columns of march. On they come, with the old swinging route step and swaying battle-flags. In the van, the proud Confederate ensign—the great field of white with canton of star-strewn cross of blue on a field of red, the regimental battle-flags with the same escutcheon following on, crowded so thick, by thinning out of men, that the whole column seemed crowned with red. At the right of our line our little group mounted beneath our flags, the red Maltese cross on a field of white, erewhile so bravely borne through many a field more crimson than itself, its mystic meaning now ruling all.

The momentous meaning of this occasion impressed me deeply. I resolved to mark it by some token of recognition, which could be no other than a salute of arms. Well aware of the responsibility assumed, and of the criticisms that would follow, as the sequel proved, nothing of that kind could move me in the least. The act could be defended, if needful, by the suggestion that such a salute was not to the cause for which the flag of the Confederacy stood, but to its going down before the flag of the Union. My main reason, however, was one for which I sought no authority nor asked forgiveness. Before us in proud humiliation stood the embodiment of manhood: men whom neither toils and

FROM Joshua L. Chamberlain, *The Passing of the Armies* (New York: G. P. Putnam's Sons, 1915), pp. 248–49, 258–65.

sufferings, nor the fact of death, nor disaster, nor hopelessness could bend from their resolve; standing before us now, thin, worn, and famished, but erect, and with eyes looking level into ours, waking memories that bound us together as no other bond;—was not such manhood to be welcomed back into a Union so tested and assured?

Instructions had been given; and when the head of each division column comes opposite our group, our bugle sounds the signal and instantly our whole line from right to left, regiment by regiment in succession, gives the soldier's salutation, from the "order arms" to the old "carry"—the marching salute. [General John B.] Gordon at the head of the column, riding with heavy spirit and downcast face, catches the sound of shifting arms, looks up, and, taking the meaning, wheels superbly, making with himself and his horse one uplifted figure, with profound salutation as he drops the point of his sword to the boot toe; then facing to his own command, gives word for his successive brigades to pass us with the same position of the manual,—honor answering honor. On our part not a sound of trumpet more, nor roll of drum; not a cheer, nor word nor whisper of vain-glorying, nor motion of man standing again at the order, but an awed stillness rather, and breath-holding, as if it were the passing of the dead!

As each successive division masks our own, it halts, the men face inward towards us across the road, twelve feet away; then carefully "dress" their line, each captain taking pains for the good appearance of his company, worn and half starved as they were. The field and staff take their positions in the intervals of regiments; generals in rear of their commands. They fix bayonets, stack arms; then, hesitatingly, remove cartridge-boxes and lay them down. Lastly,—reluctantly, with agony of expression,—they tenderly fold their flags, battle-worn and torn, blood-stained, heart-holding colors, and lay them down; some frenziedly rushing from the ranks, kneeling over them, clinging to them, pressing them to their lips with burning tears. And only the Flag of the Union greets the sky!

What visions thronged as we looked into each other's eyes! Here pass the men of Antietam, the Bloody Lane, the Sunken Road, the Cornfield, the Burnside-Bridge; the men whom Stonewall Jackson on the second night at Fredericksburg begged Lee to let him take and crush the two corps of the Army of the Potomac huddled in the streets in darkness and confusion; the men who swept away the Eleventh Corps at Chancellorsville; who left six thousand of their companions around the bases of Culp's and Cemetery Hills at Gettysburg; these survivors of the terrible Wilderness, the Bloody-Angle at Spottsylvania, the slaughter pen of Cold Harbor, the whirlpool of Bethesda Church! . . .

. . . How could we help falling on our knees, all of us together, and praying God to pity and forgive us all!

Gideon Welles Describes Lincoln's Death (1865)

Secretary of the Navy Gideon Welles kept a diary throughout most of the war that provides the greatest detail about the inner workings of the Lincoln administration. Welles was one of the most conservative members of the Cabinet, and he was jealous of the other members, whom he often judged harshly, but he was an able administrator who could recognize ability. Over the course of the war he developed a great admiration for the president and his leadership. In the following passage from his diary, Welles described the mood and reaction after Lincoln was shot and the president's subsequent death. Welles noted in particular the great public grief of the city's black population. Welles rewrote his diary after the war; the original wording of this entry, which was written on April 18, 1865, has been restored.

I had retired to bed about half past-ten on the evening of the 14th of April, and was just getting asleep when my wife said some one was at our door. Sitting up in bed I heard some one twice call to John, my son whose sleeping room was directly over the front door. I arose at once and raised a window, when my messenger James [Smith] called to me that Mr. Lincoln the President had been shot, and that Secretary Seward and his son, Assistant Secretary Frederick Seward, were assassinated. James was very much alarmed and excited. I told him his story was very incoherent and improbable, that he was associating men who were not together and liable to attack at the same time. . . .

I immediately dressed myself and against the earnest remonstrance and appeals of my wife went directly to Mr. Seward's. . . .

Entering the house I found the lower hall and office full of persons, and among them most of the foreign legations, all anxiously inquiring what truth there was in the horrible rumors afloat. . . . I found one, and I think two of the servants there checking the crowd. . . . I hastily asked what truth there was in the story that an assassin or assassins had entered the house and assaulted the Secretary. I was assured that it was true, and that Mr. Frederick was also badly injured. . . .

I asked [Secretary of War Edwin] Stanton what he had heard in regard to the President that was reliable. He said the President was shot at Ford's Theatre, that he had seen a man who was present and witnessed the occurrence. I remarked that I would go immediately to the White House. Stanton told me the President was not there but was down at the theatre. Then said I let us go immediately there. . . .

The President had been carried across the street from the theatre, to the house of a Mr. Peterson. We entered by ascending a flight of steps above the basement and passing through a long hall to the rear[.] the President lay extended on a bed breathing heavily. Several surgeons were present, at least six, I should think more. Among them I was glad to observe Dr. Hall, who, however soon left. I inquired of one of the Surgeons Dr. H., I think, the true condition of the President and was told he was dead to all intents, although he might live three hours or perhaps longer.

The giant sufferer lay extended diagonally across the bed which was not long enough for him. He had been stripped of his clothes. His large arms, which were occasionally exposed were of a size

FROM Howard K. Beale, ed., *The Diary of Gideon Welles*, vol. 2 (New York: W. W. Norton and Co., 1960), pp. 286–90.

which would one scarce have expected from his spare appearance. His slow, full respiration lifted the clothes. His features were calm and striking. I had never seen them appear to better advantage than for the first hour, perhaps, that I was there. After that his right eye began to swell and became discolored.

. . . A double guard was stationed at the door and on the sidewalk, to repress the crowd which was excited and anxious.

The room was small and overcrowded. The surgeons and members of the Cabinet were as many as should have been in the room, but there [were] many more, and the hall and other rooms in the front or main house were full. One of them was occupied by Mrs. Lincoln and her attendants. . . . About once an hour Mrs. Lincoln would repair to the bedside of her dying husband and remain until overcome by her emotion.

. . . The night was dark, cloudy and damp, and about six it began to rain. I remained until then without sitting or leaving the room, when, there being a vacant chair at the foot of the bed, I occupied for nearly two hours, listening to the heavy groans, and witnessing the wasting life of the good and great man who was expiring before me.

About 6 A.M. a fainting sickness came over me and for the first time since entering the room, a little past eleven, I left it and the house, and took a short walk in the open air. It was a dark and gloomy morning, and rain set in before I returned to the house, some fifteen minutes. Large groups of people were gathered every few rods, all anxious and solicitous. Some one stepped forward as I passed, to inquire into the condition of the President, and to ask if there was no hope. Intense grief exhibited itself on every countenance when I replied that the President could survive but a short time. The colored people especially—and there

were at this time more of them perhaps than of whites—were painfully affected.

Returning to the house, I seated myself in the back parlor where the Attorney-General and others had been engaged in taking evidence concerning the assassination. . . . The excitement and atmosphere from the crowded rooms oppressed me physically.

A little before seven, I went into the room where the dying President was rapidly drawing near the closing moments. His wife soon after made her last visit to him. The death struggle had begun. Robert his son stood at the head of the bed and bore himself well, but on two occasions gave way to overpowering grief and sobbed aloud, turning his head and leaning on the shoulder of Senator Sumner. The respiration became suspended at intervals, and at length entirely ceased at twenty-two minutes past seven.

A prayer followed by Dr. Gurley; and the Cabinet with the exception of Mr. Seward and Mr. McCulloch immediately thereafter assembled in the back parlor, from which all other persons were excluded, and signed a letter which had been prepared by Attorney-General Speed to the Vice President, informing him of the event, and that the government devolved upon him.

. . . I went after breakfast to the Executive Mansion.[1] There was a cheerless cold rain and everything seemed gloomy. On the Avenue in front of the White House were several hundred colored people, mostly women and children, weeping and wailing their loss. The crowd did not appear to diminish through the whole of that cold wet day—they seemed not to know what was to be their fate since their great benefactor was dead, and their hopeless grief affected men more than almost anything else, though strong and brave men wept when I met them.

---

[1]Welles added this paragraph at a later date.

10

Edmund Ruffin Fires the Last Shot of the Civil War (1865)

Edmund Ruffin, a leading Virginia radical and southern nationalist, had advocated secession for many years before the war began. With an eye for trouble (he had attended John Brown's execution) and a flair for the dramatic, he had gone to Charleston in 1861, following South Carolina's secession, to be at the center of the action. As an honorary member of one of the local defense units, he fired one of the first shots at Fort Sumter and was a prominent participant in the opening scenes of the war. For Ruffin, the war had ushered in period of soaring hopes, only to see his dream of an independent southern nation ultimately destroyed by the Union's military victory. Brooding about the defeat of the Confederacy and his shattered dreams, he made the following entry in his diary on June 18, 1865.

Having finished this entry, Ruffin sat down in a chair, propped a shotgun between his legs, put the barrel in his mouth, and using a forked stick pulled the trigger and committed suicide. It could be said that Edmund Ruffin fired the last shot of the Civil War.

[*June 17, 1865*] I here declare my unmitigated hatred to Yankee rule—to all political, social & business connection with Yankees—& to the Yankee race. Would that I could impress these sentiments, in their full force, on every living southerner, & bequeath them to every one yet to be born! May such sentiments be held universally in the outraged & down-trodden South, though in silence & stillness, until the now far-distant day shall arrive for just retribution for Yankee usurpation, oppression, & atrocious outrages—& for deliverance & vengeance for the now ruined, subjugated, & enslaved Southern States! May the maledictions of every victim to their malignity, press with full weight on the perfidious Yankee people & their perjured rulers—& especially on those of the invading forces who perpetrated, & their leaders & higher authorities who encouraged, directed, or permitted, the unprecedented & generally extended outrages of robbery, rapine & destruction, & house-burning, all committed contrary to the laws of war on non-combatant residents, & still worse on aged men & helpless women!

FROM William Scarborough, ed., *The Diary of Edmund Ruffin*, vol. 3 (Baton Rouge: Louisiana State University, 1989), p. 946.

11

SAMUEL T. FOSTER

A Confederate Soldier Reflects on the War's Cost and Significance (1865)

Samuel T. Foster was a captain in the Twenty-fourth Texas Cavalry. He enlisted in the fall of 1861, served in Arkansas where he was captured, and after being exchanged joined the Confederate Army of Tennessee. He fought in the major battles in the western theater in the second half of the war, including Chickamauga, Tennessee; Chattanooga (where he was wounded); the Atlanta campaign; and Franklin, Tennessee, where he was wounded again. He was back with his unit when General Joseph Johnston surrendered to Sherman in April 1865. He made the following entry in his diary after Johnston's capitulation.

April 28th [1865]

We had a dreadful night, all hands up and talking over the situation. They go over the war again, count up the killed and wounded, then the results obtained—It is too bad! If crying would have done any good, we could have cried all night.

Just to think back at the beginning of this war—and see the young men in the bloom of life—the flower of the country—Volunteering to defend their country from the Yankee hosts, who were coming to desolate their homes. Men who shut their stores and warehouses, stoped their plows, droped the axe, left their machinery lying idle, closed their law offices, churches banks and workshops; and all fall into line to defend the country.

Now where are they. As for our own Company, Regt. and Brgd.—they can be found at Ark. Post, at the prison cemetery of Camp [Butler] Springfield Ill. at Chickamauga—at Missionary Ridge—at

New Hope Church 27 May 64 at Atlanta Aug [July] 22/64 at Jonesboro Ga at Franklin and Nashville Tenn. [November–] Dec/64 and there find the remains of as noble men, and as kind hearted faithful friends as ever trod the face of the earth.

And those men who fell in 1864 even in Dec. 64 sacrificed their lives as freely as did the very first that fell in the war. There was no cooling down, no tapering off, no lukewarmness in those men, but they would brave danger when ordered as fearless of Yankee bullets as if they [had?] no power to hurt them. At Franklin Tenn. Dec Ist or Nov 30/64 was the most wholesale butchery of human lives ever witness[ed] by us. Those brave men had been taught by Genl Johnson to fear nothing when he made a fight, and expecting the same thing of [General John B.] Hood, were betrayed into a perfect slaughter pen.

Who is to blame for all this waste of human life? It is too bad to talk about. And what does it amount to? Has there been anything gained by all this sacrifice? What were we fighting for, the principles of slavery?

And now the slaves are all freed, and the Confederacy has to be dissolved. We have to go back into

FROM Norman D. Brown, ed., *One of Cleburne's Command: The Civil War Reminiscences and Diary of Capt. Samuel T. Foster, Granbury's Texas Brigade, CSA* (Austin: University of Texas Press, 1980), pp. 169–71.

the Union. Ah! there is the point. Will there ever be any more Union, as there once was?

April 29th [1865]

Men still talking politics, but it is over and over the same thing, with the same regrets for our loss, and end with the same "What does it amount to?"

Later in the day the talk is about going home, by what route, and whether we will have to walk all the way &c &c.

Men are beginning to realize their situation, and are talking about going home to Texas. . . .

April 30th [1865]

It seems curious that mens minds can change so sudden, from opinions of life long, to new ones a week old.

I mean that men who have not only been taught from their infancy that the institution of slavery was right; but men who actually owned and held slaves up to this time,—have now changed in their opinions regarding slavery, so as to be able to see the other side of the question,—to see that for man to have property in man was wrong, and that

the "Declaration of Independence meant more than they had ever been able to see before. That all men are, and of right ought to be free" has a meaning different from the definition they had been taught from their infancy up,—and to see that the institution (though perhaps wise) had been abused, and perhaps for that abuse this terrible war with its results, was brought upon us as a punishment. . . .

These ideas come not from the Yanks or northern people but come from reflection, and reasoning among ourselves.

May 3rd [1865]

After turning in our guns, and getting our parols, we feel relieved. No more picket duty, no more guard duty, no more fighting, no more war. It is all over, and we are going home. HOME after an absence of four years from our families and friends.

Actually going to start home tomorrow or perhaps this morning.

12

KATE CUMMING

A Confederate Nurse Discusses the Internal Causes of the Confederacy's Defeat (1865)

Kate Cumming was born in Scotland but had grown up in Mobile, Alabama. Her brother enlisted in the Confederate Army, and equally devoted to the South, she offered her services as a nurse with the Confederate Army after the Battle of Shiloh. Intending to serve only during the emergency following that battle, she ended up working as a nurse in several different military hospitals for the rest of the war. Cumming exemplified self-sacrifice and selfless devotion to the cause, a devotion she found lacking in many southerners. In the following passage from her diary, she criticized the behavior of the southern people during the war.

May [1]5, [1865]

To the people of the South I would also say a few words. Our doom is sealed; we are in the power of the North. . . . Have we done our duty? Have the planters given of the abundance of their harvests to the poor women and children of soldiers who were fighting to save their wealth? . . .

Have no native southern men remained at home, when their country had need of their strong arms, speculating on what the planters charged so much for, doubly taking the bread out of these same poor, yet rich, soldiers' families' mouths?

Have no native southern quartermasters and commissaries robbed these *poor*, yet *rich* soldiers, who walked boldly up to the cannon's mouth, regardless of consequences? They have starved, gone ragged and barefooted through burning suns and chilling frosts, while these delinquent commissaries and quartermasters have lived on the best of the land, and worn the finest clothes to be had.

Have the examining surgeons conscientiously worked, sending none to the field but those who were fit for field service? And none who would have served their country better and more effectively had they been left at home to till the ground, thereby making food for the army and themselves?

Have the conscript officers taken none for the army, that the surgeons had discharged some three or four times, and sent them to the field; they dying before it was ever reached?

Have the stewards and foragers, in hospitals, never speculated on food sold them, much cheaper by the farmers, because it was for the soldiers and the cause; and have they never robbed the government of the money appropriated by it to buy food for the wounded and sick soldiers? . . .

Have all the young native southerners who cried *secession*, and *war* to the *knife*, before the war broke out, gone into the field when their country was bleeding at every pore?

Have all the Christian and refined women of the South, who had no household duties to attend, gone into the hospitals, nursed the wounded and sick, preparing little delicacies . . . for the poor bedridden soldier, who had lost all but honor for his country; and, when his hours were numbered, stood by his bedside when no wife, mother, or sister was there, to soothe his last moments and lift his thoughts to . . . heaven? . . .

Have the women of the South never passed by, in disdain, a ragged and wounded soldier, who had suffered more than words can express? In a word, have the women of the South done their whole duty; and can the southern people, as a whole, say they have fully done their duty? . . .

What though we had gained our independence, while all these sins were crying out against us, could we have expected, as a nation, to go on in them and prosper? Never! We should have worked our own downfall as we have now done.

Had we been true to our God and country, with all the blessings of this glorious, sunny land, I believe we could have kept the North, with all her power, at bay for twenty years.

What I would ask now, is for the southern people to look to themselves, forgetting all the wrongs inflicted on us by our foe in the knowledge that we have sinned against each other.

FROM Kate Cumming, *A Journal of Hospital Life* (Louisville, Ky.: John P. Morton and Co., 1866), pp. 187–88.

13

ROBERT GARLICK KEAN

A Confederate Official Analyzes the Causes of the Defeat of the Confederacy (1957)

When the war began, Robert Kean of Virginia (b. 1828) enlisted in the Confederate Army and rose to the rank of captain. After a year of service, he became head of a bureau of the War Department in Richmond. Kean, who remained in this post for the duration of the conflict, kept a diary detailing from his vantage point the inner workings of the Confederate government. Shortly after the war ended, he reflected on the reasons for the defeat of the Confederacy.

The Causes of the Failure of Southern Independence

1st A bankrupt treasury. This was the prolific source of other evils: (a) high prices of all supplies, and parties unwilling to furnish even for them (b) discontent of people and army for want of payment of dues and worthlessness of it when obtained; hence *desertion*, impressment (c) decay of railroad transportation due in part to this cause, the roads not having wherewith to keep themselves up. Causes [for bankrupt treasury:] (a) belief of leaders in a short war (b) inability to deal with a very large subject; First Congress responsible as well as the President and Memminger.

2nd. Want of men; exhaustion of supply from which recruits of effective qualities to be drawn; severity of the conscription; desertion due to insufficient supply and worthlessness of money.

3rd. Shortness of subsistence, military operations fettered by; armies obliged to occupy certain fixed positions with reference to this as a main question. Due (a) to bad currency (b) to want of efficiency of transportation (c) to defective system. Behind all this the country not a food producing one.

4th. Incompetency of military men. Of the West Pointers; small, not capable of high command; promoted rapidly from grade of subalterns to command of divisions, corps and armies. Obstruction of way to command by men of capacity not bred to arms. Defective system of promotion fixed by law and President's construction of "valor and skill." Want of discernment in the selection of general officers; consequently want of discipline, especially in cavalry. Rapid destruction of best material in grade of regimental and company officers; difficult towards the last to find officers competent to command regiments and brigades. Bad selections made; losses resulting, e.g., Bragg, Pemberton, Holmes, Hindman, A. P. Hill, J. E. B. Stuart, Ewell, F. Lee, D. H. Hill. Bad system of cavalry and want of capacity to deal with the questions.

5th. Want of horses for transports and artillery; country stripped by impressment of horses, which straightway perished for want of forage; this want due to defective transportation by railroad and wagon, and limited supply in any given area of country.

6th. Difficulties of supply and recruiting aggravated by *faction*—Stephens, Toombs, J. E. Brown, Vance.

7th. Slavery an inherent weakness when deeply invaded, from desertion to the enemy and joining their army as recruits.

FROM Edward Younger, ed., *Inside the Confederate Government: The Diary of Robert Garlick Hill Kean* (New York: Oxford University Press, 1957), pp. 243–45.

To these may be added one cause which in a certain sense may be said to include them all—the absence of a Representative Man, a *leader* in the *council* as well as in the field who should comprehend and express the movement. We had no one who approached it. The country by instinct, seeking such a reliance, gave its faith to Lee in vain.

14

SARAH HINE

We Have No Future (1866)

In the following letter, Sarah Hine, who lived in Savannah, Georgia, during the war, looked back on the defeat of the Confederacy and its impact on her life. Rather than looking to internal causes to explain the Confederacy's overthrow, as Kate Cumming did, Hine emphasized the idea that, in the end, the South was overwhelmed as a means to assuage some of the pain of defeat. Her despair is readily evident.

Solitaire
Feb. 10th 1866

My dear Charlotte

. . . It had been just about a year since I had had a letter from you before, & I had so yearned to hear of your welfare & your childrens, & to tell you of our plans & prospects. I will not say hopes, for myself I have none, they are buried in the grave of my country. . . .

dear Charlotte how can we ever give up the Confederacy. One thing I shall glory in to the latest hour of my life, We never yielded in the struggle until we were bound hand & foot & the heel of the despot was on our throats. Bankrupt in men, in money, & in provisions, the wail of the bereaved & the cry of hunger rising all over the land, Our cities burned with fire and our pleasant things laid waste, the best & bravest of our sons in captivity, and the entire resources of the country exhausted—what could we do but give up. Our people certainly struggled as becomes free men who felt that every thing that was dear to man was at stake. Well may you say we lost every thing but honor & I am sure you echo the sentiments of every heart in this land when you say "I detest the United States."

I do not see a spark of love for the Union exhibited in the speeches of any of our public men neither governors messages nor any thing else. I am glad there is not, if they expressed it I should think it was duplicity. During the existence of the Confederacy my anxiety about my sons & others whom I loved in the army, & my intense yearnings for the triumph of our cause kept me in a state of continual unrest & discomfort to say the least, often times it amounted to distress, yet I would cheerfully accept the situation again if I could, with all its disturbing & distressing influences to live once more under the government of my choice.—

FROM Mauriel P. Joslyn, ed., *Charlotte's Boys: Civil War Letters of the Branch Family of Savannah* (Berryville, Va.: Rockbridge Publishing Co., 1996), pp. 310–11.

We have nothing on earth to look forward to, we have no future, no country, we are slaves to the will of others, & must do their bidding & obey their behests. May God forgive me for there are times when my heart rebels against *His* government & I feel as if I could not accept His will in the matter.

The war has left us penniless. We had a little pile of money laid up towards buying us a house when the war broke out, a good part of it was in specie. James felt & so did I that if it was put into Confederate bonds it would help sustain the government & be perhaps equally secure, & it was converted into eight per cent bonds. It is all gone of course, but I do not grieve about it I am glad we did what we could. All that James made during the war was also in Confederate money & bonds, & what little State money we had & still have is not much better than the other.

15

GEORGE TEMPLETON STRONG

We Have Lived a Century of Common Life (1865)

We have already read George Templeton Strong's accounts of the outbreak of war and the draft riots in New York City (see pp. 65, 183). At the end of the war, Strong reflected on the events of the past four years and was struck, even amazed, by the extent and significance of the changes in the nation produced by the war.

June 29 [1865]. . . . The "progress of human events" since 1860 is bewildering. Never did human events make such news before. Southern newspaper articles of three or four years ago make me feel very old. They seem medieval relics. . . . Centuries seem to have elapsed since the Richmond papers went into spasms about the invasion of Virginia and the occupation of Alexandria, and proclaimed no quarter to any black man allowed to shoulder a musket in the national army. . . .

May 22 [1865]. . . . After dinner to the Union League Club, where I spent an hour turning over volume one of Mr. Townsend's fifty or sixty dumpy folios filled with newspaper cuttings illustrating the history of the war. This volume covered December, 1860. It seemed like reading the records of some remote age and of a people wholly unlike our own. So many notions were then put forward as axioms which are now seen to have been preposterous, and so many men were molluscous and invertebrate who were so soon thereafter transmuted into mammalia that we have forgotten their indecision and gelatinous quiverings of but little more than four years ago. . . .

May 29 [1865]. . . . PEACE.

Peace herself at last, for [Kirby] Smith and [John] Magruder have surrendered, if General [Edward] Canby's dispatch to the War Department be truthful. So here I hope and believe ends, by God's great and underserved mercy, the chapter

FROM Allan Nevins and Milton Halsey Thomas, eds., *The Diary of George Templeton Strong*, vol. 2 (New York: The Macmillan Company, 1952), pp. 600–601; vol. 3, p. 14.

of this journal I opened with the heading of *War* on the night of April 13, 1861. We have lived a century of common life since then. Only within the last two months have I dared to hope that this fearful struggle would be settled so soon. . . .

What a time it has been, say from December 21, 1860, when we heard that the process of national decomposition had set in with the secession of cantankerous little South Carolina, on through disaster and depression for four years and nearly six months, till today, with its tidings that the last army Rebeldom has organized out of the many hundred thousand men it has seduced or coerced into fighting for its felonious flag, exists no longer. As I look back now to Bull Run, Fort Donelson, the Seven Days, Antietam, Gettysburg, Chancellorsville, and other battles, I wonder my thoughts have not been even more engrossed by the developments of the great tragedy, that I have been able to pay any attention to my common routine and to be interested in anything outside the tremendous chapter that history has been taking down in shorthand.

16   *NEW YORK TIMES*

The War Touches Everything (1867)

The changes wrought by the war were so profound that participants in this great struggle immediately sensed how deep and long lasting they would be. The New York Times *offered the following analysis of the war's impact on the nation.*

The truth is neither section, and but few persons in either section, appreciate fully the tremendous effect of Civil War, and especially of such a war as ours, upon every interest and every sentiment of the whole community. One might as well expect order and symmetry in the architecture of a great city after an earthquake, as to look for cool judgment and sober reason the moment the thunders of such a War have died away. The contest touches everything, and leaves nothing as it found it. Great rights, great interests, great systems of habit and of thought, disappear during its progress. It leaves us a different people in everything from what we were when it came upon us. The War created a perfect Revolution in the public mind,—in our modes of thinking on public questions and of dealing with political and social interests. Slavery once seemed to us a gigantic evil,—protected from our hatred only by the Constitution; but it disappeared so suddenly and so completely, that our respect for what was so long its bulwark is no longer what it was. The power which destroyed Slavery in spite of the Constitution, seems to us greater than the Constitution itself.

FROM *New York Times*, 9 October 1867.

Reconstruction

Abraham Lincoln Vetoes the Wade-Davis Bill (1864)

When Congress passed a bill, authored by Senator Benjamin F. Wade of Ohio and Representative Henry Winter Davis of Maryland, both antislavery radicals, establishing a program of Reconstruction, Lincoln pocket-vetoed the bill (the Constitution provides that if the president does not sign a bill after Congress has adjourned, it has the effect of a veto). Lincoln then issued the following proclamation explaining his motives. He announced that any southern state that preferred Congress's harsher program to his more lenient one was free to adopt it instead, fully realizing that this was an empty gesture (and one no doubt that added to the Radicals' fury).

[July 8, 1864]

Whereas at the late session Congress passed a bill "to guarantee to certain States whose governments have been usurped or overthrown a republican form of government," a copy of which is hereunto annexed; and

Whereas the said bill was presented to the President of the United States for his approval less than one hour before the *sine die* adjournment of said session, and was not signed by him; and

Whereas the said bill contains, among other things, a plan for restoring the States in rebellion to their proper practical relation in the Union, which plan expresses the sense of Congress upon that subject, and which plan it is now thought fit to lay before the people for their consideration:

Now, therefore, I, Abraham Lincoln, President of the United States, do proclaim, declare, and

make known that while I am (as I was in December last, when, by proclamation, I propounded a plan for restoration) unprepared by a formal approval of this bill to be inflexibly committed to any single plan of restoration, and while I am also unprepared to declare that the free State constitutions and governments already adopted and installed in Arkansas and Louisiana shall be set aside and held for naught, thereby repelling and discouraging the loyal citizens who have set up the same as to further effort, or to declare a constitutional competency in Congress to abolish slavery in States, but am at the same time sincerely hoping and expecting that a constitutional amendment abolishing slavery throughout the nation may be adopted, nevertheless I am fully satisfied with the system for restoration contained in the bill as one very proper plan for the loyal people of any State choosing to adopt it, and that I am and at all times shall be prepared to give the Executive aid and assistance to any such people so soon as the military resistance to the United States shall have been suppressed in any such State and the people thereof shall have

FROM James D. Richardson, ed., *A Compilation of the Messages and Papers of the Presidents*, vol. 4 (Washington, D.C.: Government Printing Office, 1907), pp. 222–23.

sufficiently returned to their obedience to the Constitution and the laws of the United States, in which cases military governors will be appointed with directions to proceed according to the bill.

2

BENJAMIN F. WADE AND HENRY WINTER DAVIS

The Wade-Davis Manifesto (1864)

When Lincoln pocket-vetoed their Reconstruction bill, Benjamin F. Wade and Henry W. Davis angrily responded in a manifesto that they issued on August 5, 1864. Their intemperate language, however, offended many who preferred a stricter program of Reconstruction and helped undermine their position. Rarely have members of Congress so heatedly attacked a president of their own party during a national campaign.

The President, by preventing this bill from becoming a law, holds the electoral votes of the rebel States at the dictation of his personal ambition.

If those votes turn the balance in his favor, is it to be supposed that his competitor, defeated by such means, will acquiesce?

If the rebel majority assert their supremacy in those States, and send votes which elect an enemy of the Government, will we not repel his claims?

And is not that civil war for the Presidency inaugurated by the votes of rebel States?

Seriously impressed with these dangers, Congress, "*the proper constitutional authority,*" formally declared that there are no State governments in the rebel States, and provided for their erection at a proper time; and both the Senate and the House of Representatives rejected the Senators and Representatives chosen under the authority of what the President calls the free constitution and government of Arkansas.

The President's proclamation "*holds for naught*" this judgment, and discards the authority of the Supreme Court, and strides headlong toward the anarchy his proclamation of the 8th of December inaugurated.

If electors for President be allowed to be chosen in either of those States, a sinister light will be cast on the motives which induced the President to "hold for naught" the will of Congress rather than his government in Louisiana and Arkansas.

That judgment of Congress which the President defies was the exercise of an authority exclusively vested in Congress by the Constitution to determine what is the established government in a State, and in its own nature and by the highest judicial authority binding on all other departments of the Government. . . .

A more studied outrage on the legislative authority of the people has never been perpetrated.

Congress passed a bill; the President refused to approve it, and then by proclamation puts as much of it in force as he sees fit, and proposes to execute those parts by officers unknown to the laws of the United States and not subject to the confirmation of the Senate!

The bill directed the appointment of Provisional Governors by and with the advice and consent of the Senate.

The President, after defeating the law, proposes to appoint without law, and without the advice

---

FROM Edward McPherson, ed., *Political History of the Rebellion* (Washington, D.C.: Philp and Solomons, 1864), p. 332.

and consent of the Senate, *Military* Governors for the rebel States!

He has already exercised this dictatorial usurpation in Louisiana, and he defeated the bill to prevent its limitation. . . .

The President has greatly presumed on the forbearance which the supporters of his Administration have so long practiced, in view of the arduous conflict in which we are engaged, and the reckless ferocity of our political opponents.

But he must understand that our support is of a cause and not of a man; that the authority of Congress is paramount and must be respected; that the whole body of the Union men of Congress will not submit to be impeached by him of rash and unconstitutional legislation; and if he wishes our support, he must confine himself to his executive duties—to obey and execute, not make the laws—to suppress by arms armed rebellion, and leave political reorganization to Congress.

If the supporters of the Government fail to insist on this, they become responsible for the usurpations which they fail to rebuke, and are justly liable to the indignation of the people whose rights and security, committed to their keeping, they sacrifice.

Let them consider the remedy for these usurpations, and, having found it, fearlessly execute it.

3

ABRAHAM LINCOLN

We Shall Have the Fowl Sooner by Hatching Than Smashing the Egg (1865)

On April 11, 1865, a few days before he was assassinated, Abraham Lincoln delivered a speech on the problem of Reconstruction. In it Lincoln emphasized his desire to quickly establish loyal governments in the former states of the Confederacy and place these states once again in the normal relationship with the federal government. In a clear concession to the radical members of the Republican party, Lincoln publicly endorsed for the first time limited black suffrage in the South. He went on to say, however, that he was not committed to a single plan and that he might make a new announcement on the subject of Reconstruction to the people of the South. Exactly what modifications in his program Lincoln was considering will never be known, although in his final Cabinet meeting he remarked that he might have tried to go too fast in restoring the southern states to the Union, and he authorized Secretary of War Edwin Stanton to revise a plan for the military occupation of the defeated states.

In the Annual Message of Dec. 1863 and accompanying Proclamation, I presented *a* plan of reconstruction (as the phrase goes) which, I promised, if adopted by any State, should be acceptable to, and sustained by, the Executive government of the nation. I distinctly stated that this was not the only plan which might possibly be acceptable; and I also distinctly protested that the Executive claimed no right to say when, or whether members should be admitted to seats in Congress from such States. . . . When the Message of 1863, with the plan before mentioned, reached New-Orleans, Gen. Banks wrote me that he was confident the people, with his military co-operation, would reconstruct, substantially on that plan. I wrote him, and some of them to try it; they tried it, and the result is known. Such only has been my agency in getting up the Louisiana government. As to sustaining it, my promise is out, as before stated. But, as bad promises are better broken than kept, I shall treat this as a bad promise, and break it, whenever I shall be convinced that keeping it is adverse to the public interest. But I have not yet been so convinced.

I have been shown a letter on this subject, supposed to be an able one, in which the writer expresses regret that my mind has not seemed to be definitely fixed on the question whether the seceded States, so called, are in the Union or out of it. . . . I have *purposely* forborne any public expression upon it. As appears to me that question has not been, nor yet is, a practically material one, and that any discussion of it, while it thus remains practically immaterial, could have no effect other than the mischievous one of dividing our friends. As yet, whatever it may hereafter become, that question is bad, as the basis of a controversy, and good for nothing at all—a merely pernicious abstraction.

We all agree that the seceded States, so called, are out of their proper practical relation with the Union; and that the sole object of the government,

civil and military, in regard to those States is to again get them into that proper practical relation. I believe it is not only possible, but in fact, easier, to do this, without deciding, or even considering, whether these states have even been out of the Union, than with it. Finding themselves safely at home, it would be utterly immaterial whether they had ever been abroad. Let us all join in doing the acts necessary to restoring the proper practical relations between these states and the Union; and each forever after, innocently indulge his own opinion whether, in doing the acts, he brought the States from without, into the Union, or only gave them proper assistance, they never having been out of it.

The amount of constituency, so to to [*sic*] speak, on which the new Louisiana government rests, would be more satisfactory to all, if it contained fifty, thirty, or even twenty thousand, instead of only about twelve thousand, as it does. It is also unsatisfactory to some that the elective franchise is not given to the colored man. I would myself prefer that it were now conferred on the very intelligent, and on those who serve our cause as soldiers. Still the question is not whether the Louisiana government, as it stands, is quite all that is desirable. The question is "Will it be wiser to take it as it is, and help to improve it; or to reject, and disperse it?" "Can Louisiana be brought into proper practical relation with the Union *sooner* by *sustaining*, or by *discarding* her new State Government?"

Some twelve thousand voters in the heretofore slave-state of Louisiana have sworn allegiance to the Union, assumed to be the rightful political power of the State, held elections, organized a State government, adopted a free-state constitution, giving the benefit of public schools equally to black and white, and empowering the Legislature to confer the elective franchise upon the colored man. Their Legislature has already voted to ratify the constitutional amendment recently passed by Congress, abolishing slavery throughout the nation. These twelve thousand persons are thus fully committed to the Union, and to perpetual freedom in the state—committed to the very things, and

FROM Roy P. Basler, et al., eds., *The Collected Works of Abraham Lincoln*, vol. 7 (New Brunswick, N.J.: Rutgers University Press, 1953), pp. 401–5.

nearly all the things the nation wants—and they ask the nations recognition, and it's assistance to make good their committal. Now, if we reject, and spurn them, we do our utmost to disorganize and disperse them. . . . If this course, discouraging and paralyzing both white and black, has any tendency to bring Louisiana into proper practical relations with the Union, I have, so far, been unable to perceive it. If, on the contrary, we recognize, and sustain the new government of Louisiana the converse of all this is made true. We encourage the hearts, and nerve the arms of the twelve thousand to adhere to their work, and argue for it, and proselyte for it, and fight for it, and feed it, and grow it, and ripen it to a complete success. The colored man too, in seeing all united for him, is inspired with vigilance, and energy, and daring, to the same end. Grant that he desires the elective franchise, will he not attain it sooner by saving the already advanced steps toward it, than by running backward over them? Concede that the new government of Louisiana is only to what it should be as the egg is to the fowl, we shall sooner have the fowl by hatching the egg than by smashing it? Again, if we reject Louisiana, we also reject one vote in favor of the proposed amendment to the national constitution. To meet this proposition, it has been ar-gued that no more than three fourths of those States which have not attempted secession are necessary to validly ratify the amendment. I do not commit myself against this, further than to say that such a ratification would be questionable, and sure to be persistently questioned; while a ratification by three fourths of all the States would be unquestioned and unquestionable.

I repeat the question. "Can Louisiana be brought into proper practical relation with the Union *sooner* by *sustaining* or by *discarding* her new State Government?

What has been said of Louisiana will apply generally to other States. And yet so great peculiarities pertain to each state; and such important and sudden changes occur in the same state; and, withal, so new and unprecedented is the whole case, that no exclusive, and inflexible plan can safely be prescribed as to details and colatterals. Such exclusive, and inflexible plan, would surely become a new entanglement. Important principles may, and must, be inflexible.

In the present "*situation*" as the phrase goes, it may be my duty to make some new announcement to the people of the South. I am considering, and shall not fail to act, when satisfied that action will be proper.

4

Ulysses S. Grant Affirms the Loyalty of Southern Whites (1865)

At the solicitation of President Andrew Johnson, Ulysses S. Grant made a hasty tour of part of the South in November 1865 to ascertain the attitude of southerners. Grant did not get beyond Georgia, and he did not have time to carefully formulate his impressions. Nevertheless, his enormous personal prestige gave his observations great weight. His official report stressed the loyalty of southerners in the aftermath of the war.

I am satisfied that the mass of thinking men of the south accept the present situation of affairs in good faith. The question which has heretofore divided the sentiment of the people of the two sections—Slavery and State rights, or the right of a State to secede from the Union—they regard as having been settled forever by the highest tribunal—arms—that man can resort to. I was pleased to learn from the leading men whom I met that they not only accepted the decision arrived at as final, but, now that the smoke of the battle was cleared away and time has been given for reflection, that this decision has been a fortunate one for the whole country, they receiving like benefits from it with those who opposed them in the field and in council.

Four years of war, during which law was executed only at the point of the bayonet throughout the States in rebellion, have left the people possibly in a condition not to yield that ready obedience to civil authority the American people have generally been in the habit of yielding. This would render the presence of small garrisons throughout these States necessary until such time as labor returns to its proper channel, and civil authority is fully established. I did not meet any one, either those holding place under the government or citizens of the southern States, who think it practicable to withdraw the military from the South at present. The white and the black mutually require the protection of the general government.

There is such universal acquiescence in the authority of the general government throughout the portions of country visited by me, that the mere presence of a military force, without regard to numbers, is sufficient to maintain order. The good of the country, and economy, require that the force kept in the interior, where there are many freedmen (elsewhere in the southern States than at forts upon the seacoast no force is necessary,) should all be white troops. The reasons for this are obvious without mentioning many of them. The presence of black troops, lately slaves, demoralizes labor, both by their advice and by furnishing in their camps a resort for the freedmen for long distances around. White troops generally excite no opposition, and therefore a small number of them can maintain order in a given district. Colored troops must be kept in bodies sufficient to defend themselves. It is not the thinking men who would use violence toward any class of troops sent among them by the general government, but the ignorant in some places might; and the late slave seems to be imbued with the idea that the property of his late master should, by right, belong to him, or at least should have no protection from the colored soldier. There is a danger of collision being brought on by such causes.

My observations lead me to the conclusion that the citizens of the southern States are anxious to return to self-government, within the Union, as soon as possible; that whilst reconstructing they want and require protection from the government; that they are in earnest in wishing to do what they think is required by the government, not humiliating to them as citizens, and that if such a course were pointed out they would pursue it in good faith. It is to be regretted that there cannot be a greater commingling, at this time, between the citizens of the two sections, and particularly of those intrusted with the law-making power.

FROM *Senate Executive Document,* no. 2, 39th Cong., 1st sess., 18 December 1865, p. 107.

5

Carl Schurz Questions
Southern Whites' Loyalty (1865)

Another visitor who went to the South at President Andrew Johnson's behest was Carl Schurz, the famous German Republican leader who fled Prussia after the 1848 revolution failed. Traveling in the South from July to September 1865, Schurz was more radical on the question of Reconstruction than Grant, and he reached a remarkably different conclusion concerning the state of public opinion in the region. Schurz's views sharply diverged from those of Johnson, who did not even ask him for an official report. Schurz wrote one anyway, which was published by Congress at the urging of Republicans who were opposed to the president's program.

I may group the southern people into four classes, each of which exercise an influence upon the development of things in that section:

1. Those who, although having yielded submission to the national government only when obliged to do so, have a clear perception of the irreversible change produced by the war, and honestly endeavor to accommodate themselves to the new order of things. Many of them are not free from traditional prejudice but open to conviction, and may be expected to act in good faith whatever they do. This class is composed, in its majority, of persons of mature age—planters, merchants, and professional men; some of them are active in the reconstruction movement, but boldness and energy are, with a few individual exceptions, not among their distinguishing qualities.

2. Those whose principal object is to have the States without delay restored to their position and influence in the Union and the people of the States to the absolute control of their home concerns. They are ready, in order to attain that object, to

make any ostensible concession that will not prevent them from arranging things to suit their taste as soon as that object is attained. This class comprises a considerable number, probably a large majority, of the professional politicians who are extremely active in the reconstruction movement. They are loud in their praise of the President's reconstruction policy, and clamorous for the withdrawal of the federal troops and the abolition of the Freedmen's Bureau.

3. The incorrigibles, who still indulge in the swagger which was so customary before and during the war, and still hope for a time when the southern confederacy will achieve its independence. This class consists mostly of young men, and comprises the loiterers of the towns and the idlers of the country. They persecute Union men and negroes whenever they can do so with impunity, insist clamorously upon their "rights," and are extremely impatient of the presence of the federal soldiers. A good many of them have taken the oaths of allegiance and amnesty, and associated themselves with the second class in their political operations. This element is by no means unimportant; it is strong in numbers, deals in brave talk, addresses itself directly and incessantly to the pas-

FROM *Senate Executive Document*, no. 2, 39th Cong., 1st sess., 1865, p. 5.

sions and prejudices of the masses, and commands the admiration of the women.

4. The multitude of people have no definite ideas about the circumstances under which they live and about the course they have to follow; whose intellects are weak, but whose prejudices and impulses are strong, and who are apt to be carried along by those who know how to appeal to the latter.

Much depends upon the relation and influence of these classes. . . . But whatever their differences may be, on one point they are agreed: further resistance to the power of the national government is useless, and submission to its authority a matter of necessity. It is true, the right of secession in theory is still believed in by most of those who formerly believed in it; some are still entertaining a vague hope of seeing it realized at some future time, but all give it up as a practical impossibility for the present. All movements in favor of separation from the Union have, therefore, been practically abandoned, and resistance to our military forces, on that score, has ceased. . . . This kind of loyalty, however, which is produced by the irresistible pressure of force, and consists merely in the non-commission of acts of rebellion, is of a negative character, and might as such, hardly be considered independent of circumstances and contingencies. . . .

Treason does, under existing circumstances, not appear odious in the south. The people are not impressed with any sense of its criminality. . . . There is, as yet, among the southern people an utter absence of national feeling. I made it a business, while in the south, to watch the symptoms of "returning loyalty" as they appeared not only in pri-

vate conversation, but in the public press and in the speeches delivered and the resolutions passed at Union meetings. Hardly ever was there an expression of hearty attachment to the great republic, or an appeal to the impulses of patriotism; but whenever submission to the national authority was declared and advocated, it was almost uniformly placed upon two principal grounds: That under present circumstances, the southern people could "do no better;" and then that submission was the only means by which they could rid themselves of the federal soldiers and obtain once more control of their own affairs. . . .

If nothing were necessary but to restore the machinery of government in the States lately in rebellion in point of form, the movements made to that end by the people of the South might be considered satisfactory. But if it is required that the southern people should also accommodate themselves to the results of the war in point of spirit, those movements fall far short of what must be insisted upon.

The loyalty of the masses and most of the leaders of the southern people, consists in submission to necessity. There is, except in individual instances, an entire absence of that national spirit which forms the basis of true loyalty and patriotism.

The emancipation of the slaves is submitted to only in so far as chattel slavery in the old form could not be kept up. But although the freedman is no longer considered the property of the individual master, he is considered the slave of society, and all independent State legislation will share the tendency to make him such.

6

The Mississippi Black Codes (1865)

Under Andrew Johnson's program of Reconstruction, southern state legislatures en-
acted a series of laws to regulate the black population. Reflecting ideas deeply rooted
in southern white culture, these laws were a manifestation of the widespread view
that blacks would not work without compulsion and that freedpeople posed a threat
to the security and order of society. These laws, which generally applied only to black
residents, drew upon the old slave codes as well as earlier vagrancy laws. They recog-
nized the legality of slave marriages, gave blacks access to the courts, and granted the
right to own property. In other ways, however, they severely curtailed rights and
privileges that northerners considered an essential part of freedom and, conse-
quently, alarmed northern public opinion, which saw these laws as akin to slavery.
Most of the laws were subsequently overturned by Congress and by military author-
ities stationed in the South, but they were an effective expression of southern white
attitudes in the immediate aftermath of emancipation. The Black Codes varied from
state to state, and not all were as severe as those of Mississippi, which were among
the most stringent. The Mississippi laws attracted particular attention in the North,
and the Republican Chicago Tribune *bluntly warned: "We tell the white men of*
Mississippi that the men of the North will convert the state of Mississippi into a frog
pond before they will allow such laws to disgrace one foot of soil in which the bones
of our soldiers sleep and over which the flag of freedom waves."

Vagrant Law
[November 24, 1865]

Sec. 1. . . . That all rogues and vagabonds, idle and dissipated persons, beggars, jugglers, or persons practicing unlawful games or plays, runaways, common drunkards, common night-walkers, pilferers, lewd, wanton, or lascivious persons, in speech or behavior, common railers and brawlers, persons who neglect their calling or employment,

misspend what they earn, or do not provide for the support of themselves or their families, or dependants, and all other idle and disorderly persons, including all who neglect all lawful business, habitually misspend their time by frequenting houses of ill-fame, gaming-houses, or tippling shops, shall be deemed and considered vagrants, under the provisions of this act, and upon conviction thereof shall be fined not exceeding one hundred dollars, with all accruing costs, and be imprisoned, at the discretion of the court, not exceeding ten days.

Sec. 2. . . . All freedmen, free negroes and mulattoes in this State, over the age of eighteen years, found on the second Monday in January, 1866, or

FROM Walter L. Fleming, ed., *Documentary History of Reconstruction*, vol. 1 (Cleveland: Arthur H. Clark Co., 1906–1907), pp. 281–90.

thereafter, with no lawful employment or business, or found unlawfully assembling themselves together, either in the day or night time, and all white persons so assembling themselves with freedmen, free negroes or mulattoes, or usually associating with freedmen, free negroes or mulattoes, on terms of equality, or living in adultery or fornication with a freed woman, free negro or mulatto, shall be deemed vagrants, and on conviction thereof shall be fined in a sum not exceeding, in the case of a freedman, free negro, or mulatto, fifty dollars, and a white man two hundred dollars, and imprisoned at the discretion of the court, the free negro not exceeding ten days, and the white man not exceeding six months. . . .

Sec. 7. . . . If any freedman, free negro, or mulatto shall fail or refuse to pay any tax levied according to the provisions of the sixth section of this act, it shall be *prima facie* evidence of vagrancy, and it shall be the duty of the sheriff to arrest such freedman, free negro, or mulatto or such person refusing or neglecting to pay such tax, and proceed at once to hire for the shortest time such delinquent tax-payer to any one who will pay the said tax, with accruing costs, giving preference to the employer, if there be one.

Civil Rights of Freedmen
[November 25, 1865]

Sec. 1. . . . That all freedmen, free negroes, and mulattoes may sue and be sued, implead and be impleaded, in all the courts of law and equity of this State, and may acquire personal property, and choses in action, by descent or purchase, and may dispose of the same in the same manner and to the same extent that white persons may: *Provided*, That the provisions of this section shall not be so construed as to allow any freedman, free negro, or mulatto to rent or lease any lands or tenements except in incorporated cities or towns. . . .

Sec. 2. . . . All freedmen, free negroes, and mulattoes may intermarry with each other, in the same manner and under the same regulations that are provided by law for white persons: *Provided*,

That the clerk of probate shall keep separate records of the same.

Sec. 3. . . . All freedmen, free negroes, or mulattoes who do now and have herebefore lived and cohabited together as husband and wife shall be taken and held in law as legally married, and the issue shall be taken and held as legitimate for all purposes; that it shall not be lawful for any freedman, free negro, or mulatto to intermarry with any white person; nor for any white person to intermarry with any freedman, free negro, or mulatto; and any person who shall so intermarry, shall be deemed guilty of felony, and on conviction thereof shall be confined in the State penitentiary for life; and those shall be deemed freedmen, free negroes, and mulattoes who are of pure negro blood, and those descended from a negro to the third generation, inclusive, though one ancestor in each generation may have been a white person.

Sec. 4. . . . In addition to cases in which freedmen, free negroes, and mulattoes are now by law competent witnesses, freedmen, free negroes, or mulattoes shall be competent in civil cases, when a party or parties to the suit, either plaintiff or plaintiffs, defendant or defendants; also in cases where freedmen, free negroes, and mulattoes is or are either plaintiff or plaintiffs, defendant or defendants, and a white person or white persons, is or are the opposing party or parties, plaintiff or plaintiffs, defendant or defendants. They shall also be competent witnesses in all criminal prosecutions where the crime charged is alleged to have been committed by a white person upon or against the person or property of a freedman, free negro, or mulatto: *Provided*, that in all cases said witnesses shall be examined in open court, on the stand; except, however, they may be examined before the grand jury, and shall in all cases be subject to the rules and tests of the common law as to competency and credibility.

Sec. 5. . . . Every freedman, free negro, and mulatto shall, on the second Monday of January, one thousand eight hundred and sixty-six and annually thereafter, have a lawful home or employment, and shall have written evidence thereof. . . .

Sec. 6. . . . All contracts for labor made with

freedmen, free negroes, and mulattoes for a longer period than one month shall be in writing, and in duplicate, attested and read to said freedman, free negro, or mulatto by a beat, city or county officer, or two disinterested white persons of the county in which the labor is to be performed, of which each party shall have one; and said contracts shall be taken and held as entire contracts, and if the laborer shall quit the service of the employer before the expiration of his term of service, without good cause, he shall forfeit his wages for that year up to the time of quitting.

Sec. 7. . . . Every civil officer shall, and every person may, arrest and carry back to his or her legal employer any freedman, free negro, or mulatto who shall have quit the service of his or her employer before the expiration of his or her term of service without good cause. . . . *Provided*, that said arrested party, after being so returned, may appeal to the justice of the peace or member of the board of police of the county, who, on notice to the alleged employer, shall try summarily whether said appellant is legally employed by the alleged employer, and has good cause to quit said employer; either party shall have the right of appeal to the county court, pending which the alleged deserter shall be remanded to the alleged employer or otherwise disposed of, as shall be right and just; and the decision of the county court shall be final.

Certain Offenses of Freedmen
[November 29, 1865]

Sec. 1. . . . That no freedman, free negro or mulatto, not in the military service of the United States government, and not licensed so to do by the board of police of his or her county, shall keep or carry fire-arms of any kind, or any ammunition, dirk or bowie knife, and on conviction thereof in the county court shall be punished by fine, not exceeding ten dollars, and pay the costs of such proceedings, and all such arms or ammunition shall be forfeited to the informer. . . .

Sec. 2. . . . Any freedman, free negro, or mulatto committing riots, routs, affrays, trespasses, malicious mischief, cruel treatment to animals, seditious speeches, insulting gestures, language, or acts, or assaults on any person, disturbance of the peace, exercising the function of a minister of the Gospel without a license from some regularly organized church, vending spirituous or intoxicating liquors, or committing any other misdemeanor, the punishment of which is not specifically provided for by law, shall, upon conviction thereof in the county court, be fined not less than ten dollars, and not more than one hundred dollars, and may be imprisoned at the discretion of the court, not exceeding thirty days.

Sec. 3. . . . If any white person shall sell, lend, or give to any freedman, free negro, or mulatto any fire-arms, dirk or bowie knife, or ammunition, or any spirituous or intoxicating liquors, such person or persons so offending, upon conviction thereof in the county court of his or her county, shall be fined not exceeding fifty dollars, and may be imprisoned, at the discretion of the court, not exceeding thirty days. . . .

Sec. 5. . . . If any freedman, free negro, or mulatto, convicted of any of the misdemeanors provided against in this act, shall fail or refuse for the space of five days, after conviction, to pay the fine and costs imposed, such person shall be hired out by the sheriff or other officer, at public outcry, to any white person who will pay said fine and all costs, and take said convict for the shortest time.

ANDREW JOHNSON

The Radicals Will Be Completely Foiled (1865)

Despite his rabble-rousing manner, Johnson shrank from any fundamental upheaval in southern society. Thus he quickly took a firm stand against universal suffrage. He recognized, however, the importance of politically isolating the Radical Republicans, who were keeping up a constant drumbeat for black suffrage. Consequently, in August 1865 he privately urged southern leaders to extend the franchise to a small number of blacks in order to undercut the Radicals, defuse their power, and assuage northern concern about southerners' attitudes. Johnson's southern allies, however, ignored his advice, thereby weakening Johnson and strengthening the hand of those congressmen who wanted to bar the new southern representatives from taking their seats in the next Congress.

I hope that without delay your convention will amend your State constitution, abolishing slavery and denying to all future Legislatures the power to legislate that there is property in man; also that they will adopt the amendment to the Constitution of the United States abolishing slavery. If you could extend the elective franchise to all persons of color who can read the Constitution of the United States in English and write their names, and to all persons of color who own real estate valued at not less than two hundred and fifty dollars and pay taxes thereon, you would completely disarm the adversary and set an example the other States will follow. This you can do with perfect safety, and you would thus place Southern States in reference to free persons of color upon the same basis with the free States. . . . And as a consequence the radicals, who are wild upon negro franchise, will be completely foiled in their attempts to keep the Southern States from renewing their relations to the Union by not accepting their Senators and Representatives.

FROM Walter L. Fleming, ed., *Documentary History of Reconstruction*, vol. 1 (Cleveland: Arthur H. Clark Co., 1906–1907), p. 177.

8

Virginia Blacks Petition for Suffrage (1865)

In the summer of 1865, African Americans held conventions in a number of southern states to discuss their situation under Johnson's new state governments. Detailing the abuses and wrongs blacks were subjected to in the South, the delegates called for greater civil rights for African Americans, including the right of suffrage. It is striking how quickly after emancipation blacks agitated for the right to vote. A black convention held in Alexandria, Virginia, in August 1865 adopted the following address appealing for protection and equal rights.

We, the delegates of the colored people of the State of Virginia, in Convention assembled at Alexandria, Virginia, to act and advise what is thought best to be done for the interests of the colored people of the State, and to give expression of our feelings and desires, do hereby appeal to the conscientious, sympathetic, and just judgment of the American people, solemnly declaring that we desire to live upon the most friendly and agreeable terms with all men; we feel no ill-will or prejudice towards our former oppressors; are willing and desire to forgive and forget the past, and so shape our future conduct as shall promote our happiness and the interest of the community in which we live; and that we believe that in this State we have still many warm and solid friends among the white people, and that this portion of them will do all they can for our improvement and elevation. . . .

But, while we are free to acknowledge all that we have said above, we must, on the other hand, be allowed to aver and assert that we believe that we have among the white people of this State many who are our most inveterate enemies; who hate us as a class, and who feel no sympathy with or for us; who despise us simply because we are black, and

more especially, because we have been made free by the power of the United States Government, and that they—the class last mentioned—will not, in our estimation, be willing to accord to us, as freemen, that protection which all freemen must contend for, if they would be worthy of freedom. . . .

In this state of chaos and disorganization are we assembled here to-day, to appeal to the citizens of the State of Virginia and to the Government of the United States for that protection which we so much need, and for which freemen in all ages have contended. We in our present condition are without protection, so far as the laws of the State are concerned, and but for the strong arm of the military, we feel that we have no where to look for that protection which is essential for the safety of our persons or our property, our wives or our children, for while we had in our former owners their protection, we have now in them none, and we are left to the assaults of the vile and vicious to do with us as they please, and we are left without redress.

We claim, then, as citizens of this State, the laws of the Commonwealth shall give to all men equal protection; that each and every man may appeal to the law for his equal rights without regard to the color of his skin; and we believe this can only be done by extending to us the elective franchise, which we believe to be our inalienable right

FROM *Proceedings of the Convention of the Colored People of Virginia* . . . (Alexandria: Cowing and Gillis, 1865), pp. 9–10.

as freemen, and which the Declaration of Independence guarantees to all free citizens of this Government and which is the privilege of the nation. We claim the right of suffrage:

1st. Because we can see no other safe-guard for our protection.

2d. Because we are citizens of the country and natives of this State.

3d. Because we are as well qualified to vote who shall be our rulers as many who do vote for that purpose who have no interest in us, and know not our wants.

4th. Because our representation as heretofore felt in Congress was not in accordance with our own wishes, and therefore we feel that it is right and our privilege to vote for the men who shall so represent us.

5th. Because we believe that the time has come when the colored people are to be felt as in power in this Government, either for good or evil, and that there is no way so calculated to make him subservient for good as to make him a good and loyal citizen.

6th. Because we believe it will be the means of restoring the balance of power which shall harmonize the conflicting elements which are now so rife in the South.

7th. Because we believe that if the white men will look at the subject in its proper light they will see the necessity of granting us this privilege, as they will find in us friends that will ever vote for men who shall be true to the State and loyal to the United States, and because nothing short of equality in law will ever secure to us the wants which every freeman needs and must enjoy if he will be at peace at home and in the community in which he lives. With these considerations we do most respectfully and earnestly appeal first to the citizens of Virginia that they give ear to our humble petition, that in the reconstruction of the laws of this State they do in the prayer of this Convention and before a just God so harmonize their laws as there shall be no distinction before law on account of color, and that every man may expect justice before the tribunals of the State, and then shall righteousness go forth as brightness, and truth as a lamp that burneth.

9

Andrew Johnson Reports on the Success of His Program of Reconstruction (1865)

When Congress convened in December 1865, the Senate asked President Johnson to report on the situation in the South, including the progress of Reconstruction. Johnson submitted the following message, hailing the success of his program of Reconstruction. Radicals requested this report in order to further undercut Johnson's support in Congress and the North.

Washington, December 18, 1865.

To the Senate of the United States:

In reply to the resolution adopted by the Senate on the 12th instant, I have the honor to state that the rebellion waged by a portion of the people against the properly constituted authority of the Government of the United States has been suppressed; that the United States are in possession of every State in which the insurrection existed, and that, as far as it could be done, the courts of the United States have been restored, post-offices reestablished, and steps taken to put into effective operation the revenue laws of the country.

As the result of the measures instituted by the Executive with the view of inducing a resumption of the functions of the States comprehended in the inquiry of the Senate, the people of North Carolina, South Carolina, Georgia, Alabama, Mississippi, Louisiana, Arkansas, and Tennessee have reorganized their respective State governments, and "are yielding obedience to the laws and Government of the United States" with more willingness and greater promptitude than under the circumstances could reasonably have been anticipated. The proposed amendment to the Constitution, providing for the abolition of slavery forever within the limits of the country, has been ratified by each one of those States, with the exception of Mississippi, from which no official information has been received, and in nearly all of them measures have been adopted or are now pending to confer upon freedmen the privileges which are essential to their comfort, protection, and security. In Florida and Texas the people are making commendable progress in restoring their State governments, and no doubt is entertained that they will at an early period be in a condition to resume all of their practical relations with the General Government.

In "that portion of the Union lately in rebellion" the aspect of affairs is more promising than, in view of all the circumstances, could well have been expected. The people throughout the entire South evince a laudable desire to renew their allegiance to the Government and to repair the devastations of war by a prompt and cheerful return to peaceful pursuits, and abiding faith is entertained that their actions will conform to their professions, and that in acknowledging the supremacy of the Constitution and laws of the United States their loyalty will be unreservedly given to the Government, whose leniency they can not fail to appreciate and whose fostering care will soon restore them to a condition of prosperity. It is true that in some of the States the demoralizing effects of the war are to be seen in occasional disorders; but these are local in character, not frequent in occurrence, and are rapidly disappearing as the authority of civil law is extended and sustained. Perplexing questions are naturally to be expected from the great and sudden change in the relations between the two races; but systems are gradually developing themselves under which the freedman will receive the protection to which he is justly entitled, and, by means of his labor, make himself a useful and independent member in the community in which he has a home.

From all the information in my possession and from that which I have recently derived from the most reliable authority I am induced to cherish the belief that sectional animosity is surely and rapidly merging itself into a spirit of nationality, and that representation, connected with a properly adjusted system of taxation, will result in a harmonious restoration of the relation of the States to the National Union. . . .

Andrew Johnson.

FROM James D. Richardson, ed., *A Compilation of the Messages and Papers of the Presidents*, vol. 4 (Washington, D.C.: Government Printing Office, 1907), pp. 372–73.

Thaddeus Stevens Designates the Southern States as Conquered Provinces (1865)

Thaddeus Stevens of Pennsylvania was the most important Radical Republican leader in the House of Representatives in the years immediately after the war. He was a shrewd parliamentary manager with a sharp and acid tongue that made him a feared and formidable debater. Stevens was much more advanced than most of his colleagues in his views on racial equality and his willingness to use federal power to assist the freedpeople in the South. Yet he also harbored a powerful vindictiveness toward southern whites, particularly former slaveholders. In the following speech, delivered on December 18, 1865, shortly after Congress convened, Stevens argued that the southern states were conquered provinces completely at the mercy of Congress, and he outlined the requirements for a successful program of Reconstruction. While many Republicans shared Stevens' distrust of President Johnson and his policies, few at this time were willing to embrace Stevens's far-reaching ideas.

The President assumes, what no one doubts, that the late rebel States have lost their constitutional relations to the Union, and are incapable of representation in Congress, except by permission of the Government. It matters but little, with this admission, whether you call them States out of the Union, and now conquered territories, or assert that because the Constitution forbids them to do what they did do, that they are therefore only dead as to all national and political action, and will remain so until the Government shall breathe into them the breath of life anew and permit them to occupy their former position. . . . In either case, it is very plain that it requires the action of Congress to enable them to form a State government and

send representatives to Congress. Nobody, I believe, pretends that with their old constitutions and frames of government they can be permitted to claim their old rights under the Constitution. They have torn their constitutional States into atoms, and built on their foundations fabrics of a totally different character. . . .

. . . The late war between two acknowledged belligerents severed their original compacts, and broke all the ties that bound them together. The future condition of the conquered power depends on the will of the conqueror. They must come in as new States or remain as conquered provinces. Congress . . . is the only power that can act in the matter. . . .

Congress alone can do it. . . . Hence a law of Congress must be passed before any new State can be admitted; or any dead ones revived. Until then no member can be lawfully admitted into either

FROM *Congressional Globe*, 39th Cong., 1st sess., 1865, pp. 72–75.

House. . . . Congress must create States and declare when they are entitled to be represented. Then each House must judge whether the members presenting themselves from a recognized State possess the requisite qualifications of age, residence, and citizenship; and whether the election and returns are according to law. . . .

It is obvious from all this that the first duty of Congress is to pass a law declaring the condition of these outside or defunct States, and providing proper civil governments for them. Since the conquest they have been governed by martial law. Military rule is necessarily despotic, and ought not to exist longer than is absolutely necessary. As there are no symptoms that the people of these provinces will be prepared to participate in constitutional government for some years, I know of no arrangement so proper for them as territorial governments. There they can learn the principles of freedom and eat the fruit of foul rebellion. Under such governments, while electing members to the Territorial Legislatures, they will necessarily mingle with those to whom Congress shall extend the right of suffrage. In Territories Congress fixes the qualifications of electors; and I know of no better place nor better occasion for the conquered rebels and the conqueror to practice justice to all men, and accustom themselves to make and to obey equal laws. . . .

According to my judgment they ought never to be recognized as capable of acting in the Union, or of being counted as valid States, until the Constitution shall have been so amended as to make it what its framers intended; and so as to secure perpetual ascendency to the party of the Union; and so as to render our republican Government firm and stable forever. The first of those amendments is to change the basis of representation among the States from Federal numbers to actual voters. . . .

. . . With the basis unchanged, the eighty-three southern members, with the Democrats that will in the best times be elected from the North, will always give them a majority in Congress and in the Electoral College. They will at the very first election take posession of the White House and the halls of Congress. I need not depict the ruin that would follow. Assumption of the rebel debt or repudiation of the Federal debt would be sure to follow. The oppression of the freedmen; the reamendment of their State constitutions, and the reëstablishment of slavery would be the inevitable result. That they would scorn and disregard their present constitutions, forced upon them in the midst of martial law, would be both natural and just. No one who has any regard for freedom of elections can look upon those governments, forced upon them in duress, with any favor. If they should grant the right of suffrage to persons of color, I think there would always be Union white men enough in the South, aided by the blacks, to divide the representation, and thus continue the Republican ascendency. If they should refuse to thus alter their election laws it would reduce the representatives of the late slave States to about forty-five and render them powerless for evil. . . .

But this is not all that we ought to do before these inveterate rebels are invited to participate in our legislation. We have turned, or are about to turn, loose four million slaves without a hut to shelter them or a cent in their pockets. The infernal laws of slavery have prevented them from acquiring an education, understanding the commonest laws of contract, or of managing the ordinary business of life. This Congress is bound to provide for them until they can take care of themselves. If we do not furnish them with homesteads, and hedge them around with protective laws; if we leave them to the legislation of their late masters, we had better have left them in bondage. . . . If we fail in this great duty now, when we have the power, we shall deserve and receive the execration of history and of all future ages.

Andrew Johnson Says Black Suffrage Will Lead to Race War in the South (1866)

On February 7, 1866, a delegation of African American leaders, headed by Frederick Douglass, called on Andrew Johnson in the White House. In their interview, the black leaders urged the president to adopt black suffrage as part of his Reconstruction program. Johnson responded by insisting that such a policy would lead to race war in the South because of the bitter hatred that existed between whites and blacks. While his language was reasonably restrained during the meeting, after they had left the president bitterly assailed what he termed the "darkey delegation." He remarked to his secretary, who was present at the meeting, "Those d——d sons of b——s thought they had me in a trap! I know that d——d Douglass; he's just like any nigger, and he would sooner cut a white man's throat than not."

Response of the President

In reply to some of your inquiries, not to make a speech about this thing, for it is always best to talk plainly and distinctly about such matters, I will say that if I have not given evidence in my course that I am a friend of humanity, and to that portion of it which constitutes the colored population, I can give no evidence here. . . . While I say that I am a friend of the colored man, I do not want to adopt a policy that I believe will end in a contest between the races, which if persisted in will result in the extermination of one or the other. God forbid that I should be engaged in such a work! . . .

. . . I am not willing, under either circumstance, to adopt a policy which I believe will only result in the sacrifice of his life and the shedding of his blood. I think I know what I say. I feel what I say; and I feel well assured that if the policy urged by some be persisted in, it will result in great injury to the white as well as to the colored man. There is a

great deal of talk about the sword in one hand accomplishing an end, and the ballot accomplishing another at the ballot-box. . . .

. . . We know there is an enmity, we know there is a hate. The poor white man, on the other hand, was opposed to the slave and his master; for the colored man and his master combined kept him in slavery, by depriving him of a fair participation in the labor and productions of the rich land of the country. . . .

Now, we are talking about where we are going to begin. We have got at the hate that existed between the two races. The query comes up, whether these two races, situated as they were before, without preparation, without time for passion and excitement to be appeased, and without time for the slightest improvement, whether the one should be turned loose upon the other, and be thrown together at the ballot-box with this enmity and hate existing between them. The query comes up right there, whether we don't commence a war of races. I think I understand this thing, and especially is this the case where you force it upon a people without their consent. . . .

FROM Edward McPherson, *Handbook for 1868* (Washington, D.C.: Philp and Solomons, 1868), pp. 53–56.

. . . Will you resort to an arbitrary power, and say a majority of the people shall receive a state of things they are opposed to? . . .

Each community is better prepared to determine the depository of its political power than anybody else, and it is for the Legislature, for the people of Ohio to say who shall vote, and not for the Congress of the United States. I might go down here to the ballot-box to-morrow and vote directly for universal suffrage; but if a great majority of the people said no, I should consider it would be tyrannical in me to attempt to force such upon them without their will. It is a fundamental tenet in my creed that the will of the people must be obeyed. Is there anything wrong or unfair in that? . . .

It is the people of the States that must for themselves determine this thing. I do not want to be engaged in a work that will commence a war of races. I want to begin the work of preparation, and the States, or the people in each community, if a man demeans himself well, and shows evidence that this new state of affairs will operate, will protect him in all his rights and give him every possible advantage when they become reconciled socially and politically to this state of things. Then will this new order of things work harmoniously; but forced upon the people before they are prepared for it, it will be resisted, and work inharmoniously. I feel a conviction that driving this matter upon the people, upon the community, will result in the injury of both races, and the ruin of one or the other. God knows I have no desire but the good of the whole human race. I would it were so that all you advocate could be done in the twinkling of an eye; but it is not in the nature of things, and I do not assume or pretend to be wiser than Providence, or stronger than the laws of nature. . . .

3

The Joint Committee Reports on the Status of the Former States of the Confederacy (1866)

Unwilling to accept President Johnson's program of Reconstruction, Congress appointed a special Joint Committee in December 1865 to inquire into conditions in the former states of the Confederacy and report whether they were entitled to representation in Congress. Although the committee had an overwhelming Republican majority, it was not controlled by the Radicals. In fact, Senator William Pitt Fessenden of Maine, a leading moderate Republican and one of the most respected members of Congress, was named chairman. The committee heard extensive testimony before issuing its report six months later. Its report repudiated the state governments Johnson had established in the South, concluded that the excluded southern states were not entitled to representation in Congress until certain conditions were met, and affirmed that it was the responsibility of Congress, not the president, to specify what these conditions were.

A claim for the immediate admission of senators and representatives from the so-called Confederate States has been urged, which seems to your committee not to be founded either in reason or in law, and which cannot be passed without comment. Stated in a few words, it amounts to this: That inasmuch as the lately insurgent States had no legal right to separate themselves from the Union, they still retain their positions as States, and consequently the people thereof have a right to immediate representation in Congress without the imposition of any conditions whatever; and further, that until such admission Congress has no right to tax them for the support of the government. It has even been contended that until such admission all legislation affecting their interests is, if not unconstitutional, at least unjustifiable and oppressive.

It is believed by your committee that all these propositions are not only wholly untenable, but, if admitted, would tend to the destruction of the government.

It must not be forgotten that the people of these States, without justification or excuse, rose in insurrection against the United States. . . . Whether legally and constitutionally or not, they did, in fact, withdraw from the Union and made themselves subjects of another government of their own creation. And they only yielded when, after a long, bloody, and wasting war, they were compelled by utter exhaustion to lay down their arms; and this they did, not willingly, but declaring that they yielded because they could no longer resist, affording no evidence whatever of repentance for their crime, and expressing no regret, except that they had no longer the power to continue the desperate struggle.

. . . The war thus waged was a civil war of the greatest magnitude. The people waging it were necessarily subject to all the rules which, by the law of nations, control a contest of that character, and to all the legitimate consequences following it. One of those consequences was that, within the limits prescribed by humanity, the conquered rebels were at the mercy of the conquerors. That a government thus outraged had a most perfect right to exact indemnity for the injuries done, and security against the recurrence of such outrages in the future, would seem too clear for dispute. . . .

It is moreover contended . . . that, from the peculiar nature and character of our government, no such right on the part of the conqueror can exist; that from the moment when rebellion lays down its arms and actual hostilities cease, all political rights of rebellious communities are at once restored; that, because the people of a State of the Union were once an organized community within the Union, they necessarily so remain, and their right to be represented in Congress at any and all times, and to participate in the government of the country under all circumstances, admits of neither question nor dispute. If this is indeed true, then is the government of the United States powerless for its own protection, and flagrant rebellion, carried to the extreme of civil war, is a pastime which any State may play at, not only certain that it can lose nothing in any event, but may even be the gainer by defeat. If rebellion succeeds, it accomplishes its purpose and destroys the government. If it fails, the war has been barren of results, and the battle may be still fought out in the legislative halls of the country. Treason, defeated in the field, has only to take possession of Congress and the cabinet.

Your committee do not deem it either necessary or proper to discuss the question whether the late Confederate States are still States of this Union, or can ever be otherwise. Granting this profitless abstraction about which so many words have been wasted, it by no means follows that the people of those States may not place themselves in a condition to abrogate the powers and privileges incident to a State of the Union, and deprive themselves of all pretence of right to exercise those powers and enjoy those privileges. . . . It is more than idle, it is a mockery, to contend that a people who have thrown off their allegiance, destroyed the local government which bound their States to the Union as members thereof, defied its authority, re-

FROM Joint Committee on Reconstruction, 39th Cong., 1st sess., 1866, S. Rept. 112, pp. x–xxi.

fused to execute its laws, and abrogated every provision which gave them political rights within the Union, still retain, through all, the perfect and entire right to resume, at their own will and pleasure, all their privileges within the Union, and especially to participate in its government, and to control the conduct of its affairs. . . .

. . . It is the opinion of your committee—

I. That the States lately in rebellion were, at the close of the war, disorganized communities, without civil government, and without constitutions or other forms, by virtue of which political relations could legally exist between them and the federal government.

II. That Congress cannot be expected to recognize as valid the election of representatives from disorganized communities, which, from the very nature of the case, were unable to present their claim to representation under those established and recognized rules, the observance of which has been hitherto required.

III. That Congress would not be justified in admitting such communities to a participation in the government of the country without first providing such constitutional or other guarantees as will tend to secure the civil rights of all citizens of the republic; a just equality of representation; protection against claims founded in rebellion and crime; a temporary restoration of the right of suffrage to those who have not actively participated in the efforts to destroy the Union and overthrow the government, and the exclusion from positions of public trust of, at least, a portion of those whose crimes have proved them to be enemies to the Union, and unworthy of public confidence. . . .

We now propose to re-state, as briefly as possible, the general facts and principles applicable to all the States recently in rebellion:

First. The seats of the senators and representatives from the so-called Confederate States became vacant in the year 1861, during the second session of the thirty-sixth Congress, by the voluntary withdrawal of their incumbents, with the sanction and by direction of the legislatures or conventions of their respective States. This was done as a hostile act against the Constitution and government of the United States, with a declared intent to overthrow the same. . . . From the time these confederated States thus withdrew their representation in Congress and levied war against the United States, the great mass of their people became and were insurgents, rebels, traitors, and all of them assumed and occupied the political, legal, and practical relation of enemies of the United States. . . .

Second. The States thus confederated prosecuted their war against the United States to final arbitrament, and did not cease until all their armies were captured, their military power destroyed, their civil officers, State and confederate, taken prisoners or put to flight, every vestige of State and confederate government obliterated, their territory overrun and occupied by the federal armies, and their people reduced to the condition of enemies conquered in war, entitled only by public law to such rights, privileges, and conditions as might be vouchsafed by the conqueror. . . .

Third. Having voluntarily deprived themselves of representation in Congress for the criminal purpose of destroying the federal Union, and having reduced themselves, by the act of levying war, to the condition of public enemies, they have no right to complain of temporary exclusion from Congress; but, on the contrary, having voluntarily renounced the right to representation, and disqualified themselves by crime from participating in the government, the burden now rests upon them, before claiming to be reinstated in their former condition, to show that they are qualified to resume federal relations. In order to do this, they must prove that they have established, with the consent of the people, republican forms of government in harmony with the Constitution and laws of the United States, that all hostile purposes have ceased, and should give adequate guarantees against future treason and rebellion. . . .

Fourth. Having . . . forfeited all civil and political rights and privileges under the federal Constitution, they can only be restored thereto by the permission and authority of that constitutional power against which they rebelled and by which they were subdued.

Fifth. These rebellious enemies were conquered

by the people of the United States, acting through all the co-ordinate branches of the government, and not by the executive department alone. The powers of conqueror are not so vested in the President that he can fix and regulate the terms of settlement and confer congressional representation on conquered rebels and traitors. . . . The authority to restore rebels to political power in the federal government can be exercised only with the concurrence of all the departments in which political power is vested. . . .

Eighth. . . . No proof has been afforded to Congress of a constituency in any one of the so-called Confederate States, unless we except the State of Tennessee, qualified to elect senators and representatives in Congress. No State constitution, or amendment to a State constitution, has had the sanction of the people. All the so-called legislation of State conventions and legislatures has been had under military dictation. If the President may, at his will, and under his own authority, whether as military commander or chief executive, qualify

persons to appoint senators and elect representatives, and empower others to appoint and elect them, he thereby practically controls the organization of the legislative department. The constitutional form of government is thereby practically destroyed, and its powers absorbed in the Executive. . . .

Tenth. The conclusion of your committee therefore is, that the so-called Confederate States are not, at present, entitled to representation in the Congress of the United States; that, before allowing such representation, adequate security for future peace and safety should be required; that this can only be found in such changes of the organic law as shall determine the civil rights and privileges of all citizens in all parts of the republic, shall place representation on an equitable basis, shall fix a stigma upon treason, and protect the loyal people against future claims for the expenses incurred in support of rebellion and for manumitted slaves, together with an express grant of power in Congress to enforce those provisions.

4

Andrew Johnson Vetoes the Civil Rights Bill (1866)

Fearful of the extreme ideas of the Radicals, moderate Republicans hoped to reach an agreement with Andrew Johnson concerning a program of Reconstruction. In particular, they were reluctant to endorse black suffrage, especially in the North; they had no sympathy for land redistribution; and they were unwilling to accept a long-term military occupation of the South. At the same time, they did not want former Rebels to return to power in the South, and they believed some form of protection for the freedpeople was necessary. The moderates' terms for Reconstruction were spelled out in the Fourteenth Amendment, which Congress passed and sent to the states for ratification, and in two major pieces of legislation—a bill to extend the life of the Freedmen's Bureau and a civil rights bill that made African Americans United States citizens and guaranteed them basic civil rights.

Johnson's veto of the civil rights bill, following his earlier veto of the Freedmen's Bureau bill, signaled his unwillingness to make any concessions to the moderates and heralded the beginning of a much more serious confrontation between him and Republicans in Congress over Reconstruction. In his message vetoing the civil rights bill, Johnson condemned singling out any group in society for special protection and legislation, attacked the exclusion of the southern states from Congress, and insisted that these were matters for the states and not the federal government to decide. In rejecting the idea of extending citizenship and civil rights to African Americans, Johnson forcefully invoked racist arguments and appealed to racial prejudice in the nation.

Washington, D. C., March 27, 1866.

To the Senate of the United States:

I regret that the bill, which has passed both Houses of Congress, entitled "An act to protect all persons in the United States in their civil rights and furnish the means of their vindication," contains provisions which I can not approve consistently with my sense of duty to the whole people and my obligations to the Constitution of the United States. I am therefore constrained to return it to the Senate, the House in which it originated, with my objections to its becoming a law.

By the first section of the bill all persons born in the United States and not subject to any foreign power, excluding Indians not taxed, are declared to be citizens of the United States. This provision comprehends the Chinese of the Pacific States, Indians subject to taxation, the people called gypsies, as well as the entire race designated as blacks, people of color, negroes, mulattoes, and persons of African blood. Every individual of these races born in the United States is by the bill made a citizen of the United States. It does not purport to declare or confer any other right of citizenship than Federal citizenship. It does not purport to give these classes of persons any status as citizens of States, except that which may result from their status as citizens of the United States. The power to confer the right of State citizenship is just as exclusively with the

several States as the power to confer the right of Federal citizenship is with Congress.

The right of Federal citizenship thus to be conferred on the several excepted races before mentioned is now for the first time proposed to be given by law. If, as is claimed by many, all persons who are native born already are, by virtue of the Constitution, citizens of the United States, the passage of the pending bill can not be necessary to make them such. If, on the other hand, such persons are not citizens, as may be assumed from the proposed legislation to make them such, the grave question presents itself whether, when eleven of the thirty-six States are unrepresented in Congress at the present time, it is sound policy to make our entire colored population and all other excepted classes citizens of the United States. Four millions of them have just emerged from slavery into freedom. Can it be reasonably supposed that they possess the requisite qualifications to entitle them to all the privileges and immunities of citizens of the United States? . . . It may also be asked whether it is necessary that they should be declared citizens in order that they may be secured in the enjoyment of the civil rights proposed to be conferred by the bill. Those rights are, by Federal as well as State laws, secured to all domiciled aliens and foreigners, even before the completion of the process of naturalization; and it may safely be assumed that the same enactments are sufficient to give like protection and benefits to those for whom this bill provides special legislation. Besides, the policy of the Government from its origin to the present time seems to have been that persons who are strangers to and

FROM James D. Richardson, ed., *A Compilation of the Messages and Papers of the Presidents*, vol. 4 (Washington, D.C.: Government Printing Office, 1907), pp. 405–13.

unfamiliar with our institutions and our laws should pass through a certain probation, at the end of which, before attaining the coveted prize, they must give evidence of their fitness to receive and to exercise the rights of citizens as contemplated by the Constitution of the United States. The bill in effect proposes a discrimination against large numbers of intelligent, worthy, and patriotic foreigners, and in favor of the negro, to whom, after long years of bondage, the avenues to freedom and intelligence have just now been suddenly opened. . . .

The first section of the bill also contains an enumeration of the rights to be enjoyed by these classes so made citizens "in every State and Territory in the United States." These rights are "to make and enforce contracts; to sue, be parties, and give evidence; to inherit, purchase, lease, sell, hold, and convey real and personal property," and to have "full and equal benefit of all laws and proceedings for the security of person and property as is enjoyed by white citizens." So, too, they are made subject to the same punishment, pains, and penalties in common with white citizens, and to none other. Thus a perfect equality of the white and colored races is attempted to be fixed by Federal law in every State of the Union over the vast field of State jurisdiction covered by these enumerated rights. In no one of these can any State ever exercise any power of discrimination between the different races. In the exercise of State policy over matters exclusively affecting the people of each State it has frequently been thought expedient to discriminate between the two races. . . .

. . . Hitherto every subject embraced in the enumeration of rights contained in this bill has been considered as exclusively belonging to the States. They all relate to the internal police and economy of the respective States. They are matters which in each State concern the domestic condition of its people, varying in each according to its own peculiar circumstances and the safety and well-being of its own citizens. I do not mean to say that upon all these subjects there are not Federal restraints—as, for instance, in the State power of legislation over contracts there is a Federal limitation that no State shall pass a law impairing the

obligations of contracts; and, as to crimes, that no State shall pass an *ex post facto* law; and, as to money, that no State shall make anything but gold and silver a legal tender; but where can we find a Federal prohibition against the power of any State to discriminate, as do most of them, between aliens and citizens, between artificial persons, called corporations, and natural persons, in the right to hold real estate? If it be granted that Congress can repeal all State laws discriminating between whites and blacks in the subjects covered by this bill, why, it may be asked, may not Congress repeal in the same way all State laws discriminating between the two races on the subjects of suffrage and office? If Congress can declare by law who shall hold lands, who shall testify, who shall have capacity to make a contract in a State, then Congress can by law also declare who, without regard to color or race, shall have the right to sit as a juror or as a judge, to hold any office, and, finally, to vote "in every State and Territory of the United States." As respects the Territories, they come within the power of Congress, for as to them the lawmaking power is the Federal power; but as to the States no similar provision exists vesting in Congress the power "to make rules and regulations" for them.

The object of the second section of the bill is to afford discriminating protection to colored persons in the full enjoyment of all the rights secured to them by the preceding section. . . .

. . . This provision of the bill seems to be unnecessary, as adequate judicial remedies could be adopted to secure the desired end without invading the immunities of legislators, always important to be preserved in the interest of public liberty; without assailing the independence of the judiciary, always essential to the preservation of individual rights; and without impairing the efficiency of ministerial officers, always necessary for the maintenance of public peace and order. The remedy proposed by this section seems to be in this respect not only anomalous, but unconstitutional; for the Constitution guarantees nothing with certainty if it does not insure to the several States the right of making and executing laws in regard to all matters arising within their jurisdiction, subject only to the restriction that in cases of conflict with the Constitution and constitutional laws of the United States the latter should be held to be the supreme law of the land. . . .

The fourth section of the bill provides that officers and agents of the Freedmen's Bureau shall be empowered to make arrests, and also that other officers may be specially commissioned for that purpose by the President of the United States. It also authorizes circuit courts of the United States and the superior courts of the Territories to appoint, without limitation, commissioners, who are to be charged with the performance of *quasi* judicial duties. The fifth section empowers the commissioners so to be selected by the courts to appoint in writing, under their hands, one or more suitable persons from time to time to execute warrants and other processes described by the bill. These numerous official agents are made to constitute a sort of police, in addition to the military, and are authorized to summon a *posse comitatus*, and even to call to their aid such portion of the land and naval forces of the United States, or of the militia, "as may be necessary to the performance of the duty with which they are charged." This extraordinary power is to be conferred upon agents irresponsible to the Government and to the people, to whose number the discretion of the commissioners is the only limit, and in whose hands such authority might be made a terrible engine of wrong, oppression, and fraud. The general statutes regulating the land and naval forces of the United States, the militia, and the execution of the laws are believed to be adequate for every emergency which can occur in time of peace. . . .

In all our history, in all our experience as a people living under Federal and State law, no such system as that contemplated by the details of this bill has ever before been proposed or adopted. They establish for the security of the colored race safeguards which go infinitely beyond any that the General Government has ever provided for the white race. In fact, the distinction of race and color is by the bill made to operate in favor of the colored and against the white race. They interfere with the municipal legislation of the States, with the relations existing exclusively between a State and its citizens, or between inhabitants of the same State—an absorption and assumption of power by the General Government which, if acquiesced in, must sap and destroy our federative system of limited powers and break down the barriers which preserve the rights of the States. It is another step, or rather stride, toward centralization and the concentration of all legislative powers in the National Government. The tendency of the bill must be to resuscitate the spirit of rebellion and to arrest the progress of those influences which are more closely drawing around the States the bonds of union and peace. . . .

Andrew Johnson.

5

The *Chicago Tribune* Blames Johnson for the New Orleans Riot (1866)

The New Orleans riot in 1866, in which a number of white and black delegates to a convention in favor of black suffrage were killed by the police and white residents, was a serious political blow to Johnson and his program of Reconstruction. Northern public opinion was indignant over this violence and open defiance of national au-

thority, and Republicans quickly linked the riot to Johnson himself. A powerful example of this point of view was an editorial that appeared in the staunchly Republican Chicago Tribune *shortly after the riot.*

The publication of General Sheridan's despatches concerning the New Orleans massacre lifts the veil from a ghastly scene. The principal facts of the atrocity were known before, but they had not been communicated to the public under the seal of official authority. By suppressing a part and mutilating the remainder. Andrew Johnson had succeeded in giving a false coloring to the affair and in making General Sheridan responsible, in the eyes of the people, for the falsification. General Sheridan, as we are credibly informed, threatened to resign his command and commission, if he were thus compelled to bear false testimony concerning the foul tragedy, which had moved his soul with indignation. Thus it was that Andrew Johnson, who boasted a few days ago that no power on earth could move him from his position, trembled before the honest resentment of Phil. Sheridan, and hastened to publish the evidence of his own complicity with the massacre. Like other criminals, his first effort was to hide the evidence of his guilt. In so doing he incautiously tried to make the hero of Five Forks an accessory after the fact. In this he has failed most conspicuously and ignominiously. He stands forth as the direct instigator of the massacre, without whose agency and encouragement it would never have been committed. Blood is upon his hands, the blood of innocent, loyal citizens, who had committed no crime but that of seeking to protect themselves against the rebel misrule, which he, Andrew Johnson, had foisted upon them. Henceforth let no man, who abhors treason and assassination, take him by the hand. The "thugs" of the New Orleans police, whom General Sheridan denounces, are more respectable than Andrew Johnson, and more entitled to public esteem and confidence. They do the work they were chosen to perform. He, the President of the United States, sworn to see that the laws are faithfully executed, sets these hell-hounds on the loyal men of New Orleans, and then directs the military to aid "the civil authorities," as he is pleased to denominate them. . . .

. . . But now we come to an act of baseness unparalleled in the history of any country. Union men peaceably assembling in Convention having been murdered by the rebels of New Orleans—those murders not only having been *permitted* by the President, but the army having been directed to aid the assassins; the testimony furnished by General Sheridan's despatch placing the responsibility where it properly belonged, declaring that, the more information was obtained of the affair, the more revolting it became, that it was no riot, but was an absolute massacre by the police which was not exceeded in murderous cruelty by that of Fort Pillow, that it was a murder perpetrated by the Mayor and police of the city without the shadow of necessity, premeditated and prearranged; it became necessary that the chief malefactor should relieve himself of this weight of evidence against him, and that new evidence should be manufactured to his purpose. Accordingly, on the 4th day of August, the day after Sheridan had telegraphed Grant, Andrew Johnson forwards to General Sheridan a series of leading questions, indicating the nature and kind of answers which he desires, amounting, to all intents and purposes, to an *order* to Sheridan that they be answered in the manner indicated. He says, first:

> "We have been apprised here that prior to the assembling of the illegal and unauthorized Convention elected in 1864, inflammatory, insurrectionary speeches were made to a mob composed of white and colored persons, urging on them to arm and equip themselves for protecting and sustaining the Convention in its illegal and unauthorized proceedings."

Who apprised Andrew Johnson of these facts? The rebels Herron and Voorhees. Who authorized

FROM *Chicago Tribune*, 27 August 1866.

Andrew Johnson to declare that the Convention was illegal and unauthorized and to stigmatise its members as a mob? The rebels Voorhees and Munroe. This was Andrew Johnson's authority, and upon it he acted. After laying down this platform, he proceeds to interrogate General Sheridan in this fashion, "Did the mob assemble, and was it raised for the purpose of assisting the Convention in its *usurpation.*" General Sheridan had already sufficiently given his views of the Convention and its friends. Neither of them were a mob in his estimation, but his superior declares by the wording of his interrogatories that the friends of the Convention were a mob, and that the Convention itself contemplated usurpation. He says by plain implication, "I order you to answer accordingly." He proceeds, and there is an impudence of manner and a base criminality and savagery in the question almost incredible, "*Have various individuals been shot and killed by* THIS MOB without good cause, and in violation of the public peace and good order?" The mob to which he refers was the Convention and its friends. The individuals were the police and city authorities whom Sheridan had denounced as murderers. But General Sheridan must change his views and answer the question, not according to the facts, but in harmony with the wishes of his superior. Observe, that no information is asked, whether Union men had been unneccessarily slaughtered. To these facts, to the existence of which, evidence abundant was before him, he paid no heed, and concerning them he had no care, but his anxiety was to protect the murderers whom his own hands had armed and to hide the murders that his own orders had instigated. He asks also whether steps had been taken by the civil authorities, whom Sheridan the day before had stigmatized as murderers, to arrest and try all those engaged in this riot, which Sheridan had already advised him was not a riot but a massacre. . . . Endeavoring thus to distort the facts and belie history, and being baffled in the attempt, he suppressed the despatch of General Sheridan, and awaited an answer to his own. The nation has reason to be thankful that in General Sheridan the apostate had no weak-kneed, illy-livered postmaster to deal with. General Sheridan had fought treason before, and he knew how to deal with it. Instead of answering the President's questions in the terms indicated by the latter, he proceeded to give a plain, unvarnished narrative of the whole tragedy, putting the guilt upon the head of the Mayor, and inferentially upon that of Andrew Johnson himself, who had allowed this notorious villain to assume the duties of office.

Mr. Johnson is coming to Chicago with this blood of loyal men upon his garments. We advise loyal citizens to avoid him as they would any other convicted criminal. Let those who approve of the New Orleans massacre run after him and hurrah for him. Let all others favor him with silence and yield him room.

6 Oliver P. Morton Waves the Bloody Shirt (1866)

In order to maintain their political power, Republican leaders in the years after the war routinely linked the Democratic party with treason and rebellion. In doing so, party spokesmen sought to keep the memory and hatreds of the Civil War alive as a means to win popular support. This tactic, known as "waving the bloody shirt," downplayed the issues of Reconstruction and appealed to voters to support the Republican party as the party of loyalty and the Union. A particularly powerful exam-

ple of this tactic is an 1866 speech delivered by Oliver P. Morton, Indiana's wartime governor. Originally a Republican moderate who opposed black suffrage, Morton adopted a more radical outlook on Reconstruction after Johnson refused to reach any accommodation with Congress.

The war is over, the rebellion has been suppressed, the victory has been won, and now the question is presented to us at the coming election, whether the fruits of victory shall be preserved or lost.

It is beyond doubt that the temper of the Democratic party is not changed or improved since the termination of the war, but, on the contrary, it seems to have been greatly embittered by defeat in the field and at the ballot-box. Its sympathy with those who were lately in arms against the government is more boldly avowed than ever, and it becomes argumentative and enthusiastic in behalf of the right of secession and the righteousness of the rebellion. . . .

The leaders, who are now managing the Democratic party in this state, are the men who, at the regular session of the legislature in 1861, declared that if an army went from Indiana to assist in putting down the then approaching rebellion it must first pass over their dead bodies.

They are the men who, in speeches and resolutions, proclaimed that "Southern defeats gave them no joy, and Northern disasters no sorrow." They are the men who exerted their influence to prevent their Democratic friends from going into the army, and who, by their incessant and venomous slanders against the government, checked the spirit of volunteering, and made drafting a necessity. . . .

They are the men who corresponded with the rebel leaders in the South, giving them full information of our condition, and assuring them that a revolution in public opinion was at hand, and that they had but to persevere a few months longer and the national government would fall to pieces of its own weight. . . .

FROM William Dudley Foulke, *Life of Oliver P. Morton*, vol. 1 (Indianapolis: Bowen-Merrill, 1899), pp. 470–76.

They are the men who declared in speeches and resolutions, and by their votes in Congress, that not another man nor another dollar should be voted to carry on a cruel war against their Southern brethren.

They are the men who, in the midst of the last great campaign of 1864—at the time when Sherman was fighting his way, step by step, from Chattanooga to Atlanta, and Grant was forcing Lee back into the defenses of Richmond in desperate and bloody battles from day to day; when the fate of the nation hung in the balance, and the world watched with breathless interest the gigantic struggle which was to settle the question of republican government—assembled in convention in Chicago and resolved that the war was a failure; that our cause was unjust, and that we ought to lay down our arms and sue for peace. . . .

Now, I do not mean to say that all the Democratic leaders have done all these things, but what I do say is this: that the men who have done these things are combined together, and constitute the real leaders of the Democratic party. . . .

Every unregenerate rebel lately in arms against his government calls himself a Democrat.

Every bounty jumper, every deserter, every sneak who ran away from the draft calls himself a Democrat. . . . Every "Son of Liberty" who conspired to murder, burn, rob arsenals and release rebel prisoners calls himself a Democrat. . . . Every man who labored for the rebellion in the field, who murdered Union prisoners by cruelty and starvation, who conspired to bring about civil war in the loyal states, who invented dangerous compounds to burn steamboats and Northern cities, who contrived hellish schemes to introduce into Northern cities the wasting pestilence of yellow fever, calls himself a Democrat. Every dishonest contractor who has been convicted of defrauding the government, every dishonest paymaster or disbursing officer who has been convicted of squandering the public money at the gaming table or in gold gambling operations, every officer in the army who was dismissed for cowardice or disloyalty, calls himself a Democrat. Every wolf in sheep's clothing, who pretends to preach the gospel but proclaims the righteousness of man-selling and slavery; every one who shoots down negroes in the streets, burns negro school-houses and meeting-houses, and murders women and children by the light of their own flaming dwellings, calls himself a Democrat; every New York rioter in 1863 who burned up little children in colored asylums, who robbed, ravished and murdered indiscriminately in the midst of a blazing city for three days and nights, called himself a Democrat. In short, the Democratic party may be described as a common sewer and loathsome receptacle, into which is emptied every element of treason North and South, and every element of inhumanity and barbarism which has dishonored the age.

7

ANDREW JOHNSON

I Am Fighting Traitors in the North (1866)

While Americans have traditionally displayed considerable tolerance for presidential ineffectiveness, they have been far more insistent that presidents uphold the dignity of the office. Few presidents have undermined the prestige of the office more than did Andrew Johnson. In the fall of 1866, Johnson embarked on his famous "swing around the circle" to rally popular support for his policies. In a series of speeches he delivered to northern audiences, Johnson behaved like he was on the stump back home in Tennessee, exchanging insults with hecklers and harshly assailing his critics. In the following address delivered in Cleveland on September 3, 1866, the president termed several prominent radicals traitors and accused them of seeking to destroy the government, and he tastelessly sought sympathy by wrapping himself in the mantle of a martyr. The speech is a good example of the vehemence with which Johnson expressed his views and attacked his enemies, qualities that only exacerbated his political difficulties. His behavior undermined the dignity of his office and subjected him to public ridicule, and even the president's supporters considered his campaign swing unfortunate.

I appear before you to-night and I want to say this: that I have lived and been among all American people, and have represented them in some capacity for the last twenty-five years. And where is the man living, or the woman in the community,

FROM Walter L. Fleming, ed., *Documentary History of Reconstruction*, vol. 1 (Cleveland: Arthur H. Clark Co., 1906–1907), pp. 220–26.

that I have wronged, or where is the person that can place their finger upon one single hairbreadth of deviation from one single pledge I have made, or one single violation of the Constitution of our country? What tongue does he speak? What religion does he profess? Let him come forward and place his finger upon one pledge I have violated. [A voice, "Hang Jeff Davis."] [Mr. President resumes.] Hang Jeff Davis? Hang Jeff Davis? Why don't you? [Applause.] Why don't you? [Applause.] Have you not got the court? Have you not got the court? Have you not got the Attorney General? Who is your Chief Justice, and that refused to sit upon the trial? [Applause.] I am not the prosecuting attorney. I am not the jury. But I will tell you what I did do; I called your Congress that is trying to break up the government. [Immense applause.] Yes, did your Congress order hanging Jeff Davis? [Prolonged applause, mingled with hisses].

But, fellow-citizens, we had as well let feelings and prejudices pass; let passion subside; let reason resume her empire. In representing myself to you in the few remarks I intended to make, my intention was to address myself to your judgment and to your good sense, and not to your anger or the malignity of your hearts. . . . I have heard the remark made in this crowd to-night, "Traitor, traitor!" [Prolonged confusion.] My countrymen, will you hear me for my cause? For the Constitution of my country? I want to know when, where and under what circumstances Andrew Johnson, either as Chief Executive, or in any other capacity, ever violated the Constitution of his country. . . . I would ask why Jeff Davis was not hung? Why don't you hang Thad. Stevens and Wendell Phillips? I can tell you, my countrymen, I have been fighting traitors in the south, [prolonged applause,] and they have been whipped, and say they were wrong, acknowledge their error and accept the terms of the Constitution.

And now as I pass around the circle, having fought traitors at the south, I am prepared to fight traitors at the north, God being willing with your help ["You can't have it," and prolonged confusion] they would be crushed worse than the traitors of the south, and this glorious Union of ours will be preserved. In coming here to-night, it was not coming as Chief Magistrate of twenty-five States, but I come here as the Chief Magistrate of thirty-six States. I came here to-night with the flag of my country in my hand, with a constellation of thirty-six and not twenty-five stars. I came here to-night with the Constitution of my country intact, determined to defend the Constitution let the consequences be what they may. I came here to-night

for the Union; the entire circle of these States. [A voice, "How many States made you President?"] How many States made me President? Was you against secession? Do you want to dissolve the Union? [A voice, "No."] Then I am President of the whole United States, and I will tell you one thing. I understand the discordant notes in this audience here to-night. And I will tell you, furthermore, that he that is opposed to the restoration of the government and the Union of the States, is as great a traitor as Jeff. Davis, and I am against both of them. I fought traitors at the south; now I fight them at the north. [Immense applause.]

I will tell you another thing; I know all about those boys that have fought for their country. I have been with them down there when cities were besieged. I know who was with them when some of you, that talk about traitors, had not courage to come out of your closets, but persuaded somebody else to go.

Very courageous men! While Grant, Sherman, Farragut, and a long host of the distinguished sons of the United States were in the field of battle you were cowards at home; and now when these brave men have returned, many of them having left an arm or leg on some battle-field while you were at home speculating and committing frauds upon your government, you pretend now to have great respect and sympathy for the poor fellow who left his arm on the battle-field. . . . I know who have fought the battles of the country, and I know who is to pay for it. Those brave men shed their blood and you speculated, got money, and now the great mass of the people must work it out. [Applause and confusion.] I care not for your prejudices. It is time for the great mass of the American people to understand what your designs are in not admitting the Southern States when they have come to terms and even proposed to pay their part of the national debt. . . .

But fellow-citizens, let this all pass. I care not for malignity. There is a certain portion of our countrymen that will respect their fellow-citizen whenever he is entitled to respect, and there is another portion that have no respect for themselves, and consequently have none for anybody else. I know a gentleman when I see him. And further-more, I know when I look a man in the face—[Voice, "Which you can't do."] I wish I could see you; I will bet now, if there could be a light re-flected upon your face, that cowardice and treach-ery could be seen in it. Show yourself. Come out here where we can see you. If ever you shoot a man, you will stand in the dark and pull your trig-ger. . . . And those men—such a one as insulted me to-night—you may say, has ceased to be a man, and in ceasing to be a man shrunk into the denom-ination of a reptile, and having so shrunken, as an honest man, I tread upon him. I came here to-night not to criminate or recriminate, but when provoked my nature is not to advance but to de-fend, and when encroached upon, I care not from what quarter it comes, it will find resistance, and resistance at the threshold. . . .

And let me say to-night that my head has been threatened. It has been said that my blood was to be shed. Let me say to those who are still willing to sacrifice my life [derisive laughter and cheers], if you want a victim and my country requires it, erect your altar, and the individual who addresses you tonight, while here a visitor ["No," "No," and laughter,] erect your altar if you still thirst for blood, and if you want it, take out the individual who now addresses you and lay him upon your al-tar, and the blood that now courses his veins and warms his existence shall be poured out as a last li-bation to Freedom. I love my country, and I defy any man to put his finger upon anything to the contrary. Then what is my offence? [Voices, "You ain't a radical," "New Orleans," "Veto."] . . .

Now [clamor and confusion] I never feared clamor. I have never been afraid of the people, for by them I have always been sustained. And when I have all the truth, argument, fact and reason on my side, clamor nor affront, nor animosities can drive me from my purpose. . . .

Then farewell! The little ill-feelings aroused here to-night—for some men have felt a little ill—let us not cherish them. . . . [A voice, "What about New Orleans?"] You complain of the disfranchise-ment of the negroes in the southern States, while you would not give them the right of suffrage in Ohio to-day. Let your negroes vote in Ohio before you talk about negroes voting. Take the beam out of your own eye before you see the mote in your neighbor's eye. You are very much disturbed about New Orleans; but you will not allow the negro to vote in Ohio.

8

NEW YORK TIMES

The People's Verdict (1866)

The clash between Andrew Johnson and the Republicans in Congress led both sides to take their case to the voters in the 1866 northern state and congressional elections. Hoping for a popular endorsement, Johnson made a speaking tour in the fall of 1866 in which he bitterly assailed prominent Republican leaders. Republicans responded in kind, attacking the president personally and questioning his loyalty. The result was a resounding Republican victory and thoroughgoing repudiation of Johnson and his policies. In the following editorial, the Republican New York Times, *which had earlier promoted a moderate program of Reconstruction, hailed the results of the northern elections.*

The verdict pronounced by the people of four States is merely the fullfilment of an expectation entertained by every man who has watched honestly the temper and purposes of the country. The boasting of the Democratic Press during the progress of the canvass has not misled anybody. . . . The party statistician will deem it his duty to ponder every return—to compare the figures of this year with the figures of other years, and to study the causes of every change. The people, however, have little relish for these fine-drawn distinctions. Gains or losses here or there matter comparatively little to them. They have no taste for the casuistry that would convert defeat into victory, or for the philosophy that would suck consolation out of irretrievable disaster. The general result is all that concerns them. They know that Pennsylvania, which has been the theatre of one of the hottest contests ever known, has rejected the overtures of the Democracy, and has planted itself more firmly than ever on the side of the party represented by Congress. They know that Ohio and Indiana have contributed their quota toward the maintenance of Republican supremacy, and that Iowa has not wavered in the faith which made her Congressional delegation an unit in support of the Union Party. All else is, in the popular judgment, a matter of indifference. For it concludes, rightly and reasonably, that the impulses and convictions which on Tuesday impelled four States to follow the lead of Maine and Vermont, will as surely determine the contest in New York, and in the States which have yet to pass judgment on the issues before them.

The one great result which has now been reached is the ratification by the people of the position assumed by Congress in relation to the President and the South. This has been the test to which every candidate, every platform, has been subjected. Shall the President be sustained in his plan for restoring the Union by the immediate admission of the Southern States to the Capitol? Or shall the recommendations of the President be repudiated, and the action of Congress endorsed? The question may have been more or less modified in particular localities, . . . but as a rule this has been its shape—the President or Congress? The immediate admission of the South, or the exaction of preliminary conditions, embodied in the Constitutional Amendment? And the answer leaves room neither for equivocation nor doubt. It is overwhelmingly against the President—clearly, unmistakably, decisively in favor of Congress and its policy.

Seldom, indeed, has a contest been conducted with so exclusive reference to a single issue. True, the antecedents of candidates during the war have had much to do with the question of individual eligibility. . . . But, after all, there have been few of the considerations which in ordinary times have entered into party controversy. The tariff, internal improvements, the currency, the foreign relations of the Government, have been discussed only incidentally. Everywhere the conditions of national unity and peace have formed the theme of debate and the standard by which party nominations have been weighed and judged. Minor questions, therefore, cannot be pleaded in abatement of the account as it now stands. It is a settlement which can be altered only to be made more stringent. It is a declaration of the popular determination to exact from the South guarantees for the maintenance of the Union as the war has made it, a Union assuring national citizenship to black and white, assuring equality before the law, the just representation of the sections, and the inviolability of the loyal debt, and providing effectually against the future assumption of the rebel debts or claims. This is the sum and substance of Tuesday's verdict. Not negro suffrage—not confiscation—not harsh or vindictive penalties; but the plan of restoration dictated by Congress, and designed to be a final adjustment of our national difficulties.

It is too late to say that the popular verdict hardly comes up to the rigid constitutional standard. It would avail nothing now to argue that the [proposed Fourteenth] Amendment, equitable and moderate though it be, ought not to be a condition of restoration. Equally useless were it to consider by what possible combinations and compromises

FROM *New York Times*, 11 October 1866.

the view for which we have contended might have acquired greater prominence and support. The people have been heard from, and from their decision our form of government provides no appeal. The South, if wise, will hearken and comply. And the President, if politic, will not refuse to listen to a verdict which specially concerns himself and the plan to which he is committed.

At least one source of apprehension has been removed. Had these elections ended adversely to Congress—had promises been held out of any considerable change in the complexion of that body—the idea of a second House, with the Southern representatives unconditionally admitted, might possibly have assumed dangerous dimensions. The proposition that a second Congress should be organized, and that the President should recognize the one favorable to his plan, might then have been more plausible. Fortunately this beginning of revolution has been obviated. Not the faintest pretext can now be found for impugning the validity of the Congressional decision, or for mooting the legitimacy of any other body. The

people have taken care that this threatened peril shall not be heard of more. They have decreed, not only that Congress as it now is, faithfully represents their convictions and purposes, but that the Congress which will come after shall sustain substantially the same policy. Neither the South nor the President, then, has aught to expect from delay. The South must choose between prolonged exclusion, with the probability of more stringent terms, and the acceptance of the overture already submitted to them. The President must be content to see Congress push forward its new method of settlement, despite protestations and vetoes, or must frankly accept the verdict pronounced by the people who elected him, and use his opportunities to hasten restoration on the only basis that is practicable. He has stated his own case, and the people have refused to accept it. The part of statesmanship surely is to concede graciously and promptly to the popular requirements, and to exert the influence of the Executive in support of the compromise now tendered to the Southern States.

1 Thaddeus Stevens's Land Confiscation Bill (1867)

Thaddeus Stevens was one of the most radical members of Congress when it came to the issue of racial equality. He also seethed with a hatred of Rebels and a desire to humiliate disloyal southern whites and especially the leaders of the Confederacy. Yet Stevens was also one of the few members of Congress who approached Reconstruction on its broadest terms. For Stevens, political and legal reform in the South was insufficient unless accompanied by fundamental social and economic change. As such, he was one of the leading advocates of redistributing land to former slaves as part of Reconstruction. In devising a program of Reconstruction, however, Congress rejected all proposals for confiscation and land reform, including the bill Stevens introduced for this purpose.

Whereas it is due to justice, as an example to future times, that some proper punishment should be inflicted on the people who constituted the "confederate States of America," both because they, declaring an unjust war against the United States for the purpose of destroying republican liberty and permanently establishing slavery, as well as for the cruel and barbarous manner in which they conducted said war, in violation of all the laws of civilized warfare, and also to compel them to make some compensation for the damages and expenditures caused by said war: Therefore,

Be it enacted by the Senate and House of Representatives of the United States of America in Congress assembled, That all the public lands belonging to the ten States that formed the government of the so-called "confederate States of America" shall be forfeited by said States and become forthwith vested in the United States.[1] . . .

That out of the lands thus seized and confiscated the slaves who have been liberated by the operations of the war and the amendment to the Constitution or otherwise, who resided in said "confederate States" on the 4th day of March, A.D. 1861, or since, shall have distributed to them as follows, namely: to each male person who is the head of a family, forty acres; to each adult male, whether the head of a family or not, forty acres; to each widow who is the head of a family, forty acres—to be held by them in fee-simple, but to be inalienable for the next ten years after they become seized thereof. . . .

That out of the balance of the property thus seized and confiscated there shall be raised, in the manner hereinafter provided, a sum equal to fifty dollars, for each homestead, to be applied by the trustees hereinafter mentioned toward the erection of buildings on the said homesteads for the use of said slaves; and the further sum of $500,000,000, which shall be appropriated as follows, to wit: $200,000,000 shall be invested in United States six per cent securities; and the interest thereof shall be semi-annually added to the pensions allowed by

[1]This proposed law did not apply to Tennessee, which had been readmitted to the Union in 1866.

FROM *Congressional Globe,* 40th Cong., 1st sess., March 19, 1867, p. 203.

law to pensioners who have become so by reason of the late war; $300,000,000, or so much thereof as may be needed, shall be appropriated to pay damages done to loyal citizens by the civil or military operations of the government lately called the "confederate States of America." . . .

That in order that just discrimination may be made, the property of no one shall be seized whose whole estate on the 4th day of March, A.D. 1865, was not worth more than $5,000, to be valued by the said commission, unless he shall have voluntarily become an officer or employé in the military or civil service of the "confederate States of America," or in the civil or military service of some one of said States. . . .

2

Andrew Johnson Accuses Congress of Seeking to Africanize the South (1867)

For Andrew Johnson the issue of race always was at the heart of the struggle with Congress over Reconstruction. His unwillingness to make any adjustments in his own program, which northern public opinion deemed a failure, led Congress to enact its own program of Reconstruction. In 1867 Congress approved a series of bills over his vetoes and put a new Reconstruction policy in place in the South. In his message to Congress on December 3, 1867, Johnson summarized his various objections—political, constitutional, and racial—to Congress's program of Reconstruction. This message reiterated in more condensed form many of the arguments Johnson advanced in his many messages vetoing Congressional legislation concerning Reconstruction. Notice in this message how Johnson's constitutional arguments eventually merged with his strong racial prejudice.

Washington, December 3, 1867.

Fellow-Citizens of the Senate and House of Representatives:

. . . When a civil war has been brought to a close, it is manifestly the first interest and duty of the state to repair the injuries which the war has inflicted, and to secure the benefit of the lessons it teaches as fully and as speedily as possible. This duty was, upon the termination of the rebellion, promptly accepted, not only by the executive department, but by the insurrectionary States themselves, and restoration in the first moment of peace was believed to be as easy and certain as it was indispensable. The expectations, however, then so reasonably and confidently entertained were disappointed by legislation from which I felt constrained by my obligations to the Constitution to withhold my assent.

It is therefore a source of profound regret that in complying with the obligation imposed upon the President by the Constitution to give to Congress from time to time information of the state of the Union I am unable to communicate any definitive adjustment, satisfactory to the American people, of the questions which since the close of the

FROM James D. Richardson, ed. *A Compilation of the Messages and Papers of the Presidents*, vol. 4 (Washington, D.C.: Government Printing Office, 1907) pp. 558–66.

rebellion have agitated the public mind. On the contrary, candor compels me to declare that at this time there is no Union as our fathers understood the term, and as they meant it to be understood by us. The Union which they established can exist only where all the States are represented in both Houses of Congress; where one State is as free as another to regulate its internal concerns according to its own will, and where the laws of the central Government, strictly confined to matters of national jurisdiction, apply with equal force to all the people of every section. That such is not the present "state of the Union" is a melancholy fact, and we must all acknowledge that the restoration of the States to their proper legal relations with the Federal Government and with one another, according to the terms of the original compact, would be the greatest temporal blessing which God, in His kindest providence, could bestow upon this nation. It becomes our imperative duty to consider whether or not it is impossible to effect this most desirable consummation. . . .

To me the process of restoration seems perfectly plain and simple. It consists merely in a faithful application of the Constitution and laws. The execution of the laws is not now obstructed or opposed by physical force. There is no military or other necessity, real or pretended, which can prevent obedience to the Constitution, either North or South. All the rights and all the obligations of States and individuals can be protected and enforced by means perfectly consistent with the fundamental law. The courts may be everywhere open, and if open their process would be unimpeded. Crimes against the United States can be prevented or punished by the proper judicial authorities in a manner entirely practicable and legal. There is therefore no reason why the Constitution should not be obeyed, unless those who exercise its powers have determined that it shall be disregarded and violated. The mere naked will of this Government, or of some one or more of its branches, is the only obstacle that can exist to a perfect union of all the States. . . .

It is clear to my apprehension that the States lately in rebellion are still members of the National Union. When did they cease to be so? The "ordinances of secession" adopted by a portion (in most of them a very small portion) of their citizens were mere nullities. If we admit now that they were valid and effectual for the purpose intended by their authors, we sweep from under our feet the whole ground upon which we justified the war. Were those States afterwards expelled from the Union by the war? The direct contrary was averred by this Government to be its purpose, and was so understood by all those who gave their blood and treasure to aid in its prosecution. It can not be that a successful war, waged for the preservation of the Union, had the legal effect of dissolving it. The victory of the nation's arms was not the disgrace of her policy; the defeat of secession on the battlefield was not the triumph of its lawless principle. Nor could Congress, with or without the consent of the Executive, do anything which would have the effect, directly or indirectly, of separating the States from each other. To dissolve the Union is to repeal the Constitution which holds it together, and that is a power which does not belong to any department of this Government, or to all of them united. . . .

Being sincerely convinced that these views are correct, I would be unfaithful to my duty if I did not recommend the repeal of the acts of Congress which place ten of the Southern States under the domination of military masters. If calm reflection shall satisfy a majority of your honorable bodies that the acts referred to are not only a violation of the national faith, but in direct conflict with the Constitution, I dare not permit myself to doubt that you will immediately strike them from the statute book.

To demonstrate the unconstitutional character of those acts I need do no more than refer to their general provisions. It must be seen at once that they are not authorized. To dictate what alterations shall be made in the constitutions of the several States; to control the elections of State legislators and State officers, members of Congress and electors of President and Vice-President, by arbitrarily declaring who shall vote and who shall be excluded from that privilege; to dissolve State legislatures or prevent them from assembling; to dismiss judges and other civil functionaries of the State and appoint others without regard to State law; to organize and operate all the political machinery of the States; to regulate the whole administration of their domestic and local affairs according to the mere will of strange and irresponsible agents, sent among them for that purpose—these are powers not granted to the Federal Government or to any one of its branches. . . .

The acts of Congress in question are not only objectionable for their assumption of ungranted power, but many of their provisions are in conflict with the direct prohibitions of the Constitution. The Constitution commands that a republican form of government shall be guaranteed to all the States; that no person shall be deprived of life, liberty, or property without due process of law, arrested without a judicial warrant, or punished without a fair trial before an impartial jury; that the privilege of *habeas corpus* shall not be denied in time of peace, and that no bill of attainder shall be passed even against a single individual. Yet the system of measures established by these acts of Congress does totally subvert and destroy the form as well as the substance of republican government in the ten States to which they apply. It binds them hand and foot in absolute slavery, and subjects them to a strange and hostile power, more unlimited and more likely to be abused than any other now known among civilized men. It tramples down all those rights in which the essence of liberty consists, and which a free government is always most careful to protect. It denies the *habeas corpus* and the trial by jury. Personal freedom, property, and life, if assailed by the passion, the prejudice, or the rapacity of the ruler, have no security whatever. . . .

It is manifestly and avowedly the object of these laws to confer upon negroes the privilege of voting and to disfranchise such a number of white citizens as will give the former a clear majority at all elections in the Southern States. This, to the minds of some persons, is so important that a violation of the Constitution is justified as a means of bringing it about. The morality is always false which excuses a wrong because it proposes to accomplish a desirable end. We are not permitted to do evil that good may come.

But in this case the end itself is evil, as well as the means. The subjugation of the States to negro domination would be worse than the military despotism under which they are now suffering. It was believed beforehand that the people would endure any amount of military oppression for any length of time rather than degrade themselves by subjection to the negro race. Therefore they have been left without a choice. Negro suffrage was established by act of Congress, and the military officers were commanded to superintend the process of clothing the negro race with the political privileges torn from white men. . . .

The plan of putting the Southern States wholly and the General Government partially into the hands of negroes is proposed at a time peculiarly unpropitious. The foundations of society have been broken up by civil war. Industry must be reorganized, justice reestablished, public credit maintained, and order brought out of confusion. To accomplish these ends would require all the wisdom and virtue of the great men who formed our institutions originally. I confidently believe that their descendants will be equal to the arduous task before them, but it is worse than madness to expect that negroes will perform it for us. Certainly we ought not to ask their assistance till we despair of our own competency.

The great difference between the two races in physical, mental, and moral characteristics will prevent an amalgamation or fusion of them together in one homogeneous mass. If the inferior obtains the ascendency over the other, it will govern with reference only to its own interests—for it will recognize no common interest—and create such a tyranny as this continent has never yet witnessed. Already the negroes are influenced by promises of confiscation and plunder. They are taught to regard as an enemy every white man who has any respect for the rights of his own race. If this continues it must become worse and worse, until all order will be subverted, all industry cease, and the fertile fields of the South grow up into a wilderness. Of all the dangers which our nation has yet encountered, none are equal to those which must result from the success of the effort now making to Africanize the half of our country.

The Articles of Impeachment (1868)

As the confrontation between Andrew Johnson and Congress over Reconstruction intensified, a number of Radicals urged that the president be impeached. The House resisted these calls until Johnson ignored the Tenure of Office Act and tried to remove Secretary of War Edwin Stanton without the Senate's consent. When they learned of Johnson's action, angry House members quickly voted articles of impeachment against the president. The committee charged with drafting the articles of impeachment largely focused on Johnson's violation of the Tenure of Office Act; indeed nine of the eleven articles dealt with this alleged offense. United in their desire to remove Johnson from office, House Republicans could not agree on whether to create a narrow, legalistic case or a broader one emphasizing political offenses.

[March 2–3, 1868]

Articles exhibited by the House of Representatives of the United States, in the name of themselves and all of the people of the United States, against Andrew Johnson, President of the United States, in maintenance and support of their impeachment against him for high crimes and misdemeanors in office.

Article I

That said Andrew Johnson, President of the United States, on [February 21, 1868], at Washington, in the District of Columbia, unmindful of the high duties of his office, of his oath of office, and of the requirement of the Constitution that he should take care that the laws be faithfully executed, did unlawfully, and in violation of the Constitution and laws of the United States issue an order in writing for the removal of Edwin M. Stanton from the office of Secretary for the Department of War, said Edwin M. Stanton having been theretofore duly appointed and commissioned by and with the advice and consent of the Senate of

the United States, as such Secretary. . . . Which order was unlawfully issued with intent then and there to violate the act entitled "An act regulating the tenure of certain civil offices," passed March second, eighteen hundred and sixty-seven, and with the further intent, contrary to the provisions of said act, in violation thereof, and contrary to the provisions of the Constitution of the United States, and without the advice and consent of the Senate of the United States, the said Senate then and there being in session, to remove Edwin M. Stanton from the office of Secretary for the Department of War, the said Edwin M. Stanton being then and there Secretary for the Department of War, and being then and there in the due and lawful execution and discharge of the duties of said office, whereby said Andrew Johnson, President of the United States, did then and there commit and was guilty of a high misdemeanor in office. . . .

Article IX

That said Andrew Johnson . . . [on February 22, 1868] . . . at Washington, in the District of Columbia, in disregard of the Constitution and the laws of the United States duly enacted, as commander-in-chief of the army of the United States, did bring before himself then and there

FROM Walter L. Fleming, ed., *Documentary History of Reconstruction*, vol. 1 (Cleveland: Arthur H. Clark Co., 1906–1907), pp. 458–70.

William H. Emory, a major general by brevet in the army of the United States, actually in command of the department of Washington and the military forces thereof, and did then and there as such commander-in-chief, declare to and instruct said Emory that part of a law of the United States, passed March second, eighteen hundred and sixty-seven, entitled "An act making appropriations for the support of the army for the year ending June thirtieth, eighteen hundred and sixty-eight, and for other purposes," especially the second section thereof, which provides, among other things, that "all orders and instructions relating to military operations, issued by the President or Secretary of War, shall be issued through the General of the army, and in case of inability, through the next in rank," was unconstitutional, and in contravention of the commission of said Emory, and which said provision of law had been therefore duly and legally promulgated by General Orders for the government and direction of the army of the United States, as the said Andrew Johnson then and there well knew, with intent thereby to induce said Emory, in his official capacity as commander of the department of Washington, to violate the provisions of said act, and to take and receive, act upon, and obey such orders as he, the said Andrew Johnson, might make and give, and which should not be issued through the General of the army of the United States, according to the provisions of said act, and with the further intent thereby to enable him, the said Andrew Johnson, to prevent the execution of the [Tenure of Office Act] . . . and to unlawfully prevent Edwin M. Stanton, then being Secretary for the Department of War, from holding said office and discharging the duties thereof, whereby said Andrew Johnson, President of the United States, did then and there commit and was guilty of a high misdemeanor in office.

And the house of Representatives, by protestation, saving to themselves the liberty of exhibiting at any time hereafter any further articles, or other accusation or impeachment against the said Andrew Johnson, President of the United States, and also of replying to his answers which he shall make unto the articles herein preferred against him, and

of offering proof to the same, and every part thereof, and to every other article, accusation, or impeachment which shall be exhibited by them, as the case shall require, DO DEMAND that the said Andrew Johnson may be put to answer the high crimes and misdemeanors in office herein charged against him, and that such proceedings, examinations, trials, and judgments may be thereupon had and given as may be agreeable to law and justice.

Article X

That said Andrew Johnson, President of the United States, unmindful of the high duties of his office, and the dignity and proprieties thereof, and of the harmony and courtesies which ought to exist and be maintained between the executive and legislative branches of the government of the United States, designing and intending to set aside the rightful authority and powers of Congress, did attempt to bring into disgrace, ridicule, hatred, contempt, and reproach the Congress of the United States, and the several branches thereof, to impair and destroy the regard and respect of all the good people of the United States for the Congress and legislative powers thereof, (which all officers of the government ought inviolably to preserve and maintain,) and to excite the odium and resentment of all the good people of the United States against Congress and the laws by it duly and constitutionally enacted; and in pursuance of his said design and intent, openly and publicly, and before divers assemblages of the citizens of the United States, convened in divers parts thereof to meet and receive said Andrew Johnson as the Chief Magistrate of the United States, did, on [August 18, 1866] . . . and on divers other days and times, as well before as afterward, make and deliver, with a loud voice, certain intemperate, inflammatory, and scandalous harangues, and did therein utter loud threats and bitter menaces, as well against Congress as the laws of the United States duly enacted thereby, amid the cries, jeers, and laughter of the multitudes then assembled and in hearing, which are set forth in the several specifications hereinafter written, in substance and effect. . . .

Which said utterances, declarations, threats, and harangues, highly censurable in any, are peculiarly indecent and unbecoming in the Chief Magistrate of the United States, by means whereof said Andrew Johnson has brought the high office of the President of the United States into contempt, ridicule, and disgrace, to the great scandal of all good citizens, whereby said Andrew Johnson, President of the United States, did commit, and was then and there guilty of a high misdemeanor in office.

Article XI

That said Andrew Johnson, President of the United States, unmindful of the high duties of his office, and of his oath of office, and in disregard of the Constitution and laws of the United States, did, heretofore, to-wit, on the eighteenth day of August, A.D. eighteen hundred and sixty-six, at the city of Washington, in the District of Columbia, by public speech, declare and affirm, in substance, that the thirty-ninth Congress of the United States was not a Congress of the United States authorized by the Constitution to exercise legislative power under the same, but on the contrary, was a Congress of only a part of the United States, thereby denying, and intending to deny, the power of the said thirty-ninth Congress to propose amendments to the Constitution of the United States; and in pursuance of said declaration, the said Andrew Johnson, President of the United States, afterwards, to-wit, on [February 21, 1868] . . . at the city of Washington, in the District of Columbia, did unlawfully, and in disregard of the requirements of the Constitution, that he should take care that the laws be faithfully executed, attempt to prevent the execution of [the Tenure of Office Act] . . . by unlawfully devising and contriving, and attempting to devise and contrive means by which he should prevent Edwin M. Stanton from forthwith resuming the functions of the office of Secretary for the Department of War; and, also, by further unlawfully devising and contriving, and attempting to devise and contrive means, then and there, to prevent the execution of . . . [the Army Appropriation Act and the Reconstruction Act, both of March 2, 1867] . . . whereby the said Andrew Johnson, President of the United States, did, then, to-wit, on . . . [February 21, 1868] . . . at the city of Washington, commit, and was guilty of, a high misdemeanor in office.

4

William Evarts Defends Johnson in the Impeachment Trial (1868)

After graduating from Yale, William M. Evarts studied law at Harvard and in private firms and was admitted to the bar in 1843. In the years before the Civil War, he became a distinguished New York attorney, notable Republican leader, and prominent public figure. A political ally of Secretary of State William H. Seward, Evarts agreed to be part of Andrew Johnson's legal team in the impeachment proceedings in the Senate. When the attorney general became ill, Evarts assumed the leading role in the president's defense. In his closing argument, which extended over several days, Evarts challenged the legality of the Tenure of Office Act, which he portrayed as an attempt to revolutionize the government. Contending that a president could only be removed for illegal acts and not for political transgressions, he devoted considerable attention to the political nature of the charges against Johnson. The Senate's subsequent acquittal of Johnson in effect endorsed Evarts's position and, by raising the constitutional barrier for impeachment, established a significant precedent for the future.

Supposing the law is unconstitutional, for the purpose of argument, what is the result? Is the man to be punished because he has violated the law, and the Supreme Court has not as yet declared it unconstitutional? No; he comes into court and says, "I have violated no law." The statute is read; the Constitution is read; and the judge says, "You have violated no law." That is the end of the matter. . . . I shall consider this matter more fully hereafter; and now look at it only in the view of fixing such reduced and necessarily reduced estimate of the criminality imputed as makes it impossible that this should be an impeachable offence.

Much has been said about the duty of the people to obey and of officers to execute unconstitutional laws. I claim for the President no greater right in respect to a law that operates upon him in his public duty, and upon him exclusively, to raise a question under the Constitution to determine what his right and what his duty is, than I claim for every citizen in his private capacity when a law infringes upon his constitutional and civil and personal rights; for to say that Congress has no right to pass unconstitutional laws and yet that everybody is to obey them just as if they were constitutional and to be punished for breaking them just as if they were constitutional, and to be prevented from raising the question whether they are constitutional by penal inflictions that are to fall upon them whether they succeed in proving them unconstitutional or not, is, of course, trampling the Constitution and its defence of those who obey it in the dust. Who will obey the Constitution as

against an act of Congress that invades it, if the act of Congress with the sword of its justice can cut off his head and the Constitution has no power to save him, and nothing but debate hereafter as to whether he was properly punished or not? . . .

But again, the form alleged of infraction of this law, whether it was constitutional or unconstitutional, is not such as to bring any person within any imputation, I will not say of formal infraction of the law, but of any violent, wilful use and extent of resistance to or contempt of the law. Nothing was done whatever but to issue a paper and have it delivered, which puts the posture of the thing in this condition and nothing else: the Constitution, we will suppose, says that the President has a right to remove the Secretary of War; the act of Congress says the President shall not remove the Secretary of War; the President says, "I will issue an official order which will raise the same question between my conduct and the statute that the statute raises between itself and the Constitution." . . . When the Constitution and a law are, or are supposed to be, at variance and inconsistent, everybody upon whose right this inconsistency intrudes has a right under the usual ethical conditions of conduct of good citizenship to put himself in a position to act under the Constitution and not under the law. And thus the President of the United States . . . issues an order on paper which is but an assertion of the Constitution and a denial of the law, and that paper has legal validity if the Constitution sustains it, and is legally invalid and ineffectual . . . if the law prohibits it and the law is conformed to the Constitution. Therefore it appears that nothing was done but the mere course and process of the exercise of right claimed under the Constitution without force, without violence, and making nothing but the attitude, the assertion

FROM *Trial of Andrew Johnson*, vol. 2 (Washington, D.C.: Government Printing Office, 1868), pp. 292–95, 303–4, 355–56.

which, if unquestioned, might raise the point for judicial determination. . . .

I am quite amazed . . . at the manner in which these learned managers are disposed to bear down upon people that obey the Constitution to the neglect or avoidance of a law. It is the commonest duty of the profession to advise, it is the commonest duty of the profession to maintain and defend the violation of a law in obedience to the Constitution; and in the case of an officer whose duty is ministerial, whose whole obligation in his official capacity is to execute or to give free course to a law, even when the law does not bear at all upon him or his rights, the officer may appeal to the courts if he acts in good faith and for the purpose of the public service, and with a view of ascertaining by the ultimate tribunal in season to prevent public mischiefs, whether the Constitution or the law is to be the rule of his conduct, and whether they be at variance. . . .

Now, I should like to know if the President of the United States . . . cannot appeal to the Constitution? And when he does make the appeal is the Constitution to answer him, through the House of Representatives, "We admit, for argument, that the law is unconstitutional; we admit it operates on you and your trust-right, and nothing else; we admit that you were going to raise the constitutional question, and yet the process of impeachment is the peril under which you do that, and its axe is to cut off your head for questioning an unconstitutional law that operates upon your right and contravenes that Constitution which you have sworn to protect and defend in every department of the government, on and for the legislature, on and for the judiciary, on and for the people, on and for the executive power?" . . .

And now let me urge here that all this is within the province of politics; and a free people are unworthy of their freedom and cannot maintain it if their public men, their chosen servants, are not able to draw distinctions between legal and constitutional offence and odious or even abominable politics. . . . To agree in opinion concerning the public interest is the bond of one party, and diversity from those opinions the bond of the other; and where passions and struggles of force in any form of violence or of impeachment as an engine of power come into play, then freedom has become license, and then party has become faction. . . .

I hold in my hand an article from the Tribune, written under the instructions of this trial and put with great force and skill. I do not propose to read it. I bring it here to show and to say that it is an excellent series of articles of impeachment against the President of the United States within the forum of politics for political repugnancy and obstruction, and an honest confession that the technical and formal crimes included in these articles are of very paltry consideration. That is an excellent article of impeachment, demanding by process suitable to the forum, an answer; and for the discussions of the hustings and of the election, there it belongs; there it must be kept. But this being a court, we are not to be tried for that in which we are not inculpated. How wretched the condition of him who is to be thus oppressed by a vague, uncertain shadow which he cannot oppose or resist! If the honorable managers will go back to the source of their authority, if they will obtain what was once denied them, a general and open political charge, . . . then it would be brought here; it would be written down; its dimensions would be known and understood; its weight would be estimated; the answer could be made.

And then your leisure and that of the nation being occupied with hearing witnesses about political differences and the question of political repugnance and obstructions upon the side of the President, those who should be honored with his defence in that political trial would at least have the opportunity of reducing the force of the testimony against them, and of bringing opposing and contravening proofs; and then, at least, if you would have a political trial, you would have it with name and with substance to rest upon. But the idea that a President of the United States is to be brought into the procedure of this court by a limited accusation, found "not guilty" under that, and convicted on an indictment that the House refused to sustain, or upon that wider indictment of the newspaper press, and without an opportunity to bring proof or to make arguments on the subject, seems to us too monstrous for any intelligence within or without this political circle, this arena of controversy, to maintain for a moment. . . .

And this brings me very properly to consider, as I shall very briefly, in what attitude the President stands before you when the discussion of vicious politics or of repugnant politics, whichever may be right or wrong, is removed from the case. I do not hesitate to say that if you separate your feelings and your conduct, his feelings and his conduct, from the aggravations of politics as they have been bred since his elevation to the Presidency, under the peculiar circumstances which placed him there, and your views in their severity, governed, undoubt-edly, by the grave juncture of the affairs of the country, are reduced to the ordinary standard and style of estimate that should prevail between the departments of this government, I do not hesitate to say that upon the impeachment investigations and upon the impeachment evidence you leave the general standing of the President unimpaired in his conduct and character as a man or as a magistrate. Agree that his policy has thwarted and opposed your policy, and agree that yours is the rightful policy; nevertheless, within the Constitution and within his right, and within his principles as belonging to him and known and understood when he was elevated to the office, I apprehend that no reasonable man can find it in his heart to say that evil has been proved against him here.

5

Elizabeth Cady Stanton Appeals for Universal Suffrage (1869)

Women had played a prominent role in the abolitionist movement and had worked for passage of the Thirteenth Amendment abolishing slavery. During Reconstruction, leaders of the women's rights movement linked the cause of women's suffrage to that of black suffrage and appealed to Congress to include universal suffrage in first the Fourteenth and then the Fifteenth Amendment. Even a number of their Radical Republican allies, however, balked at linking the two movements, fearing such a step would cause black suffrage to be rejected. Elizabeth Cady Stanton, one of the leaders of the women's rights movement, wrote the following reply to the famous abolitionist Gerrit Smith, who declined to sign a petition calling for universal suffrage because, he claimed, it would retard the cause of black suffrage. The refusal of Congress to give women the vote at the same time it extended it to black men was a bitter disappointment to Stanton and the other leaders of the women's rights movement, and it drove a permanent wedge between them and their previous Radical allies.

The above is the petition to which our friend Gerrit Smith, as an abolitionist, can not conscientiously put his name, while Republicans and Democrats are signing it all over the country. He does not clearly read the signs of the times, or he would see that there is to be no reconstruction of this nation, except on the basis of universal suffrage, as the natural, inalienable right of every citizen. . . . As the aristocracy in this country is the "male sex," and as Mr. Smith belongs to the privileged order, he naturally considers it important for the best interests of the nation, that every type and shade of degraded, ignorant manhood should be enfranchised, before even the higher classes of womanhood should be admitted to the polls. This does not surprise us. Men always judge more wisely of objective wrongs and oppressions, than of those in which they are themselves involved. Tyranny on a Southern plantation is far more easily seen by white men at the North than the wrongs of the women of their own households. . . .

Again; Mr. Smith refuses to sign the petition because he thinks to press the broader question of "universal suffrage" would defeat the partial one of "manhood suffrage"; in other words, to demand protection for woman against her oppressors, would jeopardize the black man's chance of securing protection against his oppressors. If it is a question of precedence merely, on what principle of justice or courtesy should woman yield her right of enfranchisement to the negro? If men can not be trusted to legislate for their own sex, how can they legislate for the opposite sex, of whose wants and needs they know nothing? It has always been considered good philosophy in pressing any measure to claim the uttermost in order to get something. . . . But their intense interest in the negro blinded our former champions so that they forsook principle for policy, and in giving woman the cold shoulder raised a more deadly opposition to the negro than any we had yet encountered, creating an antagonism between him and the very element most needed to be propitiated in his behalf. . . .

FROM *The Revolution*, 14 January 1869. In Elizabeth Cady Stanton, Susan B. Anthony, and Matilda Joslyn Gage, eds., *History of Woman Suffrage*, vol. 2 (New York: Fowler and Wells, 1881–1887), pp. 317–19.

But Mr. Smith abandons the principle clearly involved, and intrenches himself on policy. He would undoubtedly plead the necessity of the ballot for the negro at the south for his protection, and point us to innumerable acts of cruelty he suffers to-day. But all these things fall as heavily on the women of the black race, yea far more so, for no man can ever know the deep, the damning degradation to which woman is subject in her youth, in helplessness and poverty. The enfranchisement of the men of her race, Mr. Smith would say, is her protection. Our Saxon men have held the ballot in this country for a century, and what honest man can claim that it has been used for woman's protection? Alas! we have given the very hey day of our life to undoing the cruel and unjust laws that the men of New York had made for their own mothers, wives, and daughters.

. . . Politicians will find, when they come to test this question of "negro supremacy" in the several States, that there is a far stronger feeling among the women of the nation than they supposed. We doubt whether a constitutional amendment securing "manhood suffrage" alone could be fairly passed in a single State in this Union. Women everywhere are waking up to their own God-given rights, to their true dignity as citizens of a republic, as mothers of the race.

Although those who demand "woman's suffrage" on principle are few, those who would oppose "negro suffrage" from prejudice are many, hence the only way to secure the latter, is to end all this talk of class legislation, bury the negro in the citizen, and claim the suffrage for all men and women, as a natural, inalienable right. The friends of the negro never made a greater blunder than when, at the close of the war, they timidly refused to lead the nation in demanding suffrage for all. If even Wendell Phillips and Gerrit Smith, the very apostles of liberty on this continent, failed at that point, how can we wonder at the vacillation and confusion of politicians at this hour. We had hoped that the elections of '67, with their overwhelming majorities in every State against negro suffrage, would have proved to all alike, how futile is compromise, how short-sighted is policy.

6

JAMES T. RAPIER

A Black Congressman Complains about Unequal Treatment (1874)

James T. Rapier was a black congressman from Alabama. In a speech he delivered in the House of Representatives on June 9, 1874, he describes the unequal treatment he was subjected to in traveling home. Such complaints helped strengthen support for a civil rights bill banning discrimination in public accommodations and transportation.

I affirm, without the fear of contradiction, that any white ex-convict (I care not what may have been his crime . . .) may start with me to-day to Montgomery, that all the way down he will be treated as a gentleman, while I will be treated as the convict. He will be allowed a berth in a sleeping-car with all its comforts, while I will be forced into a dirty, rough box with the drunkards, apple-sellers, railroad hands, and next to any dead that may be in transit, regardless of how far decomposition may have progressed. Sentinels are placed at the doors of the better coaches, with positive instructions to keep persons of color out. . . . Tender, pure, intelligent young ladies are forced to travel in this way if they are guilty of the crime of color, the only unpardonable sin known in our Christian and Bible lands, where sinning against the Holy Ghost . . . sinks into insignificance when compared with the sin of color. If from any cause we are compelled to lay over, the best bed in the hotel is his if he can pay for it, while I am invariably turned away, hungry and cold, to stand around the railway station until the departure of the next train, it matters not how long, thereby endangering my health, while my life and property are at the mercy of any highwayman who may wish to murder and rob me.

And I state without the fear of being gainsaid,

FROM *Congressional Record*, 43rd Cong., 1st sess., 1874, pp. 4782–86.

the statement of the gentleman from Tennessee to the contrary notwithstanding, that there is not an inn between Washington and Montgomery, a distance of more than a thousand miles, that will accommodate me to a bed or meal. Now, then, is there a man upon this floor who is so heartless, whose breast is so void of the better feelings, as to say that this brutal custom needs no regulation? I hold that it does and that Congress is the body to regulate it. Authority for its action is found not only in the fourteenth amendment to the Constitution, but by virtue of that amendment (which makes all persons born here citizens,) authority is found in article 4, section 2 of the Federal Constitution, which declares in positive language "that the citizens of each State shall have the same rights as the citizens of the several States." . . . Every day my life and property are exposed, are left to the mercy of others, and will be so as long as every hotel-keeper, railroad conductor, and steamboat captain can refuse me with impunity the accommodations common to other travelers. I hold further, if the Government cannot secure to a citizen his guaranteed rights it ought not to call upon him to perform the same duties that are performed by another class of citizens who are in the free and full enjoyment of every civil and political right. . . .

Sir, there is a cowardly propensity in the human heart that delights in oppressing somebody else, and in the gratification of this base desire we always select a victim that can be outraged with safety. . . . Here the negro is the most available for this purpose; for this reason in part he was seized upon, and not because he is naturally inferior to any one else. Instead of his enemies believing him to be incapable of a high order of mental culture, they have shown that they believe the reverse to be true, by taking the most elaborate pains to prevent his development. And the smaller the caliber of the white man the more frantically has he fought to prevent the intellectual and moral progress of the negro, for the simple but good reason that he has most to fear from such a result. He does not wish to see the negro approach the high moral standard of a man and gentleman.

. . . What does the [lower] class [of whites] say? "Build a Chinese wall between the negro and the school-house, discourage in him pride of character and honest ambition, cut him off from every avenue that leads to the higher grounds of intelligence and usefulness, and then challenge him to a contest upon the highway of life to decide the question of superiority of race." By their acts, not by their words, the civilized world can and will judge how honest my opponents are in their declarations that I am naturally inferior to them. No one is surprised that this class opposes the passage of the civil-rights bill, for if the negro were allowed the same opportunities, the same rights of locomotion, the same rights to comfort in travel, how could they prove themselves better than the negro?

Mr. Speaker, nothing short of a complete acknowledgment of my manhood will satisfy me. I have no compromises to make, and shall unwillingly accept any. If I were to say that I would be content with less than any other member upon this floor I would forfeit whatever respect any one here might entertain for me, and would thereby furnish the best possible evidence that I do not and cannot appreciate the rights of a freeman. Just what I am charged with by my political enemies. I cannot willingly accept anything less than my full measure of rights as a man. . . .

This is the legitimate conclusion of the argument, that the negro is not a man and is not entitled to all the public rights common to other men, and you cannot escape it. But when I press my

claims I am asked, "Is it good policy?" My answer is, "Policy is out of the question; it has nothing to do with it; that you can have no policy in dealing with your citizens; that there must be one law for all; that in this case justice is the only standard to be used, and you can no more divide justice than you can divide Deity." . . .

I have never sought to compel any one, white or black to associate with me, and never shall; nor do I wish to be compelled to associate with any one. If a man do not wish to ride with me in the street-car I shall not object to his hiring a private conveyance; if he do not wish to ride with me from here to Baltimore, who shall complain if he charter a special train? For a man to carry out his prejudices in this way would be manly, and would leave no cause for complaint, but to crowd me out of the usual conveyance into an uncomfortable place with persons for whose manners I have a dislike, whose language is not fit for ears polite, is decidedly unmanly and cannot be submitted to tamely by any one who has a particle of self-respect.

Sir, this whole thing grows out of a desire to establish a system of "caste," an anti-republican principle, in our free country. In Europe they have princes, dukes, lords, &c, in contradistinction to the middle classes and peasants. Further East they have the brahmans or priests, who rank above the sudras or laborers. In those countries distinctions are based upon blood and position. Every one there understands the custom and no one complains. . . . But let not our friends beyond the seas lay the flattering unction to their souls that we are without distinctive lines; that we have no nobility; for we are blessed with both. Our distinction is color, (which would necessarily exclude the brahmans,) and our lines are much broader than anything they know of. Here a drunken white man is not only equal to a drunken negro, (as would be the case anywhere else,) but superior to the most sober and orderly one; here an ignorant white man is not only the equal of an unlettered negro, but is superior to the most cultivated; here our nobility cohabit with our female peasants, and then throw up their hands in holy horror when a male of the same class enters a restaurant to get a meal, and if he insist upon being accommodated our scion of royalty will leave and go to the arms of his colored mistress and there pour out his soul's complaint, tell her of the impudence of the "damned nigger" in coming to a table where a white man was sitting. . . .

Mr. Speaker, to call this land the asylum of the oppressed is a misnomer, for upon all sides I am treated as a pariah. I hold that the solution of this whole matter is to enact such laws and prescribe such penalties for their violation as will prevent any person from discriminating against another in public places on account of color. No one asks, no one seeks the passage of a law that will interfere with any one's private affairs. But I do ask the en-

actment of a law to secure me in the enjoyment of public privileges. But when I ask this I am told that I must wait for public opinion; that it is a matter that cannot be forced by law. While I admit that public opinion is a power, and in many cases is a law of itself, yet I cannot lose sight of the fact that both statute law, and the law of necessity manufacture public opinion. . . .

Suppose there had been no reconstruction acts nor amendments to the Constitution, when would public opinion in the South have suggested the propriety of giving me the ballot? . . . If you will place upon your statute-books laws that will protect me in my rights, that public opinion will speedily follow.

7

RICHARD CAIN

Equal Rights and Social Equality (1874)

The 1875 Civil Rights Act was the last major piece of Reconstruction legislation passed by Congress. Outlawing racial discrimination on public conveyances and accommodations, the law marked a dramatic expansion of federal power, and it was the first effort of the national government of outlaw segregation. Supporters dropped its provision applying to schools before it passed. Despite its sweeping provisions, the bill was largely symbolic. Passed as a tribute to Senator Charles Sumner of Massachusetts, who had died the previous year, the law was rarely enforced before the Supreme Court declared it unconstitutional in 1883. In the following 1874 speech in the House of Representatives, black congressman Richard Cain of Charleston, South Carolina, urged passage of the bill to establish equality of rights, but he carefully denied that it mandated social equality of the races.

The gentleman from North Carolina [Mr. Vance] who spoke on the question stated some objections, to which I desire to address a few words of reply. He said it would enforce social rights, and therefore would be detrimental to the interests of both the whites and the blacks of the

country. My conception of the effect of this bill, if it be passed into a law, will be simply to place the colored men of this country upon the same footing with every other citizen under the law, and will not at all enforce social relationship with any other class of persons in the country whatsoever. It is merely a matter of law. What we desire is that our civil rights shall be guaranteed by law as they are guaranteed to every other class of persons; and when that is done all other things will come in as a

FROM *Congressional Record*, 43rd Cong., 1st sess., 1874, pp. 565–67.

necessary sequence, the enforcement of the rights following the enactment of the law.

Sir, social equality is a right which every man, every woman, and every class of persons have within their own control. They have a right to form their own acquaintances, to establish their own social relationships. Its establishment and regulation is not within the province of legislation. No laws enacted by legislators can compel social equality. Now, what is it we desire? What we desire is this: inasmuch as we have been raised to the dignity, to the honor, to the position of our manhood, we ask that the laws of this country should guarantee all the rights and immunities belonging to that proud position, to be enforced all over this broad land. . . .

But, says the gentleman from North Carolina, some ambitious colored man will, when this law is passed, enter a hotel or railroad car, and thus create a disturbance. If it be his right, then there is no vaulting ambition in his enjoying that right. And if he can pay for his seat in a first-class car or his room in a hotel, I see no objection to his enjoying it. But the gentleman says more. He cited, on the school question, the evidence of South Carolina, and says the South Carolina University has been destroyed by virtue of bringing into contact the white students with the the colored. I think not. It is true that a small number of students left the institution, but the institution still remains. The buildings are there as erect as ever; the faculty are there as attentive to their duties as ever they were;

the students are coming in as they did before. It is true, sir, that there is a mixture of students now; that there are colored and white students of law and medicine sitting side by side; it is true, sir, that the prejudice of some of the professors was so strong that it drove them out of the institution; but the philanthropy and good sense of others were such that they remained; and thus we have still the institution going on, and because some students have left, it cannot be reasonably argued that the usefulness of the institution has been destroyed. The University of South Carolina has not been destroyed. . . .

I think it is proper and just that the civil-rights bill should be passed. Some think it would be better to modify it, to strike out the school clause, or to so modify it that some of the State constitutions should not be infringed. I regard it essential to us and the people of this country that we should be secured in this if in nothing else. I cannot regard that our rights will be secured until the jury-box and the school-room, those great palladiums of our liberty, shall have been opened to us. Then we will be willing to take our chances with other men. . . .

Inasmuch as we have toiled with you in building up this nation; inasmuch as we have suffered side by side with you in the war; inasmuch as we have together passed through affliction and pestilence, let there be now a fulfillment of the sublime thought of our fathers—let all men enjoy equal liberty and equal rights.

1

Alabama Blacks Voice Their Aspirations for Equality (1867)

In May 1867 a black convention adopted an address to the people of Alabama. In this address, the delegates voiced their desire for equality and rejected the argument that they should not press this issue. They also called for educational opportunities and pledged their support for the Republican party.

Fellow Citizens:

. . . As there seems to be considerable difference of opinion concerning the "legal rights of the colored man," it will not be amiss to say that we claim exactly *the same rights, privileges and immunities as are enjoyed by white men*—we ask nothing more and will be content with nothing less. *All legal* distinctions between the races are now abolished. The word white is stricken from our laws, and every privilege which white men were formerly permitted to enjoy, merely because they were white men, now that word is stricken out, we are entitled to on the ground that we are men. *Color can no longer be pleaded for the purpose of curtailing privileges, and every public right, privilege and immunity is enjoyable by every individual member of the public.*—This is the touchstone that determines all these points. So long as a park or a street is a *public* park or street the entire public has the right to use it; so long as a car or a steamboat is a public conveyance, it must carry all who come to it, and serve all alike who pay alike. The law no longer knows white nor black, but simply men, and consequently we are entitled to ride in public conveyances, hold office, sit on juries and do everything else which we have

FROM *Montgomery Daily State Sentinel*, 21 May 1867.

in the past been prevented from doing solely on the ground of our color. . . .

We have said that we intend to claim all our rights, and we submit to our white friends that it is the height of folly on their part to withhold them any longer. One-half of the voters in Alabama are black men, and in a few months there is to be an entire reorganization of the State government. The new officers—legislative, executive and judicial—will owe their election largely, if not mainly to the colored people, and every one must see clearly that the voters will then be certain to require and the officers to compel a cessation of all illegal discriminations. . . .

There are some good people who are always preaching patience and procrastination. They would have us wait a few months, years, or generations, until the whites voluntarily give us our rights, but we do not intend to wait one day longer than we are absolutely compelled to. Look at our demands, and then at theirs. We ask of them simply that they surrender unreasonable and unreasoning prejudice. . . . But they would have us pay for what we do not get; tramp through the broiling sun or pelting rain, or stand upon a platform, while empty seats mockingly invite us to rest our wearied limbs; our sick must suffer or submit to indignity; we must put up with inconvenience of every kind; and the virtuous aspirations of our children must be continually checked by the knowledge that no matter how upright their conduct, they will be looked on as less worthy of respect than the lowest wretch on earth who wears a white skin. . . .

All over the state of Alabama—all over the South indeed—the colored people have with singular unanimity, arrayed themselves under the Republican banner, upon the Republican platform, and it is confidently predicted that nine-tenths of them will vote the Republican ticket. Do you ask, why is this? we answer, because:

1. The Republican Party opposed and prohibited the extension of slavery.
2. It repealed the fugitive slave law.
3. It abolished slavery in the District of Columbia.
4. It abolished slavery in the rebellious states.
5. It abolished slavery throughout the rest of the Union.
6. It put down rebellion against the Union.
7. It passed the Freedmen's Bureau Bill and the Civil Rights Bill.
8. It enfranchised the colored people of the District of Columbia.
9. It enfranchised the colored people of the nine territories.
10. It enfranchised the colored people of the ten rebel states.
11. It provided for the formation of new constitutions and state governments in those ten states.
12. It passed new homestead laws, enabling the poor to obtain land.

In short, it has gone on, step by step, doing first one thing for us and then another, and it now proposes to enfranchise our people all over the Union. It is the only party which has ever attempted to extend our privileges, and as it has in the past always been trying to do this, it is but natural that we should trust it for the future.

While this has been the course of the Republican Party, the opposition has unitedly opposed every one of these measures, and it also now opposes the enfranchisement of our people in the North. Everywhere it has been against us in the past, and the great majority of its voters hate us as cordially now as ever before. . . . It may be and probably is true that some men acting with the Republican Party have cared nothing for the principles of that party; but it is also certainly true that ninety-nine-hundredths of all those who were conscientiously in favor of our rights were and are in the Republican Party, and that the great mass of those who hated, slandered and abused us were and are in the opposition party.

The memories of the opposition must be short indeed, to have forgotten their language of the past twenty years but we have *not* forgotten it. . . .

. . . Our opponents will become disheartened unless they can divide us. This is the great danger which we have to guard against. The most effectual method of preserving our unity will be for us to always act together—never to hold separate political meeting or caucuses. It may take some time for us to get to pulling together well, but perseverance and honest endeavor will overcome all obstacles. In nominations for office we expect that there will be no discriminations on account of color by either wing, but that the most capable and honest men will always be put in nomination. We understand full well that our people are too deficient in education to be generally qualified to fill the higher offices, but when qualified men are found, they must not be rejected for being black.

This lack of education, which is the consequence of our long servitude, and which so diminishes our powers for good, should not be allowed to characterize our children when they come upon the stage of action, and we therefore earnestly call upon every member of the Republican Party to demand the establishment of a thorough system of common schools throughout the state. It will benefit every citizen of the State, and, indeed, of the Union, for the well-being of each enures to the advantage of all. In a Republic, education is especially necessary, as the ignorant are always liable to be led astray by the arts of the demagogue.

With education secured to all; with the old and helpless properly cared for; with justice everywhere impartially administered, Alabama will commence a career of which she will have just cause to be proud. We shall all be prosperous and happy. The sad memories of the past will be forgotten amid the joys of the present and the prospect of the future.

2

South Carolina Democrats Protest against the New State Constitution (1868)

In 1868 the Democratic party in South Carolina sent a remonstrance urging Congress to reject the new state constitution drafted under the guidelines of Reconstruction. The petition, which claimed to speak for virtually all the white people of South Carolina, devoted particular attention to the insult of imposing black suffrage on the state. Affirming the state's willingness to accept the verdict of the war, including the end of slavery, it nevertheless vowed that the state's white population would continue the struggle until black rule ended.

The Respectful Remonstrance, on behalf of The White People of South Carolina, Against the Constitution of the Late Convention of that State, now Submitted to Congress for Ratification.

To the Honorable the Senate and House of Representatives of the United States, in Congress assembled:

The undersigned respectfully sheweth, that a Constitution fraught with evil to the State, and to all classes of the people thereof, is about to be submitted to your honorable body for ratification. Before your honorable body shall set upon that instrument the seal of your approval, and thus consummate upon a proud and faithful people a great and irreparable wrong, we respectfully ask a hearing at your hands, whilst with a due sense of our responsibility to God and to truth, we submit for your consideration the grave objections that may be urged against the proposed fundamental law for this State. . . .

. . . We waive all argument upon the subject of its validity. It is a Constitution *de facto*, and that is the ground upon which we approach your honorable body in the spirit of earnest remonstrance. That Constitution was the work of Northern adventurers, Southern renegades and ignorant negroes. Not one per centum of the white population of the State approves it, and not two per centum of the negroes who voted for its adoption know any more than a dog, horse, or cat, what his act of voting implied. That Constitution enfranchises every male negro over the age of twenty-one, and disfranchises many of the purest and best white men of the State. The negro being in a large numerical majority, as compared with the whites, the effect is that the new Constitution establishes in this State negro supremacy, with all its train of countless evils. A superior race—a portion, Senators and Rep-

---

FROM *The Respectful Remonstrance on Behalf of the White People of South Carolina . . .* (Columbia, S.C., 1868).

resentatives, of the same proud race to which it is your pride to belong—is put under the rule of an inferior race—the abject slaves of yesterday, the flushed freedmen of to-day. And think you that there can be any just, lasting reconstruction on this basis? The Committee respectfully reply, in behalf of their white fellow-citizens, that this cannot be. We do not mean to threaten resistance by arms. But the white people of our State will never quietly submit to negro rule. We may have to pass under the yoke you have authorized, but by moral agencies, by political organization, by every peaceful means left us, we will keep up this contest until we have regained the heritage of political control handed down to us by an honored ancestry. This is a duty we owe to the land that is ours, to the graves that it contains, and to the race of which you and we are alike members—the proud Caucasian race, whose sovereignty on earth God has ordained, and they themselves have illustrated on the most brilliant pages of the world's history.

Nor, Senators and Representatives, does the State of South Carolina merit, at your hands, the political treatment that has been meted out to her without stint.

It is true, South Carolina took the field promptly, in the late war between the States. Her people embarked their all in the struggle, because the sovereignty of the State demanded this of them. But when the war ended, and the arbitrament to which they resorted was adverse to their cause, no people ever yielded more gracefully to the decree of Providence. Quietly they laid down their arms, and, in peace, they became law-abiding, as, in war, they had been faithful to their flag. They accepted the legitimate results of the war. They were ready to abandon the claim of the right of their State peaceably to secede from the Union, and they assented, in Convention assembled, to the emancipation of their slaves. And now, were the State admitted into the Union, on a just and reasonable basis, we hesitate not to declare that again would our people greet the starry banner of the Union, and unite with their fellow-citizens of the whole country in the effort to promote the glory, wealth and prosperity of our common land.

In our relations, as proposed by us, with the black people of this State, we are not disposed to exact anything that just men may deny or Heaven disapprove.

When South Carolina assented to the act of Federal emancipation, we hold that the freed people became members of the body politic, and, as such, entitled to all civil rights that are enjoyed alike by all classes of the people. They became entitled to "life, liberty and the pursuit of happiness"—to all that the Declaration of American Independence and the English *Magna Charta* claim for man as his inalienable rights. But as it regards suffrage, we hold that this is not a political right nor a civil one for man, either white or black, but it is *trust*, a delicate trust, to be conferred by the State upon the people thereof, according to considerations of expediency, and agreeably to the sound political doctrine of the greatest good to the greatest number.

With respect, now, to the extension of this trust to the colored people, we believe that nine-tenths of our people are willing to concede it to them, duly qualified. We cannot admit universal suffrage, because the great body of the colored people are utterly unfitted to exercise it with intelligence and discretion; and because it would make the negro dominant, and thus bring about a fatal antagonism between the races. We cannot deny it altogether to the black man, because that would be neither right nor politic. Hence the policy of the mean between the two extremes, which has met with general favor in this State. The conservative party of South Carolina now stands and gathers strength, day after day, upon this proposition. The Convention of the party lately passed the following resolution:

"*Resolved*, That under the action of the State of South Carolina, heretofore taken, we recognize the colored population of the State as an integral element of the body politic; and, as such, in person and property, entitled to a full and equal protection under the State Constitution and laws. And that as citizens of South Carolina, we declare our willingness, when we have the power, to grant them, under proper qualifications as to property and intelligence, the right of suffrage."

In behalf at least of the Democratic party of South Carolina, which embraces nearly every white inhabitant, and many of the colored people, the Committee declare that this policy represents the political sentiment of the State. We offer this in good faith, as the basis of a true, a genuine and lasting reconstruction. This, we earnestly believe, is the peaceful solution of the great question of white man and black man in the South.

3

R. I. CROMWELL

An African American Leader Instructs New Black Voters (1867)

The 1867 Reconstruction Act provided that black males could vote for delegates to write new state constitutions in the former Confederate states. In the following communication to a black newspaper in New Orleans, an African American leader warned newly enfranchised black voters in that state not to vote for any supporters of the Confederacy who now professed to be their friends. Notice the writer's demand for equal privileges.

They [supporters of the Confederacy] should have nothing to do in reconstructing a State they attempted to destroy, wishing as they did at that time that you and me and all the black race be kept in bondage. Remember the Vice President of the Confederate States who said that the cornerstone of the Confederate Government was negro slavery. And yet these men, the very ones, now come to us—black men—and tell us that they are our best friends—the low debauchee, the overseer of plantations who once dared prowl around your cabins to destroy your families, the old master (so-called) now comes to tell you he is your best friend, vote for a Southerner whom you know! Yes, you do know him, and what is it you know? You know that when you were his slave the treatment he gave you, your wife, your children, your father and mother, were treated like dumb beasts, half fed, half clothed, and he deceived you on all occasions. Yes, when you volunteered to fight for the freedom of our race, what was the treatment of your families while you were fighting the battles of your country, that you and they might be free, and enjoy the freedom that you to-day enjoy? Some of them were murdered, some whipped, some starved, some half clothed, some driven into Texas. Why, my friends, these old fellows that had launched their bark on the sea of slavery, stood out until their ship was wrecked and driven ashore, on the shore of liberty, equality, justice and freedom to all loyal men. But these men or traitors find to-day you are a man on this shore of liberty, and they now come to you and ask you to trust them, elevate them into office, and they will do you good.

And will you be deceived by these old foxy fellows? You must remember how often they have deceived you; how often some of you have had to pay for yourselves; how often you have been told you should not be separated from your families, and how often you have been deceived? And you will be so again, if you trust them. Believe them not, trust them not, for if you do, we are shipwrecked.

And now, my friends, I say to you when any of that class comes to you in a Judas like manner to

FROM *New Orleans Tribune,* 25 April 1867.

ask you to vote for any of that class or him, tell him *no*; and, if he should attempt to bribe or buy your vote, report him to your club, or the Central Executive Committee. Dont be afraid of his not giving you employment, for he is compelled to have your labor. Fulfill your contracts to the letter, and vote right, and we will be sure to win. . . .

Now, in order to be ready to vote on election day, we must comply with the laws of our country. What are these laws? They are that every one must go to the register, give his name, number of his house, his ward and street, get his certificate, carry it home, put it away until election day, then take it out on that day, put it into your pocket, go to the polls and vote for some good *man*. This certificate is to show you are a citizen of Louisiana and entitled to vote FOR WHOM YOU PLEASE.

Now, the persons for whom you are to vote have to meet in a convention, to make a constitution for this State; and if we do not vote in good and true men, we will have slavery in another form, and qualified suffrage, excluding black men. That is to say that in future every man would be required to owe two hundred dollars worth of property, or to read and write, before he could vote.

Now, we want every man that is twenty one years old, and of sane mind, to vote, hold office, sit on juries, practice law, ride in any conveyance, travel on steamboats, eat in any restaurant, drink in any saloon and dine at any hotel, or educate our children at any school we may see fit or choose. We demand equal privileges with the whites in all things in our State. Let us be united in this political fight, as we were in putting down rebels and traitors, and we will have a government, under which the black man will be secure from the many discriminations that are now practiced against our race.

Now, fellow-citizens, let me say to you: Trust none who will not pledge their honor to have these principles engrafted in the Constitution of Louisiana. Then, and not until then, will the black man be in his rights secured in the State of Louisiana. We have the means in our own hands; let us use it with that good judgment that becomes all good citizens. We are the majority of loyal men in Louisiana, and if we are united and vote right, we can carry the election. And in order to become well posted and united, I would request all colored ministers, throughout the State, to lecture and enlighten, and impress upon their congregations the necessity of this great work.

We must take hold of this reconstruction matter, elect as many of our own race as we can, join in with our Southern loyalists, choose good men from among them. But be sure to vote for no Southern men that was a rebel or secessionist; for, if you do, you are pulling the hemp to hang yourself with. . . .

R. I. Cromwell.

4

HENRY CLAY WARMOTH

Who Is Responsible for Corruption? (1870)

Henry Clay Warmoth was an Illinois soldier who was stationed in Louisiana during the war. Deciding to remain in the state, he entered politics, became a leader of the state's Republican party, and was elected governor. Warmoth developed a reputation for corruption, and indeed, following his retirement, he set himself up as a wealthy planter in the state. When a group of citizens presented a petition to him in 1870 protesting corruption in the state government, he responded by emphasizing the role played by business interests seeking various government contracts and other forms of assistance.

A committee appointed by the meeting in La-fayette square on Monday night waited on Governor Warmoth this afternoon and presented their resolution. Governor Warmoth, in reply, said he was glad personally to see them. He desired, however, to say something relative to that meeting, in justice to himself and the government he represented, and stated that he had vetoed a great many bills making subsidy grants to individuals and companies, which, in a few instances, had been passed over his veto; that there were many persons in the Legislature ignorant of the manipulation of the lobbymen, [persons] who had been recently enfranchised, that would have to be instructed. He said:

"I think, gentlemen, that if you will give me the support and assistance which you ought to give from your standing in this community, we shall be able to restrain these people from running into the excesses complained of in these resolutions. Let me make one complaint against you, gentlemen, as the representatives of those in whose behalf you appear. You charge the Legislature with passing, corruptly, many bills looking to the personal aggrandizement of individuals and corporations. Let me suggest to you that these individuals and corporations are your very best people. For instance, this bank bill that is being lobbied through the Legislature now by the hardest kind of work. We have been able to defeat this bill twice in the House, and now it is up again. Who are doing it? Your bank presidents. The best people of the City of New Orleans are crowding the lobby of the Legislature continually, whispering bribes into these men's ears to pass this measure. How are we to defend the State against the interposition of these people who are potent in their influence in this community?"

The Governor went on at length, making disclosures as to how various measures were engineered through the Legislature by these same good citizens, to sign one of which he had been offered $50,000 by one party. And in addition, Mayor Conway, of this city, had offered him any consideration to sign it. The bill was vetoed. The bill here referred to was the $5,000,000 gold bond bill for redeeming the city money. He was offered $50,000 to sign the Nicholson Pavement bill, which he vetoed. The Governor complained of the refusal of the leading men of the State to counsel with him, although he had invited them, and said:

"I make this complaint to you as an individual; I make it as a citizen of Louisiana. I came here to settle among you, although by accident I have been elevated to the position I now occupy, and if you and the 2,500 citizens who were present at the meeting which sent you here would only give their support to me and the honest members of the Legislature, there will be no difficulty in restraining improvident legislation. I think I have a right to ask it, and if you will give it, I assure you that many of the evils complained of will be avoided.["] . . .

He said . . . that it was his purpose to administer the affairs of the government of the State to the best of his ability for the interest and welfare of the people, and he invited the assistance and cooperation of all good citizens.

FROM *New York World*, 4 February 1870.

5

ALEXANDER WHITE

A Defense of Carpetbaggers (1875)

In the following speech, delivered in the House of Representatives on February 4, 1875, Congressman Alexander White of Alabama discussed the background of the group of men known as carpetbaggers in southern politics and the reasons for their political prominence.

These white republicans are known by the contemptuous appellation of carpet-bagger and scalawag, names conferred upon them by the chivalry, in whose political interest prowl the bands of Ku-Klux and White League assassins in the South, and as such, especially the carpet-bagger, they have become a by-word and reproach. We of the South are not responsible for them; they are a northern growth, and unless going South expatriates them, they are still northern men, even as you are—bone of your bone, flesh of your flesh. But who are they? I can speak for my State, for I think I know nearly all in the State, and there are a good many of them. Most of them have titles, not empty titles complaisantly bestowed in piping times of peace, but titles worthily won by faithful and efficient service in the Federal armies, or plucked with strong right arm from war's rugged front upon the field of battle. Many of them bear upon their bodies scars of wounds received while fighting under your flag for the nation's life and the country's glory. These men either went South with the Union armies and at the close of the war remained there, or went there soon after, in the latter part of 1865 or early in 1866, to make cotton. The high price of cotton in 1865 and 1866, and the facility with which cheap labor could be obtained, induced many enterprising northern men, especially the officers in the Federal armies in the South

who had seen and become familiar with the country, to go or remain there to make cotton. Many purchased large plantations and paid large sums of money for them; others rented plantations, in some instances two or three, and embarked with characteristic energy in planting. This, it should be remembered, was before the civil-rights bill or the reconstruction acts, before the colored people had any part in political matters, and two years before they ever proposed to vote or claimed to have the right to vote at any election in the Southern States.

When the political contests of 1868 came on in which the colored people first took a part in politics, as near all the native population in the large cotton-growing sections were opposed to negro suffrage and opposed to the republican party, they very naturally turned to these northern men for counsel and assistance in the performance of the new duties and exercise of their newly acquired political rights, and they as naturally gave them such counsel and became their leaders, and were intrusted with official power by them.

This brief summary will give you a correct idea of the manner in which, as I believe, nine-tenths of those who are called carpet-baggers became involved in political affairs [in the] South, and dispose of a very large part of the slanders which have been promulgated against them not only by their political enemies at the South, but by the treacherous northern knaves who, under the pretense of being republicans and as correspondents of so-called republican papers at the North, have gone down South prepared in advance to stab the cause

FROM *Congressional Record*, 43rd Cong., 2d sess., 1875, Appendix, pp. 14–24.

of justice and of truth, of humanity and freedom, of the law and the Constitution, to the heart. Could these miserable miscreants have known with what ineffable contempt they were regarded by the very men whose credulous dupes they were, with what scathing scorn they regarded northern men who would lend themselves to traduce whole classes of northern men, who would allow themselves to be used as the tools to break down the political party to which they professed to belong, it would have diminished much the self-complacency with which their work was done. They could have realized that southern men, though bold and often reckless of the means by which they seek to attain political ends, that earnest and vehement, ardent and high-spirited, under the influence of one great ultimate aim to which all else is subordinated, they may reach politically to the parallel of the dogma which once prevailed in the religious world, "there is no faith to be kept with heretics," yet they can never be brought to descend to sympathy with or respect for such low-browed infamy as theirs.

These two classes, the carpet-baggers and scalawag[s], are the object of peculiar assault by the democracy, for they know that these constitute the bulwark of the republican party in the South. Without their co-operation and assistance the colored republicans could neither organize nor operate successfully in political contests, and without them the party would soon be extinguished in the Southern States.

A. B. RANDALL

Former Slaves Are Anxious to Record Their Marriages (1865)

Although most slaves were married, southern laws did not recognize the validity of slave marriages, and so slaves had to live with the constant uncertainty of whether at some point their marriage would be broken by sale. For former slaves, one of the cherished meanings of freedom was legal protection of the marriage bond. Near the end of the war, the chaplain of an Arkansas black regiment wrote the following letter to Adjutant General Lorenzo Thomas, discussing the widespread desire of freedpeople to have their slave marriages legalized and their hopes for the future protected.

Little Rock Ark Feb 28th 1865

. . . Weddings, just now, are very popular, and abundant among the Colored People. They have just learned, of the Special Order No. 15. of Gen [Lorenzo] Thomas by which, they may not only be lawfully married, but have their Marriage Certificates, *Recorded*; in a *book furnished by the Government*. This is most desirable; and the order, was very opportune; as these people were constantly loosing [*sic*] their certificates. Those who were captured . . . on the 17th of January . . . had their Marriage Certificates, taken from them; and destroyed; and then were roundly cursed, for having such papers in their posession [*sic*]. I have married, during the month, at this Post; Twenty five couples; mostly, those, who have families; & have been living together for years. I try to dissuade single men, who are soldiers, from marrying, till their time of enlistment is out: as that course seems to me, to be most judicious.

The Color[e]d People here, generally consider, this war not only; their *exodus*, from bondage; but the road, to Responsibility; Competency; and an honorable Citizenship—God grant that their hopes and expectations may be fully realized.

Most Respectfully

A. B. Randall

FROM Ira Berlin, et al., eds., *Freedom*, ser. II, *The Black Military Experience* (New York: Cambridge University Press, 1982), p. 712.

2

SIDNEY ANDREWS

Southern Whites Have No Faith in Black Free Labor (1866)

Sidney Andrews went to the Carolinas and Georgia in the fall of 1865 as a special correspondent for the Chicago Tribune *and* Boston Advertiser. *His reports on what he saw and his conversations with southern leaders were collected in a book published in 1866. In this selection, he emphasized southern whites' lack of faith in free black labor.*

The white man and the negro do not understand each other, and consequently do not work together so harmoniously as it is desirable that they should. It would seem that, one party having work to do and the other needing work, there would be such community of interest as leads to unity of purpose and action; but the fact is, that each party distrusts the other, and therefrom results bickering and antagonism. . . .

The fault unquestionably, it appears to me, lies with the white man. He is of the ruling race, and might, I feel very certain, have established a different order of things if he had pleased to do so, and had exercised good common sense in the beginning. That there are some planters who find the free negroes honest and faithful is positive proof that there might have been many more, and if many more, then without number.

Most of them began by assuming, however, that it was right to keep the negro in slavery just as long as possible, and by adding thereto the assumption that the free negro would not work. Military power has compelled the recognition of his freedom in every district, I believe, though in some of them not till within the last six weeks; but this almost universal belief that he will not work is doing a good deal to prove that he will not; and troubles which are dimly foreshadowed will come from this cause alone,—the brutal assumption that the negro cannot be controlled except by fear of the lash.

There is among the plantation negroes a widely spread idea that land is to be given them by the government, and this idea is at the bottom of much idleness and discontent. . . .

Despite the fact that nearly everybody tells me the free negro will not work, the experience of some of the better class of planters convinces me that he will work, if he is treated like a man. He is unquestionably sensitive about his freedom,—it is the only thing he has that he can call his own.

Some of the blacks are working along as heretofore, under private arrangements with their former masters; but in most cases there is a written contract between the employer and the employed,—one copy in the hands of the planter and the other at the Freedmen's Bureau office. I hear of very few cases in which the compensation is in money; in nearly all instances it is a part of the crop. The laborer's share ranges from one tenth to one half; on some small farms, where special privileges are given the negroes in the way of clothing, use of land, use of team, use of time, the share may not be over one sixth to one tenth of the regular crop; in the lower part of the State [South Car-

FROM Sidney Andrews, *The South since the War* (Boston: Ticknor and Fields, 1866), pp. 96–101.

olina], where most of the labor is done by hand, and where there are no special privileges, the share is from one third to one half; in the upper part of the State, where horses or mules are more in use, the share is from one fourth to one third. The contracts generally expire at New Year's.

It is beyond question that but little work has been done in the State this season. The free negro is the scapegoat on which the whites lay the burden of this wrong, of course; but it seems to me that the disturbed condition of the country in the early summer and through all the spring is extenuation enough.

It is, however, true that the lately freed negro has not generally been made to comprehend that there are six laboring days in each week. The railroad companies complain that they can get but three or four days' work per week from the blacks engaged in rebuilding the roads; and the contract officers of the Freedmen's Bureau quite universally concur in the statement that five days make a plantation negro's week for work. Instances in which the contract officers have been called on to go out into the country and convince the negroes that work must be done on Saturday as well as on other days are not at all rare.

The indifference which so many of the people feel and express as to the fate of the negro is shocking and to the last degree revolting to me. He is actually to many of them nothing but a troublesome animal; not a human being, with hopes and longings and feelings, but a mere animal, valuable, but altogether unlovable. "I would shoot one just as soon as I would a dog," said a man to me yesterday on the cars. And I saw one shot at in Columbia as if he had been only a dog,—shot at from the door of a store, and at midday!. . .

The whole labor system of the State is in an utterly demoralized condition. How soon it can be thoroughly reorganized, and on just what basis that reorganization will take place, are questions of no easy answering. The labor question, and not reconstruction, is the main question among intelligent thinking men of the State. Scarcely one in a dozen of the best of them have any faith in the negro. "The experiment of free negro labor is bound to be a failure; and you of the North may as well prepare for it first as last," is substantially the language of hundreds. And thereafter follow questions of, "What shall then be done with the negro?" and, "Where shall we then get our labor?"

N. B. LUCAS

Freedpeople Complain about Their Former Owners' Attempts to Cheat Them (1865)

The following communication from the Freedmen's Bureau assistant superintendent at Chattanooga, Tennessee, in 1865 is an example of the type of complaints by former slaves that the Bureau handled. In a subsequent hearing before a Bureau agent, Thomas Craighead abandoned his claim on the crop in exchange for the freedpeople paying court costs.

Chatta [Tenn], Nov. 10th 1865.

A.A. General:

I have the honor to forward the following statement, and respectfully request instructions in the matter, as Jasper is only 25 miles from this Post.

A. L. Griffith, a lawyer, and discharged Union soldier, of Jasper, Tenn., came to this Office and made the following statement:—

That T. G. Craighead, of Jasper, Tenn., owned many slaves, and, in 1863, at the approach of the Union army, he abandoned his property and fled South, giving his negroes to understand that if they remained on his farm during the war, they should be entitled to all they could make.

In August last, Craighead returned home, took possession of his farm, and sued the negroes for the rent of his farm for this year, and received judgment against the negroes for $102.50, notwithstanding the testimony of 3 white men of Jasper, (Harmon Cox, H. P. Ramsey, and John Doss) to the effect that the presence and labor of the negroes on the farm during the war, was worth more than the rents of the farm.

The case was tried by John G. Kelley, Justice of Peace, for Marion County, Tenn.

After the decision, no appeal to the Circuit Court would be granted, and the property of the Freedman has been attached to the amount of $102.50. I have the honor to be, Very Respectfully,

Your Obd't Servant,

N. B. Lucas

FROM Captain N. B. Lucas to Major Jno. H. Cochrane. In Ira Berlin, et al., eds., *Freedom*, ser. I, vol. 1, *The Destruction of Slavery* (New York: Cambridge University Press, 1985), pp. 310–11.

4

JOURDON ANDERSON

A Freedman Writes His Former Master (1865)

A few months after the war ended, Jourdon Anderson, who had fled slavery during the war, received a letter from his former master asking him to return with his family to their former home in Tennessee. Anderson reportedly dictated this reply. Whatever the letter's genesis, it succinctly expressed the meaning that freedom held for him and his family. His letter is a powerful statement of African Americans' hopes and expectations at the beginning of Reconstruction.

Dayton, Ohio, August 7, 1865.

To My Old Master, Col. P. H. Anderson,
Big Spring, Tennessee.

Sir:

I got your letter and was glad to find that you had not forgotten Jourdon, and that you wanted me to come back and live with you again, promising to do better for me than anybody else can. I have often felt uneasy about you. I thought the Yankees would have hung you long before this for harboring Rebs they found at your house. I suppose they never heard about your going to Col. Martin's to kill the Union soldier that was left by his company in their stable. Although you shot at me twice before I left you, I did not want to hear of your being hurt, and am glad you are still living. It would do

FROM *New York Tribune*, 22 August 1865.

me good to go back to the dear old home again and see Miss Mary and Miss Martha and Allen, Esther, Green, and Lee. Give my love to them all, and tell them I hope we will meet in the better world, if not in this. I would have gone back to see you all when I was working in the Nashville Hospital, but one of the neighbors told me Henry intended to shoot me if he ever got a chance.

I want to know particularly what the good chance is you propose to give me. I am doing tolerably well here; I get $25 a month, with victuals and clothing; have a comfortable home for Mandy (the folks here call her Mrs. Anderson), and the children, Milly, Jane and Grundy, go to school and are learning well; the teacher says Grundy has a head for a preacher. They go to Sunday-School, and Mandy and me attend church regularly. We are kindly treated; sometimes we overhear others saying, "Them colored people were slaves" down in Tennessee. The children feel hurt when they hear such remarks, but I tell them it was no disgrace in Tennessee to belong to Col. Anderson. Many darkies would have been proud, as I used to was, to call you master. Now, if you will write and say what wages you will give me, I will be better able to decide whether it would be to my advantage to move back again.

As to my freedom, which you say I can have, there is nothing to be gained on that score, as I got my free-papers in 1864 from the Provost-Marshal-General of the Department at Nashville. Mandy says she would be afraid to go back without some proof that you are sincerely disposed to treat us justly and kindly—and we have concluded to test your sincerity by asking you to send us our wages for the time we served you. This will make us forget and forgive old s[c]ores, and rely on your justice and friendship in the future. I served you faithfully for thirty-two years, and Mandy twenty years. At $25 a month for me, and $2 a week for Mandy, our earnings would amount to $11,680. Add to this the interest for the time our wages has been kept back and deduct what you paid for our clothing and three doctor's visits to me, and pulling a tooth for Mandy, and the balance will show what we are in justice entitled to. Please send the money by Adams Express, in care of V. Winters, esq., Dayton, Ohio. If you fail to pay us for faithful labors in the past we can have little faith in your promises in the future. We trust the good Maker has opened your eyes to the wrongs which you and your fathers have done to me and my fathers, in making us toil for you for generations without recompense. Here I draw my wages every Saturday night, but in Tennessee there was never any pay day for the negroes any more than for the horses and cows. Surely there will be a day of reckoning for those who defraud the laborer of his hire.

In answering this letter please state if there would be any safety for my Milly and Jane, who are now grown up and both good looking girls. You know how it was with poor Matilda and Catherine. I would rather stay here and starve and die if it comes to that than have my girls brought to shame by the violence and wickedness of their young masters. You will also please state if there has been any schools opened for the colored children in your neighborhood, the great desire of my life now is to give my children an education, and have them form virtuous habits.

From your old servant,

Jourdon Anderson.

P.S.—Say howdy to George Carter, and thank him for taking the pistol from you when you were shooting at me.

5

JOHN W. DeFOREST

The Tribulations of a Freedmen's Bureau Agent
(1868)

A Union Army officer during the war, John DeForest served as a Freedmen's Bureau agent in Greenville, South Carolina, from 1865 to 1868. Congress eventually decided to shut down the Bureau, and he resigned as it was nearing the end of its tenure to devote his time to writing. One of the founders of the new realist school of fiction that emerged after the war, DeForest became a major literary figure in the postwar years. His most famous work, Miss Ravenel's Conversion from Secession to Loyalty, *was published in 1867. He also wrote several articles describing the various problems and difficulties he encountered as a Freedmen's Bureau agent. As he explained in the following essay, he was not given clear guidelines, lacked sufficient power to enforce his decisions, lost valuable time on countless petty disputes, and was spread too thin to adequately handle his responsibilities. He decided that his main task was to educate white landlords and black workers alike as to the nature of free labor. DeForest's account is notable for its balanced perspective.*

*M*ost of the difficulties between whites and blacks resulted from the inevitable awkwardness of tyros in the mystery of free labor. Many of the planters seemed to be unable to understand that work could be other than a form of slavery, or that it could be accomplished without some prodigious binding and obligating of the hireling to the employer. Contracts which were brought to me for approval contained all sorts of ludicrous provisions. Negroes must be respectful and polite; if they were not respectful and polite they must pay a fine for each offense; they must admit no one on their premises unless by consent of the landowner; they must have a quiet household and not keep too many dogs; they must not go off the plantation without leave. The idea seemed to be that if the laborer were not bound body and soul he would be of no use. With regard

to many freedmen I was obliged to admit that this assumption was only too correct and to sympathize with the desire to limit their noxious liberty, at the same time that I knew such limitation to be impossible. When a darkey frolics all night and thus renders himself worthless for the next day's work; when he takes into his cabin a host of lazy relatives who eat him up, or of thievish ones who steal the neighboring pigs and chickens; when he gets high notions of freedom into his head and feels himself bound to answer his employer's directions with an indifferent whistle, what can the latter do? My advice was to pay weekly wages, if possible, and discharge every man as fast as he got through with his usefulness. But this policy was above the general reach of Southern capital and beyond the usual circle of Southern ideas. . . .

. . . I never forgot that my main duty should consist in educating the entire population around me to settle their difficulties by the civil law; in other words, I considered myself an instrument of reconstruction.

FROM John W. DeForest, "A Bureau Major's Business and Pleasures," *Harper's Magazine* 37 (November 1868): pp. 767–71.

The majority of the complaints brought before me came from Negroes. As would naturally happen to an ignorant race, they were liable to many impositions, and they saw their grievances with big eyes. . . . Of course the complaints were immensely various in nature and importance. They might refer to an alleged attempt at assassination or to the discrepancy of a bushel of pea vines in the division of a crop. They might be against brother freedmen, as well as against former slave owners and "Rebs." More than once have I been umpire in in the case of a disputed jackknife or petticoat. Priscilly Jones informed me that her "old man was a-routin' everybody out of the house an' a-breakin' everything"; then Henry Jones bemoaned himself because his wife Priscilly was going to strange places along with Tom Lynch; then Tom Lynch wanted redress and protection because of the disquieting threats of Henry Jones. The next minute Chole Jackson desired justice on Viney Robinson, who had slapped her face and torn her clothes. Everybody, guilty or innocent, ran with his or her griefs to the Bureau officer; and sometimes the Bureau officer, half distracted, longed to subject them all to some huge punishment. Of the complaints against whites the majority were because of the retention of wages or of alleged unfairness in the division of the crops.

If the case brought before me were of little consequence, I usually persuaded the Negro, if possible, to drop it or to "leave it out" to referees. Without a soldier under my command, and for months together having no garrison within forty miles, I could not execute judgment even if I could see to pronounce it; and, moreover, I had not, speaking with official strictness, any authority to act in matters of property; the provost court having been abolished before I entered upon my jurisdiction. . . .

And so the process of education went on, working its way mainly by dint of general laws, without much regard to special cases. As this is the method of universal Providence and of the War Department, I felt that I could not be far wrong in adopting it. But even this seemingly simple and easy style of performing duty had its perplexities.

Magistrates rode from ten to thirty miles to ask me how they should dispose of this, that, and the other complaint which had been turned over to them for adjudication. Their chief difficulty was to know where the military orders ended and where civil law began; and here I was little less puzzled than they, for we were acting under a hodgepodge of authorities which no man could master. I had files of orders for 1865, and 1866, and 1867; files from the Commissioner, and from the Assistant Commissioner, and from the general commanding the department; the whole making a duodecimo volume of several hundred closely printed pages. To learn these by heart and to discover the exact point where they ceased to cover and annul the state code was a task which would have bothered not only a brevet major but a chief justice. My method of interpretation was to limit the military order as much as might be, and so give all possible freedom of action to the magistrate. . . .

Although I received no precise instructions as to visiting the various portions of my district, it was probably presumed by my superiors that I would make occasional tours of inspection, and so attend to local disorders on the spot where they occurred. I did not do this; I made but a single journey of above fifteen miles; I did not absent myself more than a single night from my station, except once when summoned to Charleston. My satrapy, it must be remembered, contained two state districts or counties, and eventually three, with a population of about eighty thousand souls and an area at least two thirds as large as the state of Connecticut. Consider the absurdity of expecting one man to patrol three thousand square miles and make personal visitations to thirty thousand Negroes.

Then I had no assistant to attend to the complainants who constantly presented themselves at my office. They averaged five a day, or a total of something like two thousand during my fifteen months of duty. Moreover, they came from distances of five, ten, twenty, and even thirty miles. I planted myself firmly in Greenville and let my world come to me. Toward the end of my term of service an order was promulgated to the effect that

Bureau officers should thereafter "travel more" and that they should regularly visit the important points of their districts, giving previous notice of their tours to the inhabitants. Knowing what labor this signified and how impossible it would be to perform it in any satisfactory manner, I welcomed the decree from the headquarters of the army which mustered all volunteer officers out of the service, and declined an appointment as civilian agent of the Bureau.

6

NEW ORLEANS TRIBUNE

They Are the Planter's Guards (1867)

The degree to which the Freedmen's Bureau protected African Americans' rights very much depended on the attitude of Bureau officials in the different southern states. As a result, the Bureau was more aggressive in protecting blacks' rights in some states than others. The following editorial in the New Orleans Tribune, *one of the leading black newspapers in the country, charged that the Bureau in Louisiana was basically an ally of the planters in enforcing labor contracts.*

Justice for All.

Among the questions that will come up before the Convention will be that of securing justice for all. Under the present state of things, there is hardly any justice for a poor man. The laborer on the plantations is, to a very great extent, in the clutches of his employer. Should he be abused or wronged what are the means of redress? Practically he has none.

If he goes to the Bureau's agent, he finds there an officer who rides with his employer, who dines with him, and who drinks champaign with him. He is not likely to receive impartial justice at the hands of such a prejudiced officer. The case of the poor freedman is hurried up and slighted, not to say more. Most of the Agents think their particular business is to furnish the planters with cheap hands, and as a consequence to retain at any cost the laborers on the plantation. They are, in fact, the planter's guards, and not nothing else. Every person acquainted with the regime of our country perishes knows what has become of the Bureau's agencies and the Agents.

It is, therefore, perfectly useless for the poor laborer to look at the Freedmen's Bureau for relief. He knows in advance that the Bureau will send him back to his unjust or exacting employer. He will not be assisted to get his pay, or to get redress; but will be told to go back to his master and do his work.

FROM *New Orleans Tribune*, 31 October 1867.

The Contested Meaning of Freedom (1880)

In testimony before a congressional committee, Henry Adams, a former Louisiana slave who served in the Union Army after the war, later described the situation freedpeople encountered in the first months after the war. Note in his account the contrast Adams draws between the privileges of freedom and the requirements of slavery, and the ways the notion of freedom precipitated conflict with his former owners. Adams was a local office holder during Reconstruction and after 1874 devoted his energies to promoting black migration from the South. (Paragraphing has been supplied.)

In the parish of De Soto, La., near Logansport, on a plantation owned by a man named Ferguson, the white men read a paper to all of us colored people, telling us that we were all free, and that we colored people could go where we pleased and manage our own affairs, and could work for who we pleased. The man I belonged to, or who had me in charge, told me I could work there, or work wherever I wanted to; but it was best to stay there with him and his family on his plantation, because . . . the bad white men was mad with all the negroes, because they were free, and they would kill you all for fun; for, said he, I do not want them to meddle with you; if they do they will have me to kill. . . . He said . . . but stay where we were living, and we could get protection from our old masters.

I told him I thought that every man when he was free could have his rights and protections and protect himself. He said that was true, but the colored people could never protect themselves among the white people. There was too many bad white men that would all the time be killing colored people, for no other reason than because they were free and may get well off. . . . So you all had better stay with the white people who raised you, and not leave them, but make contracts to work for them

by the year for one-fifth you all make, and next year you can get one-third, and the next you may work for one-half you make, and by that we may be able to protect you from the bad white men, and keep them from killing you all so much. We have contracts for you all to sign, and to work on for 10¹/₂₀ you make from now until the crop is ended, and then next year you all can make another crop and get more of it.

I told him that I would not sign anything, for I am a slave, and belong to a white girl about fourteen years of age; her name is Nancy Emily Adams, and I expect to work for her until God frees me, and then I will go where I pleases, and will go to some free State where I can be free. The boss man was named W. M. C. Carrods. He then said to me, you are all as free as I am. Sign this paper and get yourselves another home if you want to, or keep the same. I said if I cannot do like a white man I am not free. I see how the poor white people do. I ought to do so too, or else I am a slave. You says we must carry a pass to keep the white men from killing us, or whipping us, so I think still we are all slaves, and I will sign no paper. I might sign to be killed, and I believe that the white people is trying to fool us to see if we are fools enough to go off to work for ourselves, and then everywhere they see one of us they will kill us and take all of our money away what we work for, and everything that we

FROM U.S. Senate, *Negro Exodus from Southern States*, 46th Cong., 2d sess., 1880, S. Rept. 693, pt. II, pp. 190–92.

may have. But he said again, "You all are as free as I am, and as any white man, and sign this contract so I can take it to Mansfield to the Yankees and have it recorded." So all of our colored people signed it but myself and a boy named Samuel Jefferson, and Manuel Adams, and John Jefferson; all who lived on the place was about sixty, young and old. My mother lived at one of my young master's place, and belonged to him. . . .

On the same day or the next after all had signed the papers or contracts, we went to cutting oats. I asked the boss could we get any of the oats? He said no; the oats were made before you were free. I said it is some of the crop we made, but we did not get any of it. We made about eight hundred bushels. After that he told us to get timber to build a sugar-mill to make molasses; we did so. On the 13th day of July, 1865, we started to pull fodder. I asked the boss would he make a bargain with me to give us half of all the fodder we would pull and save. He said we may pull two or three stacks and then we could have all the other. I told him we wanted to make a bargain for half, so if we only pulled two or three stacks we would get half of that. He said, "All right." We got that and part of the corn we made. We made five bales of cotton, but we did not get a pound of that. We made two or three hundred gallons of molasses and we only got what we could eat. We made about fifty or seventy-five bushels of pindar; we got none of them. We made about seven or eight hundred bushel of potatoes; we got a few to eat. We split rails three or four weeks, and got not a cent for that.

So in September of same year I asked the boss to let me go to Shreveport. He said, "All right; when will you come back?" I told him "next week." He said "You had better carry a pass." I said, "I will see whether I am free by going without a pass."

So the next day I left, and got about six or seven miles from home. . . . I . . . met four white men about six miles south of Keachie, De Soto Parish. One of them asked me who I belonged to. I told me no one; so him and two others struck me with a stick, and told me they was a going to kill me and every other negro who told them that they did not belong to any one; but one of them who knew me told the others to "Let Henry alone, for he is a hard-working nigger, and a good nigger, and I will fight for him." They left me, and I then went on to Shreveport. . . .

Sunday I went back home. . . . When I got home, the boss was not at home. I asked the madame where was the boss? She says, "Now, the boss; now, the boss; now, the boss! You should say master, and say mistress—and shall, or leave this place; we will not have no nigger here on our place who cannot say mistress and master; and you shall, for you all are not free yet, and will not be until Congress sits, for General Butler cannot free any one, and you shall call every white lady misses, and every white man boss, master."

During the same week the madame, Mrs. Frances Carrods, taken a stick and beat one of the young colored girls, who was about fifteen years of age, and who is my sister, and split her back. The boss came next day, and take this same girl (my sister), whose name is Katie Carter, and whipped her nearly to death; but in the contracts he was to hit no one any more. So, after the whipping, a large number of the young colored people, all kin to her, taken a notion to leave, and the next day she left. . . .

On the 18th of September, I and eleven men and boys left that place and other places in the same settlement and started for Shreveport. We all got to Keachie, a little town. I had my two hundred dollar horse along; my brother was riding him, and all of our things was packed on him. Out come about forty or fifty armed men (white) into the public road and shot at us all, and taken my horse; said they were going to kill every nigger they found leaving their masters, and taking all of our clothes and bed-clothing and our money. I had my pocket-book in my saddle-bags on my horse with one hundred and fifty dollars in gold, and they got it all; so I had to work away to get a white man to my boss to get my horse.

Then I took my horse and another horse and got a wagon and went to peddling, and had to get a pass, according to the laws of the parishes, to do so. In October and November and December I was searched for pistols and was robbed of $250 in goods and money by a large crowd of white men

. . ., and the law would do nothing about it. This was at or near Thomas' place, near the line of Texas and De Soto Parish, and they shot at me twenty times during the same day. The same crowd of white men broke up five churches (colored) and from time to time broke up churches everywhere the colored people held them; and when any of us colored people would leave the white people, they would take everything we had, during the year of 1865; and when any of us left we had to run away. I ran away, as also did most of the rest, and the white people did not sympathize with us; they would take all the money that we made on their places when we went to leave; and they killed many hundreds of my race when they were running away to get freedom.

After they told us we were free—even then they would not let us live as man and wife together. And when we would run away to be free from slavery, the white people would not let us come on their places to see our mothers, wives, sisters, or fathers. We was made to leave the place, or made to go back and live as slaves. To my own knowledge there was over two thousand colored people killed trying to get away, after the white people told us we were free, which was in 1865.

8

HENRY ADAMS

Planters Insist That Black Women Work in the Fields (1880)

When the war ended, white planters were psychologically unprepared to deal with free black labor and wanted to retain as much of the old system of slavery as possible to regulate black labor. Black workers, in contrast, were determined to assert their new rights of freedom in both major and minor matters. Only with time did the two groups work out a new relationship in freedom. One source of conflict was black husbands' desire to remove their wives and children from working in the fields. In his testimony before a congressional committee, former Louisiana slave Henry Adams recounted planters' attitudes immediately after the war.

I seen on some plantations on Red River where the white men would drive colored women out in the fields to work, when the husbands would be absent from their home, and would tell colored men that their wives and children could not live on their places unless they work in the fields. The colored men would tell them they wanted their children to attend school; and whenever they wanted their wives to work they would tell them themselves; and if he could not rule his own domestic affairs on that place he would leave it and go somewhere else. So the white people would tell them if he expected for his wife and children to live on their places without working in the field they would have to pay house rents or leave it; and if the colored people would go to leave, they would take everything they had, chickens, hogs, horses, cows, mules, crops, and everything, and tell them it was for what his damn family had eat, doing nothing but sitting up acting the grand lady and their daughters acting the same, for I will be damn if niggers aint got to work on my place or leave it.

FROM U.S. Senate, *Negro Exodus from Southern States*, 46th Cong., 2d sess., 1880, S. Rept. 693, pt. II, p. 182.

9

MARIAH BALDWIN AND ELLEN LATIMER

Two Black Workers Settle Accounts at the End of the Year (1867)

One source of conflict between white landlords and black agricultural workers was the annual settling of accounts at the end of the year. Landlords deducted a whole host of charges from their workers' wages, including items they purchased on credit at the plantation store, fines for disobedience, days lost from sickness or other causes, and absenteeism. Since the vast majority of freedpeople were illiterate, they had no way to check the accuracy of the landlord's books. Contracts often required employees to work Saturdays, and many of the deductions for being absent stemmed from freedpeople's refusal to work on Saturdays and Sundays. Below are two accounts with J. R. Thomas, a Georgia planter, in 1867. Mariah Baldwin, who had been promised $60 in wages, had so many deductions that, at the end of the year, she received only $3.15 (the first three months of her "deducts" are given). Ellen Latimer fared even worse. She purchased more items during the year, and as a result ended the year with a debt of $9.43 to her employer.

1867 Mariah Baldwin Dr			
To James P. Thomas			
January 19th	Lost time & rations 1 Day by sickness		50
" 22	" " " 1 Day " "		50
" 25	Half Plug of Tobacco		25
" 27	Lost time & ration by sickness ½ day		25
" 31	" " " " 1 day		50
" "	3 Yds of Osnaburg[1]		1 30
Feb. 2	Lost time & rations 1 Day by sickness		25
" 4	" " " by sickness		50
" 5	" " " 1 Day		50
" 6	" " & rat by sickness		50
" 7	" " " "		50
" 8	Lost time & rat by sknss		1 00
" 9	" " " 1 Day		50
" 16	" " " ⅓ day		25

[1]A coarse cloth.

FROM Dorothy Sterling, ed., *We Are Your Sisters* (New York: W. W. Norton, 1984), pp. 329–30.

″	23	″ ″ ″	1 Day	50
″	27	″ ″ ″	1 day by day	50
Mch	2	Lost time & rations	1 day do	50
	8	″ ″ ″	1 Day Do	50
	9	″ ″ ″	1 Day Do	50
	15	″ ″ ″	1 Day Do	50
	18	″ 1 Plug of tobacco		25
	21	Lost time & rations	1 Day	50
	27	Lost time & rations	1 Day	50
	28	½ Gal of syrup		60
	30	Lost time & rations	1 Day	50

$11.65
−9.25
2.40

1867 Ellen Latimer—
         To Helsman & Ely Dr-

May 8.	1 blank book 12½—8 yds calico $2	2.12½
Sept 15	1 pr shoes—1.75 Nov 9 1 pr do 3.00	4.75
Mch 30	order W W. Kendrick	5.00
June 1st	1 pr shoes 3.00 5 yds homespun 1.25	4.25
″	1 umbrella	1.50
	Coleman & Doughtys Act	21.50
	39½ day sick & lost & rations a 40^c	15.80
Nov 30	cups saucers & plates	2.75
Dec 28	Cash paid	1.76

10

NEW ORLEANS TRIBUNE

A Black Newspaper Calls for Integrated Schools in New Orleans (1867)

The New Orleans Tribune *advanced the following argument in support of integrating the city's schools. New Orleans was the only southern city to establish integrated public schools during Reconstruction.*

This experiment [in integrating the city's trolley cars] well illustrate[s] the fact that absurd distinctions are not of the essence of human society. Such discriminations may be maintained by pride, prejudices, or hatred. But as soon as they are dropped, the whole community perceive that they were not necessary, and that the social machinery works better and in a simpler way after they have disappeared; they even experience a sense of relief by the introduction of any reform that benefit the masses of the people. No one is really and truly benefited by the rules which prescribe, in certain aristocratic countries, discriminations in dress; and at the overthrow of these discriminations everybody feels relieved.

But now that the car question, which was a minor one, is settled, the time has come to consider the propriety, justice and simplicity of admitting all children into the public schools. The distinction kept up in the schools has no different, and therefore no better ground, than that which was made in the cars. It originated from the same source, slavery, which has now disappeared. It was kept up much more by pride than by prejudice, just as was the star car system.[1] There is not a single reason that can be given to abolish the distinction on railroads, that cannot apply as well to the abolition of a similar distinction in schools.

We do not see why the city should go to the expense of organizing twenty or thirty new schools, when she has already a sufficient number of public schools to receive all the children to be educated. Discriminations among children, on account of religion and on account of language, would certainly be better justified than a distinction based on their complexions. The mere mention of this last discrimination would be laughed at, the world over. The idea of having schools over the doors of which will be inscribed the words "for children of fair complexion only," or "for children with blue eyes only," and of other schools set apart "for children of dark complexion," and "for children with dark eyes," is of itself ridiculous, and brings a smile on the lips of every reader, outside the Southern States.

Even a distinction based on the social condition, occupation, or respectability of parents, would be better justified than a distinction on color. Yet nobody thinks of setting apart, in distinct schools, children of merchants and of mechanics, of tradesmen and of laborers. It is not proposed to separate bad children from good ones. Why? Because such distinctions are against the Democratic principle of American society; because they would be a source of injustice; and also because they would give rise to endless troubles, petitions and protests. . . .

. . . We have to make this community one nation and one people, where two nations and two people previously existed. We had better begin at the root, and first of all unite the children in the public schools, than to unite at once the grown persons in the city cars. But when parents agree to sit together, children can as well sit close to each other. When parents are conciliated, children can attend the same schools.

---

[1]The city's trolley lines were initially segregated, and black passengers rode in jim crow cars designated with a star.

FROM *New Orleans Tribune*, 9 May 1867.

11

A Sharecropping Contract (1886)

The system of sharecropping eventually became the dominant mode of organizing agricultural labor in the South. This system evolved in the first years of Reconstruction after a period of experimentation with other systems of compensation. Below is a typical sharecropper contract between a white landlord and a black farmer made in January 1886. Note that the sharecropper was illiterate.

This contract made and entered into between A. T. Mial of one part and Fenner Powell of the other part both of the County of Wake and State of North Carolina—

Witnesseth—That the Said Fenner Powell hath barganed and agreed with the Said Mial to work as a cropper for the year 1886 on Said Mial's land on the land now occupied by Said Powell on the west Side of Poplar Creek and a point on the east Side of Said Creek and both South and North of the Mial road, leading to Raleigh, That the Said Fenner Powell agrees to work faithfully and dilligently without any unnecessary loss of time, to do all manner of work on Said farm as may be directed by Said Mial, And to be respectful in manners and deportment to Said Mial. And the Said Mial agrees on his part to furnish mule and feed for the same and all plantation tools and Seed to plant the crop free of charge, and to give the Said Powell One half of all crops raised and housed by Said Powell on Said land except the cotton seed. The Said Mial agrees to advance as provisions to Said Powell fifty pound of bacon and two sacks of meal pr month and occationally Some flour to be paid out of his the Said Powell's part of the crop or from any other advance that may be made to Said Powell by Said Mial. As witness our hands and seals this the 16th day of January A.D. 1886

Witness

W. S. Mial [signed]

A.T. Mial [signed] [Seal]

his
Fenner **X** Powell [Seal]
mark

FROM Roger L. Ransom and Richard Sutch, *One Kind of Freedom* (New York: Cambridge University Press, 1977), p. 91.

1

Ulysses S. Grant Signals a Retreat from Reconstruction (1874)

In an interview in 1874, President Grant expressed irritation at having to constantly deal with violence and disorder in the southern states and expressed his opinion that the Republican party should stop trying to sustain the Republican governments in the South. In an editorial, the New York Herald commented on what it termed Grant's "New Departure" and on its implications for the future of American politics. Grant's desire to distance himself and the party from Reconstruction grew stronger with time. Two years later, Grant privately declared that the Fifteenth Amendment "had done the Negro no good, and had been a hindrance to the South, and by no means a political advantage to the North."

General Grant's New Departure— Notice to the Republican Party and Its Monstrosities.

General Grant is reported to have said on Friday last to some prominent republicans who called upon him at the White House:—"I begin to think it is time for the republican party to unload. There has been too much dead weight carried by it. The success of our arms during the rebellion and the confidence that the republican party was strong enough to hold up any burden have imposed all the disaffection in the Gulf States on the administration. I am tired of this nonsense. Let Louisiana take care of herself as Texas will have to do. I don't want any quarrel about Mississippi State matters to be referred to me. This nursing of monstrosities has nearly exhausted the life of the party. I am done with them, and they will have to take care of

themselves." These words from such a speaker are of the sort to "give us pause." There is, of course, no doubt that they were spoken as indicated, and in the absence of definite statement to the contrary it is to be supposed they were remembered by some one of the prominent republicans referred to and repeated outside with substantial accuracy. The authenticity of the words being thus reasonably clear of doubt, we are of opinion that none of General Grant's famous utterances will prove more memorable than this one. From the time when Grant informed a rebel commander that he proposed "to move immediately on his works"—when the country first became clearly acquainted with his name—the few words of this silent man have had a greater effect upon the popular mind than the orators, with all their speeches. . . . They are neat statements of thoughts that find general acceptance because of the keen perception they indicate, or because of their apt relation to existing circumstances. And the utterance given above is in character with those heard before, and will have

FROM *New York Herald*, 20 January 1874.

equal influence in giving definite direction to a wide and vague public opinion on the subject it handles. It is a summary of the condition of the dominant political party, and it indicates the most threatening symptom and the practical remedy, and deals with the subject, too, in a tone of resolute impatience that is in sympathy with the feelings of the people.

From a potential source, therefore, we have these points:—That the republican party has been "nursing monstrosities," and that these have nearly exhausted its life; that in future these monstrosities, which are reconstruction difficulties, "must take care of themselves," as the official head of the party means to cut them loose; that the party has been carrying a great deal of dead weight—that is to say, that it has been playing false with its supporters by foisting into the party purposes and programmes various issues and facts, that had no relation whatever to those principles which alone the people supposed they were supporting when they voted republican tickets; that the leader is of opinion the party ought to unload this dead weight and turn honest; that Louisiana, as well as Texas, "must" govern herself; and, finally, greatest point of all, that General Grant is "tired of this nonsense." The phrase "nursing monstrosities" describes accurately the general activity of the republican party. If that party addresses itself to the subject of reconstruction it solves no vexed problem, pacifies no excitement, lays the foundation of no useful progress; it only nurses some monstrosity conceived by profligate wretches eager to utilize for their own advantage public misfortune or national ruin. If it turns to the subject of great national enterprises, urged by the needs of communication with the Pacific Coast, it does not stimulate and encourage a healthy material progress; it nurses the Credit Mobilier monstrosity. And so through the category. One cannot touch a topic of public interest but the action of the republican party in regard to it resolves itself at once into the mere nursing of some monstrosity instead of the honest performance of some legitimate function. Neither need one go far into the measures with which the party is identified to find the dead

weight that threatens to carry it down. Indeed, it is difficult to say what is not dead weight—to indicate any one purpose which the party advocates now earnestly urge that may fairly be called a vital, throbbing portion of the party principle. All the financial policy is dead weight, because the party principle would require a strict economy and the administration of the Treasury in the interest of the people. But it is all done in the interest of jobbers. All the nominations are dead weight, for they are bargains. Reconstruction, the carpet-baggers, the usurpation of power supported by troops—all this is dead weight, a millstone, that if not speedily disengaged will carry republicanism to the bottom. Was there ever in the history of politics a party whose leaders had so crippled it with gratuitous loads of issues not related to its principles and outrageously offensive to the people?

But General Grant, being "tired of this nonsense," thoroughly disgusted with the antics of the party leaders, is not the man patiently to countenance and assist a policy whose inevitably ruinous consequences he clearly perceives; and he indicates the tendency of his revolt against the enormities that are loosening the hold of his party on the people. He intends to separate himself entirely from the Congressional policy and to inaugurate a policy of his own, at the risk of any probable issue with the leaders in Congress; to cut away the dead weight and carry the party nearer to the popular impulse. It is a project that, if wisely acted upon and successfully carried out, will add to his laurels as a soldier the fame of a great political leader. . . . An issue between Grant and the leaders in Congress is the imminent fact of the day. . . . Should General Grant's endeavor to free his party from the burdens that it unprofitably bears receive the co-operation of any considerable portion of the party leaders success in the admirable project proposed would be certain and easy; but it is far more likely that he will awaken the hostility and meet the furious opposition of the party leaders, and then his ultimate success will be gained in a struggle that may make its triumphs all the more precious to the public. It is clear why the party leaders will oppose him. They are no longer interested in the successes of the party, but only in the net result that such successes may secure to them individually—that is to say, they are more interested in the dead weights than in the legitimate party vitality; and the proposition to cut away all the grand schemes of plunder and all that corrupt system of administration that is the ruin of the party North and South is simply a proposition to cut away that which they hold more precious than all beside. Any new departure in this direction, therefore, they will oppose with characteristic ferocity. . . . But the result will be an exposure of their motives and the public exhibition of the fact that the leaders care nothing for the purposes that the people have at heart in party victories. This will be fatal to their standing in popular esteem, and we may see almost as marvellous a political mortality as we saw in 1860. Inevitably such a disintegration would result in the formation of a middle party; for which, indeed, on altogether different reasons,

the time is ripe. All the legitimate purposes of the original republican party are gained, and its dismemberment must follow the loss of its objective unless it changes ground, and the only ground it can take is to move a little nearer the opposition, dropping its extreme on one hand as the democrats drop theirs on the other. This would be to repeat the liberal movement of the last campaign, or the frame of that movement; but the animating spirit would be different, for here the impulse would not be captious or personal. This would not be an intrigue of candidates, but would be inspired by the generous patriotic purposes of the need of good government. And in the machinery of this new party General Grant could dictate the succession, and he would have the glory of restoring and reinvigorating with fresh purpose the party that has saved the country from armed foes and may yet save it from the assault of insidious plunderers.

2

JAMES S. PIKE

Society Turned Bottom-Side Up (1874)

James S. Pike was a reporter for the Republican New York Tribune. *Although he had opposed slavery, Pike held strong racist sentiments against blacks. In 1874 he published a famous and influential account of South Carolina's radical government entitled The* Prostrate State. *Pike's repudiation of Reconstruction and the radical government of the state was in tune with the shifting mood of northern public opinion. Even Republicans were increasingly willing to write off Reconstruction as a mistake and allow southern whites to regulate race relations in their section. Pike's racial feelings, which so powerfully fueled his hostility to the South Carolina government, are apparent in his description of the state legislature.*

Yesterday, about 4 P.M., the assembled wisdom of the State, whose achievements are illustrated on that theatre, issued forth from the State-House. About three-quarters of the crowd belonged to the African race. They were of every hue, from the light octoroon to the deep black. They were such a looking body of men as might pour out of a market-house or a court-house at random in any Southern State. Every negro type and physiognomy was here to be seen, from the genteel serving-man to the rough-hewn customer from the rice or cotton field. Their dress was as varied as their countenances. . . .

Here, then, is the outcome, the ripe, perfected fruit of the boasted civilization of the South, after two hundred years of experience. A white community, that had gradually risen from small beginnings, till it grew into wealth, culture, and refinement, and became accomplished in all the arts of civilization; that successfully asserted its resistance to a foreign tyranny by deeds of conspicuous valor, which achieved liberty and independence through the fire and tempest of civil war, and illustrated itself in the councils of the nation by orators and statesmen worthy of any age or nation—such a community is then reduced to this. It lies prostrate in the dust, ruled over by this strange conglomerate, gathered from the ranks of its own servile population. It is the spectacle of a society suddenly turned bottom-side up. The wealth, the intelligence, the culture, the wisdom of the State, have broken through the crust of that social volcano on which they were contentedly reposing, and have sunk out of sight, consumed by the subterranean fires they had with such temerity braved and defied.

In the place of this old aristocratic society stands the rude form of the most ignorant democracy that mankind ever saw, invested with the functions of government. It is the dregs of the population habilitated in the robes of their intelligent predecessors, and asserting over them the rule of ignorance and corruption, through the inexorable machinery of a majority of numbers. It is barbarism overwhelming civilization by physical force. It is the slave rioting in the halls of his master, and putting that master under his feet. . . .

Deducting the twenty-three members referred to, who comprise the entire strength of the opposition, we find one hundred and one remaining. Of this one hundred and one, ninety-four are colored, and seven are their white allies. Thus the blacks outnumber the whole body of whites in the House more than three to one. . . . As things stand, the body is almost literally a Black Parliament, and it is the only one on the face of the earth which is the representative of a white constituency and the professed exponent of an advanced type of modern civilization. But the reader will find almost any portraiture inadequate to give a vivid idea of the body, and enable him to comprehend the complete metamorphosis of the South Carolina Legislature, without observing its details. The Speaker is black, the Clerk is black, the door-keepers are black, the little pages are black, the chairman of the Ways and Means is black, and the chaplain is coal-black. At some of the desks sit colored men whose types it would be hard to find outside of Congo; whose costume, visages, attitudes, and expression, only befit the forecastle of a buccaneer. It must be remembered, also, that these men, with not more than half a dozen exceptions, have been themselves slaves, and that their ancestors were slaves for generations. . . .

One of the things that first strike a casual observer in this negro assembly is the fluency of debate, if the endless chatter that goes on there can be dignified with this term. . . . Sambo can talk on these topics and those of a kindred character, and their endless ramifications, day in and day out. There is no end to his gush and babble. The intellectual level is that of a bevy of fresh converts at a negro camp-meeting. Of course this kind of talk can be extended indefinitely. It is the doggerel of debate, and not beyond the reach of the lowest parts. . . .

But underneath all this shocking burlesque upon legislative proceedings, we must not forget

---

FROM James S. Pike, *The Prostrate State* (New York: D. Appleton and Company, 1874), pp. 9–21, 58–65.

that there is something very real to this uncouth and untutored multitude. It is not all sham, nor all burlesque. . . . They have an earnest purpose, born of a conviction that their position and condition are not fully assured, which lends a sort of dignity to their proceedings. The barbarous, animated jargon in which they so often indulge is on occasion seen to be so transparently sincere and weighty in their own minds that sympathy supplants disgust. The whole thing is a wonderful novelty to them as well as to observers. Seven years ago these men were raising corn and cotton under the whip of the overseer. To-day they are raising points of order and questions of privilege. They find they can raise one as well as the other. They prefer the latter. It is easier, and better paid. Then, it is the evidence of an accomplished result. It means escape and defense from old oppressors. It means liberty. It means the destruction of prison-walls only too real to them. It is the sunshine of their lives. It is their day of jubilee. It is their long-promised vision of the Lord God Almighty. . . .

The rule of South Carolina should not be dignified with the name of government. It is the installation of a huge system of brigandage. The men who have had it in control, and who now have it in control, are the picked villains of the community. They are the highwaymen of the State. They are professional legislative robbers. They are men who have studied and practised the art of legalized theft. They are in no sense different from, or better than, the men who fill the prisons and penitentiaries of the world. They are, in fact, of precisely that class, only more daring and audacious. They pick your pockets by law. They rob the poor and the rich alike, by law. They confiscate your estate by law. They do none of these things even under the tyrant's plea of the public good or the public necessity. They do all simply to enrich themselves personally. The sole, base object is, to gorge the individual with public plunder. Having done it, they turn around and buy immunity for their acts by sharing their gains with the ignorant, pauperized, besotted crowd who have chosen them to the stations they fill, and which enable them thus to rob and plunder. . . .

Those who suppose that any thing short of a good government in the State of South Carolina, and, we may add, of any other State similarly situated in the South, is going to long stand, or be tolerated, may well take heed, if their judgments are ever to find expression in action. . . . Where there is actual injustice, or radical wrong in the government, it breeds resistance. . . . The present government of South Carolina is not only corrupt and oppressive, it is insulting. It denies the exercise of the rights of white communities, because they are white. The city of Charleston is an example. . . . The black government of the State denies it the right to superintend its own voting, or to count its own votes.

3

THE NATION

This Is Socialism (1874)

The Nation had been an early supporter of Congressional Reconstruction, but by the 1870s it was increasingly disillusioned with the whole experiment. Alarmed by the growing corruption in American politics and the fiscal policies of urban political machines like Tammany Hall, the magazine was sympathetic to the complaints of

South Carolina property holders, as evidenced in the Taxpayers' Petition to Congress about high taxes, government waste, and fraud. In an extremely influential article in 1874, The Nation accused the Radical regime in the state of representing the interests of those without property by conducting a campaign against property rights.

Socialism in South Carolina.

The present condition of South Carolina can only be understood by a consideration of the character of the population and the changes which have taken place in it since the close of the war. There are now about three hundred thousand whites in the State to four hundred thousand blacks. The general effect of the Reconstruction acts may be put in a few words. They left the property of the State in the hands of the disfranchised whites, and the governing power in the hands of the negroes. From that time to this, politics in South Carolina have consisted of determined efforts on the part of a few designing men, with the aid of the negro vote, to plunder the property-holders. The first set who succeeded in doing this were the carpet-baggers, who from 1868 to 1872 ruled the State through the negroes. . . . There is undoubtedly a great deal of difference among the South Carolina negroes in intelligence and morality. Among the small number of negroes in the cities who have always been free there is a good deal of industry, intelligence, and good conduct. But the average of intelligence among the rest is very low—so low that they are but slightly above the level of animals. On the sea-coast and on the rivers they talk an out-landish idiom which is so different from English that in the witness-box they are with difficulty understood by judge or jury, and when on the jury itself they must certainly be very far from understanding either the address of counsel or the charge of the judge. As they are ignorant, they are of course credulous. The quality of their minds and their fitness for the discharge of delicate political duties may be gathered from the fact that in one of the State elections held since the war, in

which Judge Carpenter, an old South Carolinian and a Republican, ran against the carpet-bag candidate, the two most serious charges brought against him were, first, that if he was elected, he would return them to slavery again, and, second, failing that, he would not allow their wives and daughters to wear hoop-skirts. On the other hand, the great argument used on the carpet-bag side— an argument which was urged on the stump from one end of the State to the other—was that the real owners of the lands, dwelling-houses, gin-houses, and everything in the State were not the white rebels, but the loyal blacks; or, as Senator Beverly Nash, himself a negro leader, . . . said in a speech at Columbus to six or eight thousand men, after the taxpayers had begun their attempt at reform, "The reformers complain of taxes being too high. I tell you that they are not high enough. I want them taxed until they put these lands back where they belong, into the hands of those who worked for them. You worked for them, you labored for them, and were sold to pay for them, and you ought to have them." Such was the "key-note" of the campaign during the carpet-bag period.

The Convention of 1868 which drew up a State constitution, was composed of seventy-two negroes and forty-nine whites. This convention made provision for a levy of $2,230,950, yet only 13 of these 72 negroes paid taxes. In the Legislature of 1869, there were 12 black and 20 white senators. Eight of these 12 paid no taxes. In the House, there were 86 black and 37 white members; 68 of the 86 paid no taxes. This was the machinery which was set in motion to produce the South Carolina of to-day. It would be a waste of time to attempt to trace in detail the operation of these causes in producing their legitimate results. We will state the results themselves.

The days of the carpet-baggers are gone by.

FROM *The Nation*, 16 April 1874.

South Carolina is governed by its own native-born citizens as much as Massachusetts or Illinois. In the House of Representatives (we quote the observations of Mr. J. S. Pike, who travelled through the State only a year ago), sit 124 members. Of these, 30 are pure white men, and the remainder black; but as 7 out of the 30 white men vote with the black, the real strength of the opposition is only 23. The Speaker is black, the clerk is black, the door-keepers are black, the pages are black, the chairman of the committee of ways and means is black, and the chaplain is black. The Lieutenant-Governor, the President of the Senate, the Speaker of the House, the Treasurers, are all blacks. The Governor alone is a white, elected by black votes.

The helpless condition of the judiciary may be inferred from this account of the legislature: Last year a judge was threatened with impeachment, and was telegraphed to appear before the legislature at Columbia, because it was alleged that in a case tried in Charleston, involving a claim for damages against a railroad, he "had made improper reflections on a colored woman of doubtful character." Two or three months since, in a trial for larceny, a colored man had been proved guilty of larceny by three respectable witnesses of his own color. The jury (black) acquitted him, but as none of them could write, and, after the verdict had been rendered, several of them declared it was not their decision, the judge came to the conclusion that they were incompetent and discharged them. A resolution was immediately introduced into the legislature for impeaching the judge, on the ground that he had denied to blacks the right to sit on juries. The judge was R. B. Carpenter, not a suspected character, but a Republican, who cast his vote for Grant in 1872.

The finances of the State are involved in hopeless confusion. D. T. Corbin, United States District-Attorney, a leading Republican senator, was obliged to admit in 1872, and in a speech in favor of the re-election of General Grant, that under Governor Orr, the first reconstruction governor, the bonded debt amounted to $5,500,000, with a floating debt of $1,500,000 more, while at the time of his speech the State was saddled with a bonded debt of $16,000,000 and a floating debt of two or three millions more. The money was obtained in New York by a man named Kimpton, who acted as financial agent of the State, who had been required by the Governor to give good bonds for the faithful performance of his duties, and who had accomplished this end, it was understood, by getting as sureties Henry Clews & Co. of this city. Henry Clews & Co., however, in reality only signed as witnesses to Kimpton's signature. Kimpton managed his business so well that in 1871 the interest, commissions, and stamps paid on short loans made in New York amounted to nearly as much as the entire interest on the State debt, with a large commission account in favor of Kimpton still unsettled. There is no use, however, in going into details. It is enough that the taxable property in the State before the war was $490,000,000, and is now assessed at $180,000,000, while good judges are of opinion that it is not worth $100,000,000; that the taxes levied before the war were not over $500,000, and are now $2,700,000, while the legislative expenses have crept up from $40,000 a year to $291,000, and the public printing, for a government which can neither read nor write, from $5,000 to $450,000; that land assessed at $15,000 is offered in the market for $5,000. The sum and substance of it all is confiscation. Property is no longer owned in South Carolina under the protection of the laws or Constitution; it is held until it is taken away by Beverly Nash, or [Governor Franklin] Moses, or any one of the gang who govern the State by means of the votes of the colored race. Farms are sold to pay taxes; the old, rich plantations are broken up; the whites are driven out of the State or disfranchised, and a queer aristocracy of color is set up, with the rich Congo thief on top and the degraded Anglo-Saxon at the bottom.

This is what socialism has done for South Carolina. It is not a question any longer about the more or less good government of the State, or the rights of minorities, but whether the whites can stay in the State at all. The taxpayers have appealed to Washington for moral support, and they have been dismissed by the President with surly anger and contempt, and are now actually engaged in begging General [Benjamin F.] Butler, the greatest socialistic demagogue of our day, to have a little mercy on them. It is not a mistaken instinct which leads them to him, for they know very well that the South Carolinian imitators derive their power from the steady-moving and merciless machinery which fills the custom-houses and post-offices with his tools; and it is this machinery which makes so-cialism in America the dangerous, deadly poison it is. Left to themselves, the whites of South Carolina would find some means to govern the State. But they are not left to themselves. They are gradually being driven out of the State, and the only question remaining to be settled is how long it will take to make the once "sovereign State" of South Carolina a truly loyal, truly Republican, truly African San Domingo.

South Carolina Black Leaders Defend the State Government's Fiscal Record (1874)

As part of the drive to overthrow Reconstruction in the state, South Carolina whites organized a Taxpayers' convention in 1874 which appealed to Washington for relief. Accusing carpetbaggers and black politicians of looting and plundering the state on an unprecedented scale, the convention alleged that taxes had risen twentyfold since the war. The Associated Press disseminated the full text of the convention's petition to newspapers, and many northern papers responded sympathetically. Recognizing the potential damage the issue of high taxes posed, a group of black leaders in the state issued a reply, written by F. L. Cardozo, to the Taxpayers' memorial. This document carefully demonstrated how emancipation, by increasing the number of citizens served by the state, necessitated an expansion of state programs and thus state expenditures. The Associated Press refused to distribute this document, and it therefore appeared only in black newspapers.

Certain citizens of South Carolina, styling themselves "The Taxpayers' Convention," have memorialized your honorable bodies to grant them relief from unjust burdens and oppressions, alleged by them to have been imposed by the Republican State government, we, the undersigned, members of the State Central Committee of the Union Republican party of South Carolina, beg

leave most respectfully to submit . . . the following counter statement and reply: . . .

The statement that "the annual expenses of the government have advanced from four hundred thousand dollars before the war to two millions and a half at the present time," is entirely incorrect, and the items of expenditures given to illustrate and prove this statement are wholly inaccurate and untrue, and skillfully selected to deceive. . . .

We present a true statement of the appropriation of the fiscal year before the war, beginning

FROM *New National Era,* 16 April 1874.

October 1, 1859, and ending September 30, 1860, and the fiscal year beginning November 1, 1872, and ending October 31, 1873, that are properly chargeable to those respective fiscal years:

	1859–60	1872–[73]
Salaries	$81,100	$194,989
Contingents	73,000	47,600
Free schools	75,000	300,000
State Normal School	8,704	25,000
Deaf, dumb, and blind	8,000	16,000
Military academies	30,000	—
Military contingencies	100,000	20,000
Roper Hospital	3,000	—
State Lunatic Asylum	—	77,500
State Normal and High School	5,000	—
Jurors and Constables	50,000	—
State Orphan House (colored)	—	20,000
State Penitentiary	—	40,000
Sundries	184,427	444,787
Total	$618,231	$1,184,876

. . . By the census of 1860, there were in South Carolina at that time 301,214 free population, and 402,406 slaves. By the census of 1870 there were 705,606 free population. Now "remember . . . that in 1860, 402,406 souls, now a part of the body politic, . . . the cost of governing whom is now chargeable to the Government of our State, were, in 1860, chattels. . . . In 1860, the slave was no charge on the State Government, save when he was hung for some petty misdemeanor, and the State compelled to pay his loss."

It would be, therefore, but just and fair to divide the amount appropriated in 1859–60, viz.: $618,231, by the then free population, 301,214, and it will be found that the cost of governing each citizen was $2.05; and then divide the amount appropriated in 1872–73 by the free population now, viz.: 705,606, and it will be found that the cost of

governing each citizen is $1.67—$2.05 in 1859–60, during the boasted Democratic period, and $1.67 in 1872–73, under the so-called corrupt Radical rule—a different of 38 cents *per capita* in favor of the latter. So that if the Democrats had the same number of free citizens to govern in 1859–60 that the Republicans had in 1872–73, it would have cost them $261,616.30 more than it has cost us.

The State having been organized on a free basis necessarily created a larger number of officers, and, therefore, a larger amount of salaries. We are not ashamed of the fact that our appropriation for schools in 1872–73 is four times greater than in 1859–60. Ignorance was the corner-stone of slavery, and essential to its perpetuity. . . .

Now in every hamlet and village in our state, "the schoolmaster is abroad."

In 1857 the number of scholars attending the free schools was only 19,356, while in 1873 the number of scholars attending the schools was 85,753 (of which 37,218 were white, 46,535 colored).

It will be observed that there were no appropriations for the State Lunatic Asylum and Penitentiary in 1859–60. The Lunatic Asylum was then supported by the friends of its wealthy inmates and the counties, but in 1872–73 . . . the State assumed its support and made liberal appropriation for its unfortunate patients.

The erection of the Penitentiary was not begun until after the war, and there was, therefore, no appropriation for it in 1859–60.

The appropriation in 1872–73 for military purposes was but $20,000. We had no occasion to appropriate $130,000 for military academies and contingencies, in order to furnish nurseries to train the young to strike at the nation's life, and to purchase material for the war of secession.

There was no appropriation in 1859–60 for a colored State Orphan Home. The colored orphans that were then uncared for were free, but their parents, when living, were heavily taxed to support white orphans, while their own children, after their death, were neglected. . . .

The statement that "it has been openly avowed by prominent members of the Legislature that taxes should be increased to a point which will compel the sale of the great body of land and take it away from the former owners," is not correct.

It is, however, a fact that the present system of taxation, like that of almost all civilized countries, is based chiefly upon real estate. In the days of slavery before the war it was not so. Taxes were levied by the large planters, who absolutely controlled the State, upon trades, professions, free colored persons, a mere nominal *per capita* tax upon slaves, and upon the lands assessed at one-tenth their true value.

This method of taxing lands enabled the planters to acquire and retain large and uncultivated tracts of land, and thus form that most dangerous of all oligarchies—a landed aristocracy.

It was from this class that secession and the war sprung. Our present method of taxation very naturally and properly prevents the perpetuation of this system, which is so repugnant to our Republican institutions. . . .

The statement that "the appropriations made in one year for the work (*i.e.* printing) done, or to be done, . . . amounted to $475,000 exclusive of $100,000 for publishing the laws," is wholly incorrect.

The present Legislature during the session of 1872–73 made appropriations for $450,000 for printing and advertising the laws. . . .

It will be seen that these appropriations, though made in one year, are for work ordered and performed during a period of three years. . . .

It is stated that the total appropriations for public printing made by the Legislature of South Carolina, during a period of sixty years, from 1800 to 1859, is $271,180. This statement is not correct; but even if it were, is it a cause for boastfulness, that but that amount was expended for printing during the sixty years that the people were kept in ignorance, and no public information disseminated amongst them for their enlightenment and elevation? We think not.

It is stated that "the committees have received large sums as compensation for reporting favorably on private bills." Whatever corruption may exist in the Legislature is to be attributed to the Democrats as well as the Republicans. They never hesitate to offer bribes when they have a private bill to pass. But corruption existed long before the advent of the Republican party of this State into power, only it was carried on then with the artistic skill of more experienced operators, and not easily seen.

The gentlemen who have assembled in this [convention], constituting themselves . . . representatives of the so-called taxpayers, are not what they would have the country believe. They are the prominent politicians of the old *regime*—the former ruling element of the State—who simply desire to regain the power they lost by their folly of secession. . . .

The Republicans admit the existence of evils among them. They acknowledge they have committed mistakes and errors in the past which they deeply regret. But those mistakes and errors are being daily corrected, and they see no necessity whatever to resort to the desperate remedies asked for by the convention of the so-called tax-payers. There are enough able and good men among those who have the present charge of the government in their hands to right every existing wrong. They are determined to do so.

In this work the difficulties under which they have labored have been naturally great, and have been increased ten-fold by the determined hostility and opposition of the Democratic party ever since reconstruction. This is their third effort to regain power. First they expected it through the election of Seymour and Blair [in 1868]; second, through the midnight murders and assassinations of Ku-Kluxism; and now, thirdly, by the distortion and misrepresentation of facts, in order to create a public sentiment in their favor and obtain relief from Congress.

Ulysses S. Grant Vetoes the Currency Act (1874)

During the war, the Union had issued over $400 million of paper currency, known as greenbacks, to finance the war; these notes were backed only by the faith of the federal government and could not be redeemed for gold or silver (specie). After the war, the currency question divided those who favored a return to specie-based currency and those who wanted to expand the currency supply by keeping greenbacks in circulation and even increasing the amount the Treasury Department issued. The depression that began in 1873 gave new urgency to the currency question in American politics, and in 1874 Congress, hoping to stimulate the economy, provided for the issuing of $100 million in additional greenbacks. In his veto message, President Grant listed the reasons for his opposition to this bill. Grant's veto pleased eastern conservatives, but the protest against it signaled a growing public interest in economic issues unrelated to Reconstruction.

Executive Mansion, April 22, 1874.

To the Senate of the United States:

Herewith I return Senate bill No. 617, entitled "An act to fix the amount of United States notes and the circulation of national banks, and for other purposes," without my approval. . . .

Practically it is a question whether the measure under discussion would give an additional dollar to the irredeemable paper currency of the country or not, and whether by requiring three-fourths of the reserve to be retained by the banks and prohibiting interest to be received on the balance it might not prove a contraction.

But the fact can not be concealed that theoretically the bill increases the paper circulation $100,000,000, less only the amount of reserves restrained from circulation by the provision of the second section. The measure has been supported on the theory that it would give increased circulation. It is a fair inference, therefore, that if in practice the measure should fail to create the abundance of circulation expected of it the friends of the measure, particularly those out of Congress, would clamor for such inflation as would give the expected relief.

The theory, in my belief, is a departure from true principles of finance, national interest, national obligations to creditors, Congressional promises, party pledges (on the part of both political parties), and of personal views and promises made by me in every annual message sent to Congress and in each inaugural address. . . .

As early as December 4, 1865, the House of Representatives passed a resolution, by a vote of 144 yeas to 6 nays, concurring "in the views of the Secretary of the Treasury in relation to the necessity of a contraction of the currency, with a view to as early a resumption of specie payments as the business interests of the country will permit," and pledging "cooperative action to this end as speedily as possible."

The first act passed by the Forty-first Congress, [approved] on the 18th day of March, 1869, . . . remains as a continuing pledge of the faith of the United States "to make provision at the earliest

FROM James D. Richardson, ed., *A Compilation of the Messages and Papers of the Presidents*, vol. 7 (Washington, D.C.: Government Printing Office, 1907), pp. 269–71.

practicable period for the redemption of the United States notes in coin."

A declaration contained in the act of June 30, 1864, created an obligation that the total amount of United States notes issued or to be issued should never exceed $400,000,000. The amount in actual circulation was actually reduced to $356,000,000, at which point Congress passed the act of February 4, 1868, suspending the further reduction of the currency. The forty-four millions have ever been regarded as a reserve, to be used only in case of emergency, such as has occurred on several occasions, and must occur when from any cause revenues suddenly fall below expenditures; and such a reserve is necessary, because the fractional currency, amounting to fifty millions, is redeemable in legal tender on call.

It may be said that such a return of fractional currency for redemption is impossible; but let steps be taken for a return to a specie basis and it will be found that silver will take the place of fractional currency as rapidly as it can be supplied, when the premium on gold reaches a sufficiently low point. With the amount of United States notes to be issued permanently fixed within proper limits and the Treasury so strengthened as to be able to redeem them in coin on demand it will then be safe to inaugurate a system of free banking with such provisions as to make compulsory redemption of the circulating notes of the banks in coin, or in United States notes, themselves redeemable and made equivalent to coin.

As a measure preparatory to free banking, and for placing the Government in a condition to redeem its notes in coin "at the earliest practicable period," the revenues of the country should be increased so as to pay current expenses, provide for the sinking fund required by law, and also a surplus to be retained in the Treasury in gold.

I am not a believer in any artificial method of making paper money equal to coin when the coin is not owned or held ready to redeem the promises to pay, for paper money is nothing more than promises to pay, and is valuable exactly in proportion to the amount of coin that it can be converted into. While coin is not used as a circulating medium, or the currency of the country is not convertible into it at par, it becomes an article of commerce as much as any other product. The surplus will seek a foreign market as will any other surplus. The balance of trade has nothing to do with the question. Duties on imports being required in coin creates a limited demand for gold. About enough to satisfy that demand remains in the country. To increase this supply I see no way open but by the Government hoarding through the means above given, and possibly by requiring the national banks to aid.

It is claimed by the advocates of the measure herewith returned that there is an unequal distribution of the banking capital of the country. I was disposed to give great weight to this view of the question at first, but on reflection it will be remembered that there still remains $4,000,000 of authorized bank-note circulation assigned to States having less than their quota not yet taken. In addition to this the States having less than their quota of bank circulation have the option of twenty-five millions more to be taken from those States having more than their proportion. When this is all taken up, or when specie payments are fully restored or are in rapid process of restoration, will be the time to consider the question of "more currency."

U. S. Grant.

6

JAMES G. BLAINE

The Blaine Amendment (1875)

Damaged by corruption and scandal, hurt by hard times, and weakened by the growing northern disillusionment with Reconstruction, the Republican party gave renewed attention to ethnocultural issues in the 1870s. In 1875 James G. Blaine of Maine, who was an important Republican leader in Congress and would be the party's presidential candidate in 1884, proposed a constitutional amendment to prohibit the use of any tax money to support religious schools. The intended target of this amendment was the Catholic Church, which had long sought public money to support its parochial schools. Blaine had been sympathetic to the Know-Nothing party in the 1850s, and one purpose of this amendment was to revive ethnocultural issues in northern politics and thereby strengthen the Republican party's hold on its traditional Protestant voting base. The amendment was also evidence that party leaders feared that traditional sectional issues, which had been the party's mainstay for many years, were losing their political salience in the North. Grant endorsed such an amendment in his annual message later that year.

Augusta, Me., October 20, 1875.

My Dear Sir:

The public-school agitation in your late campaign is liable to break out elsewhere; and, occurring first in one State and then in another, may keep the whole country in a ferment for years to come. This inevitably arouses sectarian feeling and leads to that bitterest and most deplorable of all strifes, the strife between religious denominations. It seems to me that this question ought to be settled in some definite and comprehensive way, and the only settlement that can be final is the complete victory for non-sectarian schools. I am sure this will be demanded by the American people at all hazards and at any cost.

The dread of sectarian legislation in this country has been felt many times in the past. It began very early. The first amendment to the Constitution, the joint product of Jefferson and Madison,

FROM *Appleton's Annual Cyclopedia for the Year 1875* (New York: D. Appleton and Co., 1876), pp. 79–80.

proposed in 1789, declared that "Congress shall make no law respecting an establishment of religion, nor prohibiting the free exercise thereof." At that time, when the powers of the Federal Government were untried and undeveloped, the fear was that Congress might be the source of danger to perfect religious liberty, and hence all power was taken away from it. At the same time the States were left free to do as they pleased in regard to "an establishment of religion," for the tenth amendment, proposed by that eminent jurist, Theophilus Parsons, and adopted contemporaneously with the first, declared that "all powers not delegated to the United States, by the Constitution, nor prohibited by it to the States, are reserved to the States respectively, or to the people."

A majority of the people in any State in this Union can, therefore, if they desire it, have an established Church, under which the minority may be taxed for the erection of church-edifices which they never enter and for the support of which they do not believe. This power was actually exercised in some of the States long after the adoption of the

Federal Constitution, and, although there may be no positive danger of its revival in the future, the possibility of it should not be permitted. The auspicious time to guard against an evil is when all will unite in preventing it.

And in curing this constitutional defect all possibility of hurtful agitation on the school question should be ended also. Just let the old Jefferson-Madison amendment be applied to the States by adding the following to the inhibitory clauses in section 10, Article I, of the Federal Constitution, viz.:

No State shall make any law respecting an establishment of religion, or prohibiting the free exercise thereof; and no money raised by taxation in any State, for the support of the public schools or derived from any public fund therefor, shall ever be under the control of any religious sect, nor shall any money so raised ever be divided between religious sects or denominations.

This, you will observe, does not interfere with any State having just such a school system as its citizens may prefer, subject to the single and simple restriction that the schools shall not be made the arena for sectarian controversy or theological disputation. This adjustment, it seems to me, would be comprehensive and conclusive, and would be fair alike to Protestant and Catholic, to Jew and Gentile, leaving the religious faith and the conscience of every man free and unmolested.

Very sincerely yours,

J. G. Blaine.

7

EDWARDS PIERREPONT

The Public Is Tired of These Outbreaks in the South (1875)

General Adelbert Ames, who was of New England origins, was stationed in Mississippi after the war. Married to the daughter of former Union General Benjamin F. Butler, who was now a Radical leader in the House of Representatives, Ames served as senator and then governor of Mississippi. He never had any particular attachment to the state and viewed his mission as primarily to protect black residents and uphold their rights. Ames was in office in 1875 when Mississippi Democrats launched a concerted campaign of violence and intimidation against blacks and Republicans in the state election. When he requested federal assistance to restore order and safeguard the polls, the attorney general sent the following reply. After the election, which produced an overwhelming Democratic victory, Ames resigned to avoid impeachment on trumped up charges and permanently left the state.

FROM Edward McPherson, *Handbook for 1876* (Washington, D.C.: Philp and Solomons, 1876), pp. 42–43.

Department of Justice
Washington, Sept. 14, 1875.

To Governor Ames, Jackson, Miss.:

This hour I have had dispatches from the PRESIDENT. I can best convey to you his ideas by extracts from his dispatch.

"The whole public are tired out with these annual autumnal outbreaks in the South, and the great majority are ready now to condemn any interference on the part of the Government. I heartily wish that peace and good order may be restored without issuing the proclamation. But if it *is not*, the proclamation must be issued, and if it *is*, I shall instruct the commander of the forces to have *no child's play*.

"If there is a necessity for military interference, there is justice in such interference as to deter evil doers. . . . I would suggest the sending of a dispatch (or better by private messenger) to Gov. Ames, urging him to strengthen his own position by exhausting his own resources in restoring order, before he receives government aid. He might accept the assistance offered by the citizens of Jackson and elsewhere. . . . Gov. Ames and his advisers can be made perfectly secure.

"As many of the troops now in Mississippi as he deems necessary may be sent to Jackson. If he is betrayed by those who offer assistance, he will be in a position to defeat their ends and punish them."

You see by this the mind of the President, with which I and every member of the Cabinet who has been consulted are in full accord. You see the difficulties; you see the responsibilities which you assume.

We cannot understand why you do not strengthen yourself in the way the President suggests; nor do we see why you do not call the Legislature together, and obtain from them whatever powers and money and arms you need. The Constitution is explicit that the executive of the State can call upon the President for aid in suppressing *"domestic violence"* only *"when the Legislature cannot be convened."* And the law expressly says: *"In case of an insurrection in any State against the government thereof, it shall be lawful for the President, on application of the Legislature of such State, or of the Executive when the Legislature cannot be convened, to call, etc."* It is the plain meaning of the constitution and the laws, when taken together, that the executive of the State may call upon the President for military aid to quell "domestic violence" only in case of an insurrection in any State against the government thereof, when the Legislature cannot be called together. You make no suggestion even that there is any insurrection against the government of the State, or that the Legislature would not support you in any measures you might propose to preserve the public order.

I suggest that you take all lawful means and all needed measures to preserve the peace by the forces in your own State, and let the country see that the citizens of Mississippi, who are largely favorable to good order, and who are largely Republican, have the courage and the manhood to *fight* for their rights, and to destroy the bloody ruffians who murder the innocent and unoffending freedmen.

Everything is in readiness. Be careful to bring yourself strictly within the Constitution and the laws; and if there *is such resistance to your State authorities as you cannot by all the means at your command suppress*, the President will swiftly aid you in crushing these lawless traitors to human rights.

Telegraph me on receipt of this, and state *explicitly* what you need.

Yours very respectfully,
Edwards Pierrepont, Attorney-General.

8

JAMES W. LEE

The Mississippi Plan in Action (1876)

James W. Lee was the Republican sheriff of Monroe County, Mississippi. In a letter to Governor Adelbert Ames, he described the methods used by Democrats to carry the 1875 state election in the county, which contained a large black majority.

Office of U.S. Commissioner,
Aberdeen, Miss., Feby. 7, 1876.

To His Excellency A. Ames, Gov.

Dr. Sir: In answer to your excellencie's letter of the 17th, I have to say: That the deep-seated opposition to republican rule in Mississippi developed fully & powerfully immediately succeeding the Vicksburgh municipal election, and was the occasion of two or three large out-door political meetings in Aberdeen, at which the speakers took very extreme grounds in favor of the color-line policy and social ostracisum, and they declared even then that they intended to cary the next general election in this State at any cost; the policy there foreshadowed culminating in the great political campaign of 1875, through which we have recently passed. At the commencement of that campaign the policy was far more aggressive and intolerant than on any former occasion since the late war; their speakers made the most extravagant declarations on all occasions and at the same time there were local organizations of infantry & artillery, the former being armed with "needle-guns" and the latter with a sword and one 24-pound cannon; at the opening of the campaign large sums of money were subscribed, paid & placed under the control of the democratic Co. Ex. Com. by some in this Co.; . . . at first every influence that could be brought to bear on the colored men was used to get them to

renounce their party and go with the democrats, but they stood firmly & truly to the republican party; seeing that nothing but intimidation would enable them to carry the election they resorted to it in every possible way, and the republicans at once found themselves in the midst of a perfect organized armed opposition that embraced the entire democratic party, & hundreds of boys under 21 participating actively in all their movements, &c. Near the close of the campaign the republican speakers were followed & met at their regular appointments by large numbers of democrats and the artillery co., until about the 22 of Oct. At Sulphur Springs they came very near precipitating a bloody riot by beating colored men over the heads with pistols, & by cutting the heads out of drums, &c. The republicans, seeing what would be the result, at once revoked the balance of their appointments running up to the election, and did not attempt to hold any more meetings in the Co. We barely escaped several bloody riots in Aberdeen the last ten days immediately preceeding the election, almost always using colored democrats to provoke & bring it on. On the night before the election armed bodies of men visited almost every neighborhood in the county, threatening death to all who voted the "radical" ticket. . . .

The policy of intimidation had been so successfully managed that many colored men kept away from the polls, and 1 U.S. supervisor of election kept away from the election through actual fear of being killed if he went. On the morning of the election in Aberdeen about 1,300 men assembled at the "C. H." [Court House] to vote, and when the

FROM U.S. Senate, 44th Cong., 1st sess., S. Rept. 527, vol. 3, pt. 2, pp. 67–68.

proclamation was made announcing the polls open for votes the White-Liners took possession of the polls & held them until the infantry, armed with "needle-guns," came upon the ground; at the same time the artillery came up to the N. corner of the "C. H." square, and was unlimbered & placed in position, at first bearing on the jail; about the same time about 100 armed mounted men passed between the C. H. & jail, & they drove a large body of colored men from the town. The colored men who had gathered immediately around the "C. H." to vote were told if they did not leave the town within five minutes that the last man would be shot dead in his tracks, and that not a man could vote that day unless he voted the democratic ticket. These orders were given by the commanders of the infry., cavalry, & artillery. In the mean time the cannon was brought down to the gate opening to the west of the "C. H.," where a large crowd had gathered to vote at the west door. The cannon was placed in position bearing on the large crowd, when one of the officers called out, "If there are any democrats in that crowd get out, for we are going to fire the cannon," when the whole crowd broke & run in confusion, then the infantry & cavalry had no trouble in driving everything from town; and there are over 1,300 men in this county, & mostly in this beat, No. 4, who will swear that they were driven from the polls & could not vote. The night before the election the iron bridge draw was turned & left in that condition on the 2 of Novbr., election-day; all the fords on the river were guarded by White-Liners, who drove every man back unless he was going to vote the democratic ticket.

The foregoing instances are only a few that occurred in the county before & at the election.

Yours, truly,

James W. Lee.

9

MARGARET ANN CALDWELL

The Assassination of an African American Political Leader (1876)

Violence, intimidation, and assassination were standard tactics used by white Democrats to overthrow Reconstruction in the South. Republican leaders, both white and black, became marked men in the South in the 1870s as the movement to drive the Republicans from power intensified. A former slave who had received some education, Charles Caldwell was a Republican leader in Hinds County, Mississippi, and served in the state senate. During the tumultuous 1875 campaign, Caldwell boldly led a black militia unit through the town of Clinton in order to bolster blacks' courage and intimidate local whites. He subsequently had to flee the county for his personal safety, but he returned on election day. Two months later, as his widow recounted in testimony before a congressional committee, he was assassinated by local whites. Caldwell's fate, and that of other Republicans in the South, made a mockery of Democrats' claims to represent the forces of democracy and purity of elections in the South.

Jackson, Miss., June 20, 1876.

Mrs. Margaret Ann Caldwell (colored) sworn and
examined.

By the Chairman:

The Widow of Senator Caldwell.

Question. What is your name?—Answer. Margaret Ann Caldwell.

Q. Where do you live?—A. In Clinton, Hinds
County.

Q. Was Mr. Caldwell, formerly senator, your
husband?—A. Yes, sir.

Q. What was his first name?—A. Charles.

Q. When did he die?—A. Thursday night, in
the Christmas. Him and his brother was killed.

Q. You may state to the committee what you
know of his death.—A. I know when he left the
house on the Thursday evening, in the Christmas,
between dark and sundown. . . .

Mr. Nelson said that Buck Cabell . . . persuaded
him [Caldwell] to go out and drink; insisted upon
his taking a drink with him, and him and Buck Cabell never knowed anything against each other in
his life; never had no hard words. My husband told
him no, he didn't want any Christmas. He said,
"You must take a drink with me," and entreated
him, and said, "You must take a drink." He then
took him by the arm and told him to drink for a
Christmas treat; that he must drink, and carried
him into Chilton's cellar, and they jingled the
glasses, and at the tap of the glasses, and while each
one held the glass, while they were taking the
glasses, somebody shot right through the back
from the outside of the gate window, and he fell to
the ground.

As they struck their glasses, that was the signal
to shoot. They had him in the cellar, and shot him
right there, and he fell on the ground.

When he was first shot, he called for Judge
Cabinis, and called for Mr. Chilton; I don't know
who else. They were all around, and nobody went
to his relief; all them men standing around with
their guns. Nobody went to the cellar, and he
called for Preacher Nelson, called for him, and
Preacher Nelson said that when he went to the
cellar-door he was afraid to go in, and called to
him two or three times, "Don't shoot me," and
Charles said, "Come in," he wouldn't hurt him,
and "take him out of the cellar"; that he wanted to
die in the open air, and did not want to die like a
dog closed up.

When they taken him out, he was in a manner
dead, just from that one shot; and they brings him
out then, and he only asked one question, so Par-
son Nelson told me—to take him home and let
him see his wife before he died; that he could not
live long.

It was only a few steps to my house, and they
would not do it, and some said this.

Nelson carried him to the middle of the street,
and the men all hallooed, "we will save him while
we've got him; dead men tell no tales. . . ."

Whether he stood up right there in the street
while they riddled him with thirty or forty of their
loads, of course, I do not know, but they shot him
all that many times when he was in a manner dead.
All those balls went in him.

I understood that a young gentleman told that
they shot him as he lay on the ground until they
turned him over. He said so. I did not hear him.

Mr. Nelson said when he asked them to let him
see me they told him no, and he then said, taking
both sides of his coat and bringing them up this
way so, he said, "Remember when you kill me you
kill a gentleman and a brave man. Never say you
killed a coward. I want you to remember it when I
am gone."

Nelson told me that, and he said that he never
begged them, and that he never told them, but to
see how a brave man could die.

They can find no cause; but some said they
killed him because he carried the militia to Edwards, and they meant to kill him for that. The
time the guns were sent there he was captain under
Governor Ames, and they said they killed him for
that; for obeying Governor Ames.

FROM U.S. Senate, 44th Cong., 1st sess., S. Rept. 527, vol. 3,
pp. 435–39.

10

JAMES LUSK

A Southern White Leader Abandons the Republican Party (1913)

In order to overthrow the Republican state governments in the South, southern Democrats sought to draw the race line in politics as tightly as possible. At one time southern whites accounted for perhaps one-fifth of the total Republican vote in the South. As they came under increasing social and political pressure, however, a growing number of these whites abandoned the Republican party. Colonel James Lusk of Alabama, who left the Republican party following the 1874 election, explained to a former political associate his reasons for switching parties.

No white man can live in the South in the future and act with any other than the Democratic party unless he is willing and prepared to live a life of social isolation and remain in political oblivion. While I am somewhat advanced in years, I am not so old as to be devoid of political ambition. Besides I have two grown sons. There is, no doubt, a bright, brilliant and successful future before them if they are Democrats; otherwise, not. If I remain in the Republican party,—which can hereafter exist at the South only in name,—I will thereby retard, if not mar and possibly destroy, their future prospects. Then, you must remember that a man's first duty is to his family. My daughters are the pride of my home. I cannot afford to have them suffer the humiliating consequences of the social ostracism to which they may be subjected if I remain in the Republican party.

The die is cast. I must yield to the inevitable and surrender my convictions upon the altar of my family's good,—the outgrowth of circumstances and conditions which I am powerless to prevent and cannot control. Henceforth I must act with the Democratic party or make myself a martyr; and I do not feel that there is enough at stake to justify me in making such a fearful sacrifice as that. It is, therefore, with deep sorrow and sincere regret, Henry, that I am constrained to leave you politically, but I find that I am confronted with a condition, not a theory. I am compelled to choose between you, on one side, and my family and personal interests, on the other. That I have decided to sacrifice you and yours upon the altar of my family's good is a decision for which you should neither blame nor censure me. If I could see my way clear to pursue a different course it would be done; but my decision is based upon careful and thoughtful consideration and it must stand.

FROM John R. Lynch, *The Facts of Reconstruction* (New York: The Neale Publishing Co., 1913), pp. 122–23.

Rutherford B. Hayes Outlines His Southern Policy (1877)

In his inaugural address on March 5, 1877, Rutherford B. Hayes discussed his southern policy. The anticipated results from his policy of conciliation failed to materialize, and before long Hayes was denouncing southern whites for failing to honor their pledge to protect the rights and liberties of African Americans.

The sweeping revolution of the entire labor system of a large portion of our country and the advance of 4,000,000 people from a condition of servitude to that of citizenship, upon an equal footing with their former masters, could not occur without presenting problems of the gravest moment, to be dealt with by the emancipated race, by their former masters, and by the General Government, the author of the act of emancipation. That it was a wise, just, and providential act, fraught with good for all concerned, is now generally conceded throughout the country. That a moral obligation rests upon the National Government to employ its constitutional power and influence to establish the rights of the people it has emancipated, and to protect them in the enjoyment of those rights when they are infringed or assailed, is also generally admitted.

The evils which afflict the Southern States can only be removed or remedied by the united and harmonious efforts of both races, actuated by motives of mutual sympathy and regard; and while in duty bound and fully determined to protect the rights of all by every constitutional means at the disposal of my Administration, I am sincerely anxious to use every legitimate influence in favor of honest and efficient local *self*-government as the true resource of those States for the promotion of the contentment and prosperity of their citizens. In the effort I shall make to accomplish this purpose I ask the cordial cooperation of all who cherish an interest in the welfare of the country, trusting that party ties and the prejudice of race will be freely surrendered in behalf of the great purpose to be accomplished. In the important work of restoring the South it is not the political situation alone that merits attention. The material development of that section of the country has been arrested by the social and political revolution through which it has passed, and now needs and deserves the considerate care of the National Government within the just limits prescribed by the Constitution and wise public economy.

But at the basis of all prosperity, for that as well as for every other part of the country, lies the improvement of the intellectual and moral condition of the people. Universal suffrage should rest upon universal education. To this end, liberal and permanent provision should be made for the support of free schools by the State governments, and, if

FROM James D. Richardson, ed., *A Compilation of the Messages and Papers of the Presidents*, vol. 7 (Washington, D.C.: Government Printing Office, 1907), pp. 443–44.

need be, supplemented by legitimate aid from national authority.

Let me assure my countrymen of the Southern States that it is my earnest desire to regard and promote their truest interests—the interests of the white and of the colored people both and equally—and to put forth my best efforts in behalf of a civil policy which will forever wipe out in our political affairs the color line and the distinction between North and South, to the end that we may have not merely a united North or a united South, but a united country.

2

Governor Daniel Chamberlain Surrenders the South Carolina Governorship (1877)

After President Hayes ended federal support for the Radical government in South Carolina, the Republican regime promptly collapsed and Governor Daniel Chamberlain left the state. Chamberlain understandably was bitter, for if Hayes carried the state in the 1876 election, then Chamberlain certainly did as well. In this address to the Republicans in South Carolina on April 10, 1877, Chamberlain discussed the causes that produced his downfall and explained his decision not to prolong the contest over the governorship.

To the Republicans of South Carolina:

By your choice I was made Governor of this State in 1874. At the election on the 7th of November last, I was again, by your votes, elected to the same office. My title to the office, upon every legal and moral ground, is to-day clear and perfect. By the recent decision and action of the President of the United States, I find myself unable longer to maintain my official rights, and I hereby announce to you that I am unwilling to prolong a struggle which can only bring further suffering upon those who engage in it.

In announcing this conclusion, it is my duty to say for you, that the Republicans of South Carolina entered upon their recent political struggle for the maintenance of their political and civil rights.

Constituting, beyond question, a large majority of the lawful voters of the State, you allied yourselves with that political party whose central and inspiring principle has hitherto been the civil and political freedom of all men under the Constitution and laws of our country. By heroic efforts and sacrifices which the just verdict of history will rescue from the cowardly scorn now cast upon them by political placemen and traders, you secured the electoral vote of South Carolina for Hayes and Wheeler. In accomplishing this result, you became the victims of every form of persecution and injury. From authentic evidence it is shown that not less than one hundred of your number were murdered because they were faithful to their principles and exercised rights solemnly guaranteed to them by the nation. You were denied employment, driven from your homes, robbed of the earnings of years of honest industry, hunted for your lives like wild beasts, your families outraged and scattered, for no offence except your peaceful and firm determination

FROM Walter Allen, *Governor Chamberlain's Administration in South Carolina* (New York: G. P. Putnam's Sons, 1888), p. 504.

to exercise your political rights. You trusted, as you had a right to trust, that if by such efforts you established the lawful supremacy of your political party in the nation, the Government of the United States, in the discharge of its constitutional duty, would protect the lawful Government of the State from overthrow at the hands of your political enemies. From causes patent to all men, and questioned by none who regard truth, you have been unable to overcome the unlawful combinations and obstacles which have opposed the practical supremacy of the Government which your votes have established. For many weary months you have waited for your deliverance. While the long struggle for the Presidency was in progress, you were exhorted by every representative and organ of the National Republican Party, to keep your allegiance true to that party, in order that your deliverance might be certain and complete.

Not the faintest whisper of the possibility of disappointment in these hopes and promises ever reached you while the struggle was pending. To-day—April 10, 1877—by the order of the President whom your votes alone rescued from overwhelming defeat, the Government of the United States abandons you, deliberately withdraws from you its support, with the full knowledge that the lawful Government of the State will be speedily overthrown. By a new interpretation of the Constitution of the United States at variance alike with the previous practice of the Government and with the decisions of the Supreme Court, the Executive of the United States evades the duty of ascertaining which of two rival State Governments is the lawful one, and by the withdrawal of troops now protecting the State from domestic violence, abandons the lawful State Government to a struggle with insurrectionary forces too powerful to be resisted. The grounds of policy upon which such action is defended are startling. . . .

It is said that if a majority of a State are unable by physical force to maintain their rights, they must be left to political servitude. Is this a doctrine ever before heard in our history? If it shall prevail, its consequences will not long be confined to South Carolina and Louisiana. It is said that a Democratic House of Representatives will refuse an appropriation for the army of the United States, if the lawful Government of South Carolina is maintained by the military forces. Submission to such coercion marks the degeneracy of the political party or people which endures it. A Government worthy the name, a political party fit to wield power, never before blanched at such a threat. But the edict has gone forth. No arguments or considerations which your friends could present have sufficed to avert the disaster.

No effective means of resistance to the consummation of the wrong are left. The struggle can be prolonged. My strict legal rights are, of course, wholly unaffected by the action of the President. No Court of the State has jurisdiction to pass upon the title of my office. No lawful Legislature can be convened except at my call. . . .

But, to my mind, my present responsibility involves the consideration of the effect of my action upon those whose representative I am. I have hitherto been willing to ask you, Republicans, to risk all dangers and endure all hardships until relief should come from the Government of the United States. That relief will never come. I cannot ask you to follow me further. In my best judgment I can no longer serve you by further resistance to the impending calamity.

With gratitude . . . to you for your boundless confidence in me, with profound admiration for your matchless fidelity to the cause in which we have struggled, I now announce to you and to the people of the State that I shall no longer actively assert my right to the office of Governor of South Carolina.

The motives and purposes of the President of the United States in the policy which compels me to my present course are unquestionably honorable and patriotic. I devoutly pray that events may vindicate the wisdom of his action, and that peace, justice, freedom, and prosperity may hereafter be the portion of every citizen of South Carolina.

D. H. Chamberlain,
Governor of South Carolina.

3

Frederick Douglass Assesses the Mistakes of Reconstruction (1880)

Frederick Douglass was the most important African American leader in the country during the era of the Civil War and Reconstruction. He had been a vocal advocate of making emancipation a Union war aim, and after the war he lobbied for civil rights for blacks, including the right of suffrage. In a speech delivered in 1880, he looked back on the experience of Reconstruction and analyzed the fundamental errors that led to its collapse, emphasizing especially the failure to provide freedpeople with economic independence. Yet he assured his audience that a better day was coming.

How stands the case with the recently-emancipated millions of colored people in our own country? What is their condition today? What is their relation to the people who formerly held them as slaves? These are important questions, and they are such as trouble the minds of thoughtful men of all colors, at home and abroad. By law, by the Constitution of the United States, slavery has no existence in our country. The legal form has been abolished. By the law and the Constitution, the Negro is a man and a citizen, and has all the rights and liberties guaranteed to any other variety of the human family, residing in the United States.

He has a country, a flag, and a government, and may legally claim full and complete protection under the laws. It was the ruling wish, intention, and purpose of the loyal people, after rebellion was suppressed, to have an end to the entire cause of that calamity by forever putting away the system of slavery and all its incidents. In pursuance of this idea, the Negro was made free, made a citizen, made eligible to hold office, to be a juryman, a legislator, and a magistrate. To this end, several amendments to the Constitution were proposed, recommended, and adopted. They are now a part of the supreme law of the land, binding alike upon every state and territory of the United States, north and south. Briefly, this is our legal and theoretical condition. This is our condition on paper and parchment. If only from the national statute book we were left to learn the true condition of the colored race, the result would be altogether creditable to the American people. . . .

We have gone still further. We have laid the heavy hand of the Constitution upon the matchless meanness of caste, as well as upon the hell-black crime of slavery. We have declared before all the world that there shall be no denial of rights on account of race, color, or previous condition of servitude. The advantage gained in this respect is immense.

It is a great thing to have the supreme law of the land on the side of justice and liberty. It is the line up to which the nation is destined to march—the law to which the nation's life must ultimately conform. It is a great principle, up to which we may educate the people, and to this extent its value exceeds all speech.

But today, in most of the southern states, the fourteenth and fifteenth amendments are virtually nullified.

The rights which they were intended to guarantee are denied and held in contempt. The citi-

FROM Frederick Douglass, *Life and Times of Frederick Douglass* (Boston: De Wolfe, Fiske and Co., 1892), pp. 609–15.

zenship granted in the fourteenth amendment is practically a mockery, and the right to vote, provided for in the fifteenth amendment, is literally stamped out in face of government. The old master class is today triumphant, and the newly-enfranchised class in a condition but little above that in which they were found before the rebellion.

Do you ask me how, after all that has been done, this state of things has been made possible? I will tell you. Our reconstruction measures were radically defective. They left the former slave completely in the power of the old master, the loyal citizen in the hands of the disloyal rebel against the government. Wise, grand, and comprehensive in scope and design as were the reconstruction measures, high and honorable as were the intentions of the statesmen by whom they were framed and adopted, time and experience, which try all things, have demonstrated that they did not successfully meet the case.

In the hurry and confusion of the hour, and the eager desire to have the Union restored, there was more care for the sublime superstructure of the republic than for the solid foundations upon which it could alone be upheld. To the freedmen was given the machinery of liberty, but there was denied to them the steam to put it in motion. They were given the uniform of soldiers, but no arms; they were called citizens, but left subjects; they were called free, but left almost slaves. The old master class was not deprived of the power of life and death, which was the soul of the relation of master and slave. They could not, of course, sell their former slaves, but they retained the power to starve them to death, and wherever this power is held there is the power of slavery. . . . The Negro today . . . is in a thralldom grievous and intolerable, compelled to work for whatever his employer is pleased to pay him, swindled out of his hard earnings by money orders redeemed in stores, compelled to pay the price of an acre of ground for its use during a single year, to pay four times more than a fair price for a pound of bacon and to be

kept upon the narrowest margin between life and starvation. Much complaint has been made that the freedmen have shown so little ability to take care of themselves since their emancipation. Men have marvelled that they have made so little progress. I question the justice of this complaint. It is neither reasonable, nor in any sense just. To me the wonder is, not that the freedmen have made so little progress, but, rather, that they have made so much—not that they have been standing still, but that they have been able to stand at all.

We have only to reflect for a moment upon the situation in which these people found themselves when liberated. Consider their ignorance, their poverty, their destitution, and their absolute dependence upon the very class by which they had been held in bondage for centuries, a class whose every sentiment was averse to their freedom, and we shall be prepared to marvel that they have, under the circumstances, done so well.

. . . When the serfs of Russia were emancipated, they were given three acres of ground upon which they could live and make a living. But not so when our slaves were emancipated. They were sent away empty-handed, without money, without friends, and without a foot of land upon which to stand. Old and young, sick and well, were turned loose to the open sky, naked to their enemies. The old slave quarter that had before sheltered them and the fields that had yielded them corn were now denied them. . . .

Taking all the circumstances into consideration, the colored people have no reason to despair. We still live, and while there is life there is hope. The fact that we have endured wrongs and hardships which would have destroyed any other race, and have increased in numbers and public consideration, ought to strengthen our faith in ourselves and our future. Let us, then, wherever we are, whether at the North or at the South, resolutely struggle on in the belief that there is a better day coming, and that we, by patience, industry, uprightness, and economy may hasten that better day.

United States Constitution

We the People of the United States, in Order to form a more perfect Union, establish Justice, insure domestic Tranquility, provide for the common defence, promote the general Welfare, and secure the Blessings of Liberty to ourselves and our Posterity, do ordain and establish this CONSTITUTION for the United States of America.

Article 1

Section 1. All legislative Powers herein granted shall be vested in a Congress of the United States, which shall consist of a Senate and House of Representatives.

Section 2. The House of Representatives shall be composed of Members chosen every second Year by the People of the several States, and the Electors in each State shall have the Qualifications requisite for Electors of the most numerous Branch of the State Legislature.

No Person shall be a Representative who shall not have attained to the Age of twenty-five Years, and been seven Years a Citizen of the United States, and who shall not, when elected, be an Inhabitant of that State in which he shall be chosen.

Representatives and direct Taxes shall be apportioned among the several States which may be included within this Union, according to their respective Numbers, which shall be determined by adding to the whole Number of free Persons, including those bound to Service for a Term of Years, and excluding Indians not taxed, three-fifths of all other Persons. The actual Enumeration shall be made within three Years after the first Meeting of the Congress of the United States, and within every subsequent Term of ten Years, in such Manner as they shall by Law direct. The Number of Representatives shall not exceed one for every thirty Thousand, but each State shall have at Least one Representative; and until such enumeration shall be made, the State of New Hampshire shall be entitled to chuse three, Massachusetts eight, Rhode-Island and Providence Plantations one, Connecticut five, New York six, New Jersey four, Pennsylvania eight, Delaware one, Maryland six, Virginia ten, North Carolina five, South Carolina five, and Georgia three.

When vacancies happen in the Representation from any State, the Executive Authority thereof shall issue Writs of Election to fill such Vacancies.

The House of Representatives shall chuse their Speaker and other Officers; and shall have the sole Power of Impeachment.

Section 3. The Senate of the United States shall be composed of two Senators from each State, chosen by the Legislature thereof, for six Years; and each Senator shall have one Vote.

Immediately after they shall be assembled in Consequence of the first Election, they shall be divided as equally as may be into three Classes. The Seats of the Senators of the first Class shall be vacated at the Expiration of the second Year, of the second Class at the Expiration of the fourth Year, and of the third Class at the Expiration of the sixth Year, so that one-third may be chosen every second Year; and if Vacancies happen by Resignation, or otherwise, during the Recess of the Legislature of any State, the Executive thereof may make temporary Appointments until the next Meeting of the Legislature, which shall then fill such Vacancies.

No Person shall be a Senator who shall not have attained to the Age of thirty Years, and been nine Years a Citizen of the United States, and who shall not, when elected, be an Inhabitant of that State for which he shall be chosen.

The Vice President of the United States shall be

President of the Senate, but shall have no vote, unless they be equally divided.

The Senate shall chuse their other Officers, and also a President pro tempore, in the absence of the Vice President, or when he shall exercise the Office of President of the United States.

The Senate shall have the sole Power to try all Impeachments. When sitting for that purpose they shall be on Oath or Affirmation. When the President of the United States is tried, the Chief Justice shall preside: And no person shall be convicted without the Concurrence of two thirds of the Members present.

Judgment in Cases of Impeachment shall not extend further than to removal from Office, and disqualification to hold and enjoy any Office of honor, Trust, or Profit under the United States: but the Party convicted shall nevertheless be liable and subject to Indictment, Trial, Judgment, and Punishment, according to Law.

Section 4. The Times, Places and Manner of holding Elections for Senators and Representatives, shall be prescribed in each State by the Legislature thereof; but the Congress may at any time by Law make or alter such Regulations, except as to the Places of Chusing Senators.

The Congress shall assemble at least once in every Year, and such Meeting shall be on the first Monday in December, unless they shall by Law appoint a different Day.

Section 5. Each House shall be the Judge of the Elections, Returns and Qualifications of its own Members, and a Majority of each shall constitute a Quorum to do Business; but a smaller number may adjourn from day to day, and may be authorized to compel the Attendance of absent Members, in such Manner, and under such Penalties, as each House may provide.

Each House may determine the Rules of its Proceedings, punish its Members for disorderly Behaviour, and, with the Concurrence of two thirds, expel a Member.

Each House shall keep a Journal of its Proceedings, and from time to time publish the same, ex-

cepting such Parts as may in their Judgment require Secrecy; and the Yeas and Nays of the Members of either House on any question shall, at the Desire of one fifth of those Present, be entered on the Journal.

Neither House, during the Session of Congress, shall, without the Consent of the other, adjourn for more than three days, nor to any other Place than that in which the two Houses shall be sitting.

Section 6. The Senators and Representatives shall receive a Compensation for their Services, to be ascertained by Law, and paid out of the Treasury of the United States. They shall in all Cases, except Treason, Felony, and Breach of the Peace, be privileged from Arrest during their Attendance at the Session of their respective Houses, and in going to and returning from the same; and for any Speech or Debate in either House, they shall not be questioned in any other Place.

No Senator or Representative shall, during the Time for which he was elected, be appointed to any civil Office under the Authority of the United States, which shall have been created, or the Emoluments whereof shall have been increased, during such time; and no Person holding any Office under the United States shall be a Member of either House during his continuance in Office.

Section 7. All Bills for raising Revenue shall originate in the House of Representatives; but the Senate may propose or concur with Amendments as on other bills.

Every Bill which shall have passed the House of Representatives and the Senate, shall, before it become a Law, be presented to the President of the United States; If he approve he shall sign it, but if not he shall return it, with his Objections, to that House in which it shall have originated, who shall enter the Objections at large on their Journal, and proceed to reconsider it. If after such Reconsideration two thirds of that House shall agree to pass the bill, it shall be sent, together with the objections, to the other House, by which it shall likewise be reconsidered, and if approved by two thirds of that House, it shall become a Law. But in all such Cases the Votes of both Houses shall be determined by Yeas and Nays, and the Names of the Persons voting for and against the Bill shall be entered on the Journal of each House respectively. If any Bill shall not be returned by the President within ten Days (Sundays excepted) after it shall have been presented to him, the Same shall be a Law, in like Manner as if he had signed it, unless the Congress by their Adjournment prevent its Return, in which Case it shall not be a Law.

Every Order, Resolution, or Vote to which the Concurrence of the Senate and House of Representatives may be necessary (except on a question of Adjournment) shall be presented to the President of the United States; and before the Same shall take Effect, shall be approved by him, or being disapproved by him, shall be repassed by two thirds of the Senate and House of Representatives, according to the Rules and Limitations prescribed in the Case of a Bill.

Section 8. The Congress shall have Power To lay and collect Taxes, Duties, Imposts and Excises, to pay the Debts and provide for the common Defence and general Welfare of the United States; but all Duties, Imposts and Excises shall be uniform throughout the United States;

To borrow money on the credit of the United States;

To regulate Commerce with foreign Nations, and among the several States, and with the Indian Tribes;

To establish an uniform rule of Naturalization, and uniform Laws on the subject of Bankruptcies throughout the United States;

To coin Money, regulate the Value thereof, and of foreign Coin, and fix the Standard of Weights and Measures;

To provide for the Punishment of counterfeiting the Securities and current Coin of the United States;

To establish Post Offices and post Roads;

To promote the Progress of Science and useful Arts, by securing for limited Times to Authors and Inventors the exclusive Right to their respective Writings and Discoveries;

To constitute Tribunals inferior to the Supreme Court;

To define and punish Piracies and Felonies committed on the high Seas, and Offenses against the Law of Nations;

To declare War, grant Letters of Marque and Reprisal, and make Rules concerning Captures on Land and Water;

To raise and support Armies, but no Appropriation of Money to that Use shall be for a longer Term than two Years;

To provide and maintain a Navy;

To make Rules for the Government and Regulation of the land and naval forces;

To provide for calling forth the Militia to execute the Laws of the Union, suppress Insurrections and repel Invasions;

To provide for organizing, arming, and disciplining the Militia, and for governing such Part of them as may be employed in the Service of the United States, reserving to the States respectively, the Appointment of the Officers, and the Authority of training the Militia according to the discipline prescribed by Congress;

To exercise exclusive Legislation in all Cases whatsoever, over such District (not exceeding ten Miles square) as may, by Cession of particular States, and the acceptance of Congress, become the Seat of the Government of the United States, and to exercise like Authority over all Places purchased by the Consent of the Legislature of the State in which the Same shall be, for the Erection of Forts, Magazines, Arsenals, Dock-yards, and other needful Buildings;—And

To make all Laws which shall be necessary and proper for carrying into Execution the foregoing Powers, and all other Powers vested by this Constitution in the Government of the United States, or in any Department or Officer thereof.

Section 9. The Migration or Importation of such Persons as any of the States now existing shall think proper to admit, shall not be prohibited by the Congress prior to the Year one thousand eight hundred and eight, but a tax or duty may be imposed on such Importation, not exceeding ten dollars for each Person.

The privilege of the Writ of Habeas Corpus shall not be suspended, unless when in Cases of Rebellion or Invasion the public Safety may require it.

No bill of Attainder or ex post facto Law shall be passed.

No capitation, or other direct, Tax shall be laid unless in Proportion to the Census or Enumeration herein before directed to be taken.

No Tax or Duty shall be laid on Articles exported from any State.

No Preference shall be given by any Regulation of Commerce or Revenue to the Ports of one State over those of another: nor shall Vessels bound to, or from, one State, be obliged to enter, clear, or pay Duties in another.

No Money shall be drawn from the Treasury, but in Consequence of Appropriations made by Law; and a regular Statement and Account of the Receipts and Expenditures of all public Money shall be published from time to time.

No Title of Nobility shall be granted by the United States: And no Person holding any Office of Profit or Trust under them, shall, without the Consent of the Congress, accept of any present, Emolument, Office, or Title, of any kind whatever, from any King, Prince, or foreign State.

Section 10. No State shall enter into any Treaty, Alliance, or Confederation; grant Letters of Marque and Reprisal; coin Money; emit Bills of Credit; make any Thing but gold and silver Coin a Tender in Payment of Debts; pass any Bill of Attainder, ex post facto Law, or Law impairing the Obligation of Contracts, or grant any Title of Nobility.

No State shall, without the Consent of the Congress, lay any Imposts or Duties on Imports or Exports, except what may be absolutely necessary for executing its inspection Laws; and the net Produce of all Duties and Imposts, laid by any State on Imports or Exports, shall be for the use of the Treasury of the United States; and all such Laws shall be subject to the Revision and Control of the Congress.

No state shall, without the Consent of Congress, lay any duty of Tonnage, keep Troops, or Ships of War in time of Peace, enter into any Agreement or Compact with another State, or with a foreign Power, or engage in War, unless actually invaded, or in such imminent Danger as will not admit of delay.

Article II

Section 1. The executive Power shall be vested in a President of the United States of America. He shall hold his Office during the Term of four years, and, together with the Vice President, chosen for the same Term, be elected, as follows:

Each State shall appoint, in such Manner as the Legislature thereof may direct, a Number of Electors, equal to the whole Number of Senators and Representatives to which the State may be entitled in the Congress: but no Senator or Representative, or Person holding an Office of Trust or Profit under the United States, shall be appointed an Elector.

The Electors shall meet in their respective States, and vote by Ballot for two persons, of whom one at least shall not be an Inhabitant of the same State with themselves. And they shall make a List of all the Persons voted for, and of the Number of Votes for each; which List they shall sign and certify, and transmit sealed to the Seat of the Government of the United States, directed to the President of the Senate. The President of the Senate shall, in the Presence of the Senate and House of Representatives, open all the Certificates, and the Votes shall then be counted. The Person having the greatest Number of Votes shall be the President, if such Number be a Majority of the whole Number of Electors appointed; and if there be more than one who have such Majority, and have an equal Number of Votes, then the House of Representatives shall immediately chuse by Ballot one of them for President; and if no Person have a Majority, then from the five highest on the List the said House shall in like Manner chuse the President.

But in chusing the President, the Votes shall be taken by States, the Representation from each State having one Vote; a quorum for this Purpose shall consist of a Member or Members from two-thirds of the States, and a Majority of all the States shall be necessary to a Choice. In every Case, after the Choice of the President, the Person having the greatest Number of Votes of the Electors shall be the Vice President. But if there should remain two or more who have equal votes, the Senate shall chuse from them by Ballot the Vice President.

The Congress may determine the Time of chusing the Electors, and the Day on which they shall give their Votes; which Day shall be the same throughout the United States.

No person except a natural-born Citizen, or a Citizen of the United States, at the time of the Adoption of this Constitution, shall be eligible to the Office of President; neither shall any Person be eligible to that Office who shall not have attained to the Age of thirty-five years, and been fourteen Years a Resident within the United States.

In Case of the Removal of the President from Office, or of his Death, Resignation, or Inability to discharge the Powers and Duties of the said Office, the same shall devolve on the Vice President, and the Congress may by Law provide for the Case of Removal, Death, Resignation, or Inability, both of the President and Vice President, declaring what Officer shall then act as President, and such Officer shall act accordingly, until the disability be removed, or a President shall be elected.

The President shall, at stated Times, receive for his Services a Compensation, which shall neither be increased nor diminished during the Period for which he shall have been elected, and he shall not receive within that Period any other Emolument from the United States, or any of them.

Before he enter on the execution of his Office, he shall take the following Oath or Affirmation:—"I do solemnly swear (or affirm) that I will faithfully execute the Office of President of the United States, and will, to the best of my Ability, preserve, protect, and defend the Constitution of the United States."

Section 2. The President shall be Commander in Chief of the Army and Navy of the United States, and of the Militia of the several States, when called into the actual Service of the United States; he may require the Opinion, in writing, of the principal Officer in each of the executive Departments, upon any subject relating to the Duties of their respective Offices, and he shall have Power to Grant Reprieves and Pardons for Offenses against the United States, except in Cases of Impeachment.

He shall have Power, by and with the Advice and Consent of the Senate, to make Treaties, provided two-thirds of the Senators present concur; and he shall nominate, and by and with the Advice and Consent of the Senate, shall appoint Ambassadors, other public Ministers and Consuls, Judges of the supreme Court, and all other Officers of the United States, whose Appointments are not herein otherwise provided for, and which shall be established by Law: but the Congress may by Law vest the Appointment of such inferior Officers, as they think proper, in the President alone, in the Courts of Law, or in the Heads of Departments.

The President shall have Power to fill up all Vacancies that may happen during the Recess of the Senate, by granting Commissions which shall expire at the End of their next Session.

Section 3. He shall from time to time give to the Congress Information of the State of the Union, and recommend to their Consideration such Measures as he shall judge necessary and expedient; he may, on extraordinary occasions, convene both Houses, or either of them, and in Case of Disagreement between them, with respect to the Time of Adjournment, he may adjourn them to such Time as he shall think proper; he shall receive Ambassadors and other public Ministers; he shall take care that the Laws be faithfully executed, and shall Commission all the Officers of the United States.

Section 4. The President, Vice President and all civil Officers of the United States, shall be removed from Office on Impeachment for, and Conviction of, Treason, Bribery, or other high Crimes and Misdemeanors.

Article III

Section 1. The judicial Power of the United States, shall be vested in one supreme Court, and in such inferior Courts as the Congress may from time to time ordain and establish. The Judges, both of the supreme and inferior Courts, shall hold their Offices during good Behaviour, and shall, at stated Times, receive for their Services, a Compensation, which shall not be diminished during their Continuance in Office.

Section 2. The judicial Power shall extend to all Cases, in Law and Equity, arising under this Constitution, the Laws of the United States, and Treaties made, or which shall be made, under their Authority;—to all Cases affecting ambassadors, other public ministers and consuls;—to all cases of admiralty and maritime Jurisdiction;—to Controversies to which the United States shall be a Party;—to Controversies between two or more States;—between a State and Citizens of another State;—between Citizens of different States—between Citizens of the same State claiming Lands under Grants of different States, and between a State, or the Citizens thereof, and foreign States, Citizens, or Subjects.

In all Cases affecting Ambassadors, other public Ministers and Consuls, and those in which a State shall be Party, the supreme Court shall have original Jurisdiction. In all the other Cases before mentioned, the supreme Court shall have appellate Jurisdiction, both as to Law and Fact, with such Exceptions, and under such Regulations as the Congress shall make.

The trial of all Crimes, except in Cases of Impeachment, shall be by Jury; and such Trial shall be held in the State where the said Crimes shall have been committed; but when not committed within any State, the Trial shall be at such Place or Places as the Congress may by Law have directed.

Section 3. Treason against the United States, shall consist only in levying War against them, or in adhering to their Enemies, giving them Aid and Comfort. No Person shall be convicted of Treason unless on the Testimony of two Witnesses to the same overt Act, or on Confession in open Court.

The Congress shall have power to declare the Punishment of Treason, but no Attainder of Treason shall work Corruption of Blood, or Forfeiture except during the Life of the Person attainted.

Article IV

Section 1. Full Faith and Credit shall be given in each State to the public Acts, Records, and judicial Proceedings of every other State. And the Congress may by general Laws prescribe the Manner in which such Acts, Records and Proceedings shall be proved, and the Effect thereof.

Section 2. The Citizens of each State shall be entitled to all Privileges and Immunities of Citizens in the several States.

A Person charged in any State with Treason, Felony, or other Crime, who shall flee from Justice, and be found in another State, shall on demand of the executive Authority of the State from which he fled, be delivered up, to be removed to the State having Jurisdiction of the crime.

No Person held to Service or Labour in one State, under the Laws thereof, escaping into another, shall, in Consequence of any Law or Regulation therein, be discharged from such Service or Labour, but shall be delivered up on Claim of the Party to whom such Service or Labour may be due.

Section 3. New States may be admitted by the Congress into this Union; but no new State shall be formed or erected within the Jurisdiction of any other State; nor any State be formed by the Junction of two or more States, or parts of States, without the Consent of the Legislatures of the States concerned as well as of the Congress.

The Congress shall have Power to dispose of and make all needful Rules and Regulations respecting the Territory or other Property belonging to the United States; and nothing in this Constitution shall be so construed as to Prejudice any Claims of the United States, or of any particular State.

Section 4. The United States shall guarantee to every State in this Union a Republican Form of Government, and shall protect each of them against Invasion; and on Application of the Legislature, or of the Executive (when the Legislature cannot be convened) against domestic Violence.

Article V

The Congress, whenever two-thirds of both Houses shall deem it necessary, shall propose Amendments to this Constitution, or, on the Application of the Legislatures of two-thirds of the several States, shall call a Convention for proposing Amendments, which, in either Case, shall be valid to all Intents and Purposes, as part of this Constitution, when ratified by the Legislatures of three-fourths of the several States, or by Conventions in three-fourths thereof, as the one or the other Mode of Ratification may be proposed by the Congress; Provided that no Amendment which may be made prior to the Year One thousand eight hundred and eight shall in any Manner affect the first and fourth Clauses in the Ninth Section of the first Article; and that no State, without its Consent, shall be deprived of its equal Suffrage in the Senate.

Article VI

All Debts contracted and Engagements entered into, before the Adoption of this Constitution, shall be as valid against the United States under this Constitution, as under the Confederation.

This Constitution, and the Laws of the United States which shall be made in Pursuance thereof; and all Treaties made, or which shall be made, under the Authority of the United States, shall be the supreme Law of the Land; and the Judges in every State shall be bound thereby, any Thing in the Constitution or Laws of any State to the Contrary notwithstanding.

The Senators and Representatives before mentioned, and the Members of the several State Legislatures, and all executive and judicial Officers, both of the United States and of the several States, shall be bound by Oath or Affirmation to support this Constitution; but no religious Tests shall ever be required as a qualification to any Office or public Trust under the United States.

Article VII

The Ratification of the Conventions of nine States shall be sufficient for the Establishment of this Constitution between the States so ratifying the same.

Done in Convention by the Unanimous Consent of the States present the Seventeenth Day of September in the Year of our Lord one thousand seven hundred and Eighty seven, and of the Independence of the United States of America the Twelfth. In Witness whereof We have hereunto subscribed our Names.

Articles in Addition to, and Amendment of, the Constitution of the United States of America, Proposed by Congress, and Ratified by the Legislatures of the Several States, Pursuant to the Fifth Article of the Original Constitution

Amendment I

Congress shall make no law respecting an establishment of religion, or prohibiting the free exercise thereof; or abridging the freedom of speech, or of the press; or the right of the people peaceably to assemble, and to petition the Government for a redress of grievances.

Amendment II

A well regulated Militia, being necessary to the security of a free State, the right of the people to keep and bear Arms shall not be infringed.

Amendment III

No Soldier shall, in time of peace, be quartered in any house, without the consent of the Owner, nor in time of war, but in a manner to be prescribed by law.

Amendment IV

The right of the people to be secure in their persons, houses, papers, and effects, against unreasonable searches and seizures, shall not be violated, and no Warrants shall issue, but upon probable cause, supported by Oath or affirmation, and particularly describing the place to be searched, and the persons or things to be seized.

Amendment V

No person shall be held to answer for a capital or otherwise infamous crime, unless on a presentment or indictment of a Grand Jury, except in cases arising in the land or naval forces, or in the Militia, when in actual service in time of War or public danger; nor shall any person be subject for the same offence to be twice put in jeopardy of life or limb; nor shall be compelled in any criminal case to be a witness against himself, nor be deprived of life, liberty, or property, without due process of law; nor shall private property be taken for public use, without just compensation.

Amendment VI

In all criminal prosecutions, the accused shall enjoy the right to a speedy and public trial, by an impartial jury of the State and district wherein the crime shall have been committed, which district shall have been previously ascertained by law, and to be informed of the nature and cause of the accusation; to be confronted with the witnesses against him; to have compulsory process for obtaining witnesses in his favour, and to have the Assistance of Counsel for his defence.

Amendment VII

In suits at common law, where the value in controversy shall exceed twenty dollars, the right of trial by jury shall be preserved, and no fact tried by a jury, shall be otherwise reexamined in any Court of the United States, than according to the rules of the common law.

Amendment VIII

Excessive bail shall not be required, nor excessive fines imposed, nor cruel and unusual punishments inflicted.

Amendment IX

The enumeration of the Constitution, of certain rights, shall not be construed to deny or disparage others retained by the people.

Amendment X[1]

The powers not delegated to the United States by the Constitution, nor prohibited by it to the States, are reserved to the States respectively, or to the people.

Amendment XI[2]

The Judicial power of the United States shall not be construed to extend to any suit in law or equity, commenced or prosecuted against one of the United States by Citizens of another State, or by Citizens or Subjects of any Foreign State.

Amendment XII[3]

The Electors shall meet in their respective States and vote by ballot for President and Vice-President, one of whom, at least, shall not be an inhabitant of the same State with themselves; they shall name in their ballots the person voted for as President, and in distinct ballots the person voted for as Vice-President, and they shall make distinct lists of all persons voted for as President, and of all persons voted for as Vice-President, and of the number of votes for each, which lists they shall sign and certify, and transmit sealed to the seat of the government of the United States, directed to

[1] Amendments I–X adopted 1791.

[2] Adopted in 1798.

[3] Adopted in 1804.

the President of the Senate;—The President of the Senate shall, in the presence of the Senate and House of Representatives, open all the certificates and the votes shall then be counted;—The person having the greatest number of votes for President, shall be the President, if such number be a majority of the whole number of Electors appointed; and if no person have such majority, then from the persons having the highest numbers not exceeding three on the list of those voted for as President, the House of Representatives shall choose immediately, by ballot, the President. But in choosing the President, the votes shall be taken by states, the representation from each state having one vote; a quorum for this purpose shall consist of a member or members from two-thirds of the states, and a majority of all the states shall be necessary to a choice. And if the House of Representatives shall not choose a President whenever the right of choice shall devolve upon them, before the fourth day of March next following, then the Vice-President shall act as President, as in the case of the death or other constitutional disability of the President.—The person having the greatest number of votes as Vice-President, shall be the Vice-President, if such number be a majority of the whole number of Electors appointed, and if no person have a majority, then from the two highest numbers on the list, the Senate shall choose the Vice-President; a quorum for the purpose shall consist of two-thirds of the whole number of Senators, and a majority of the whole number shall be necessary to a choice. But no person constitutionally ineligible to the office of President shall be eligible to that of Vice-President of the United States.

Amendment XIII[4]

Section 1. Neither slavery nor involuntary servitude, except as a punishment for crime whereof the party shall have been duly convicted, shall exist within the United States, or any place subject to their jurisdiction.

Section 2. Congress shall have power to enforce this article by appropriate legislation.

Amendment XIV[5]

Section 1. All persons born or naturalized in the United States, and subject to the jurisdiction thereof, are citizens of the United States and of the State wherein they reside. No State shall abridge the privileges or immunities of citizens of the United States; nor shall any State deprive any person of life, liberty, or property, without due process of law; nor deny to any person within its jurisdiction the equal protection of the laws.

Section 2. Representatives shall be apportioned among the several States according to their respective numbers, counting the whole number of persons in each State, excluding Indians not taxed. But when the right to vote at any election for the choice of electors for President and Vice-President of the United States, Representatives in Congress, the Executive and Judicial officers of a State, or the members of the Legislature thereof, is denied to any of the male inhabitants of such State, being twenty-one years of age, and citizens of the United States, or in any way abridged, except for participation in rebellion, or other crime, the basis of representation therein shall be reduced in the proportion which the number of such male citizens shall bear to the whole number of male citizens twenty-one years of age in such State.

Section 3. No person shall be a Senator or Representative in Congress, or elector of President and Vice-President, or hold any office, civil or military, under the United States, or under any State, who, having previously taken an oath, as a member of Congress, or as an officer of the United States, or as a member of any State legislature, or as an executive or judicial officer of any State, to support the Constitution of the United States, shall have engaged in insurrection or rebellion against the same,

[4] Adopted in 1865.

[5] Adopted in 1868.

or given aid or comfort to the enemies thereof. But Congress may by a vote of two-thirds of each House, remove such disability.

Section 4. The validity of the public debt of the United States, authorized by law, including debts incurred for payment of pensions and bounties for services in suppressing insurrection or rebellion, shall not be questioned. But neither the United States nor any State shall assume or pay any debts or obligation incurred in aid of insurrection or re-bellion against the United States, or any claim for the loss or emancipation of any slave; but all such debts, obligations, and claims shall be held illegal and void.

Section 5. The Congress shall have the power to enforce, by appropriate legislation, the provisions of this article.

Amendment XV[6]

Section 1. The right of citizens of the United States to vote shall not be denied or abridged by the United States or by any State on account of race, color, or previous condition of servitude—

Section 2. The Congress shall have power to enforce this article by appropriate legislation.

---

[6] Adopted in 1870.

Confederate Constitution

We, the people of the Confederate States, each State acting in its sovereign and independent character, in order to form a permanent federal government, establish justice, insure domestic tranquillity, and secure the blessings of liberty to ourselves and our posterity—invoking the favor and guidance of Almighty God—do ordain and establish this Constitution for the Confederate States of America.

Article I.

Section 1. All legislative powers herein delegated shall be vested in a Congress of the Confederate States, which shall consist of a Senate and House of Representatives.

Section 2. 1. The House of Representatives shall be composed of members chosen every second year by the people of the several States; and the electors in each State shall be citizens of the Confederate States, and have the qualifications requisite for electors of the most numerous branch of the State Legislature; but no person of foreign birth, not a citizen of the Confederate States, shall be allowed to vote for any officer, civil or political, State or Federal.

2. No person shall be a Representative who shall not have attained the age of twenty-five years, and be a citizen of the Confederate States, and who shall not, when elected, be an inhabitant of that State in which he shall be chosen.

3. Representatives and direct taxes shall be apportioned among the several States, which may be included within this Confederacy, according to their respective numbers, which shall be determined by adding to the whole number of free persons, including those bound to service for a term of years, and excluding Indians not taxed, three-fifths of all slaves. The actual enumeration shall be made within three years after the first meeting of the Congress of the Confederate States, and within every subsequent term of ten years, in such manner as they shall by law direct. The number of Representatives shall not exceed one for every fifty thousand, but each State shall have at least one Representative; and until such enumeration shall be made, the State of South Carolina shall be entitled to choose six; the State of Georgia ten; the State of Alabama nine; the State of Florida two; the State of Mississippi seven; the State of Louisiana six; and the State of Texas six.

4. When vacancies happen in the representation from any State the executive authority thereof shall issue writs of election to fill such vacancies.

5. The House of Representatives shall choose their Speaker and other officers; and shall have the sole power of impeachment; except that any judicial or other Federal officer, resident and acting solely within the limits of any State, may be impeached by a vote of two-thirds of both branches of the Legislature thereof.

Section 3. 1. The Senate of the Confederate States shall be composed of two Senators from each State, chosen for six years by the Legislature thereof, at the regular session next immediately preceding the commencement of the term of service; and each Senator shall have one vote.

2. Immediately after they shall be assembled, in consequence of the first election, they shall be divided as equally as may be into three classes. The seats of the Senators of the first class shall be vacated at the expiration of the second year; of the second class at the expiration of the fourth year; and of the third class at the expiration of the sixth year; so that one-third may be chosen every second year; and if vacancies happen by resignation, or otherwise, during the recess of the Legislature of any State, the Executive thereof may make temporary appointments until the next meeting of the Legislature, which shall then fill such vacancies.

3. No person shall be a Senator who shall not have attained the age of thirty years, and be a citizen of the Confederate States; and who shall not, when elected, be an inhabitant of the State for which he shall be chosen.

4. The Vice-President of the Confederate States shall be president of the Senate, but shall have no vote unless they be equally divided.

5. The Senate shall choose their other officers; and also a president *pro tempore* in the absence of the Vice-President, or when he shall exercise the office of President of the Confederate States.

6. The Senate shall have the sole power to try all impeachments. When sitting for that purpose, they shall be on oath or affirmation. When the President of the Confederate States is tried, the Chief Justice shall preside; and no person shall be convicted without the concurrence of two-thirds of the members present.

7. Judgment in cases of impeachment shall not extend further than to removal from office, and disqualification to hold and enjoy any office of honor, trust, or profit under the Confederate States; but the party convicted shall, nevertheless, be liable and subject to indictment, trial, judgment and punishment according to law.

Section 4. 1. The times places and manner of holding elections for Senators and Representatives shall be prescribed in each State by the Legislature thereof, subject to the provisions of this Constitution; but the Congress may, at any time, by law, make or alter such regulations, except as to the times and places of choosing Senators.

2. The Congress shall assemble at least once in every year; and such meeting shall be on the first Monday in December, unless they shall, by law, appoint a different day.

Section 5. 1. Each House shall be the judge of the elections, returns, and qualifications of its own members, and a majority of each shall constitute a quorum to do business; but a smaller number may adjourn from day to day, and may be authorized to compel the attendance of absent members, in such manner and under such penalties as each House may provide.

2. Each House may determine the rules of its proceedings, punish its members for disorderly behavior, and with the concurrence of two-thirds of the whole number expel a member.

3. Each House shall keep a journal of its proceedings, and from time to time publish the same, excepting such parts as may in their judgment re-

quire secrecy; and the yeas and nays of the members of either House, on any question, shall, at the desire of one-fifth of those present, be entered on the journal.

4. Neither House, during the session of Congress, shall, without the consent of the other, adjourn for more than three days, nor to any other place than that in which the two Houses shall be sitting.

Section 6. 1. The Senators and Representatives shall receive a compensation for their services, to be ascertained by law, and paid out of the Treasury of the Confederate States. They shall, in all cases, except treason, felony, and breach of the peace, be privileged from arrest during their attendance at the session of their respective Houses, and in going to and returning from the same; and for any speech or debate in either House, they shall not be questioned in any other place.

2. No Senator or Representative shall, during the time for which he was elected, be appointed to any civil office under the authority of the Confederate States, which shall have been created, or the emoluments whereof shall have been increased during such time; and no person holding any office under the Confederate States shall be a member of either House during his continuance in office. But Congress may, by law, grant to the principal officer in each of the Executive Departments a seat upon the floor of either House, with the privilege of discussing any measures appertaining to his department.

Section 7. 1. All bills for raising revenue shall originate in the House of Representatives; but the Senate may propose or concur with amendments, as on other bills.

2. Every bill which shall have passed both Houses shall, before it becomes a law, be presented to the President of the Confederate States; if he approve, he shall sign it; but if not, he shall return it, with his objections, to that House in which it shall have originated, who shall enter the objections at large on their journal, and proceed to reconsider it. If, after such reconsideration, two-thirds of that House shall agree to pass the bill, it shall be sent,

together with the objections, to the other House, by which it shall likewise be reconsidered, and if approved by two-thirds of that House, it shall become a law. But in all such cases, the votes of both Houses shall be determined by yeas and nays, and the names of the persons voting for and against the bill shall be entered on the journal of each House respectively. If any bill shall not be returned by the President within ten days (Sundays excepted) after it shall have been presented to him, the same shall be a law, in like manner as if he had signed it, unless the Congress, by their adjournment, prevent its return; in which case it shall not be a law. The President may approve any appropriation and disapprove any other appropriation in the same bill. In such case he shall, in signing the bill, designate the appropriations disapproved; and shall return a copy of such appropriations, with his objections, to the House in which the bill shall have originated; and the same proceedings shall then be had as in case of other bills disapproved by the President.

3. Every order, resolution or vote, to which the concurrence of both Houses may be necessary (except on a question of adjournment) shall be presented to the President of the Confederate States; and before the same shall take effect, shall be approved by him; or being disapproved by him, shall be repassed by two-thirds of both Houses, according to the rules and limitations prescribed in case of a bill.

Section 8. The Congress shall have power—

1. To lay and collect taxes, duties, imposts, and excises for revenue, necessary to pay the debts, provide for the common defense, and carry on the Government of the Confederate States; but no bounties shall be granted from the Treasury; nor shall any duties or taxes on importations from foreign nations be laid to promote or foster any branch of industry; and all duties, imposts, and excises shall be uniform throughout the Confederate States:

2. To borrow money on the credit of the Confederate States:

3. To regulate commerce with foreign nations, and among the several States, and with the Indian tribes; but neither this, nor any other clause contained in the Constitution, shall ever be construed to delegate the power to Congress to appropriate money for any internal improvement intended to facilitate commerce; except for the purpose of furnishing lights, beacons, and buoys, and other aids to navigation upon the coasts, and the improvement of harbors and the removing of obstructions in river navigation; in all which cases such duties shall be laid on the navigation facilitated thereby as may be necessary to pay the costs and expenses thereof:

4. To establish uniform laws of naturalization, and uniform laws on the subject of bankruptcies, throughout the Confederate States; but no law of Congress shall discharge any debt contracted before the passage of the same:

5. To coin money, regulate the value thereof and of foreign coin, and fix the standard of weights and measures:

6. To provide for the punishment of counterfeiting the securities and current coin of the Confederate States:

7. To establish post-offices and post-routes; but the expenses of the Post-Office Department, after the 1st day of March in the year of our Lord eighteen hundred and sixty-three, shall be paid out of its own revenues:

8. To promote the progress of science and useful arts, by securing for limited times to authors and inventors the exclusive right to their respective writings and discoveries:

9. To constitute tribunals inferior to the Supreme Court:

10. To define and punish piracies and felonies committed on the high seas, and offenses against the law of nations:

11. To declare war, grant letters of marque and reprisal, and make rules concerning captures on land and water:

12. To raise and support armies; but no appropriation of money to that use shall be for a longer term than two years:

13. To provide and maintain a navy:

14. To make rules for the government and regulation of the land and naval forces:

15. To provide for calling forth the militia to execute the laws of the Confederate States, suppress insurrections, and repel invasions:

16. To provide for organizing, arming, and disciplining the militia, and for governing such part of them as may be employed in the service of the Confederate States: reserving to the States, respectively, the appointment of the officers, and the authority of training the militia according to the discipline prescribed by Congress:

17. To exercise exclusive legislation, in all cases whatsoever, over such district (not exceeding ten miles square) as may, by cession of one or more States and the acceptance of Congress, become the seat of the Government of the Confederate States; and to exercise like authority over all places purchased by the consent of the Legislature of the State in which the same shall be, for the erection of forts, magazines, arsenals, dockyards, and other needful buildings: and

18. To make all laws which shall be necessary and proper for carrying into execution the foregoing powers, and all other powers vested by this Constitution in the Government of the Confederate States, or in any department or officer thereof.

Section 9. 1. The importation of negroes of the African race, from any foreign country other than the slave-holding States or Territories of the United States of America, is hereby forbidden; and Congress is required to pass such laws as shall effectually prevent the same.

2. Congress shall also have power to prohibit the introduction of slaves from any State not a member of, or Territory not belonging to, this Confederacy.

3. The privilege of the writ of habeas corpus shall not be suspended, unless when in cases of rebellion or invasion the public safety may require it.

4. No bill of attainder, *ex post facto* law, or law denying or impairing the right of property in negro slaves shall be passed.

5. No capitation or other direct tax shall be laid, unless in proportion to the census or enumeration hereinbefore directed to be taken.

6. No tax or duty shall be laid on articles exported from any State, except by a vote of two-thirds of both Houses.

7. No preference shall be given by any regulation of commerce or revenue to the ports of one State over those of another.

8. No money shall be drawn from the Treasury, but in consequence of appropriations made by law; and a regular statement and account of the receipts and expenditures of all public money shall be published from time to time.

9. Congress shall appropriate no money from the Treasury except by a vote of two-thirds of both Houses, taken by yeas and nays, unless it be asked and estimated for by some one of the heads of departments and submitted to Congress by the President; or for the purpose of paying its own expenses and contingencies; or for the payment of claims against the Confederate States, the justice of which shall have been judicially declared by a tribunal for the investigation of claims against the Government, which it is hereby made the duty of Congress to establish.

10. All bills appropriating money shall specify in Federal currency the exact amount of each appropriation and the purposes for which it is made; and Congress shall grant no extra compensation to any public contractor, officer, agent or servant, after such contract shall have been made or such service rendered.

11. No title of nobility shall be granted by the Confederate States; and no person holding any office of profit or trust under them shall, without the consent of the Congress, accept of any present, emolument, office, or title of any kind whatever, from any king, prince, or foreign state.

12. Congress shall make no law respecting an establishment of religion, or prohibiting the free exercise thereof; or abridging the freedom of speech, or of the press; or the right of the people peaceably to assemble and petition the Government for a redress of grievances.

13. A well-regulated militia being necessary to the security of a free State, the right of the people to keep and bear arms shall not be infringed.

14. No soldier shall, in time of peace, be quartered in any house without the consent of the

owner; nor in time of war, but in a manner to be prescribed by law.

15. The right of the people to be secure in their persons, houses, papers, and effects, against unreasonable searches and seizures, shall not be violated; and no warrants shall issue but upon probable cause, supported by oath or affirmation, and particularly describing the place to be searched and the persons or things to be seized.

16. No person shall be held to answer for a capital or otherwise infamous crime, unless on a presentment or indictment of a grand jury, except in cases arising in the land or naval forces, or in the militia, when in actual service in time of war or public danger; nor shall any person be subject for the same offense to be twice put in jeopardy of life or limb; nor be compelled, in any criminal case, to be a witness against himself; nor be deprived of life, liberty, or property without due process of law; nor shall private property be taken for public use, without just compensation.

17. In all criminal prosecutions the accused shall enjoy the right to a speedy and public trial, by an impartial jury of the State and district wherein the crime shall have been committed, which district shall have been previously ascertained by law, and to be informed of the nature and cause of the accusation; to be confronted with the witnesses against him; to have compulsory process for obtaining witnesses in his favor; and to have the assistance of counsel for his defense.

18. In suits at common law, where the value in controversy shall exceed twenty dollars, the right of trial by jury shall be preserved; and no fact so tried by a jury shall be otherwise re-examined in any court of the Confederacy, than according to the rules of common law.

19. Excessive bail shall not be required, nor excessive fines imposed, nor cruel and unusual punishments inflicted.

20. Every law, or resolution having the force of law, shall relate to but one subject, and that shall be expressed in the title.

Section 10. 1. No State shall enter into any treaty, alliance, or confederation; grant letters of marque and reprisal; coin money; make anything but gold and silver coin tender in payment of debts; pass any bill of attainder, or *ex post facto* law, or law impairing the obligation of contracts; or grant any title of nobility.

2. No State shall, without the consent of the Congress, lay any imposts or duties on imports or exports, except what may be absolutely necessary for executing its inspection laws; and the net produce of all duties and imposts, laid by any State on imports or exports, shall be for the use of the Treasury of the Confederate States; and all such laws shall be subject to the revision and control of Congress.

3. No State shall, without the consent of Congress, lay any duty on tonnage, except on seagoing vessels, for the improvement of its rivers and harbors navigated by the said vessels; but such duties shall not conflict with any treaties of the Confederate States with foreign nations; and any surplus revenue, thus derived, shall, after making such improvement, be paid into the common treasury. Nor shall any State keep troops or ships of war in time of peace, enter into any agreement or compact with another State, or with a foreign power, or engage in war, unless actually invaded, or in such imminent danger as will not admit of delay. But when any river divides or flows through two or more States they may enter into compacts with each other to improve the navigation thereof.

Article II.

Section 1. 1. The executive power shall be vested in a President of the Confederate States of America. He and the Vice-President shall hold their offices for the term of six years; but the President shall not be reeligible. The President and Vice-President shall be elected as follows:

2. Each State shall appoint, in such manner as the Legislature thereof may direct, a number of electors equal to the whole number of Senators and Representatives to which the State may be entitled in the Congress; but no Senator or Representative or person holding an office of trust or profit under the Confederate States shall be appointed an elector.

3. The electors shall meet in their respective States and vote by ballot for President and Vice-President, one of whom, at least, shall not be an inhabitant of the same State with themselves; they shall name in their ballots the person voted for as President, and in distinct ballots the person voted for as Vice-President, and they shall make distinct lists of all persons voted for as President, and of all persons voted for as Vice-President, and of the number of votes for each, which lists they shall sign and certify, and transmit, sealed, to the seat of the Government of the Confederate States, directed to the President of the Senate; the President of the Senate shall, in the presence of the Senate and House of Representatives, open all the certificates, and the votes shall then be counted; the person having the greatest number of votes for President shall be the President, if such number be a majority of the whole number of electors appointed; and if no person have such majority, then from the persons having the highest numbers, not exceeding three, on the list of those voted for as President, the House of Representatives shall choose immediately, by ballot, the President. But in choosing the President the votes shall be taken by States—the representation from each State having one vote; a quorum for this purpose shall consist of a member or members from two-thirds of the States, and a majority of all the States shall be necessary to a choice. And if the House of Representatives shall not choose a President, whenever the right of choice shall devolve upon them, before the 4th day of March next following, then the Vice-President shall act as President, as in case of the death, or other constitutional disability of the President.

4. The person having the greatest number of votes as Vice-President shall be the Vice-President, if such number be a majority of the whole number of electors appointed; and if no person have a majority, then, from the two highest numbers on the list, the Senate shall choose the Vice-President; a quorum for the purpose shall consist of two-thirds of the whole number of Senators, and a majority of the whole number shall be necessary to a choice.

5. But no person constitutionally ineligible to the office of President shall be eligible to that of Vice-President of the Confederate States.

6. The Congress may determine the time of choosing the electors, and the day on which they shall give their votes; which day shall be the same throughout the Confederate States.

7. No person except a natural-born citizen of the Confederate States, or a citizen thereof at the time of the adoption of this Constitution, or a citizen thereof born in the United States prior to the 20th of December, 1860, shall be eligible to the office of President; neither shall any person be eligible to that office who shall not have attained the age of thirty-five years, and been fourteen years a resident within the limits of the Confederate States, as they may exist at the time of his election.

8. In case of the removal of the President from office, or of his death, resignation, or inability to discharge the powers and duties of the said office, the same shall devolve on the Vice-President; and the Congress may, by law, provide for the case of removal, death, resignation, or inability, both of the President and Vice-President, declaring what officer shall then act as President; and such officer shall act accordingly until the disability be removed or a President shall be elected.

9. The President shall, at stated times, receive for his services a compensation, which shall neither be increased nor diminished during the period for which he shall have been elected; and he shall not receive within that period any other emolument from the Confederate States, or any of them.

10. Before he enters on the execution of his office he shall take the following oath or affirmation:

"I do solemnly swear (or affirm) that I will faithfully execute the office of President of the Confederate States, and will, to the best of my ability, preserve, protect, and defend the Constitution thereof."

Section 2. 1. The President shall be Commander-in-Chief of the Army and Navy of the Confederate States, and of the militia of the several States, when called into the actual service of the Confederate States; he may require the opinion, in writing, of the principal officer in each of the Executive Departments, upon any subject relating to the duties of their respective offices; and he shall have power to grant reprieves and pardons for offenses against the Confederate States, except in cases of impeachment.

2. He shall have power, by and with the advice and consent of the Senate, to make treaties; provided two-thirds of the Senators present concur; and he shall nominate, and by and with the advice and consent of the Senate, shall appoint ambassadors, other public ministers and consuls, judges of the Supreme Court, and all other officers of the Confederate States whose appointments are not herein otherwise provided for, and which shall be established by law; but the Congress may, by law, vest the appointment of such inferior officers, as they think proper, in the President alone, in the courts of law, or in the heads of departments.

3. The principal officer in each of the Executive Departments, and all persons connected with the diplomatic service, may be removed from office at the pleasure of the President. All other civil officers of the Executive Departments may be removed at any time by the President, or other appointing power, when their services are unnecessary, or for dishonesty, incapacity, inefficiency, misconduct, or neglect of duty; and when so removed, the removal shall be reported to the Senate, together with the reasons therefor.

4. The President shall have power to fill all vacancies that may happen during the recess of the Senate, by granting commissions which shall expire at the end of their next session; but no person rejected by the Senate shall be reappointed to the same office during their ensuing recess.

Section 3. 1. The President shall, from time to time, give to the Congress information of the state of the Confederacy, and recommend to their consideration such measures as he shall judge necessary and expedient; he may, on extraordinary occasions, convene both Houses, or either of them; and in case of disagreement between them, with respect to the time of adjournment, he may adjourn them to such time as he shall think proper; he shall receive ambassadors and other public ministers; he shall take care that the laws be faithfully

executed, and shall commission all the officers of the Confederate States.

Section 4. 1. The President, Vice-President, and all civil officers of the Confederate States, shall be removed from office on impeachment, for and conviction of treason, bribery, or other high crimes and misdemeanors.

Article III.

Section 1. 1. The judicial power of the Confederate States shall be vested in one Supreme Court, and in such inferior courts as the Congress may, from time to time, ordain and establish. The judges, both of the Supreme and inferior courts, shall hold their offices during good behavior, and shall, at stated times, receive for their services a compensation which shall not be diminished during their continuance in office.

Section 2. 1. The judicial power shall extend to all cases arising under this Constitution, the laws of the Confederate States, and treaties made, or which shall be made, under their authority; to all cases affecting ambassadors, other public ministers and consuls; to all cases of admiralty and maritime jurisdiction; to controversies to which the Confederate States shall be a party; to controversies between two or more States; between a State and citizens of another State, where the State is plaintiff; between citizens claiming lands under grants of different States; and between a State or the citizens thereof, and foreign states, citizens, or subjects; but no State shall be sued by a citizen or subject of any foreign state.

2. In all cases affecting ambassadors, other public ministers and consuls, and those in which a State shall be a party, the Supreme Court shall have original jurisdiction. In all the other cases before mentioned, the Supreme Court shall have appellate jurisdiction both as to law and fact, with such exceptions and under such regulations as the Congress shall make.

3. The trial of all crimes, except in cases of impeachment, shall be by jury, and such trial shall be

held in the State where the said crimes shall have been committed; but when not committed within any State, the trial shall be at such place or places as the Congress may by law have directed.

Section 3. 1. Treason against the Confederate States shall consist only in levying war against them, or in adhering to their enemies, giving them aid and comfort. No person shall be convicted of treason unless on the testimony of two witnesses to the same overt act, or on confession in open court.

2. The Congress shall have power to declare the punishment of treason; but no attainder of treason shall work corruption of blood, or forfeiture, except during the life of the person attainted.

Article IV.

Section 1. 1. Full faith and credit shall be given in each State to the public acts, records, and judicial proceedings of every other State; and the Congress may, by general laws, prescribe the manner in which such acts, records, and proceedings shall be proved, and the effect thereof.

Section 2. 1. The citizens of each State shall be entitled to all the privileges and immunities of citizens in the several States; and shall have the right of transit and sojourn in any State of this Confederacy, with their slaves and other property; and the right of property in said slaves shall not be thereby impaired.

2. A person charged in any State with treason, felony, or other crime against the laws of such State, who shall flee from justice, and be found in another State, shall, on demand of the executive authority of the State from which he fled, be delivered up, to be removed to the State having jurisdiction of the crime.

3. No slave or other person held to service or labor in any State or Territory of the Confederate States, under the laws thereof, escaping or lawfully carried into another, shall, in consequence of any law or regulation therein, be discharged from such service or labor; but shall be delivered up on claim

of the party to whom such slave belongs, or to whom such service or labor may be due.

Section 3. 1. Other States may be admitted into this Confederacy by a vote of two-thirds of the whole House of Representatives and two-thirds of the Senate, the Senate voting by States; but no new State shall be formed or erected within the jurisdiction of any other State, nor any State be formed by the junction of two or more States, or parts of States, without the consent of the Legislatures of the States concerned, as well as of the Congress.

2. The Congress shall have power to dispose of and make all needful rules and regulations concerning the property of the Confederate States, including the lands thereof.

3. The Confederate States may acquire new territory; and Congress shall have power to legislate and provide governments for the inhabitants of all territory belonging to the Confederate States, lying without the limits of the several States; and may permit them, at such times, and in such manner as it may by law provide, to form States to be admitted into the Confederacy. In all such territory the institution of negro slavery, as it now exists in the Confederate States, shall be recognized and protected by Congress and by the Territorial government; and the inhabitants of the several Confederate States and Territories shall have the right to take to such Territory any slaves lawfully held by them in any of the States or Territories of the Confederate States.

4. The Confederate States shall guarantee to every State that now is, or hereafter may become, a member of this Confederacy, a republican form of government; and shall protect each of them against invasion; and on application of the Legislature (or of the Executive when the Legislature is not in session) against domestic violence.

Article V.

Section 1. 1. Upon the demand of any three States, legally assembled in their several conventions, the Congress shall summon a convention of all the

States, to take into consideration such amendments to the Constitution as the said States shall concur in suggesting at the time when the said demand is made; and should any of the proposed amendments to the Constitution be agreed on by the said convention—voting by States—and the same be ratified by the Legislatures of two-thirds of the several States, or by conventions in two-thirds thereof—as the one or the other mode of ratification may be proposed by the general convention—they shall thenceforward form a part of this Constitution. But no State shall, without its consent, be deprived of its equal representation in the Senate.

Article VI.

1. The Government established by this Constitution is the successor of the Provisional Government of the Confederate States of America, and all the laws passed by the latter shall continue in force until the same shall be repealed or modified; and all the officers appointed by the same shall remain in office until their successors are appointed and qualified, or the offices abolished.

2. All debts contracted and engagements entered into before the adoption of this Constitution shall be as valid against the Confederate States under this Constitution, as under the Provisional Government.

3. This Constitution, and the laws of the Confederate States made in pursuance thereof, and all treaties made, or which shall be made, under the authority of the Confederate States, shall be the supreme law of the land; and the judges in every State shall be bound thereby, anything in the constitution or laws of any State to the contrary notwithstanding.

4. The Senators and Representatives before mentioned, and the members of the several State Legislatures, and all executive and judicial officers, both of the Confederate States and of the several States, shall be bound by oath or affirmation to support this Constitution; but no religious test shall ever be required as a qualification to any office or public trust under the Confederate States.

5. The enumeration, in the Constitution, of certain rights shall not be construed to deny or disparage others retained by the people of the several States.

6. The powers not delegated to the Confederate States by the Constitution, nor prohibited by it to the States, are reserved to the States, respectively, or to the people thereof.

Article VII.

1. The ratification of the conventions of five States shall be sufficient for the establishment of this Constitution between the States so ratifying the same.

2. When five States shall have ratified this Constitution, in the manner before specified, the Congress under the Provisional Constitution shall prescribe the time for holding the election of President and Vice-President; and for the meeting of the Electoral College; and for counting the votes, and inaugurating the President. They shall, also, prescribe the time for holding the first election of members of Congress under this Constitution, and the time for assembling the same. Until the assembling of such Congress, the Congress under the Provisional Constitution shall continue to exercise the legislative powers granted them; not extending beyond the time limited by the Constitution of the Provisional Government.

Adopted unanimously by the Congress of the Confederate States of South Carolina, Georgia, Florida, Alabama, Mississippi, Louisiana and Texas, sitting in convention at the capitol, in the city of Montgomery, Ala., on the eleventh day of March, in the year eighteen hundred and sixty-one.

PERMISSIONS ACKNOWLEDGMENTS

p. 3 From *A Russian Looks at America* by Aleksandr Borisovich Lakier, translated by Arnold Schrier and Joyce Story. © 1979 by The University of Chicago. All Rights Reserved. Published 1979. **p. 47** Permission courtesy of the Abraham Lincoln Association. **p. 66** Reprinted with the permission of Scribner, a Division of Simon & Schuster from *The Diary of George Templeton Strong*, Volume III, by Allan Nevins and Milton Halsey Thomas. Copyright © 1952 by Macmillan Publishing Company, renewed 1980 by Milton Halsey Thomas. **p. 77** Permission courtesy of the Abraham Lincoln Association. **p. 78** Permission courtesy of the Abraham Lincoln Association. **p. 88** Permission courtesy of the Abraham Lincoln Association. **p. 89** Reprinted from "The Civil War Diary of C. F. Boyd, Fifteenth Iowa Infantry," edited by Mildred F. Throne, *Iowa Journal of History* 50 (1952), 70–82. Copyright 1952 State Historical Society of Iowa. Reprinted with the permission of the publisher. **p. 93** Permission courtesy of the Abraham Lincoln Association. **p. 102** From *Fighting for the Confederacy: The Personal Recollections of General Edward Porter Alexander* edited by Gary W. Gallagher. Copyright © 1989 by the University of North Carolina Press. Used by permission of the publisher. **p. 126** Permission courtesy of the Abraham Lincoln Association. **p. 130** Permission courtesy of the Abraham Lincoln Association. **p. 147** Permission courtesy of the Abraham Lincoln Association. **p. 151** Reprinted from *The Cormany Diaries: A Northern Family in the Civil War*, James C. Mohr, Editor, by permission of the University of Pittsburgh Press. © 1982 by University of Pittsburgh Press. **p. 155** From *John Dooley, Confederate Soldier: His War Journal*, edited by Joseph T. Durkin (Georgetown: Georgetown University Press, 1945). **p. 157** From *The Boys from Rockville*, edited by Robert L. Bee (Knoxville: University of Tennessee Press, 1998). **p. 163** From *The Journals of Josiah Gorgas, 1857–1878*, edited by Sarah Woolfolk Wiggins (Tuscaloosa: University of Alabama Press, 1995).

p. 165 Permission courtesy of the Abraham Lincoln Association. **p. 173** Permission courtesy of the Abraham Lincoln Association. **p. 176** Permission courtesy of the Abraham Lincoln Association. **p. 177** Permission courtesy of the Abraham Lincoln Association. **p. 183** Reprinted with the permission of Scribner, a Division of Simon & Schuster from *The Diary of George Templeton Strong*, Volume III, by Allan Nevins and Milton Halsey Thomas. Copyright © 1952 by Macmillan Publishing Company, renewed 1980 by Milton Halsey Thomas. **p. 189** From *South after Gettysburg: Letters of Cornelia Hancock from the Army of the Potomac 1863–1865*, edited by Henrietta Stratton Jaquette. Copyright © 1937 University of Pennsylvania Press. Reprinted by permission. **p. 198** North Carolina Division of Archives and History. **p. 208** Reprint courtesy of *The Register of the Kentucky Historical Society*. **p. 210** From *The Secret Eye: The Journal of Ella Gertrude Clanton Thomas, 1848-1889*, edited by Virginia Ingraham Burr. Copyright © 1990 by Virginia Ingraham Burr and Gertrude D. Despeaux. Used by permission of the publisher. **p. 214** From *Mary Chesnut's Civil War*, edited by C. Van Woodward (New Haven: Yale University Press, 1981). © 1981 by C. Vann Woodward, Sally Bland Metts, Barbara G. Carpenter, Sally Bland Johnson, and Katherine W. Herbert. **p. 224** Letter in the Clement C. Clay Papers dated September 5, 1863, from Susanna C. Clay to her son. **p. 235** North Carolina Division of Archives and History. **p. 236** From *Hard Marching Every Day: The Civil War Letters of Private Wilbur Fisk, 1861–1865*, edited by Emil and Ruth Rosenblatt, Modern War Studies series, Theodore A. Wilson, general editor. Published by University Press of Kansas © 1983, 1992 by Emil Rosenblatt. All rights reserved. **p. 238** Thomas W. Chadwick, ed., "The Diary of Samuel Edward Burges: 1860–1862," *South Carolina Historical and Genealogical Magazine* 48 (October 1947), p. 216. **p. 238** From *Far, Far from Home: The Wartime Letters of Dick and Tally Simpson, Third South Car-*